P9-DTG-951

DATE DUE

~~OC 1 5 '98~~			
NO 2 4 '98			
~~JA 5 0 '02~~			

DEMCO 38-296

PARIS

CAPITAL OF EUROPE

Frontispiece. *The Eiffel Tower, erected between 1885 and 1889 in the Champs de Mar, was designed by the engineer Gustave Eiffel, who in this photograph stands at the top of the tower's spiral staircase.*

CAPITAL OF EUROPE

From the Revolution to the Belle Epoque

JOHANNES WILLMS

TRANSLATED BY EVELINE L. KANES

HOLMES & MEIER
NEW YORK / LONDON

Anna Mariani
Notre Dame des Fenêtres
Paris-Rome

Published in the United States of America 1997 by
Holmes & Meier Publishers, Inc.
160 Broadway
New York, NY 10038

Originally published under the title *Paris: Hauptstadt Europas 1789–1914*, copyright © C. H. Beck, Munich, 1988.

Map sources appear on pages 343–346.

Book design by Michael Mendelsohn

This book has been printed on acid-free paper.

Library of Congress Cataloging-in-Publication Data
Willms, Johannes.
    [Paris. English]
    Paris: from the Revolution to the Belle Epoque / Johannes Willms; translated by Eveline L. Kanes.
        p.   cm.
    Translation of: Paris: Haupstadt Europas, 1789–1914.
    Includes bibliographical references and indexes.
    ISBN 0-8419-1245-9
    1. Paris (France)—History—1789–1900. 2. Paris (France)—History—1870–1940. I. Title.
    DC731.W5513   1997   95-38075
    944'.36—dc20   CIP

Manufactured in the United States of America

$\mathscr{L}$es lieux que nous avons connus n'appartiennent pas qu'au monde de l'espace où nous les situons pour plus de facilité. Ils n'étaient qu'une mince tranche au milieu d'impressions contigues qui formaient notre vie d'alors; le souvenir d'une certain image n'est que le regret d'un certain instant; et les maisons, les routes, les avenues, sont fugitives, hélas! comme les années.

$\mathscr{T}$he places we have known do not belong merely to the spatial world in which, for convenience, we locate them. They were merely a narrow strip of the dense impressions that formed our life at that time; the memory of a certain image is but the nostalgia for a certain moment; and the houses, roads and avenues are as fugitive, alas, as the years.

—Marcel Proust, *A la recherche du temps perdu*

Contents

BOOK SEVEN
FROM COMMUNE TO BELLE EPOQUE, 1871–1914

Preface

*T*his book stresses the importance Paris acquired in the nineteenth century. Much of what happened here had repercussions throughout Europe. It was Paris and not London or even Berlin that became the vast stage on which the paradoxical history of the century was played out.

Paris is filled with history and stories. It was therefore very difficult to find a cutoff point, even though the account is limited essentially to the nineteenth century. I have tried my best to make an adequate selection of the vast amount of material at hand. I chose not to go into a lengthier discussion of the history of the theatrical or religious life of the city; nor did I do more than touch upon the intellectual movements, or the various schools and styles in literature and art. This work aims to inform the reader about the transformation of the city, the changes affecting its internal and external life in the course of the nineteenth century. Paris is shown as an arena continually transformed by the interplay of the political, social, and economic processes of the period. These changes were recorded by contemporaries with critical attention. I have used their testimony in the form of novels, memoirs, official protocols, reports, pamphlets, travel descriptions, diaries, and letters. The book is arranged chronologically, each of the seven sections of the book being devoted to a specific period within the century.

The notes and bibliography indicate the sources of all the material used. As many of the texts can only be consulted as originals in one of the Paris libraries, I decided to quote frequently and more fully than is usually the case, to give the reader a direct impression of the source material.

This is the first time that a history of Paris in the nineteenth century is presented in German in this sort of detail. I alone am responsible for any shortcomings in the book, and I hold with Goethe that "The historian has a dual duty: first to himself, then to the reader. As for himself, he must evaluate accurately what might have happened; and for the sake of the reader he must determine what actually happened. As for himself, he must answer to his colleagues; but the public must not be let into the secret of how little there is in history that can be considered decisive."

I extend my thanks to everyone who gave support and advice during the creation of this work. However, special gratitude is due my wife, who once again has demonstrated her understanding for a time-consuming project that had to be completed along with my commitment to journalism.

JOHANNES WILLMS

BOOK ONE

Paris on the Eve of the Revolution

Il est temps que ceux qui sont à la tête de la plus oppulente capital de l'Europe la rendent la plus commode et la plus magnifique. . . . Fasse le ciel qu'il se trouve quelque homme assez zélé pour embrasser de tels projets, d'une âme assez ferme pour les suivre, d'un esprit assez éclairé pour les rédiger, et qu'il soit assez accrédité pour les faire réussir.

It is time for those in charge of the wealthiest capital of Europe to make it the most commodious and the most magnificent. . . . May heaven grant that a man can be found who is energetic enough to undertake such projects, sufficiently strong-willed to follow them up, far-sighted enough to organize them, and of sufficient stature to carry it all off.

—Voltaire, *Des Embellissements de Paris* (1749)

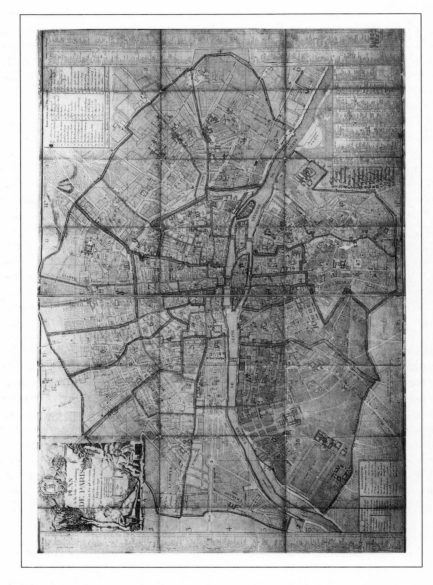

Plan of the city and its districts (in a 1791 print) as specified by the decree of the Convention of June 22, 1790.
ARCHIV FÜR KUNST UND GESCHICHTE, BERLIN

The Growth of Paris

*P*ARIS WAS THE CULTURAL AND ECONOMIC CAPITAL of France until the end of the Old Regime. In 1789 it became the focal point of a nation embroiled in a revolution, the course of which was largely identical with the city's growth. Only in the Revolution did Paris truly become the political, cultural, and economic nucleus that directly controlled the future development of France and, indirectly, that of Europe. From that moment city and country had parallel histories.

The year 1789 marked a turning point in the city's history, giving it an importance unlike that of any other capital. Its evolution began in the thirteenth century; in fact its social topography then resembled, on a small scale, the image it would have by the end of the eighteenth century. It gradually spread out more and more from the Ile de la Cité to the two banks that flanked the Seine. The university's *grandes écoles* were concentrated in the south, on the Left Bank known as the Latin Quarter; while the bourgeois districts where trade and commerce were carried on developed in the north, on the Right Bank. Descriptions of the social topography of Paris in the eighteenth century still reflect the older separations into *Cité, Université*, and *Ville*; the interplay of these elements led to the city's growing prominence as a seat of worldly and intellectual power.[1]

The significance of Paris under the Old Regime was inseparably linked to the degree of power possessed by the crown. Each royal victory over the specific interests and demands of the Estates increased the tendency toward centralization and consequently the importance of Paris. The city finally attained its political, cultural, and economic supremacy over the rest of France under Henry IV. As of this time it also began to loosen its ties to royal patronage and to follow its own dynamics. This is underscored by the crown's repeated attempts to restrict the growth of Paris. In 1638 Louis XIII had boundary-stones erected at the building limits of the fourteen suburbs, the faubourgs de Paris, beyond which it was forbidden to construct houses or new streets. The pointlessness of this attempt became evident when Louis XIV had to move the barriers a considerable distance farther out in 1672. Other attempts, including those of Louis XV, to curb the growth of the suburbs by setting *justes limites*, were equally futile. All were prompted by the same fear that once the city became too large it would escape the social and political control of the crown and present a constant threat.[2]

But the crown itself was partly to blame for its failure to halt the growth of Paris. In particular it was Louis XIV's decision to eliminate the fortifications encircling Paris, and to replace them with wide boulevards, that encouraged further expansion of urban living space. In 1698 a visitor to Paris commented that an entirely new city had replaced the old one over the last forty years; there had been so many improvements since Louis XIV ascended the throne that everything seemed different.[3]

3

Even if this statement was exaggerated, it contained a prophetic truth: under Louis XIV a new concept of the city as living space emerged. Paris, the most important city in France, was to testify to the grandeur of French power and culture. The destruction of the ramparts erected by Charles V, of which only the Bastille remained, signaled that in future the security of Paris would be defended at the country's frontiers. But this measure also symbolized the crown's final subjugation of a city that had once taken up arms against Henry IV to preserve its political independence. Paris had become the jewel in the crown of absolute monarchy.

This new function of the city was emphasized in various ways. The old city gates that had been eliminated along with the ramparts were replaced by magnificent triumphal arches. Like the statues of French kings in public places, they had as their model the structures of ancient Rome. The monument of Henry IV on a horse on the Pont Neuf, of Louis XIII in the place Royale (now the place des Vosges); the statues of Louis XIV in the place des Victoires and the place Vendôme, all characterize the areas or buildings erected or restored by those kings.

Beginning with Louis XIV, a new urban esthetic evolved, derived from an idealized antiquity and designed to make Paris the symbol of the monarchy's greatness. Its main characteristics were a strict geometric arrangement of the buildings, symmetry of the structures emphasized by line, and above all a calculated harmony expressed in the proportions of open areas to the height of the uniform constructions around them.

The building activity inspired by various sovereigns came to a halt in the eighteenth century, when the court settled permanently in Versailles. Paris was no longer needed as an effective backdrop for its power and splendor.[4] The royal promotion of urban development was now taken over by private speculators, who engaged in an unparalleled volume of construction in the thirty years preceding the Revolution. More than ten thousand houses were built between 1760 and 1783, according to Louis-Sébastien Mercier. As he noted in 1783, "In the last twenty-five years the building trade has given one-third of the capital a completely new face." But he added the criticism that

> if this building activity served the convenience of the general public, one would have to praise it; but it is solely the building trade itself that benefits and not the architecture: the parvenu wants to reside in roomy quarters and the merchant wants to live like a prince. While all sorts of theaters spring up, while the opera, the Théâtre-Français, and the Théâtre des Italiens are being built, the Hôtel-Dieu remains enclosed by its run-down neighborhood. . . . The speculators convinced the entrepreneurs who, holding the construction plans in one hand and the cost estimates in the other, fanned the desire of those who wanted to invest their capital. Gardens turned to stone and one now sees tall buildings where only vegetables grew previously. The urban image of the city has been completely transformed by the mason's indefatigable trowel: the Quinze-Vingts Hospital has disappeared and in its place there now stands a whole batch of ordinary new houses.[5] The Invalides, thought to be at peace in its open spaces, has been surrounded by new houses; the old Mint has been sacrificed for two streets, and an entirely new residential section has sprung up along the Chaussée d'Antin.[6]

The Palais-Royal: Capital of Paris

*O*F THE MANY SPECULATIVE VENTURES the most famous, and the one destined to be of greatest importance, was the enlargement of the Palais-Royal. It was undertaken by the duc de Chartres, who later became the duc d'Orléans but was better known as Philippe-Egalité.

Richelieu had been in charge of its original construction, and after the cardinal's death the building had become the property of the crown. Louis XIV then left it to his younger brother, the duc d'Orléans, as an appanage. Until its rebuilding and expansion the Palais-Royal consisted of only one wing, to which large parklike gardens were attached, intended exclusively for the use of the aristocracy.[7] Baron de Frénilly described them in his memoirs:

> The large gardens were bounded by the Palais on the west side and on the other three sides by houses that were quite unaffordable because of their location. Straight avenues, reflecting pools, and flower borders divided these gardens; on the southern side there was a large avenue lined with chestnut trees that were unique in all of France for their size and age; they formed a magnificent canopy that the sun's rays could not penetrate. At the end of this avenue of chestnut trees stood the Orangerie. This very spacious gallery had been the meeting place of Parisian high society since the days of Anne of Austria. . . . The gardens of the Palais-Royal served as a promenade to display luxury, festivity, and good manners. . . . In short, the Palais-Royal was the heart and soul, the center and preferred meeting place of the aristocracy of Paris.[8]

In 1780 the duc de Chartres, plagued by great financial difficulties, decided to rebuild the Palais-Royal, paying no attention to the loud public protest at his plans.[9] He wanted to interest investors in turning this property, situated not far from the Opera, into a good source of income.[10] The architect Victor Louis was commissioned to make a design based on St. Mark's Square in Venice. A row of two-story houses was to enclose the gardens on three sides, and would tie in with the new wing of the palace on the south side. Covered arcades were to run along the entire length of the gardens of this right-angled complex of buildings, and would form columned halls under the old as well as the new Palais, according to the duc de Chartres' instructions. The arcades would have stores in them, like the ones in St. Mark's, with windows facing the gardens. Deliveries to these stores, as well as access to the apartments on the two floors above them, would be from the streets to be constructed along the rear of the new buildings.[11]

To ensure the social exclusiveness of his investment and its commercial success, the duc de Chartres insisted on tenants in keeping with an aristocratic atmosphere. Only luxury businesses and places of entertainment catering to a refined public were considered suitable for the "Palais-Marchand," as the Palais-Royal soon came to be known. Merchants and artisans whose trade involved noise, dirt, or smells—and the list ran from blacksmiths to dealers in smoked meat—were specifically excluded.[12] Furthermore, until the outbreak of the Revolution visitors were carefully screened by Swiss Guards, dressed in the king's livery and stationed at the entrances to the gardens. The guards refused entry to "soldiers, domestics, or persons who wore caps or jackets, students, street urchins, beggars, dogs, and artisans."[13]

When the arcades were completed in 1784, and the trees of the gardens around them once more shaded strollers and idlers, the Palais-Royal became the place where fashionable society liked to meet; the duc de Chartres' venture began to bear fruit. Melchior von Grimm gave this description of the scene:

> It is difficult to describe the interesting picture offered by this promenade once the sun sets and ladies are tempted to walk about in the fresh air, and to enjoy looking around this garden of pleasures and, better still, being looked at. The chairs, which are placed two or three deep all along the walks, hardly suffice to accommodate all these women who are so beautiful to look at in the waning light and who provide such a varied and tempting feast for the eyes. The most beautiful, or at least the most elegant, saunter, with a natural grace that marks a Parisian woman, past those lined up along the paths. Never before have our lovely women appeared more attractive. Their presence lends this promenade an irresistible charm; one never tires of watching the changing scene which the eye views with constant pleasure; and it is almost regrettable that when night falls the spectacle is replaced by another, although it, too, enchants the senses and is even more seductive.
>
> The 180 lamps that hang from the 180 arches of the arcades surrounding the gardens, as well as the lights of the cafés, restaurants, and shops, bathe this promenade in a soft glow—a sort of twilight that makes the beautiful still more interesting and even improves what is ordinary. This half-light encourages decency but also desire, as its magical effects seem to fill the air with sensuality. This is the moment all our lovely courtesans choose for their rendezvous. The exquisite elegance of their attire, the excessively free and easy way in which they walk here, attract a noisy crowd of young people. They swarm about these women ceaselessly, hastening from one to another, following and overtaking them with an eagerness that is tiresome even to the objects of this attention. The ebb and flow of activity is controlled by these young beauties themselves, who are anxious to steer this movement into the broad avenues, well aware that the artificial light there shows off their beauty to greater advantage than in other sections of the garden.[14]

The popularity of the new Palais-Royal was not affected by the duc de Chartres' inability promptly to add the planned *corps de logis*, with its majestic columned hall. Because of a shortage of funds, a provisional wooden structure was built on the foundations to close off the complex on the south side. This "Camp des Tartares," as it came to be known, was opened in January 1785 and contained two covered galleries accommodating a hundred additional stores. Their exteriors resembled those of the three completed wings of the complex. The duc de Chartres leased the Camp des Tartares for 50,000 livres a year to a sieur Romain.[15]

This new investment by the duc de Chartres immediately angered owners of existing stores, who had to pay a considerably higher rent to the duke than those who opened their businesses in the Camp des Tartares.[16] It also increased the already strong competition among retailers of luxury goods in the Palais-Royal. "Each item," commented Mercier, "costs three to four times more here than elsewhere."[17] He went on to say that the atmosphere in the Palais-Royal was so tempting, "it made everyone spend their money, especially foreigners, who were so enchanted by the various costly items that they could not resist them." On the other hand, Mercier also noted that "the high rents for the stores tended to increase the mad competition," a fact that contributed to bankruptcies: "Bankruptcies were a normal happening; they occurred by the dozen."[18]

But the failed businesses of some in no way affected the illusions of others. It seemed no longer possible to think of commerce and profit anywhere but in the Palais-Royal. Anyone who wanted status in the business world had to have a shop in the "Palais-Marchand." Anything tempting that involved craftsmanship, luxury, or fashion was sold there. Finely crafted goods made of the rarest and most precious raw materials—clocks, jewelry, wardrobes, canes, toys, perfumes, gloves, liqueurs made from tropical fruits, pictures, prints, engravings, aquatints, etchings, and naturally books, brochures, and pamphlets as well—were displayed under the arcades in windows large enough to admit the daylight. The convexity of the glass made the items glow and shine and appear still more mysterious and attractive to the passersby. Nikolai M. Karamzin, a young Russian nobleman, who spent a few months in Paris prior to the Revolution as part of his grand tour, described his impressions of the variety of the goods displayed in the Palais-Royal:

In short, should an American savage come to the Palais-Royal, in half an hour he would be most beautifully attired and would have a richly furnished house, a carriage, many servants, twenty courses on the table, and, if he wished, a blooming Lais who each moment would die for love of him. Here are assembled all the remedies for boredom, and all the sweet banes for spiritual and physical health, every method of swindling those with money and tormenting those without it, all means of enjoying and killing time. One could spend his entire life, even the longest, in the Palais-Royal and, as in an enchanting dream, dying, say: "I have seen and known all!"[19]

The stores with their luxurious goods were only a part of the great fascination the Palais-Royal exerted over the public. Excellent restaurants certainly contributed to its general popularity. Foremost among them was Beauvilliers, elegantly appointed with mahogany tables and chairs, silver cutlery, and porcelain dishes. Then there was the less lavish La Barrière, which could accommodate twenty guests at one sitting; or the somewhat more modest Restaurant Huré. An even simpler place was the Couvert Espagnol, a table d'hôte where one could eat for 4 francs. And more appealing to the general public than these rather expensive establishments were the cafés, especially the Café de Foy and the Café du Caveau. The elegant Café de Foy, with its small marble tables and mirrored walls, was spread over seven arcades in the Galerie Montpensier. Its owner, Jousserand, was the only proprietor given the privilege of serving his refreshments in one of the covered garden pavilions as well. According to a contemporary gossip-sheet, the *Chronique scandaleuse*, the duc de Chartres bestowed this favor on Jousserand because of the beauty of his wife.[20]

The Café du Caveau, as its name indicates, was situated in the basement. This café, famous for the quality of its ices and an interior featuring the busts of famous musicians, was preferred by stockbrokers and literary men. As a place where news was exchanged and discussed, where rumors were started and intrigues of all sorts carried on, it played an important part in forming public opinion in prerevolutionary Paris. Besides these two cafés, where the unique atmosphere of the Palais-Royal and its public was concentrated, there were others like the Café de Valois and the Café Italien, both of which were especially popular with chess- and domino-players; foreigners living in the city, particularly Germans and Englishmen, frequented the Café de Chartres. At the beginning the Café Mécanique was a well-attended object of curiosity. Everyone admired the specially constructed moving-belt system, located in the central support of each table, that automatically brought the customer his drink.[21]

In addition to luxury shops, cafés, and restaurants, there were various other temptations such as puppet and vaudeville theaters, a wax museum run by a German named Curtius, billiard salons, and even the medicinal baths of the sieur Sérain, to whom the duc de Chartres had given the title of Master of the Baths (which were approved by the Royal Society of Medicine). The *Almanach du Palais-Royal*, which was constantly updated, kept the public informed of what the "Palais-Marchand" had to offer.

One of the favorite attractions, though, was free. It took place at noon on clear days between May and October, and dandies and onlookers eagerly awaited it holding their pocket watches in their hands. The duc de Chartres had installed a sundial to which a burning glass was fixed; it caught the concentrated heat of the sun and caused the attached gunpowder-filled shell to explode with a loud gun-like salute at midday. This sundial, with its daily explosion, was so popular that it became the subject of numerous lithographs titled *Midi ou le Coup de Canon du Palais Royal*.

A number of clubs and societies modeled on those in England also established themselves in the Palais-Royal, adding to the choice of diversions. One of these was the *Salon des Arcades* which was really a front for high-stakes gambling, something not permitted to private promoters. However, two groups were exempt from this prohibition. The first was the *Club des Chevaliers de Saint-Louis*, whose members belonged to the exclusive circle of holders of the Order of St. Louis, the highest order bestowed by the Old Regime. The other was the *Salon de la Comédie-Italienne*, which did not meet in the Palais-Royal. The most fashionable club of all was the *Club Olympique*, to which even ladies could belong; in February 1785 its membership list included over a hundred society women, among them three princesses, and about four hundred gentlemen who were part of court society and of *Tout Paris*. The purpose of this illustrious organization was of course banal, consisting as it did of arranging festivals, concerts, balls, and dinners. Clubs that were specifically for men included the *Salon des Arts*, an intellectual group to which scientists, artists, and writers belonged; the *Club Politique* and the *Club des Américains* attracted a similar membership.

The popularity of these clubs and the great overall success of the Palais-Royal revealed a far-reaching change in society. People had simply grown tired of the highly differentiated etiquette of the Old Regime. Clubs in which persons of various social ranks mingled—the *gens de roture* and *gens de noblesse*, as bourgeois and aristocrats were called—did away with artificially preserved, outdated social differences. In the closed society of the clubs an individual's heredity or social standing was no longer important, and etiquette was reduced to a polite minimum. These fops thought nothing was more ridiculous than *l'air vieille-cour*, the wig that suggested antiquated formality and outmoded gallantry.[22]

Just as people of differing social standing but of common outlook and interests came together in clubs, all social distinctions—still obstinately observed by the Old Regime in its laws and politics—merged in the colorful dressed-up crowd that daily filled the Palais-Royal. The Palais-Royal's resounding success certainly demonstrated that social hierarchy had become a fiction. It no longer coincided with social reality, with the way in which Parisian society saw itself prior to the Revolution. The barriers had become largely obsolete between the old aristocracy on the one hand, and the *noblesse de robe* and *gens de condition* (the bankers or rich merchants who could afford an aristocratic life-style) on the other.[23]

Fashion and hairstyles, both of which became progressively simpler, were the external symbols of social change. "In the year 1787," baron de Frénilly wrote in his memoirs,

> priests and prelates wore only simple brown or purple cassocks except on special ceremonial occasions; presidents of the court or government agencies dressed in tails or frock-coats. Even the differently styled wigs formerly worn by judges, bankers, doctors, laywers, or merchants disappeared; instead it was customary to powder one's hair.[24]

As the political, economic, and social crisis of the Old Regime approached its climax, the Palais-Royal also acted as the fuse that fired all political opinions and currents. Those who gathered there—*gens de condition* as well as stock-market speculators, courtesans, literary men, lawyers, schemers, ideologues, and all who wanted to change the world—met informally for discussion and debate. They were the critical public that shaped the intellectual content of the revolutionary actions against the Old Regime in July 1789. Even then Anne-Henri de Dampmartin could predict that "the Palais-Royal is so influential in the kingdom that nineteenth-century historians will have to study it very carefully, and perhaps they will manage to disentangle all the forces hidden there."[25]

Whatever was said, whispered, maintained, or spread about as rumor or truth in cafés, restaurants, and clubs of the Palais-Royal found its way into the press—the *Journal général de la France*, or the *Journal de Paris*. The Palais-

Royal served as a news agency and rumor mill; this was where everyone in Paris went if they wanted firsthand information. Eventually, in the summer of 1789, it also became the center of increasingly heated and radical agitation against the royal government.

It was not pure chance that led to the Palais-Royal's unique function in the final phase of the Old Regime. Like the eye of a hurricane that was about to destroy the old order, it had concentrated within itself the entire force of Parisian life. In his letters Karamzin referred to the Palais-Royal as the heart, soul, brain, and essence of the entire city. Mercier described it as "La capitale de Paris," and said:

> It attracts a steady stream of foreigners and leaves the other side of the city too empty. Far too much activity is concentrated around the Palais-Royal, so that the faubourg Saint-Germain is rapidly becoming less important. It would therefore be desirable to have something to balance it; the money of the bourgeoisie would certainly benefit, and the two halves of the city could compete in wealth, splendor, number of residents, and profit from trade.[26]

Probably nothing could have competed with the Palais-Royal. The advantages of its central location could not be reproduced in any other district of the city. It was situated at the point where the economic activities of the stock exchange and banks on one side met those of the markets and their accompanying industries on the other. Moreover, it was linked to the area dominated by the Louvre and the Tuileries. In short, the Palais-Royal lay just between the newly developed and attractive residential neighborhoods of the rich in the west, and the more densely populated city sections to the north and east. These latter districts still possessed their medieval characteristics, in terms of social mix as well as topography.[27]

Dark and Light

ACLEAR DIVISION OF THE CITY into separate neighborhoods for the wealthy and the workers did not develop until the nineteenth century. Yet various parts of the city differed in their social makeup and economic structure well before the onset of the Revolution. For instance the court's move to Versailles led many members of the aristocracy to give up their residences in the Marais, the heart of old Paris, in exchange for homes in the newer western sections. Under Louis XIV the area between the place des Victoires and the place Vendôme was preferred by the nobility; under Louis XV the faubourg Saint-Honoré and the equally elegant faubourg Saint-Germain on the Left Bank became the aristocratic areas.[28] In 1789 more than half the dukes and peers in Paris owned houses in the faubourg Saint-Germain; another third of the upper nobility as well as numerous members of the *cours souveraines*, or high courts of justice, had properties in the place des Victoires and the Palais-Royal.[29] On the other hand the Marais, a stronghold of the nobility under Louis XIII, became the chosen quarter of the *noblesse de robe*, a great many of whom lived in Paris. Many members of the lower aristocracy who could not afford, or did not like, the more fashionable new districts also lived here. Mercier considered residents of the Marais to be especially conservative:

> The Marais is to the magnificent Palais-Royal what Vienna is to London. Though you find no poverty here, there is quite a concentration of all the old prejudices, brought along by those who are not really wealthy. Here you have the old argumentative types, the sworn enemies of all new ideas. These rather opinionated judges criticize authors they have only heard of and describe the philosophes as people who ought to be burnt.[30]

Other sections of Paris, though, remained very much as they had been in the Middle Ages, and reflected the trades practiced by their inhabitants. The unique character of the food markets of Les Halles was preserved until the 1970s; goldsmiths had their shops in the heart of the city, along the quai des Orfèvres and in the place Dauphine on the Ile de la Cité. The actual business center of Paris, however, lay to the east of Les Halles, in an area bounded by the rue des Lombards, the rue Saint-Denis, and the rue des Gravilliers. People who worked at home for the textile industry also lived here. Around the Hôtel de Ville and the place de Grève one found porters, dockers, and seasonal laborers. The furniture industry was concentrated in the faubourg Saint-Antoine, as were some breweries and a glass factory that employed several hundred individuals between them. An even more varied scene, involving all sorts of small trades, characterized the faubourg Saint-Marcel and the adjoining faubourgs of Saint-Jacques and Saint-Victor. The reason was that any craft or trade could be practiced there without the guild membership or qualifications required in the inner city. But the consequent overcrowding in the various trades led to great poverty in these districts. By far the largest amount of welfare relief distributed during the Old Regime and the Revolution went to the poor of these suburbs.[31]

Despite the feverish building activity of the final decades of the Old Regime, medieval Paris was on the whole preserved in a state that was not to alter radically until the Second Empire. There were earlier changes, to be sure, but these were largely due to growth and expansion across the Paris basin. The hills of Ménilmont, Belleville, and the Buttes-Chaumont surrounding Paris were not developed until the nineteenth century. The appearance of Paris from Montmartre has been described by Friedrich Schulz, who was there at the outbreak of the Revolution:

> From up here, to right and left and as far as the eye can see, you have roof upon roof, gable upon gable. The highest towers emerge like chimneys from this roofed-over area. You cannot tell one street from another, or recognize any squares, or distinguish any of the palaces. It is a connected surface of tiles on which, or so it appears, one could walk as on an immense terrace, and through which a stream has been diverted that one could easily leap across. In the fore-

ground the whole view descends to the Seine and then rises up again beyond it like an amphitheater. It is encircled and ornamented by hills—some small, some large—that are partly decorated with windmills, summer residences, or woods, and are partly bare and barren.[32]

Construction of a wall that would encircle Paris was begun in 1784; it was known as the wall of the *fermiers-généraux*, or tax farmers [the financiers who purchased from the government the concession—or "farm"—to collect the taxes]. Its dimensions give us a rough idea of the overall size of Paris at that time: it was eighteen miles long and ten feet high, and linked fifty-four municipal customs posts. In the reign of Louis XIII the city limits had followed a line marked by the inner boulevards; however, the Tax Farmers' Wall also enclosed certain suburbs, making them part of Paris in matters of taxation. To the south on the Left Bank, these included the old faubourgs of Saint-Victor, Saint-Marcel, Saint-Jacques, Saint-Michel, and Saint-Germain; in the west it took in the villages of Passy and Chaillot; in the north the suburbs of Saint-Martin and Saint-Denis; and the faubourg Saint-Antoine to the east.[33] Moreover, the wall also included areas that were at a considerable distance beyond the city's building limits: in this way fields, gardens, vegetable patches, and huge uncultivated sections were added to the actual area of the city.[34]

The main purpose of the wall was not to define the city limits with an eye to future growth, but to increase existing tax revenues and cut off smuggling.[35] This measure, dictated by the crown's chronic shortage of money, proved fatal to the Old Regime. Until then, residents of the faubourgs paid fewer duties and taxes than the citizens of Paris. Now they were taxed at the same rates which, along with the great economic crisis, plunged an increasingly large number of them into what they considered unbearable misery. The building of the wall united the faubourgs and the city in their resistance to the Old Regime even before the Revolution began: "*Le mur murant Paris rend Paris murmurant*" (The wall around Paris makes Paris complain), as the saying went.[36] The *Parlement* of Paris [i.e., the city's royal court of justice] kept condemning the illegality of these new customs posts at the city boundaries and those who shaped public opinion voiced their criticism more and more harshly. Together with the *peuple* who were burdened by the increased taxation, they formed a coalition of the discontented. This was the force behind the revolutionary storm that was gathering over the royal government's ineffectual economic policy. Even prior to the attack on the Bastille on July 14, 1789, forty of the fifty-four customs posts were set on fire and destroyed by the mob.[37]

While the wall represented a geographically exact demarcation of the city limits shortly before the Revolution, only an approximate estimate can be given of the city's population. Estimates vary from a low of 524,186 to a high of 800,000, a figure that is surely exaggerated.[38] Necker's 1784 estimate of 640,000 to 680,000 is probably closest to the actual figure.[39] Privileged or propertied members of society represented only a small part of these figures.

The First Estate—the clergy—numbered around 10,000 in Paris in the middle of the eighteenth century. The aristocracy—including all family members—comprised no more than 5,000 individuals, and the bourgeois and their families amounted to 40,000.[40] Thus the majority of the inhabitants of Paris of those times, 600,000 people, belonged to the lower and even very lowest social strata.

Great discrepancies characterized the social structure of Paris, organized as it was according to the system of Estates. But the class differences only became defined as opposing political views in the course of the Revolution. One extreme was the decadent luxury of the Palais-Royal, the elegance displayed on the boulevards and promenades, the elaborate and beautiful new residential sections to the west of the old city. The other consisted of malodorous, dark, damp, and overcrowded alleys and neighborhoods in the city center, choked with dirt and trash, and the depressing suburbs that resounded with the noise of workshops, and were polluted by the fumes of forges and boiling-houses. Foreigners coming to Paris for the first time were deeply impressed by the stark contrasts, the juxtaposition of wealth and poverty, and the clash of the beautiful and the ugly. Looking out over Paris from the Tuileries terrace, Karamzin wrote:

> You ascend to the vast terrace and look to right and left. You see enormous buildings everywhere, palaces, churches, the beautiful banks of the Seine with its granite bridges over which thousands of people swarm and scores of coaches rumble. You look at everything and ask: What is Paris? Clearly it is not enough to call it the first city in the world, the capital of splendor and enchantment. Stop here, if you do not wish to change your opinion, for if you go farther you will see crowded streets, and an outrageous confusion of wealth and poverty. Close by a glittering jewelry shop lies a pile of rotten apples and herrings; filth is everywhere and even blood streaming from the butchers' stalls.[41] You must hold your nose and close your eyes. The picture of a splendid city grows dim in your thoughts, and it seems to you that the dirt and muck of all the cities in the world is flowing through the sewers of Paris. Take but one more step, and suddenly the fragrance of happy Arabia or, at least, Provence's flowering meadows, is wafted to you, for you have come to one of the many shops where perfume and pommades are sold. In a word, every step brings a new atmosphere, new objects of luxury or the most loathsome filth. Thus you must call Paris the most magnificent and most vile, the most fragrant and the most fetid city.[42]

Hygienic conditions were worst in the medieval center of Paris, with its twisting streets, filth, poverty, stench, and overcrowding. Restif de la Bretonne described the *Cité* as "barbaric and gothic," and felt it resembled "a tangled labyrinth" rather than a city.[43] In the market of Les Halles and around the old Hôtel de Ville every available square foot of ground had been covered. The houses there had been patched, added on to, and built up over the centuries.[44] Tiny shops were squeezed into the ground floors of narrow houses. Behind them, facing the dark inner courtyards, there was often another small shop bathed in half-light, next to which were warehouses and storage areas. In the back of one of these inner courtyards, there was often yet another building just like the one in front. The houses in the rear generally towered over the ground levels, creating pitch black passages and corridors, culs-de-sac that ended in rank darkness. The rue Mouffetard and the rue Quincampoix, for instance, were flanked by dark, dank mazes like these. Light, air, and cleanliness were absent. All human activities took place in these narrow areas and limited spaces: work, eating and drinking, and sleeping. Large families were herded together in the smallest of spaces—such as rooms made by partitioning off part of an attic with a few boards. Buildings housed up to four tenants on each floor, with the main tenant leasing space to a subtenant, the subtenant in his turn leasing to another, and so on.[45] Several men—usually seasonal workers, unmarried masons, porters, or apprentices— would share one of the *chambres garnies*, the dirty, flea-ridden furnished rooms in boardinghouses. These were mostly located in the rue de la Mortellerie near the Hôtel de Ville, or in the rue Garlande and rue des Jardins not far from Notre Dame.

The shocking account given by Mercier of the rue du Pied-de-Boeuf provides some idea of the horrible conditions in the center of Paris:

> Compare the rue du Pied-de-Boeuf, which lies in the center of Paris, with neat streets like the rues Saint-Honoré, Saint-Antoine, or Saint-Louis-au-Marais: it is by far the worst-smelling place in the whole world. There is a courthouse, the Grand-Châtelet; beyond it are dark cavernous structures and the tumult of a dirty market. Adjoining that is a building where the decaying corpses retrieved from the Seine or the city environs are stored. Then there is a prison, a butcher shop, and a slaughterhouse; all these form a polluted and filthy row of houses where the Pont-au-Change begins. Coaches wanting to get from this bridge, lined with dilapidated houses, to the rue Saint-Denis, need to make a detour through an alley which has a reeking sewer running down it. The rue du Pied-de-Boeuf lies opposite this sewer and has a number of dirty little alleys branching off it that are soaked in the blood of slaughtered animals. Some of this collects in puddles, the rest trickles down to the Seine in small rivulets. A pestilential stench always hangs over this area, and the miasma that rises from this small alley near the Pont Notre-Dame and the rue de la Planche-Mibray is so stifling that one has to hold one's breath and pass through quickly.[46]

Mercier belonged to the minority that was shocked by these disgusting conditions and demanded change.[47] Most of the others had long taken them for granted; in fact respect for tradition, as questionable or unbearable as it might become, was one of the most important characteristics of the Old Regime. This shows an increasing structural weakness in the absolute monarchy, a fatal inability to initiate necessary reforms in time. The monarchy was encouraged in its undiscerning attitude by all those who stood to gain from leaving things as they were, especially the two privileged Estates, the clergy and the nobility.

For instance, the clergy, which owned considerable property that it was unwilling to give up, blocked all attempts by Louis XV to rehabilitate the inner city so as to create more light and air by building new streets and squares. Such modifications would also have eliminated the worst of the obstacles that prevented efficient circulation of traffic, especially in an east-west direction.[48] But it proved impossible to make any changes until the Revolution, when all the property held by the church was confiscated. The monarchy showed similar consideration for owners of private property. If a house collapsed or was destroyed by fire, the occasion was rarely used to improve the cluttered condition of the area by putting a street through it; property owners were merely obliged to observe the building line when replacing the structure.[49]

This sort of consideration was given property owners by the royal administration because no laws existed for the expropriation of private holdings, even when it was in the public interest. Furthermore, ownership of property in the medieval center of Paris was as difficult to disentangle as the arrangement of the houses themselves.[50] It made compensation to individual owners an expensive matter, for which there was no money in the royal treasury.[51] There was an additional factor that always influenced the crown's political attitude toward Paris: it feared that any change would cause unrest that would be difficult to stop. A major rehabilitation of inner-city neighborhoods would immediately present the enormous task of transferring the many people who lived and worked there. This problem was more than the Old Regime could begin to handle and was only solved—in a brutal if effective manner—during the Second Empire.

The Gradual Discovery of Hygiene

*T*HE SAINTS-INNOCENTS CEMETERY was an example of the difficulties faced by the Old Regime. While the government was aware of the urgent need for improving the foul living conditions in the overcrowded inner city neighborhoods, it also recognized that any measures undertaken would conflict with age-old religious customs and habits.[52] During the Old Regime, burial was the exclusive concern of the church. However, the establishment of new cemeteries by no means kept pace with the continuous growth in the population of Paris. Since the Middle Ages it was customary to bury people inside the churches or in the adjacent churchyards. One can therefore assume that by the end of the eighteenth century the number of cemeteries corresponded to the 200 churches then in existence.[53] Actual burial space, though, was very limited, as churches and cemeteries were squeezed in among the maze of houses. Additional space could only have been gained by sacrificing what was needed by the living.

This highly obnoxious system of packing the living and the dead so closely together produced the most macabre analogies. In overpopulated sections of the city cemeteries were also overcrowded; hence it is not surprising that trade and commerce in those areas eventually spilled over onto the small open spaces intended for the dead. For instance, public scribes conducted their business in the Saints-Innocents charnel house, the largest Parisian cemetery in the the hub of the city, right by the markets.[54] Charlatans, quacks, peddlers, secondhand dealers, prostitutes, and hawkers also plied their trades there.

In these cemeteries, the dead were normally buried in mass graves, the *fosses communes*. Since only very few people could afford coffins, the naked corpses were wrapped in sheets before the undertaker and his assistant laid them side by side in the trench and covered them with a shovelful of quicklime.[55] Once a horizontal row was filled, it was covered with a layer of earth in the expectation that the corpses would decompose within a week; then the next row would be set out, and so on until the mass grave—the largest of which were filled with up to 1,500 corpses—could be closed off with a mound of earth. Mass graves that were not yet completely full were temporarily covered with wooden planks, which did not prevent the sickly odor of decaying bodies from seeping through the thin layer of earth and permeating the cemetery as well as the surrounding area. Once all the graves were filled the oldest ones were excavated, skeletons were transferred to charnel houses, and the burial process could begin all over again.

The unavoidably overcrowded condition of inner-city cemeteries soon had some serious consequences. This was especially the case in Saints-Innocents, which had to accommodate around 3,000 corpses each year in its limited space of about 68,000 square feet.[56] Petitions for the elimination of these intolerable conditions were made to the authorities as early as the beginning of the eighteenth century.[57] However, the growing protest had little effect because, as Mercier pointed out, "these deplorable conditions are so closely linked to, and deeply rooted in, religious practices that even the law could not immediately put an end to it."[58] Mercier was referring to two acts passed by the *Parlement* of Paris. The first of these was based on a report by the *premier avocat général* (principal attorney general), Le Peletier de Saint-Fargeau, dated March 12, 1763, and states:

> Several cemeteries that formerly caused no unhealthy conditions are now doing so to an unprecedented degree. Their stifling vapors were previously dissipated by the circulation of air; today they are surrounded by houses that prevent such circulation and cause a concentration of the vapors.[59]

These conclusions prompted an investigation of all Paris cemeteries.[60] After considering this report, the *Parlement* issued a second decree, stating that as of January 1, 1766, there were to be no more interments in inner-city cemeteries, with the exception of distinguished people. The ruling also stipulated that eight spacious burial sites be established outside the city limits. At first this turned out to be ineffective as it continued to be difficult to overcome ingrained customs.[61]

But these two decrees did focus public concern on the issue. The authorities managed to put an end to one of the worst problems by closing the Saints-Innocents, complaints and protests by area residents at last having had some effect. The *Lieutenant général de police* made the following report to the *Parlement on* December 5, 1780:

> In May of last year the condition of the Saints-Innocents cemetery caused residents of neighboring houses to complain. Reports as well as inspection at that time determined that the cellars of these houses were filled with a pestilential odor, endangering workers who had to go in there. It finally became quite impossible to enter the cellars and retrieve goods stored there, because the suffocating atmosphere extinguished any lit torches.[62]

The closing of the Saints-Innocents was ordered by the *Parlement* on September 4, 1780; no further burials were permitted as of November 1 of that year.[63] Parishes affected by this ruling had difficulty finding alternate burial space within the allotted time; so the *Parlement* had to extend the period to December 1. It was obvious that this problem could not be resolved in so short a period. According to the same police report, three of the twenty parishes that had used the Saints-Innocents buried their dead in the "Caveau Cul-de-Sac de Sainte-Marie"; three other parishes used their respective churches, and four additional parishes shared the "Chapelle basse de Saint-Luc."

Still, the closing of Saints-Innocents had set an example. In 1781 the cemeteries of the Chaussée d'Antin (Saint-Roch), of the rue Saint-Joseph (Saint-Eustache) and of Saint-Sulpice were closed, as was the burial site on the Ile Saint-Louis in 1782. Other existing cemeteries, like the Clamart cemetery on the Left Bank, were enlarged and new ones were opened outside the building limits of Paris, such as the Vaugirard cemetery in 1784, or the Sainte-Marguerite cemetery at the foot of Montmartre in 1787.[64]

Once the Saints-Innocents was closed, it took another five years before the archbishop of Paris gave his formal consent to the secularization of the area.[65] Only then was a complete clearing of the cemetery possible; the skeletons of those buried there were exhumed and transported to the catacombs located in the south of Paris. The work was begun in December 1785 and took until January 1788 with some interruptions.[66]

If the Saints-Innocents stood for the medieval city, then the Palais-Royal symbolized the new Paris. Between them they expressed the radically different concepts and contrasting social worlds characteristic of Paris on the eve of the Revolution. In his twelve-volume work *Le Tableau de Paris*, Louis-Sébastien Mercier, that tireless stroller, faithfully described all the incongruities of Paris in those days: the confusion of light and dark, splendor and dirt, wealth and misery, greatness and provinciality. It has frequently been said that his description of Paris was highly unsystematic; that it was really nothing more than a collection of haphazard impressions and arbitrarily arranged notes. But that is precisely what gives it its substance and authenticity. For his much-criticized unsystematic approach faithfully reflected the city's diversity as he saw it. His testimony was definitely subjective; his judgment was based on a philosophy of enlightenment aimed at making practical improvements. No doubt he exaggerated a great deal and was biased—

still, Mercier's account provides an almost cinematic rendition, *avant la lettre,* of prerevolutionary Paris.

It was not by chance that Mercier kept coming back to the topic of public hygiene—the ubiquitous dirt, stench of excrement, and decaying refuse. For although the closing of the Saints-Innocents meant that one of the most serious problems was solved, other, far worse conditions persisted.

The vehemence with which Mercier kept attacking inadequate hygiene reflected an almost hysterical sensitivity to the odors and vapors that rose up continuously from the ground. The stench polluting the air was acknowledged not so much because it bothered people but because it was considered to be exceedingly hazardous to life and health. Until Pasteur's and Koch's research into bacteria as carriers of disease in the last third of the nineteenth century, bad odors and polluted air were thought to cause all sorts of sicknesses.[67] According to some observers, the reek of decay emanating from Saints-Innocents undoubtedly caused food to spoil in adjacent houses; it was thought to be responsible for everything from the rusting of metal to the loss of good looks on the part of young girls living there. Areas like cemeteries, knacker's yards, sewers, cesspools, latrines, hospitals, prisons, butcher shops, and fish markets, as well as marshes and stagnant water—in short, anything emitting odors of greater or lesser intensity—were considered dangerous and health-threatening.[68]

In the course of the eighteenth century doctors and chemists developed a number of strategies to combat the threat of polluting vapors. These were publicized by men like Mercier and were part of official regulations. Their common purpose was to seal off the sources of the stench; or else to move problem-producing sites outside the city gates to avoid contamination of the atmosphere in urban residential neighborhoods.[69] Preventive actions included the "privatization of excrement" by means of toilets and cesspools inside the houses; the closing of inner-city cemeteries; and the paving over of streets and squares (to stop vapors rising up from the polluted ground) as well as their constant cleaning with water.

One great obstacle to the success of this preventive hygiene was a highly inadequate water supply. There were no springs in the city because the Paris basin was covered with a thick layer of porous chalk. The greater part of the population therefore had to obtain its drinking and household water from the Seine, either drawn directly from the river or from artesian wells that could easily be dug close by. With few exceptions, the public wells—about fifty-six of them were scattered throughout Paris—were also supplied with water from the Seine, brought by old-fashioned pumps located in the Samaritaine near the Pont Neuf. However, Mercier maintained that most of these public wells were dry for half of the year.[70] The water had to be brought to those households that could afford such modest luxuries by water-carriers, who hung buckets on a yoke across their shoulders and charged a sou per bucket. Mercier estimated the number of water-carriers in Paris to be between 12,000 and 15,000.[71]

A decisive step was taken to improve the water-supply system in 1781, when the Compagnie des Eaux de Paris, a joint-stock company, was founded by the Périer brothers. Two steam engines drove the water pumps—installed near Chaillot—that delivered Seine water free of coarse particles to individual households through a network of conduits.[72] Ironically, however, it was not the pollution of the Seine that disturbed eighteenth-century experts on hygiene, but rather they looked with suspicion on the notion that availability of water in some way could help prevent pollution.[73] The connection between the quality of drinking water and repeated outbreaks of cholera in nineteenth-century Paris was not made until after 1892.

It was also very characteristic that obsessions with hygiene in the late eighteenth century were closely linked to social fears. The new sensitivity to odors and rank vapors was an expression of social status. The bourgeoisie's disgust with refuse contrasted with the indifference of the working class, which lived its whole life in filth. In his *Lettre sur les moyens d'amener l'eau à Paris*, the chemist Lavoisier notes:

> It is frightening to realize that by far the greatest number of Parisians are supplied with water from the river, brought by carriers on their shoulders or on carts; there can be little doubt that such a shortage of water is the decisive factor in keeping the working class in its filthy condition, which in turn contributes considerably to the unhealthy air in the capital.[74]

Fresh water was an expensive luxury and a daily bucket of the Périer brothers' drinking water cost 50 livres a year, a sum that very few households could afford.[75] Still there were enough of them for the Compagnie des Eaux de Paris to become an economic success.[76]

Refuse and sewage also presented problems. Household refuse was collected by trash carts several times a week; animal cadavers and the offal from butcher shops and slaughterhouses were gathered by knackers concentrated around Montfaucon.[77] Residents were required to sweep the street in front of their houses every morning, and to refrain from emptying chamber pots out of the windows; they were also forbidden to block the sewers running down the middle of the street with rubbish heaps. Especially severe penalties awaited those who connected residential latrines and cesspools to the city's drains.[78]

However, practically all these regulations were ignored. Animal cadavers, and even sections of human corpses used in anatomy classes, were simply thrown into the Seine, and houses situated along underground sewers that were not opened frequently connected their cesspools to them. Mercier claimed that this abuse was normal procedure for houses above the city's large subterranean sewer, the Egout Turgot.[79] Residential cesspools were frequently in bad condition; their fecal content seeped into nearby artesian wells, from which bakeries drew their water.[80] Regulations were also broken quite often when cesspools had to be emptied, a task that had to be completed at night. As Mercier notes,

> to save themselves the labor of carting the excrement outside the city, the sewage collectors dumped their carts into the sewers and gutters at daybreak. This awful mess then made its way slowly down to the Seine, polluting the banks along

which the water-carriers fill their buckets in the morning; this was the water insensitive Parisians then had to drink.[81]

The unbelievable sanitary arrangements inside the houses are also described by Mercier:

> Three quarters of all the toilets are filthy, horrible, and disgusting; but the eyes and sense of smell of Parisians are thoroughly used to that. The narrow and interlocking structure of the houses forced builders to install the sewage pipes haphazardly; hence nothing shocks a foreigner more than the sight of an amphitheater of toilets, one on top of another out on the landings, next to the apartment doors and right by the kitchens, which emit an unbearable odor. . . . The pipes are much too narrow and easily get clogged up; they are not cleaned; the excrement becomes piled up until it reaches the toilet seats; the overloaded pipes burst; the houses get flooded; the odor spreads everywhere but no one seems to care: Parisian noses are completely insensitive to such poisonous emanations.[82]

Street Life

ALL OF PARIS was filled with the stench of human excretions. In the summer the penetrating odor of stale urine polluted the Palais-Royal gardens; sludge and fecal matter piled up as people relieved themselves in the avenues, along the boulevards, by the customs posts, and even in coaches and hackneys.[83] Strolling in the more than 950 inner-city streets and alleys of Paris required the greatest dexterity; the ground was entirely covered with animal or human feces, and murky puddles of water and excrement collected everywhere. Despite the 900,000 francs allocated annually by the royal administration for maintaining the public streets and squares, Paris was considerably dirtier in 1783 than it had been earlier.[84]

These observations by Mercier were confirmed by various other travelers who were present in Paris on the eve of the Revolution. Arthur Young, an Englishman, notes on October 27, 1787:

> The streets are very narrow and a great many of them are overloaded with traffic; in nine out of ten streets you sink into excrement and dirt, and none of them have any kind of pavement.[85] The promenading that is so agreeable and done without any qualms in London, where even ladies are able to indulge in this pleasure, demands effort and exertion from a man over here and is quite out of the question for a well-dressed woman.[86]

Friedrich Schulz mentions similar experiences:

> But even the wider and more elegant streets in the center of the city, though quite spacious, are perpetually covered in dark black sludge which is less hazardous when it rains than when the sun has dried it to a certain consistency. It

then becomes impossible to find firm ground and you are always forced back into the middle of the street, where puddles—some small, some larger—are constantly stirred up as hackney upon hackney, and cart upon cart roll or bump through them.[87]

In rainy weather the sewers, known as *ruisseaux*, turned into wide, racing streams in the middle of the streets. They were fed by cascades falling steadily from waterspouts high up on the buildings.[88] Whenever someone had to cross from one side of the street to the other in such weather, he either had to risk a daring leap or wait until one of the many rogues or panhandlers came rushing over with a wooden plank, which the pedestrian could use as a bridge and for which he had to pay 1 sou. As if this were not awkward enough, the situation was made downright life-threatening by the busy traffic of coaches, carts, and light carriages that rattled through the streets day and night. "There are a great many vehicles," Arthur Young remarks,

> and the worst thing is the tremendous number of one-horse carriages driven by young fops (and others who emulate them and are no less dangerous fools), at such breakneck speed that they are a real menace and extremely dangerous for any pedestrian not constantly on the lookout. I witnessed a child being run over and probably killed, and was myself frequently splashed with sludge from the sewer.[89]

The dirt to which helpless pedestrians were exposed in Parisian streets created a separate trade: the *décrotteurs*, itinerant boot-scrapers and clothes-cleaners. They were generally to be seen on the Pont Neuf; some of them also knew how to trim the dogs fashionable women liked to take for walks.[90] The miserable condition of the capital's streets helped the hackney business to flourish as well.[91]

All the hazards and dangers that threatened pedestrians by day in the narrow, dirty, and traffic-laden streets became much worse at night, though by the end of the Old Regime street lighting had been considerably improved. In fact in 1782 Mercier remarked that oil lamps had replaced the former inadequate candle lanterns as of 1766, and noted that their brightness was considerably increased by polished reflectors. At the very least each shed a strong even light on the area immediately around it. However, the new system was still marked by considerable inefficiency. The more than 8,000 streetlights were lit each evening when it grew dark and extinguished at dawn the next morning. This procedure and other aspects of streetlight maintenance were put into the hands of a private company by the royal administration in 1789.[92]

Lack of adequate street lighting led to the formation of a separate trade known as the *falots* (lantern-carriers), who accompanied and provided light for pedestrians at night in return for a small fee. Mercier describes the *falots'* service as

> useful and secure for anyone returning home late at night; the lantern-carrier accompanies a person to his house, and to his apartment even if it is on the seventh floor, and lights the customer's candles if he has no servants, or if he lacks

matches or tinder—not unusual among those bachelors who frequent the theaters and stroll along the boulevards. Moreover, lantern-carriers scare off thieves
and for that reason are no less welcome to the public than are the police
patrols.[93]

No matter what time of day or night it was, or what the weather was like,
Paris streets were anything but a pleasant place for a leisurely stroller. That
alone accounts for the great throngs in the Palais-Royal by the end of the Old
Regime, and explains why the arcades and covered galleries that came into
existence at the beginning of the nineteenth century were so popular. People
could walk about there and be protected from rain and downspouts, or the
contents of chamber pots, and not be bothered by the traffic of coaches and
carriages; nor did they run the risk of having their clothes or even their health
ruined; above all, they could be part of a social group less motley than that
in the streets.

The diversity of the people; the professions and trades practiced on the
streets, whose number and complexity are vividly conveyed by illustrations
depicting the street criers of the times; the markets and booths; the calls with
which goods and services were offered and which rose to a clamorous
cacophony at certain particularly busy and sought-after corners and squares;
the shapes and colorful variety of goods for sale that competed with the fanciful and grotesque shop signs—all of this was part of the street experience
of the period. Trading, haggling, measuring out, cheating, arguing, and
shouting went on in just about every Paris street, except for those in the elegant and quiet sections in the west and south of the city. Paris was one gigantic bazaar, in which every square was a market, and no building respected.
Mercier reports, for instance, that a secondhand market had even established
itself in the place du Louvre, along the base of the majestic columned facade,
and was doing a brisk trade in used clothing and rags.[94]

Such secondhand markets were scattered over the entire area of the inner
city. Booths selling used clothes were set up under the arcades of the old markets; in the place de Grève a market known as the *Foire du Saint-Esprit* was
held every Monday and was devoted to the sale of women's and children's
clothing. "It is said," writes Mercier,

> that this market sells clothing that had once belonged to the women of an
> entire province, or was the booty of a tribe of Amazons. Petticoats, hooped
> skirts, house dresses are all mixed up or set out in a large pile in which you can
> rummage to your heart's content. Here is a sumptuous dress of the deceased wife
> of a presiding judge, which is bought by a public prosecutor's spouse; over there
> a *grisette*—a young shop girl—adorns herself with a bonnet that had been worn
> by the chambermaid of a marquise. Clothes are tried on in full view of the
> public. . . . [95]

The sale of used clothing was also the preferred trade of the markets in
the rue Tirechappe, and of the booths along the quai de la Feraille, as well
as on the Pont Neuf. "You see," Mercier comments,

just as in nature's eternal cycle, nothing is wasted in Paris. The most trivial of items—be it a torn slip, a pair of pantaloons full of holes, or an old down-at-heel shoe—does not simply disappear without a trace; nothing is wasted; there is always someone who likes these things and whom they fit as if they were made to measure.[96]

But not only used clothing was traded on the streets; whatever was left over or discarded from the tables of the rich was sold to others: the kitchen boys from wealthy houses delivered these leftovers to the *regrattiers*, as they were known, who sold them to the poor and the hungry.[97]

Although the dealers in used clothing and *regrattiers* were set up in permanent locations, other *métiers de la rue*, or street trades, were to be found everywhere: the roast-chestnut and doughnut vendors, and those selling brandy or coffee, all of whom carried small stoves on which they prepared these products. Knife-grinders offered their services, as did quacks and extractors of teeth; others dealt in fish, oysters, vegetables, flowers, and fruits, or sold combs and children's toys. Ragmen carried large baskets on their backs; men who bought up rabbit skins were hidden under their burden. According to Mercier, the latter were surrounded by a rankness that heralded their approach even before their hoarse, throaty call "*peaux de lapins*" (rabbit skins), could be heard.[98] These were all as much part of the street scene as those who sold hats or went door to door with a small barrel of vinegar on a handcart. Water-carriers, coalmen and porters, chimneysweeps, and wig-barbers hurried to their customers' houses; pastry-shop delivery boys balanced cakes on their heads, while waiters carried trays with coffee or lemonade through the streets. Together they created the rhythm of this Parisian street symphony that continually prompted visitors to describe its rich variety.

All goods and services were announced by special street cries. Each trade had an unmistakable call, modulated in different keys, with varying cadences and pitch, now ceremonially slow like an adagio, now fast and hasty, resembling an allegro—sounds that merged with the noise and multitudinous shouts resounding in the narrow streets and squares. Only occasionally did the gloomy, attention-claiming voice of a public crier break through the clamor with any clarity, as he announced a recently decreed death sentence. Blended into this chaotic portrait in sound were the mournful voices of the blind of the Quinze-Vingts Society who sang religious songs at carriage entrances, the sad litanies of penitents walking behind a cross, the tunes played by itinerant musicians, or the declamations of groups reciting ballads and stories. Finally, and at first barely discernible in this pandemonium, there were the ubiquitous beggars and streetwalkers who leaned against houses and squatted in various recesses and corners, persecuted by the police with unrelenting severity; with their quiet plaintive voices they also tried to attract the attention of passersby.[99]

In addition to the daily confusion and cacophony, Parisian streets were occasionally the stage for special events: funerals of important and influential personalities with all the ponderous and somber splendor such a ceremony merited, or church processions that displayed hardly less lavish ritual. The annual procession of the Knights of the Holy Sepulcher was a curious event, during which debtors who had been redeemed from prison were led through the streets. An even stranger and rarer spectacle, seen only once every thirty years, was the procession of those who had been freed from imprisonment or enslavement by the Moors through charitable contributions. Three hundred and thirteen freedmen participated in the last of these processions on October 19, 1785.[100]

The greatest number of pageant-watchers and curiosity-seekers lined the streets of Paris when the king and queen, coming from Versailles, made their ceremonial entry into Paris. On these occasions the whole court ritual was played out in all its extravagant splendor; the long succession of state carriages surrounded by mounted guards and liveried lackeys drove past the gaping populace that lined the streets.

Still another scene, though horrifying when compared with the rest, was equally irresistible to the crowds. This was the public executions, in which delinquents were guillotined, broken on the wheel, or drawn and quartered, and which took place in the place de Grève in the city center. Shoulder to shoulder, in uneasy suspense, the people followed every move made by the executioner and his assistants as they went about their harrowing task. Once it was accomplished and death had finally released the guilty man from his dreadful torture, the executioner—"*le grand acteur tragique pour la populace*" (a great tragic actor in the eyes of the people)—washed his bloody hands, descended from the platform, and disappeared into the crowd of onlookers who slowly emerged from their trance.[101]

The Estates

*T*HE EBB AND FLOW of people in the streets and squares varied according to the time of day and location. A careful observer could therefore come to certain conclusions about the complex social division of Parisians on the eve of the Revolution. Indeed Mercier has left a highly typological but charming account of what he witnessed on workdays and holidays.[102]

Princes of the blood and the wealthy old nobility formed the uppermost layer of Parisian society. Members of the *noblesse de robe* also belonged to this group, especially those who were judges or presidents of one of the *cours souveraines*, the royal high courts of Paris. By and large these important positions had, over several generations, been allocated to a few families frequently allied to the *noblesse d'epée* (the old aristocracy) by marriage.

The line dividing the aristocracy and the *noblesse de robe* from the Parisian upper bourgeoisie was rather vague and fluid, especially as many of the latter managed to buy their way into the nobility. With the acquisition of a noble property, it was also possible to usurp its feudal title. Thus the former court banker Jean-Joseph de la Borde had the titles vidame de Chartres, marquis de la Borde, and baron vicomte et haut châtelain de Méréville, and was moreover seigneur of several other domains; his daughters had all married into the old aristocracy. Certain successful lawyers and notaries, doctors, scientists, artists, and writers joined this rather small upper bourgeois group of bankers and financiers. They were eligible because of their extravagant life-style, or on account of their intellect and intelligence, both of which gave them access to the literary salons of the times where "good society" gathered.

Nor were the distinctions between the upper bourgeoisie and the middle layer, the *bourgeoisie des affaires*, very clear. The very complex relationship of the aristocracy and upper bourgeoisie to the middle bourgeoisie, that "group of honorable, professional people whom neither wealth nor poverty have corrupted," as a brochure entitled *Le Paris d'aujourdhui* put it in 1789, was of great importance for future events.[103] The interconnection was expressed in all sorts of common business, political, and social interests. Members of the middle class—most lawyers, notaries, doctors, and pharmacists, middle-level functionaries in administrative offices and ministries, writers and journalists, book dealers, printers and publishers, painters, sculptors, and architects, in short all who had a higher education and a guaranteed income—took as their social model those in the level above them. They could strive to attain that level by hard work, talent, useful marriages, or the acquisition of a position with a hereditary title.[104] Their interests, education, and openness to new ideas and projects, their relatively large number, and their key positions in society prepared members of this middle layer for an active and self-confident role in the great social upheaval of the Revolution.

Moreover, lack of specific social barriers permitted members of this ambitious middle class to look for support from either the upper class or the great mass of the petite bourgeoisie—whichever circumstances or tactical considerations demanded—in the pursuit of their political, social, and economic mobility. The intellectual leaders of the Revolution all came from this middle class—men like Danton, Marat, Robespierre, and Desmoulins who initiated the Revolution in Paris by the spoken or printed word and who eventually guided events in a direction far removed from that envisaged by their original allies, the liberal aristocracy and the upper bourgeoisie.

Besides belonging to various clubs and academies, members of these social strata met and associated with one another in literary salons and gatherings. Heinrich Jacob Meister, a Swiss clergyman who worked as a private tutor in Paris for a few years prior to the Revolution, nostalgically recalls the "charms of this society that no longer exists and that most probably will never be reconstituted in the same way anywhere else"; and he notes that

at least in Paris all privileges of rank, estate, or birth were considered less important in social intercourse than whether a person was amiable. It was enough to
demonstrate this one attribute to be admitted to the most elegant circles and
be accepted there in a most flattering manner. At these gatherings one met . . .
people of every rank, all of whom were treated as equals as long as they were
equally interesting or knew how to please.[105]

The salons and gatherings of Mmes Helvétius, Suard, de Condorcet, or
Necker were famous, and the *gens à talents*, the intellectual elite of which
there were a goodly number, met there to discuss their theories and exchange
their literary, philosophical, and political points of view. Meister recalled that
"one of the most noteworthy advantages of these societies . . . was that those
who wanted to succeed were forced to use a language understood by everyone, so that their work and intentions were made clear enough to enrich the
general conversation."[106]

It is not without a certain irony that it was in these salons and gatherings,
a sociocultural phenomenon that was in its decline by the end of the Old
Regime, that the rhetorical talents of the Revolution were given their final
polish. In his memoirs Jacques de Norvins quoted ironists who said, "Long
trousers and short waistcoats made the Revolution."[107]

But despite the interlocking network that linked members of individual
social groups to form the *Tout Paris*, the importance of social differences
could not be overlooked. This applied to distinctions between the aristocracy and the bourgeoisie, which continued to be characterized by established
privileges and order of rank. Even the richest banker could not expect to be
given a position reserved for the nobility. Although the bourgeoisie was by far
the most powerful class in terms of its economic, intellectual, and entrepreneurial resources, its expectations for further advancement were increasingly frustrated on the eve of the Revolution by the political barriers the Old
Regime continued to erect. Over and above these frustrations lay the serious economic and financial crisis of the Old Regime. True, the Estates
General were convened in Versailles, and the government appeared willing to
go along with certain reforms and the correction of some of the worst conditions. Such measures were advised by more moderate elements who hoped
to stave off the crisis. But they had precisely the opposite effect and provoked
the Revolution; the old order was overthrown by the working class, with the
intellectual guidance of a radical elite drawn from the bourgeoisie.

A contemporary writer characterizes the *peuple* in 1783 as "the lowest
level of the citizens, those who must work in order to live and who do menial
labor for wages."[108] This straightforward definition does not adequately
describe the intricate connections between the lower middle class and the
"Fourth Estate." Mercier categorizes the petite bourgeoisie as "the lowest
level [of that class] which is linked to the one below called *le petit peuple*—
the ordinary people—under which are the *populace* or common people."[109]
Independent artisans or proprietors of small businesses, though they owned
their materials and provided work for a few apprentices or employees, did the
same work and lived in conditions similar to those of their men. They were

therefore considered to be part of the same lower level of the working class.[110]

The *peuple*, the working class that earned its living manually, was by far the largest segment of the population of Paris; under the Old Regime no other city in the country had as great a concentration, and nowhere else was the difference between rich and poor as vast. The collapse of the economy in 1786 increased the steady stream of newcomers from the provinces who hoped to find work and food in Paris. This addition of uprooted individuals swelled the "Fourth Estate" to a disproportionate size; it enlarged the gray army of the unemployed: the beggars, the prostitutes, the poor and hungry, as well as the generally dissatisfied.[111]

Yet the *peuple* by no means constituted a homogeneous segment of the population, for it was itself broken up into a number of distinct categories. The social standing of a member of the *peuple* was determined by the trade he practiced, or the guild to which he belonged. It did not depend on the training he had received, or on the economic importance of that trade.[112] Nor was any distinction made between master and apprentice, a circumstance reflected by current usage which classified both of them as *ouvriers* or workers.[113]

The *ouvriers*, workers who were either masters or apprentices in a craft or trade that belonged to a guild, were distinct from the *manouvriers*, laborers who learned how to do certain jobs requiring no specialization. Next in descending order on the social ladder were the unskilled laborers, who earned their living as *hommes de peine et de main*—that is to say, those who did heavy labor and were wage earners independent of guilds or corporations.[114] Of even lesser account were domestic servants and lackeys, who were especially numerous in a city like Paris and whose status did not depend on that of the household in which they worked.[115] Finally, on the very lowest rung were the beggars, the unemployed, petty criminals, and prostitutes, individuals who had been forced out of the working class.[116]

The lower layer of society, which was quite separate from the Three Estates and itself divided into *peuple*, *populace*, and *canaille*, was permanently in fear of being overwhelmed by abject poverty. Workers earned a precarious living and that only by being perpetually overworked. As Mercier puts it:

> The traveler, who can judge better at first glance than can we whose impressions are dulled by familiarity, makes it very clear that the *peuple* of Paris are those who work the hardest and at the same time are the worst-nourished and the saddest sight of all those on earth. . . . The impoverished man in Paris, bowed by the eternal burden of his hard work, who erects, builds, and forges, who slaves in quarries or high up on roofs, who carries incredible loads, who is at the mercy of any powerful person, who is squashed like an insect the minute he opens his mouth, exerts himself by the sweat of his brow to gain his pittance—just about enough to live on but not enough to guarantee him a better lot in his old age.[117]

As a rule a working day lasted fourteen to sixteen hours. In the building trades it began at 5:00 A.M. in the summer months and did not end until 7:00 P.M., while in the winter it lasted from 6:00 A.M. to 8:00 P.M. Working conditions in the workshops and factories defied all description. Noise, heat, and stench prevailed. Mercier, who visited the royal mirror and glass factory in Paris, transmitted a horrifying picture of it, especially since the mercury fumes to which the workers were exposed quickly destroyed their health: "A very strong man can earn up to three livres a day when he first works there; but the same man loses half of his strength in six months as his health dwindles rapidly due to the murderous amount of work he has to complete each day, as well as to the unhealthy air he has to breathe."[118]

Two to 3 livres was the wage for a fourteen-to-sixteen-hour workday for comparatively less specialized workers such as masons, roofers, carpenters, and cabinetmakers. More specialized and qualified workers like the engravers or designers who worked in Réveillon's wallpaper factory, earned up to 6 livres a day, while goldsmiths and jewelers received a daily wage of up to 8 livres. Laborers and unskilled workers were condemned to starvation wages: in the building trades, which were still the best paid at the end of the Old Regime, unskilled workers made between 1 livre and 1 livre 15 sous a day.[119] Printers, foundrymen, and carpenters, in contrast, earned between 25 and 50 sous per day at Réveillon's, as against the 25 to 30 sous paid to porters, paint-mixers, packers, and cleaners; children between the ages of twelve and fifteen received only 8 to 15 sous for the same work.[120]

For the majority of Paris workers, whose nominal average daily wage was 1 livre, it was a hopeless situation, though understandable if one compares the cost of living with real wages.[121] According to estimates made by Ernest Labrousse, nominal wages rose an average 22 percent between 1726–41 and 1771–89, against a median price increase of 62 percent for basic foodstuffs, rent, heating, and light in the same period.[122] In other words, the poorer social groups had to contend with an ever-widening gap between wages and basic living expenses in the course of the eighteenth century—a disastrous condition that neither hard work nor thrift could improve.

A comparison between real wages and the price of bread makes it obvious that even those who worked and had a regular income were condemned to end in poverty sooner or later. Those who earned a nominal wage of 25 sous per day and worked for no more than 250 days annually had a real wage of 15 sous. The normal price for a four-pound loaf of bread, the staple diet of the lower classes, was 9 sous, so that it represented 60 percent of the real wage.[123] If the price of bread rose to 14 sous and 6 deniers (i.e., 14½ sous) because of a poor harvest or other crisis, as happened in the spring and summer of 1789, then no less than 97 percent of real wages had to be spent on its purchase.[124]

These few examples suggest the extent of the destitution that characterized late eighteenth-century Paris alongside the luxury flaunted by the rich. Sickness, loss of work, large families, or even a sudden increase in the price of bread sufficed to turn a worker into a beggar. The uncontainable spread of poverty robbed those who lived under its threat of all hope and crushed their feelings of self-esteem. Mercier expresses this in one sentence: "In London one refers to the majesty of the English people; in Paris, on the other hand, one does not know how to characterize the *peuple*."[125] Mercier's perplexity was significant; for neither the worsening economic crisis at the end of the Old Regime, nor the increase in the number of factory workers held to a rigidly uniform routine, produced anything like a collective consciousness. The reason for this lay in the absence of social cohesion among Parisian workers. The economic problems, which threatened all of them with dire poverty, gave them a certain social identity. But this was not as strong as their corporate identity, which had its roots in the traditional artisan mentality. This corporate yet extremely individualistic attitude grew out of the careful distinction still being made between "honorable" and "less honorable" trades. Spontaneous collective acts, like revolts caused by hunger, or strikes by individual branches of trades to protest further deterioration in their living conditions, were rare prior to 1789. It was customary, instead, for individuals to act separately and ensure they had the bare minimum for their survival. One terrible example of such action is the correlation between the rise in bread prices and the number of small children abandoned by their parents.[126]

Repressing the Helpless

HOSE WHO BELONGED to the upper and middle levels of society were not concerned by the pitiful condition of the working class; for them work and deprivation were necessary and effective means of disciplining the masses.[127] The views of Restif de la Bretonne echoed those of the bourgeoisie: "The mob is like a group of savages who live just for the present. If the mob can earn what it needs to live in three days, then they will only work those three days and spend the other four in idleness and dissipation."[128] And even the more circumspect Mercier, who so movingly reports and speculates on the causes of the "culture of poverty" at the end of the eighteenth century in his *Tableau de Paris*, was himself convinced of the people's immaturity.[129] This view was confirmed by the people's strong religious faith marked by syncretist elements.[130] The people's faith had its worldly parallel in their respect for the king and the royal family: they saw their ruler as a benevolent father. News of the dauphin's birth in 1781 was greeted with a joy that overcame all the irritation caused by the dismissal of the popular minister Necker and the increase in taxes and duties. The aspirations of the working class were of a decidedly apolitical nature, in that they did not threaten the social order which they firmly believed to be ordained by God.[131] The spontaneous demonstrations that broke out from time to time were easily put down because of their very spontaneity, and because it was not the demonstrators' intention to establish a new political or social order. Besides, the government kept a constant eye on the mood of the *peuple*; in fact it tried where possible to produce a favorable atmosphere and prevent any likely uprising.[132]

There was therefore good reason not to fear what later observers would see as inevitable: that the dissatisfaction born of need and desperation would one day induce the workers to use violent means to obtain their ends. Contemporaries were more appalled and disgusted by the growing mass of *gens sans feu ni lieu*—the needy, the unemployed, and the beggars who were uprooted and made homeless by economic hardship, and who flooded Paris where they were treated harshly by the authorities.[133] "The excuse given," Mercier writes, "was that need produces criminality, that revolts were being plotted by this mass of people who had nothing more to lose."[134] Anyone caught begging by the police and considered employable was put into one of the five *Dépôts de mendicité* which had been established in the *Généralité de Paris* in 1767.[135] Conditions in the *Dépôts*, which had attached workhouses and workshops, were beyond all description. Yet Mercier, who had still been indignant over the cruel and barbaric treatment of the poor in 1782, comments in 1788:

> It is wise to use harshness in tracking down the system of begging to its hid-ing-places; because it represents the complete opposite of our present social order. To eliminate this weed one must use hard, yes even inhuman measures, foreign to our nature; but this cancer threatens the tree and its leaves. . . . It is to be hoped that one day the last of this pitiful race (the beggars) will have disap-peared from France's beautiful soil for ever. . . . Instead of beggars and the needy there will then be only those diligent poor who are eager to work, who alone rep-resent the true wealth of kingdoms, and who therefore require all attention and care from wise governments; for whoever produces something interests govern-ments in quite a different way from the epicure, who only consumes.[136]

In this respect Mercier agreed with the public opinion of his time, which considered beggars as people "for whom doing nothing is a profession and who live at the expense of others; who know neither order nor duty nor obe-dience; and who not only are free of all ties but, what is more, are aware that people fear them and do their bidding."[137] Beggars and vagrants, the *gens sans aveu*, were a serious threat to the bourgeois society of the Enlightenment because they refused to obey the first and most important duty of the peo-ple, namely the willingness to work. And because they did not fulfill their obligation to be productive and to contribute to the general welfare, they were considered no more than a social evil, a useless burden that forced other members of society to work all the harder so as to indulge their decadent lazi-ness. In short, begging was denounced mainly because it offended the bour-geois sense of order, which was based on such values as work, thrift, and sobriety.[138]

The beggars' lot was shared by those forced by poverty into prostitution, or by those who were unable to earn their living on account of sickness or old age. The welfare and health systems of the Old Regime that cared for the poor and indigent were in no way set up to rehabilitate or reintegrate them into society; their aim was to isolate and control them. Several large institu-tions in and around Paris served this purpose; they were a horrible combi-

nation of hospital for the poor, prison, insane asylum, and isolation facility for
incurable diseases; the *Courier de l'Europe* once described them as "cloaques
de l'humanité" (cesspools of humanity).[139] The most notorious was Bicêtre,
which lay outside the city limits, between the villages of Ville-Juif and
Gentilly. Mercier considered it the "reservoir of the worst scum of society."[140]
Criminals, thieves, forgers, and pederasts were incarcerated there together
with cripples and beggars; epileptics and the mentally ill were shut up in large
cages like animals. Bicêtre also acted as a hospital for the terminally ill and an
isolation facility for men and women with sexual diseases. Having such a disease was considered a crime and anyone suffering from one was whipped
upon being admitted.

The Salpêtrière, which Restif de la Bretonne classified as a "cul-de-sac of
hell," served the specific purpose of social hygiene: incurable, blind, and
mentally disturbed women were kept there under conditions unfit for human
beings. While the insane and epileptic vegetated in chains in special cubi-
cles, the sick and terminally ill were put in vast wards in which up to five people shared one bed. The Salpêtrière also functioned as a women's prison and
house of correction for prostitutes, beggars, and female criminals, and as a
school for girls whose parents had sent them to this inferno.

Those inmates who were capable of working—there were on average
4,000 inmates in Bicêtre and 7,000 in the Salpêtrière—were forced to contribute to their upkeep. The generally heavy physical labor, the inadequate
daily ration of a pound of bad bread and some wine, and the very limited
medical care produced an expectably high average yearly mortality rate of
6,000 persons.

Conditions were hardly better in the Hôtel-Dieu, the hospital for the
poor near Notre Dame, which took in victims of accidents and where members of working-class families could get minimal medical care. There were
generally around 3,000 patients who shared 1,200 beds; those who were only
slightly ill often became infected with deadly diseases.[141] In this hospital the
average annual death rate was between 3,500 and 4,500 patients, a number
that disturbed even contemporaries who tried, without success, to initiate a
sweeping reform of the hospitals for the poor.[142]

The Hôtel-Dieu, Bicêtre, or Salpêtrière were the final and most miserable resting places in the short and pitiful lives of many of the working class;
and even after their death the poor and needy were deprived of the final
respect due to them. The dead from the Hôtel-Dieu were buried in mass
graves in the Clamart cemetery. Mercier reports:

> The mob never misses visiting this vast cemetery on All Souls Day, where
> all of them will eventually end up with their fathers anyway. They kneel down
> and pray and then get drunk afterwards. There are no monuments or grave-
> stones, no inscribed plaques or mausoleums, and the ground is completely bare.
> Young surgeons-in-training come at night to this pasture full of corpses to steal
> bodies on which to practice their techniques. Thus the poor are even robbed of
> their own bodies after their death. The disrespectful treatment they receive does
> not end until they have lost the final traits that define them as human beings.[143]

The social sphere of the working class was not on the edge of but outside that of the Estates; as Mercier puts it: "Le peuple semble un corps séparé
des autres ordres de l'état" (the people seem to be a group isolated from other
segments of society).[144] They had, as Mercier notes elsewhere, to live by the
laws made by the rich and powerful.[145] The working class was disregarded
because it had nothing; it had neither the means nor the right to lead a bourgeois life. The *peuple* lived within their own culture, characterized by shortage rather than abundance. It was a culture that fostered fatalism, awareness
of impotence, dependence, and inferiority. The people's patience despite
injustice, and their indifference to the persecution and suffering to which
they were exposed, led the Estates to regard them with distaste and fear, and
to treat them with cynical arrogance. A poor man who belonged to the working class did not have the slightest chance of changing his social status under
the Old Regime. Without any hope, without the vision of a better future
under improved social conditions, their only certainty was that death would
put them out of their misery sooner or later. They took some minimal comfort from the saying "*La mort saisit sans exception*" (death makes no distinction). For as long as anyone could remember it had always been the same:
children were born and died, the increase in prices was always greater than
the increase in wages. That was the way of the world and there was no more
to be said.

This fatalism, produced over several generations by helplessness in dealing with the Estates, enabled the *peuple* to come to terms with their situation. In turning their backs on the Estates from which they were excluded,
they developed their own social culture. The culture of poverty in which the
working classes lived filled a dual function: on the one hand it protected them
from daily hardships; on the other hand it was an effective buffer against the
threat of their destruction by society. The obverse side of this culture was that
it intensified marginalization; those who were part of it were prevented from
developing any feeling of self-esteem, any sort of class or collective consciousness that would have helped them to take the initiative in changing
their circumstances. In other words, the working classes had no conception
of what they were; working people were prevented from knowing that they
belonged to a certain class because of the diversity of their respective lives as
workers or unemployed, as residents or vagrants, as poor men or beggars. Yet
they were never so apathetic or blind that they could not react from time to
time against their hopeless position. They also had an extremely simple and
highly inaccurate idea of the mechanisms of their oppression. Individual ministers and especially the tax farmers were always accused of being responsible for any crisis that severely affected the people. Criticism directed at individuals rather than the social system was bound to be ineffectual, or to die out
in easily dispersed expressions of grievance and revolts.

But their protests gained increasing coherence as their living conditions
worsened and as the gulf between the powerful and the powerless widened in
the final years of the Old Regime. United by a common fear, the poor and
disenfranchised, who were convinced society had betrayed them and threat-

ened their very lives, grew more and more rebellious. One example of their feverish state of mind was the famous *pacte de famine*, the rumor of a secret plan to starve the people that circulated in Paris in the course of the severe winter of 1788–89. However, the extreme threat felt by the people was diffused because at least some of the skilled workers in Paris had been exposed to the political ideas being debated by the Third Estate. Still, the event was of great importance as it began a process during which the *peuple* abandoned their traditional fatalistic concepts. George Rudé describes this as follows:

> Once these ideas began to permeate the common people, as they did in the spring of 1789, a new direction and purpose were given to popular unrest, already nurtured on economic hardship and traditional grievances. The very realization, indeed, that the States General [*sic*] were about to meet and that the people's complaints, as voiced in the *cahiers de doléances*, should be heard, aroused what historians have called "la grande espérance."[146]

Important though the force behind that great hope was as a phenomenon, it had little effect on the expression of revolutionary feelings. Of far greater significance was the fact that the impact of the economic crisis, from which the Third Estate had first profited, now caught up with it and it began to close ranks against the Old Regime. Members of the Third Estate already held key economic positions in society, giving them a decisive role in the political system, as Mercier recognizes:

> Civilized nations that are characterized by civilized behavior require a humane government. It is therefore unnecessary to control the capital's inhabitants with the full weight of authority. Aside from the fact that they are all peaceful and unarmed, and are fully occupied with their businesses and pleasures, they have a tendency to like order, amicable coexistence, and quiet, especially as educated citizens are in the majority. Moreover the upper classes, who enjoy leisure and culture and are engaged in their pursuit, are the ones who most effectively control an angry mob. For the mob constantly tests the mood of the bourgeois classes and as long as they merely smile the mob will be incapable of continuing an insurrection for more than two weeks.[147]

Once the Third Estate was itself affected by the economic crisis, it was no longer inclined to placate the working class, nor did it show a smiling face. Instead it articulated its own dissatisfaction with and criticism of existing conditions loudly enough to be heard. The Third Estate's revolutionary proclamation that it was entirely legitimate to change a supposedly God-given order based on inequality and injustice showed the people a way out of the vicious circle to which fate had assigned them until then. What the bourgeoisie really had in mind was careful political reform to benefit itself; it saw the *peuple* as a very useful ally to achieve this. However, the stone thus dislodged started an avalanche that could not be guided, let alone stopped. Desire for political reform brought on a political revolution, which in its turn provoked a social revolution. In setting it in motion the people of Paris freed themselves of their fatalistic mind-set.

BOOK TWO

Capital of the Revolution

1789–1799

Mais pour nous à qui la vie civile est nécessaire et qui ne pouvons plus nous passer de manger des hommes, l'intérêt de chacun de nous est de fréquenter les pays où l'on en trouve le plus. Voilà pourquoi tout afflue à Rome, à Paris, à Londres. C'est toujours dans les capitales que le sang humaine se vend à meilleur marché.

As for us, for whom urban life is now indispensable and who must feed on other men, we are interested in frequenting those places where men are found in profusion. That is why everything flows toward Rome, Paris, and London. It is always in the great cities that human blood can be had at bargain prices.

— Jean-Jacques Rousseau, *Emile*

The Parisian Market Women's march on Versailles on October 5, 1789:
The Important Day of Versailles. *A period colored etching from the Bibliothèque collection, Paris.*
ARCHIV FÜR KUNST UND GESCHICHTE, BERLIN.

Revolutionary Forces and Centers

CONTEMPORARY HISTORIANS no longer hold with the former view of Paris as the primary source of the French Revolution. And yet the city developed into the most significant site of revolutionary activity. It was there that the goals and directions of the Revolution were established, and that the king tried to stop the insurgent movement before being swallowed up by it.

On the eve of the Revolution Paris already functioned as the capital of France. The dominant political discourse was reflected in an ever-growing number of pamphlets published there; and the seeds of revolutionary ideas and theories spread from there into the farthest corners of the provinces.[1] This was confirmed by the unanimity of grievances voiced by the Third Estate in various parts of the country. The city that Louis XIV had once disempowered regained its importance well before the establishment of the Estates General in Versailles and their subsequent forced move to Paris. It had assumed the role it was to play time and again in the nineteenth century—that of the European capital of revolution.

Strict property qualifications considerably curtailed both active and passive voting rights of the Third Estate, and show that the royal authorities were by no means blind to the threat Paris presented.[2] The purpose of the qualifications is obvious: the poor and uneducated *peuple* were to be prevented from dominating the bourgeoisie by their sheer number.[3] But that in itself was not considered adequate. Fear of possible demonstrations and unrest during electoral meetings of the Third Estate led to the city's division into sixty zones that were to serve as original voting districts of the delegates who constituted the Paris Assembly.[4] Twenty deputies were then chosen from their ranks to represent the Third Estate of Paris in the Estates General.

The Parisian working class, though prevented from voting by property qualifications and hence from having direct influence on the organization of the Estates General, managed to add its own fuel to the revolutionary mood of the bourgeoisie.[5] There were uprisings on April 27 and 28, 1789, in which over a hundred people were killed. These bloody events were caused by the rumor that two Parisian manufacturers, Henriot and Réveillon, had attended the electoral meetings of the Third Estate to protest the ruinous wages they had to pay on account of the continued market crisis.[6] This senseless and horrible bloodbath was caused by the bungling of the authorities, who reacted only after an excited crowd had forced its way into the two men's homes and plundered them. The Gardes françaises were then sent into the narrow alleys of the faubourg Saint-Antoine where they fired on the closely packed crowd without warning.[7]

The Réveillon affair remained a spontaneous revolt without further consequences. Peace returned to the city on April 29 and apparently the prior two days' events made no great impression on the voting citizens of the

Third Estate. No one saw the writing on the wall announcing a social revolution.[8] Soon after the bloody affair, on May 5, 1789, the Estates General were ceremonially inaugurated at Versailles.

Located only twelve miles from the gates of Paris, Versailles found itself in the capital's deep and threatening shadow right from the start. Everything discussed at the meetings of the Estates General was followed with great attention and commented on in Paris. It was quite natural, therefore, for the Third Estate of Paris to decide, on May 10, 1789, not to dissolve its Assembly once the twenty deputies had been elected to the Estates General, but to meet for as long as the deliberations of the Estates General continued in Versailles.[9] The electoral councils of the sixty districts also decided to continue meeting though their task was completed.[10]

This revolutionary decision heralded the coming confrontations with the crown. At first nothing happened, as the king avoided deciding on the way in which voting would be conducted in the Estates General. His indecision lasted the whole of May, during which economic hardship continued in Paris along with expectations of what the Estates General would accomplish. On June 10 those representing the Third Estate in Versailles finally took some action. They invited deputies of the two privileged Estates, the nobility and the clergy, to unite with them and thereby to unite the mandates of "all the representatives of the nation." Events now moved quickly: on June 17 the Third Estate formed a "National Assembly," and on June 19 a majority of the clergy decided to join the Third Estate, followed by eighty members of the aristocracy. On June 27, after some vacillation, Louis XVI requested his "faithful clergy and his faithful nobles" to meet with the Third Estate. This request was really a capitulation—the king had accepted the will of the National Assembly. After this date France was no longer an absolute monarchy.

Two days earlier, on June 25, 1789, the Paris Assembly of the Third Estate had met again, in keeping with its decision of May 10.[11] The purpose of the meeting was to send a vote of thanks to the National Assembly in Versailles for their "steadfast and patriotic attitude"; they also assured the National Assembly of their unconditional support of all decisions taken, especially those of June 17.[12]

The political changes formulated by the National Assembly on June 17 were thus approved by the body that was soon to become the Commune. That Commune represented not only the wealthy bourgeoisie, the liberal aristocracy, and the lower clergy, but also the general public—especially the working class of Paris, that great mass of petty artisans, shopkeepers, and tradesmen, as well as the skilled and unskilled workers who feared for their existence in the face of continuing economic problems. This fear lent the *peuple* a purposefulness that counterbalanced the king's military power over Paris. Nothing had yet been conclusively decided since the latter had given in to the National Assembly on June 27. But it had become clear that Versailles, not Paris, was the place where decisions would have to be made—and made promptly as tension steadily mounted.

In its resolution of June 25 the Paris Assembly indicated its willingness to undertake initiatives—all the more important because the National Assembly in Versailles appeared to be dazed and overwhelmed by its own courage. Moreover, the latter had been surrounded by troops since June 23 and the public was excluded from its meetings. Its members felt threatened but their protests remained weak and initially ineffectual. All signs seemed to point to the king's decision to orchestrate a coup, a civil war that would stifle the coming Revolution at its birth. Paris was a rumor mill, and the continued increases in bread prices caused anxiety that could easily turn to panic. Anything seemed possible, the most diverse premonitions were experienced as real. What was to be done? The general fear made people want to sell their lives as dearly as possible. On June 25 the call to arms was heard for the first time in the Paris Assembly. One of the delegates requested the formation of a citizens' militia that would guard against "local unrest, the shortage of food, and the blind enthusiasm that can incite the young who want action." This, too, was a new and revolutionary idea. Why were the citizens of Paris to arm themselves? Not only to to protect their property, their houses, and their families, but above all to assert their rights to a constitution preventing ministerial despotism, as the speaker went on to explain.[13] He called for willingness to sacrifice their very lives for a constitution and the decisions and purposes of the National Assembly. But this was to misjudge entirely the revolutionary spirit of the wealthy bourgeoisie who dominated the Paris Assembly. They were not about to fight for the Revolution but rather to defend their property. Still, on that June 25 they did not yet fully realize what extreme dangers lay ahead.[14]

Such hesitations deprived the representatives of the Third Estate of their chance to influence and control the growing revolutionary mood in Paris which was constantly nourished by the most contradictory rumors and hopes. The people's *grande espérance* was mixed with fear of an aristocratic plot to starve and subjugate Paris. Those who shaped public opinion now took over. Pamphleteers, writers of brochures, and journalists, who made the Palais-Royal their headquarters, set the topics of discussion. A varied group gathered there on balmy summer evenings in 1789, to hear the latest slogans, proclamations, and gossip. The Palais-Royal became the center of agitation and action. It was there that the fires of the Revolution were kindled while the Third Estate of Paris discussed and formulated lengthy protocols in its Assembly, and tried to disguise its helplessness. Those of the bourgeoisie who gathered in the Palais-Royal incited the Gardes françaises, and undermined their morale and discipline by treating them to wine and brandy so that should they be transferred to Versailles, as the bookseller Hardy noted in his diary on June 25, 1789, "they would refuse to move against the bourgeoisie."[15]

It made sense to co-opt the Gardes françaises since they enforced the power of the crown in Paris. The freeing of eleven guards from the Abbaye prison on June 30 by a crowd that rushed over from the Palais-Royal was therefore of inestimable propaganda value. The guards had been imprisoned

for their refusal, on June 23, to take action against the crowd that had sur-
rounded the National Assembly building and the palace at Versailles.[16]
Following their release the soldiers were led in triumphal procession to the
Palais-Royal, where they were lodged and kept for several days until the
National Assembly, after being bombarded with requests from the public,
obtained their pardon from the king on July 3.[17]

Although the crown gave in to the Palais-Royal in this instance, no one
was under any false illusions, for Versailles and Paris were both surrounded
by troops—not the Gardes françaises but foreign regiments, mostly Swiss
and German mercenaries. What the king had in mind was obvious even to
the most naïve observer. A police spy reported on July 2, 1789, that the mob
in the Palais-Royal suspected the government of planning a coup and had
decided to defend itself.[18]

Meanwhile the ever-rising bread prices aggravated the already tense situation. Hardy noted in his diary on July 4 that military patrols on streets and
in the squares had been increased "to maintain order despite the rising cost
of bread." On Monday, July 6, Hardy noticed that detachments of troops
were on hand in the morning during the distribution of bread.

> It seems, and many people are firmly convinced, that the government alone was
> responsible for causing a shortage of bread grains, and that measures have
> already been taken to hoard the new crops and to keep increasing the price of
> bread; that way considerable sums of money could continue to be collected to
> pay the state's debts if the recommendations of the Estates General were not fol-
> lowed . . . .

On July 9 Hardy reported that the inhabitants of Paris were agitated over
the constant movement and reinforcement of troops, from which they concluded the city was going to be occupied. On July 20 he noted that the previous evening several detachments of cavalry had galloped through the city
with drawn sabers in the direction of the faubourg Montmartre. A group of
the unemployed, who had been assigned to excavation work there by an *atelier de charité*, had stopped working in order to free two of their comrades
from a nearby prison. As Hardy further explained, the irritation of these
unemployed men, who earned 20 sous per day, was caused above all by the
poor quality of the bread to which they were entitled as their nourishment.
Faced by a determined crowd that threatened and insulted them, the troops
did not dare to quell the riot by force. [19]

Such incidents and events, news of which spread quickly and led to yet
further rumors and anxieties, helped to fuel the tension. But it was the crown
that hastened the escalation by its rash action: Louis XVI dismissed Necker,
his minister of finance, on the evening of July 11. The following morning,
when this became known in Paris, it was seen as a clear intimation of the
royal countermeasures that had been expected for weeks. The wealthy, who
had invested their income in high-yielding state bonds, considered Necker's
dismissal as an admission of the state's bankruptcy and its unwillingness to
pay them any restitution.[20]

Around noon on July 12—it was a bright sunny day—a large, excited crowd of individuals gathered around several speakers in the Palais-Royal, one of whom was Camille Desmoulins, who counted among the most talented and hotheaded journalists influencing public opinion. Standing on a table in front of the Café de Foy, Desmoulins made the following statement:

> Citizens, we cannot waste a moment. I've just come from Versailles. M. Necker has been dismissed. This gesture by the crown sounds the alarm for a new St. Bartholomew's Night of the patriots. This evening all German and Swiss regiments will leave the Champ de Mars to come and murder us. We have no choice but to arm ourselves and to pin on cockades, so that we shall be able to recognize each other.[21]

Desmoulins was only expressing openly what others had been fearing for days: that foreign mercenaries would enter the city under cover of night and transform Paris into a heap of rubble. That had to be prevented at all costs. Versailles with its self-congratulatory discussions of lofty ideals intended to bring happiness to all mankind now seemed very far away; those ideals were nothing but literature and philosophy. Life itself—whether pitiful and full of anxiety, or easy and carefree—was now at stake. Unity and a common desire for action were not created by well-intentioned statements on basic rights and paper achievements; nor by the promising pronouncements on freedom and equality with which the National Assembly wanted to please everyone. They were created, rather, by the collective awareness of an existential threat. Paris prepared itself for a resistance that was to produce a revolution. Of course the intention was not to bring about the change for which the Enlightenment had paved the way, and which had been called for in the Versailles debates. The sole aim right now was to prevent the destruction that supposedly lay ahead. In the end it amounted to the same thing. The determined opposition by Paris, the revolt of July 14, brought about the long-awaited changes to which members of the National Assembly had also dedicated themselves.

At first, however, there was complete confusion. Word had gone out from the Palais-Royal but beyond that there was no leadership to guide those who wanted action. The evening saw groups of individuals, armed with tools and sticks, milling around aimlessly in different sections of Paris. In the place Louis XV clashes took place between an originally peaceful crowd and a regiment of the Royal Allemand Dragoons. Meantime an enraged mob collected in front of the Hôtel de Ville, making ever more urgent demands for arms. Soon, under cover of night, mercenaries would attack the unarmed city and create a horrible bloodbath. Finally the aroused mob stormed and plundered the city's arsenal while Besenval, the commander of the Paris garrison, took whatever troops remained—many of the Gardes françaises had deserted during the day and disappeared—and left Paris. Members of the Paris Assembly gradually began to arrive at the Hôtel de Ville, but it was not until eleven o'clock at night that they reinstated some sort of order—forced by circumstances rather than their own volition to reach some administrative decisions.

They alerted the various districts, and some of their more courageous members were dispatched to persuade any armed citizens they met to stay away from large crowds "in the name of *la patrie*."[22] A request of this sort was as ineffective as it was ridiculous; the gathering storm could hardly be stopped by persuasion and the evocation of *la patrie*. The armed hordes that had gathered everywhere refused to disperse simply because the Paris Assembly requested them to do so.

But things could not go on like this much longer. The mob had already taken advantage of the existing anarchy to put forty of the fifty-four hated customs posts to the torch.[23] Still more dangerous was the fact that all sorts of shady characters forced their way into the Saint-Lazare monastery that same night, searching for food and weapons and finally plundering and setting fire to it.[24]

The events of the night of July 12–13 clearly showed that some authority, however improvised and temporary it might be, had to be established to prevent further excesses and to deal with the already difficult task of maintaining the city's food supply. Members of the Paris Assembly therefore met at the Hôtel de Ville on the morning of July 13, to establish a Permanent Committee empowered to take over the administrative control of Paris. Furthermore, all citizens who had acquired arms were required to hand them over to their respective local administrations, so that they could be distributed to the citizens' militia that was still to be organized.[25]

The Paris Assembly met amid chaos. Ever since the morning the place de Grève had been occupied by a steadily swelling mass of people, pushing their way into the Hôtel de Ville and even into the meeting room, settling on stairs and landings, and constantly demanding arms. By early afternoon the Permanent Committee announced its decision to form a citizens' militia of 4,800 men, to which each district was expected to contribute 600 volunteers.

These were revolutionary decisions for the Paris Assembly to take. The formation of a Permanent Committee and a citizens' militia were illegal acts, given an appearance of legality by the appointment of the *Prévôt des marchands* (the royal government's senior magistrate of the city of Paris) to head the Committee. The bourgeois citizens considered their actions simply a way of preventing further chaos rather than an expression of radical fervor. As a matter of fact, membership in the citizens' militia was to be limited to those regarded as *citoyens connus*, individuals who owned their homes, a condition that would guarantee their reliability.

However, the decisions reached on July 13 were at first no more than the promise of a new order, a promise whose effects were limited by the existing confusion and excitement. Although the district councils approved all the measures taken by the Paris Assembly, they themselves were only islands in a sea of anarchy. The general obsession with weapons persisted: local districts demanded them from the Permanent Committee so as to arm the citizens' militia, and the general public kept up its own strident requests for arms. In its search for weapons the mob stormed the La Force prison later that morning and freed all its prisoners.[26]

The general hysteria and the urge to take up arms became even greater when news came that the king had again refused to order the withdrawal of the troops surrounding Paris, or to sanction the formation of a citizens' militia. The Permanent Committee had no way of enforcing its mandate, so it tried to hold on to its precarious authority by making promises. Around midday the *Prévôt des marchands* announced that 12,000 muskets would be delivered and distributed to the districts by five o'clock at the latest.[27] A few boxes marked "artillery" actually did arrive at the Hôtel de Ville in the late afternoon, but when it was discovered that they contained only old rags the people directed their anger at the Permanent Committee, and especially at the *Prévôt des marchands*, whom they suspected of having betrayed them.

Despite considerable difficulties the citizens' militia was formed very quickly—the duc d'Aumont and the marquis de Lasalle were nominated to be its commanders.[28] By the evening of July 13 its soldiers, recognizable by their blue-and-red cockades, were patrolling everywhere.[29] The Permanent Committee noted in its minutes that this new authority had managed to "impose order and obedience on disorder and anarchy."[30]

By the following day it became evident that the Permanent Committee had overestimated the extent to which it controlled the situation. The *bon bourgeois* was satisfied with a militia composed of his own kind that would protect his property, so he was willing to wait and see what would happen. But that was not enough for the *peuple*, who took any bit of news, however ghastly, at face value.

There was one false rumor, for instance, on the night of July 13, that the 15,000 mercenary troops surrounding Paris had entered the faubourg Saint-Antoine and embarked on a bloody massacre. Hearsay of this kind—even if it usually turned out to be untrue—magnified everyone's fears of an unknown peril lying ahead. On the morning of July 14 the people identified the Bastille as the immediate source of their imagined danger.

The Bastille had long been used by the Old Regime as a fortified prison. Its massive stone structure with eight towers, each approximately ninety-five feet high, was situated between the inner city and the faubourg Saint-Antoine. To be sure, the enlightened Third Estate had called for its destruction in their *cahier de doléances*, and its replacement by a column that would symbolize a new regime. But the people did not think in terms of symbols; they believed in their saints and the goodness of their king. And they accepted the Bastille just as they had taken their miserable lot for granted all this time. But on July 14 they suddenly saw the fortress for what it was. Its cannon were trained on the faubourg Saint-Antoine; there lay the real threat.

July 14 and Its Consequences

*O*N THE MORNING OF JULY 14 the place de Grève was again filled with people demanding weapons. Those who had gone to various monasteries the previous evening, expecting to find arms hidden there, had returned empty-handed. That quickly became known and the Permanent Committee was faced with dire threats by the excited crowd. The Committee realized that guns now had to be given priority over bread if it did not want to be overwhelmed by an angry mob. In desperation it sent one of its members, Ethis de Corny, Procureur du Roi et de la Ville, to the Hôtel des Invalides at about 7:00 A.M., to "collect whatever weapons were thought to be stored there and bring them back to the Hôtel de Ville."[31] Around 8:00 A.M. news reached the Hôtel de Ville that the Bastille's cannon were trained on the rue Saint-Antoine. The Committee immediately sent three emissaries to the commander of the Bastille, de Launey, "to avoid the massacre indicated by this news." They asked him to pull back the cannon and to promise that he would not use force. For its part the Committee guaranteed that "the people of Saint-Antoine and the surrounding area would not engage in destructive actions against him and his fortress."[32]

The Permanent Committee tried to hold on to its precarious authority by fruitless negotiations, but the people realized instinctively that only a firm stand could help them now. Several thousand citizens gathered in front of the gate of the Hôtel des Invalides in the course of the morning.[33] When Ethis de Corny returned from his mission without having accomplished anything, the mob stormed the poorly protected Invalides and helped themselves to the firearms and muskets stored there, as well as to some cannon.[34]

The weapons captured in this surprise attack gave the crowd additional courage, and though they lacked gunpowder they expected to find plentiful supplies of it in the Bastille vaults. Now they had weapons and a goal; but as they rushed toward the fortress shouting their slogan, "à la Bastille," they had no actual plans to take it by force. In the general confusion, however, and through a series of misunderstandings, this was precisely what happened in the end.

Various eyewitnesses have described the fall of the Bastille—in the early afternoon of July 14—in what is an unavoidable mixture of myth and reality. One of the most complete and reliable depictions was included in the minutes of the Paris Assembly.[35] It seems that the Permanent Committee's delegation arrived at the Bastille around ten o'clock and was received by its commander, de Launey, and offered refreshments. This delayed the delegation's mission and caused the crowd outside to grow restless. People suspected that a trap had been laid and spoke of betrayal; finally there were loud calls for the fortress to surrender or be attacked. To cool the hotheaded mob two representatives of the Saint-Louis-la-Culture district, Boucheron and Thuriot de la Rosière, were dispatched to the Bastille to request the commander to pull back the cannon pointing at the faubourg Saint-Antoine and to hand over the fortress. These two emissaries were also admitted to de Launey, who declared that he would only give the order to fire if the mob attacked the Bastille. This information was transmitted to the Permanent Committee, which immediately ordered it to be made public. Just as the town crier was about to do so, the firing of a cannon was heard. The crowd was convinced it had been betrayed and shortly thereafter two wounded people were brought by. Rumor had it that fifteen to twenty other injured individuals were being cared for in the rue de la Cérisaie. Further news came that the mob had managed to cross a drawbridge and enter the outer courtyard of the Bastille, where it had been fired upon.

Entrance from the outer to the inner courtyard of the Bastille was also protected by a drawbridge which, though it was up, was left unguarded. Two men using an adjacent rooftop climbed the wall and released it. Believing he was being attacked, de Launey ordered the three cannon in the inner courtyard to fire on the mob in the outer courtyard.[36]

Meantime the Permanent Committee had completely lost control of the situation. Two additional delegations sent out to request the Bastille's surrender returned without achieving anything. The confusion of the fighting and the presence of agitated crowds had prevented their getting through and arranging for a peaceful surrender. The Bastille fell in a battle waged and won by the *peuple*. From now on their strength, revolutionary fervor, and determination were factors to be reckoned with.

What was militarily decisive in the prompt fall of the Bastille was the fact that two divisions of the Gardes françaises joined the fray with five cannon. Together with several hundred civilians they forced their way to the inner courtyard. The commander offered to surrender on condition that his forces would not be attacked. But the crowd, having suffered severe losses and suspecting de Launey of trickery, was unwilling to make concessions and continued fighting. De Launey now lost his nerve. He ordered the gunpowder supplies in the fortress vaults to be blown up, so that defenders and attackers would be buried under the rubble. The garrison refused to obey this insane order. In desperation he then gave instructions for the main drawbridge to be let down, thus sealing the fate of the Bastille.[37] "The fortress that Henry IV and Louis XIV had attacked unsuccessfully," Hardy notes in his diary, "was taken in less than three hours."[38]

Intoxicated with its success, the crowd now rushed into the Bastille. Given the tension in which the rioters had been living for days, their fear of sudden attack against which they would be defenseless, and the many who were killed or were wounded in the fighting, it is amazing that only 6 or 7 of the more than 110 troops stationed in the Bastille were massacred. Among those killed was de Launey who, though assured of safe-conduct to the Hôtel de Ville, had been sacrificed to popular justice. Another who later fell victim to the angry mob in the Palais-Royal was de Flesselles, the *Prévôt des marchands*.

These murders, as well as those of Foullon and Berthier committed a week later—whose lurid details were endlessly repeated—were often cited to discredit the conquerors of the Bastille and picture them as a band of criminals and vagabonds, the scum of the people.[39] This interpretation, which was endlessly repeated and seemed firmly entrenched, was finally refuted by George Rudé's careful research into source material. According to him, about two-thirds of the approximately 800 to 900 persons who were given the honorary title of *vainqueur de la Bastille* (conqueror of the Bastille), following an investigation in 1790, were proprietors of small workshops, craftsmen, journeymen, petty tradesmen, and wage earners from over thirty different trades employed primarily in the faubourg Saint-Antoine.[40] These conquerors of the Bastille were far from representing the lowest levels of society; in fact the majority belonged to the citizens' militia of their districts.

The storming of the Bastille on July 14, 1789, was, as Michelet so aptly writes, "contrary to all reason. It was an act of faith."[41] It saved the Revolution, it freed the National Assembly in Versailles from its ineffectual deliberations and forced the king to accept the situation. But the *peuple* only gradually understood the events of that day and what they could expect from them. At first they were unable to see their victory as a cause for celebration, being afraid that an attack on the city was now more certain than ever. Even the king's order to withdraw, issued to the troops stationed around Paris, was met with skepticism and mistrust. The *peuple* sensed a false peace, and new rumors were floated of incredible terrors that would befall the city. There was talk of subterranean passages from which attackers would emerge at night, in the middle of Paris, to surprise and massacre the citizens in their sleep. Other conjectures claimed that these tunnels were filled with gunpowder that would be set alight to destroy the whole city.

The Bastille was the centerpiece of all these fears. It was typical of the people's imaginative powers that they only perceived the dragon's evil nature once it had been slain. Hence it is understandable that the district of Saint-Louis-la-Culture asked the Permanent Committee on July 16 to "pull down the Bastille immediately so as to eliminate all cause for mistrust and terror." The request was promptly granted.[42]

Whereas the Bastille had been an imagined danger, the real threats facing Paris were hunger and unemployment. Supplies of grain and flour were soon exhausted; fresh deliveries intended for the capital disappeared in the provinces where people also suffered from hunger. The price of bread, which had risen to the exorbitant level of $14^{1}/_{4}$ sous on July 14, had to be lowered if the Paris Assembly and the Permanent Committee were to strengthen their still shaky authority. They feared a hunger revolt by the people—who had retained their weapons despite all appeals, and who had just had their first taste of power and strength—that would end in catastrophe. One did not have to be a prophet to foresee that. To prevent people from hoarding and to avoid panic the Committee announced that the city had sufficient grain supplies for more than two months In actual fact, though, everyone in Paris was living from day to day.[43]

Popular frustration ended in the summary killing of large-scale grain speculators like Foullon de Doué and his son-in-law Bertier de Sauvigny.

Both were seen as ringleaders in a new *pacte de famine* (agreement to starve the people). These desperate actions once again pointed to the need for an overall authority to eliminate street terror.[44] But that could only succeed if the problem of the citizens' militia was resolved. In the general excitement of the days when this new instrument of power had been approved, there had not been time to plan the complete organization of the National Guard, as it was now called. The Permanent Committee had originally decided that only *citoyens connus*, established citizens, were to be included in it; but many districts had simply ignored this stipulation so that a considerable number of employed artisans and even apprentices had joined the militia. This could not be annulled—an order to that effect, issued July 26, 1789, was protested by about twenty districts.[45] Eventually a compromise was found: in future only "active citizens" would be allowed to serve in the National Guard. However, "passive citizens," who had belonged to the citizens' militia from the beginning of the Revolution, could remain in it. As an "active citizen" could also buy his way out of National Guard service, it meant that from the very start this body was not the homogeneous social group envisioned by its creators. The National Guard always contained a "proletarian core."[46]

It was far more important, though, to reorganize what was still a provisional city administration and to give it as legitimate a basis as possible. The idea was to replace the Paris Assembly and the Permanent Committee with an elected Commune, whose constitution and organization were to be determined by a deliberative body to which each district would send two representatives.[47] But the first Paris Assembly, or *Assemblée des Représentants de la Commune*, was replaced by a different body on September 18. Now each district was to have five representatives, for whom anyone could vote who had resided in Paris for at least one year and who paid a *subside direct et personnel* (a direct personal tax). This was decidedly a more tolerant approach than had been the case with the election rules for the first Paris Assembly. The idea was to establish closer ties between the new Assembly and the districts—which had shown considerable independence as long as the state of anarchy existed—and so to subject them to the political control of the Hôtel de Ville.

But this did not work out in practice as the sixty districts had long since built up administrative machines that made their own decisions and rules.[48] Hardly a day went by without numerous delegations from the districts appearing before the Paris Assembly to complain about the most diverse matters, or to present requests and petitions. While this was evidence of the political consciousness of these quasi-autonomous bodies, it eventually became too much for the Assembly. On September 23, 1789, the enervated Assembly requested the districts to refrain from sending any further delegations.[49] Even so the work for which the 300 Assembly members had been elected—to organize the city's administration and to develop a communal constitution—did not proceed any faster. The districts had meantime found ways to make their influence felt; despite its important-sounding name, *Assemblée des Représentants*, the mandate of Assembly members was very limited and there was no end to the fights over its scope. The districts constant-

ly strove to influence the authority of the Assembly in their own favor. All
in all it was November before the new communal constitution was completed; it remained in force until October 1790, when the Constituent Assembly
passed a law on municipalities that applied to the whole country.[50]

The many arguments in which the districts involved the Assembly, and
which ended in the promulgation of numerous *arrêts* (decrees), were discussed everywhere. They were debated in the newspapers—which had mush-
roomed since July—and at district meetings; they were discussed in the
Palais-Royal and criticized in pamphlets in an increasingly aggressive and
turbulent style. This public discussion contributed greatly to the political
education of the masses; it made them familiar with the concepts, techniques,
and strategies of political action. All of this occurred against the backdrop of
an onerous food shortage, whose duration was at first unpredictable. The
regulations, prohibitions, and threats with which the Assembly flooded grain
producers, suppliers, and bakers had no effect. Grain supplies destined for
Paris were constantly stopped and plundered en route. There were more and
more frequent confrontations in the Paris markets over the distribution of
flour, and the National Guard had to protect bakeries as well as grain transports.

Now the specter of mass unemployment joined the threat of famine. The
luxury goods and building trades, two important industries that had flourished before the outbreak of the Revolution, were particularly affected. After
July 14 there had been sizable emigration and flight of capital. This, together with the general dread of bankruptcy, slowed the overall monetary circulation.[51] *Atéliers de charité* (charitable workhouses) were established in May
1789 to deal with joblessness following the harsh winter of 1788–89. They
supplied 22,000 workers for excavation work in Vaugirard, Reuilly, and especially in Montmartre. But with the deepening of the economic crisis and
escalating unemployment, it became quite clear that this was no way to solve
the problem. Bailly wrote that more than anything it was feared that "this
horde of people could turn into quite a frightening army if it lacked bread for
even a short time."[52] It was, therefore, out of pure fear that the Commune
closed these charity workhouses on August 31.[53]

On the other hand, even Bailly should have known what the baron de
Staël notes about the food scarcity, that it could "foster and bring about a second revolution more quickly."[54] In other words, a mere shortage of bread was
not in itself enough to bring about a new upheaval; but the continued threat
of hunger and dire misery made the people more receptive to the social and
political agitation to which they were exposed. Hunger and deprivation were
familiar conditions, of course, but they were now being experienced quite differently. The summer's events, in which the people had been the most active
participants, had roused them from their lethargy and given them something
of a new political awareness.[55] The district assemblies alone—which were in
continual session and to which access was not nearly as restricted as pre-
scribed by property qualifications—provided an excellent object lesson in
politics. But the Palais-Royal was and continued to be the ultimate training

ground in agitation. It was not a place where the petty affairs of local districts were debated, but where the actions or failures to act of the National Assembly in Versailles were knowledgeably discussed and harshly criticized.

Of course the Paris Assembly was suspicious of all this political activity it could not control. A ruling was issued on August 7 stating that enfranchised citizens were permitted to participate only in organized district sessions; all other public meetings were prohibited and the National Guard was empowered to break up any *attroupements séditieux* (seditious gatherings).[56] While the Palais-Royal was not specifically referred to, there can be no doubt that the decree was aimed at it; and though the decree was reissued three more times by September 1, the Paris Assembly failed to curb controversial discussion there.[57] That was where the heart and mind of the Revolution were united, a union that could not be destroyed by prohibitions from a powerless group.

Paris Replaces Versailles

*T*HE APPARENT CALM AFTER THE FALL of the Bastille grew more unpredictable as the chronic food shortage and bad economic conditions became harder to bear. Meantime the Constituent Assembly in Versailles continued to work on the Constitution. Between August 4 and 11 the feudal system and all privileges were abolished; on August 26 the Rights of Man were ceremonially proclaimed. It seemed that all was going well and the Revolution's aims were being enforced. But this impression was misleading because the king obstinately refused to sanction the decisions reached by the Assembly. The longer the political stalemate lasted, the more suspicious the crown's intentions appeared. When the Flanders regiment arrived in Versailles on September 23, it was seen as part of the crown's counterrevolutionary plans and Paris felt threatened again.[58] At the end of September Loustalot wrote in *Les Révolutions de Paris*, "The coalition is using regular troops in Versailles. It is afraid of the armed citizens who want to defend their freedom. What sort of conspiracy is being hatched against us? We must be on guard. . . . Patriotic fervor is dying out. A new revolutionary stimulus is needed."[59]

Revolt requires stronger provocation than well-meant appeals. Incitement of this sort was provided by a banquet given in Versailles on October 1, at which aristocratic officers tore the red-white-and-blue cockades off their uniforms, trampled on them, and replaced them with the monarchy's traditional white rosette. News of this reached Paris on October 3, in the *Courrier de Versailles*, and was generally regarded as proof of the royal counterrevolutionary plans that journalists and pamphleteers had been predicting. Several districts immediately pressured the Paris Assembly to take action. The National Guard was put on alert, and a solemn decree was put out emphasizing that the red-white-and-blue cockade was the only one that citizens

were allowed to wear.[60] This decree not only gave official recognition to the
Versailles incident, but increased the agitation in Paris still further. There was
frequent talk of going to Versailles.[61]

Demonstrations broke out simultaneously in the central markets and the
faubourg Saint-Antoine on the morning of October 5.[62] In contrast to July
14, however, it was largely women who took the intitiative and who, as the
reports unanimously show, came from various levels of society.[63] As the tocsin rang out a crowd gathered in front of the Hôtel de Ville from all parts of
town. The minutes of the Assembly on the morning of October 5 read:

> A large gathering of people and unusual excitement filled the square in
> front of the Hôtel de Ville, when several large groups of women, who had gath-
> ered in the districts, began to arrive; they asked to be admitted to the Hôtel de
> Ville and stated that they wished to speak to the mayor and representatives of the
> Commune, to inform them that they had decided to march to Versailles. They
> added that they would not permit any men to join them.[64]

Indeed it was exclusively women, several thousand of them, ranging from
market fishwives to *femmes à chapeau* (middle-class women), who set out for
Versailles later that cold and rainy morning on October 5.[65] Their prime
motivation was the chronic shortage of bread, rather than any of the important political questions of current concern. What inspired them was the old
faith in the goodness of their king, who would supposedly take care of his
people as soon as he learned of their misery. Paradoxically, it was this prepo-
litical faith that helped to secure the gains of the political Revolution of 1789.

The women's procession to Versailles encouraged the National Guard to
follow their example. When Lafayette arrived at Hôtel de Ville around noon
he tried to gain some time by dissuading the good citizens, who actually
looked martial in their handsome blue uniforms, from carrying out their
plan. But Lafayette had to give in to the National Guard. The Paris Assembly
then took Lafayette's advice and instructed the National Guard to march to
Versailles, in order to conceal their refusal to obey orders.[66]

In the revolutionary history of Paris there had not been, nor was there
ever again anything like that mass action of October 5. All of Paris went to
Versailles—for reasons that varied greatly—and saved the Revolution by
bringing the king back to Paris in triumph. On the evening of October 5
Louis XVI gave his written agreement to the decrees issued by the National
Assembly between August 4 and 11. Not many hours earlier he had said he
would never consent to these regulations. The following morning he
promised the women, the National Guard, and the rest of the crowd that had
camped outside the palace that he would accept their request and move to
Paris. The National Assembly then decided to follow the king to Paris.

An enormous procession set out for Paris in the early afternoon of
October 6, and that evening the king arrived in the capital as a prisoner of his
people. This ominous spectacle has been described frequently; it symbolized the victory of Paris over the Versailles of Louis XIV, of the Revolution
over the Old Regime.[67]

The royal family then took up residence in the Tuileries and their presence established a new configuration of political forces: the king now had the National Assembly, the Commune, and the districts to contend with.[68] At the same time the National Asssembly found itself more and more under the population's revolutionary influence. Comte d'Escherny noted, prophetically, "Paris will become the secret engine of all that is about to happen; the invisible instigator of a second revolution that will have to be considered a necessary complement to the first one."[69]

Meantime the royal family's move to Paris brought about a deceptive lessening of tension as the people expected the bread shortage to end. But the October Terror was too deeply ingrained in the memories of the Commune's deputies for them to see this peaceful interlude as permanent. They knew that events had moved beyond their control again recently, and that the National Guard had been unable to restore order.

The Commune and the monarch were not the only ones afraid of the people of Paris; many members of the National Assembly shared those fears. More than 200 delegates requested their passports in a stormy session on October 8, so that they could return to their homes.[70] After their request had been denied by a majority of the Assembly, the latter quickly issued an explanation on October 10 to reassure the fearful delegates.[71] In addition the Assembly issued a proclamation to the inhabitants of Paris on October 15, begging them not to jeopardize their newly won rights by starting fresh disturbances.[72]

The effect of these solemn entreaties depended primarily on the capital's food supply. As long as the flour promised by the king on his return was available in sufficient quantity and of good quality, everything remained calm. But the situation could change quickly, and as soon as there were delays in the supply, new protests broke out in the faubourg Saint-Antoine on the evening of October 18.[73] Three days later a baker called François was murdered by an angry crowd. This event, which presaged worse to come, induced the authorities to act promptly: a law was passed by the National Assembly declaring a state of emergency.[74] The Commune established a *comité des recherches*, a special police unit that was to follow up all information on conspiracies, and to arrest and question suspects.[75]

These measures immediately encountered much reaction. Robespierre argued against martial law, stating that it would be more useful to improve the grain distribution than to shoot at those protesting the food shortage.[76] A number of Paris districts, controlled by the *peuple*, also criticized the imposition of martial law. They pointed out that the National Guard, which was recruited from among "active citizens," should not be allowed to open fire on the lower classes. On the other hand, the more bourgeois districts welcomed the new law.[77]

The declaration of the state of emergency revealed the political and social differences that were to lead to bloody confrontations and begin a new phase of the Revolution in less than two years. But this development was not foreseeable at the end of 1789, and for the time being it seemed that previous gains could now be consolidated under peaceful conditions.

The years 1790–91 were the "happy years" of the Revolution. The bourgeoisie had achieved those political reforms conceived by the Enlightenment
critics. Now society and state had to be organized so that the country as well
as Paris conformed to the new requirements. But reshaping the capital as
the political center of the country did not proceed without conflict and friction. That was not surprising as too many competing "sovereign" forces were
gathered there: the National Assembly, the Commune, the districts, the king,
the political clubs that gained more and more influence on public opinion
and, finally, the *peuple*, whose role remained problematical. All of them
mistrusted each other and coexisted in a state of delicate balance, the stability of which depended largely on the apparent elimination of the two worst
dangers—lack of food and counterrevolutionary plots.

Paris was now the seat of legislative and executive power in France and
this affected the way the city developed. The area around the Tuileries
became the political center, with the National Assembly meeting in the *salle
de manège* in the palace gardens, which was hastily remodeled for this purpose. Its offices were set up in barracks on the garden terrace of the
Feuillantine monastery. Other offices, as well as the National Assembly's
printing press, were installed in the Feuillantine monastery itself and in a
Capuchin friary on the other side of the place Louis Le Grand (now the place
Vendôme). The Jacobin Club was right near the place Louis Le Grand; the
Palais-Royal was just a few steps away from there, and so were various min-
istries, which together formed a concentration of power.

Districts on the Right Bank of the Seine, containing the city administration, thus became part of the new section in which government offices
were housed as of October 1789. The mayor and some of the city administration were established in the rue Neuve des Capucines, formerly the headquarters of the *Lieutenant générale de police;* and the commander of the
National Guard operated out of the Hôtel de Longueville, which stood
among the maze of alleys east of the Tuileries. The city administration's main
office, the Hôtel de Ville, was still further east in the place de Gréve; various other city offices were accommodated in the Marais.

This east-west axis, which still marks the topography of Paris, reflected
a need that was to last beyond the revolutionary period. Close cooperation
between state and city government was to their mutual advantage. It was an
effective way of dealing with the *peuple*, considered a latent threat. The possibility of future revolt also dominated the National Assembly debates, in
the spring of 1790, which preceded the writing of a new constitution for the
whole of France. Several deputies supported another state-of-emergency
regulation for Paris. Maximilien Robespierre was again one of those who
strongly opposed it, as shown by his speech of May 3, 1790.[78]

A compromise had to be found between the position of those who felt
enough had been gained from the revolt in 1789, and others, like Robespierre, who considered the work of the Revolution far from complete. The
Assembly tried to work out such a compromise in its far-reaching decree of
May 21, 1790.[79] The decree consisted of three provisions: first, the poll tax

was lowered from 6 to 3 livres, which meant that the number of voters in Paris increased from 50,000 to 80,000 "active citizens"; second, the 60 districts were abolished and replaced by 48 sections that were to function as primary voting districts. The newly constituted sections were, however, allowed a certain amount of maneuverability, in the hope that their political activity could be controlled. But as later events showed, this expectation was thoroughly disappointed. The sections in fact became the political bases for the *sans-culotte* movement.[80]

The third provision required all cities to be under the legal control of the departmental authorities and their executive bodies. In concrete terms this meant the Commune of Paris was subject to the direction of the department when it came to making up its budget or determining other "important matters." The political intent of this regulation was to dilute the feared radicalism of Paris voters with the more moderate vote of the department.

In the summer of 1790 it seemed as if the revolutionary energies of Paris had been exhausted. Even the elimination of the sixty districts—which these themselves tried to oppose—hardly provoked any reaction.[81] A spirit of reconciliation, of peaceful coexistence and brotherhood prevailed, which was reflected in the big *fête de la fédération* with which the first anniversary of the storming of the Bastille was ceremonially celebrated on July 14, 1790.

This festival marked the high point of a movement that had meantime caught the attention of the entire country. Within a very short time the Revolution had brought the French people into the political mainstream; and hardly had the first enthusiasm for the new freedom spent itself than it was felt that something had been irrevocably lost in the process. The immediate reaction to this feeling of loss was that cities and communities wanted to become "federated," a desire expressed quite specifically in numerous petitions and requests made by the provinces to the Commune of Paris as of the autumn of 1789.

These wishes, together with the example of the *pacte fédératif* (pact of federation)—concluded by the provinces of Anjou and Brittany in February 1790—suggested the following idea to the Paris districts.[82] It was decided to have a big celebration in the capital, to be attended by all eighty-three departments, at which everyone would solemnly swear allegiance to the freely chosen unity of the nation.[83] But the wary National Assembly was afraid that it would once again be overwhelmed by an autonomous movement of the people. It therefore limited attendance at this "civic and fraternal meeting of all citizens" to representatives of the National Guard from the various departments.[84]

The population of Paris was undeterred by this regulation and enthusiastically began preparing for the festivities to be held in the Champ de Mars, in the west of Paris. In the space of a month stages were erected and in the center of the area a huge mound of earth was built up for an altar to *la patrie*. Thousands of Parisians from all classes took up picks and shovels to get the work done in time. This helped to make the site a scene of spontaneous reconciliation for Parisians before national unity was celebrated on July 14.[85]

Festivities began on July 12 with the arrival of National Guard members from all over France. The painter Jacques-Louis David—who was to have frequent opportunity in the future to plan revolutionary spectacles—was in charge of the celebration.[86] The taking of the Bastille was commemorated at Notre Dame the following day with an *hiérodrame*, a musical drama in which over 600 musicians performed religious compositions by Désaugiers.[87] On July 14 a procession set out from the Bastille toward the Champ de Mars. It was headed by companies of the Paris National Guard; these were followed by representatives of the Commune and leaders of the sections, behind which came deputies of the National Assembly. They were accompanied by children and veterans, and the rest of the procession consisted of department delegates and National Guard units from provincial cities.

In spite of bad weather that day a sizable crowd waited patiently at the Champ de Mars for the procession which did not arrive until noon.[88] Talleyrand, the bishop of Autun, first held a mass "to celebrate unity, brotherhood, peace and freedom," at the altar of *la patrie*, which ended with a Te Deum.[89] Lafayette, representing everyone present, then came up to the altar to take the oath affirming national unity in freedom. Bailly de Virieu writes:

> At the same moment the National Guards said, in unison, "I swear." The clink of sabers and daggers made this oath particularly solemn, and all the spectators, as though prompted by an unknown force, also lifted their right hand and said "I swear." One cannot express in words the deep emotions this oath produced in everyone's soul. It was inconceivable to remain unmoved by this moment which sparked the fire of patriotism in everyone's heart.[90]

Radicalization and Repression

*T*HE FESTIVAL OF JULY 14, 1790, was far more than a symbolic spectacle artfully arranged by the painter David, the cynical Talleyrand, and the ambitious Lafayette to confuse the participants while capturing their hearts. No, the *fête de la fédération* was a truly popular event for the nation to celebrate itself. But once this high point in the "happy years" of the Revolution was over, whatever differences had been masked by the joy of that day reappeared with even greater clarity. A year later, almost to the day, any remaining illusions vanished when the Paris National Guard opened fire on the people, assembled in that very same Champ de Mars to show their support of the republic!

Results of the mayoral and local elections on August 2, 1790, were an early signal that the patriotic fervor expressed on July 14 had been a brief phenomenon. Bailly's reelection as mayor for a further two years, by an overwhelming majority of more than 12,000 of the 14,000 votes, ratified the existing balance of power. But what provided food for thought was that voter turnout amounted to less than 20 percent—the majority of the 80,000 "active citizens" having abstained.[91]

As those who were comparatively well off had thus turned their backs on the Revolution, the radical minority now stood a chance of one day taking over the helm. Future revolutionary positions were quietly being staked out behind the impressive front of unanimity and reconciliation that had been forged on the Champ de Mars on July 14. However, it was not until the spring of 1791 that the mist cleared to reveal a new political configuration. There were the moderate elements associated with Bailly and Lafayette, who wanted to curb the Revolution and ensure bourgeois order. Opposing them were the radicals—the Jacobins and their auxiliary troops, the future *sans-culottes*—who wanted to continue the Revolution.

The *sociétés populaires* or *sociétés fraternelles*, which sprang up in the petit bourgeois residential districts, became a very useful instrument for the mobilization of the *sans-culottes*.[92] The latter came from among the radicalized skilled workers whose livelihood was threatened by new regulations giving individuals the right to choose and practice any trade. Jean-Paul Marat was one of the first to recognize and capitalize on the fears and wishes of the petite bourgeoisie, who were disappointed by the outcome of the Revolution. He devoted himself emphatically to the establishment of such societies. Whereas the existing political clubs accepted only "active citizens," the new ones were open principally to "passive citizens," that is, those who were prevented by the property qualifications from influencing politics. Marat and some of the other demagogues aimed to politicize these disenfranchised and inexperienced people, who were filled with fervent revolutionary patriotism and whose deteriorating economic condition was driving them to express their discontent. The societies were a way of channeling this energy, of shaping a new revolutionary movement that would help its intellectual leaders come to power.

Discontent among workers was stimulated by the proclamation on April 1, 1791, abolishing the guilds and allowing workers freely to choose their trade. The title of master was discontinued, as were registers and employment records that had been effective measures of police control. This encouraged journeymen and apprentices to take a more inflexible stand on wages, leading to frequent confrontations. The growing dissatisfaction over wages was hardly surprising in view of the continual increase in prices, as well as the steady fall in value of the assignats. These had replaced the scarce silver money in December 1789 and were supposed to be backed by the sale of confiscated church properties. What was new, however, was the aggressivity with which the demands were expressed, and the strategies and methods used to carry them out.

Printers, considered the intellectual elite among workers, were the first to act. An *assemblée encyclopédique* (an association of owners of print-shops) informed the *Conseil Général de la Commune* that the typographers had determined to limit the number of apprentices and to fix a minimum wage.[93] Similar goals were pursued by the *union fraternelle des ouvriers en l'art de la charpente*, which was formed by Parisian carpenters on April 18, 1791.[94] The employers in this branch of industry requested the Commune to take action against the *union fraternelle*, as it represented a clear violation of rules forbidding combinations issued repeatedly under the Old Regime. At first the municipality merely issued an *avis aux ouvriers* (a notice to the workers) on April 26, advising them of the relevant labor legislation.[95] This notice had no effect whatever and by April 30 the master carpenters again requested the city authorities to take stronger measures against their employees. They pointed out that the union had meantime reached agreement to ask for a minimum wage of 50 sous per working day, and threatened to use force against anyone willing to work for less. As a result there had been active confrontations at various building sites in Paris since April 18.[96] Only now did the Commune become alarmed, and on May 4 it prohibited the carpenters' union.[97] Agitation continued, however, and work stoppages and confrontations took place with increasing frequency.[98] Unable to control the growing unrest, the Commune approached the administration of the department, which agreed that the matter should be turned over to the National Assembly.[99]

The National Assembly took prompt action, announcing the Chapelier Law as early as June 14, 1791. This law denied workers the right to form unions even if they worked in the same trade; it emphasized the principle of freedom of contract (the old guild system having been abolished); and it made illegal any form of agreement, any collective action or petition, or even strikes.[100] By means of these restrictions the Chapelier Law, which also had the support of the Left, quickly put an end to the strikes.

Various other measures were also enacted, all of which reflected a policy of social repression. The *ateliers de charité*, which had been reopened in October 1789, were closed again in the summer of 1791.[101] As of May 18, clubs, societies, and sections were forbidden to submit petitions to the National Assembly. Finally the Assembly ordered the municipalities to deal only with issues and problems that fell within their political and administrative competence.

All these repressive acts, passed without much resistance, gave the misleading impression that the revolutionary movement had been put down before it had the chance to become properly organized. What contributed to this view was that the *sans-culottes*, those of the *peuple* who were revolutionary democrats, formed isolated and easily controlled groups; as for the mass of the workers, they had been forced into even greater obedience by the new regulations and economic hardship. Under these circumstances, continued agitation by the left-wing press, as well as by the *sociétés fraternelles* and the radical political clubs, was largely ineffective. Lafayette and his National Guard controlled the scene and it appeared as if nothing could upset the seeming stability of what had been achieved.

But this situation began to look questionable on the morning of June 21, 1791, when news of the king's flight reached Paris. The Commune, however, had received the information in time to plan extensive safety measures.

At first everything remained quiet in Paris thanks to its precautions. But there was ferment beneath the apparently calm surface, and a vehement republican spirit was developing. Soon excited groups of people were to be seen everywhere in Paris, destroying pictures of the king, or his crest and other insignia of the monarchy.[102] At first spontaneous antimonarchical demonstrations were stirred up by the left-wing press, particularly Marat's and Fréron's papers which let loose a violent campaign against the king.[103] It was impossible to halt the effects of the agitation either by confiscations and prohibitions, or by the very obvious official tactic of explaining the king's flight as an abduction, so as to save the monarchy and the Constitution of September 1790. In fact the Assembly clung to the fiction of the king's abduction to avoid losing what it had gained thus far.

But the myth of the monarchy had been irretrievably compromised for the people since June 21. The circumstances under which Louis XVI entered Paris as a prisoner on June 25 made this abundantly clear. The National Guard had been instructed to protect the king from possible attacks by the waiting crowd, which turned out to be quite subdued.[104] The depressing spectacle possessed a deep symbolism that prefigured coming events: the bourgeois National Guard, which served the Commune and the National Assembly, were protecting a king whose people expressed their contempt for him. The gulf between the bourgeoisie and the *peuple* grew even wider and their basic political attitudes proved irreconcilable. The *peuple* now gave pride of place in their hearts to the Republic, preferring its promise of social and political equality. The bourgeoisie, on the other hand, were forced by their material interests to continue supporting the politically bankrupt monarchy.

Meanwhile the National Assembly noted the spreading republican ferment with ever greater mistrust. On July 16 it expressly requested the Commune to do everything in its power to quell the unrest in Paris before it became more serious.[105] This request hid a senseless political calculation: it aimed to force public opinion to accept the Assembly's previous transparent explanation of the king's flight as an abduction. The Commune was to proclaim martial law at the least provocation and end the republican unrest in bloody confrontation. An incident that was probably set up occurred a day later, on a fine summer's day, when a motley crowd came together in the Champ de Mars to sign a republican declaration on the altar of *la patrie*.

Two men, an unemployed wigmaker and a disabled war veteran, had hidden under the altar during the night, probably out of curiosity. The two were discovered on the morning of July 17, pulled from their hiding place, and murdered by an enraged crowd, which accused the men of wanting to blow up the altar.[106] Later the bloody heads of the two miserable creatures were spiked on lances and carried to the Palais-Royal. News of this act of lynch law had hardly been made known before the National Assembly convened and used the Champ de Mars murders as a welcome excuse to carry out their plans. Deputy Regnault de Saint-Jean-d'Angely expressed their intention: "I demand the imposition of martial law. It is the duty of this Assembly to regard as enemies of the state those who, by individual or collective petitions, incite the people."[107]

The Assembly considered that it had two good motives for its action: the republican declaration, which the Jacobins had originally supported; and the murder of two "good citizens," who wanted to make the people respect the law (as one speaker in the Assembly noted in all seriousness). These enabled the Assembly to classify any gathering of the people as a riotous mob of potential murderers, who had to be stopped by any available legal means. A corresponding order was sent to the Commune, which waited until early afternoon, however, before sending National Guard units to the Champ de Mars.

When Lafayette arrived at the head of his troops he saw a peaceful crowd dispersed over the area. Some were looking for protection from the heat of the July day among the trees and bushes; others were gathered around the altar of *la patrie* to sign the declaration. Only a few hotheads, grouped around the notorious agitator Fournier l'Américain, acted as though they wanted to engage the National Guard in a skirmish. But the crowd maintained its relaxed behavior so that nothing further happened.[108] The peaceful atmosphere of the Champ de Mars did not conform to the National Assembly's strategy, so they quickly had to find a new excuse to prevent the republican movement from developing. A rumor that a fast-growing crowd planned to make its way to the Assembly from the Champ de Mars gave them the necessary pretext. The municipality disregarded the reports by Lafayette and two members of the Commune who had also visited the Champ de Mars, all of whom agreed that it was nothing but hearsay. In the afternoon of July 17 martial law was declared and additional troops were sent to the Champ de Mars to disperse the crowd by force.[109]

The troops approached the Champ de Mars from different sides late that afternoon and were at first greeted with innocent curiosity by the crowd. But once it became obvious what they were there for, confrontations and loud insults resulted, and eventually some stones were thrown as well. Then the real trouble began: without showing the red flag, or issuing three requests to the crowd to disperse, as required by law, Lafayette's elite paid troops, mostly headed by aristocratic officers, opened fire on the unarmed people around the altar of *la patrie*.[110]

The massacre in the Champ de Mars, in which at least fifteen were killed and more than thirty wounded, irrevocably widened the gulf between the bourgeoisie and the *peuple*, and divided moderates from radicals. It was no longer possible to bridge this division, the hatred and mistrust being too great. Those who bore the responsibility for the massacre—the majority of the National Assembly, the Commune, and the propertied bourgeoisie they represented—had won a pyrrhic victory that day. Their use of force did not manage to restore respect for the monarchy, nor did their subsequent repressive actions accomplish anything.[111]

The Revenge of the Sans-Culottes

*B*Y SEPTEMBER THE DEMOCRATIC-REPUBLICAN FORCES had recovered from the shock of July 17. Preparations for the elections to the Legislative Assembly, interrupted by the king's flight, were resumed and helped to raise people's spirits. Three of the 48 sections that functioned as primary voting districts were controlled by the democrats: the Théâtre-Français section, where the Cordeliers Club met, the Quinze-Vingts in the faubourg Saint-Antoine, and the Ile-Saint-Louis. In 4 other sections democratic- or republican-oriented delegates were in the majority; the moderates (Feuillants), who wanted things to remain as they were, prevailed in the rest. The election results reflected this pattern, giving the moderates a major victory. Their success was repeated in October and November when deputies were elected to the representative bodies of the Paris department. This made the outcome of the mayoral election on November 15, 1791—Bailly having resigned—all the more surprising. Lafayette had given up his position as commander of the National Guard to be the candidate of the moderates. But he received only a third of all the votes, while Jérôme Pétion, a Jacobin lawyer from Chartres, was elected by a solid majority of 63 percent.

What brought about this surprising result was the massive number of moderate "active citizens" who had abstained: only a tenth of the approximately 100,000 eligible voters had voted. This very limited turnout helped the radicals to mobilize their members. For instance, Pétion received 70 percent of all the votes in the Théâtre-Français section, and almost 90 percent in the faubourg Saint-Antoine. Two other democrats obtained important city positions as well as Pétion: Louis-Pierre Manuel became municipal magistrate of the Commune, and Danton was made his deputy.

In contrast to the administration of the Commune, now controlled by democrats, the Legislative Assembly which met for the first time on October 1, 1791, was in the hands of the moderates. Its members were largely newcomers—Robespierre having made sure that no one from the Constituent Assembly was reelected to the new one—who showed far less understanding of the city's needs and problems than did their predecessors.

By now the suffering caused by the continual economic recession was far greater than the city's financial resources could handle. But the Legislative Assembly remained obstinate and refused to approve the necessary funds. The honest deputies considered it "a great injustice" to require their voters "to finance expenditures whose only purpose is to promote the well-being and comfort of the Parisians. Paris is a bottomless pit."[112]

The legislators' attitude was bound to create a heightening of the crisis sooner or later, and to encourage agitation by those sections now possessing greater political self-confidence. In October 1791, for instance, the *Proceedings of the Commune* cited an *Adresse aux Parisiens*, expressing the following sentiments: "Because of its large population, the capital of the realm is capable of defying the final gestures of the tyrants on its own; it made the Revolution."[113] But this newfound political awareness still had to prove itself in action. The grain supply problem, in spite of a good harvest in 1791, provided the needed motivation. The sections kept up a steady attack on grain speculators and even accused the city administration of complicity. They managed to get the Jacobins and some of the *sociétés populaires* to support their campaign, which began at the beginning of October. At that time thirty-two sections sent delegates to a general meeting, whose purpose was to reorganize grain distribution then controlled by the city administration. Their attempt was resisted by the authorities, and the sections tried again at the end of the month, when their deputies turned to the Legislative Assembly.[114]

This conflict between the sections and authorities of both city and department lasted for three months but was by no means as fruitless as it seemed. Though the sections did not get what they wanted, their persistence proved their strength and they regained the ground they had lost in the July elections. Evidence of the good harvest of 1791 reached the Paris market just in time to prevent the sections from inciting any further unrest against grain speculation and increased bread prices. However, the precarious condition of food supplies and prices remained a prime incentive for provocation. A good example of this was the increment in the price of sugar shortly thereafter, which rose from 22 sous a pound in the autumn, to 3 francs in January 1792.[115]

Reaction to that increase was unanimous. As of January 21, 1792, whatever sugar was found in warehouses, at wholesalers, and at times even in individual retail stores was stolen and sold for betweeen 20 and 25 sous a pound. Such an arbitrary method of setting a maximum price for a basic food was geared to the disposable income of the *peuple*. In contrast to previous occasions, when they had taken drastic countermeasures, this time the authorities showed tolerance. It was significant for the way in which the antagonism between *sans-culottes* and Jacobins was minimized in the interest of political unity. The sections, the Jacobin Club and Mayor Pétion, all of whom believed in the principles of free trade, simply referred to the relevant regulations but bowed to popular demand for a "maximum price."

But the unrest and lawbreaking sparked by the rise in sugar as well as coffee prices were only of limited importance. Of far greater consequence were the conflicts developing among various factions of the national government in the winter of 1791–92. They affected the basis of the Revolution itself and their resolution made a radical change in the structure of political power. The conflicts were provoked by the suspicion that the king's flight was part of a counterrevolutionary plot by European states. Jacques Pierre Brissot, who headed the so-called Girondins, now campaigned for the idea of a great European revolutionary war. He fervently believed it would destroy the enemies of the Revolution and bring the blessings of freedom to all the oppressed peoples of Europe.

It was certainly a persuasive idea, appealing to the revolutionary nationalism of the *peuple*, as well as to the Legislative Assembly. It would transfer the still unresolved confrontation between supporters and opponents of the Revolution from France to Europe, and achieve a quick and triumphant victory there. Robespierre, leader of the Jacobins, warned of the problems: the revolutionary goals had not even been consolidated in France and the country was unprepared for a big war. Brissot's European crusade posed a great risk that could end in a terrible disaster for the Revolution's cause. Still the idea of a crusade for the freedom of all nations—supported by Brissot and others—was filled with such revolutionary romanticism that any misgivings broached by Robespierre, Marat, or Danton went unheeded. The other side, the monarchist Feuillants together with the king, wanted a European war in the hope that it would save the throne. Thus reactionaries as well as revolutionaries played the war card to hedge their bets, though for entirely different reasons.

Along with the disagreement over war or peace that polarized the revolutionary camp, there was the matter of who was to lead the Revolution in the future—the Girondins around Brissot, or Robespierre's Jacobin followers. In terms of political strategy there was not much difference between them, both groups being democrats. Their rivalry owed more to personal animosities and incompatible temperaments, and especially to their ambition for power. But leadership of the movement would only go to the one who had the support of the *peuple* of Paris—the sections, the *sociétés fraternelles*, and the *sans-culottes*.

In this contest the Girondins proved to have better political instinct at first. Their plan for staying in power was based on two issues: one was the popular demand for war, the other was the energetic pursuit of reconciliation between bourgeoisie and *peuple*. The latter involved reconstituting a government representing all levels of society, which had not existed since July 17, 1791, but was indispensable to the Revolution's successful continuation. Given this background it becomes clear why the Girondins expressed so much support for the people's demands for weapons. They believed that all those too poor to join the National Guard should at least be supplied with pikes.

It took a further six months, though, until the democrats finally accepted the solution made plain since the Champ de Mars massacre of July 17. The people were given arms; they would resist the Counterrevolution by their sheer number. As of January 1792 the pike, red cap, and long pants instead of the "feudal" knee-length *culotte* became the symbols of the *sans-culotte* movement.

The emergence of the newly self-confident *peuple* as another political force marked a fresh stage in the Revolution. Their strength lay in the *sans-culotte* movement's large membership, making Paris the seat of revolutionary power. The group's political goals were largely those of the democrats, but they had very different social and economic objectives. They stood for large-scale reform of the economy, so that everyone would have work and a livelihood, according to his "natural" needs. These loosely developed concepts were based on a utopian ideal of social equality. But the group lacked the ideological coherence to maneuver their own political advancement. This was reflected in the diversity of its followers—the shopkeepers, artisans, and skilled workers, who came mostly from the petite bourgeoisie.

Lack of an ideology inclined the *sans-culottes* to react spontaneously rather than initiate their own plans. That made them an unpredictable but potentially useful force. Their ability to mobilize masses of people, as the fall of the Bastille had shown, could become an invaluable tool in the hands of the right person—someone who would know how to manipulate and direct their limited concepts. Robespierre was the first to understand this and to use the *sans-culottes* for his political objectives. He outlined his plan to the Jacobin Club on February 10, 1792: the Jacobins were to work through the sections to gain influence in the National Assembly.[116]

This scheme was put into effect within a few months. Its success was due mainly to the declaration and mismanaged conduct of the war against the King of Bohemia and Hungary, from April 1792 onward. The Girondins had succeeded in convincing the Legislative Assembly to wage the war, while the Jacobins still considered it disastrous for the Revolution. It soon became clear, however, that the generals heading the French armies were defying their orders. Instead of a quick offensive, to help the population of the Austrian Netherlands revolt, they appeared to have plans of their own. They were pursuing a defensive campaign in order to keep an eye on Paris. The Girondins found themselves desperately trying to cover up the officers' independent and contrary strategies. That proved an irrevocable mistake on their part, contributing greatly to the betrayal psychosis in Paris. For the *sans-culottes* saw the generals' cautious tactics—particularly the pullback of troops without even engaging the enemy—as outright treason to the revolutionary cause. When the three commanding generals, Biron, Rochambert, and Lafayette, decided to cease fighting altogether on May 18, it was considered the final treacherous blow. Now it was no longer possible to gloss over and conceal their actions. Clearly they were willing to let the Austrian troops advance on Paris without any interference.

The sections and the *sans-culottes* recognized and wanted to prepare for this emergency. On May 29 residents of the faubourg Saint-Marceau took up arms and a group of demonstrators from the Gobelins section, armed with pikes, forced their way into the Legislative Assembly. That set an example. In the days that followed more and more sections requested they be allowed to meet in permanent session and to arm themselves. But the feeling that these measures would be inadequate led to a call for 200,000 volunteer troops to be moved to Paris from the provinces. The reason given for such a transfer, and to make it look harmless, was that a communal celebration was to take place on July 14. As the Girondin leadership was unwilling to refuse this public demand, the king expressed his veto and on June 12 he also dismissed the Girondin ministers who had served since March 10. These actions pointed to a coup from the "top," especially when Lafayette asked the king on June 16 to prohibit meetings of the Jacobin Club. Everything was at stake now, but the Legislative Assembly as well as the political clubs appeared to be in a state

of paralysis. Only the sections remained firm. On June 20 they armed themselves and advanced on the Assembly's meeting hall in the Tuileries Gardens.

The events of June 20 were neither influenced nor directed by Jacobins
or Girondins, but by "leaders of the people"—men like the wealthy brewer
Antoine-Joseph Santerre from the faubourg Saint-Antoine, the bizarre marquis de Saint-Huruge, or Claude-François Lazowski, son of a nobleman who
belonged to the politicized aristocracy. In the course of the morning the *sans-
culottes* who had come from the suburbs surrounded the Assembly. A group
representing the demonstrators was admitted into the meeting hall. They
submitted a resolution that ended in the threat that the people would continue to bear arms until all parts of the Constitution had been enacted.[117]

After the group left the hall the waiting crowd gathered in front of a
locked gate at the entrance to the Tuileries Gardens. The gate gave way
under the pressure and the demonstrators flooded the terrace of the
Feuillantine monastery. They then moved to the place du Carrousel where
they regrouped. Encouraged by Santerre and Saint-Huruge, they forced
their way into the palace without interference from the National Guards stationed there. All was confusion as the mob swept through the royal apartments. For over two hours the king was trapped in a window recess as they
shouted their demands, always ending in the refrain "down with the veto."
Though he put on the red Jacobin cap, offered him on the point of a saber,
and drank several toasts to the health of the nation, he remained quite
adamant in his refusal to grant their requests.[118] Toward evening Mayor
Pétion finally put an end to the horrible spectacle and the National Guards
cleared the palace and the Tuileries Gardens without meeting any resistance.

This first direct encounter between the *sans-culottes*, who stood for a
democratic and social revolution, and the counterrevolutionaries, represented by the king and his court, seemed to have ended without any major gains
for either side. It was true that the king had stood firm, and the counterrevolutionaries even felt encouraged enough to relieve Mayor Pétion and
Manuel (the municipal magistrate) of their positions. But none of that was
really signficant; what mattered was that none of the forty-eight sections dis-
approved of the events of June 20. It revealed a basic unanimity and determination on fundamental revolutionary issues. What appeared like a stalemate had in fact strengthened and intensified the pressure from below.

The strong impression of that day, that *la patrie* and the Revolution were
in utmost danger, induced the Paris sections and provincial administrations
to disregard the royal veto. They decided to act independently and order volunteer troops to proceed to Paris. This autonomous action was sanctioned by
the Legislative Assembly on July 2 and quickly brought about other events.
On July 3 Pierre-Victurien Vergniaud, one of the most powerful Girondin
orators, severely criticized the politics of the executive, especially the
ambiguous behavior of Louis XVI.[119] The following day the *Declaration du
danger de la patrie* was formulated. On July 11 the Assembly approved this
declaration—meantime Prussia had entered the war as Austria's ally—and it
was duly announced on July 22. The Paris sections had been meeting in per-

manent session for some time now, with all citizens participating regardless of property qualifications. The National Guards were put on alert and new volunteer battalions were recruited. On July 17 Manuel, who had been reinstated as municipal magistrate, arranged that the sections be given a central office in the Hôtel de Ville so that their decisions could be coordinated.

These measures were taken with outside threats in mind, as well as to revive the revolutionary cause. They were intensified when the arrogant manifesto by the Duke of Brunswick, commander of the Allied armies, was made known in Paris. This bragging document threatened the capital with the most terrible reprisals. All members of the Legislative Assembly, of the department, the sections, the Commune, and the National Guard, as well as numerous others, would be dealt with by a military tribunal and shown no mercy. The declaration promised that if as much as a hair on the king's head were harmed, Paris would be completely destroyed by the victors.

However, such threats had an entirely different effect from what was intended. Rather than intimidate the revolutionaries, the manifesto provoked them to express what they had not dared to do previously. The Mauconseil section made a start by issuing a proclamation, signed by over 600 citizens, stating that it was impossible to defend the nation's freedom effectively under existing laws. The section therefore declared its loyalty oath void and refused to acknowledge the sovereignty of Louis XVI. Finally, it announced that it intended to contact the Legislative Assembly, to find out what measures were planned to save *la patrie*. Furthermore, regardless of what the Assembly answered, the section reserved the right to act in whatever way it saw fit; that its citizens were even willing to be buried under the ruins of freedom, should that become necessary.[120]

Now it was out in the open: one of the forty-eight Paris sections had declared its intention not to wait any longer. It was willing to risk rebellion against crown and constitution to defend the Revolution and *la patrie* against all danger. This was a signal and by August 3 all Paris sections, except for that of the Temple, sent a joint request to the Assembly demanding the king's deposal.[121] There was no longer any doubt that Paris had decided to revolt again and to complete what it had begun. When the eruption occurred on August 10 it was indeed "un grand acte du peuple" ("a great undertaking by the people"), as Michelet writes.[122] It completed what had been begun on October 6, 1789, when the women of Paris forced the king to move back to the old capital. And this time, just as before, it was not the work of Jacobin or Girondin deputies of the Assembly; neither was it the Cordeliers, nor members of the Commune who were directly responsible for the surge of revolutionary indignation. It was brought about by the sections, various nameless individuals who had come together in the *sans-culotte* movement.

The court had known for days what was being planned and had made extensive preparations. The Tuileries had been turned into a fortress and Swiss mercenaries had been added to the National Guards already guarding the court. Cannon were set up at strategic points and lead and gunpowder supplies were increased. In short everything was ready to meet the threat and the court, more splendid than ever in those final days, basked in the vanity of an assured victory. It was anticipated that the *peuple*—the *sans-culottes* and the volunteer troops—and the entire revolutionary movement would be destroyed by the Tuileries. This seemed a certainty because the insurgents, though superior in number, were inexperienced and poorly equipped to take on the massed military force of the court. The *peuple* were driven by anger and frustration, and their enthusiasm for the Revolution at first blinded them to the dangers that lay ahead.

When the time came, and the tocsin sounded on the night of August 9, their naïve fervor was shaken by the reality of what seemed a hopeless fight from the start. Even harder to contemplate than attacking the well-defended Tuileries was the uncertainty over how many different battles would have to be waged. After all, the revolt planned for the following day was not only against the court in its fortified palace but the Parisian bourgeoisie as well. Its members formed the elite National Guard battalions they would have to face; and the Guards had long regarded the *sans-culotte* movement with open hostility. Fortunately, though, the Legislative Assembly and the administration of the department—both of which clearly supported the monarchy in this crisis—were incapable of controlling the situation as it developed.

At first the revolutionaries had no central authority and were slow to organize events. On the evening of August 9 each of the sections had agreed to appoint three commissioners, "to join the Commune in saving *la patrie*," as their duties were vaguely described.[123] But these stalwart commissioners took their time getting to the Hôtel de Ville, arriving only in the early hours of August 10. A similar delay occurred in the formation of the marching columns that were to set out from the suburbs. Santerre, who was in command there, had difficulty in planning his strategy. Finally, he decided to order the volunteer troops from Marseilles to set out for the Tuileries.

At the Hôtel de Ville things were also in disarray. The Commune's representatives had disappeared and the new commissioners were loath to act without authorization. After lengthy deliberations they constituted themselves as the new revolutionary Commune of the *peuple*. Now the revolt had a central executive to direct action. One of their first operations was to remove the crown's loyal battalion of National Guards, whose members belonged to the wealthy goldsmithing district, from the Pont Neuf. That was very important strategically, giving the revolutionary marching columns from the faubourg Saint-Marceau and the Cordeliers district clear access to the Right Bank of the Seine, where they joined the others from the faubourg Saint-Antoine. The revolutionaries also gained command over the National Guard after killing Mandat. Santerre then became its new commander.

Groups of the angry mob arrived at the Tuileries palace in the course of the morning of August 10. The king and his family had already left to seek refuge in the nearby National Assembly. After initial strong resistance by the Swiss Guards, who fired on the crowd and killed or wounded more than 370 men, the situation improved for the revolutionaries. They were helped by partially trained and well-armed volunteer troops from Marseilles and Brest;

and by the fact that the National Guards assigned to the palace abstained from fighting.

To avoid any further senseless bloodshed the king finally ordered his men to give up their arms and surrender. Now the infuriated revolutionaries took revenge for their own losses. They attacked and brutally massacred the defenseless Swiss Guards.[124] Many commentators ascribed this horrible act of popular justice to criminal elements, who had supposedly used the opportunity to vent their murderous instincts. But such explanations, intended to defame the revolutionary movement as the creation of common felons, were not borne out by the facts. The social background of the insurgent dead and wounded was revealed in the information later given by their dependents claiming compensation. Even Michelet points out that all identifiable combatants were blameless citizens, most of them artisans who had a permanent residence and place of work. Whole groups of individuals from a particular trade—cabinetmakers, for instance, from the same street or building in the faubourg Saint-Antoine—often fought as a unit. Moreover, most of the casualties were over thirty, old enough to be influenced by motives other than the sheer pleasure of a fight.[125] These men belonged to the Parisian *sans-culottes* and their struggle that day brought some of the concessions they had been demanding for so long.

Victory and Dictatorship of the Sans-Culottes

THE EVENTS OF AUGUST 10, 1792, altered the character of the Revolution so radically as to create a completely new and democratic phase, the one that really gave the Revolution its great historical importance. The change was not brought about by the forced abdication of the king and his imprisonment in the Temple, or by his replacement by a provisional executive. Neither was it due to the premature dissolution of the Legislative Assembly in favor of a National Convention charged with working out a new republican constitution. Rather, it resulted from the Assembly's decision of August 11 that the election of a new Convention be based on the vote of all citizens over twenty-one who had lived at the same address in a municipality for one year and who were not lackeys or servants. This did away with the discrimination between "active" and "passive" citizens against which the *sans-culottes* had been fighting for so long. Indeed, the old system had been abolished in the sections since June 10. Now that all citizens were declared politically equal, various positions in the state and Commune were open to competent individuals. Anyone with an unblemished record could join the National Guard; and as well-to-do Parisians increasingly preferred to forgo what they considered a tiresome obligation, the Guard soon became the armed force of the *sans-culottes*.

Not only the king, now confined in the Temple like an ordinary bankrupt, but also the Legislative Assembly lost all power as a result of the events of August 10. It was unable to give Louis XVI the protection he sought and had to hand him over to the insurgents. The power vacuum thus created was filled by the revolutionary Commune of Paris which was now the only and highest authority in the country, superior even to the Legislative Assembly. To give the Commune greater legitimacy, its executive committee was now enlarged to consist of 288 section members. Membership in this new and permanent *conseil général* consisted largely of the middle and petite bourgeoisie. Aside from 2 workers there were 100 shopkeepers and artisans, 54 professionals such as journalists, actors, and doctors, 20 civil servants, 23 lawyers, and 5 priests.[126] The social composition of this committee typified the *sans-culotte* ideal, and its leaders were men who would soon form the radical core of the *Montagne*, the so-called Mountain party in the Convention: Robespierre, Marat (though he was only co-opted after September 2), the lawyer Billaud-Varenne, Chaumette the "professional revolutionary," the actor Collot d'Herbois, and Tallien the ex-priest.[127]

However, the general elation at the success of August 10 was marred by the feeling that at the very moment of the Revolution's greatest triumph— its undeniable move toward democracy—it faced the threat of suppression. This was not mere imagination. The monarchy and its counterrevolutionary allies had lost another battle on August 10, but they had by no means lost the war. Their chances of winning were not at all bad, because the Austrian and Prussian troops had already entered France and appeared ready to march on Paris to punish it.

The revolutionaries' fear of this threat paved the way for the policies of repression and terror that were to come. The Commune took the lead and the helpless Legislative Assembly went along with it—albeit unwillingly—and sanctioned the requested measures. As early as August 11 a decree was passed that gave municipal administrations the right to engage in police investigations. In Paris this task was shared by a fifteen-man Committee of Surveillance (which also served as an executive body in place of the mayor who had become a figurehead), and individual sections that had formed their own surveillance groups. These were given far-reaching authority and were gradually taken over by the *sans-culottes*, who used them for their own political purposes.[128]

When the town of Longwy's capitulation to the advancing Prussian troops became known on August 26, the fear that had inspired the politics of terror turned to hysteria. The Prussians advancing on Paris were seen as the scourge of God, or the coming of the Last Judgment. Wild rumors of atrocities committed by the Prussians and Austrians—whose victims had naturally been supporters of the Revolution—were spread about and caused the masses to invent ever more frightening scenes. It was said that the inhabitants of Paris would be herded together before the kings of Europe on a large uncultivated plain—perhaps that of Saint-Denis—where they would be mercilessly punished. According to gossip, it had long been decided to destroy the whole country, to lay all its cities to waste because the European monarchs had agreed that a wasteland was preferable to an insurgent people.[129]

The impression of real danger conveyed by the approaching armies was heightened by the supposed threat of a large conspiracy planned by the Church within the country. The uprising and unrest in the Morbihan and in the Deux-Sèvres, as well as the plot by the nobility of Grenoble, were considered proof positive. People were convinced that Paris was full of traitors and conspirators, who were awaiting their moment of triumph with joyful impatience and who would see to it that no one escaped their revenge. The masses were suddenly obsessed with finding and destroying these traitors in time, an obsession that neither the Commune nor the moribund National Assembly could dispel.

After Longwy's capitulation Paris was quickly turned into a fortress. The gates were barred, horses and coaches were requisitioned, and the Legislative Assembly decided to enlist 30,000 men in the city and its environs. That not being sufficient, Danton appeared in the Assembly on the evening of August 28 and requested the immediate approval of a whole catalog of emergency measures for the defense of Paris and the Revolution. In addition to arming all able citizens, he demanded that house searches be sanctioned to eliminate royalist conspirators. In situations of this sort the Revolution had to be informed about everything; as Danton put it: "I know the means, I know the obstacles; I know the men and I know where they are; I also know where the weapons are hidden. When *la patrie* is in danger everything belongs to it."[130]

These house searches, begun the afternoon of August 29 with only limited results, were intended to have a psychological effect: royalist plotters were to be made to feel insecure as Danton had indicated. Moreover, the searches were now given the stamp of legality to prevent further arbitrary "wild searches" by sections acting autonomously. But whatever the motivations for these *visites domiciliaires*, their real effect was to increase the psychosis of fear which had already seized the capital's population. When news of the Prussian army's occupation of Verdun was received in Paris on September 2, the Commune immediately decided of its own accord to intensify defense measures, to organize a volunteer army of 60,000 men in the Champ de Mars, to arm them and send them into battle. That raised public excitement to such a pitch as to provoke the September massacres—the massive slaughter of the defenseless inmates of Paris prisons by delirious bloodthirsty crowds. The latter were by no means the dregs of society but rather decent storekeepers and artisans who were the backbone of the *sans-culotte* movement, and their actions constituted one of the most horrifying chapters of the entire history of the Revolution.

There had been indications that excesses might take place, but precautionary regulations, such as the creation of special revolutionary tribunals, were of no avail. Responsibility for the dreadful event was later repeatedly blamed on certain elements, so as to discredit a specific revolutionary party or even individual leaders like Danton or Marat. It is true that Fréron, who numbered the "bloodsucker" Marat among the regular contributors to his ultraradical paper *L'Orateur du Peuple*, had hardly let an opportunity pass after August 10 without drawing his readers' attention to the "conspirators" in the prisons. It is also a fact that the Poissonière section had believed the summary execution of the prisoners to be necessary for the common good before the volunteers left for the front.[131] This section represented the *sans-culottes* who actively feared reprisals against their wives and children while they were away fighting the enemy. No outside encouragement had been needed for this mass execution which claimed more than a thousand victims—mostly criminals, but also numerous priests who had refused to take the August 14 oath of "freedom and equality" demanded of all citizens. Under the pressure of extreme danger, long pent-up fears were released in the form of atavistic, bloodthirsty murders of even such inmates of the Salpêtrière as prostitutes, victims of venereal diseases, and orphans.[132] The murders were the terrible expression of a *grande peur* that had accumulated in the chaos of revolutionary Paris, whose population had been subjected to three years of alternating hope and disappointment, of misery and deceptive promises of happiness. Now they reacted with the savagery of a raw force of nature and did not stop until its strength was spent.[133]

Behind the inaction of the authorities, who did nothing to prevent the pogrom, lay worries about the fate of Paris and the Revolution to be decided by the battle following the fall of Verdun. As Danton admitted with undisguised cynicism, the prisoners' terrible end counted for little in view of the fateful development of the military situation. While the prisons turned into slaughterhouses where inmates were stabbed, cut up, and clubbed like mad dogs, life went on as usual outside and elections were even held for deputies to the National Convention.

The new Convention assembled on September 20 for its organizational meeting, immediately following which it conducted a trial of Louis XVI. The sentence of death he received was the logical conclusion to the great massacre that was supposed to stamp out the Counterrevolution. But the plan to decapitate the king like a common criminal struck many contemporaries not only as an unheard of, truly revolutionary action, but as quite impossible—a deed that would taint everyone with the blood of the victim.

In spite of such sentiments the Provisional Executive Committee instructed the Commune to take the necessary security measures for Louis XVI's execution on January 21, 1793. The Commune followed the instructions in a way that reflected their fears quite openly. The sections were called to arms; various entrances to the city were provided with double their number of guards; the sections were declared permanent bodies; instructions were given for all streets to be lit; and a general curfew was imposed for the hours preceding the king's execution. These measures resulted in an unusually quiet, seemingly threatening atmosphere in the streets in the early morning of January 21. Following official orders all shops were closed, as were all gates, doors, and windows. The streets were empty. In complete contrast to the somber silence in most parts of the city, there was feverish activity in the streets leading from the Temple to the place de la Révolution, lined on both sides by National Guards who stood four deep.

Santerre, commander in chief of the National Guards, arrived at the Temple at 8.30 A.M. to conduct the king to his execution. Accompanied by his confessor, Louis XVI got into the closed coach waiting in the courtyard. The king's final journey took more than an hour. Detachments of the various sections armed with pikes and muskets, and National Guards on horseback escorted the coach. The king arrived at the foot of the six-foot-high guillotine structure around ten o'clock. Two thousand federal volunteers and National Guards were stationed around the scaffold; behind them a crowd of thousands of onlookers had gathered. When he arrived the king waited motionless in the coach for a few moments before descending, his eyes on the metallic silhouette of the guillotine outlined against the gray, rainy Paris sky. After he had taken off his outer clothes himself, he allowed his hands to be tied behind his back and let executioner Sanson cut his hair. Then, leaning on his confessor, Louis XVI climbed the steep steps up to the platform of the guillotine. Once he was there he wanted to address the onlookers, but a roll of drums began immediately and drowned his words. Shortly thereafter the blade severed Louis XVI's annointed head. That released the tension of the crowd which shouted "Long live the Republic! Long live the Nation! Long live freedom!" The king's corpse, like that of other guillotined victims, was taken to the cemetery of the Madeleine church and unceremoniously interred in a mass grave.

The people accepted the king's execution without a word. So much had happened so rapidly that they had become fatalistic and unimpressionable. Their initial revolutionary fervor had been sobered by various threats. The Revolution, which had originally been limited to finding practical use for the critical principles of Enlightenment philosophy, forfeited its innocence once the September massacres revealed its dark passions and secret, vengeful urges. Its former idealism was replaced by the political necessity of accommodating the new force of the *sans-culottes* who were indispensable to the final victory of the bourgeois Revolution. This fact, together with the fluctuating course of the war, and above all, the ever-present economic crisis and inadequate food supply, increasingly influenced events in the Convention. It was there that the Mountain party expressed its growing radical-democratic views which were diametrically opposed to those of the Girondins who, as Michelet said aptly, were becoming more "royalized." The developing conflict between two parties now out to destroy each other was eventually settled by a new uprising of the Paris sections and the *sans-culottes*. Only four months elapsed from January 21 to the Girondins' loss of power on June 2, 1793, but time enough for the aims of the Revolution to be thoroughly transformed.

By the end of May it was clear that the sections were preparing an uprising. But it was predictable that this was not going to be the great demonstration envisaged by the Jacobins. They hoped to assert the political and moral integrity of the *peuple* and thus force the Convention to rid itself of its corrupt Girondins. Instead the uprising turned out to be a violent revolt that neither Commune nor Jacobins nor the Mountain would be able to control.

At this point it was the *sans-culottes* and the radical revolutionary *enragés*—a group that had come into being in the spring of 1793 and whose vociferous agitation found favor with the *sans-culottes*—who had the most influence in the sections. A central committee, located in the archbishop's palace, coordinated the action being planned by thirty-four of the forty-eight sections.[134] On the evening of May 30 it was decided to begin the revolt on the following day, to arrest the "suspects," and to order the National Guard to advance on the Convention, which had meanwhile moved to the Tuileries. The aim was to force the Convention to expel the twenty-two Girondins from its ranks and to hand them over to the revolutionary tribunal. François Hanriot took over as commander of the National Guard from Santerre, who was to head the Vendée army.

Objections raised to the plans by thirty-four of the sections did not bother the central coordinating committee. It claimed to have been given complete authority by the sovereign people of Paris, as expressed by the majority vote of the sections.[135] The committee informed the Commune on the morning of May 31 that it was dissolved and would be reconstituted with the unlimited powers then held by the people's commissioners. In other words the municipal council of Paris, which until then had been subject to the Convention, was to be replaced by a Commune legitimized by the sovereignty of the people.

However, hardly had the alarm been sounded at daybreak when it became apparent that the committee did not have the expected broad support for its plans. A great deal of confusion resulted and the revolt almost ended before it had begun. The only thing the committee accomplished—after much effort and not until five o'clock in the afternoon—was to have the Convention surrounded by a few armed contingents. Several petitions were handed to the Convention, the most radical of which was worked out by the committee itself but presented in the name of the Commune. It called for the arrest not only of the twenty-two Girondins and the ministers Clavière and Lebrun, but also of various members of the so-called Commission of Twelve who had been appointed to the Convention on May 18 at the bidding of the Girondins to investigate the Paris Commune. Included in the petitions was the list of demands submitted by the *sans-culottes* at every opportunity since August 10, 1792. Although these demands were basically supported by the Mountain deputies, the majority of the Convention managed only to agree on the dissolution of the Commission of Twelve. That was little enough and did not alter the fact that May 31 was a fiasco for those who had prepared the uprising. Still the Jacobins could claim success that day. They had not been defeated, as they feared they would be, and political leadership of the Revolution was still in their hands.

But the insurgents' committee did not give up its efforts and used Saturday June 1 to set up a systematic plan for further action the next day. The events of May 31 had shown that it could only mobilize some of the sections, so that it had to concentrate its forces this time.

A crowd of several thousand people surrounded the Convention early in the afternoon of June 2, though most of them had come out of sheer curiosity. The committee arranged for battalions of the National Guard, whose loyalty to its cause was assured, to take up position in front of the crowd so as to prevent any contact between the deputies and the moderate sections. When several deputies wanted to leave the Convention around five o'clock, they were prevented by Hanriot's troops, whose cannon were pointed at the Tuileries. The Convention was being held prisoner by Paris. To safeguard its dignity and independence, all the deputies left the palace with the exception of thirty members of the Mountain including Robespierre and Marat. Hanriot confronted them again and ordered the president, Hérault de Séchelles, to give up the guilty members. When Hérault refused, Hanriot ordered the cannoneers, "Take up your positions!" Faced with this threat the deputies fled back to the assembly hall and decided, after a long and heated debate, to agree to the insurgents' terms insofar as it meant putting the Girondin deputies and the two ministers, Clavière and Lebrun, under house arrest. That sealed the political fate of the Girondins; the Mountain, backed by the people of Paris, had triumphed over its political opponent in the Convention. This marked the beginning of a new chapter in the Revolution.

Indeed June 2, 1793, became an important date in the revolutionary history of Paris, with the *sans-culottes* having become the strongest political force in the capital. Their new position of strength enabled them to obtain economic, social, and political concessions from the Mountain that the latter would never have made of its own accord. Nevertheless, the movement was no more than an influential minority able to dominate the revolutionary committees in certain sections. These committees, consisting of no more than twelve members—all proven *sans-culottes*—managed to fill the power vacuum left by the disappearance of the Girondins. Because neither the Convention, nor the Committee of Public Safety (that did not become fully effective until September), or even the Paris Commune, the Jacobin or the Mountain parties were now in complete control. Even the mysterious central committee that had coordinated recent events was disbanded on June 6 and vanished from the scene.

After June 2 the real strength lay in the revolutionary committees that knew how to terrorize other members of the sections to compensate for their own minority position. Not until extensive purges were carried out in the summer of 1793 did the militant *sans-culottes* gain full control of the sections. Each member of a revolutionary committee was paid for attendance—3 francs at first and then 5 francs—and this tended to encourage primarily petty artisans to volunteer.

The committees' control over their fellow-citizens was as complete as it was terrible. They were the ones who received the innumerable denunciations and who decided what action to take. They were also responsible for the arrests, house searches, and *cartes de sûreté* (identity documents) without which a person was automatically suspect. But it was precisely the despotism and terror practiced by these committees that made them an indispensable tool of the Revolution. In the months of its greatest crisis they prevented the Revolution from sinking into anarchy.

Meantime the chronic food shortage had become even worse, providing additional incentive for the introduction of the Reign of Terror. The *sans-culottes* had long considered that grain speculators deserved the death penalty, and they now pressed for it still more strongly. The *enragé* group acted as the main spokesmen in this campaign. Of course the situation was particularly complicated in Paris; though the price of bread could be kept at 3 sous a pound due to a subsidy by the Convention, other foodstuffs had become considerably more expensive and some items, such as soap, were almost impossible to obtain. However, even bread grains and flour became scarce after the maximum price for grain was announced in May, and once the assignats dropped to 30 percent of their nominal value by July 1793. A police report dated June 17, 1793, refers to the possibility of famine, a concern that was shared by many residents of the capital and ended in much more forceful measures being taken against speculators and profiteers. On June 15 the militant *Droits de l'homme* section (in which Jean Varlet of the *enragé* party was an important figure) demanded that price controls be set for all goods, and decrees issued concerning racketeers and hoarders. Jacques Roux (the other leader of the *enragés*) also flooded the Convention with petitions. They ended with the extremely disturbing conclusion that unless the Convention came up with the requisite measures "the *peuple* would feel that the cause of the poor is further from your hearts than that of the rich, and it would give them unmistakable proof that you are engaged in a counterrevolution."[136]

Marat's murder on the evening of July 13 added such momentum to the *sans-culottes'* agitation—manipulated by the *enragés* and now supported by the power-hungry Hébert—that the unity of those who favored the continuation of a free economy began to crack.[137] In any case, the people had seen Marat as the guiding light of the Revolution. His radicalism, his incorruptibility, the simple life he was known to lead, and not least the hatred with which all previous revolutionary governments had persecuted him, made him more popular than anyone else. This had led to his election to the Convention despite the undisguised aversion shown him by most members of the Mountain and especially by Robespierre. Desmoulins once gave a fitting description of Marat's importance: "On the other side of Marat lies territory similar to the unexplored regions that ancient geographers used to refer to as *terra incognita* on their maps."[138] With his death this *terra incognita* acquired contours.

Aside from being under more pressure from the *sans-culottes*, the Convention found itself facing growing problems on the various battle fronts. The entire northern frontier was lost, Mainz had to capitulate, Landau was besieged, and Alsace surrendered to the enemy. As all of this restricted its ability to act freely, the Convention decided on various expedients, the most spectacular of which was the call for a *levée en masse*, or national conscription, on August 23, 1793. It was an action the *sans-culottes* had been clamoring for since the beginning of July.[139]

The *levée en masse* and further conciliatory gestures taken with the psychology of the *sans-culottes* in mind did not suffice, however, to prevent another, justly feared revolutionary movement from forming.[140] The Jacobins and the Mountain now had trouble holding on to their political gains, acquired with so much effort on June 2. The problems they faced ranged from the chronic food shortage to the war being conducted simultaneously against the rebels in the Vendée and the powerful European coalition; and from the anarchy of the sections to the radical demands of the *enragés* and the Hébertists.

The Hébertists were far more dangerous than the *enragés* who, though they enjoyed the support of the *peuple*, had no followers in the Convention or the executive. Marat's murder was the signal for the Hébertists to begin their fight for power.[141] They, too, could depend on the *sans-culottes*, whose demands they had incorporated into their program. But in contrast to the *enragés* their great strategic advantage lay in the number of powerful supporters they had in the Convention as well as the executive; in fact they completely controlled the Paris Commune. Moreover, through Hébert's paper, *Le Père Duchesne*, they were able to influence public opinion.

It was especially easy to incite the suburbs to unrest, and Hébert had the means to do it. Men, women, and children of the faubourg Saint-Antoine formed a demonstration in the streets on the morning of September 4, "pour aller démander du pain" ("to ask for bread"). The crowd arrived in the place de Grève around 2:00 P.M., where they delivered their petition expressing anger with the Commune's *comité des subsistances*. They requested that all food supplies be officially inventoried, and that ownership of private property as well as profits from trade and commerce be curtailed.[142] But that was only the beginning. The following morning the Convention was surrounded by demonstrators, as in August 1792 and June 1793, and the *peuple* belabored the deputies. Chaumette and Mayor Pache conveyed the demands of the insurgents, almost all of which were granted by the Convention. Ceilings would be set for prices and wages; a revolutionary army was to be set up; and a *loi des suspects* (a law of suspects) would be enacted. The Convention refused to sanction only the *guillotines ambulantes* (portable guillotines) and the traveling tribunals associated with them.

Two additional decrees, issued by the Convention under the cover of concessions made to the *sans-culottes*, were expected to be very important. The first of these permitted the arrest of suspects, already the practice of the revolutionary committees. However, this approval was linked to the condition that the Commune purge the committees and appoint new members.[143] That ended the committees' ability to act autonomously and the violence of the *sans-culottes* came under control of the Commune.

The second decree reduced the fee paid to section members for their attendance at meetings to 40 sous a day, and limited meetings to twice a week.[144] The intention was to use the sections to counterbalance their respective revolutionary committees. Although many of the sections tried to circumvent these regulations by describing additional meetings as gatherings of a *société populaire* (a people's society), these maneuvers could not prevent the loss of their political importance.[145] The speed with which this occurred became apparent in January 1794, when the so-called important committees of the Commune, backed by the *comité du salut publique* (the Convention's Committee of Public Safety), purged and reorganized the section assemblies as well as the sections themselves. These bodies therefore lost the last remnant of their former autonomy and became dependencies of the city administration, which was itself already firmly linked to the strictly centralized hierarchy of the Terror.

The Terror

HE *SANS-CULOTTES* WERE AT THE HEIGHT of their power in the September riots of 1793, when they managed to impose their conditions on the Convention for the second time that year. In putting their political concepts into practice, however, they soon embarked on a reign of terror that for sheer horror was unlike any other period of the French Revolution. And despite their gains it was already possible to foresee their political demise. For they had not managed to render the Convention or even the Committee of Public Safety powerless; the latter had managed to become the chief decision-making body following September's events. In the winter of 1793–94, the intellectual leadership of the *sans-culotte* movement tried to use the population's growing dissatisfaction over new food price increases for its own ends. But these efforts failed to get the support of the Paris sections whose revolutionary enthusiasm had been worn out by economic hardship.[146] On 24 Ventôse, year II (March 14, 1794; one month after the Terror began the Convention adopted a new calendar), Hébert and seven other leading "Patriots of 1793" were arrested. They were tried from 1 to 4 Germinal (March 21–24), and then executed.

Their execution robbed the *sans-culottes* of their leaders and began a time of ruthless suppression of the movement. But to safeguard their own political existence, the powerful committees of the revolutionary government—particularly the Committee of Public Safety—went about this gradually at first so as not to weaken the radical Left too much.[147]

By eliminating the *sans-culotte* movement, the revolutionary government freed itself from the pressure exerted by the *peuple*; but it soon became clear that this had also destroyed the balance that represented its political raison d'être. The government's desperate attempt to redress the imbalance between radicals and moderates by arresting the leaders of the *Indulgents* party—Danton, Delacroix, Desmoulins, and Philippeaux—on 10 Germinal (March 30), and trying and executing them on 16 Germinal (April 5) did not alter the situation. Urged on by Robespierre, the Committee of Public Safety continued to lash out left and right in an effort to hold on to its political autonomy. But it only accelerated the Revolution's terrible process of self-destruction. Robespierre was digging his own grave—the grave that was to receive him on 9 Thermidor (July 27, 1794).

The final months of that regime of virtue and terror announced by Robespierre in his speech of 17 Pluviôse were dominated by a series of measures all designed to relieve the *sans-culottes* of their power. Immediately after the Hébertists were removed on 7 Germinal, the Committee of Public Safety requested the Convention to dissolve the revolutionary army that had been one of the *sans-culottes'* most successful tools for achieving their political and social goals.[148] The Ministry of War, also a *sans-culotte* stronghold, was eliminated five days later. Meantime all radicals suspected of being *sans-culottes* were removed from the Paris Commune, a procedure that took until Prairial (May–June 1794). This official action was supplemented by a Jacobin offensive against the *sociétés populaires* that ended in their abolition in the month of Prairial.[149]

These repressive measures left the *sans-culotte* movement without any hope of resuming its political activity in the foreseeable future. But what really destroyed this Parisian movement was the new economic policy introduced by the Committee of Public Safety. On 1 Germinal (March 21, 1794) new maximum prices were announced for basic foods and supplies, set at a far higher level than they had been. It was also decided to do without the commissioners who had been inspecting the quality of the merchants' goods; and, finally, a more lenient attitude was adopted toward those guilty of hoarding. All in all these additional steps in the liberalization of the economy were designed to accommodate the merchants rather than the *sans-culottes*.

Furthermore, the authorities began to intervene actively in labor conflicts, enabling employers to keep wages stable.[150] It was on account of this new economic and wage policy that the *sans-culottes* would not react to Robespierre's eventual downfall on 9 Thermidor. There was no sense in defending a regime that had so blatantly disregarded their own needs and interests.

The Terror lasted beyond Germinal, unaffected by the liberalization of the economy; in fact it turned into a *Grande Terreur*. The basis for this was the law of 22 Prairial (June 10, 1794) that eliminated almost all guarantees of civil rights and ordered the death penalty for anything remotely considered "hostility toward the Revolution." Between June 10 and July 27, 1794, 1,300 death verdicts were handed down in Paris alone.[151] The regime of virtue and terror thus became involved in the blind slaughter of its political opponents. This created a paradoxical situation: in the *Grande Terreur* the decentralized democratic system built up by the *sans-culottes* was completely destroyed. Its sections and committees were integrated into the strictly centralized power structure of the Jacobin dictatorship, and reabsorbed into the state.[152]

Moreover, the Terror resulted in a thorough depoliticization of the masses, who sank back into the lethargy from which the Revolution had roused them. Robespierre and his *Grande Terreur* thus performed an invaluable service for the Thermidor regime that was to follow. This dictator—not yet honored with a monument—took on the bloody and compromising work of defending the gains of the bourgeois revolution of 1789 against the greatest danger it faced at the time: the rise of the *sans-culottes*.

That bourgeois *damnatio memoriae* is one bitter irony; the other is that Robespierre ended up a victim of his own reign. The more mercilessly the *Grande Terreur* was carried out, the more trite virtue became. Terror paralyzed the very virtue that was supposed to assure the regime's existence. Repugnance for that regime and the desire to make a quick end of it increased as the men who embodied the Revolution disappeared at an ever-increasing rate, and were replaced by bureaucrats who administered the Terror with businesslike monotony. It is significant that this mounting public disgust manifested itself in a growing sensitivity to the daily spectacle provided by those unhappy creatures on their way from the Conciergerie to the place de la Révolution, where the "razor of equality" awaited them. They were transported in large open tumbrils, surrounded by screaming mobs. There was even greater aversion to the custom of transporting the decapitated bodies on low carts that left trails of blood as they rolled through the streets of the fashionable faubourg Saint-Honoré on their way to the mass graves of the Madeleine cemetery.

The longer these public spectacles lasted the more unbearable they became. Residents of the faubourg Saint-Honoré complained, as did storekeepers who maintained that the bloody carts stopped customers from coming. As of February 1794, individuals who lived in the neighborhood of the Madeleine cemetery objected that they were bothered by the putrid odor of the corpses and feared for their health.[153] It was uncertain whether these complaints were justified or not. But it expressed a sensitized awareness, a reluctance to tolerate much longer this place of terror where all who had been executed since August 1792 lay buried. At first the authorities turned a deaf ear to the protests, but at the end of March 1794 they finally decided to close the cemetery. What may have changed their minds was a police informer's report that it had become "a place of aristocratic and counterrevolutionary activity."[154] Louis XVI as well as various other personalities were buried there, and could easily have inspired a martyr cult.[155]

To prevent this the Commune designated a new burial site, in an uncultivated area, right by the wall of the *fermiers-généraux* and close to a large dump that adjoined the Folie de Chartres (now the Parc Monceau). Between March 24 and June 9, 1794, almost a thousand corpses were interred there in mass graves. At first this was done secretly, giving rise to a rumor that guillotine victims were being buried in a cemetery in the rue Pigalle.[156] The first to be sacrificed to the guillotine during this period were the Hébertists, who were followed by the Dantonists on April 5. The *cimitière des errancis*, as the burial site was popularly known, was closed as early as 21 Prairial (June 9, 1794). It seemed that the Commune was reacting to the ongoing protests of the faubourg Saint-Honoré district, through which the carts bearing the dead still passed. But they were probably willing to do so knowing that the number of executions would accelerate following the law of 22 Prairial dealing

with the "enemies of the Revolution." Presumably this decision was also connected with the plan to move the guillotine from the place de la Révolution
to the place de la Bastille.

The authorities thought that by changing the guillotine's location they
could count on more tolerance of the repulsive spectacle. They expected the
stalwart revolutionaries of the faubourg Saint-Antoine to be less squeamish
about the growing number of public executions than the well-to-do residents
of the western districts. But the Commune was greatly disappointed: after
only three days, in which 73 people were executed in the place de la Bastille
and interred in the Sainte Marguerite cemetery, emphatic protests by the residents forced another change in location.[157] On June 13 the site was finally
changed to one on the outskirts of the city in the place du Trône-Renversé,
now the place de la Nation.[158] The choice of this spot, where 1,306 executions took place by 9 Thermidor, was not without importance for the sudden end of Robespierre's dictatorship. The moving sight of the helpless victims being driven through half of the city, from the Conciergerie to the place
du Trône-Renversé, had to affect even the most eager revolutionaries.[159]
Scenes like the one preceding the execution of 16 Carmelite nuns from
Compiègne, on 29 Messidor (July 17, 1794), were particularly heartrending
although not unusual. During the entire long way from their prison to the
execution site the nuns sang the Miserere, which silenced even the most
hardened furies who had at first accompanied their progress with jeers.

The executions in the place du Trône-Renversé were worse than anything else done in public "in the name of justice" since the agonizing, drawn-
out torture-death of Ravaillac, the murderer of Henry IV. On 29 Prairial
(June 17, 1794) Sanson, the executioner, outdid himself when he decapitated 54 people in less than half an hour, an "achievement" for which he was
given an extra payment by the Committee of Public Safety. And even on the
last day of the Great Terror, 9 Thermidor, 46 people were executed there.

Having learned from previous experience, the Commune now made sure
that corpses were buried with all discretion. Assistants loaded the dead onto
low carts that followed the inner path along the wall of the *fermiers-généraux*.
They were soon out of sight of anyone who happened to be in the fields and
vegetable patches. The corpses were buried in the small cemetery of Picpus,
the only place among the numerous revolutionary sites in Paris that still looks
as it did in those weeks of the Terror.

Picpus was a monastery that had been closed during the Revolution and
acquired by the state in May 1792. Five months later the Administration of
Domains leased the property to a sieur Riédain, who in turn rented the
greater part of the buildings as well as the adjacent park to a sieur Coignard.
The latter established a sort of private asylum there for the wealthy, whose
supposed illnesses and infirmities prevented their being put into a state
prison. A similar establishment was tolerated by the authorities in Paris, in
the rue de Charonne. Considerable freedom was given to inmates of these
private prisons; their accommodations were quite appropriate to their status
and the food was excellent. For this, however, they paid fees. These *maisons*

de santé also had the great advantage that almost all of the residents were forgotten by the authorities and so managed to avoid execution.

The idyllic way of life in the remote monastery of Picpus came to an abrupt end on 25 Prairial (June 13, 1794). On that day two members of the Commune went to see Riédain, wanting to look at the park but without explaining their intentions. The next day the Commune sent workmen who made an opening in the garden wall wide enough for a cart to pass through. They also began excavating a trench in one corner of the park that was 18 feet deep, 24 feet long and 15 feet wide. Only then did Riédain learn that by a decree of the Commune on 26 Prairial, the former monastery garden was to become the burial site of those executed in the place du Trône-Renversé. Neither his protests nor those of Coignard, who pointed out the terrible effects such use of the garden would have on the inmates of his *maison de santé*, made the least impression on the Committee of Public Safety.

The first mass grave was barely ready when a second, equally large one was begun. The markings for a planned third trench are still visible today. This part of the garden was then divided off from the rest by a high wooden fence, the remains of which can also still be seen. The opening in the northern wall was closed off with a solid wooden gate to prevent anyone from looking in. As soon as the cart had passed through the gate the corpses were removed from it and Sanson's assistants undressed the bloody bodies. Large quantities of juniper twigs and thyme stems were burned while this disgusting business was going on, to cover the odor of decay and dried blood made more penetrating by the summer heat. Once the corpses had been stripped, the naked bodies were dragged to the open mass graves where they were packed together as closely as possible. At first the graves were left open, which meant that a pestilential smell was released, polluting the entire area. This required the further installation of a wooden cover for the trenches. The cover contained a locked trap door through which the corpses were lowered.

After 9 Thermidor, when the executions in the place du Trône-Renversé ceased and the inmates of the *maison de santé* had fled from their comfortable prison, the Picpus cemetery was consigned to oblivion. The mass graves were not covered over with earth until June 1795, when the ground was graded and the gate in the wall closed off again. The entire complex was sold to two private individuals in 1796, who then resold the section of garden containing the mass graves to a princess of Hohenzollern-Sigmaringen, whose brother the prince of Salm-Kirburg had been interred there on July 23, 1794.

In 1802 the marquise de Montaigne—whose mother and grandmother had both been buried in Picpus—founded an association limited to those who could prove that members of their families had been guillotined and buried there during the Terror. The aim of this macabre exclusivity was to buy back the entire monastery property with members' contributions and thus prevent any desecration of the area. The purchase was in fact accomplished a year later, with the exception of that garden section which remained the property of the House of Hohenzollern-Sigmaringen until 1920. The association also acquired another parcel of about 3,000 square meters that adjoined the garden. The area is still used as a private cemetery and is administered by what must be the oldest and most exclusive private burial society in France. According to the regulations of the society, only descendants of the victims of the Terror may be buried there.[160]

While the victims are still remembered today, their executioners were forgotten. Robespierre, Saint-Just, and several others who belonged to the inner circle of the dictators were guillotined without trial early in the evening of 10 Thermidor, in the place de la Révolution. At daybreak the following day their bodies were added to the mass grave in the Errancis cemetery that contained Hébert, Danton, and their followers. No evidence remains of this final resting place of all the leaders of the Jacobin revolution. Having served four Paris districts since the previous August, the cemetery was closed on April 27 following complaints by area residents, and the site soon returned to its former natural and idyllic appearance. During the Restoration a restaurant and dance hall called the *Bal de la Chaumière* opened in the neighborhood of the erstwhile cemetery and remained in existence until 1860.[161]

Jules Michelet, the historian of the Revolution, paid a visit to the Plaine des Errancis in 1852. According to his description, right next to the restaurant there was

> an area that was infertile, sandy and full of stones, with which nothing could be done and that had therefore been leased to some Parisians who need soil of that sort to cultivate gardens. . . . In this barren region there is one section along the wall [of the *fermiers-généraux*], right by the customs post [of Monceau] that is even more unfruitful than the rest. During some digging there, to set up foundations for rabbit hutches, human skeletons and skulls were found. They were the remains of those who had been executed in the Place de la Révolution during the Terror.[162]

The fast-changing events that took place in Paris between 1789 and 1793 also had some lasting effects on the public life of the city. For instance, religious festivals and processions that marked the year's progress were banned during the Revolution. As of 1792 processions could only take place inside churches, and religious festivals were gradually replaced by revolutionary festivities with a secular emphasis.[163] These symbolic events were celebrated with virtuous boredom and soon degenerated into sterile performances.

The process of suppressing traditional religious observance was hastened by the campaign of radical dechristianization. Church bells were melted down to make cannon; most of the churches, which had once been islands of stately splendor in the labyrinth of narrow and dirty alleys, now stood robbed of their ornaments. They were either left empty or used as warehouses, workshops, or stables. Many church buildings fell into such disrepair they had to be torn down during the First Empire. Numerous inner-city monasteries and other church-owned properties secularized in May 1792 suffered a similar fate. Some were used as clubs and meeting halls, others became offices, barracks, or prisons; many were simply destroyed with pickaxes.

Vacant aristocratic townhouses that had once been brilliant centers of social life were used for the most banal purposes. The Hôtel Biron and the Hôtel d'Orsay, for instance, were turned into cheap dance-halls; the Hôtel Villeroy functioned as a telegraph office; and book auctions were held in the Hôtel de Brissac. The Hôtel de Luynes was actually used as an orphanage, and the de la Rochefoucauld mansion became a warehouse for general merchandise. However, most of the aristocratic houses stood empty and were up for sale. The Swiss clergyman Heinrich Meister, who paid Paris a visit in 1795, notes his impressions as follows:

> Entire city districts appear to be completely devoid of people and you can well imagine that the beautiful faubourg Saint-Germain has suffered the most; only a few of the mansions that line the streets are occupied by offices of the Republic. If you enter one of the empty buildings, after having read the notice in large red and black letters that says "National Property: For Sale," you are inevitably shocked by the desolate conditions you encounter. Because not only have all furnishings been removed, but even the mirrors, the wainscoting, and the moldings have been stripped off the walls. The wooden ceilings and parquet floors were also frequently removed under the pretext of salvaging lead from the roofs and saltpeter from the cellars.[164]

Cultural life came to a gradual halt as well. Theaters were muzzled by strict censorship that was particularly hard on the opera—already quite suspect because of its aristocratic past. All stage characters detested by the Revolution—kings, princesses, gods, and priests—had to be eliminated before performances were authorized. Sometimes the censorship had very bizarre results. In the opera *Le Déserteur* by Jean Michel Sedaine, the word *"roi"* had to be replaced by *"loi,"* so that the libretto read: " La loi passsait et le tambour battait aux champs" ("the law passed and the drums rolled").[165] Other works, including most of the classical repertory of the Théâtre Français (renamed Théâtre du Peuple), were completely sacrificed to censorship. Schiller's *William Tell* had to be given the strange title *Sans-Culottes Suisses!*

Normal social intercourse was also affected by the Terror. Denunciations bred mistrust so that people preferred their immediate family circle and behaved as unobtrusively as possible outside their own four walls. In his memoirs baron Frénilly describes what life was like for the few aristocrats who had remained in Paris during the Terror:

> The women hardly ever left the house; the men rarely did so and those whom one met in the street were all dressed in the *carmagnole* style. That is, they wore pants and coats of a gray-brown material and neckties of the same color; their hair was cut short in a plain style, they wore caps and hobnailed shoes, and carried heavy sticks. That was what etiquette demanded.[166]

Insistence on such a uniform contributed to the drab aspect of the once-lively streets. Daily life in the revolutionary period was a monotonous routine. As Meister records it:

> Any foreigner who knew the city in better days would be amazed by the *tristesse* and deprivation that exist in Paris, especially when the theaters close around ten o'clock at night, for that used to be the hour when the bustling crowds were at their liveliest. People were on their way to suppers or other entertainments and the rattle of thousands of coaches made the streets echo with the effusive joy of life expressed by frivolous, pleasure-seeking inhabitants. . . . Today when the theaters close there is deathly silence in all the districts; it's an event if you meet a coach, and you rarely see anyone out on foot.[167]

The streets now belonged to those whom the Revolution had brought to the forefront, especially the *sans-culottes*, whose dress and speech advertised their political leanings. They wore a red cap over their long hair combed in the plain Jacobin style, a *carmagnole* (short vest), a cloth coat, and long cloth pants. Aside from his dress, a militant member of the *sans-culottes* could be identified by his language studded with vulgar epithets and his habit of addressing everyone in the familiar form.[168] Their female counterparts were the notorious *tricoteuses de Robespierre*, the women who sat knitting in the bleachers of the Convention and who accompanied the executioner's cart to the guillotine. After the general callup of August 1793, the streets were filled with officers and soldiers who stopped off in the capital to enjoy the pleasures of civilian life on their way to the front. In fact in 1793 and 1794 the physiognomy of Paris was defined more and more by the many requirements of war. Churches, convents, requisitioned mansions, even public areas and a number of ships anchored in the Seine were all used as sites to mix gunpowder, forge weapons, or sew uniforms.[169] Everyone was asked to collect and deliver the saltpeter—an important ingredient of gunpowder—that formed on damp cellar walls, and in churches and crypts. Inscriptions reading "The inhabitants of this house have made their supply of saltpeter available to bring death to the tyrants" could be seen frequently.[170]

But despite considerable change, in a certain sense Paris remained true to its former self. The city that had proudly claimed to be the capital of a revolution intended to improve the lot of all men was still in danger of being stifled by its filth and trash. It is unnecessary to detail all the dreadful conditions revealed by piecing together relevant police reports and travelers' tales.[171] One such example is the decline of the Palais-Royal; after it was closed down by the puritanical regime, the once-fashionable place was filled with a penetrating smell of urine that blended with the bestial odor from a neighboring pigsty and was especially noticeable in the summer months.[172] It appears there were repeated complaints and protests that pigs ran wild in this district.[173]

Regulations against keeping domestic animals did not prevent pigs from being raised in the middle of Paris.[174] They were even stuck and singed in the Petite-Pologne district on the edge of the faubourg Saint-Honoré.[175] Similar conditions existed on the Montagne Saint-Geneviève and in other neighborhoods. The pollution of the Seine and its banks was even more disgusting and constituted a permanent health hazard, since the river supplied most of Paris with its drinking water. Just between the rue de la Bièvre and the

Petit-Pont, four large sewers discharged their contents discolored by excrement, blood, and waste from the slaughterhouses. This mixed with dirty, soapy water from the numerous laundry boats, creating a permanent miasma. Paris water-carriers filled their buckets on the opposite bank, where various sewers also emptied out, completely disregarding the river's unsanitary state. The revolutionary Commune had not been bothered by such circumstances and even the city administrations of the Thermidor and Directory governments would be preoccupied with other problems.

Thermidor

EACTION TO THE DOWNFALL of the virtuous tyrants on 9 Thermidor was one of general relief. The Great Terror (which had actually lasted only six weeks but had seemed like an eternity), had weighed people down and taken all the joy out of life. No dances were held during this time.[176] But now, with Robespierre, Saint-Just, and Couthon having just been beheaded and the Terror having come to an end by its own terrible means, residents of the capital were seized by a wild craving for entertainment that expressed their relief at having survived once more.[177] Georges Duval, who was a notary's clerk at the time, paints a vivid picture of the dance craze that became an obsession:

> After the day of salvation (9 Thermidor) a violent and terrible dance craze suddenly broke out. The scaffold had hardly been dismantled, the trough that caught the blood of the guillotined victims along the barrière du Trône still gaped open for horrified passersby to see and polluting miasmas floated in the air; the ground around it had not yet soaked up all the human blood it had been given to drink for almost two months, when balls began to be organized all over the capital. The merry sounds of clarinet, violin, tambourine, and fife tempted the survivors of the Terror to join the dance, and people flocked there in droves. The lovely garden owned by the tax farmer Boutin . . . given the Italian name of Tivoli by its new owners, was the first of the places of entertainment to open its doors. The second of these establishments was set up in the Jardin Marbeuf at the head of the Champs-Elysées. I can testify that people danced with abandon in both places, without considering that the skeletons of those who had created these enjoyable spaces . . . had hardly been buried. The lawns in the Jardin Marbeuf were dug up without anyone realizing that the marquise de Marbeuf had paid with her life on the scaffold for ignoring Chaumette's request that she turn this very lawn into potato fields, as had been done in the Tuileries gardens and the park of the Luxembourg Palace.[178]

Not infrequently the profanation of a site revealed a shocking lack of sensitivity. For instance, dances were held in the former novitiate of the Jesuits, in the convents of the Carmelites of the Marais and the Filles Sainte-Marie, in the Saint-Sulpice seminary, and in the Jardin des Carmes where the orchestra was set up on the steps of the former sacristy—the spot where several priests had been slaughtered by the mob in September 1792. Duval who once visited the latter place, known as the *Bal champêtre des Tilleuls*, and who also claims to have witnessed the priests' murder from the window of a neighboring house, mentions in his memoirs that traces of blood were still visible on the steps.[179] The *Bal des Zéphyrs* was held in another, highly macabre location: the old Saint-Sulpice cemetery, which was closed in 1784![180]

Ironically there were some who actually benefited from the Reign of Terror, proof of which were the *Bals des Victimes*. These did not come into fashion until the beginning of 1795, when a series of restitution laws compensated family members of guillotine victims whose property had been confiscated. In this way young aristocrats—who would normally not have come into a rich inheritance for many years, or who might not have received anything because of other direct heirs—suddenly found themselves quite wealthy. These nouveaux riches, whose good fortune was solely due to the excesses of the guillotine, were drawn together by the dance craze and generally held their exclusive *Bals des Victimes* in the faubourg Saint-Germain. Only those who had lost relatives to the guillotine were admitted, and the greetings exchanged and invitations to dance were made *à la victime*: they imitated the movement made by the victims when they bowed their heads under the blade.[181]

A curious situation was created by 9 Thermidor; for while the Parisian public openly showed its relief that the Terror had ended, the Thermidoreans took care not to outlaw or give up the instruments of terror. Robespierre's fall had only been a settling of accounts among the terrorists; in no way was it a carefully planned coup or revolution. In a certain sense it was no more than a highly coincidental coming together of fears that focused upon the virtuous dictator.

It soon became apparent what sort of policy the Thermidoreans planned to follow, though their first decisions only affected Paris. Using Robespierre's methods, they brutally condemned ninety-six members of the Commune to be executed on 10 and 11 Thermidor. That ended the revolutionary Commune of May 31, 1793. However, it lived on in the collective memory of the French Left where it became the great myth that even the bloody events of 1871 failed to blot out. But the hard, uncompromising line was soon relaxed. The Convention wanted to hold on to the unaccustomed popularity it now enjoyed. It therefore gave in to public pressure and passed a law on 18 Thermidor freeing all prisoners who were not guilty under the Law of Suspects of September 17, 1793.[182]

At the time over 7,000 prisoners lingered in the overcrowded prisons; by 23 Thermidor 478 of them were freed.[183] This encouraged a flood of petitions. The Committee of General Security was besieged by petitioners; many of them persuaded Convention deputies to support their wishes and requests.[184] According to a man released at the time, certain women seem to have been particularly influential in these matters. "Those Thermidoreans who were under the gentle influence of several charming women freely issued permits for release, and they did so with so much warmth and grace that they were blessed even by those who had every reason to curse them."[185] Among these women the lovely Thérésa Tallien stood out particularly; as the guardian angel of the former Feuillants and Girondins she was given the honorary title of "Our Lady of Thermidor," and "Our Lady of merciful deliverance."[186]

The hotheads in the Convention, who had compromised themselves in the Reign of Terror by their speeches and actions, felt this was going too far. By 23 Thermidor (August 10, 1794) they saw to it that the revolutionary tribunal was reorganized, thereby emphasizing their intention of continuing the strict application of the Law of Suspects. On the other hand, there were some groups in the Convention that wanted to win over public opinion and come to power; they were willing to make large concessions and this led to long-lasting conflicts. All the decisions taken at that time had a thoroughly two-sided aspect and could be interpreted in various ways. The upshot was that the public experienced a great sense of insecurity, torn as it was between the fear that everything would remain the same and the hope for greater liberalization of the government.

Taking power away from the Commune was only the first step in eliminating the city's independence and subjecting it to the political will of the Thermidor regime. The decision to stop the payment of 40 sous for attendance at the section assemblies was part of the same plan. In addition it was decided that these assemblies should be held only once every ten days. The radical *sans-culottes* who had controlled these meetings soon lost interest in them and withdrew, and were replaced by more moderate members.

The *sans-culottes* had always defended the independence of Paris tooth and nail; any limitation on that independence represented a serious blow to their own political dominance. But now two laws were passed on 4 and 7 Fructidor (August 21 and 24) eliminating the notorious revolutionary committees of the individual sections. These had become a symbol of the Terror and of *sans-culotte* power and were henceforth to be taken over by twelve *comités de surveillance*, whose members came from the ranks of the more moderate middle-level bourgeoisie.[187] The newly created *comités de surveillance* were to serve as organs of the government. They were no longer to be under the influence of the section assemblies and were instead to be directly responsible to the government's Committee of General Security.

Finally, these laws changed the way in which the administration of Paris was to be set up. Instead of the former forty-eight sections, twelve arrondissements or districts were envisaged, so that four sections would form one of the new administrative units. Elimination of the individual sections destroyed the organizational basis of the *sans-culotte* movement—a measure made even more effective by ensuring that socially or politically homogeneous sections were not combined to form an arrondissement. Thus the faubourg Saint-Antoine and the Marais were to be combined into one arrondissement; however, the faubourgs Montmartre and Poissonière were separated. Sections that were not even adjacent to each other were now linked together—the faubourgs Saint-Denis and Saint-Martin were added to

Bonne-Nouvelle and Montorgueil. And the *Cité* was arbitrarily divided between the ninth and the eleventh arrondissements.[188]

The purpose of these administrative changes was left unclear as long as the political conflict went on between the moderates, the neo-Hébertists, and the Jacobins.[189] Confrontations not only occurred in the Convention and the important committees but carried over to the streets of Paris as well. There the radicals had the advantage at first, having organized a group of followers in their clubs. The moderates soon matched that by enlisting the help of the Parisian *jeunesse dorée*, the wealthy youths who were rudely called *Muscadins* (fops) by their opponents.[190]

The *Muscadins* or *jeunesse dorée* (also called the *jeunesse de Fréron* after Fréron, editor of the extremely demagogic paper *L'Orateur du Peuple*) had existed prior to Thermidor, but only showed their political strength now. They fought the *sans-culottes* as well as the Jacobins. They were immediately recognizable by their exaggeratedly elegant clothing. Their hair was frequently set in small curls, and they wore voluminous neckties and tight-fitting coats with large lapels and long tails. Their outfits were completed by pointed, soft leather boots and a knobby walking stick called, in their special jargon, "executive power," and used to "hunt terrorists."[191]

They were characterized by a shared militant ideology rather than by social homogeneity, and first attracted attention in 1793. At that time several hundred of them banded together in Paris and refused to join the army.[192] During the Terror they disappeared, only to reappear immediately after 9 Thermidor, in greater numbers and behaving more impertinently than before. Now they formed the spearhead of an anti-Jacobin campaign that was backed by a great flood of brochures and newspaper articles.[193]

Disclosure of the atrocities committed in Nantes by Jean-Baptiste Carrier, the infamous revolutionary commissioner, set off the anti-Jacobin campaign.[194] The revelation of the crimes of this former proconsul of the Revolution—also a prominent member of the Parisian Jacobin Club and of the Convention—gave the moderates a welcome excuse to disparage all Jacobins as "vampires" and "mass murderers." As the campaign grew fiercer the Convention found itself pressured to take special action against Carrier and to deal with the Jacobins as well. At first the Convention tried to divert attention with various maneuvers. One such effort involved transferring the remains of Marat, "the saint of the Revolution," to the Pantheon on September 21, 1794. It was a pompous ceremony in which the public showed a noticeable lack of interest.[195] On September 29 the Convention finally got around to indicting General Turreau, one of Carrier's accomplices in the Nantes murders; and on October 14 the indictment was broadened to include members of the Revolutionary Committee of Nantes, with the exception of Carrier.

Two days later, these desperate attempts by the radicals to protect Carrier involved them in a setback that was to prove fatal. On October 16 the Convention passed a law that forbade all collective petitions and addresses, as well as gatherings of and correspondence between clubs and societies.[196] It effectively cut off the Jacobins from contact with their sister societies in the provinces. This, and their growing isolation within the section assemblies and the *sans-culotte* movement in Paris, explains their powerlessness vis-à-vis the witch-hunt being conducted against them. The Revolution had left them behind and even the old slogans with which they tried to give each other courage at their club meetings could no longer hide what was in store for them.

As the extent of the atrocities committed in Nantes was uncovered, public pressure concentrated on bringing Carrier to justice. On 9 Brumaire, year III (October 30, 1794), the Convention appointed a committee to look into lifting Carrier's parliamentary immunity. The longer the committee's deliberations lasted the more aggressive were the public expressions of displeasure with the Jacobins.[197] Things finally came to a head on the evening of 19 Brumaire (November 9, 1794), when groups of the *jeunesse dorée* went from the Palais-Royal to the nearby Jacobin Club, smashed its windows, stormed the meeting hall, and beat up some of the club members who tried to block their way.[198] This drama was repeated in the evening hours of 21 Brumaire, when the arrest of Carrier became known.[199]

That was the end of the Jacobin Club: the same evening the Committees of Public Safety and Security, which had not interfered with the *jeunesse dorée*, ordered the club closed. This decision to destroy the heart of the Revolution of 1793 was confirmed by the Convention on 22 Brumaire.[200] The only thing that still prevented the victory of the reactionary elements was their uncertainty of being in the majority in the Convention. Many of them also feared that they, like Carrier, would be held accountable for their deeds.

The Revolution and Its Aftermath

*F*ASHIONABLE LIFE RETURNED TO NORMAL in Paris once the Terror ended and the Jacobins fell from power. A cadet called Bonaparte, who was then at the Ecole militaire, writes in a letter:

> Luxury, entertainment, and the arts have made an astonishing comeback. Yesterday there was a benefit performance of *Phèdre* at the Opera; from two o'clock in the afternoon onward an enormous crowd arrived, even though the ticket prices were more than three times normal. Elegant people in their carriages have reappeared or, to put it better, people can no longer remember—as if they had been having a long dream—that they had ever lost their splendor.[201]

But that only described one side of the coin; the other was that in the *Thermidor* period the contrast between rich and poor became greater than ever. Those who had money—other than the assignats, whose value had plunged from 31 percent of that of the silver currency in July 1794 to 8 percent in March 1795—could afford every luxury.

The rapid devaluation of the assignats and the chronic shortage of food grew worse as the winter of 1794–95 became more severe. In January and February 1795 temperatures dropped below zero and the Seine froze.[202] Wood and coal, needed for home heating and industrial use, also grew scarcer and therefore more expensive. All of this brought an increase in prices that the majority of the population was unable to meet. The hardest hit were of course those who had to spend the greater part of their income on food.[203] But investors and petty capitalists, whose interest payments were made in assignats, also suffered; only a small number of manufacturers, speculators, army suppliers, and wholesalers lived in high style.[204] Georges Duval gives a good description of these contrasts in his memoirs: "There were balls along with the famine. If you left a dance-hall between midnight and one o'clock, the first thing you saw in the dim light of the streetlamps were long lines of people that had already formed in front of the bakeries."[205] The shortage of bread was so great that most Parisians had to make do with black bread. Duval continues:

> Bread was nothing but a lovely memory. A few people could remember having seen it once, but that was all. Who would have dared to refer to the few ounces of a blackish and unappetizing mass, tiny portions of which were sold in bakeries, as bread? You could still see it at the tables of some of the aristocrats, and in a few of the well-to-do bourgeois households like that of M. Chavet [the notary for whom Duval worked], who had paid pure gold for the flour he bought and had his bread baked secretly in his own house. It would not have been advisable to have it baked at the bakery; he would not have seen one slice of it! All dinner invitations at that time ended with the request: "Bring your own bread." Guests who were unable to do so were obliged to eat boiled potatoes like M. Chavet's employees.[206]

The severe cold weather at the beginning of 1795 brought all excavating work to a halt. At first only the building trades were affected; but the shortage of fuel and other raw material that could not be transported on the frozen Seine soon forced further workshops and factories to close. This caused rapid growth in unemployment and greater deprivation as conditions forced people to migrate from the provinces. Duval reports that "On the streets you only met gray starved figures, whose bodies were marked by hunger." Soon that hunger and the terrible cold took their toll.[207] In October 1794, 1,900 Parisians died. In January 1795 that figure increased to more than 2,600, and in February it reached its peak at 3,000.[208] Many sought to make an end of their suffering by making an end of themselves and their families.[209]

A sure sign of the miserable condition of the population was the large number of dealers in secondhand goods. As Meister notes:

> In front of almost all the houses and along the large boulevards, at least in the more lively neighborhoods, innumerable booths have sprung up where furniture, clothes, paintings, engravings, and other goods are for sale. You see the same things that were previously sold only on the Pont Saint-Michel, the quai de la Ferraille, or under the arcades of Les Halles. You get the impression that sud-

denly everything that used to be inside the houses is now displayed out on the street. The capital of the world looks like a junk shop. . . . Everywhere you go you meet people of both sexes, of every age and social level, with packages under their arm—do they contain coffee, sugar, cheese, oil, soap, or something else? In most cases they contain the last bit of furnishings or clothing that some unhappy person has decided to sell so that he can buy himself or his family something to eat.[210]

The hardship that affected just about everyone this time—workers and craftsmen, and even those who thought they were better off because they had a steady income—created anger and desperation that turned into a rebellious mood in the month of Germinal.[211]

The *peuple*—passive observers of the loss of power of the revolutionary Commune, of the sections and their committees, of Robespierre's fall and the demise of the Jacobins—began to stir once again under the pressure of the dire conditions. The Thermidor regime became increasingly nervous as each day brought further signs that something was brewing in the faubourgs.[212] Those who felt that their very existence was threatened grew more desperate; they were abetted by socially conscious, revolutionary journalists like Babeuf or Lebois, who awakened them from their lethargy to unite under the slogan "Du pain et la constitution de 1793" ("Bread and the Constitution of 1793").

As of the end of Ventôse (the middle of March 1795) police reports mentioned revolts in one or the other of the sections. On March 21 the Convention passed a law that imposed deportation on all those calling for rebellion. In addition it was stressed that any demonstration would be countered with the immmediate proclamation of martial law, and anyone committing violence against the Convention would be subject to the death penalty. But the threats had no effect. Debates by the Convention on 5 Germinal on the question of trying four former members of the Committee of Public Safety—Barère, Billaud-Varenne, Collot d'Herbois, and Vadier—incited the people further.[213] At the same time the *jeunesse dorée* became active again and there were confrontations between them and members of the working class.[214] However, incidents in several locations of the city that made the authorities fear a bloody crisis turned out to be merely preliminary skirmishes. They were followed by a misleading period of calm, used by the regime to formulate broad measures to cope with any possible uprising.[215] Finally a revolt was attempted in the Gravilliers section, when the daily bread ration was reduced to half a pound per person, on the morning of 7 Germinal. As with so many other *journées révolutionnaires*, it was the women *de mince vertu* (of little virtue) who once again led a crowd of several hundred people to the Convention, where they demanded bread and the Constitution of 1793.[216]

This spontaneous protest by the Gravilliers section was a signal to the sections that met three days later. The shortage of bread and the proclamation of the democratic Constitution of 1793 were the subject of excited debate, as was the freeing of the imprisoned patriots, the reopening of the *sociétés fraternelles*, and further protest.[217] Although the authorities were kept informed of the proceedings by informers, and even knew when the uprising was to take place, they lacked enough loyal troops to cope with the situation. Their desperate attempts to add more volunteer units to the National Guard in the moderate sections revealed how bad things were for the Thermidor government. On the evening of 11 Germinal, various deputies turned to the *jeunesse dorée*, requesting them to defend the Convention, thus revealing the embarrassing situation in which the government found itself.[218]

The uprising erupted on the Ile de la Cité on the morning of 12 Germinal. As in Gravilliers five days earlier, it was the women who called for a march to the Convention. This was formally endorsed at a meeting held in the "Temple of Reason," as Notre Dame was known. When the demonstrators, swelled by numerous individuals from the faubourgs, arrived at the Tuileries in the middle of the day, the *jeunesse dorée* on guard there were simply pushed aside. The crowd forced its way into the meeting hall of the Convention and occupied it for several hours. Meantime additional demonstrators gathered in the gardens of the Tuileries, and there were disturbances in other city districts where carts carrying food supplies were stopped and plundered. Around two o'clock the Committee of General Security finally alerted the National Guard of the forty-eight sections; those battalions that seemed the most loyal were ordered to go to the area around the Convention.[219] Having just finished lunch when the call came, the good citizens took a while to turn themselves into National Guardsmen and reach their place of assembly. These afternoon hours were the most critical period for the Convention; during that time it was held captive by a crowd that fortunately confined itself to words. If violence had erupted, the desperate mob would have gone wild. Even the loyal National Guard battalions that gradually arrived around five o'clock could not have averted bloodshed, and Paris would have sunk into a state of anarchy.

As it turned out, it was not the incompetent *jeunesse dorée* or the loyal battalions of the National Guard who saved the Convention that afternoon. It was the peaceful behavior of a severely demoralized and leaderless crowd that limited itself to inundating the Convention with petitions. But the *peuple* of Paris were going to have to pay for their weakness on 12 Germinal for over a hundred years. Ironically it was the left-wing deputies who, though they supported the petitions of the demonstrators, were the very ones who managed to persuade them to leave the assembly hall.[220]

But the unharmed deputies were planning a terrible revenge, a foretaste of which was contained in the decisions made at the meeting the protesters had temporarily disrupted. The first of these was the immediate expulsion of Barère, Billaud-Varenne, Collot d'Herbois, and Vadier from the Convention, without any sort of prior hearing. A second action, approved by a majority and accompanied by applause from the visitors' benches [now occupied exclusively by the *honnêtes gens* or solid citizens], called for the arrest of eight of the left-wing delegates who were now seized by a "terreur coupable," according to Levasseur's description of the meeting.[221] Finally, the Convention declared a state of emergency in Paris and nominated General Pichegru as commander in chief of the forces of law and order.

Yet neither the failure of the Germinal uprising nor the accompanying harsh treatment of Jacobins and *sans-culottes* by the authorities managed to destroy the popular movement in Paris. The continuing food shortage turned into a famine in Floréal (May–June 1795) and led to a coalition of the desperate. The extent of the terrible conditions was reflected in the unvarnished prose of police reports that contained increasing references to suicides.[222] These reports also described individuals so weak from starvation that they collapsed and remained lying in the streets.[223] What made the *peuple* especially bitter was the pronounced social character of the famine: shortages affected the poorer sections of the population almost exclusively, whereas the wealthy could afford to buy anything they needed. The reason, police reports state repeatedly, was that "Les Halles and the markets were well stocked, but the food could only be bought at excessive prices." This was a paradoxical situation due to the government's refusal to ration basic foods.

The attitude of the Thermidoreans soon aggravated general dissatisfaction to the point where people were driven to plunder and demonstrate. Matters finally reached boiling point on the morning of 1 Prairial (May 20, 1795). As they had done earlier, demonstrators from the city's central and eastern districts called for the Constitution of 1793 and demanded bread as they made their way to the Convention. And again it was the women, headed by Théroigne de Méricourt, who formed the vanguard and filled the spectators' benches.[224] The bulk of the insurgents, who had been joined by several battalions of National Guards, reached the Palais National around half past three. Deputy Féraud, who tried to block their way, was killed by a pistol shot; his head was severed, put on a pike, and carried around. Once more the protesters held the Convention hostage and the few left-wing delegates tried to get their requests accepted. Again it was all in vain. Once the angry crowd had dispersed that evening, it took only two battalions of the National Guard to force their way into the meeting hall and put an end to things there. Saved from this renewed threat, the Convention reacted by having fourteen members of the Mountain arrested that very night.

Next morning the drama was repeated. The National Guard from the faubourg Saint-Antoine had now joined the agitators, surrounded the Convention as of 7:00 A.M. and trained its guns on the meeting hall. In the course of the morning their numbers were increased by additional mutinous troops. The Convention was now in a very precarious position since it no longer had the protection of sufficient loyal National Guards. It therefore found a way out through negotiations and concessions. In the evening the rebellious crowd again withdrew to the suburbs.[225] What had at first been a successful popular uprising failed quickly for the second time. Once more the failure was due to the insurgents' political weakness. They lacked leadership and strategy, and hence had no idea of how to make use of a favorable situation; that is, how to send the Convention packing and establish a dictatorship of the people.

The dissolution of the uprising and dispersal of the insurgents in the suburbs by no means made the Thermidoreans more lenient; on the contrary, they now began to consider a plan that would finally destroy the faubourg Saint-Antoine, the seat of unrest. Preparations were begun immediately. Regular troops were assembled in the center of the city during the night of 3–4 Prairial. A battalion of about 1,200—consisting of selected volunteers as well as a large number of the *jeunesse dorée* who could hardly wait to get even for what had been done to them recently—was to conduct the first attack on the faubourg. This formation, strengthened by a detachment of 200 dragoons and commanded by two army generals, moved into the faubourg on 4 *Prairial* where it experienced a humiliating defeat. The men who had started out so sure of their victory were bombarded by flowerpots, chamber pots, refuse, and stones; moreover, a hastily erected barricade prevented their retreat.[226] The pitiful outcome of this punitive expedition sealed the fate of the *jeunesse dorée*, who no longer had a role to play. Large formations of regular troops who then marched on the faubourg forced a peaceful capitulation of the rebels by issuing an ultimatum.[227]

Capture of the bastion of the former *vainqueurs de la Bastille* ended the people's revolution; there were no further uprisings in the capital until July 1830. The severe repressive measures immediately carried out by the Thermidoreans and subsequent regimes made this peaceful respite possible. After 4 Prairial the prisons, from which victims of the Terror had only lately been released, rapidly filled up again. Those who had taken part in the demonstrations, and others who had been denounced for making disparaging remarks, were arrested indiscriminately. This fate was shared by a number of the Convention's deputies, as well as by all members of former government committees with the exception of Carnot. In addition, over 1,700 people were deprived of their civil rights. The National Guard was reorganized on 28 Prairial by a decree that excluded from service anyone who was not a property-owning citizen.[228] But the crowning glory of these repressive acts was a new constitution replacing that of 1793, which had never been in force. It received an overwhelming majority vote in a plebiscite in September 1795. The vote made it clear that Jacobinism had lost its importance as a political force. On the other hand, the moderate bourgeoisie had learned a lesson since 1792: it was now willing to use politics as a means to gain its ends.

The Directory

*T*HE THERMIDOR ERA ENDED with an ironic twist unique in the annals of history. The same Convention that had torn the country apart with its execution of Louis XVI decreed in its final session on 4 Brumaire, year IV (October 26, 1795), that the place de la Révolution be renamed the place de la Concorde. The symbolic meaning of the decision was obvious: the Revolution was to be put to rest and relegated to the past. The bourgeoisie, having overcome the Terror and emerged as the clear victor in the Revolution, became the group that set the political and social tone of the Directory. They had good reason to forget the past, even though they owed it their success. But this act of suppression did not result from the guilty conscience of those who had benefited from the misfortunes of others. It was, rather, a collective sublimation in the depths of social consciousness. Balzac's novel *Une Ténébreuse affaire* describes it this way:

> Those who now read histories of the French Revolution will never know what incredibly long intervals public awareness established between the closely occurring events of that time. The overall longing for peace and tranquillity that everyone felt after the violent upheavals produced a total obliteration of the most sinister prior occurrences. History aged very quickly, its aging accelerated by ever new and burning interests.[229]

Typically, this process of collective sublimation sought refuge from its own historic reality in the masquerade of antiquity. Fashion and furniture design expressed this with particular naïveté. Members of the Council of Five Hundred, as the Directory's Chamber of Deputies was called, wore official dress in the colors of the Republic. The outfit consisted of an ample white garment reaching down to the feet, covered by a red toga edged with an ornamental border, and a blue beret.[230]

Women's fashions made this an especially unforgettable period; viewed retrospectively fashions seemed to express a moral corruption that is still considered the main characteristic of the Directory. The preference of the time was for flowing, semitransparent, extremely fine gowns of silk or satin, artfully cut so low in imitation of Greco-Roman simplicity that they revealed more than they hid of the wearers' bodily charms.[231] Notwithstanding the grace that has frequently been ascribed to it, this style was simply another of the vulgar distractions indulged in by a nouveau riche society to keep boredom at bay. The ostentatious furniture of the period still tends to put off any sensitive person. All the recamiers (a useless and uncomfortable combination of chair and sofa), all the bulky chests of drawers and curule chairs overloaded with heavy fittings of fire-gilt bronze, completely lacked the balance between material, form, and function of the antique models they were trying to copy.

In a strictly formal, art-historical, and morphological sense the Directory style continued the classicism that had emerged at the end of the Old Regime. At that time, though, the severity of antique form had been softened by a baroque influence. A marked preference for classical models had also characterized the revolutionary period, though its intellectual leaders had used their borrowings from antiquity as propaganda tools. This was true of their rhetorical references as well as the republican symbols in which they clothed their populist politics.[232] While the Directory now assumed a seemingly similar facade, it lost all concepts of political emancipation. The result was a tasteless and sterile classicism; it served a morally bankrupt society as a screen behind which the former victims and their executioners shared a mutually beneficial oblivion of their unsavory past.

The life-style of the nouveaux riches, that small sector of unscrupulous wheeler-dealers who now occupied center stage, was wasteful and superficial. The famous *Fête du Directoire*, to which the Goncourt brothers dedicated one of their best works on cultural history, was a unique celebration of the good life.[233] Jean-Nicolas Demeunier, a former deputy of the Constituent Assembly who returned to Paris from his American emigration in 1797, describes the colorful Paris scene in a letter to his friend Moreau de Saint-Méry:

> [There were] scintillating parties at which the whole splendor of Greek and Roman fashion was revealed to perfection. How little resemblance there is between this Paris under its new administration and that of the Revolution! Balls, spectacles, and fireworks have replaced prisons and revolutionary committees. . . . The court ladies have disappeared; the newly rich ladies have taken their place and are surrounded, as were their predecessors, by courtesans who compete with them in extravagance and extreme fashion. These sirens are in their turn courted by a swarm of fools, who used to be called *petits-maîtres* and who are now known as *merveilleux*. They talk about politics as they dance, and express their longing for the return of the monarchy as they eat ices or watch fireworks with affected boredom.[234]

This *Tout Paris*, the moneyed upper bourgeoisie in Greco-Roman clothing, imitated the way the aristocracy had lived under the Old Regime. The debris and pawned remnants of an extinct world were now used to create new palaces.[235] And just as in the long-gone gallant society of the Old Regime, women played a dominant role during the Directory.[236] Though their background was often humble, their freely displayed bodily charms and their cleverness in choosing and changing lovers gave them much influence in society. The air of wickedness and immorality that surrounded them, so different from the virtuous moral code of the puritanical Terror, steeped the Directory in a musk of depravity with which it is still associated. And yet any narrow judgment of that period misses an important point: the Directory's worship of exchange value in its brute form marked the beginning of the bourgeois nineteenth century. Hence feminine beauty became just as much of an exchange value as money. Both could be used to gain power and influence now that the Revolution had torn down the barriers of privilege and class.

In fact Directory society resembled the stock exchange. Individual position and reputation were not permanent but depended on supply and demand. That required relatively broad social dynamics and explains the close relationship between *Tout Paris* and the *demi-monde*—the dozens of dancers and actresses, speculators and young good-for-nothings from the provinces who wasted their parents' money in Paris.[237]

Members of the old aristocracy who had hidden or emigrated during the Revolution reemerged or returned during the Directory. Though frequently impoverished, they tried to rebuild a suitable social life. But they cut themselves off from the society of nouveaux riches by their strict etiquette and offensive arrogance. Baron Frénilly gives a wonderful description of them in his memoirs:

During the Directory the remnants of good society, which had flown off in all directions, began returning to the dovecote. They looked for each other, made contact, even met socially, but it all happened without fanfare because informers had replaced the executioners. Neither horse nor carriage were used, so as not to offend the sovereign (that is the *peuple*), who went on foot. Even silver table settings were no longer used because supposedly everything had been given up to the mint. And even in public one indulged in the charming luxury of poverty by using only earthenware plates, as if faience were too expensive. It was considered good form to claim to be completely ruined, to have been pursued, suspected, and imprisoned. Unless a person claimed the latter, he was neither greeted nor respected in society. It was also customary to express firm regret at not having been guillotined, and hastily to add the claim that this would have been bound to happen on the morrow, or the day after the morrow, of 9 Thermidor.[238]

As always there were a few exceptions—members of the nobility who felt it was to their advantage to get along with those in control of the new society. Talleyrand, who returned from his American exile in September 1796, is merely the best-known example. He was named minister of foreign affairs—for which he had to thank Mme de Staël, who campaigned for him with the full power of her charms.[239] Her salon was said to have a certain influence on the style of men's fashions, as the *Courier Républicain* ironically noted. Mme de Staël put considerable effort into introducing members of the old nobility to Directory society.[240] Her rival in these endeavors was the lovely Joséphine de Beauharnais. Pasquier, who later became chancellor, recalls in his memoirs:

> It was mostly emigrants who used her magnanimity and helpfulness, to get out of the clutches of a court-martial, or to be taken off the list of emigrants who were still banished, or to have their property returned to them. At that time they were beginning to hurry back. Most of them had either used up their money or could no longer bear to be dependent on the help of strangers. The hope of recovering some of their fortune, to save one or another inherited item, the longing for their loved ones and their home, made them defy whatever danger they might face in returning.[241]

The Directory completed the process of political and social change begun by the Revolution. The nobility and clergy, once elements of stability, had been defeated along with the Old Regime and had been replaced by new social groups that owed their existence and status to the Revolution. The most important of these was the new class of landowners on whom the Directory could rely because they were the ones who had the most to fear from a restoration of the monarchy. They were the beneficiaries of the enormous redistribution of wealth that occurred during the Revolution. Two factors had contributed to this. The first was the rapid devaluation of money as a result of the disastrous financial policy of the revolutionary governments whose attempt to finance war with paper money turned everything upside down. Large numbers of investors who lived in the cities were ruined, while debtors and speculators profited. The second reason was the sale of nationalized Church and aristocratic properties for less than their true value. This was especially the case after "territorial mandates" were issued to replace the worthless assignats in February 1797. Nationalized properties were sold for next to nothing since they were priced at the nominal rate of the rapidly devaluing mandates (35 francs in paper money at the official rate corresponded to 1 franc in territorial money, or merely 3 sous in hard currency).[242]

Changes wrought by the new social order were also reflected in the topography of Paris. The faubourg Saint-Germain, which had been the stronghold of the nobility, was deserted and only came alive again under the First Empire. The opulent aristocratic mansions in the rue de Varennes, the rue de Grenelle, and the rue de Tournon had long since fallen prey to real-estate sharks. Many of them had been rebuilt as apartments—a circumstance that explains why so few houses were built under the Directory although the renting of individual apartments had just been developed as a lucrative source of income.[243] Speculation under the Directory therefore completed a trend begun by Robespierre's virtuous Terror.[244] On the other hand, some of these mansions now became the setting for the vulgar pleasures of the newly rich, who had no notion of the aristocratic enjoyment of life under the Old Regime with its sensuousness dominated by wit and intellect. Those who now set the tone were men like Hanet-Cléry, the son of a gardener from Versailles; or Corbigny, who was a former vintner; or Claude Lenthereau, who had advanced from being a hairdresser to supplying the army and who gave the most extravagant parties in the Hôtel de Salm.[245]

The new world of *Tout Paris* tried to adopt the brilliant life-style of the former aristocratic society, but preferred to exhibit its wealth in the Chaussée d'Antin district on the Right Bank. That helped to make the Champs-Elysées fashionable, with popular garden cafés being opened and public dance-halls established in the Hôtel de Beaujon and the Elysée palace.[246] The frivolous smart set of the Directory also filled the Palais-Royal with renewed feverish activity; speculation, gambling, and prostitution again found a home there. In addition to the old, well-known cafés, ten new restaurants competed for the favor of delicate palates, their openly displayed gluttony adding a special fillip to the sharp contrast between rich and poor.[247]

Thus trends that had already been apparent at the end of the Old Regime became even more firmly established during the Directory. The wealthy lived in the west of Paris, around the Chaussée d'Antin and the Tuileries, and to a somewhat lesser extent in the faubourg Saint-Germain on the Left Bank. The majority of the population, the poor, spent their lives in the east, in the crowded faubourgs of Saint-Antoine and Saint-Marcel. This is clearly shown by property taxes for the year 1799 which ranged between 2,000 and 4,000 francs per dwelling in the west, and from 765 to 1,000 francs in the east.[248] As well as this obvious social hierarchy, there was also political differentiation. During the Revolution a political division had developed for the first time that was to remain practically unchanged for the rest of the nineteenth century. The Paris of the rich and the Paris of the poor grew into two separate cultural and political worlds divided by a wall of fear and mistrust.

Abolition of the universal right to vote and its replacement by a property qualification was a first step toward preventing the political integration of the two parts of Paris. For to be nominated as an elector at all, that is, to be a candidate for the assembly from which deputies and important administrative officials of the department were appointed, one now had to pay a fee of 200 francs. This guaranteed that the electoral body would consist exclusively of members of the bourgeoisie. Accordingly the petty *peuple*, though participating in primary elections, were unable to influence the choice of deputies and soon lost all interest in political involvement.[249] The office of mayor of Paris was also discontinued and the city was put under the control of the Department of the Seine. The twelve administrative bodies of the city's individual districts retained only subsidiary functions. After having long and successfully defended its communal autonomy against the powerful centralizing tendencies of the Revolution, Paris now came under direct governmental control in the person of a commissioner in the administration of the department.

The new administration managed to straighten out the chaos of the city's finances. The system of taxation was thoroughly overhauled; property, income, and trade taxes were restructured and collected relentlessly. Anyone who did not pay promptly was fined, a procedure no one would have dared enact under the Old Regime. The working class was also subject to taxation; however, their average personal tax rate only amounted to 3 francs 75 centimes. The indirect taxes that particularly burdened the poorer levels of society yielded considerably more money. The wall of the *fermiers-généraux* served its hated purpose again as of October 22, 1798; duty had to be paid at the customs posts on all goods brought into the city. Only grain and flour were exempt from this regulation.

Both the Consulate and the Empire were to reap the benefit from these sweeping tax reforms that now brought order to the city's finances.[250] At last it was possible to improve some of the worst conditions affecting public hygiene and the water supply. While the will to make improvements had existed during the revolutionary years, the time and means to make the needed changes did not. The *Commission des Artistes* and the *Plan des Artistes* were proof of these good intentions.[251] The Committee of Public Safety had passed a law on June 28, 1794, under which a comprehensive plan for public buildings was to be developed. Architects who already had appropriate designs ready were invited to submit them to the *Commission des travaux publics* within fifteen days of the passage of this law. A jury appointed by the Convention was to evaluate the proposals and develop an overall plan for the redevelopment and beautification of Paris. The aim was to

> improve the living conditions of its citizens to such an extent that there is a sufficient supply of drinking water; to create large public squares, wells, markets, cultural facilities, baths, theaters, wide streets with pavements, sewers, cesspools, and cemeteries. In short, to see that everything is done that will contribute to public hygiene and comfort.[252]

But 9 Thermidor and subsequent political and social crises prevented this truly grandiose scheme—to turn Paris into the model city of a new society—from developing beyond its initial planning stage. The heritage of the Revolution began to be realized with the First Empire, and even more so in the Second Empire, when the system of large inner-city avenues was laid out whose imperial grandeur still characterizes the French capital today. The Revolution had created an enormous horizon of expectation that was to last for the entire nineteenth century. In turning Paris into the political and cultural center of France, the Revolution transformed the city into a stage on which the splendors and miseries of all of French society were played out. Michelet writes, "Every epoch dreams the next one"; thus the French Revolution dreamed the nineteenth century that was to take shape in Paris, as nowhere else, in all its baffling disparity.

BOOK THREE

Capital of Europe

1800–1815

Si j'étais maître en France, je voudrais faire de Paris, non seulement la plus belle ville qui existât, la plus belle ville qui ait existé, mais encore la plus belle qui puisse exister.

If I were the master of France, I would like to make Paris not only the most beautiful city in the world, the most beautiful that ever existed, but also the most beautiful that could ever exist.

—Bonaparte, 1798

The Card Game. *A Paris soirée around 1801 during the Consulate period (1799–1804).*
Colored etching by Jean-François Bosio (1764–1827), from the Bibliothèque Nationale collection.
ARCHIV FÜR KUNST UND GESCHICHTE, BERLIN.

The Consulate

*T*T IS DIFFICULT TO IMAGINE a greater contrast than that between revolutionary and Napoleonic Paris. During the Revolution the city had been the center of historic events that were to affect all of Europe. But after the Directory had undone the achievements of the Revolution, and once the Consulate and Empire periods were under way, Paris lost its extraordinary status. Attention was no longer focused on the problems of the Revolution but on the pageantry and festivities celebrating Napoleon's many victories.

The dramatic transformation of the city's role reflects a significant internal change. The Terror had been able to save the Revolution only at the price of compromising it in the eyes of most of its contemporaries. Despite this obvious fact, the men of the Directory tried to follow the same path. Their policy (dictated by weakness and fear), though uncompromising in its intent, was in form a rather more moderate version of revolutionary concepts; its result was that they soon lost all public support. All the broad political issues that had aroused excitement just a few years earlier were now met with silent indifference and a general desire for peace and distraction. This desire manifested itself in diverse ways ranging from the craze for dancing and general immoral behavior, to preoccupation with preserving fortunes amassed during the Revolution. Everyone, however, hoped the regime would bring political stability. Their hope was increasingly focused on a man of whom Ségur once said that no one loved him, but everyone preferred him.[1] That man was General Bonaparte, whose campaigns in Italy and Egypt had brought him great personal prestige and whose qualities as a statesman were already being speculated on by the public.

Most important, Bonaparte's successful coup d'état on 18 Brumaire guaranteed the quiescence of those who had passionately supported the Revolution—the *sans-culottes*, the artisans, workers, and ordinary people, and all those who had to pay for their former involvement once Robespierre was finished. That experience killed their enthusiasm, made them suspicious of all illusions and revolutionary promises. Although they could influence events through sheer numbers they had long since left center stage and gone into the wings, where they awaited the future with great disinterest.[2] But there was a further reason for their remarkable apathy. Because the Revolution had destroyed the hierarchy of the trades and given many apprentice artisans their economic freedom, the latter had become independent and established themselves as bourgeois. These new petty capitalists, who had benefited from the Revolution in their own way, became rabid conservatives during the economic crisis of the Directory. Even when the situation was precarious, nothing was further from their minds than going into the streets to fight for a cause that had long ceased to concern them. Given the overall contempt in which the Directory was held, it was also significant that those who turned

against it were the very ones who had profited the most from it: revolutionary profiteers, speculators, and buyers of nationalized property who, though
they were a heterogeneous group, found common interests once their profits
were threatened by the financial measures of the Directory.[3] For instance
the introduction of progressive property and income taxes caused considerable insecurity in the capital market. The price of government bonds
experienced a particular decline—a trend that was immediately stopped
by Bonaparte's coup d'état. Whereas they traded for 11.38 francs on 17
Brumaire, the price rose to 14.38 on 19 Brumaire, and five days later it had
reached 20 francs.[4]

The 18 Brumaire was also an expression of protest against the political
changes that the Directory had all too irresponsibly made. It now became
clear that the regime had been no more than the administrator of a politically bankrupt situation, without the vision or force to substitute a stable social
order for the one destroyed by the Revolution. The republicanism of the
Directory turned out to be lacking in republicans, an empty concept that was
simply kept in place by the fear of change as long as it was not challenged by
a convincing alternative. That alternative was now personified by Bonaparte.[5]

Not that history is made by individual men. But Bonaparte appeared on
the scene at a time when collective relief at having escaped the multiple horrors of the Terror had died down, thereby removing the actual foundation on
which the Directory was built. To secure his own position, Bonaparte had
already cultivated the various forces that brought about the end of the
Directory, thereby ruling out any possibility of its restoration. He was especially successful in shaping the process of social change that the Directory
had been unable to manage—a change that Chateaubriand characterizes as
"the metamorphosis of republicans into followers of the Empire, and of the
tyranny of the many into the despotism of an individual."[6]

A clear sense of how the ideals of the Jacobin Revolution were abandoned can be obtained by studying the society of the times. Miot de Melito,
who returned to Paris in April 1798 after being absent for three years,
describes the external characteristics of this transformation as follows:

> Except for the simplest exchanges, the common speech of the Convention
> had been replaced by politeness of expression; the same held true for manners and
> dress, which now became quite refined. The familiar form of address was no
> longer in use, and the *carmagnole* was not considered a suitable garment. The
> women, especially, eagerly returned to their former tastes: fashion ruled again and
> a passion for antiquity took hold without any regard for modesty. Of course the
> atmosphere could not yet be compared to the splendor of the court; more had to
> be done to attain that. But etiquette unmistakably showed a rejection of the com-
> mon habits that had existed for so long. Society had not yet been organized, the
> individual layers had not been separated from one another. There was great con-
> fusion and salons were indiscriminately attended by suppliers to the army and gen-
> erals; by men of science and mere knights of industry; by fast women and noble
> ladies; by patriots and returned emigrants. These individuals, whose heredity and
> education were so varied, were all possessed by a single idea: to make money, to
> grow rich; and they approved of any means for reaching that single goal.[7]

The Consulate's political stability not only helped create completely new social strata, whose higher ranks were filled with revolutionary profiteers and former Jacobins, but also permitted members of the old nobility to return to Paris from their exile.[8] Gradually the aristocracy reestablished its social life. Salons that had long been closed were reopened and soon became the focal points of a scene that was as intellectual as it was worldly. For instance, in the rue de Luxembourg, Mme de Beaumont entertained a circle of individuals of which Chateaubriand, Pasquier, Fontanes, Mme de Staël, and Joubert, to name just a few, were members. In his memoirs Pasquier evokes the attraction of these evening gatherings: "The great charm of our meetings lay in the consideration as well as the complete freedom that existed there; the happiness of seeing each other again made everything very easy. People forgot all the differences and disagreements that they would hardly have countenanced prior to 1791. . . . "[9]

However, these new salons and circles, in which members of the old aristocracy met during the Consulate, dispensed with that wasteful opulence that had distinguished them under the Old Regime. Too many of the nobility had been partially or completely ruined by the Revolution. Baron de Frénilly was one of the few lucky ones who had not been reduced to poverty. His account of the amount of effort required to lead a life that more or less conformed to one's rank—it was required to give a dinner for six good friends every Wednesday—is most revealing:

> In those days I had an excellent cook, Mlle Victoire, the daughter of my worthless gardener, who had been raised in my house. We lived well, thanks to a carrier from La Ferté–Milan, who brought us game, poultry, guinea fowl, ducks, doves, vegetables, etc. from Bourneville [where Frénilly owned a castle] every week, so that we had only to pay for our bread and meat. Fruit and firewood, hay and oats were supplied to us at the beginning of the winter across the Ourcq, and I believe it was hardly possible to exist in greater abundance than we did then, though we were very thrifty as well. Our only servants were a ladies' maid, a children's nurse, a cook and a kitchen help, a coachman and two lackeys. That was a very modest household; still, it was considered very lavish at the time.[10]

The extremely difficult financial situation of most of the nobility under the Consulate partly explains a marginal social life that made them strangers in their own country. *La bonne compagnie*, as the old aristocracy was still called, underscored this tendency by its snobbery and observation of a rigid etiquette.[11] It is not surprising, therefore, that the nobility's attitude toward Bonaparte was at first extremely reserved, although it avoided open opposition. Instead it was content to live on its memories and to hope for a better future. The conferment upon Napoleon of the life consulship, and above all the establishment of the Empire, gradually destroyed this unity of silent rejection. For Napoleon was enough of a psychologist to reintroduce offices and appointments that added a veneer of court life to his consulship, and of course to his imperial regime. Many aristocrats were soon enticed.[12]

At first the *bonne compagnie* punished deserters from its ranks with contempt and ostracism.[13] However, as the number of proselytes increased, these
unbending attitudes were relaxed, until only the most important noble families continued to boycott the Empire. Altogether members of the old nobility provided about a quarter of the new aristocracy of the Empire.[14]

Though the *bonne compagnie* never completely lifted its ostracism of
deserters, the latter were eventually allowed to participate in social events
on condition that they observed the prevailing etiquette. In these circles they
were not permitted to wear uniforms or any insignia of the Empire.[15] This
social exclusivity, to which some of the old nobility clung until the end of
the Empire, meant that their influence on the new social order was nil, especially since this attitude ran completely counter to the spirit of the times
which held that the past—that is, the Revolution—should be forgotten.

As has been shown, a similar mood had existed in the Directory period.
But it only became clearly visible in the Consulate, that regime having put a
firm end to the political vacillations of the Directory. The renaissance of
fashionable social life, centered in Paris and strongly supported by the first
consul, reflected the desire to repress the past.[16] The emigrés who returned
home in large numbers after 18 Brumaire could only register their amazement at this unexpected change in the situation.[17]

Aside from the changes in etiquette, the most striking feature of the new
society was the way in which people who had been irreconcilable adver-
saries—monarchists and former Jacobins—now gathered in the same circles.
A reception of this sort of "mixed society" was given by Talleyrand on
February 25, 1800, while he was serving as foreign minister in the Consulate,
and caused a sensation.[18] Members of the "old" and "new" society even met
regularly in the salon of the influential Mme de Montesson, as well as in
other salons that soon imitated hers. This was possible because Consulate,
and later Empire etiquette forbade mention of the Revolution as a topic of
conversation. The subject was only permitted if limited to complaints about
the material hardships suffered during that time.[19]

Bonaparte made clever use of this taboo, and by encouraging national reconciliation he consolidated his own position. His political priority was to obtain
the allegiance of the former opponents of his tightly controlled central government. And because of the great prestige of his military and civil bureaucra-
cies—which grew to mammoth size along with the Empire itself—nothing was
more sought after than a position in this hierarchy, were it ever so humble.[20]

Indeed, the army of civil servants formed a completely new social stra-
tum, unknown even in the Old Regime with its practice of selling positions.
Anyone who had the right qualifications could belong to this new group. Its
reputation increased as the government extended its control over ever greater
areas. Twelve ministries, centered in Paris, were created in year VIII of the
Republic (1800) under the newly organized administrative system. These
ministries had about 25,000 employees, and each was made to feel that he was
participating in the decision-making process of the first consul or later of
the emperor—or at least that he was the executive organ of those decisions.

The new bureaucrats and the new aristocracy (they overlapped to some extent) formed the backbone of Napoleonic society. In contrast, the profiteers and the Jacobins—who had trimmed their sails to the wind and called the tune during the Directory—forfeited their influence under the Consulate. The new wealth they flaunted, clearly derived from the Revolution, defied the unspoken agreement to forget the past.[21] They were regarded with growing contempt—Bonaparte himself in the lead—because of their frequent vociferous statements about the evils of the Revolution. They naïvely believed they were offering proof of having always acted honorably.[22] Unaffected by the ostracism of "good society," these nouveaux riches established a luxurious world of their own that cast an affluent glow over the Consulate. That is, it did so until its brilliance was diminished by the decline of many not very solidly established fortunes; or until it was overshadowed by the still greater luxury at the imperial court.

One must exempt from this group of newly rich, ridiculous imitators of the life-style and manners of the *bonne compagnie*, those bankers whose wealth predated the Revolution. Such a one was the banker Récamier from Lyons, who had bought Necker's former mansion in the Chaussée d'Antin and refurbished it extravagantly in the prevailing classic style. But it was neither his wealth nor the opulence of his parties—which other rich magnates possibly even outdid—that made his house such a popular gathering place. The appeal lay in the legendary beauty of Mme Juliette Récamier, whose face and figure incarnated the period's ideal of feminine beauty.

Indeed, Juliette Récamier's appearance was one of the chief attractions of Paris during the Consulate. Although there were many enthusiastic descriptions of her figure and personality by her contemporaries, Johann Friedrich Reichardt conveys the best impression with his more prosaic and straightforward account:

> Mme Récamier has . . . such a thoroughly translucent skin that one can see the blood course through her veins; yet she is more white than red. She was dressed all in white, too, in satin and delicate Indian materials—her beautiful neck and back were bare. Her face and her entire being have a unique, naïve character, charming in an almost childlike way; she has lovely light eyes, with which she often looks up, and her beautiful mouth, full of fine teeth, is always half-open; she seems to find it quite natural that people like to look at her in the same position and pose for hours on end. Her lovely brown hair was simply styled in large curls and tied up fairly high with a broad black velvet ribbon that covered her forehead almost down to her eyes on one side.[23]

The way in which Mme Récamier presented herself, her simple yet carefully chosen outfits together with the open and easy manner she adopted toward everyone, could as easily have been calculated as truly unpretentious. She became a model for many others.[24]

The magic of her person reflected on her immediate environment as well. Because of her the mansion in the Chaussée d'Antin became a worldly shrine, and its interior decoration set the fashion for the Empire style. The bedroom and adjoining bathroom (an unheard–of rarity in those days) of the mistress of the house, which all guests were keen to see, were considered the sanctuary of this temple of good taste.[25] This curiosity, peculiar even in the context of current etiquette and customs, was satisfied by the lovely Juliette with the greatest willingness. Reinhardt reports:

> The first thing Mme Récamier did with each newly arrived lady was to say "Voulez vous voir ma chambre à coucher?" ("Would you like to see my bed-room?"). Then she would take her arm and lead her to the bedroom. I don't have to tell you that she was followed by a swarm of young and old men each time. This bedroom with its adjacent dressing- and bathroom is the most elegant one there is. The bedroom is very spacious, the main walls are almost entirely covered with high, wide mirrors. Between the mirrors and the tall doors made of multicolored, beautifully paneled wood, the walls are decorated with brown and white wood-work with a great deal of carefully wrought bronze detail. The back wall of the room, across from the windows, consists almost entirely of mirrored glass. In front of this sits the ethereal bed of the gods; it is all in white, covered with the finest of Indian fabrics: everything looks as if it had wafted there. The bedstead has a lovely classic form and the lower part is richly but tastefully decorated with the finest bronze detail. Finely shaped classic vases stand on the edge of the bed which is two steps high. Two very high candelabra, each holding six to eight tall candles, stand farther back. The knot or crown of the bed is fastened to the beams practically at the very highest point of the room, and delicate white curtains hang down from it almost to the ground, one on each side but only at the head of the bed. The background, moreover, consists of a heavy purple damask drape that hangs in elegant pleats, but is pulled back to the sides to leave the mirrored wall bare so that when Mme Récamier lies in bed she is reflected from head to toe.[26]

Many of the old aristocracy used Juliette's extraordinary charms as an excuse to visit the Récamier salon. They did so "almost ostentatiously and as though to emphasize their absence from the regime's festivities," as Mathieu Molé puts it.[27] The salons and receptions held by other financial magnates did not have any special reputation.[28]

The social morphology of *Tout Paris*, according to which contemporaries distinguished between a *beau monde* and a *grand monde*, made it clear that the Consulate had by no means lived down the heritage of the Directory.[29] On the contrary, it was a transitional period of flux before the emergence of the new social hierarchy of the Empire. The uncertainty in matters of taste and social behavior corresponded to the uncertainty of the political situation and proved that the loss of tradition brought about by the Revolution was grave indeed.

These initial attempts to restore private social relationships correspond-ed to a similar development in public life.[30] In February 1800, Napoleon established his official headquarters in the Tuileries, which had stood aban-doned since August 10, 1792. In appointing his own consular retinue in imi-tation of the royal model, he emphasized the marked antirepublican tenden-cy that had developed. Immediately after the Peace of Amiens he also rein-stated the court dress worn in the Old Regime. Women again had to wear extravagant gowns at gatherings in the Tuileries, and men had to dress in breeches, silk stockings, and buckled shoes. [31]

With the gradual reintroduction of prerevolutionary etiquette the Consulate found itself in general agreement with the wishes and ideas of bourgeois Paris. People everywhere addressed each other as *Monsieur* and *Madame*, though the official form of address was still *Citoyen* and *Citoyenne*. The familiar republican *tu* was replaced by the seigneurial *vous*. And the many balls that were held during the Directory and remained in fashion far into the Consulate awakened a desire for the more frivolous pleasures of the Carnival—forbidden since the beginning of the Revolution.[32] Despite the misgivings of Fouché, the minister of police, four masked balls were permitted in 1800 at the Opera, known as the *Théâtre de la République et des Arts*.[33] The first of these, well attended because of the fairly low entry fee of 6 francs, does not appear to have produced the sort of pleasure that had been longed for. The other balls were a financial failure for their organizers.[34]

What was permitted to the bourgeoisie could not be denied the *peuple* if one wanted to avoid being accused of favoritism. So it was only natural, for instance, that laundresses were allowed to have masked festivities on 29 Ventôse "on their boats as well as at other locations."[35] The following winter—that of 1801–02, by which time the Consulate was well established—the authorities were even more lenient. They allowed masked celebrations during "les jours dits du Carnaval" to be held in the streets and public places.[36] In the spring of 1800 a custom of the former *Tout Paris* was revived: that of going to the abbey of Longchamp on Good Friday in a festive procession of carriages, under the pretext of attending Vespers. In reality it was an excuse to show off new carriages and outfits.[37] The fact that the abbey had been closed during the Revolution, thereby removing the cover of religious observance for worldly pleasure, made no difference.

Social Life and Customs

*T*HE PARTIAL REINTRODUCTION of prerevolutionary etiquette and customs must not obscure the widespread and far-reaching social changes that were nevertheless the real legacy of the Revolution. Such changes were especially evident in the structure of everyday life. Gastronomy provides a good example, the Revolution having democratized the refined luxury of the aristocratic cuisine.

Public restaurants as they exist today were unknown until 1789. Of course the Palais-Royal had had a variety of coffeehouses, some of which served small meals. But people had not thought of eating a real meal in a café or inviting their friends to dine there. Distinguished foreigners ate at the tables d'hôte of their hotels; local residents dined in their own houses or at private parties. It was the Revolution that first encouraged a radical change, having generally opened up the public sphere at the expense of the private one.

As the aristocracy lost power, cooks and other domestic staff became unemployed. Many of them were master chefs who now became independent and opened restaurants, or worked in the coffeehouses whose number increased in proportion to demand.[38] These restaurants were frequented by members of the National Assembly, who tended to lived modestly as lodgers and did not have the money for extravagant households. Many foreigners who had been attracted by the spectacle of the Revolution also ate there. Moreover, the endless round of gatherings in revolutionary clubs, debating societies, and other meetings led to new habits suited to changing circumstances: spending hours in a café or having dinner before or after these sessions was an integral part of it.

It is not surprising, therefore, that the Palais-Royal became the center of the rapidly developing *haute cuisine*. There one could find such previously unheard-of delicacies as turtle soup, or truffles steamed in champagne. Many previous owners of what had been luxury stores now tried their luck with "grande cuisine"—generally with success.[39] All in all, the Palais-Royal attracted the many people who valued enjoyment of life above all else and who could afford it even in the dire times of the Directory—the speculators.

Like true gourmets the brothers Goncourt include in their social history an account of these culinary sanctuaries and their delectable offerings; they also speak of the galaxy of delicatessens, pastry shops, ice-cream parlors, butcher and cheese shops that were established in the Palais-Royal area.[40] As political and economic conditions stabilized under the Consulate, further culinary refinements became possible and were available to a broader segment of society. Fashionable social life was no longer confined to the private sphere and was soon centered in some of the famous restaurants of the period.[41] This favored the development of the gourmet, that *arbiter elegantiae* of all questions concerning the pleasures of the table, and whose judgment was law.[42] It was also a time when dozens of cookbooks appeared: Viard's *Le Cuisinier imperial*, *Le Nouveau cuisinier universel* by Magiron, or *La Cuisine élémentaire et économique* by Leriguet, to name only the best-known ones. Then there were those like *L'Antigastronomie* by Gouriet, or *Le Gastronome à Paris* that even praised the culinary arts in verse. The enormous success of Grimod de la Reynière's book *Almanach des Gourmands* also testified to the public's great interest in all questions relating to the kitchen and the table.[43]

Clearly the level of subtlety and refinement of the food enjoyed by various parts of society was different. The differences lay in the more or less sophisticated choices of dishes and their preparation, in the types of restaurants chosen, as well as in the size and variety of menus. As far as the latter is concerned, the *Almanach des Gourmands* concluded that five hours was an appropriate amount of time to spend over a rich dinner.[44]

Social differences were revealed very clearly when it came to the question of the correct hour for various meals. The habit of eating the main meal at midday had gone out of fashion long before the Revolution. During the last years of the Old Regime it was customary to sit down to lunch at two o'clock in the afternoon—something only the *bourgeoisie du Marais* continued to do, and they were thought hopelessly old-fashioned in the Consulate and the Empire.[45] In circles that considered themselves to be the progressive elements of society, the hour of the midday meal—then called *diner*—was set later and later in the afternoon. Parisian restaurants were always filled between two and seven o'clock, an indication that each person determined the hour of his own principal meal according to his habits, preferences, or professional needs.[46] But new fashionable attitudes required official dinners to be held as late as possible, frequently not before seven o'clock. It did not take long for this rule to set the social *bon ton*. In the Empire no one who valued good manners had his dinner at four o'clock. "The earliest one should dine," Prudhomme writes in 1807, "is six o'clock, if one wants to be different from the bourgeoisie."[47]

A highly ridiculous custom developed in the matter of letting guests know the time of an official dinner. There were three types of invitation, and those who were unable to divine their real intention were shown up as provincials. According to this "protocol" made public in the indispensable guide to good taste, the *Almanach des Gourmands*, an invitation for "five o'clock" actually meant that one was not expected until six o'clock. An invitation that read *cinq heures précises* indicated that dinner would begin at half past five; and *cinq heures très précises* meant that the meal really would be served at five o'clock.[48]

The late hour at which the main meal began meant that the long interval between it and breakfast had to be broken by a second breakfast, the so-called *déjeuner* or lunch, which took place between ten and eleven o'clock in the morning. In contrast to the early-morning *petit déjeuner*, which consisted merely of a cup of coffee or chocolate, the *Almanach des Gourmands* describes the *déjeuner* as a real meal.[49] As a rule guests were not invited for the *déjeuner*; still, for those who could not afford lavish evening dinners, it was a good way to invite friends and acquaintances. The *Almanach des Gourmands*, the infallible expert on table etiquette, has this to say on the subject: "Lunch is a meal without specific obligations, one that anyone can give—be it someone who prefers not to reveal his income, a bachelor with no home of his own, or a gourmet who makes no special demands—without annoying his guests or provoking their contempt."[50]

Because gourmets and gourmands filled and overstuffed their stomachs at these late dinners during the Consulate and Empire, the prerevolutionary habit of gathering for a supper after going to the theater or other evening entertainment was abandoned. Instead the fashionable world, which had begun to adopt English customs, served tea late in the evening. Of course tea was only one of many ingredients used to brew a strong punch; a richly varied buffet was offered with it, ranging from turkey with truffles, to roast beef and ham, to petits-fours and other sweet delicacies.

This food fetish, the *grande bouffe* of the Consulate and Empire, is quite revealing about the inner values of Napoleonic society. It comes as no surprise that the spirit and refinement of previous centuries had been destroyed by the Revolution. But what is astonishing is that they had been replaced by an exaggerated, superficial enjoyment of life whose banality was emphasized by infantile behavior. It had become widespread fashion to enliven these stupefyingly gluttonous occasions with all sorts of trite pranks. For instance, one sprayed one's table companions with water, exploded small fireworks, or let a live fox run around under the table.[51] It was also popular to invite a paid buffoon, who was supposed to entertain the guests with all sorts of nonsense, or who pretended to have a tic.[52] Most of the guests were discreetly informed about this beforehand, except for one individual, who became more and more embarrassed to everyone's amusement.[53] The famous "funeral repast," given by the Prince of Ysenburg in Paris in the spring of 1810, at which the guests drank out of skulls and the food was shaped like human bones, also belongs to this tradition of foolishness.[54]

The mood of the times, alternating between serious, ceremonial stiffness and childish exuberance, was also reflected in fashions. In contrast to the cleverly cut gowns of the *merveilleuses* (as the women were called) showing off their bodily charms to best advantage, men's fashion was remarkable for its intentional sloppiness.[55] It was considered the very latest style to wear badly fitting outer garments that clearly bore the marks of long wear and tear. And in further contrast to the ladies who were forced by the prevailing trend to present themselves as youthfully as possible— something that did not always correspond to reality—the *élégants* or *incroyables* (as the men were known) tried to appear far older than they actually were. They stooped and walked with a dragging gait and examined the world through enormous spectacles or lorgnettes. The latest men's fashion also required that they never dress in keeping with the weather. Thus if it was raining the *incroyables* promenaded in white silk hose that promptly got splashed from the deep mud. In the summer, on the other hand, they never left off wearing their top boots and underneath their thick cloth coats they wore two or three layers of waistcoats.[56] Sir John Dean Paul notes during his stay in Paris in 1802, that the restaurant Frascati "serves as the meeting place of good society. However, the men's unkempt look clashes so obviously with the elegance of the beautiful women, that it takes away any semblance of good taste from this sort of public place."[57]

Once the Empire began, the exaggerated styles disappeared; the taste for nudity and carelessness now yielded to the other extreme. The imperial court dictated fashion for Parisian society. Bodices that had been abandoned after the fall of the Bastille came back again, and women's charms were hidden from men's eyes by swathes of fabric. Men's clothing also changed from its previous faddishness to a studied elegance.[58]

The extent to which the Revolution had destroyed not only the structure of society but its accepted values can be seen in the great changes affecting the choice of partners in marriage. In certain aristocratic and bourgeois circles it was still customary to have arranged marriages without consultation of the future spouses. But that was the exception in the Empire; most marriages were agreed to rather hastily, a very few weeks after the couple met. These "love marriages" were part of the feverish postrevolutionary desire to enjoy life to the hilt without worrying about what was to come.

If a person grew tired of a spouse, nothing was easier than getting rid of him or her. Divorce had been made legal in 1792 and was granted as soon as both partners wanted it. By far the most frequent cause given was *incompatibilité d'humeur* (mental incompatibility), hardly surprising given the speed with which most marriages were contracted.[59]

Marriages between partners of greatly disparate ages became increasingly common. Contemporary memoirs make particular reference to the marriages of Napoleon's generals and marshals. Thus General Mouton was twenty years older than his wife; General Legrand, who was over fifty, married a seventeen-year-old; d'Oudinot surprised his daughters of his first marriage with a stepmother of their own age; and the aged Marshall Kellermann, long past seventy, thought nothing of wooing Mlle de Chastenay who was thirty years his junior.

There were numerous reasons for such marriages: the lack of time during the hectic years of the Revolution to find a suitable partner; the fact that it was no longer necessary to wait until one acquired a certain position or status to make a good match; and the general change in values. All of this meant that the choice of partners, like that of other marketable items, depended on supply and demand. Under the Directory a certain Liardot had already had the brilliant idea of starting a marriage bureau. It was located in the ill-famed rue de la Tixanderie and, according to one of its advertisements, it "offered satisfactory matches by giving accurate information about character, habits, income, and all other questions pertinent to each case."[60] The prompt success Liardot had with his marriage bureau soon led to competition. A paper devoted exclusively to advertisements by persons wishing to get married, the *Indicateur des Mariages*, began to appear every Tuesday and Friday.[61] There was also a firm that arranged for prospective marriage partners to meet at balls, three days a week.[62]

Many for whom the Old Regime represented the good old days saw undeniable signs of overall moral decay in this. And the often repeated assertion by self-appointed apostles of morality—men like Geoffroy, who wrote for the feuilleton of the *Journal des Debats*—that even marital fidelity had been sacrificed to the Revolution, has long become part of the ineradicable legend of degeneracy that surrounds the Directory as well as the Consulate and Empire periods. Stendhal, to whom love and women meant a great deal if not all of what there was to life, maintains in a letter to Edouard Mounier in 1803 that the law of conjugal fidelity "only exists in books now, and even in a novel you can no longer find a man and wife held together by faithfulness."[63] That statement is contradicted by Savary duc de Rovigo, who replaced Fouché in 1810 at the Ministry of Police; thanks to his informers he had accurate information about the most intimate relationships and events.[64] However, both accounts must be taken with a grain of salt; for while Stendhal was obviously exaggerating, Savary—who assumed his position at a critical moment for the Empire—was more inclined to gloss things over. In any case, there was a seven-year interval between 1803 and 1810 during which much had changed. The society that had still been in its formative

stage in 1803 was well established by 1810. Moreover, as a result of the gradual official return to religious life, Catholicism (with the help of official,
imperial bigotry) had not only regained but increased its influence. Another
indirect, though reliable indicator of the changing moral attitude is the relationship between marriages and divorces. In 1800 there were 3,315 marriages
in Paris and 698 divorces; in 1801, of 3,842 marriages, 808 ended in divorce.[65]
But the proportion changed again in 1804, when there were 3,676 marriages
but only 316 divorces.[66]

The double moral standard adopted by the Consulate and Empire when
it came to divorce is rather typical of prevailing attitudes. Divorced persons
were not socially ostracized; in fact anyone who criticized the principle of
divorce risked rebuke. On the other hand, the consequences were far worse if
anyone praised the system of divorce. That is, what was generally accepted as
a necessary evil was not to be mentioned in public. Mme de Staël had this
experience following the publication of her novel *Delphine*, in which she
made a strong case for divorce. It provoked a severe reaction by contemporary critics.

It is not surprising, therefore, that even the comedies of manners of
Napoleonic times hypocritically condemned adultery or divorce. A reader
of these now long-forgotten pieces very aptly scoffs that one comes away
with the impression that "all spouses were faithful to one another and all
marriages were indissoluble."[67] The theatrical scandal of February 1801, the
performance of *L'Aimable vieillard* in the Théâtre-Français, is also of interest here. The story of this play—a highly dubious one from any point of view
other than moralistic—concerns a sixty-year-old man who marries a young
girl but discovers almost immediately that she loves someone else. He
promptly gets a divorce so that the two lovers can get married. . . . According to a report by a police agent who attended the performance, the audience began to protest and demonstrate as soon as the protagonist's unselfish
intention became clear. "This, as well as the way in which it was carried out,
upset the public which failed to see any sort of moral in it; hardly had the
word divorce been uttered when the audience turned into a storm-tossed
sea."[68]

The Socialization of Death

*A*PORTRAIT, EVEN A SKETCH of postrevolutionary ethics would be
incomplete if it did not shed some light on the attitude toward
death. As in other areas, the Revolution had destroyed old traditions without replacing them with new ones. During the Terror, when
death was a constant presence, no secure or special place was allocated that
would protect the dead from the disrespect of the living, and free the living
from the horrible burden of the dead. Unidentified corpses were simply

thrown into the trenches of knackers' yards, while guillotine victims were interred in anonymous mass graves in out-of-the-way places.[69] Nor did the churches offer any safeguard against profanation, especially if they contained the remains of members of the royal family. Even burial in the Pantheon could not guarantee the peace of the dead, as was shown by the examples of Mirabeau and Marat.

Cemeteries turned into neglected wastelands during the campaign against Christianity that denied the dead any religious ritual. Instead of the republican equality that many had hoped would apply to burial in uniform graves, naked bodies were still being transported to these sites in wretched carts and hastily deposited in mass graves, with no family members present.[70]

Suggestions for changing the ubiquitous plight of the dead had already been put forward during the Directory.[71] Burial customs were to be reintegrated into a firm social structure so as to eliminate the uncivilized procedures associated with them.[72] However, despite a campaign for reform by the Institut de France, nothing changed during the Directory. The architect Antoine Quatremère de Quincy set out the growing dangers that this situation presented to the "harmonie du tableau social" (harmony of the social structure), as he called it, in a detailed report in August 1800.[73]

In contrast to the Directory, the Consulate began to deal with such matters promptly once it came to power. On February 24, 1800, Lucien Bonaparte, the minister of the interior, instructed the Institut de France to organize a public competition to solve the problem of new rituals and the establishment of cemeteries.[74] The fact that forty suggestions were made in the course of the competition indicated how strong public interest was in settling this question.[75]

One of the first practical results of these proposals was the appointment of undertakers in each of the twelve Paris arrondissements.[76] As of the spring of 1800 a private joint-stock company tried to take advantage of this change in attitude by offering four different categories of burial service. Frochot, the prefect of the Seine, eventually signed a comprehensive decree outlining Parisian burial requirements. The importance he attached to this document, the individual regulations of which were based on the competition's suggestions, is shown in its ceremonial preamble:

> Burial institutions are of utmost importance to mankind.
> The rites that were completely abandoned as a result of the Revolution used to provide a final tribute to the wealthy, whereas the poor were consigned to misery and oblivion.
> Today's ceremonies treat rich and poor with the same indifference; and public opinion, which is equivalent to a moral attitude, condemns the austerity of contemporary graves. It is proper for the capital of the Republic to lend dignity to burials by its example, and above all to show concern for the interment of the poor as an obligation and sign of communal respect.[77]

Under Frochot's regulations funeral corteges were permitted only if they were led by a hearse drawn by two horses. A hearse was limited to one coffin, and had to proceed at a walking pace. The funeral procession following the hearse was not to be stopped or interrupted by other traffic. Finally, the temporary coffins used solely to transport corpses to the cemeteries were no longer to be used. Instead everyone, including the indigent, was now entitled to his own coffin and shroud.

The new burial ordinance went into effect on 1 Floréal of the year IX (April 21, 1801) and met with public approval.[78] But it only solved a small part of the problem as the condition of the cemeteries was still horrifying. While efforts had been made at the end of the Old Regime to improve their worst aspects, plans to open new cemeteries outside the city were shelved once the Revolution began.[79] At that time the inner city cemeteries, with the exception of Sainte Marguerite, were closed. But new ones in outlying districts or outside of the tax wall—such as the one near the tax post of Clichy at the foot of Montmartre—soon fell into a state of neglect.[80] The condition of mass graves for the poor and needy was appalling, as they were left uncovered until completely filled. Cambry, in a report prepared for the department of the Seine at the end of the Directory on these places—more like knackers' yards than burial sites—actually felt obliged to resort to Latin when describing their most disgusting aspects. Among things noted were roving dogs chewing at the cadavers, and grave-diggers assaulting female corpses.[81] There was also the persistent problem of the odor in these areas. Baudin des Ardennes, who was present at a funeral in the Montmartre cemetery on November 3, 1798, at which the Institut de France organized a protest demonstration, reports: "There was an unbearable stench that choked the participants, although it was a cold time of year and a completely clear day."[82]

Although now, in the Consulate, all were entitled to their own wooden coffin, these were still placed in anonymous mass graves. In a confidential account in 1801 Frochot notes:

> Most of the cemeteries have long suffered from such a condition of overcrowding that they can neither hold more corpses nor decompose those that are there. All decomposition takes place practically in the open. The ground has become a fetid black mire from the constant process of decay.[83]

Another report issued four years later again stressed similar conditions.[84] Even newly established cemeteries, like that in Montmartre, ended up with the same problems on account of mass graves. This is pointed out in a report of March 18, 1806, by Dubois, the Paris prefect of police, to the minister of the interior: "To save space coffins are piled closely together in mass graves. They are are then covered over with a few inches of soil insufficient to eliminate the fumes of decay, especially in the warm season."[85]

Frochot had long since realized that thorough reform could only be undertaken if three cemeteries were established outside the city limits, each occupying an area of at least fifteen hectares. But it took another two years before the city received permission to acquire the necessary land.[86] A law passed on 17 Floréal, year XI, finally enabled Frochot to buy property for the future eastern and southern sites; he expected to enlarge the existing one, at the foot of Montmartre, to become the projected northern cemetery.

The first property to be acquired lay to the east of the city on the hills of Ménilmontant, "au lieu dit la maison du Père la Chaise"—named after the country house of the Jesuit Father François de la Chaise, one of Louis XIV's confessors.[87] A year later, on May 1, 1804, Frochot closed Sainte Marguerite, the last of the inner-city cemeteries; the new eastern cemetery was opened on May 21 of the same year.[88]

Meanwhile Frochot realized that the many problems of hygiene could not be solved merely by establishing newer and larger cemeteries. He therefore came up with the brilliant idea of discontinuing the system of mass graves and instead making burial a matter of private, individual concern, as in antiquity.[89] In a decree issued on 23 Prairial, year XII, which at first applied only to the new eastern cemetery, he allowed private individuals to acquire "permanent" concessions for graves, and to decorate these with individual monuments. A further law of 15 Ventôse, year XIII, set a very moderate price of 100 francs per square meter for the plots.

Frochot's proposals, which eventually turned Père-Lachaise into one of the most beautiful and most sought-after Parisian cemeteries, were far ahead of their time. Wealthy residents at first had reservations, probably because it was far from the city; but a more important reason was surely that a private cult of death was quite alien to the mentality of the times. After all, during the revolutionary period disdain for death had been a way of exorcising it. So it was that up to December 1805 only three concessions in perpetuity were sold for Père-Lachaise; in 1806 the number rose to five and in 1807 to nine. Altogether a total of 530 graves was sold from the opening of the cemetery to the end of 1815. Not until the Restoration and the beginning of Romanticism, when the motif of death began to play an important role, did the situation change. Then Père-Lachaise was discovered as a place where romantic feeling found expression in landscape and nature.[90] By 1835 11,259 plots had been bought and embellished with tombstones.[91]

The southern burial site, also approved in the Decree of 17 Floréal, year XII, was developed more slowly. Ground for it had been purchased on the other side of the boulevard Montparnasse adjoining the La Charité cemetery, but it was not enclosed until 1810. For some strange reason it was not walled off; instead a deep ditch was dug around it. No one was buried there for another fourteen years. The delay was due to the fact that an area established during the Revolution near the Vaugirard tax post still had sufficient space for the dead from the Left Bank. The Sainte-Catherine cemetery—better known by its popular name of Clamart—to which corpses from the faubourg Saint-Marcel were taken, was also located there.

When the Prefecture revealed its plans to close the Clamart cemetery once the new Montparnasse site opened, residents of the faubourg Saint-Marcel voiced strong resentment that their dead were to be buried so far away.[92] A different view was expressed by the wealthy residents of the Chaussée d'Antin, who tried to stop the proposed enlargement of the north-

ern cemetery in Montmartre. In numerous petitions and protests they pointed out the danger they would be exposed to from the poisonous vapors
spread by the decomposing bodies. "If one were to be deterred by complaints
of this sort," Frochot writes to the minister of the interior on April 23, 1806,
"it would become completely impossible to establish any new cemeteries in
Paris. Every property owner would try as best he could to have an institution of this sort kept as far away from his neighborhood as possible."[93] Still
the protests from the Chaussée d'Antin district did prevent expansion of the
Montmartre site from being decreed until August 13, 1811.

In the end it was Frochot who continued the work begun before but halted during the Revolution. Thirteen inner-city cemeteries were shut down
between 1804 and 1813, and the remains transferred to the subterranean
quarries near the Enfer tax post.[94] In 1810 and 1811 Frochot had the skeletons and skulls decoratively arranged on both sides of the subterranean passages. In addition, tablets bearing inscriptions such as *Haec ultra metas requi-
escunt beatam spem exspectantes* were put up. When the work was completed
the catacombs were opened to visitors and soon became one of the most popular sights in Paris.[95]

The Laboring Classes

*T*HOSE WHO BELONGED TO THE "GOOD SOCIETY" of Paris, who
visited the subterranean realm of the dead in the catacombs with
morbid curiosity, took care not to set foot in the poorer sections.
A completely different social reality existed there from that of the fashionable
sections along the Chaussée d'Antin, or the bustling streets and alleys around
the Palais-Royal. It was a far cry, too, from the ambiance of elegance and nostalgia for the past in the faubourg Saint-Germain; or from the Marais, where
bourgeois social etiquette was strictly observed. By and large the social topography of the Consulate and Empire still corresponded to that of prerevolutionary times. But an 1801 study of the poor of Paris showed certain changes:
the number of those dependent on public welfare was especially large in the
Quinze-Vingts district, in Popincourt, in the Quartier de la Fidélité around
the Hôtel de Ville, as well as in the Jardin des Plantes and Finistère sections.[96]
The latter two, better known as the faubourg Saint-Marcel, were considered
to be the center of the worst kind of deprivation until the extensive incorporation of suburban municipalities in 1860. A contemporary observer notes
that even "the working class of the faubourg Saint-Antoine was offended if
one lumped it together with that of the faubourg Saint-Marcel."[97]

A clear demarcation of districts inhabited exclusively by workers, such
as developed during the Second Empire, existed in only a limited way in the
Napoleonic period. "The proletariat," as they began to be called at the time,
preferred to live near their work. These locations, varying in density, were

dispersed over the entire city except for the few purely residential quarters of the rich and the aristocrats that evolved at the end of the Old Regime. Social status could still be determined according to the floor on which one lived: the cheapest living quarters were on the upper floors of houses, serving the common people and the poor.[98]

Living conditions of the lower classes had not been affected much by the Revolution—the poverty that had long governed their existence had outlasted all upheavals. Yet wage earners who, along with their families, amounted to half the inhabitants of Paris were materially better off than before or during the Revolution.[99] The main reason for this was that the unemployment rife under the Old Regime was replaced by a relative shortage of workers in the Consulate and Empire due to the Napoleonic wars.[100] Furthermore, the economic boom that lasted until 1810 led to a rise in real wages that averaged 25 percent over the level of 1789.[101]

The scarcity of workers, at times very noticeable in specific trades, was alleviated by the massive influx of seasonal laborers; stone-cutters came from the western provinces, textile workers from the north and from the French section of Flanders; chimney sweeps, shoe-cleaners and porters arrived from Savoy, and bricklayers from the Massif Central.[102]

Seasonal workers, who mostly came to Paris in small groups, kept in close touch in the capital and hence looked for modest lodgings in specific sections. Bricklayers and stone-cutters preferred the area around the place de Grève, the other trades chose the network of alleys around the Châtelet or near the Bastille. They frequently lived in simple inns run by compatriots, where they rented beds in twenty-bed dormitories.

The relatively great instability of their situation—anyone who was ill or unemployed was soon swallowed up by poverty—was responsible for the easy transition from *classes laborieuses* to *classes dangereuses*. Begging occupied the gray zone between poverty and criminality. There were over a hundred thousand beggars in Paris in 1802, a number that had not decreased by the end of the Empire.[103] The two *Dépôts de Mendicité* in Saint-Denis and Villers-Cotterêts, used by the police to intern those caught begging, were totally inadequate to solve the social problem whose victims represented a blight in the streets of Paris. As Reichardt puts it:

> A good German, who has a heart in his body and who really paid attention to the various stages of the Revolution and still remembers them—something that rarely happens with a Frenchman—is moved by the horrible, endless begging in the streets. . . . In bad, dirty weather, when one cannot step too far away from the houses without ending up in a sea of sludge, or when one is in danger of falling under a wheel, one has to make one's way through long rows of beggars who cannot be avoided. Generally they tend not to be too importunate; but they make one feel all the more compassionate toward their meaningful, imploring voices and their pitiful gestures.[104]

Prostitution also fell between poverty and criminality. "If the police were aware," Henrion writes, "that it is due to lack of work that female workers are driven into prostitution, they would make an effort to establish public work-shops for women, similar to those for men."[105] Actually, female unemploy-ment caused by seasonal and economic conditions was only one of the rea-sons for prostitution. What was more important was that women were paid so little that a female worker hardly earned enough to feed herself. Furthermore, the influx of seasonal laborers who came to Paris without their families increased the demand for paid sex.

Theft was the most frequently cited offense in the crime statistics of the Empire. On the other hand, aggravated robberies and capital offenses such as murder were committed far less often. For instance, in 1801 13 murders were registered; in 1808 the number increased to 17 and to 18 in 1811.[106] All in all, these statistics provided neither justification for, nor confirmation of, the fears constantly expressed by the authorities—especially since the army's need for manpower saw to it that criminal elements were deployed on the battlefields of Europe.[107] The exaggerated estimate of criminality particularly current in the first two years of the Consulate may have have been linked to the experience of the revolutionary Terror. Moreover, the great public interest in the few really spectacular capital offenses was part of the same morbid curiosity that also inspired the public's Sunday visits to the Paris morgue to view the corpses.[108]

But what was a constant source of anxiety to the bourgeoisie, and the administrative bodies drawn from its ranks, was the large working class of Paris. Uneasiness was expressed in various ways, such as the open contempt with which the middle classes reacted to and described the alien world of the workers, especially the poor hygienic conditions in districts inhabited by the proletariat:

> The extreme overcrowding of residents in certain quarters, and the stench of household animals blended with that of excrement, decaying animal cadavers, and rotting food, all create extensive atmospheric pollution in which people live and eat. The fetid air is a visible haze that generally covers Paris and there are districts over which it is particularly thick.[109]

Also revealing of the arrogant and unfeeling attitude is the pitiless language of a police report on the *condition morale* of workers employed in various trades.[110]

It is obvious why the Paris bourgeoisie feared the workers; they had not forgotten the lesson learned in the days of the Revolution. Even Napoleon is known to have made the following statement during a depressed period in the furniture industry: "The workers have no work, consequently they will listen to any conspirator and are open to incitement. I fear revolts caused by a shortage of bread far more than going into battle against two hundred thousand men."[111]

In fact one of Napoleon's main concerns was to make sure that the capi-tal's proletariat always had work and could buy its bread at affordable prices.[112] Orders were given to provide employment for 3,000 workers in the first winter of the Consulate. These measures became superfluous once the economy improved and the beautification and restoration of Paris was under-taken. The prefect of police is only echoing his lord and master when he states on July 13, 1801: "It would be of great significance if construction of the bridges were to begin now, because many workers are unemployed and the entire economy is stagnant."[113] Time and again, however far from Paris he happened to be and whatever other problems concerned him, Napoleon encouraged his ministers and officials to see that the workers of Paris were kept busy. For instance, on 19 Fructidor, year XI, (September 6, 1803), he writes to the minister of the interior: "The winter is going to be hard, citizen minister, and meat will be expensive. You have to make sure that work is available in Paris."[114] And eight years later, during the unmistakable recession, he repeatedly requests Montalivet (then minister of the interior) to increase state building activity and thus create more work: "Take whatever measures seem appropriate to ensure that the police do not have to seize workers and put them in workshops supported by the state."[115]

In return for this precarious security workers gave up their freedom. The Law of 22 Germinal, year XI, introduced the *livret* or work book that all employees were obliged to have. A consular regulation issued on 9 Frimaire, year XII, set out the details: the *livret* was issued and controlled by the police; it had to be given to the employer when the individual was hired; any worker who left one job for another without his *livret* risked having to appear in court as a vagrant.[116] In other words, introduction of the work book strengthened the employer's position considerably, especially as the strict prohibition against worker associations—already enforced by the Constituent Assembly and the National Convention—was reinstated.[117]

Behind everything that was ostensibly done to protect them, the real aim was to create safeguards against the workers. But the regime's assumptions were false. At no time did the Paris working class present a serious threat to Napoleon's administrative system. It was not social repression that kept them in check but rather their vivid memory of the Revolution that had disappointed their hopes. The numerous strikes that kept breaking out under the Empire despite repressive measures were essentially nonpolitical protests against working hours and wages.[118] The workers lacked the leadership of the sort of bourgeois intellectuals who had inspired them during the Revolution, and who could have coordinated and expanded their demands into a political strategy.

Besides, and there is a certain irony in this, the workers remained completely pro-Bonaparte to the bitter end of the Empire. They regarded Napoleon with the same blind trust they had previously had in the king. They naïvely believed that a sovereign's sole concern was with his subjects, and that any political decision that shattered this belief was not taken by him. Napoleon was quite aware of this loyalty and always tried not to destroy the irrational attachment to his person. "It is important to make sure," he writes from the Schönbrunn Palace in occupied Vienna to Fouché, the minister of police, "that no new regulations be issued for or against the workers while I am away from Paris, and that their habits and customs not be interfered with. For they believe that they are being treated badly only because I am not there and they cannot complain to me; that is why they feel that an injustice is being done to them."[119]

New Administration—Little Change

*N*APOLEON'S OLDEST AND GREATEST PASSION, one that was to last to the end of his life, was the beautification of Paris. Even in exile on St. Helena he spoke often and with obvious pleasure of the projects he had wanted to complete in the capital—a center that he had wanted to make the most beautiful in the world. This passion of the Corsican Bonaparte was by no means love at first sight. He was in Paris for the first time from October 1784 to October 1785 as a cadet at the Ecole militaire, but the strict discipline of the academy prevented him from getting to know the city properly. When he came to Paris in the autumn of 1787 for the second time, he was entirely taken up with exploring the Palais-Royal where, on November 22, he had his first romantic adventure with a young prostitute from Nantes.

Even during his third stay in Paris in 1792, when he witnessed the storming of the Tuileries, the city did not win his heart. And the conditions of his fourth visit were hardly conducive to his seeing Paris in a more friendly light. He was on half-pay because of his differences with the Committee of Public Safety, and as he roamed aimlessly through the streets of Paris he memorized their layout. This knowledge of the area was to stand him in good stead when the royalist insurgency of 13 Vendémiaire was put down. Later, as commander in chief of the territorial army with headquarters in Paris he had ample opportunity to familiarize himself with the complex problems of a metropolis. However, he grew tired of the power struggles and political intrigues of the Directory and applied for the chance to head the Italian campaign, which revealed his military genius in all its brilliance for the first time. It was only when he returned to Paris as a much-celebrated hero that he conceived the passion to make that city a monument to himself.

After the coup d'état of 18 Brumaire Bonaparte at first devoted his whole attention to reorganizing the ineffficient city administration.[120] He did away with the system of incompetent and powerless elected bodies that had been prevented from carrying out their work by continual political machinations. The new organization established by the Law of 28 Pluviôse, year VIII, created a clearly structured administrative hierarchy. It was headed by the prefect of the Department of the Seine, who also served as mayor and was directly responsible to the minister of the interior.

The Prefecture of the Seine, located as of 1803 in the Hôtel de Ville, consisted of a general administrative department with four subsections. These were responsible for public works, financial administration, state properties, culture and welfare, military establishments, and prisons and workhouses. Because of the capital's special importance, it had its own prefect of police parallel to the prefect of the Seine. The former, also under the direct jurisdiction of the minister of the interior, was responsible for everything connected with the city's security. In this way, the city administration not only had two independent heads but also two administrative structures—an organizational system almost identical with that of the Old Regime. The prefect of the Seine filled the function of the previous *Prévôt des Marchands*, while the police prefect had the position of the former *Lieutenant Général*. And just as then, this double-headed setup was the cause of repeated differences in matters of authority between the prefect of the Seine and the prefect of police; usually, however, the latter could make decisions on his own.[121]

Given the power of these two representatives of the regime, the other "major administrative officials" of the city were condemned to be mere figureheads. This was true of the mayors of the twelve arrondissements or districts into which the city had been divided by the law of 19 Vendémiaire, year IV, as well as of the prefect's advisory committee, the *Conseil de la Préfecture*. The *Conseil Général du Département de la Seine*, whose twenty-four members were supposed to "represent the eyes of the government, of which the prefect was the arm," according to Bonaparte's instructions, shared the same fate.[122]

In conjunction with this reform, the city finances were also reorganized. A series of revenue sources were added to the hated *octroi*, the tax on goods levied at the city limits that had already been reinstated by the Directory.[123] The subsequent balancing of the city's notorious deficit did not last very long. This was because the estimated costs of Napoleon's vast construction projects were always too low. Moreover, Napoleon liked to control the capital's budget himself, a fact that was anything but advantageous for the accounts.[124]

Napoleon's administrative system was designed to prevent the people from having any say in the election of administrators or the decision process. This was not merely a matter of his preference for prerevolutionary institutions. What was decisive for the first consul was the experience of the Revolution and the lesson he drew from it—that no independent force able to challenge the government's authority be allowed to establish itself in the capital. Besides, an administration that was directly responsible to the government provided assurances that the grandiose plans he had for the city's embellishment would be carried out promptly.

In these ways the Paris of 1800 essentially resembled that of 1789, with the difference that the city had deteriorated even further in the ten years since the Revolution.[125] For instance the condition of the streets defied all description. The account by Reichardt is only one of many:

> Night frosts have made the disgusting mud that formed in the streets after some rainy days easier to negotiate; once again one can walk to outlying areas. For however good a pedestrian one is, and however little one cares about wet and discomfort along the way, it is impossible to walk in such dirty streets for any length of time. Apart from having to step on stones covered with thick sludge, and getting very tired and losing time by having to work one's way through the crowd constantly milling about near the houses, the stench in the streets causes nausea and a very unpleasant sensation in one's stomach not experienced anywhere else. I can honestly say that for the first time in my life I became aware of my stomach.[126]

This was not an exaggeration. A leisurely stroll in Paris during the Consulate was out of the question. There were no pavements on which a person could make his way so as not to be bothered by the heavy coach traffic. The absence of pavements meant that the Palais-Royal continued to be very popular. So were the various pedestrian arcades erected during the Empire: the Passage Delorme connecting the rue Saint-Honoré with the rue de Rivoli in an "elegant and convenient fashion," or the Passage des Panoramas that opened in 1800.[127]

Even under the Empire the condition of the streets remained much the same, part of the general chaos that struck visitors to Paris.[128] There was the densely built center of the *Cité*, with its twisting alleys, from which rose no less than eighteen church spires. On the Left Bank, the mansions of the faubourg Saint-Germain and their gardens contrasted starkly with the dark streets of the overcrowded faubourg Saint-Marcel.[129] A similar situation existed on the Right Bank, where houses stood squeezed together between the Seine and the interior boulevards, and where a network of dark little alleys and crooked streets crisscrossed the area. On the other side of the interior boulevards and the tax wall, however, there were great uncultivated areas and gardens in which separate clusters of houses sat like islands in a green sea.

What this almost organically developed cityscape needed was large connecting streets to provide better circulation of traffic and relieve the cluttered and overpopulated center. Moreover, such an improvement would make individual districts of the city equally accessible. A cleanup of inner-city conditions and the construction of new, wider streets had already been planned during the Old Regime and the Revolution. The monarchy, for its part, continually put off implementation because of the many property owners whose rights would have been affected. But once the extensive Church properties were expropriated in the Revolution, one of the main obstacles to rehabilitation was suddenly removed. At that time, though, the will and money needed to realize the plans were lacking.

Napoleon was familiar with some of these earlier projected improvements that were inspired by a taste for classical symmetry and harmony. They served as models for his own partially realized urban architectural vision.[130] The work for which Napoleon was directly responsible can be classified as follows: renewal of inner-city districts by large-scale demolition, new construction of streets and squares in the center, erection of monuments to commemorate his rule or military successes, and systems for improving the city's supply of food and fresh water (see map 1, page 343).

A special bureaucracy was established to coordinate the work of architects, engineers, and administrators and see that all was carried out according to the wishes and conceptions of the imperial sovereign and planner in chief. In addition a Department of Public Works was set up in the Ministry of the Interior, to supervise the construction of new streets and squares in Paris. Besides these two bodies there were also the *conseils d'administration* or advisory committees, over which Napoleon himself presided; their membership varied according to the subject being discussed. As a rule these meetings were attended by a number of city councilmen and the minister whose special domain was being considered; very often engineers and architects were present to give explanations and evaluations. The conclusions were frequently summarized by Napoleon himself in detailed orders, in which he also expressed his own opinions and wishes.[131]

But in spite of this elaborate apparatus and his own tireless efforts, Napoleon failed to turn Paris into a city of unique size and splendor. He had to abandon his original intention of a systematic and large-scale transformation of the capital and content himself with a few smaller improvements. Not that he lacked a broad vision or a concrete plan—the basis for various projects was the so-called *Plan des Artistes*, referred to earlier; but what was missing was the time and means to create the metropolis that would anchor his fame in the memory of mankind as lastingly as the pyramids had done for their creators.

Still, even if Napoleon's accomplishments were modest in terms of his overall plans for Paris, even if much of what he envisaged was reduced or eliminated during the Second Empire, he did set an example after more than a century of ineffective planning. It was an example to which his nephew and Baron Haussmann still felt committed. Napoleon knew that shortage of funds and the interests of wealthy property owners (including the Church) had prevented urban reforms. He therefore went about creating the necessary financing and expropriation laws with the same intensity as in the planning, design, and building of his projects. Concerning financing he still maintained on St. Helena that his plans would not have cost the city one sou.[132] He never seems to have realized that this did not correspond to reality because, especially in the later years of the Empire, his budget planning was characterized by higher estimates of revenues than what was eventually received. At the same time the estimated costs for new buildings were always too low. He was particularly disappointed when public buildings like covered markets, warehouses, and slaughterhouses did not show the expected profits after amortization. These profits were calculated in the costs, but failed to materialize during his lifetime.[133]

Another peculiarity of the Napoleonic financial system was that certain revenues were allocated to specific projects, so as to avoid having to detail income and expenses. Thus he conceived of making the city pay for the inner-city street system, in return for which it would receive a portion of the road toll levied at the city gates. Similarly he decided that the police, profiting handsomely from gambling concessions, should contribute 100,000 francs each month to public projects in Paris. In 1806 he also instructed the city administration to pay a yearly sum of up to 2 million francs for new construction and beautification projects. The sums actually contributed, though, were far less: police and city administration could only contribute 200,000 francs each. To make up the difference it was necessary to float a loan of 8 million francs in November 1807.[134]

In a letter to Minister of the Interior Cretet, emphasizing the importance of the loan, Napoleon indicates how much he disliked this type of financing which he had to resort to more and more often:

I assume you will take the necessary steps so that the projected work can be finished promptly and the city's revenues be increased accordingly. Some of these constructions will not yield much income and will only serve to beautify the area; but others, like the galleries in the markets and slaughterhouses, should produce a profit, and it is therefore important to act quickly.[135]

Finally, it was due to Napoleon's initiative that an expropriation law was passed on March 8, 1810, despite the stubborn resistance of the *Conseil d'Etat*, whose members were opposed to it.[136]

Napoleon as Architect

A NEAR-FATAL BOMB ATTACK on Napoleon's life in the narrow rue Saint-Niçaise, on the evening of 3 Nivôse, year IX (December 24, 1800), convinced him to begin restoring this district directly adjoining the Tuileries.[137] On 15 Nivôse (January 5, 1801) he ordered the two houses damaged by the explosion to be demolished, along with the Hôtel de Coigny and several other buildings in the neighborhood if they could be acquired without too much expense.[138] This important redevelopment effort enlarged the place du Carrousel considerably and met with general approval. It caught the public imagination and sparked a desire for the demolition work to continue—which is what Napoleon had counted on.[139] However, additional groups of houses were not bought and pulled down until 1806, when the Louvre was expanded. With some interruptions, this work continued until 1813.

The most significant urban improvement under the Consulate and the Empire involved the area bounded by the Jardin des Tuileries, the place de la Concorde, and the interior boulevards. To begin with four new streets were built: the rue de Rivoli, the rue de Castiglione, the rue de la Paix and the rue des Pyramides. Somewhat later three more streets—Mondovi, Cambon, and Mont-Thabor—were created between the rue de Rivoli and the rue Saint-Honoré. The many expropriated Church properties in this district created an ideal situation for thorough urban renovation that would express Napoleon's vision. According to a consular decree of 17 Vendémiaire, year IX (October 9, 1801), private builders who wanted to erect houses along the new streets could do so only "if they observed the plans and projections for the facades designed by government architects."[140] The Manège meeting hall, in which the first three National Assemblies had met, was torn down in the summer of 1802; and plans for the rue de Rivoli were drawn the following year.

After a lively debate, in which the public also participated, a decree was issued permitting houses to be built along the side of the street facing the Terrace des Feuillants. This was what gave the rue de Rivoli its great charm. Yet despite the new street becoming one of the most scenic locations of its time, there was only limited interest. Even when the wall obstructing the view over the Terrace des Feuillants and the adjoining Jardin des Tuileries was replaced by a railing in the summer of 1806, there was still little enthusiasm for it.[141] This was because the architects—Pierre Fontaine and Charles Percier, Napoleon's two most important artistic advisers—had designed the houses along the rue de Rivoli with arcades. Construction was thus bound to be more expensive than usual; and the street had to be elegant since it was so close to the Tuileries. Therefore the shops under the arcades could not be rented to "artisans using hammers," or to butchers or bakers—restrictions that were bound to scare off interested buyers.[142]

Those who decided to build a house regardless of the restrictions were immediately exempted from taxes for twenty, and eventually for thirty years, but this proved only a small incentive. By the end of the imperial regime very few houses graced the rue de Rivoli. Chateaubriand, who had an apartment there, describes the street as it looked in 1813: "In this street you only saw the arcades built by the government, and a few houses rising here and there with their lateral connecting stones still exposed."[143]

In those days the rue de Rivoli ended just beyond the place des Pyramides at the Passage Delorme. Between it, the Palais-Royal, and the Tuileries there was still a maze of dilapidated houses, sheds, and workshops that were not to be removed until after 1848. It would have made sense to continue the rue de Rivoli parallel to the Louvre, as it is today, and to restore the area. But at the time there were other, far more grandiose and fascinating plans so that this obvious project was simply ignored. The idea was to build a triumphal way that would run in a straight line from the Bastille, or even from the more distant barrière du Trône—the present place de la Nation—past the Hôtel de Ville, and end in a gigantic square in front of the columned facade of the Louvre.

However, though surveying was begun in the autumn of 1809, Napoleon then decided not to go ahead with the actual opening-up of this long street and the construction of the enormous square. He outlines the reasons for his seemingly paradoxical decision in a memorandum to Montalivet, the minister of the interior, on September 14, 1810:

> If the idea [of this street] were new, then His Majesty could easily pass a law that would authorize it; but the idea is as old as the city of Paris. . . . Therefore this great undertaking can only be decided on when one is really ready to go ahead with it. But before embarking on it, one has to know what the whole project will cost. It is highly probable that it will cost more than 20 million. . . . Hence this enormous task can only be considered once the fresh-water supply of Paris has been secured, and when sewers, slaughterhouses, markets, granaries, etc., have been built.

In the same memorandum Napoleon hints that it might be possible to realize part of the project by constructing the place de la Bastille, aligning the building line of the projected street with the northern facade of the Hôtel de Ville, and opening up the space in front of the Louvre. That would have meant demolishing the church of Saint-Germain l'Auxerrois: "If such preparations were made, all of which would indicate the foreseeable construction of the large street, this project would become known and accepted as a fact. At the same time it would avoid having to go through the ridiculous motions of passing a law that might not have any practical results for a long time."[144] But the emperor was soon so busy with other projects—such as the Palais du Roi de Rome on the hill of Chaillot, of which only the foundations were ever built—that except for the place de la Bastille the plan was never even partially implemented.[145]

Even the extensive rehabilitation envisaged for the Ile de la Cité eventually shrank to quite modest proportions. Just before Napoleon's coronation as emperor in Notre Dame, the old cloister of Notre Dame as well as a number of neighboring houses were razed to make room for the lavish coronation procession. Only then was the square built that extended from the portico of the cathedral to the Pont de la Cité, giving the onlooker "an impressive view of an architecture that is as remarkable for its daring as for its age."[146]

Esthetic considerations also determined the destruction of the old seminary buildings that hid the main facade of Saint-Sulpice designed by Servandoni. The creation of a square in front of the church improved the effect of its architecture.

Notre Dame and Saint-Sulpice are about the only exceptions to the general rule that old buildings—neglected during the Revolution and fallen into disrepair—were simply torn down. A long list exists of sacred buildings and cloisters that disappeared without a trace—they "died of the Revolution during the Empire."[147] Far fewer secular buildings were eliminated during the Napoleonic era. Besides the previously mentioned Manège hall, which had to make way for the rue de Rivoli, the Châtelet and Temple were also destroyed. The Châtelet, that dark medieval fortress, "cette masse hideuse et nuisible," as Frochot describes it with much revulsion, had already been pulled down during the Consulate to make room for a square that did not acquire its present form until the Third Republic.[148] The Tour du Temple, that other medieval relic in which Louis XVI was imprisoned prior to his execution, was demolished in 1811. It seems that this was done as a political expedient: Napoleon wanted to avoid its becoming a royalist pilgrimage site.[149]

Someone like Napoleon, who had set his sights on beautifying Paris in an eighteenth-century tradition, was bound to pay attention to the Seine. It was undoubtedly the most important communication route in the city—its lifeline in the truest sense of the word, being the main artery for the transportation of all vital goods—as well as the source from which Paris obtained its water supply. But it was also the biggest obstacle to transportation; apart from the Pont Neuf, the few bridges spanning it were hardly adequate for the ever-growing traffic. The Law of 24 Ventôse, year IX (March 15, 1801), ordered the construction of three more bridges: one between the Jardin des Plantes and the Arsenal (the Pont d'Austerlitz); another between the Ile de la Cité and the Ile Saint-Louis (the Pont Saint-Louis); and a third between the Louvre and the Collège des Quatre-Nations (the Pont des Arts). All three (the Pont des Arts being designed exclusively for pedestrians) were to be ready for use within eighteen months.

The speed required for their construction, and Napoleon's idea that private joint-stock companies should finance the construction in return for a bridge toll for twenty-five years, had unfortunate results. The Pont Saint-Louis, completed in early 1803, soon proved to be so flimsily constructed that despite additional strengthening of its wooden arches loaded wagons were forbidden to use it. The problem was unresolved until the Restoration, in 1819, when the bridge was rebuilt.[150]

On the other hand the Pont des Arts, the first iron bridge to be erected in France, was ready on September 24, 1803, and was an immediate success. When it officially opened, 64,000 pedestrians crossed it, each of whom paid a toll of 1 sou. And the success continued—about 11,000 people used the bridge each day—so that in ten months the revenue amounted to the considerable sum of 160,000 francs.[151]

The Pont du Jardin des Plantes (the Pont d'Austerlitz) eventually became the one most important to the traffic pattern. It created a direct link between the faubourgs Saint-Antoine and Saint-Marcel, for which reason it had already been projected under the Old Regime. But it took the longest to build because of financing and construction difficulties. Work on it was only begun in the autumn of 1804 and the bridge was not ready for use until January 1, 1806.[152]

Napoleon encouraged the building of yet a fourth bridge, the Pont d'Iena. It took from 1806 to 1813 to construct and connected the Ecole militaire with Chaillot on the other bank of the Seine. Two years later, when the Allies marched into Paris, Blücher threatened to blow it up because its name recalled one of Prussia's most disastrous defeats. This senseless act was prevented by the intervention of Tsar Alexander I and the protests of Louis XVIII. But in deference to the feelings of the victorious Prussians the bridge was given a different name for several years.[153]

Houses and shacks lining the Pont Saint-Michel made passage on that old bridge rather difficult and were scheduled to be pulled down as of 1806. However it took until the spring of 1808 before these parasitical buildings were actually removed.[154]

At the beginning of the nineteenth century, medieval urban elements were still much in evidence on both sides of the Seine. Laundry barges were anchored to the banks as they always had been.[155] Then there were numerous storage areas for bulk goods; and various mills lay along the river or out in the middle of the riverbed so as to maximize the water power.[156] All these barges and mills created obstructions for inland shipping, already an important supply source before the English blockade of the Continent. In his *Exposé de la situation de l'Empire* of March 5, 1806, Napoleon therefore orders the Seine to be cleared of "obstacles of all kinds that spoil the view and make navigation through Paris practically impossible."[157] But even this plan was only partially realized. Most of the main obstacles, such as the mills, did disappear, but the two water pumps—the Samaritaine and the Pompe Notre-Dame—were retained so as not to endanger the city's fresh-water supply.[158]

Flooding was a far greater, though less frequent danger. Since the river banks were unstable, whole sections of the city were flooded when the tide was high. The floods that occurred in the winter of 1801-02 were the worst anyone in Paris had seen since 1740. Parts of the Champs-Elysées were under water, as were the place de Grève and even sections of the rue du Faubourg Saint-Honoré, the rue du Faubourg Saint-Antoine and the place Maubert.[159] The extent of the floods provided a ready argument for a plan Napoleon had long harbored for esthetic reasons: the erection of high embankment walls to contain the Seine. He ordered the immediate construction of the quai d'Orsay between the Pont National (now the Pont Royal) and the Pont de la Révolution (now the Pont de la Concorde) on 13 Messidor of the year X (July 2, 1802).[160] By 1813 a total of three kilometers of quais lined both banks of the Seine.[161]

The construction of quais, bridges, new streets, and squares that brought light, air, and order to the maze of houses was surely welcomed by the public. Unfortunately Bonaparte's passion for building—at first devoted to a radical transformation of the entire city—eventually began to be concentrated on a few projects of self-glorification as his regime assumed a more imperial character. Consequently the idea of doing something for the common good became a side issue. Of course a number of factors came into play here, some beyond his control and others that he lacked the will or energy to tackle. Most important, though, he was always short of funds. Then there was also the city administration which tended to let things take their course whenever Napoleon left the capital. And that happened frequently: between 1805 and 1809 the emperor spent only 900 days in Paris. Though he never forgot the capital's interests even when he was far away, and though he kept issuing instructions and urging their prompt execution—perhaps in subconscious awareness that there was not much time left for him to realize his concepts— written directives could hardly replace the authority of his physical presence. His unproductive restlessness masked an anguish that becomes evident if one considers those of his plans that were completed.

In fact his obsession with construction was focused more and more on imperial palaces and monuments commemorating his military victories. The sheer effect of the majestic coldness of these neoclassical structures was supposed to compensate for all his uncompleted grandiose schemes.

Maybe that is also why Napoleon—legendary for his ability to analyze complex situations more quickly than others, and celebrated for his enjoyment of political and military decision-making—was seen by his architects as an indecisive procrastinator. Hardly had a project been agreed upon and work begun than he desired major changes to be made, revealing an insecurity not generally associated with his person. The rebuilding of the Tuileries and the Louvre which were his immediate concerns provide many examples of this.

The Tuileries had served as a sort of prison for Louis XVI for almost three years; it then stood empty during the Directory except for brief use by the National Assembly. By 1800 it had reached a state of practically irreversible deterioration.[162] Some repairs were quickly undertaken at the beginning of the Consulate. David and his students touched up the faded ceiling paintings; and the rooms on the second floor had to be entirely redecorated. Even in the winter as many as 3,000 workmen were employed there day and night.[163] In spite of all efforts and the considerable cost of almost 2 million francs, only the most neccessary repairs could be completed so as to make the Tuileries more or less livable for the first consul. But as the imperial atmosphere of the regime developed, Bonaparte had extensive rebuilding done to accommodate his sizable retinue.[164]

The renovations carried out over the years confirmed the opinion of the two imperial architects, Percier and Fontaine, that "during his fourteen-year stay in the Tuileries, Napoleon was more concerned with the splendor and beauty of the restored building than with his personal comfort."[165] Napoleon himself confirms this view in his unique and terse style on being shown the plans for the Palais du Roi de Rome: "The royal apartments should not ordinarily be comfortable; for someone who has to uphold his standing that is always a burden. The dignity of a sovereign and the petty comforts of life are not easily reconciled."[166] But as the years went by and the burdens of state increased, it became progressively more difficult for Napoleon to subordinate his personal life to his official position. In the Tuileries conditions were crowded; the public had access to the gardens so that he was unable to use them. Even if he merely appeared at a window he was greeted by the strolling throng. On his short visits to Paris he therefore sought refuge in his more isolated palace at Saint-Cloud, or in the Elysée palace which he liked to call his "maison de santé."[167]

Despite all its inadequacies, the Tuileries remained the official seat of the imperial court for the entire Napoleonic period. The obvious solution of using the directly adjoining Louvre was impractical, not only because this vast complex of buildings was much too big for the relatively modest life of the imperial household, but above all because the Louvre was considered "a shrine of the monarchy and therefore less suitable as the normal residence of the sovereign than as a place for large receptions, parties, and public ceremonies."[168] This conclusion by Percier and Fontaine—who were in charge of the work at the Louvre—reflected Napoleon's own views, as, for example, when he had pompous celebrations held there on the occasion of his church wedding to Marie-Louise.

In order to make the Louvre usable for functions of that sort, large-scale work was begun in 1806. The intention, not to be realized in the Napoleonic era, was to complete the enormous, half-finished structure and to combine it with the Tuileries to form a single, grandiose entity unequaled in the world for its size and splendor. A start was made by tearing down the miserable houses and shacks close to the Louvre. Furthermore, all artists and scholars who had their studios and studies in the Louvre, were evicted—a "cleansing of the Augean stables," which had needed the iron will of a Bonaparte according to Etienne-Jean Delécluze.[169]

Once it stood free of the pitiful hovels that had hidden it from view for so long, the Louvre's architectonic and stylistic image was seen to be unbalanced. Its exterior had undergone several modifications in the generations since Francis I, changes that were bound to displease the contemporary taste fixated on a rule-bound classicism. Percier and Fontaine therefore suggested that the various facades be rebuilt to harmonize with the style of the seventeenth century and the design of the architect Perrault. If their concepts had been approved, all traces of the Renaissance would have been eliminated and the Pavillon de l'Horloge built by Pierre Lescot would have been completely altered. Because of the great expense as well as an unusual respect on his part for the past, Napoleon consistently opposed these ideas. "The architects," he writes on February 6, 1806, "want to create harmony and, so it is said, change everything. However, thrift, common sense, and good taste dictate the contrary; all existing sections of the Louvre should retain their long-standing characteristics and one should opt for the most affordable execution of any new construction."[170]

The eventual compromise was to restore and complete the Pavillon de l'Horloge in Renaissance style, while the other facades were to be replaced using Perrault's design.[171] Hardly had this solution been found when Napoleon's imagination began to be filled with another, grander scheme. As already noted, he wanted to complete the *grand dessein* of the Old Regime and combine the Louvre with the Tuileries. Louis XIV, who had built the wing of the Louvre paralleling the Seine, was the model Napoleon wanted to surpass by the time he reached the end of his own building activities. His decree of February 26, 1806, briefly described the status of the plan and ordered a widening of the place du Carrousel as well as construction of a street, about fifty-one feet wide, between the Louvre and the Tuileries.[172] But the first consul soon dropped this project that had occupied him since 1802 in favor of yet another, more extensive one.[173] The new idea was to build a second wing along the rue de Rivoli, to link the old Louvre with the Tuileries. This would have presented considerable design problems that would have taken Napoleon and his architects several years to solve; it would have created an enormous rectangular space fringed by massive buildings. As a result the project was never undertaken in the Napoleonic period, just as the skeptical Prince Clary-Aldringen had foreseen.[174]

Monuments and Other Improvements

O*N EXAMINING ALL THE BUILDING ACTIVITY* inspired by Napoleon, one soon realizes that it was more often "mere" restoration than new construction.[175] The Bourbons' enormous architectural heritage certainly stimulated his imagination, but it also overwhelmed his initiative. The deciding factor for him was a constant shortage of funds, producing a discrepancy between what he wanted and what he could actually do. He compromised by limiting his plans to embellishment, something that looked imposing but was affordable. This compromise was expressed in the columns, triumphal arches, or temples commemorating the ruler's victories. But even for such comparatively modest projects more was plannned than was usually carried out. This is well illustrated by the history of a memorial that was supposed to be dedicated to General Desaix.

Under the Convention the famous monument to Louis XIV that had dominated the place des Victoires was taken down and replaced with a pyramid in memory of Pelletier de Saint-Fargeau. Pelletier had been murdered by an ex-member of the Garde du Corps for having voted for Louis XVI's execution. But the subject of the monument as well as its unimaginative execution soon made it inappropriate for one of the most beautiful squares in Paris. Two weeks after the coup d'état of 18 Brumaire, the Consuls announced their intention of replacing it with a new one to commemorate the Italian campaign. Its most important ornament was to be the classic group of bronze horses brought back from Venice as a trophy.[176] But work on the monument was not begun right away. Fresh incentive was then provided by the news that General Desaix had lost his life on June 14, 1800, at the battle of Marengo, and that General Kléber had been murdered in Eygpt on the same day. That called for a different theme and it was decided to replace the pyramid with a memorial to the two generals. The foundation stone was laid on 1 Vendémiaire, year IX (September 23, 1801), although none of the various design proposals had yet been approved.[177] Meantime, as Léon Lanzac de Laborie surmises,

> the regime's political tendencies veered more and more toward a monarchical system. Kléber suddenly began to seem a *frondeur*, an unreasonable Jacobin, whose glorification was inappropriate. On the other hand Desaix, that model of a deputy who had sacrificed himself to secure Napoleon's military prestige and political sovereignty, seemed worthier than ever of being honored.[178]

On August 15, 1810, ten years after the battle of Marengo, a monument to Desaix was finally unveiled. A stele of red granite, beside a nude, life-size representation of Desaix, was supposed to evoke the Egyptian campaign. Public criticism of it was as unanimous as it was scathing. The monument soon disappeared and the statue of Desaix was melted down. The bronze was later used for the equestrian statue of Henry IV that was placed on the Pont Neuf under the Restoration.[179]

It was not because of public prudishness that Desaix had to vacate his pedestal but because the taste in icons had changed. The Revolution had been concerned to honor generals who had fallen for the Republic and the fatherland; now it was time to deal with other matters. Napoleon had already pointed this out to Artistic Director Daru in 1805: "I intend to encourage the fine arts, in particular to select subjects that will commemorate what has taken place over the last five years."[180] Of course he was referring to his military victories, and many contemporaries believed that like his Roman predecessors he intended to erect monuments to himself in his own lifetime. At first he was against any such ideas, as when it was suggested in 1808 that the triumphal arch in the place du Carrousel be decorated with a statue of himself. At the time he commented tersely, "Ce n'est pas à moi de me faire des statues" ("it is not for me to build statues to myself").[181] Two years later, when he was at the height of his imperial splendor, this modesty had vanished. On August 15, 1810, a bronze pillar topped with the figure of Napoleon in an imperial Roman toga, his head wreathed in a crown of laurel, was inaugurated in the place Vendôme.

This tribute to the Grand Army created by Chaudet, and the triumphal arch in the place du Carrousel, were in fact the only two monuments planned and actually completed during the Empire. Others never got beyond the planning stage or were begun but only finished much later.[182] The wars that inspired such art also delayed execution of these projects.

But while Napoleon desired to honor his own fame and the achievements of the Grand Army, he also envisioned an imperial art carried out by officially commissioned artists. He was only able to see a small part of his plans carried out, but an imperial memorandum of May 14, 1806, indicates his intentions:

> I want to provide work for French sculptors for the next ten years with these triumphal arches. M. Denon is to work out the necessary plans for me. The minister of the interior will see to it that another triumphal arch is erected in the Etoile. The designs will have to be voted on. One arch is to be dedicated to Marengo (the arch in the place du Carrousel), the other to Austerlitz (in the place de l'Etoile). In addition I shall give orders for an *arc de la paix*, as well as a fourth one to be known as the *arc de la religion*, to be erected in other parts of Paris.[183]

Napoleon never managed to build four colossal triumphal arches in Paris, but he did transform the city into the unrivaled center of art and culture in France. Indeed, the Revolution had already destroyed certain smaller cultural centers that had grown up around provincial parliaments and academies under the Old Regime. Napoleon's system of political and administrative centralization merely completed the process. Paris became the magnet for all talent and ideas, and dominated the intellectual climate of the times.

In addition to theaters and the opera which the public had already enjoyed under the Old Regime, museums and art exhibitions now became especially popular. Chroniclers of the period found it remarkable that those interested in the arts came from all segments of society.[184] To be sure entrance to museums was free and Parisians were known to be curious. What was undoubtedly responsible for the great overall public interest was the fact that under the Directory Paris had become the art capital of Europe. On the heels of the victorious French troops had come the art commissioners, who acquired the most valuable artworks in conquered countries and had them taken to Paris. First Flanders was plundered, then Italy and Eygpt; finally the German states and Spain.[185] Their treasures were stored and exhibited in the Louvre. On Saturdays and Sundays, between two and four o'clock, curious crowds poured in to see everything. Soon the space became too limited; between 1806 and 1810 the exhibition area had to be enlarged.[186] The major social and artistic event of the season, however, was the Paris Salon. It was an official exhibition of the best works of art by contemporary French painters and sculptors, held once a year until 1802, after which it took place twice a year.[187]

But all the esthetic innovations, and the construction and restoration that went on, were only part of what contemporaries considered *embellissements*. They also included measures that were of direct public benefit. Here, too, Napoleon had great plans though again many could only be partially realized. Chaptal has a famous anecdote about this in his memoirs. Once while walking in Malmaison with his minister of the interior, the first consul turned and asked: "I would like to do something important and useful for Paris; what do you think I should do?" "Supply its inhabitants with water," was the answer.[188]

The water supply of Paris was still a major problem. For apart from numerous wells that belonged to private houses, and the low-yield springs of Arcueil, Belleville and Pré-Saint-Gervais, the city's inhabitants continued to depend on the Seine for their fresh water. The quality of the water was praised by contemporaries, though there were constant complaints about its short supply.[189] The fact is that at the beginning of the Consulate there were only fifty-six public wells in the entire city.[190] These were filled by four water pumps, two of which were rather old and of correspondingly limited efficiency; the Samaritaine pump had been in use since 1608 and the Notre-Dame pump dated back to 1680. The other two, driven by steam, had been built at the end of the Old Regime by the Périer brothers, as mentioned earlier. They were near Gros-Caillou and supplied the Left Bank.

In view of this situation Napoleon dictated a memorandum on April 10, 1806, which states: "My aims are: 1. As of May 1, the fifty-six wells in Paris are to be kept supplied with water day and night, and water is no longer to be sold. Everyone is entitled to take as much as he wants. 2. Any other wells that exist in Paris are to be restored as promptly as possible to provide additional water."[191] An imperial decree of May 2, 1806, ordering the construction of nineteen new wells, also gives instructions that "as of July 1 Paris wells are to have a steady water supply, sufficient not only for the needs of the general public and the special requirements of trades, but for keeping the air fresh and cleaning the streets."[192]

But even the emperor's will could not bring this about in so short a time, because the city still had only four pumps in the Seine. They were unable to keep all wells constantly supplied. The emperor came closer to seeing his wishes met by March 1812, when the Canal de l'Ourcq, the large reservoir of drinking water at La Villette, the necessary aqueducts and water mains, as well as the pump at Château-d'Eau were completed.[193]

It turned out to be exceedingly costly. Construction of the canal alone— designed to carry water from the small river Ourcq ninety-six kilometers to Paris—absorbed the fantastic sum of 38 million francs. This meant that money was unavailable for other projects; and there were some who were not impressed by the substantial improvement in the water supply. Petit-Radel sees it as a great danger to Paris morality: "An abundance of water at first encouraged the use and then the misuse of the baths in Rome. . . . Won't the ease of having water in one's own home lead to the same moral decay, once this oriental luxury is developed?"[194] But Petit-Radel was far ahead of actual developments with his strange apprehensions. *L'eau à l'étage* (water on every floor of a building) only became available in certain newly constructed luxury apartments in the July Monarchy. At first none but the courtesans of the *grande monde* could afford the luxury of having their own baths.

Aside from improvements in the fresh-water supply, other city services remained much as they had been. This was especially true in the case of street cleaning and refuse collection, which were handled with even greater carelessness than at the end of the Old Regime. The reason was that such work was not controlled by the administration of the department but had been assigned to a private contractor.[195] Even the maintenance of street paving, which mostly consisted of uneven slabs of sandstone, was in the hands of a private company. According to a police report of 1801, maintenance left much to be desired.[196] As for street lighting, that had not improved either. Ill-lit streets continued to be a hazard for pedestrians under the Empire even though Napoleon himself occasionally complained strongly about this problem.[197]

Ever-increasing traffic made the unpleasant condition of the streets even worse. People kept their own carriages, as status and wealth could once more be openly displayed. Police statistics for 1807 refer to 1,460 *carosses bourgeois*, 339 *carosses de remise*, 3,100 *cabriolets bourgeois*, 1,212 *fiacres*, 1,673 *cabriolets de louage*, as well as 6,000 carts and commercial vehicles.[198]

In comparison with the heavy traffic of our time these figures appear very modest; but one has to consider that in those days Paris knew nothing of traffic regulations. Many streets were so narrow that a coach could barely pass through and as there were many culs-de-sac unsuitable for horse carriages, traffic was limited to relatively few thoroughfares. That, along with the fashion of having light, easily maneuverable, and fast-moving carriages, quickly multiplied the number of traffic accidents. It also gave some poor souls the incentive to let themselves be deliberately run over so as to be able to claim a few francs in damages.[199] The police tried vainly to put a stop to this state of affairs by issuing rules and regulations. They allocated very few spaces for carriages to stop, and obliged every vehicle to have an official registration number prominently displayed behind the driver's seat.[200]

Another problem, even for residents of the city, was that of locating a specific address. Many street names had been changed during and after the Revolution, and the numbering of houses was in a state of complete chaos.[201] Everyone had trouble finding his way, as this account shows: "In the rues Saint-Denis, Saint-Honoré and others there are four, five, even six identical house numbers. In the rue Saint-Denis I went to three houses with the number 42 before I found the one I wanted."[202] A regulation issued by the prefect of police on February 4, 1805, finally introduced a clear system of numbering. Even-numbered houses were on one side of the street, odd-numbered houses on the other side. Numbering either began at the Seine or, in streets paralleling the river, corresponded to the direction of its flow. House numbers in streets that ran parallel to the Seine were painted red; numbers in streets at a right angle to the Seine were painted black.[203]

Then there was the matter of establishing an efficient fire-fighting system. This was a service that had been badly neglected though the frequent chimney fires could easily have caused enormous conflagrations in the overcrowded inner-city districts. Whatever regulations existed—and they were highly inadequate—dated back to the Old Regime. For instance owners of wells and cisterns were ordered to keep buckets and ropes handy for fire purposes. Water-carriers were supposed to have their buckets filled at night and were expected to proceed immediately to the site of a fire. There had even been a sort of volunteer fire brigade since the time of Louis XV. Its members were mostly petty artisans, who gathered whenever a fire broke out and fought it with much energy but little experience.[204] Such arrangements were totally inadequate for a city the size of Paris, as the events of July 1, 1810, made quite clear.[205] A fire broke out at a ball given by the Austrian ambassador, Prince Schwarzenberg, and even Napoleon and the empress barely managed to escape the flames. That finally jolted officials out of their lethargy and they took action. A professional group of firefighters, known as *sapeurs-pompiers*, was apppointed to replace the capital's original volunteer brigade. The battalion was equipped with all the necessary tools and was divided into four barracked companies.[206]

Trade and Commerce

*N*APOLEON CONSIDERED IT IMPORTANT to pay close attention to the question of food supply. There is a famous comment he once made to the prefect of police, "Je veux que les Halles soient le Louvre du peuple" ("I want the food markets to be the people's Louvre"). And even in his exile on St. Helena he remarks: "It is unfair to keep the price of bread lower in Paris than elsewhere; but it has to be subsidized because that is where the government has its seat, and the soldiers don't like to fire on women who line up outside the bakeries with their infants on their backs."[207] The latter statement aptly describes his intent: the capital had always to be kept supplied with bread and other foodstuffs at reasonable prices to avoid revolt. It was one of the most significant lessons that Napoleon had learned from the Revolution, and the prefect of police had to give him a daily report on prices and the amount of provisions available.

Thanks to Napoleon's careful supervision of these matters Parisians were able to enjoy an abundance of inexpensive foodstuffs during the Consulate and Empire, with the exception of two crises in 1801 and 1811–12. Moreover, the quality and choice of these goods improved for all sections of the

population. Meat, especially, became a regular item in even the simplest journeyman's and worker's diet; and more and more people were able to afford
imported products such as tea, coffee, and sugar.

This came about as agricultural production and imports increased, once
domestic tariffs were abolished, and as a result of large-scale expansion of
national transportation routes. The fact that greater care was taken with food
storage and distribution in Paris was also decisive. Les Halles, "the stomach
of Paris" as the markets were called, were of special importance, though they
were not nearly as well organized as they were to become during the Second
Empire. Lanzac de Laborie describes them as follows:

> In Paris, "les Halles" refers to the various squares, streets and passages
> between the church of Saint-Eustache, the rue Saint-Denis, and the rue de la
> Ferronnerie, where food and other daily needs are sold. Some of the food is dis-
> played in airy buildings, like the fish market. Other items are sold outside, where
> certain stalls are protected by oilcloth umbrellas; while butter, eggs, cheese,
> fruits and clothing are sold in the Piliers des Halles, a series of unstable, low-
> ceilinged and uncomfortable, irregular covered galleries.[208]

This account of the markets at the end of 1813 describes a situation
Napoleon would gladly have consigned to the past. Two imperial decrees had
been issued in February 1811 ordering considerable expansion of the market area as well as construction of a large market building that would put an
end to unhygienic conditions. The worst of these were to be found in the fish
market, as J.-B. Poujoulx describes so vividly:

> There is nothing more disgusting than the Halle à la Marée, the entrance to
> which is popularly known as the *porte merdeuse*. A stranger will hardly fail to
> agree that the entrance to the most important food market in Paris rightfully
> deserves its name. Even the sewers are cleaner than this fish market. The rot-
> ten planks of the stalls have been soaked for more than a century with the efflu-
> via of decaying fish; fetid miasmas have seeped into the ground. . . . All in all it
> is a cesspool lying in one of the least airy districts of Paris.[209]

Napoleon wanted the new market complex to be ready by the end of
1814.[210] Once again budget and time estimates fell short, and when the
Empire ended nothing had been done. A similar fate befell the slaughterhouses Napoleon wanted to erect on the periphery of Paris. A decree ordering the immediate construction of five slaughterhouses was issued on
February 9, 1810.[211] Four years later, as battles were raging around Paris, two
of the still unfinished buildings were used as auxiliary hospitals.[212] The five
slaughterhouses were not put to their destined use until September 15, 1818,
under the Restoration.[213] They were a novelty at the time and served as a
model for similar establishments in other countries.[214]

By ensuring that sufficient supplies of food were available at stable prices,
Napoleon's authoritarian regime could count on the loyalty of the lower strata of Parisian society. As long as improved economic conditions lasted, and
business, trade, and manufacturing sectors managed to recover from the

effects of the Revolution, he had more general support as well. Lacuée, the *Conseiller d'Etat*, comes to a sobering conclusion in his analysis of the economic situation directly after 18 Brumaire:

> Prior to the Revolution expenditures in Paris amounted to a sum of 260 million; at the same time, revenues brought in 300 million. That means there was a yearly surplus of 40 million. During the Revolution no one was able or willing to determine the relationship of revenues to expenses. However, it is revealing that although expenses decreased during this period, income from taxation was also considerably lower, so that there was an annual deficit or, at best, a balance. Though there have been some distinct changes since 18 Brumaire, it is not possible at present to conclude that there is a noticeable surplus.[215]

During the Old Regime the economic status of Paris had been based on three factors: on a relatively large domestic market created by the demands of a population of almost 700,000 inhabitants and numerous wealthy foreign visitors; on the exchange of goods between Paris and the provinces; and, finally, on the export of manufactured and crafted items to European and oversea countries. The Revolution destroyed the basis of the economic prosperity of Paris. It brought the flourishing commerce with northern and central Europe to a halt, and the internal confusion paralyzed reciprocal trade with the provinces. Local demand also declined rapidly on account of the flight of capital, and the constant fall in the value of the assignats and territorial paper money. Not until Napoleon's coup was the necessary psychological and political climate created for a more vigorous economy. Here the centralized political system, ratified by the Constitution of 1799, was of great benefit with its emphasis on the functional duties of Paris as capital. Stabilization of the government improved local demand, which in turn encouraged the formation of capital and stimulated business.

Napoleon's military achievements were also of great importance to the economy. The farther the influence of the Empire extended, the larger were the markets for French products in Europe. A characteristic consequence of this boom was that the number of Paris retailers and storekeepers increased. Artisans could not resist the temptation to borrow money to open shops of their own and sell their products themselves. This sudden industrial and commercial regrouping, which was to become even more pronounced during the Restoration and the July Monarchy, caught the attention of contemporary observers. For instance, Louis Prudhomme notes in 1804:

> While our Revolution slowed business in most of the cities of France, the economy of Paris seems to have undergone enormous improvement. The number of owners of stores has increased considerably within the last five years; in some sections, where there was only a single store previously, you can now find a great many. Paris is like a trade fair; never before were there such extravagantly beautiful shops as there are in the rues Vivienne, Saint-Honoré, du Roule, and Saint-Denis.[216]

If retail stores multiplied to such an extent as to arouse contemporary comment, it stands to reason that business was bound to become more competitive. This led to many bankruptcies, but even those able to cope with greater challenges had to adapt to new trends. Goods had to be of better quality and meet the changing taste of the public; they had to be displayed more attractively so as to whet the buyer's appetite. Above all, attention had to be paid to the buyer's comfort and his ability to browse in peace. This is where the weatherproof covered passages developed under the Empire proved so successful, along with the again-popular Palais-Royal. In both places exorbitant rents and the pressure of competition led store owners to outdo each other in their displays. Pierre Jouhaud provides an interesting account of this situation in the Palais-Royal:

> Paris residents know that each storekeeper has to pay at least one thousand écus rent in the arcades, and there are a few shops that occupy three or even four arcades. It is obvious that such high rents have to be paid for by the customers. That applies especially to foreigners: everything is done to tempt them to buy and great care is taken to set out goods and products to best advantage. Over here Cabasson and Quielet display a valuable sparkling diamond or some skilfully crafted piece in gold; over there the imaginative Leroy offers strolling beauties his elegant hats. Elsewhere Alexandre has arranged his tempting pyramids in which transparent gauze vies with gold and silk.[217]

The improved economy of the Consulate was bound to help Parisian manufacturers of luxury items, a type of goods for which demand had dropped during the Revolution.[218] Police reports even noted a shortage of qualified workers, as well as distinct increases in orders received by individual manufacturers.[219] Finally, the production of armaments and the fact that English finished goods were no longer being imported stimulated the Paris economy as well. A most enthusiastic eyewitness account of its growth is given by Nemnich, a visitor from Hamburg:

> Before the Revolution a considerable number of highly regarded products were manufactured in Paris: tapestries by Gobelin, carpets by La Savonnerie, objects crafted by goldsmiths, as well as porcelain, glassware, jewelery, and various less important items. Manufacture of such articles has not only multiplied and become perfected over the last twelve years, but a great many new workshops have been opened for quite different goods. Thus the industrial development of Paris progresses all the time. New inventions, new production methods barely allow the freshly created businesses enough time to benefit from increased profits—for as soon as an important branch of industry has become successfully established, a whole group of competitors appears right away, who are more or less able to hold their own.[220]

Despite indisputable progress in the manufacture of luxury and cotton goods, Paris was somewhat of a weak plant compared with English industrial centers for it lacked the humus of adequate capital.[221] That these industries managed to enjoy some years of feverish economic growth was largely due to a strict protectionist trade policy against English competition, and to Napoleon's military victories, which opened up European markets for French goods.

How precarious such an economic trend actually was became apparent in the crisis of 1806. Brought on by the bankruptcy of the *Négociants réunis,* a syndicate of Paris bankers, it led to a general flight of capital.[222] The result was that money became so scarce in Paris that "manufacturers, artisans, and all who had to pay their workers in ready cash had to start giving notice to individuals. The movement of goods decreased daily. Manufacturers of cotton fabrics decided to pay lower wages so as to sell their products more cheaply."[223]

A more deep-seated cause for the problem of overproduction had been the additional spurt in the demand for luxury items at the beginning of December 1804, when Napoleon became emperor. Members of the new court had to be equipped then for the pomp of the new empire; and the many dignitaries and foreigners who rushed to Paris for the inaugural celebrations also increased the demand for goods and services. This boom in the luxury trade came to a sudden end in March 1805, when Napoleon set out for Italy to crown himself in Milan with the bronze crown of the kings of Lombardy, and Pope Pius VII returned to Rome. The market suddenly dried up and the effects were felt barely two weeks later. According to a police report of April 18, 1805, in Paris alone the daily loss of business after the court's departure was 200,000 francs![224]

However, conditions only became really serious with the collapse of the *Négociants réunis* and the Récamier bank, when the shortage of capital and credit put an end to demand for goods of all types. The whole industrial sector was affected and there was no letup until November 1806, when the Continental System was introduced and competition from English imports was finally eliminated. That marked the beginning of a new three-year boom, an economic complement to the political and military brilliance of the Empire. During that time Napoleon was at the height of his power, in control of the whole of Europe with the exception of England and Russia. The situation could not have been more advantageous—but it was fraught with perils that were to bring the general upswing to a sudden end.

The impending decline of the Napoleonic empire was later signaled by the critical economic crisis of 1810. Actually there were three different crises telescoped into, and adversely influencing, each other. An initial financial crisis caused the collapse of many businesses and brought about a general economic recession. This in its turn increased and worsened the agricultural crisis occasioned by the poor harvest of 1811.

The germ responsible for the initial financial debacle was speculation in high-risk commodity futures trading, involving a small, closely connected group of European financiers. The special virulence of this germ stemmed from the contradictions of Napoleonic economic protectionism. While the blockade of English imports had greatly increased the price of colonial goods, comparatively large numbers of wealthy Parisian consumers did not want to do without them. This created such demand that despite the considerable risk of privateer attacks on merchant ships, speculation in coffee, sugar, tea, and spices promised very high returns.[225]

Along with these highly precarious transactions, speculators used the greater part of their profits to make more permanent investments in real estate. This meant that in a sudden liquidity crisis their capital was immobilized—a great risk for those involved in this kind of business.[226]

No one realized the hazards involved in all this because everyone labored under a misapprehension. As a member of the *Conseil de commerce* (commerce committee) put it: "Paris has become the trade depot for the whole of France and the hub of European commerce. The other cities of the empire place their orders here thus creating new profits, and the large European trade and financial centers that once competed with each other for credit business now turn to Paris for their capital."[227]

It was an apt description of Paris as the most important European financial center; but it needed only one serious insolvency to destroy the speculation-based house of cards of the money market. As of July 1810 there were frequent signs of an impending disaster; in September it struck in earnest with the collapse of the Lübeck Rodde Bank. That bankruptcy ruined Parisian banks like Laffitte, Fould, Tourton, and Doumerc, causing a chain reaction that brought on a general economic crisis.[228] By December 1810 there were so many bankruptcies that other banks were affected.[229] The recession that now began increased the number of unemployed, to which Napoleon reacted promptly and successfully by placing large-scale public orders.[230]

Though business failures decreased by May 1811, and the economy's downward trend gradually ended, its cyclical effects lasted somewhat longer owing to a poor harvest. Bad weather destroyed a promising crop in the Paris basin, while the south of France suffered from an unusual drought. However, there was no immediate threat to the Paris grain supply. The two granaries of the capital, the regions of the Beauce and the Brie, harvested enough to satisfy its needs.[231] But the overall poor yield first caused grain prices to rise in the Loire region, and then led to shortages and an increase in the price of bread grains in Paris. The situation was promptly aggravated by speculation. On August 10, 1811, Pasquier, the prefect of police, describes the city's supplies as "needing some attention."[232] Napoleon took these first signs of a supply emergency very seriously and issued a decree on August 28, 1811, intended to reorganize the food supply system. A *Conseil des subsistances* (food supply committee) was created, to meet once a week under the direction of the minister of the interior.[233]

Mere administrative plans for dealing with this projected shortage accomplished little, however, when its effects began to be felt by the middle of September. Moreover, the same old mistakes were still being made in setting low bread prices, which merely encouraged the hoarding of grain and flour supplies. The only useful way to counteract this speculation was to decontrol the price of bread—a measure the authorities came to accept very reluctantly for fear of uprisings. Indeed, their hesitation merely served to prolong and increase the problem. In the middle of December the official price of bread rose from 14 to 16 sous, and in mid-January 1812 it reached 17 sous. But these increases came too late and were too small to make speculation less lucrative. At the beginning of March Napoleon finally agreed to raise the price to 18 sous and at least satisfied the bakers. But unrest grew among the poor sections of the population because even at that price bread was already sold out in the early morning hours. The bakers preferred to bake better-quality bread that they could then sell at their own prices![234]

Even the free distribution of vegetable soup to the needy, ordered by Napoleon on March 24, 1812, could not hide the bread shortage or calm the people's growing dissatisfaction. "The unrest," Pasquier writes, "developed into terror," an evaluation that required energetic measures.[235] On April 16, 1812, the warehouses of several known speculators were put under police jurisdiction and their supplies were confiscated. But this merely warned speculators that in future it would be somewhat more risky to make a quick profit.

Two other attempts were made to deal with the ever more obvious shortage of grain, but they only helped to make matters worse. On May 4, 1812, the grain trade was limited to licensed markets; furthermore, a law passed on May 8 set official price ceilings on bread grains in Paris and surrounding departments for a period of four months.[236] But by the end of June the authorities, having run out of ideas, had to admit the failure of both measures. Better crops were needed to end the grain crisis, but even the plentiful harvest of 1812 was slow to ease the situation. The market was in such a state of disarray that things did not return to normal until after the unusually good harvest of 1813. By September 1, 1813, the official price of bread had once again leveled off at 15 sous.[237]

The economic difficulties of these two years gradually caused a profound shift in public opinion.[238] Napoleon had managed to retain the faubourgs' loyalty by ordering public construction to continue; but the bourgeoisie, engaged in trade and industry, withdrew its once-willing support. It did so with cold calculation: as long as its well-being outweighed the sacrifices made for Napoleon's politics, it saw the regime in positive terms. But as of 1810 Napoleon's actions were considered too adventurous; moreover everyone was sick of the never-ending wars. "When the guns fired the victory salute for a battle," writes the Comtesse de Boigne,

> some were sad about it, a somewhat larger number showed their pleasure, while the great mass of the population remained indifferent. They had had enough of glory and knew that fresh successes inevitably meant fresh burdens. A victorious battle was the signal for further recruitment, and the conquest of Vienna was no more than the signal for an offensive against Warsaw or Pressburg. Beyond that, people had little faith in the bulletins from the battle front and their publication was hardly cause for jubilation.[239]

Seen against this sort of background it becomes clear why preparations for the Russsian campaign were followed with great misgivings. Everyone recognized the twenty- ninth *Bulletin de la Grande Armée*—describing the full extent of the terrible disaster in which the campaign had ended—as the writing on the wall for the Napoleonic empire. The more frequent and precise the news of the retreat of the Grand Army and its heavy losses, the faster stocks fell, the more the credit market and stock exchange stagnated, and the faster the public became depressed.[240] In his account of one of Napoleon's visits to Paris toward the end of 1813, the duke of Bassano, who was then foreign minister, gives a memorable picture of the deep dejection in the capital:

> A steady fall of fine, dry snow had coated the pavement. . . . We could only move very slowly. Not a greeting was to be heard; the few pedestrians who crossed the bridge at this hour simply acknowledged us silently, because thanks to his gray cloak and small hat it was almost impossible to recognize the emperor. The sad, gray sky and the deep silence surrounding the emperor's path were very moving.[241]

The Downfall of the Empire

HE END OF THE EMPIRE seemed imminent and yet no one had enough imagination to picture what it would be like. That was particularly true of the inhabitants of Paris, whose only information about the war came from the triumphantly worded bulletins published in the *Moniteur* and read out in theaters and schools. Nor did they learn the true extent of the horrible events from the colorful military parades in the place du Carrousel, or the boastful tales of veterans and officers on leave. Parisians got an approximate idea of what war was about from paintings of battles by artists such as Horace Vernet, who produced stylized heroic tableaus of the battle inferno with its seething mass of human and animal bodies, its dirt, blood, mutilation, and death. Many a good Parisian looking at these in a warm gallery might have experienced the bourgeois sentiment that is always felt when news comes that, "far off, in Turkey, nations are fighting each other."

Even the invasion by Allied troops, who crossed the Rhine on January 6, 1814, did nothing to change the attitude that war was always a distant happening that never directly affected the capital. In his memoirs the duc de Broglie writes:

> The rapid change from victory to defeat during the short campaign on French soil had confused everyone to such an extent, and was so contrary to all forecasts, that no one wanted to believe the news of the Allies' advance. Only the roar of the cannon and the sight of peasants who had fled to the suburbs with their families, belongings and domestic animals, overcame the general disbelief.[242]

In any case Paris was not prepared for defense. The efforts made since January to improve the situation—such as the restoration of the National Guard—were of merely symbolic significance. The tax wall, still incomplete in some sections, could hardly serve as a fortification; nor could the 200 cannon mounted at the tax posts and manned by veterans and students from the

Ecole Polytechnique be considered a serious defense measure.[243] None-theless, what was probably the most senseless of all the Napoleonic battles, the battle for Paris, began before dawn on March 30, 1814.[244] Over 100,000 well-armed attacking troops—aware they were close to final victory—faced 40,000 defenders who had absolutely no moral support. The flight of the imperial court from the capital was a clear indication the cause was lost. That should have been the decisive factor but Generals Marmont and Mortier, who were the commanders in chief of the Paris area, felt that their honor demanded that they continue what had been a hopeless resistance from the start. Not until the attackers had taken Ménilmontant, the Buttes-Chaumont, Belleville, and Montmartre after a bloody battle, and the city lay open to their cannon, were the defenders willing to settle for a cease-fire. Following difficult negotiations Paris capitulated and placed itself at "the mercy of the Allies."

News of the capitulation spread like wildfire early in the morning of March 31 and was accepted with overall relief.[245] At least the Parisians had avoided the fate of the Muscovites who had seen their city turn to rubble and ashes . . . But how would the victors—the Cossacks and Prussians—behave? Shocking reports had been received of their many atrocities as they made their way through France. Could one trust Tsar Alexander's promise to place Paris and its residents under his personal protection? Pierre Fontaine notes in his diary:

> I would never have believed that the capital of an empire that had made the whole of Europe tremble for about two years would yield in such an unusual way—after an unequal battle in which National Guards and students were forced to fight. I was just as unprepared to believe that a victorious army—consisting of troops from twenty nations and a large number of wild hordes—an army that had been promised the chance to plunder, would take Paris without force or other excesses. Who could have imagined that the actual event would then resemble a festival that did not disturb public peace and order?[246]

The Allied troops' entry into the city had still another surprise effect on the population. News of the capitulation had hardly made the rounds on the morning of March 31, 1814, when some young men gathered in the place de la Concorde wearing white cummerbunds and rosettes as a token of their support for the monarchy. After breaking up into several small groups they marched to various parts of the city calling out "Vive le Roi! Vivent les Bourbons! A bas le tyran!" They were joined by a few passersby who waved white handkerchiefs to show their royalist feelings, but general reaction to this demonstration was very unfriendly on the whole. There was even a fight in the place de Grève that had to be broken up by the National Guard.[247] However most Parisians, whether they had rejected or been openly hostile to these royalist expressions, put aside their feelings once the Allied troops passed the Barrière de Pantin in orderly formation, at 11:00 A.M.[248] What surprised the population was that each of the soldiers and officers wore a white armband; it convinced everyone that the victors planned to reinstate the

Bourbon monarchy.[249] This complete misunderstanding—for the Allies were wearing white armbands simply to produce a uniform effect and avoid fatal mixups—prompted many Parisians to wear white armbands as well to avoid being attacked. The Allies in their turn got the false impression that royalist sympathies prevailed in Paris, an impression that royalist agents cultivated for their own advantage.[250]

But these misunderstandings were not the real reason why the Allies eventually restored the Bourbons; for that was not what Tsar Alexander I or Metternich had originally intended.[251] What prompted their decision was the power vacuum in Paris and, not least, Napoleon himself who had reached Fontainebleau. Unwilling to give up yet, he was ready to throw himself into a new battle with the courage born of desperation. This threat, together with Talleyrand's intrigues, led to a bloodless coup in which the Senate declared the emperor deposed on April 2.[252] After some hesitation but recognizing the hopelessness of his cause Napoleon announced his abdication on April 6. Shortly thereafter the Senate decided to bring back the Bourbons. Louis XVIII entered Paris on May 3, 1814.

The change in regime had fewer effects than were feared by some and hoped for by others. The new government took over the old administrative machine with the exception of the prefecture of police, whose reputation had been ruined by its many arbitrary actions. It was abolished along with the Ministry of the Interior, and replaced by a police directorate. Only in very few instances was there a change in personnel.[253] Louis XVIII was afraid of sweeping reforms, as shown by the weak but politically astute way in which he handled these matters. Hence the public accepted him with resignation and expectant goodwill. What else could they do? Bonapartism no longer presented a viable political alternative and a new regime generally meant new opportunities for new people. Opposition to the Bourbons came at first from only two, clearly defined sources: the soldiers and the unemployed.

In the army the old officers were primarily the ones to remain loyal to Napoleon, not least because they had been dismissed or put on half-pay.[254] Helped by strict police surveillance the authorities were able to control this opposition promptly. But it was more difficult to deal with the problem of the unemployed, especially since their numbers kept increasing. The collapse of the Empire put 4,000 construction workers out of work; these were now joined by several thousand more from cotton factories that had been bankrupted by the opening of the French market to cheaper English goods.[255] However, this group's Bonapartist sympathies cooled off somewhat once a series of new measures created more employment for them. They were also pacified by a prohibition on seasonal workers coming to Paris from the provinces; and in the autumn of 1814 their hopes were raised by what later turned out to be a false improvement in the economy.[256]

The commercial and industrial bourgeoisie, which had originally greeted the Restoration with relief if not actual enthusiasm, now began to withdraw its support. It had become too used to Napoleon's economic protectionism, and many enterprises began to experience difficulties under the newly established free-trade system. Retailers' earnings were also reduced by the departure of the Allied troops from Paris; and the law passed on June 7, 1814, forbidding Sunday and holiday commerce caused further resentment.[257] Furthermore, the bourgeoisie was especially angered by the behavior of the nobility, and the fact that their demands were granted as a matter of course. Baron de Barante writes:

> There is nothing wrong with a nobleman becoming a minister or officer, but one is outraged when a member of the landed gentry—who has an income of two or three thousand francs and no knowledge of spelling or any other competence—thinks he can treat a landowner, lawyer or doctor condescendingly. And who then feels insulted if he is asked to pay taxes, because he is convinced that he would be giving up his rank if he paid them.[258]

However, this growing dissatisfaction did not dispose the bourgeoisie more kindly toward Napoleon, from whom they expected nothing but further adventures with uncertain outcomes. That is why Paris remained calm when news came on March 7, 1815, that Napoleon had landed near Fréjus. There were neither manifestations in favor of Louis XVIII nor signs of uprising in the suburbs, nor even a revolt by the army. Contrary to all experience since 1789, this time Paris remained completely passive; its population permitted a change of regime in the provinces without being involved in any way. "The government and society," notes the duc de Broglie in his memoirs, "presented an abject picture. False news was exchanged without anyone believing any of it. Passions were roused by speeches anyone could see through. Everyone prepared for resistance while firmly resolving to avoid any confrontation. All proclaimed their hatred for the tyrant while secretly making their arrangements."[259]

The Hundred Days

ITH NAPOLEON'S RETURN, a drama that everyone had considered finished looked as if it were about to begin all over again. For the prominent bourgeois it was cause for dismay and unhappiness.[260] Louis XVIII and his ministers left the Tuileries on the night of March 19, 1815, and went into exile in Ghent.[261] His departure left Paris and France without a government but the experienced bureaucracy continued to function smoothly. It was child's play for small groups of Napoleon's followers to take over the key positions the following morning; and the monarchy disappeared as quietly and casually as it had come to power a year earlier. "Dear friend," Napoleon said to Mollien a few days after he arrived in Paris, "they let me come back just as easily as they let the others go."[262] The symbols of the Restoration disappeared like faded leaves in the wind of Napoleon's continuing magic. Pictures and insignia of the king were removed from Paris streets; in the Palais-Royal, a large crowd celebrated Napoleon's expected return; a tricolor flag of a size never seen before rose over the Tuileries, and soldiers marched through the city singing the Marseillaise.[263]

When the emperor's dust-covered coach arrived at the Tuileries from Fontainebleau around nine o'clock in the evening, enthusiasm turned to delirium. Hundreds of officers from all regiments carried the emperor on their shoulders to his room—each one wanted to touch him, to kiss his coat. With some effort Napoleon eventually managed to calm the frenzy and to get away from his followers who spent half the night outside the Tuileries singing songs and cheering.[264]

The great contrast between the loud jubilation and songs echoing in the immediate neighborhood of the Tuileries and the total darkness of the desolate, outlying districts of the city was a foretaste of things to come. As had happened when Napoleon made his way through the provinces, so also in Paris, only soldiers and veterans, suburban workers, and the petite and middle bourgeoisie celebrated his return. They did so for various reasons—some were still taken in by his magic, others nostalgically thought of past victories, and then there were those who felt that compared to the Restoration a Napoleonic regime was the lesser of two evils. But those who were concerned for their business interests feared the abrupt change in government and Napoleon's political adventurism, and continued to feel as depressed as when they first learned that he had landed.[265] They were not reassured when he promptly and energetically filled executive and administrative positions with his faithful followers, thus eliminating the danger of the kind of betrayals that had cost him his rule in the spring of 1814.[266]

Napoleon's initiative impressed his followers but did not win over the prophets of doom who waited for things to take their course. In a notation in his diary, Pierre Fontaine manages to convey an excellent impression of the prevailing mood:

> It was impossible for us to reimmerse ourselves in the illusion of a dream once we had awakened from it. Nothing could make us believe in the return of a hitherto unknown good fortune. Instead we remained convinced that all was over and that is why we were content simply to carry out the orders we were given.[267]

From the very start Napoleon's chances were nonexistent. He had the bureaucracy's passive or precarious loyalty; but the legitimate aristocracy and the bourgeoisie rejected him in more or less undisguised fashion. Other than his faithful troops, Napoleon could rely only on those very elements that he both feared and despised: the workers and the petite bourgeoisie. And even their loyalty had its price.[268]

The sudden return to power of the man who had just been exiled considerably heightened the threat of war in Europe. This had an immediate adverse effect on an economy barely recovered from recession and a low-tariff policy. By the end of March the alarm signals became more frequent: unemployment increased in the building trade and among cabinetmakers as

orders decreased in the faubourg Saint-Antoine.[269] Napoleon overlooked the
dangers facing his regime from that quarter and promptly gave instructions
in keeping with his tried and true remedies. On March 25 he wrote a letter to
Montalivet, who was the *Intendant général de la Couronne*, instructing him to
come up with an employment program overnight; he indicated that work
could begin immediately on the Louvre and other royal buildings.[270]

Though time had passed, the emperor was still convinced that he could
take up his projects where he had left off; he was equally certain that his old
solutions were still effective. Just how wrong he was has been very percep-
tively described by Chateaubriand.[271] And whatever popularity he did enjoy,
the big demonstration on March 14, 1815, in which workers from the faubourg Saint-Antoine marched from the place de la Bastille to the Tuileries,
was not at all a spontaneous expression of patriotic enthusiasm for the emper-
or.[272] It was an event organized by the authorities in which veterans were the
major participants.[273] As a matter of fact, the demonstration could not even
produce the desired effects because, as the *peuple* of Paris suspected and as
Chateaubriand shows, "the emperor's progress from Cannes to Paris consumed all that was left in the old man: the talisman was broken in Paris."[274]

But what really prevented the reestablishment of Napoleon's rule on a
permanent basis was not unemployment—which he tried to relieve as best he
could—or rising food prices. Two other events made him lose credit among
the bourgeoisie: the referendum on the articles to be added to the
Constitutions of the Empire, and the unavoidable resumption of the war once
the European powers formed a new alliance on March 25, 1815.

The plebiscite on the additions to the Constitutions made Napoleon's
problem very clear. In Paris alone more than half of those eligible refrained
from casting their votes.[275] It was a massive rejection not only of the content
of the articles, but of Napoleon's politics in general. And the major reason for
this rejection was the bourgeoisie's uncertainty over what another war might
bring. It confirmed the conclusion reached by the prefect of police in 1814 as
the Allies were advancing. At that time he had attacked the egoism that is
"the sickness of large cities," an egoism that made Parisians dread war
because they had much to lose and nothing to gain from it.[276] And what,
other than self-interest, could have produced such a horrified reaction among
the Parisian bourgeoisie following a speech at the veterans' mass demonstration on May 14, 1815? The veterans, who generally led a pitiful existence as
suburban artisans and workers, had been told of a new war that would free
the oppressed peoples of Europe.[277] "That smacked of republicanism," comments Antoine Thibaudeau in his memoirs.[278]

Though Napoleon made no reference to any such popular revolutionary war in his answering speech, it did not assuage the bourgeoisie's concern.[279] Napoleon himself was known to have a deep antipathy to the *peuple*
and everything he considered to be revolutionary disorder. The extent of his
mistrust of the faubourgs' patriotic fervor became even more evident in his
decree of May 15, 1815, ordering the formation of 24 battalions, each to consist of 720 men. They were to be recruited from among residents of Paris and

its environs, as long as they were not subject to service in the National Guard (limited to members of the bourgeoisie). Not only did Napoleon intentionally keep the number of these *Tirailleurs-fédérés* low—conscription of double the number would easily have been possible—but he ordered that weapons and munitions for these troops be kept stored in arsenals![280]

These *Tirailleurs-fédérés* were greatly inspired by Napoleon and his cause, though completely inadequate militarily. They and the National Guard were the only ones available to defend Paris once the emperor left on June 12, 1815, to engage the Allied troops far from the capital. There were plans to fortify the city, but there had been neither time nor means to do so.[281]

News of Napoleon's defeat at Waterloo produced some expressions of loyalty from his *fédérés* and the Imperial Guard, when he returned to Paris on June 21, 1815. But that did not blind him to the true feelings of the public. The egoism of the large cities was much stronger than Napoleon realized when he undertook his vast reorganization of administrative personnel. His opponents no longer made the slightest effort to hide their joy over his debacle at Waterloo—the end of the empire as they saw it. Fouché was particularly busy scheming Napoleon's abdication.[282] The emperor's announcement on June 22 that he would abdicate in favor of his son—a last desperate attempt to salvage his dynasty—brought him fresh declarations of loyalty. But they could neither change his decision nor save what he himself had given up as lost. He left Paris on June 24, never to return; Fouché had won.

Everything now hinged on the speed with which the Allied troops would reach the capital. Civil and military authorities gave the appearance of being ready to come to its defense, not because they really felt obliged to do so but to safeguard their own interests.[283] The fact that Fouché headed the provisional government formed after Napoleon's departure guaranteed that this time around there would not be another senseless battle over Paris as in the previous year. Fouché had long since reached an agreement with Davout, commander in chief of the French troops massed around Paris, that any military resistance against the Allies outside the gates of Paris would be useless.[284] From now on everything else was merely a face-saving device. On July 2 the Allies surrounded Paris at a distance of three kilometers; the following day the first negotiations began that led to a cease-fire and the withdrawal of French troops behind the Loire. On July 4 Allied troops moved into Saint-Denis, Saint-Ouen, Clichy, and Neuilly; on July 5 Montmartre was handed over to them.[285] The next day the last imperial troops left Paris as the Allied occupation forces took over.

Louis XVIII returned to Paris early in the afternoon of July 8. The day before the king had ordered Chabrol—the former and now the new prefect of the Department of the Seine—to reinstate all officials in the positions they had held up to March 1, 1815. In the welcoming address Chabrol prepared for this occasion, the term "Hundred Days" appears for the time. It has been used since then to refer to the interim rule by Napoleon: "A hundred days have gone by since the fatal moment when Your Majesty was forced to tear

Yourself away from everyone's heartfelt affection and to leave the capital amid the public's tears and laments."[286]

The Hundred Days only confirmed what had been quite evident in the spring of 1814: Paris was more than sick of that "little man who had increased his stature with a hundred victories," as the duc de Broglie put it. Paradoxically it was Napoleon himself who had dug his own grave; his solutions and methods no longer corresponded to the expectations of the society he had created. There was general dissatisfaction over continual and increasingly rash military campaigns, over the economy's ongoing decline, over the ever-receding chances for peace and improvement. A prime example of this was the rejection (discussed earlier), especially in bourgeois circles, of the articles added to the Constitutions of the Empire. Compared to the relatively liberal Charter of Louis XVIII—a clever compromise between the Old Regime and the new France—the bourgeoisie saw these additions as a step backward. After all, they had consolidated their revolutionary gains under the Consulate and Empire. In their new political maturity they recognized the articles as expressions of excessive autocratic self-aggrandizement—something they now found distasteful.

Napoleon had tried to annul the Revolution but ended by becoming its unwitting executor. The great push for centralization encouraged by the Terror presented Paris with a challenge whose dynamics the Directory was incapable of handling. Napoleon, on the other hand, understood how to make use of it because it fitted in with his concept of government. He created a disciplined, centralized, and hierarchical system, able to execute his orders promptly anywhere in the country. This system, together with his clearly formulated *Code Civil*, produced the framework for a modernization of society—a process initiated by the abolition of privilege by the Revolution. But the saying *unda fert, nec regitur* ("The wave flows on and cannot be guided") held true for Napoleon as well. Many of the important social developments during his regime, such as the beginning of the great migration from the provinces, or the creation of a new aristocracy, were not at all what he had intended. He had not anticipated the emergence of a subtly differentiated bourgeoisie, quite unlike what it had been under the Old Regime; or of a new proletariat—whose full political and revolutionary impact would be felt in the Revolution of 1830.

In his exile on St. Helena Napoleon once remarked to the Comte de Las Cases, "I wanted Paris to become a city of two, three, or four million inhabitants, that is, something wonderful, powerful, and never experienced before our time. . . . If the heavens had granted me another twenty years and some leisure, you would have looked in vain for the old Paris; you would not have been able to see the slightest trace of it. . . . "[287] Indeed it was his dream to turn Paris into a gigantic monument to the fame and greatness of his rule. But this vision contained a contradiction probably sensed by Napoleon himself, a contradiction fed by the same anxieties that had already plagued the Bourbons and were confirmed by the Revolution. Paris was not supposed to become too big, or overpopulated; it was especially important to prevent the *peuple* from becoming too numerous, so as to avoid unrest and strikes that might paralyze the political center or, still worse, spark a revolt.

Though the Consulate and the Empire held exhibitions to encourage the growth of industry, everything had in fact been done to slow its progress in and around Paris. The city's disadvantages as an industrial site—its distance from raw material and energy sources—were always given as reasons; but in reality it was fear of having too great a concentration of workers. Prefect Frochot himself once openly admitted this in asking: "Is it good politics for the administration to want to increase the number of industries in Paris and so add a large number of easily incited workers to a city that already has its share of unruly elements?"[288]

There is no question that Napoleon shared his prefect's apprehensions. His constant concern that Paris should always be supplied with sufficient, reasonably priced food and that unemployment should be held in check is ample proof of this. But as the further growth of Paris in the nineteenth century was to show, Napoleon's dreams of the capital's attraction could only come true at the cost of accepting industry and a large working class.

BOOK FOUR

Growth and Stagnation

1815–1830

Paris est toujours cette monstrueuse merveille, étonnant assemblage de mouvements, de machines et de pensées, la ville aux cent mille romans, la tête du monde.

Paris is still that monstrous marvel, that astonishing assemblage of movements, of machines, of thoughts, the city of a hundred thousand novels, the center of the world.

Honoré de Balzac, *Ferragus*

The July Revolution, when Louis Philippe succeeded Charles X. A caricature of the enthusiastic peuple: "Oh by God, Thérèse, there's a good man of the government . . . and one who's not at all stuck up . . . I shook his hand just like I'm talking to you . . . and he called me comrade . . ." (July 31, 1830). A period lithograph by Hippolyte Bellange (1800–1866).
ARCHIV FÜR KUNST UND GESCHICHTE, BERLIN

Liquidation of the Empire

*W*HEN LOUIS XVIII ENTERED PARIS around three o'clock on July 8, 1815, the city looked odd. English and Prussian soldiers, who had taken over the streets on the previous day, were stationed at strategic points and intersections, and along the bridge ramps. Countrypeople who had fled their villages with their cattle and possessions as the Allies approached were camped here and there; trash had collected on the streets, giving off an unpleasant smell.

When he reached the Tuileries the king could see a demonstration by his supporters, who had come there to express in song and dance their joy at their monarch's return; meantime Prussian troops were bivouacked in the place du Carrousel, their cannon trained on the palace.[1] Under the Arc de Triomphe—the only monument successfully completed by Napoleon's architects Percier and Fontaine—Prussian soldiers had set up a field kitchen. Paris was overrun by foreign troops, a sight that embarrassed the comte d'Allonville when he arrived, as he writes in his memoirs.[2]

It has been said that Louis XVIII followed in Napoleon's footsteps. That is a good description of the nature and extent of the Restoration's administration of the capital. The new regime took over the administrative system and personnel of the Consulate with its two independent prefectures, both supervised by the central government.[3] For example, Gilbert-Joseph-Gaspard comte Chabrol de Volvic was prefect of the Seine, a position he had held uninterruptedly since 1812.[4] After Napoleon's return Chabrol was removed from his post on account of his disloyalty, a decision that Louis XVIII countermanded by an order of July 7, 1815. Chabrol kept this position until the end of the regime in 1830.

In contrast to the continuity in the Prefecture of the Seine, there was greater turnover at the top of the Prefecture of Police. In the fifteen years of the second Restoration there were five police prefects in the rue de Jerusalem. This instability in the administration of one of the most important departments of the capital was due to the fact that the prefect of police was directly responsible to and chosen by the minister of the interior. Within the complex political system of the constitutional monarchy, this gave the prefect of police considerable independence of action, but the drawback was that he was automatically a victim of every political change.[5]

The advisory bodies of the city administration—the twenty-four-member *Conseil municipal* chosen by the king which met once a month; and the *Conseil général* that only met once a year and whose task it was to advise the two prefectures on their budgets—were also taken over by the regime.[6] The personnel of these organizations were kept on except for those who had compromised themselves during the Hundred Days. However, those who stayed on soon experienced what Charles de Remusat describes in his memoirs as follows:

153

> The Restoration was a first lesson for the arrogant officeholders of the Empire. The representative regime was a still better lesson. One had to learn the art of hiding one's own prejudices, suppressing resentments, of restraint in expressing one's views and of cultivating other people's vanities in dealing with the court and its various factions, and with the rapid changes that altered coalitions from one day to the next.[7]

This continuity of institutions and their staffs—regardless of the radically altered political conditions—ensured that they functioned normally while concentrating on the liquidation of the Empire's enormous legacy. This included a mountain of debts caused by Napoleon's highly individual financial policies. There were also immense expenditures due to the Allies' twice-repeated occupation of Paris, which could only be met by loans that would add to the debt and have to be financed by increasing taxes.[8]

A depressed economy was another Napoleonic legacy; it did not respond to the change in political regime and was made still worse by the poor harvest in 1816.[9] The previous harvest had only been an average one and had to feed the occupation troops as well, so that no reserves had been put by. As a result some parts of France actually suffered from a famine in 1816.

The strategies used by the government and administration to deal with the crisis were the same as those of the Napoleonic period. The king appointed a *Commission des subsistances* on September 5, 1815, to be directed by the minister of the interior.[10] But the commission had barely achieved its first results when they were canceled by the bad harvest of 1816. The price of a hectoliter (2.84 bushels) of wheat rose from 21 francs in January 1816 to more than 50 francs in June 1817. In view of this increase the store price for a loaf of bread weighing two kilograms should have been 1 franc 70.[11] But political considerations, and the fear of revolts and plunder, forced the Restoration government to keep the price of bread relatively low in Paris at least. The magic limit that was not to be exceeded under any circumstances was 1 franc for a four-pound loaf. A state subsidy had to make up the difference between this and the real market price. In view of the unforeseeable costs involved in this subsidy, Chabrol suggested that the price of bread be split in the Paris market. Only those considered needy by the authorities were to enjoy subsidized bread; the rest of the population was to purchase its bread at uncontrolled prices. Louis XVIII was against this solution and insisted on a general subsidy, with the result that inhabitants from areas around Paris went there to buy their bread at lower prices than in their own regions. In addition, many seasonal workers stayed on in Paris in the autumn and winter of 1816, contrary to their normal practice. Consequently the daily demand for flour rose rapidly from 1,450 sacks to over 1,800 sacks.[12]

The authorities kept the price of bread at 90 centimes until May 1817, when they set a ceiling price of 1 franc for it; at first they subsidized it by supplying the bakers from state flour reserves. But by the beginning of October 1816 these supplies were used up except for what was considered an emergency reserve of a little more than five thousand sacks, so that other means had to be found. There was only one way to deal with this, given existing conditions and previous experiences. Individual bakers would have to receive a subsidy to make up the difference between the price set by the government and the real market price of flour. The question was, who was to pay for the enormous costs which would average about 10 francs per sack of flour?

Chabrol and the *Conseil municipal* argued that the necessary sums be allocated from the state budget because "Paris is the capital of France; it is therefore in the interests of the entire nation that peace and order be maintained in this city. Hence it is the country's duty to express its political solidarity by contributing to the amount needed to accomplish this goal."[13] But this argument had no effect, nor did the fact that Paris was already carrying a heavy debt amounting to more than three times its annual income, and that imposing new taxes was not politically wise. Paris itself was made to pay for the bread subsidy dictated by the government, thus increasing its debt by 24 million francs.[14]

As had been the case in 1811, the lower levels of society were the ones to suffer the most since the food-supply crisis coincided with an economic slump. Not only was the cotton trade badly affected by the lifting of tariffs on competing English goods, but cabinetmakers in the faubourg Saint-Antoine had to adjust to a sudden change in public taste with the onset of the Second Restoration. The Empire style with its marked preference for furniture decorated with fire-gilded bronze was replaced by English-inspired neo-Gothic monstrosities. The demand for luxury goods also slowed down, the overall result being lower wages or bankruptcies, which not only increased the number of unemployed but contributed to the worsening of living conditions of the poor. Further aggravation was caused by a massive immigration of workers from the provinces who hoped to find work on public building projects.[15] These widely differing causes created a condition of unchanging hardship that lasted until 1820 and whose genesis Balzac masterfully describes in his tale "*La Vendetta.*"[16]

In order to deal effectively with the various aspects of this crisis that could affect the political stability of the Restoration, especially in Paris, the authorities followed the old Napoleonic prescriptions. Building projects were undertaken on a large scale; for example, the five slaughterhouses that had been approved in 1810 were completed by 1818 in Rochechouart, Roule, Ménilmontant, Grenelle and Villejuif.[17] Furthermore, construction of the markets at Blancs-Manteaux and Saint-Germain was begun, and construction continued on the Ourcq and Saint-Denis canals, as well as on the Pont de Sèvres. Finally the openings in the tax wall that had permitted a lively smuggling trade were closed. The most important work done in this connection was the erection of an entirely new piece of wall between the posts of Italie and of la Gare. This was completed in 1819 and united a piece of land containing the Salpêtrière complex, the slaughterhouse of Villejuif, and the hamlet of Austerlitz—formerly part of the community of Ivry—with the municipality of Paris.

Measures to create work as well as the lower food prices that followed the bountiful harvests of 1818 and 1819 helped to alleviate the effects of unem-

ployment and wage cuts, and prevented the reactions feared by the
Restoration government. But, as a police report of March 21, 1819, points
out, it was really more due to "the working class not participating in political discussions because it is no longer used to questioning the decisions of the
government, rather than its having become content and peaceful."[18] This
conclusion describes a condition that the Paris prefect of police had already
described with relief back in April 1817, when he remarked, "Le peuple n'est
plus révolutionnaire" ("the *peuple* are no longer revolutionary").[19] In contrast
to some places in the provinces, where the effects of the crisis were more
severe and where hunger revolts and plunder had taken place, the privations
of the *peuple* in Paris had not been expressed in terms of opposition to the
Bourbon regime.[20] The disappointment of the population over its failure to
achieve its political and social ambitions in the Revolution apparently outlasted the changeover from the Napoleonic Empire to the Bourbon
Restoration.

The crisis of the years 1815–20 shielded the Restoration regime and
enabled it to establish itself. An additional diversion was provided by the
presence of the Allied troops, which amounted to more than 300,000 men
by the beginning of April 1815, who were stationed in Paris and its environs.[21] The English troops camped in the Champs-Elysées, while their
Hanoverian and Dutch auxiliaries occupied the Bois de Boulogne (which was
completely cut down during the occupation). The Prussian troops had been
moved from the place du Carrousel to the Champ de Mars, the esplanade of
the Invalides, and into specially erected barracks in the Jardin du Luxembourg; their officers were housed in requisitioned private apartments. Only
the Russian troops were accommodated in the city barracks.

But apart from the enormous costs occasioned by this second occupation of Paris—amounting to more than 42 million francs—and the daily
inconveniences occasioned by such a massive concentration of soldiers in the
life of a city, it was by no means an oppressive yoke.[22] There was the material compensation provided by Allied officers, who spent their money lavishly
in the restaurants, gambling clubs, and shops in the Palais-Royal, where the
proprietors doubled and tripled their prices out of sheer patriotism.[23] But this
did not change the fact that the presence of the Allied troops was especially
resented by the old nobility, the *bonne compagnie*, gathered around the
restored Bourbon throne. Although there was social contact with the mostly
aristocratic officers of the occupation forces, who were also considered allies
in the fight against the Revolution, these relationships remained tenuous.
Finally there was friction when the Allies demanded in earnest the return of
the artworks Napoleon had stolen from all over Europe. The comtesse de
Boigne, for instance, expresses disgust in her memoirs at the behavior of the
duke of Wellington, commander in chief of the Allied troops in Paris,

> who, under the pretense that the English had no claims to make in this respect,
> was willing to remove paintings from our museums, triumphantly and with his
> own hands. That is by no means a rhetorical statement, but a description of what

actually took place. He was seen on a ladder, setting an example. And on the day the Venetian horses were removed from the Arc du Carrousel, he spent the entire morning standing on the monument, across from the windows of the royal apartments, observing the work being carried out. On the evening of that day he was at a small party given by Madame Duras in honor of the king of Prussia. We were unable to hide our indignation from him at this gathering; but he just made fun of his actions. That put him completely in the wrong as our anger was only too justified and far more diplomatic than his behavior. The foreigners were here as our allies; but their acts reflected on the royal family.[24]

This curious-sounding indignation of the *bonne compagnie* over the behavior of the Allies—who only wanted to return the stolen artworks to the nations to which they rightfully belonged—revealed a pharisaic attitude that was to become characteristic of this class. Its members had themselves been preoccupied with regaining possession of their *hôtels particuliers* (their mansions) in the faubourg Saint-Germain.[25]

Meantime some decisive actions were taken to protect the Second Restoration. In complete contrast to Marseille, for instance, where numerous individuals had fallen victim to the "White Terror," in Paris the reckoning with those functionaries of the First Restoration who had gone over to Napoleon on March 20, 1814, took place in orderly fashion. The *Chambre des Cent-Jours* had already been dissolved on July 13. A royal ordinance of July 24 exiled thirty-eight important people who had compromised themselves too deeply. Furthermore, a number of generals were tried by courts martial, and all those who had been part of the *Chambre des pairs* (the upper house) during the Hundred Days were replaced by men faithful to the Bourbon regime.[26]

For the new elections to the lower house that took place in the middle of August, the voting age was lowered to twenty-one years, and that of the deputies to twenty-five years. At the same time the composition of the electoral body (under the system of indirect election, whereby the voters chose electors who then chose the actual deputies) was changed only insofar as the number of electors for Paris and the Department of the Seine was increased from 215 to 231.[27] This had the foreseeable result that Paris registered an overwhelmingly liberal vote; most of the ten deputies who represented the capital in the lower house were former Napoleonic administrators, as were members of the electoral bodies of the individual districts and the Department of the Seine. The voting reform law of February 1817, by which the minimum age of active and passive suffrage was changed to thirty and forty years respectively, did nothing to alter the fact that Paris generally voted for the liberal opposition. This is proved by the social composition of the electoral body of Paris, consisting of 9,677 electors chosen by a population of 14,000: 62 percent of the Paris electors paid property tax, while only 15 percent paid business taxes![28]

Until about 1822 the usually liberal vote of these electors conformed to government policy. And at first this policy was devoted to transforming the Charter, a paper compromise between the Old Regime and the new France of 1789, into a working, liberal reality. Even the persecution, trial, and execution of a few followers and prominent adherents of Napoleon, such as the shooting of Marshall Ney on December 7, 1815, spectacular and moving though they were, did nothing to alter that intention.[29]

The fifteen-year period of the Restoration was a thoroughly Janus-like epoch. Napoleon had cleverly channeled and controlled the dynamics of the Revolution to accomplish the quick expansion of his empire; but those forces were by no means destroyed when the empire collapsed. The real peace that followed, the prompt stabilization of internal as well as external politics, together with the reorganization of the country's depleted finances and the revival of the economy—developments that had to be credited to the Restoration and its representatives—were simply one side of the coin. The other was that the various forces of those dynamics were all concentrated in Paris, developing there without interference or control by the Restoration, thus initiating processes that eventually overwhelmed the regime with a new revolution. This was bound to happen, the Restoration simply leaving things as they were under Napoleon and doing nothing to let the provinces benefit from the centralized political, economic, and cultural status of Paris. That is why during the Restoration Paris, without being affected by the loss of the enormous hinterland of the Napoleonic Empire, developed into the monstrous concentration of people and talents, of wealth and poverty, of power and crime that all through the nineteenth century fascinated, influenced, and frightened contemporaries far beyond the frontiers of France.

Paris—a Moloch

*T*HE POPULATION OF PARIS GREW RAPIDLY: it increased from 713,966 in 1817 to 785,862 in 1831, a rise of 10.7 percent.[30] But most likely it actually numbered far more than 800,000 by the middle of the 1820s. After that there was a decline due first to the economic crisis that began in the winter of 1825–26, and then to the July Revolution of 1830. Reliable figures, only available again in 1831, therefore do not show a continuous growth.[31]

Though the figures indicated a considerably more rapid increase in the number of inhabitants than during the Empire period, there was no corresponding growth in living space. Detailed statistics collected in the capital in 1828 by Daubenton, the *Inspecteur général de la voirie de Paris*, show the population growth in relation to the number of available houses and the area of the individual arrondissements. The figures indicate the growing density of the population and the subsequent continuously deteriorating housing situation. This was a highly characteristic trend in Paris during the Restoration and the July Monarchy.[32]

According to Daubenton's findings, the disproportion between the increase in population and the number of new houses in the period 1817–26 was especially unfavorable in the third, fourth, fifth, sixth, seventh, ninth, eleventh, and twelfth arrondissements. Conditions in the first and second arrondissements were the exact opposite. Private speculation created a supply of housing there that was far greater than the increase in inhabitants. Only in the eighth arrondissement was the relationship between residents and housing more or less balanced. In other words, living conditions were far worse in the older and fastest-growing sections of the city where the poorer people lived.[33]

Between 1817 and 1831 arrondissements with relatively few residents, such as the fifth and sixth arrondissements situated on the far side of the interior boulevards along the northeastern periphery, experienced greater growth. But any study based only on that information would ignore the fact that there was a dramatic increase in population in the built-up inner city, primarily working class in composition.[34]

Daubenton calculated that there was a shortage of no fewer than 3,242 houses in Paris in 1827.[35] This, of course, affected rents. While the average rent for a household of three persons came to 267 francs in 1817, ten years later an apartment of similar size cost 333 francs, far in excess of the sum set aside for rent by working-class families.[36] The lack of sufficient living space, together with the resulting increase of 25 percent in rents, created a vicious circle. More than two-thirds of the Parisians of that time were forced to live in ever more crowded conditions in rooms that often had to be used as workshops as well.

The growth experienced during the Restoration was exacerbated by people moving to Paris from the provinces; the natural increase of the capital's population was only secondary.[37] This type of increase, so characteristic of Paris, also affected the city's age composition in relation to the national pattern, there being far more in the 15- to 40-year-old group and considerably fewer under the age of 15.[38] The greater number of individuals in the 15-to-40 age group is easily explained by the large annual influx of those seeking work in Paris. The underrepresentation of children and young people of less than 15 years was due to the fact that two-thirds of all newly born infants were sent to the country by their parents—or, if they were orphans, by the *assistance publique*—to be raised by wet-nurses or foster parents.[39] This barbaric practice cost many of these poor children their lives.[40] In addition, there was a high infant mortality rate among the poorer sections of the population.[41]

The continual metamorphosis and mixing of members of different social strata and groups—who became lost in the anonymity typical of large cities—frightened as well as fascinated the people of the Restoration and the July Monarchy. The lawyer Derville, in Balzac's story "Le Colonel Chabert," ends his list of despicable human behavior he witnessed in Paris by saying, "I shall move to the country with my wife; Paris frightens me."[42] And Heinrich von Kleist, who spent some weeks in Paris in the summer of 1801, writes to Luise von Zenge:

Two antipodes could not seem more alien and unknown to each other than
two neighbors in Paris, and a poor foreigner cannot find anyone to befriend him,
no one pays attention to him. Sometimes I walk through the long, crooked, narrow, dirty, malodorous streets, I make my way through a crowd of people who
scream, run, pant, push past and into others, and turn them around without anyone taking offense; I look at someone, he looks at me, I ask him a few questions,
he answers me politely, I become friendly, he gets bored, we're both sick of each
other, he says goodbye, I bow and we've forgotten one another as soon as we've
turned the corner.[43]

This inhuman monstrosity of Paris, its diabolical nature, its sirenlike temptations that no one can avoid or survive, is the theme of the *Comédie humaine*. In
no other work does Balzac evoke the infernal nature of the metropolis as thoroughly and intensely as at the beginning of his novel *La Fille aux yeux d'or*.[44]

For Balzac, Paris is the center of an enormous maelstrom whose ines-
capable pull can be felt in the most remote corner of the country:

Aristocracy, ambition, and talent are always attracted to Paris, a city that swal-
lows up gifted individuals born everywhere in the kingdom, makes them part of
its strange population, and dries out the intellectual capacities of the nation for
its own benefit. The provinces themselves are responsible for the force that
plunders them. Should a young man show promise, they call out to him, "Go
to Paris!" And as soon as a merchant has amassed a fortune, he thinks only of
taking it to Paris, the city that thus comes to epitomize all of France.[45]

Balzac's description sketches a process of social evolution that produced
two classes, the bourgeoisie and the proletariat, whose confrontation was to
influence the future history of the city. But despite the decided partiality of
Balzac's contemporaries for statistics and quantified research in all areas of
social life, it is no simple matter to describe the complex tableau of the inhabitants of Paris of the Restoration and the July Monarchy. As before, the poor and
needy majority formed the broad basis of the social pyramid. However, poverty and need are imprecise categories of only relative value, since they depend on
a number of parameters such as age, habits, origin, and opportunity for social
mobility. Moreover, it is necessary to distinguish between misery and poverty,
a difference defined by the dividing line between the hopelessness of a human
condition that has robbed the individual of all chance of a moral and dignified
life, and the assurance of some sort of existence even if precarious.

Quantitative information as to what proportion of the population of
Paris was constituted by the lower classes can be gleaned from the distribution of the yield from the *taxe mobilière*, a tax combined with the personal
income tax and based on the yearly rental of apartments. All apartment owners who paid less than 150 francs annually were exempt from this tax until
1825. Apartments that were more expensive were taxed at a rate that varied
from 5 to 80 francs, depending on the rent. Following considerable increases in Paris rents, the tax-free ceiling of the *taxe mobilière* rate was raised to 200
francs in September 1825.[46]

The *taxe mobilière* made it possible to divide the entire population of
Paris into two categories: those who could only afford or wanted to pay less

than 200 francs a year in rent; and those who paid a higher rent and were thus considered to be wealthy and to belong to the bourgeoisie.

But the *taxe mobilière* was in itself not a reliable gauge for differentiating between poor and rich. For it applied neither to the thousands of individuals who lodged cheaply in *chambres garnis*, nor to those who lived a marginal life with their families. Nor was the variation in rents in different arrondissements taken into consideration, so that the basis for assessment of the *taxe mobilière* did not always match the actual financial situation of the taxpayers. The *Directeur des contributions directes* of the Department of the Seine was completely aware of this state of affairs when he wrote in his report of 1829:

> One gets an idea . . . of the relationship between the wealthy segment of the population, the simple artisans and journeymen—all of whom live in poverty to a greater or lesser extent—and the truly poor, if one considers that in spite of the extraordinary rent increases in the 233,583 apartments situated in the 26,080 houses in Paris, the rents paid for 136,127 apartments amount to between 40 and 200 francs. . . and that of the 87,465 apartments that cost more than 201 francs and for which tax has to be paid, 31,956 apartments belong in the rent category that ranges from 201 to 399 francs. . . . Doubtless, however, a number of those living in the 136,127 apartments whose rents amount to 200 francs or less have an income that would require them to pay the personal tax; on the other hand, there is surely a far greater number of tenants who pay 201 to 399 francs, who are not subject to this tax according their earnings.

On the basis of these analyses the writer concludes "that of the 224,000 households in Paris at least 136,000 must be classified as being poor, and a further 32,000 households as living on the edge of poverty . . . while the percentage of the population who could be considered well-off or rich does not amount to more than a quarter of all the households."[47]

This approximate determination arrived at from tax analyses of those living in poverty is confirmed by burial statistics. Of the 261,360 deaths registered in Paris between 1821 and 1830, the number of paid burials—that is those that took place according to the graduated tariff set by Frochot— amounted to only 17 percent. The conclusion drawn is that the other 83 percent of the deaths were poor individuals "not one of whom knew how he would have survived on the following day, for he had not even set aside the 15 francs required for his burial."[48]

But if one considers that the life expectancy of the poor was generally shorter than that of the rich and, furthermore, that fewer people normally lived in the smaller apartments not subject to the *taxe mobilière;* and if one also considers that economic fluctuations affected the hordes of the poor and needy, one can estimate the size of the petite bourgeoisie to have been between 65 and 75 percent in the period 1815–48. Louis Chevalier describes what poverty under the Restoration and July Monarchy really was:

> . . . all in all [it was] an enormous and lasting misery that increased tenfold during times of crisis and then forced almost half of the inhabitants of Paris, and that means just about the entire working class, to experience hunger, sickness, or

death; a situation that prevailed even in normal times and from which no less than a quarter of the entire population of Paris had to suffer.[49]

Even if it is impossible to determine the gradations of poverty all the way down to deepest misery, it is certain that the statistics on needy individuals in Paris—available because such persons came to the attention of public welfare officials—provide an approximate idea of the extent of the poverty. In 1818 and 1830 the figures vary between 84,461 and 78,325 persons. The fact that the number of poor was as high as 85,357 individuals in 1819, and as low as 54,371 in 1822, only proves the close correlation between the endemic poverty in Paris and the effects of economic fluctuation.[50]

The misery and poverty under which two-thirds to three-quarters of the capital's population lived did not concern the public in the Restoration, although the sheer numbers and obvious presence of the poor could not be ignored. The pathology of this condition, the potential dangers it held for society as a whole, only began to bother the bourgeoisie in the July Monarchy. Two events in particular focused attention on these problems and turned them into a real obsession, behind which hid naked fear: the July Revolution of 1830 and the great cholera epidemic of 1832.

Work and Wages

*A*S WAS NOTED EARLIER, those who belonged to the lower level of society and led very precarious lives, and those whose comparatively stable existence marked them as petits bourgeois, shared the same marginal economic basis. The difference was that the daily deprivation faced by the poorer segment was merely a more distant threat for the others. This explains why there was considerable social mobility between the two strata. In times of prosperity it was not unusual for some members of the deprived to work their way up into the higher ranks by means of thrift and skill; in times of crisis this trend was reversed, forcing those who were better off to lose their status.

Membership in one or the other social class did not depend on whether an individual was "independent" or "employed," but on the relationship between wages and cost of living, both being unstable and variable. Women and children received far lower wages than men, and daily wage rates varied greatly in different trades. Wages were lowest in large-scale manufacturing enterprises such as the textile industry, where mechanization had replaced certain operations. For a twelve-hour day, men received between 2 francs 50 and 3 francs; women got between 1 franc 20 and 1 franc 30; children were paid between 40 and 70 centimes! The pay was equally low in other mechanized industries, the only exception being the metalworking "industry," where trained workers could earn up to 5 francs a day. The pay scale was fairly good for artisans in the building trade; and cabinetmakers, clock- and instrument-makers, as well as printers, earned even higher wages, ranging from 7 francs 50 to 15 francs a day.[51] Wage rates were generally tied to economic trends: times of crisis and low demand regularly produced lower wages in those trades most susceptible to them.

But in themselves wage rates have little meaning unless they are compared to the cost of living. In the Restoration a simple standard of living required between 500 and 600 francs per person annually, which means that even a poorly paid worker receiving 2 francs a day had an assured income provided he worked at least 300 days a year.[52] However, this is an unrealistic abstraction, for a yearly income of 600 francs was not sufficient to feed a wife and children as well—even if they contributed to the family income—let alone to put something aside for the sickness or periodic unemployment of the principal breadwinner. Loss of work or illness could change this level of poverty to one of total deprivation from which it was frequently impossible to escape. It was not so much the pay scale that determined social status as the number of days a year that an individual was able to work.

Two severe crises affected the economy, and increased unemployment during the Restoration. The impact of this development was hardest on the petite bourgeoisie and the lower classes. The first crisis, lasting from 1816 to 1820, was followed by an upswing that continued until the summer of 1826. While this phase improved demand in the Parisian building trade, it was followed by a sudden slump that lasted until the end of the Restoration and affected all branches of trade and industry. It was characteristic of this depression that while wages decreased, prices for basic foods rose considerably.[53] The unemployment problem was further aggravated by an increase in bankruptcies and the growing mechanization of industry.[54] One important example of this was the royal tobacco factory, the largest employer in the capital, where 310 workers were made redundant by the installation of a machine in December 1827.[55]

The influx of workers from the provinces—as always in time of economic crisis—who expected to find better job opportunities and pay in the city also added to unemployment. A greater number of people came to Paris during the Restoration and the July Monarchy than before, without there being sufficient work available.

But the obvious decline of the economy, aside from the five years of prosperity between 1820 and 1825, did not bring about greater political unrest among the petite bourgeoisie and the lower classes. On the contrary, at the height of the economic crisis in 1829, the prefect of police comments on this unusually quiet period with these words: "The working class seems never to have been more willing to avoid anything that might disturb the existing order. One must conclude that this class has undergone a sort of moral improvement."[56]

This peacefulness was all the more paradoxical in view of the numerous strikes that took place, especially in the years 1825 and 1826 of the economic boom. These confrontations were generally limited to questions of pay;

political demands were not at issue. Of course it would have made little sense
to fight for higher wages in times of economic crisis, as many of the unemployed would have been willing to work at cut rates. It seemed as if the
depoliticization of the former *sans-culottes*, actively pursued by the Napoleonic
regime, was not affected by their deteriorating situation under the Restoration.
But this was in fact a mistaken conclusion, which had fatal consequences first
for the Restoration and then for the July Monarchy. The revolutionary volcano most contemporaries believed to have become extinct was merely
renewing its force for another gigantic eruption. But everyone denied or
ignored its existence.

The number of immigrants who continued to flood into Paris despite the
worsening living conditions was bound to threaten the capital's social stability in the long run. It increased the proportion of uprooted individuals who
formed the lumpenproletariat, a group that fell between the *classe laborieuse*
(the laboring class) and the *classe dangereuse* (the dangerous class). This group
had been less significant in the Napoleonic era, when its members as a rule
were dispatched to the European battlefronts; but now that the safety valve
of war was missing and there were far more pauperized immigrants, the
problem was of greater importance.

This phenomenon daily became more evident in the Paris streets as is
confirmed by numerous reports in the "picturesque literature" of the Restoration. All those types, which Jules Janin describes so colorfully in his contribution to the collection *Paris ou le Livre des Cent-et-Un*—the tricksters,
panhandlers, and itinerant merchants; the peddlers, barkers, bootblacks,
porters, chimneysweeps, lottery-sellers, knife-grinders, acrobats, fortune-
tellers, and charlatans—came together in the zone where poverty and petty
crime converged. It is impossible to determine the size and social composition of this group that was so characteristic of the population in the
Restoration and the July Monarchy. For the authorities of the times only paid
attention to certain individual professions of this lumpenproletariat, such as
newspaper vendors and billposters.[57] Possibly most of these itinerant trades
masked forms of begging and were tolerated by the authorities because the
problem could not have been dealt with otherwise. Sheer numbers made it
hopeless to use police measures.[58] The two *dépôts de mendicité* in Villers-
Cotterêts and Saint-Denis, where beggars and vagrants were imprisoned
after being convicted, were always overcrowded; but severe treatment had no
effect. Nor did deportation of the vast army of preindustrial paupers back to
their places of origin make any difference. It is also interesting that the
authorities were not concerned about the misery of the overall group, but
singled out certain segments that were especially noticeable for social-phe-
nomenological or moral-hygienic reasons. Aside from those who were a nui-
sance because they made no effort to hide their begging, ragpickers and prostitutes received most attention.

Though the ragpickers belonged to the category of itinerant trades, their
repugnant, filth-encrusted outward appearance and their penetrating odor
created fear among their contemporaries. It was said that ragpickers com-

mitted all sorts of crimes at night as they roamed Paris alleys and rummaged through trash piles looking for useful items, which they then put in their baskets and took to their hideaways.[59] It was also widely believed that these city nomads were oblivious of social ties—that they behaved like uncivilized beings and lived together in complete promiscuity; and that despite their extreme poverty they had numerous children whom they trained to serve as lookouts and helpers. The police decree of September 1, 1828, ordering rag-pickers to register and forbidding them to engage in their trade between midnight and 5:00 A.M., was a clear indication that the authorities shared the public's fears.[60]

Prostitutes formed the other social layer between the *classes laborieuses* and the *classes dangereuses*. Official preventive and repressive measures against prostitution in the capital were based on the assumption that prostitutes were the natural allies and helpmates of vagabonds and thieves.[61] It followed, therefore, that all companions of criminals had to be prostitutes; and this led to the conclusion that restricting and controlling prostitution would prove effective in fighting and preventing crime.[62]

But neither the prostitutes nor the *classes dangereuses* and their connection with the poverty-stricken *classes laborieuses* bothered the public and the administration nearly as much in the Restoration as under the July Monarchy. The almost obsessive concern in that period with the darker side of human misery gave it its unique character. The Restoration was merely a time of incubation for the fears and conflicts that afterward dominated public consciousness during the July Monarchy.

Social and Economic Topography

S LARGE WAVES OF IMMIGRANTS from the provinces caused a rapid growth in population, each of the city's districts began to acquire a unique character. This was determined by the concentration of economic activities as well as by the varied social status of the residents. Even in the early years of the Restoration tax revenues revealed a clear east-west social differentiation within Paris.[63] However, during both the Restoration and the July Monarchy residence in a certain neighborhood was only a relative indication of a person's status. In fact individual areas of nineteenth-century Paris never achieved the same degree of homogeneity as the boroughs of central London.[64] There were islands in almost all of the Paris arrondissements that often contrasted strongly with their dominant social grouping. The Petite-Pologne section, that "succursale du faubourg Saint-Marceau" ("anteroom of the faubourg Saint-Marceau"), as Balzac called it, was an excellent example of this social divergence. It lay between the rue de la Pépinière, the Parc Monceau, the rue de Courcelles, and the rue du Rocher, in the middle of the fashionable residential quarter that had sprung up between the Chaussée d'Antin, the Champs-Elysées, and the boulevards.[65]

Even if the contrasts between rich and poor were rarely as marked as in those particular neighborhoods, they did determine the heterogeneous aspect of Paris evoked by Auguste Luchet:

> Paris, more than other capitals, presents a strange picture that makes one feel as if different cities lay encircled by one wall and were connected by streets lined with houses instead of ditches and trees. Indeed each arrondissement has residents who in no way resemble those in the neighboring one. The aristocratic manners of the faubourg Saint-Germain are completely different from the no less aristocratic behavior one encounters in the Chaussée d'Antin, the faubourgs Montmartre, Poissonnière, du Roule and Saint-Honoré. The working class of the faubourg Saint-Antoine is offended if it is mistaken for that of the faubourg Saint-Marcel. An inhabitant of Chaillot, or one from Gros-Caillou remarks, when he crosses the Champs-Elysées or the Esplanade des Invalides: "I'm going to Paris." What do the rows of houses and dark, narrow alleys that form the *Cité*, have in common with the lordly palaces in the place Vendôme? What should one say of the Marais, the Paris of Louis XIV and of Madame de Sévigné? What about the Ile Saint-Louis, that perfect replica of a green provincial town that chance seems to have set down in the middle of the restless capital? Here there are houses with up to seven floors, over there others with only two storeys; a superb colonnade [stands] next to a miserable hovel; the most beautiful street in the world, the rue de Rivoli, is lined with houses like those in the rue Saint-Louis and the rue du Dauphin; [there are] arcades paved with marble, galleries of stores in which the glitter of gold and glass compete, and which open onto malodorous squares filled with trash. Everything in this bizarre city forms a unique contrast, it is a baffling mixture of colors that clash and repel and yet form a breathtaking whole that charms a person without his being able to give the real reason for it.[66]

This confusing contrast between poverty and wealth had always existed in Paris; but it had never before been as stark as it was now, due to the socioeconomic changes that took place under the constitutional monarchy. In 1821 P.-J.-S. Dufey comes to the conclusion that:

> Paris is no longer the abyss that devours provincial agricultural and manufactured products without compensation. Rather Paris has become an industrial city and is today the manufacturing center of France. Factories of all kinds employ numerous artisans and workers, and there is no longer any place in France that is not in constant touch with the capital.[67]

However, the traditional commercial system did not disappear overnight and it took some time before a new type of national economy took hold. And yet Dufey's overall conclusion is justified insofar as political centralization was accompanied and supplemented by an economic centralization that directly affected the socioeconomic structure of Paris. It could be taken as a rule of thumb that in all those Paris districts where trades employing artisans continued to exist, the social structure was more varied because commerce and trade were closely linked in symbiotic interdependence. An example of this was the Saint-Denis district, right near the Halles area, which Auguste Luchet describes so well:

This is where most of the products known in France by the label *fabrique de Paris* come from. In order to give the reader an idea of the amazing industry of the residents of the streets of Saint-Denis and Saint-Martin, I shall describe just one house that is not even as large as many others in the same area.

On the ground floor of this house there are a fabric shop and one that sells haberdashery; on the mezzanine level is another fabric store as well as one devoted to lingerie and dressmaking. On the first floor there is another haberdashery; on the second floor there is a place where bird's feathers are processed; on the third floor metal jewelery, fans, and garters are made; on the fourth floor they gild copper; on the fifth floor a clockmaker has a workshop where he makes clocks out of alabaster: fifteen workers are employed there, in a room that is as big as a boudoir in the rue Chantereuse. The assistants from the fabric and haberdashery shops live on the sixth floor; and three tailors and a shoemaker have opened their workshops next to the chimney flues in the attic. All in all this house has eighty occupants, all of whom work, all of whom have useful occupations. . . . [68]

Even if this district continued to exist until the Second Empire as described by Luchet, it had already lost some of its substance and importance under the Restoration when the wholesale trade began to move to the west of the city and to reestablish itself in the vicinity of the Bourse. The exodus of the wholesale trade from its traditional habitat was a direct result of changes in the socioeconomic structure. For the wholesalers had close business and at times financial ties to manufacturers and producers in the provinces, for whom Paris served as the most important outlet for the entire home and export market.[69] At the same time, the wholesalers often had business connections with the major banks of Paris, which were located near the stock exchange as well, in the areas along the place Vendôme, the Chaussée d'Antin, or the faubourg Montmartre.[70]

Structural change also meant that the traditional concentration of crafts and commerce, of workers, artisans, entrepreneurs, and merchants, disappeared from specific streets and neighborhoods. This development was particularly noticeable in the Paris textile trade. While textile factories were spread over the neighborhoods to the east of the rue Saint-Denis, which were mainly worker-populated, the textile business was concentrated primarily in the rues de Clery and de Bourbon-Villeneuve.[71]

Other industries showed similar separation between manufacture and commerce. There was also some diversification in the types of products manufactured in any one district; so that whereas the faubourg Saint-Antoine had formerly been devoted to the furniture industry, it now accommodated a variety of other manufacturers as well. Though goods continued to be produced in their traditional home in the east of Paris, the retail trade began to spread out over the entire city—a development that rather surprised observers at the time.[72] A plausible explanation is that the rapid rise in population increased the demand for goods which, together with the new independence of artisans, produced more retailers. This created more competition than needed, which in turn forced greater specialization and diversification of products, as well as disruption in their distribution. For example, businesses that dealt in luxury items and nonessential goods, known as the *magasins de nouveautés*, followed their wealthier clientele to the newer residential sections in the northwest of Paris.[73]

The Triumph of Commerce: The Arcades

*G*REATER COMPETITION OBLIGED the *magasins de nouveautés* in the "better districts" of the city to display their wares with an extravagance not seen hitherto. At first this was reflected in the more or less fantastic names drawn from politics or literature, and especially from stage plays, which served as themes for large signs and painted or carved panels for the facades of stores.[74] About 250 of these store signs were described in the *Dictionnaire des Enseignes de Paris* (erroneously ascribed to Balzac), by G. L. Brismontier, which appeared in 1826. This by no means covered all the varieties of a phenomenon that was no longer new but had become quite widespread. It was characteristic of these names and signs that almost none referred to the actual products; their creators tried to outdo one another in appealing to the customers' sense of humor and curiosity. Thus Jean-Baptiste Gouriet tells of a "demigod of antiquity armed with a club, shown on the sign of a woman selling artificial flowers; and a saint sunk in her prayers fulfilled the same purpose for a milliner."[75] In the Passage des Panoramas a glove-maker's shop was called *Au ci-devant jeune homme* (The Young Ex-Aristocrat), after a comedy by the playwrights Brazier and Merle; another glovemaker sold his goods under the name *A la Lampe merveilleuse* (The Magic Lamp), the title of numerous plays of the period. And in the same arcade there was also a pastry shop called *Aux Armes de Werther* (Werther's Coat of Arms), a name particularly attractive to romantic customers.[76]

These early attempts at advertising, already noticeable in the Palais-Royal before the Revolution, were soon supplemented and eventually replaced by more effective methods. But even these announcements and posters—especially those promoting cosmetics in flowery language—and the use of extravagant packaging or elaborate flasks for such items, were not in the long run considered sufficient by shopkeepers to keep abreast of the competition.[77]

The Palais-Royal provided a typical example of the kind of rivalry existing among stores; considerable sumptuousness was soon used there to display goods. There were large shop windows, and clever and elaborate ways of dressing them to draw the attention of passersby; in the evening hours, when there were many idle strollers, this was acccomplished by all sorts of lighting effects. But the large shop windows required renovation of the facade as well as changes in the interior decoration. The aura of the products had to reflect the ambiance in which they were sold. Shops like the fabric store described by Balzac in *La Maison du Chat-qui-pelote* (At the Sign of the Cat and Racquet), owned by M. Guillaume in the rue Saint-Denis, made a decidedly dated impression in the Restoration:

> It would have been difficult for a passerby to guess what M. Guillaume sold. Behind thick iron bars that protected his shop from outside, one could hardly see the packages wrapped in brown canvas, which were as numerous as herrings swimming in the ocean. Despite the seeming simplicity of this Gothic facade, of all the Paris fabric merchants M. Guillaume was the one whose storeroom always had the best supplies, who had the widest contacts, and whose business ethics were beyond all doubt.[78]

The new luxurious arcade store, which developed as a result of heightened competition during the Restoration, was exactly what César Birotteau had in mind when he told his wife:

> I shall burn our old shop sign *La Reine des Roses* and have the firm's name *César Birotteau; Marchand Parfumeur, Successeur de Ragon* painted over and then substitute a short and concise *Parfumeries* in gigantic golden letters. I'll put the main office, the cash desk and a nice office for you on the mezzanine. The back room, the present dining room, and the kitchen will become storerooms. I shall rent the first floor of the house next door, make a door by breaking through the wall, and have our stairs turned around in the back, so that we can go directly from one house to the other. That way we'll have a large apartment that we can have beautifully furnished. There'll also be a room for you. You'll have a small parlor and Césarine will have a pretty room as well. The saleslady you're going to hire, the senior salesman, and a ladies' maid—yes, yes my good wife, you shall have one!— will live on the second floor. The kitchen and bedrooms for the cook and the delivery boy will be on the third floor. The fourth floor will house our bottles, the crystal and porcelain supplies, and our workshop will be in the attic. That way people won't be able to look in from the street and watch us sticking the labels on, sorting the little bottles, making up the small bags, and putting corks in the vials. That may be all right for the rue Saint-Denis, but it makes a bad impression in the rue Saint-Honoré. Our shop has to look like a comfortable parlor.[79]

But even more obvious than the changes in the internal organization of retail trade—involving the strict separation of salesroom, storeroom, manufacturing space, and living quarters—were the exterior features with which the shops altered the look of the facades facing the streets. The clumsy older window and doorjambs became slender pilasters and columns of wood or cast iron that gave seemingly fragile support to the ever larger and more numerous window surfaces. The buildings were decorated in a variety of colors at the level of the shop premises; the embellishments imitated precious materials such as red, yellow or green marble, lapis lazuli, bronze, gold, or ancient bas-reliefs. The elaborate signs intended for advertising purposes were replaced by ornaments and symbols. For instance, the facade of a butcher in the rue du faubourg Saint-Denis was decorated with steer heads, as well as cleavers and other professional tools. In the same way the front of a music shop was decorated with lyres and medallion portraits of famous composers.[80] Frequently entire fronts were decorated with banners that drew attention to a shop on the ground floor:

One sees houses decorated with banners all the way from top to bottom like ships on a holiday. The inscription *Grands Magasins à prix fixe* is repeated again and again on the same facade from the ground level to the chimneys. The house number is imprinted on the left and right, above and below, in the front and in the back, in letters three feet high. For these festoons they must have used at least two hundred to three hundred yards of cloth.[81]

The new world of commerce that came into being with the advent of the *magasins de nouveautés*—shops stuffed with fashionable, extravagant, sophisticated, or exotic finery—created its temples and cathedrals in the arcades. These provided the most varied and tempting specimens of color and form, of light and shade, of materials and smells, all vying to outdo one another in a jungle of sensations. The Palais-Royal had proved that a dense concentration of shops, cafés, restaurants, gambling clubs, theaters, and houses of ill repute, situated in an elegant area, and protected from wind and weather, the dirt and traffic of the streets, increased sales and profits. It provided the impetus for the design and construction of the shopping arcades and glass-covered galleries that had their heyday under the constitutional monarchy. As these arcades became the centers of the luxury trade and as competition encouraged the refinement of the appeal to the senses, the attraction of the Palais-Royal diminished.[82]

This unleashing of commerce which transformed an anonymous clientele into a group of individualized customers, needed the artificial climate of the glass-covered arcades, something that Auguste Luchet recognized and described at the time:

> It was not enough for [the arcades] to protect the passerby from the dangers of the streets; they had to hold him, to enslave him, body and soul; and as soon as he entered the corrupting arcades he was supposed to feel so enchanted that he forgot everything: his wife, his children, the office, and his dinner; the arcade was no longer allowed to be a convenient shortcut for him—it had to become a meeting place like the Palais-Royal, where people from all over the city arrived and left again by carriage. The following problem had to be solved: the arcade had to be as light as it was outside on the street; it had to be be warm in the winter and cool in the summer; it had to provide shelter in all seasons; and it was never to become dusty or covered in dirt from the streets. An enormous fortune awaited the first one who understood the purposes of the arcade and managed to design it accordingly. All of Paris knew this man; his name was Delorme and his masterpiece links the rue Saint-Honoré with the Tuileries. He had the honor of having invented the glass-covered arcade.[83]

Like the Palais-Royal, the arcades were built by private speculators, though with the noteworthy difference that they were primarily financed by bourgeois capital. The best-known example is the Galerie Véro-Dodat near the Palais-Royal, completed in 1826; the dual name of its builder-owners, the rich butchers Véro and Dodat, is still a monument to them.[84] Originally, this speculation owed its success to the great improvement in circulation (Paris had yet to undergo Haussmann's vast redevelopment), as it provided a direct and convenient connection between the Halles and the Palais-Royal.[85] The

Galerie Véro-Dodat met the stipulations that were essential to the commercial success of such a project. It had to be located in the center of the city to serve the greatest possible number of people at any time of the day or night, whatever their class, or purpose in being there. Second, the arcade had to link two important and heavily used urban streets.[86] Finally, the arcade had to provide a special attraction, which meant that its architect had to plan for it to hold as many retail stores as possible. This was not merely in the interest of the speculators whose profit depended on the number of shops, but corresponded to the secret wishes of the public. The more stores that lined the arcade, the more varied were the goods and services offered, and the greater was the diversity of the display for the pleasure of the jaded strollers. As Johann Friedrich Geist points out in his magisterial work on the arcades as an example of nineteenth-century architecture, the variety of wares offered served to

> guarantee the arcade a life of its own, like that of a street, for the entire day. Places of entertainment, or ones to fill culinary and cultural needs, belonged in the arcade, to turn the passerby into a user and to become indispensable to the public life of the city. In the ideal case the arcade has to become a kaleidoscopic, smaller version of the city.

Finally, it was important that "the arcade space resemble street space with external facades and use this illusion so that the strollers never have the feeling of being in an interior space, because an interior space is always entered with a goal, with a recognizable purpose in mind."[87]

The Galerie Véro-Dodat seems to have managed to create this illusion ideally according to eyewitnesses. At any rate, in 1837 Thiollet and Roux write:

> Among the various commercial arcades that have been built in Paris in recent years, the Passage Véro-Dodat deserves first place on account of its richness and the regularity of its decoration. Without being colored, an engraving could provide only an incomplete impression of the beautiful effect of this double row of individual shops, of their glass windows set in polished copper frames that glitter like gold, and their glass doors over which there are arrangements of gilded palmettos and rosettes, or their marble floors, etc., etc. One cannot praise this display enough, the purity of the profiles, the painterly and glowing effect created by the glass globes of the gaslights hanging between the capitals crowning the pair of columns on either side of each of the shops, the spaces in between them being decorated with mirrors. . . . Nothing has been omitted to make this arcade a jewel. The floor is made of marble slabs and the ceilings— insofar as they are not part of the glass roof—are painted with landscapes and other subjects and are framed with gilded molding.[88]

Its ingenious displays, which combined speculative interests and merchandising psychology, made the Galerie Véro-Dodat the architectural pinnacle of Parisian arcades. However, it could not maintain its popularity as its location began to be less desirable under the Restoration. Arcades like the Galerie Vivienne (1825) and the one parallel to it, the Galerie Colbert

(1826), built in the business district around the Bourse, were far more successful.[89] Interestingly enough the Passage de l'Opéra (1823–25) and the
Passage des Panoramas (1800), which were not only near the Bourse but
opened onto the boulevard des Italiens and the boulevard Montmartre,
respectively, were even more prosperous.

The Passage de l'Opéra, a dual passage—one branch of which was called
the Passage de l'Horloge and the other known as the Passage du Baromètre—
was the first one of its kind built for speculation during the Restoration. Its
prompt and great commercial success provided the incentive for the building
of fifteen more arcades and galleries that were completed by 1829.[90] The
Passage de l'Opéra, which had to make way for the boulevard Haussmann
in 1925, owed its popularity to its location on the boulevard des Italiens near
the Chaussée d'Antin, an arrondissement that eventually became the preferred residential neighborhood of the wealthy.[91]

By far the most famous arcade, and the one whose success lasted well
beyond the constitutional monarchy, was the Passage des Panoramas.[92] Along
with the Palais-Royal it can be considered as the archetypical Parisian arcade.
Because it connected with the boulevard Montmartre in the latter's heyday
between 1815 and 1848 when its cafés, theaters, dance-halls, baths, and
hotels competed with the Palais-Royal as a fashionable entertainment center,
the Passage des Panoramas soon became the place chosen by strollers and
wealthy idlers. The three panoramas that accounted for its name were created at the same time and were its major attraction.[93]

The great and long-lasting popularity of the Passage des Panoramas
again illustrates the importance of location and variety of goods and services.
These made shopping arcades unique and lively places for generation after
generation of all kinds of people fleeing from their boredom to the luxury
shops and cafés. Their flight was encouraged by the fairy-tale world that the
brilliantly lit arcades simulated so well, transfiguring the value and usefulness
of their goods. This magical effect is described by Amédée Kermel in his contribution to the book *Paris ou le Livre des Cent-et-Un:* "The arcades of this
Paris hemisphere [he is referring to the Passage de l'Opéra and the Passage
des Panoramas] need to be under the fabulous influence of an atmosphere
that imposes its special magic—the magic of gold as well as filth, of passion as
well as pangs of conscience—on all the objects it surrounds."[94]

Some of the businesses and establishments in the Passage des Panoramas
were world-famous in their time and were mentioned in literary works. One
such store was that of Susse, the stationers, in which all kinds of caskets,
jewelry boxes, cases, leather wallets, or valuable desk sets were sold. The
magic of gold and filth invoked by Kermel was the very thing to be found in
these luxury items of unusual refinement, because such knickknacks were
produced by workers in miserable workshops like those described by Balzac
in his portrayal of the speculator Gigonnet.[95] Another store there was the
chocolate shop Marquis, known for its extravagantly packaged products
and made famous by Heinrich Heine's poem "Yehuda ben Halevy" in the
Romancero:

> Yehuda ben Halevy,
> She said, has been
> Faithfully encased
> In handsome cardboard
>
> Elegantly oriental are
> Its patterns, like the pretty
> Sweetmeat boxes of Marquis
> In the Panorama Arcade.

Heinrich Heine was one of the many who regularly went to the Passage des Panoramas according to August Lewald:

> His favorite walk was the Passage des Panoramas, a place one avoids walking through in the evening if one is accompanying a lady. . . . Heine strolled up and down, his hands in his pockets, with his head thrown back and his spectacles on. He liked to watch the Parisian world go by, and was attracted by the "Zoës, Aglaës, Desirées, Clarissas, Amélies, etc." who constantly promenade up and down, and to whom he dedicated the pretty songs he included in the first section of his *Salons*.[96]

The public patronizing the arcades was identical to the one that had once favored the Palais-Royal:

> In the arcades around the Bourse and the Chaussée d'Antin—neighborhoods long inhabited by the moneyed aristocracy—one finds an atmosphere of prosperity and luxury that decreases as soon as one leaves these sections; and since gold is the coveted power that irresistibly tempts all dubious types and venal consciences, the underworld of the big city is to be found there, too: pickpockets and tricksters, mistresses, libertines and spendthrifts, prostitutes, beggars and panhandlers, who make the most of the people idling around—that is to say, theft, vice, and fraud in all its guises and disguises.[97]

This truly mixed society that met in the arcades accounts for their ultimate attraction: they assured complete anonymity. It was possible to observe the colorful scene without seeming to participate, or to indulge one's passions and desires secretly and yet in full view of the public. Only a major city could offer the public a space free from social control like the open world of commerce concentrated in the arcades. Charles de Forster is yet another observer of what went on in the arcades during the July Monarchy:

> The Passage des Panoramas next to the Théâtre des Variétées is the one preferred by all the idlers. A lively crowd is sure to be found there at any time of day. . . . Numerous strollers also gather in the Passage Choiseul to watch the beautiful women pass by; it may be impossible to explain by what mysterious coincidence more of them are to be found here than elsewhere, but I know someone who comes here just to be with them. This is where he keeps his appointments, where he takes his breakfast; he also has his dinner in the Café de Choiseul. Here he writes his articles for his paper, smokes his cigars, and waits for lovely women at the exit of the Opéra italien. As vanity and the desire to please are nourished by everything around them, many of the female fre-

quenters of this theater find special pleasure in walking through the arcade after instructing their coachmen to meet them either in the rue de Petits-Champs or the rue Choiseul. They enjoy showing off their outfits specially made for this promenade—wrapped in a plaid or a fanciful shawl, or with a scarf draped over their head in picturesque fashion and decorated with sparkling jewels. . . . As for the dandies, with their dark suits, their white ties, and their topcoats draped over one shoulder, they believe there is nothing more pleasant to do after a performance in the Opéra italien than to buy a cigar in the Passage Choiseul and to behave like a groom while dressed in evening clothes.[98]

Dynamism and Inertia

*B*UT THIS TYPE OF PUBLIC was not to be found in every arcade. The fabulous world of luxury and fashion was governed by its location and its patrons: "The difference depends on industry and the bourgeoisie. The Vendôme, Bourg l'Abbé and Saucède arcades, like all others situated in this part of the city, represent the stable section of our society. A frequenter of these dark arcades would feel as if he were in a foreign country in the Passage de l'Opéra."[99]

The enormous popularity of these arcades complemented the uniform social characteristics that were developing in different parts of the city. Thus the fashionable arcades, whose sumptuous interiors and mixed clientele have already been described, were confined to the wealthy neighborhoods. Their only similarity to those that lay to the east of streets like the rue de Louvre, the rue Montmartre, and the rue du faubourg Montmartre, was their external architecture.[100] Often these were not actual shopping arcades but covered passages in which artisans had opened workshops. The Passage Saucède was an exception on account of the numerous dressmakers who had rented shops there, making it for some time a center of Paris fashion. Such petit-bourgeois arcades were separated from more luxurious and pleasant ones by more than distance: the two were worlds apart.

This stratification demonstrated the extent to which the Estates had developed into the class society designed by the *Code Napoléon*. In the second half of the century it was still thought that tenants of Parisian apartment houses represented a cross section of society; that storekeepers and their families still lived on the mezzanine level just above their businesses; that the first floor, known as the *bel étage*, still belonged to the wealthy; that the higher up one went the poorer the occupants became and the more humble their living quarters.[101] As late as 1873, the London magazine *The Architect* could present the following clichéd description to its readers:

It would be difficult to quote any custom of the French which English people might less readily fall in with than that which assigns the tenancy of the half dozen successive storeys of the same house to just as many utterly dissociated and indeed discordant people, ranging from a jaunty viscount on the *premier étage* —not merely to a very small *rentier* on the *troisième*, but to a little nest of the humblest workpeople on the *cinquième*, all meeting on the common stair.[102]

But this sort of social mix had been eliminated by Haussmann's time. Even during the constitutional monarchy it existed only in a limited way. It was generally found where traditional economic structures made a mingling of work and living space necessary; where journeymen, store help, artisans, and storekeepers lived in close proximity. Even Balzac's rich speculator Gigonnet lived among merchants and artisans in the district of Saint-Denis—not so much out of miserliness but because they were his clients and victims, and he made his living from them.[103] Moreover, the social divide between a journeyman or an artisan and a petit-bourgeois storekeeper, and the latter from a really rich speculator like Gigonnet, was not very stark. In fact, the contrasts in the economic symbiosis of mentalities and forms of existence were exaggerated in picturesque literature:

> In Paris, wealth and poverty form dreadful contrasts that are separated only by thin wooden partitions. The noisy entertainments in the salons disturb and taint the monotonous sadness on the top floors. The rich man is aware of it and is resigned to it. The unhappy workers die of exhaustion on their miserable pallets and their last sighs are blended with the sounds of festivities on the first floor—the voices, the clattering of china and of silver cutlery.[104]

Most of the residential buildings in Paris—apart from the palatial homes of the aristocracy and rich bankers, and the dwellings in the central and eastern districts limited to worker and artisan occupants—were divided into apartments of varying comfort and rents, whose tenants belonged to different social classes. But already in Napoleonic times and certainly during the Restoration it was evident that the actual social gap between those living under one roof was narrowing. In sections of the city preferred by the petite bourgeoisie there were houses accommodating mostly small investors, workers, and artisans, just as there was a similar homogenization in the neighborhoods favored by the rich. The latter, of course, had to provide living quarters for the servants and personnel on whom their life-style on the *bel étage* depended, which meant that there was no longer room on the top floors for members of the lower classes. In those instances where the upper floors of luxury residences were rented out, the tenants were bourgeois by profession, life-style, or social aspiration. Similarly, there were buildings shared by *rentiers* (individuals living on their investments) and surgeons who lived downstairs, while workers and artisans lived on the upper floors with their families. Whereas the former qualified as petits bourgeois on account of their life-style, the income of the latter also put them in this class.[105]

This trend determined the character of different districts, and was especially noticeable in the new residences built by large speculators:

> Almost all houses built recently consist of two parts: in the rear is a courtyard and the main building, while the front section opens onto the street. Instead of the walls that used to enclose the old townhouses, this front section has sev-

eral elegant storefronts between which a no less elegant staircase leads to the mezzanine: in this way vanity makes way for business, for if the front section does not contain shops, it is occupied by offices or rooms for domestics.[106] Such are the results of progress made by trade and commerce that have brought into being the fashion, or rather the mania, for establishing shops in all new buildings and in many of the old mansions. . . . The first, the second, even the third floors in these new buildings that are by no means *hôtels garnis* are occupied by storekeepers, bank clerks, stock exchange speculators, financiers, ministry employees, actresses, kept women, doctors, or those who, for professional purposes, have to live in houses whose exteriors are somewhat ostentatious and which are located in sections preferred by financiers or wealthy foreigners. As the rooms in these apartments are not very large and are decorated in the latest style with parquet flooring, mirrors, or wallpaper, their tenants have to spend considerable sums on furnishings; on the other hand, the rent for these candybox-size apartments is very high. . . . As can be imagined, that is why these apartments are beyond the reach of those who live by the work of their hands . . . from which one can deduce that the owners are interested in renting the space from cellar to attic only to rich tenants.[107]

A number of fashionable new residential neighborhoods were established between 1820 and 1826 in the northwest and west of Paris by a few large banks and private finance companies. This speculation was not intended to produce a favorable, long-term return on the capital invested; rather, it looked to gain a quick profit by selling the finished houses promptly to interested private buyers. This was also the practice of those who invested in most of the arcades and galleries, which were rented out as soon as they were finished and then sold off building by building.[108] Though the high rents guaranteed buyers of these arcade sections and apartments an immediate premium on their capital, it was precisely this expectation that hastened their financial collapse: the supply of expensive luxury apartments soon outran demand.[109] Moreover, the sudden rise in building costs decreased the profit margins.[110]

On the other hand, ownership of rental apartments in the poorer sections of the city yielded good returns. The demand for moderately priced space there was countered by a rapidly decreasing amount of new construction. The usual and far more lucrative practice was to herd the residents into ever smaller units, whose rents rose all the same.[111] According to official statistics, the average rent during the Restoration increased by 25 percent.[112] The result was that those who belonged to the poorer segments of the population were driven out of the city and had to find accommodations in nearby suburbs.[113] That set off an exodus that grew during the July Monarchy and increased noticeably following Haussmann's sweeping rehabilitation of the inner city.[114]

The large-scale speculation that subdivided the open areas between the inner and outer boulevards in the north and west of Paris, and the concurrent banishment of the working population to the suburbs, created a mechanism that was to be typical of the future history of Paris in the nineteenth century. It was also significant that Chabrol, the prefect of Paris, encouraged this development by avoiding any urban planning priorities that might have solved the problem of dangerous overpopulation of the inner city. His policy of letting things take their course boiled down to his wish that "it would be welcome if the speculations and business interests of the building companies helped the administration."[115]

Finally, it is worth noting that this speculation was financed primarily by bourgeois capital. The banker Jonas Hagermann and the entrepreneur Sylvain Mignon founded a society in 1824 to develop an area that became known as the Quartier de l'Europe, after each had independently acquired parts of the property.[116] The land of the former monastery of Saint-Lazare, as well as the adjoining gardens, also situated to the north of Paris, provided additional arenas for building speculation. The André & Cottier and Jacques Laffitte banks had already reached agreement to develop the Poissonière area in 1812.[117] The two investments in the west of Paris that created the sections Beaujon and François Ier to the right and left of the Champs-Elysées were much smaller ventures.[118]

A speculative craze seized the Paris bourgeoisie and led it to invest its savings blindly in what looked to be profitable building schemes. Many were ruined in the process, as Balzac's César Birotteau so dramatically exemplified. In his memoirs the banker Gabriel-Julien Ouvrard also gives a vivid picture of this period:

> At that time everyone succumbed to a building mania. . . . A man would go to bed in his miserable hut and wake up rich the next morning. Everyone knew the story of the property owner in the plain of Sablons, who had six acres of completely barren land and who considered himself lucky to rent the area—which had a capital value of about 4,800 francs—for 240 francs a year to a laundry in Neuilly that used it for its bleaching process. One day he received a visit from a rich speculator. "How much do you want for your six acres?" he was asked. Completely taken aback by this unknown person's offer, the owner thought he was asking a highly inflated amount when he answered: "I'm asking 30,000 francs." "Thirty thousand francs per acre!" the speculator said, "that's expensive!" "Do you think so?" the completely amazed owner responded. "The devil take it, that comes to 180,000 francs . . . ah well, it's a deal, send your deeds of ownership to my notary, M. Chaulin."
>
> This transaction could be a tale out of *A Thousand and One Nights*, if similar things had not happened elsewhere.
>
> In connection with this general building craze all the old quarries were exhausted, new ones had to be opened up in the vicinity of Paris, and people were so ignorant that they were unaware that buildings erected at such high costs could be neither sold nor rented. When you saw these empty houses and unpopulated districts you would have supposed that the speculators had been advised of a gigantic migration that was to settle an entirely fresh group of residents in the middle of Paris.[119]

Indeed this was the reason for the failure of most of these investments. The new districts had been planned in anticipation of wealthy, interested clients without consideration of actual demand. The very residents speculators hoped to attract preferred two of the older sections: the faubourg Saint-Germain and the Chaussée d'Antin. The legitimate aristocracy was concentrated in the former neighborhood, where it created a closed-off world for itself, while the wealthy bourgeoisie chose the latter section.[120] Furthermore the new sections were too far from the centers of commerce and entertainment to attract these classes. On the average, these new developments turned out to be bad investments. In his novel *Béatrix* Balzac describes the Quartier de l'Europe development, as it appeared to a visitor in the July Monarchy:

> Were it not for the high-class prostitutes of the Notre-Dame de Lorette neighborhood, fewer houses would be built in Paris. Pioneers of fresh stucco, they are drawn by speculation along the hills of Montmartre, pitching their tents in those wastelands of masonry that grace streets named for Amsterdam, Milan, Stockholm, London, and Moscow—architectural steppes where the wind agitates innumerable signs that point up the emptiness with the words: Apartments for rent! The situation of these ladies is determined by where they lodge in these apocryphal neighborhoods. If her dwelling is near the rue de Provence, the lady has an income and a generous budget; but if she lives further out, near the exterior boulevards or near the infamous suburb of Batignolles, she has no regular income. Now when M. de Rochefide met Mme Schontz, she occupied the fourth floor of the only building in the rue de Berlin, in other words, she was perching on the edge of Paris and poverty.[121]

This neighborhood did not come alive until the Second Empire, when the boom anticipated by Restoration speculators set in. The same held true for other residential sections planned and partially completed during the Restoration.

It can be assumed that the failure of these large-scale investments explains why a more thorough rehabilitation of Paris was not undertaken in the period of the constitutional monarchy. Having had this sobering experience, the bourgeoisie was loath to invest its capital in similar enterprises. Yet the plans conceived at the time, some of which had been realized, served as an urban example later on.

In addition to private investments in urban living space in the north and west of the city, various other changes were made under the Restoration. But as these were not particularly remarkable, later generations paid them little attention. Thus André Morizet saw Prefect Chabrol's achievements as limited to the administration and completion of the Napoleonic legacy.[122] But such a verdict is hardly justified. Chabrol completed much of what Napoleon planned or started in Paris, including the slaughterhouses, the new stock exchange building (1824), the canals of Saint-Denis (1821) and Saint-Martin (1822), the Montparnasse cemetery (1824), grain silos, the Halle aux Vins, and the markets of Saint-Martin, Saint-Jacques, Carmes, Blancs-Manteaux and Saint-Germain. Further work was done on the Madeleine and in 1823 construction was begun again on the Arc de l'Etoile after it had been stopped for quite some time. It was no mean task to complete these projects despite the heavy national and municipal debts created by Napoleon, and the severe economic crisis in the early years of the Restoration. And in fact, considerably more was spent on public construction in Paris during the Restoration than in Napoleon's time.[123]

But what was missing were the large concepts and designs, and an overall plan for Paris that would solve the problem of a constantly growing population and an increasingly chaotic inner-city traffic system. Instead, administrators limited themselves to working on the symptoms and trying to interfere as little as possible with property rights and private economic interests. The Restoration was as scrupulous about this as the Old Regime had been; and it was characteristic of this attitude that all plans to relieve the hopelessly overburdened traffic system by creating newer and wider thoroughfares were shelved. In 1823 Chabrol submitted a plan for increasing the surface devoted to inner-city traffic by 500,000 square meters.[124] But, as Chabrol admitted in September 1828, only a tiny fraction of it was actually completed: between 1816 and 1828 traffic surface was expanded by 25,000 square meters.[125] The greater part of this expansion consisted of streets and squares laid out in the new parts of the city, where their peripheral location was irrelevant to the traffic problem.[126] Chabrol's plan could only have been realized by means of extensive expropriation of property. But this was something the Restoration regime was loath to do, for financial as well as political reasons.

The traditional respect for private property also prevented inner-city streets from being paved. Those whose properties fronted on the streets refused to contribute to the costs. But progress was made in the matter of sidewalks, larger-scale construction of which began in 1825. By 1829 at least twenty kilometers of the wider streets were bordered by them.[127]

However, such modest improvements were negated by the fact that Restoration Paris still had not dealt with the problem of filth and trash. Trash collection and street cleaning were as inefficient as before; and though a growing and densely housed population produced considerably more trash, the problem was treated with customary nonchalance:

> Trash and rubbish of all sorts are simply deposited daily on the streets by more than two hundred thousand households and remain lying there for an indeterminate time. Refuse from workshops is added to this, and the constantly passing horses, carriages, and pedestrians break up, scatter, and turn the mess into black sludge that liquefies in the rain and domestic sewage, making it difficult or impossible for the cleaners to dispose of it. Hardly has half of it been swept up when the rest is scattered in the gutters, blocking the water from draining away; it only disappears when strong rains flood the drains.
>
> Bad gases and pestilential miasmas rise up from the places where the trash collects, not to mention that the sludge gets stuck between the paving stones. But that is not all. A far worse and unhealthier stench streams from the underground sewers that benumbs passersby, and forces residents to leave their houses. The sewage that runs into the Seine creates a swamp on the banks that pollutes the water used for washing or drinking by half the inhabitants of Paris.[128]

It was impossible to change these unsanitary conditions though the administration constantly issued new regulations. Expansion of the underground sewer system was urgently needed; failing that, their measures made little difference.[129]

Restoration Society

*L*IKE ALL CONSTITUTIONAL MONARCHIES, the Restoration was a transitional regime; it used up its energies in self-made contradictions and was incapable of planning any sort of future for itself. This is demonstrated by the largely uncontrolled demographic, economic, and urban development of Paris up to 1848. The royalist reaction of 1822, following the liberal phase of the regime, unleashed a period of internal political instability masked only by an economic boom that lasted until 1826. Having to confront the liberal opposition and deal with the economic recession, the government simply marked time. This was bound to have an adverse effect on the situation in Paris.

The helplessness of the government was matched by the complete indifference of the governed to all social and political questions. The art critic Etienne-Jean Delécluze refers to this at various times in his diary.[130] Even the most important political questions, such as the law concerning restitution for returning emigrants, failed to arouse public discussion. A general apathy overtook public, cultural, and political life, and created the strangely empty atmosphere that Stendhal describes with almost photographic precision in his novels *Armance* and *Le Rouge et le Noir*.

Not that there was a dearth of talent, or of new movements in literature and art. Quite the contrary: disciples of two diametrically opposed theories of art and life, spread over three different generations, were caught up in diverse and lively intellectual debates with each other. The older generation—in its forties at the beginning of the Restoration, consequently about sixty at the time of the July Revolution—was still dedicated to the classical tradition. In the controversy surrounding Victor Hugo's drama *Hernani ou l'honneur castillane* at the Théâtre-Français on February 25, 1830, this aging rearguard was the target of Préault's taunt: "Bald heads to the guillotine!"[131] The next generation, between twenty and forty-five years old in 1815, was deeply affected by the events of its lifetime. Its members were those who mourned the passing of Napoleonic grandeur, a loss that had robbed them of their chance for advancement. Finally, the third and youngest generation had experienced Napoleon's defeat, and anticipated limited opportunities in the social stagnation of the Restoration. This group was therefore all the readier to question traditional ideas and concepts, or to reject them as unsuitable. The view of life held by these individuals, who considered themselves a lost generation, was expressed in Alfred de Musset's *La Confession d'un Enfant du Siècle*.[132]

The endless intellectual feuds between these three generations led to many public lectures on the most varied subjects and to the formation of numerous literary circles; the feuds also fed the paradoxically dynamic stagnation that characterized the Restoration.[133] It was quite typical of the intellectual climate of those years as well that many people became dilettantes in intellectual or artistic spheres other than those for which they were gifted or trained. For instance Ampère, the scientist, tried to gain acceptance as a philosopher; the painter Delacroix and the composer Berlioz wanted to be considered writers; and Hugo and Mérimée attempted sketching. This intellectual or artistic nomadism, this striving to make a name for oneself in various fields of cultural endeavor was, from a superficial point of view, consistent with the romantic concept of genius. In reality, though, it only reflected a reaction to the social emptiness that was the bane of all these efforts.

Much of this intellectual bustle did not amount to anything, but it left its mark on the social life of the Restoration. The many Parisian literary salons of the Restoration have been immortalized by Mme Ancelot and the duchesse d'Abrantes in their memoirs. Reading them today still gives one the impression that the social life of those times possessed an enviable intellectual and cultural liveliness, and that it basked in a fashionable radiance.

The world of the salons was divided into different spheres. These spheres were defined first in social terms and then by their different interests. The old aristocracy of the faubourg Saint-Germain was, with few exceptions, based on strict exclusivity.[134] As under the Empire, this tended to intensify its social marginality.[135] On the other hand, anyone who possessed a modicum of talent, elegance, wit, or intellect had access to the world of the bankers, the newly rich, and the parvenus of finance and commerce. There were also several salons and groups of a decidedly intellectual nature, such as those of the painter Gérard in the rue Bonaparte and the critic Delécluze in the rue de Chabanais; or the most famous and most influential of them all, Charles Nodier's salon in the Bibliothèque de l'Arsenal, which was especially favored by the Romantics. And then there was Juliette Récamier's salon in the Abbaye-aux-Bois in the rue de Sèvres, which was hardly less famous or influential.[136]

This seemingly unchanged and animated social world, in which members of different intellectual spheres and social backgrounds mingled—and which supposedly mirrored the splendor of prerevolutionary conviviality—was brought to an abrupt end in 1830 by three factors. In the first place there was the matter of the political and ideological convictions that had dominated public debate since the Revolution, splitting it into two opposing camps. The irreconcilable polarization had a distinctly negative influence on the charm, gallantry, intellectual diversity, and freedom that had been characteristic of prerevolutionary salon culture.

The second problem was that while the salons and gatherings had previously been the sole venue of public debate, they now faced competition from a growing and partisan press. These newspapers were available only on expensive yearly subscriptions, and their print runs were comparatively small.[137] To deal with this difficulty, readers either formed subscription groups, or went to cafés or *cabinets de lecture* (public reading rooms) where they could browse in a wealth of national and international journals. Stendhal admits in his *Souvenirs d'Egotisme* that in the 1820s (which he spent in Paris) he liked above all to indulge in a "very innocent pleasure": "Quand il faisait chaud, aller lire les journaux anglais dans le jardin de Galignani" ("When it was hot, I liked to go and read the English papers in the Jardin de Galignani").[138]

Through these methods of distribution, which were typical of the period, readerships were considerably larger than the thousand or so copies in which papers were printed. This meant that the press created a much wider and more varied, as well as better-informed, public than the older salon culture had been able to do. Furthermore, the press was more capable than the salon of instructing and influencing the public because it was accessible to members of all parties and movements without their having to fear social sanctions. A traditional liberal could read a royalist paper, just as an ultra-royalist could find out what the views of his opponent were by reading a liberal journal. And newspapers created a battlefield by enabling members of opposing parties to express their arguments, a confrontation that would promptly have ruined a salon. Finally, because of its wide audience the press gave talented writers or those with trenchant opinions a quicker chance to become known, and to flatter themselves that their influence was effective. In this connection it is revealing to read the critic Delécluze, who confided his concerns for the intellectual exclusivity of his regular Sunday gatherings to his diary:

> These incredible intellectual intrigues, this constant exchange of ideas available in print, this fickleness in tastes, habits, and morals that lets everything flit past us with the speed of lightning, deny the intellect and the heart the time really to become attached to anything. The multiplicity of sensations prevents any single one from enduring, and everyone suffers from the sickness that used only to befall the rich: no passions, no desire, and no hope. . . .
> The only though not especially stimulating thing that at least manages to exist in this ocean of boredom is the brilliant *esprit* that has meantime also become public property in France. But this *esprit* is rather sterile as soon as more than just current matters are involved; I for my part am sick of this sort of thing and especially of the way in which it is dealt with. These days everyone is writing something and almost everyone is writing for newspapers; and all these writer-experts give the impression that they only visit the salons to get material for another article. When it concerns matters of *esprit* they behave like traveling salesmen who arrive at the feeding grounds and are not afraid to betray the most intimate secrets of a friendship just to get an alleged bon mot into print, or have a scandalmongering anecdote published.[139]

Delécluze is in effect describing the structural change in the public world that rendered the old aristocratic salon culture obsolete. After all, it was closed to those whom the Revolution had emancipated into politically aware *citoyens*. Only the bourgeoisie had access to the salons, which ultimately degenerated into marriage markets, or served as rumor mills and news agencies. It was precisely the misuse of social gatherings, combined with a general desire for more widely disseminated information, that created a more sophisticated public. The new public was superior to that of the salons; Etienne de Jouy describes the boredom experienced at the salon gatherings:

> I am astonished by the sterility of the discussions in society; and the vain emptiness of the new speakers in the salons amazes me no less than the unshakable patience of those who listen to them. Today a bon mot is an extraordinary event in the capital; one fights not over the honor of having coined it, but over having been the first one to repeat it.[140]

The third factor to influence the decline of the salon was the development of classless public spaces. The motley crowd for which the Palais-Royal had become too small and which flooded the arcades, cafés, restaurants, public reading rooms, theaters, balls, gardens, and boulevards proved that everyone who could afford it now had the right to enjoy recreation and entertainment. Free of the constraints of social etiquette, members of a pluralistic and largely bourgeois public could arrange to meet in these places according to their political inclination, individual preference, or daily itinerary. Thus Stendhal, who was unemployed during the Restoration and therefore led a precariously idle life in Paris, spent his day in cafés and public reading rooms. For nine years, he reports in the *Souvenirs d'Egotisme*, he breakfasted every morning with his friend Lussinge in the Café de Rouen. When he grew tired of his friend's company, he chose the famous liberal Café Lemblin in the Palais-Royal.[141] And even after dinner, he writes, "I enjoyed being at the café. Much more so than walking along the boulevard de Gand, which was very popular but also very dusty.[142] It was a real torture for me to spend time where dressed-up shop assistants, officers of the Garde, first-class prostitutes, and their elegant bourgeois rivals frolicked around."[143]

The arcades and the better cafés, whose comfort and luxury satisfied even the most demanding customers, also attracted a clientele that did not have access to exclusive private circles and salons, as Stendhal's example shows.[144] Stendhal frequented the fashionable cafés as well as numerous Restoration salons. In the less constrained atmosphere of the cafés or public reading rooms, among a mixed group of friends and acquaintances, it was possible to air all sorts of topics—including politics, which were strictly forbidden in most salons. Moreover, one could avoid the boredom of the sort of conversation to which one was exposed, for better or worse, the minute one entered a salon. "Spent the evening with Louise," Delécluze notes in his diary on July 4, 1825,

> where Mme la comtesse d'Hautpoult-Beaufort, the poetess, was present, who bored us for two hours by raving on about the wonderful times in Barèges and Toulouse before the Revolution! There really is nothing worse than people of that class talking about their social life. It is only a series of banalities, just like those that all the other classes experience daily; but in this case they acquire a somewhat artificial importance from the resounding names of counts and duchesses; and afterwards one is all the more aggravated for having paid so much attention.[145]

The question arises as to why this old-fashioned salon culture continued to exist at all in Restoration Paris, when there were so many other possibilities for freer and certainly more stimulating social encounters; why men like Delécluze, Stendhal, *e tutti quanti* favored these more or less exclusive circles although they were often terribly bored. There is a simple answer: despite the changes, real Parisian society still existed. In cultural and above all economic terms, the bourgeoisie may have played the dominant role; but the aristocracy still controlled social status. Free talents like Delécluze and Stendhal could find general acceptance in this society only if they could count on sponsorship. The bestowing and receiving of approval was the whole point of the salon. One had to find an entrée and to prove oneself; so that if one had sufficient talent and the right opportunity, one would at some point be rewarded for all the hours suffered there and be accepted by "society."

With the clairvoyance that is sometimes born of hate, Philarète Chasles chronicles the rapid social advance enjoyed by François Villemain, François Guizot, and Victor Cousin through the protection they enjoyed in Restoration salons:

> All three were just ordinary bourgeois without social distinction . . . or any connections to the salons or to elegant society. They made these only after they had done their homework; despite their more than careless manners, a few ladies permitted them to visit their salons, which was the indispensable first step for any man who wanted to succeed in France. The two pedants, Villemain and Cousin, accomplished this through the university and through friendships—one as a friend of M. de Narbonne, the other as the protégé of M. de la Romiguière. As for M. Guizot, he achieved all of this much faster; he also passed through the needle's eye of salon society (without which there is no luck) with greater ease because he was a Protestant: Madame de Rumfort, whose circle intersected with the salons of Madame Garat, Madame Récamier, Madame de Staël and other ladies then in fashion, took the young Protestant under her wing.[146]

Whatever its political implications, the Restoration saw a reorganization of society which also made it an "intellectual-moral turning point," as evidenced by the renewed vigor of the salon culture. There was, however, a visible revival of class consciousness that erected unsurmountable barriers between the families of the old aristocracy and the rest of society. Members of the faubourg Saint-Germain treated the *noblesse d'Empire* (the Napoleonic administrative nobility), as well as those who had been ennobled under the Restoration, with ostentatious contempt. An example of this was the experience of the former minister Antoine Roy one evening in January 1829. Roy had become very rich as a supplier to Napoleon's army, and Louis XVIII had created him a count: "M. Roy gave a big ball last night. The entire court had been invited, but was noticeably absent. . . . M. de Polignac was the only one who ignored the ostracism provoked by the plebeian name of M. Roy."[147]

The old aristocracy's snobbery marked the point to which the social pendulum had returned under Charles X, after having moved so far to the other side during the Revolution and the Empire. This backward movement could be observed in almost all areas of social life. Universal immorality, that seductive legacy of the Directory still enjoyed by the Empire, was at times replaced under the Restoration by bigoted piety. The Catholic Church, which had been raised to the level of state religion by the Charter of 1814, actually became the basic institution of the restored Bourbon monarchy. Sick of the godless cult of reason, people now desired a society with Christian ethics, and looked to intellectuals like Chateaubriand, whose very popular work *Le Genie du christianisme* provided a social plan based on Christianity. It is not surprising, therefore, that at first the dominant role assigned to the Catholic Church was passively accepted; for example, there was no resistance to the abolition of divorce, which was not reintroduced until the secular Third Republic.

It is also symptomatic of the times that the architectural legacy left by the Restoration was largely one of churches: Notre-Dame-de-Lorette, Saint-Ambroise and Saint-Vincent-de-Paul. But the most striking church of all erected in that period was the monumental Chapelle Expiatoire, designed by Fontaine and Percier in memory of Louis XVI and Marie-Antoinette, and situated on the site of the former revolutionary cemetery in which the corpse of Citizen Capet had been buried.[148] The reerection of monuments removed by the Revolution was also characteristic of the program of Christian dynastic renewal: the equestrian statues of Henry IV on the Pont Neuf, of Louis XIII in the place Royale, of Louis XIV in the place des Victoires, and the bas-relief of the Sun King on the facade of the Invalides. The bridges known as Concorde and Austerlitz were renamed Pont Louis XVI and Pont du Jardin du Roi. The quai Montebello became the quai Saint-Michel, and the Lycée Bonaparte turned into the Lycée Bourbon. Saints and aristocrats gave their names again to the streets that had once carried them.

These and similar efforts to reestablish the historic continuity and legitimacy disrupted by the Revolution failed, as had those of other restoration regimes, to obliterate the historic forces that had been at work. The changes were too deep-seated for the world of the Old Regime to be resuscitated one generation after its disappearance. The Restoration, in fact, perpetuated the legacy of the Revolution and the Empire.

For the most vivid example of this one must look to gastronomy. During the Restoration the pleasures of the table attained their ultimate triumph: since that time *grande cuisine* belongs to the patrimony of French civilization. The culinary arts, which had been democratized by the Revolution and had seen their first flowering in the Palais-Royal restaurants, now gained a firm foothold in Restoration society where they were truly assimilated. "Most memories of wit, friendship, business, yes, even the reminiscences of extraordinary happenings or political events," writes the scintillating Docteur Louis-Désiré Véron, one of the frequenters of the Café de Paris, "are associated with those dinners."[149]

The reputation of French cuisine actually dates back to the Paris of the Empire; but it was only through the long peaceful period beginning with the Restoration that this renown spread to the farthest corners of the world. Paris and French cuisine became synonymous, and it was impossible to imagine life in Paris without its restaurants:

> No other capital of Europe can boast of such luxurious establishments open day and night with varied menus, in which one can have a meal at any time, and where one can enjoy peace and solitude among the crowd. Writers, princes, artists, judges, ministers, deputies, soldiers, foreigners from all over, Croesuses of all classes and ages, beauties from the north or south—how many races and eccentrics the viewer sees, as they meet at tables, *inter pocula*, which anyone can join! And there is no longer a single Parisian who does not indulge himself on certain days, by dining at the Café de Paris, at the Frères Provençaux, at the Café Anglais, at Riche, Véry, or Véfour.[150]

In those days the pleasures of the table were considered works of art, to be celebrated with unheard-of extravagance in spite of their ephemerality. Every dinner, whether enjoyed at one of the restaurants famous for its cuisine or at a private home, became an event awaited with much anticipation and recalled with relish. The importance of gastronomy in the life and consciousness of society comes through in the literature of the period. In Balzac such depictions become a veritable topos of bourgeois or aristocratic life. For instance in *Le Père Goriot*, the impoverished Eugène de Rastignac, who lives in a scruffy *pension*, is invited to dinner at the house of a very rich relative for the first time:

> They went into the dining room, where the vicomte awaited his wife and where the table glowed in magnificent splendor, with a luxury which, as everyone knows, reached its height under the Restoration. M. de Beauséant, like other bored people, no longer had any pleasures save those of the table. As a gourmet he belonged to the school of Louis XVIII and the duc d'Escars. His table therefore offered a double luxury: that of the settings as well as of the food.[151]

Here Balzac once more proves himself a careful observer of his times. Doubtless the Restoration was the heyday of extravagant cuisine, whereas during the July Monarchy one ate out of necessity rather than enjoyment. That, at any rate, is the essence of reports from that period.[152] But perhaps such generalizations should be taken with a grain of salt, for while it is true that the tradition of *grande cuisine* began with the Restoration, it has survived over the centuries.

Though the Restoration was a period of stagnation, it did introduce two technical innovations that were to change the face of Paris in the nineteenth century: gas lighting and the municipal bus. But gas lighting, that quietly humming marvel that was to give the nights in the capital a magical brightness, took twelve years to become operative because of public fears and administrative inactivity.

Gas lighting was a French invention—coal gas was discovered by the engineer Philippe Lebon in 1791—but its technology was first developed in England and used in London. The method became known in Paris in 1816, and the *Chambre des Pairs* in the Palais du Luxembourg was the first institution in the capital to enjoy its use. At the beginning of 1818 a gasometer was installed in a former church near the rue d'Enfer, with sufficient capacity to illuminate the Théâtre de l'Odéon as well. A second, larger gasworks was built in the rue du faubourg Poissonière by an English company in 1822, so that the new Opera as well as the Saint-Louis hospital had gas lighting. There were no further installations until 1829, when a few gas streetlights were put up in the place Vendôme, the rue de la Paix, and the rue Castiglione. But the real victory of gas street lighting did not occur until after 1835, when the inner-city oil lamps were rapidly replaced.[153]

The second important innovation, which also heralded a new age, was the introduction of the horse-drawn omnibus in 1828—the first means of mass public transportation. These buses, which drove along specific inner-city routes at regular intervals, were an invention that was in the air, so to speak. Paris had been expanding continuously; and though most residents still confined their activities to their immediate neighborhoods, this custom no longer corresponded to the city's diversified economic reality.[154] In the wake of the social homogenization of the arrondissements, merchants and artisans no longer found their clientele in their immediate vicinity. But it was very laborious and time-consuming to cover longer distances on foot, the streets of those times still being narrow, congested, and filthy. Only the wealthy could afford carriages, or the lighter and more maneuverable cabriolets; the same applied to the hackneys, cabs, and cabriolets of concessionaires, which were available all over the city for 3 francs 50 per hour in the daytime and 5 francs at night.[155]

This privileged transportation system for those who could afford it was destroyed by the establishment of bus lines with a uniform tariff of only 25 centimes. Depending on its construction, a horse-drawn bus could carry between twelve and twenty passengers. The new system was so successful that eight lines were established by 1828; they immediately had competition from similar enterprises with names like *Dames-Blanches, Favorites, Citadines, Hirondelles,* and *Parisiennes,* which took care of another twenty-six routes.[156]

Of course the development of horse-drawn buses was not as great a revolution in transportation as that of the railroads which not only created a new country but a new human type.[157] Still, buses heralded this vast development. Paris with its gas lighting and public transportation was no longer the old city of Charles X, unchanged since the *grand siècle* of Louis XIV. The outlines of a new Paris were now visible in the gentle glow of the gas lights; with the advent of horse-drawn buses, the city entered modern times.

The July Revolution

*T*HE STRANGE, JANUS-HEADED, paradoxical period of the Restoration ended in the mighty convulsions of another revolution that resulted from the combination of a backward-looking Bourbon regime and the modernization symbolized by gas lighting and buses. It became obvious that the Restoration had only been an interlude that had failed to kill the hopes and desires awakened by the Revolution and the Empire. The change in regime and administration, and the wide influence of Catholicism on state and society, were not sufficient to blot out the history of a generation that had been moved by so many expectations and disappointments. For however contradictorily the Revolution and the Empire had been experienced, they had shaped everyone's aspirations. The Bourbon government was sheltered from discontent as long as the population was still stunned from the catastrophe and decline of the Empire. This state of affairs was soon undermined by an economic recession which set in at the end of 1826, and the subsequent agricultural crisis.

As noted in the discussion on work and wages, the number of bankruptcies increased in Paris in 1826; in fact the number doubled as against the preceding year.[158] Overall unemployment rose and wages, especially those in the building trades, were cut by up to 20 percent.[159] Lack of work did not prevent the influx of seasonal workers which added to the army of unemployed.[160] By 1828, a recession originally limited to certain sections of industry affected the entire economy.[161]

Once again as in 1811, poor harvests contributed to the general downward turn of the economy. A rainy summer in 1828 destroyed most of the grain harvest. The result was that after some years of abundance, during which the price of a four-pound loaf of bread stayed between 60 and 65 centimes in Paris, wheat prices rose 40 percent over those of 1825; in May 1829 the difference reached 60 percent. Thus, while the average price of a four-pound loaf was 95 centimes in the autumn of 1828, by the following May it cost 1 franc 5 centimes. The price never fell below 75 centimes until August 1830.[162] The Paris administration decided to subsidize the price of bread so that the maximum cost to the working class—already suffering from wage cuts and unemployment—would not rise above 80 centimes. But this subsidy was only intended to benefit the *classe nécessiteuse* (the needy), proving that the authorities had learned from the expensive mistakes made under similar conditions at the beginning of the Restoration.[163] According to Chabrol's statistics, this group numbered 100,000 at the beginning of January 1829 and reached its absolute ceiling of 227,399 in the first half of July of that year.[164]

The misery brought on by rising bread prices, wage cuts and mass unemployment was further aggravated by bad weather. The winters of 1828-29 and 1829-30 saw many weeks of severe cold that were particularly hard on the poor and needy. Soup kitchens and heated shelters were promptly organized and helped somewhat, but the signs of suffering were similar to those of the early famine winters of the Revolution. There were more suicides, as well as a frightening increase in the number of abandoned children, who roamed the streets cold and hungry.[165]

To the relief of the authorities this gloomy picture quickly changed in the spring of 1830. The price of bread began to fall, and demand in the important building trades improved to such an extent that work was always available for the hundreds of people who showed up daily in the place de Grève. Business improved in other trades as well, which in turn improved wage rates. The crisis of the past four years began to seem like a bad memory. This optimism even informed the daily police reports, which kept referring to the *tranquillité la plus parfaite* ("the utmost tranquility"); the statement by Police Prefect Mangin, on July 26, 1830, confirms this as being the case "everywhere in the city. The reports I have received contain no mention of any event worth noting."[166]

Apparently the administration and the prefect of police, whose spies and informers had infiltrated the most varied social groups in the capital and who made daily reports on what they observed, remained in complete ignorance of the situation. No one noticed the signs, or heard the rumbling of the volcano about to erupt. The revolution of July 1830 seemed to break out with the suddenness of a summer storm.

There is one plausible explanation for everyone's inability to predict the portentous events of the *Trois Glorieuses* (the so-called Three Glorious Days of July 27, 28, and 29), which signaled the reemergence of Paris on the political stage of France and Europe. It is that the happenings were of a purely political nature, leading to an abrupt change of regime. This is precisely where the July Revolution contradicted the lesson of the experiences of 1789; namely, that if the misery of the *classes laborieuses* were kept at a minimum they would not resort to revolt. Officials and contemporary observers who held this view were relieved to see an improvement in the economy as of the spring of 1830 and hoped it would keep violent reactions at bay. This general expectation was transformed to the point of certainty in police reports, especially since earlier and no less severe economic crises had not generated unrest among the *classes laborieuses.*

Even the prime minister, Prince Jules de Polignac, whom Charles X had appointed to head an ultra-royalist cabinet in 1829, concluded mistakenly that the opposition to king and government in the spring of 1830 was limited to a small, ineffective liberal minority. Liberal attempts to stir up the masses had failed and would not succeed in the future because, as Polignac set out in a paper of April 14, 1830, the *peuple* were interested only in their material welfare which was well taken care of by the crown.[167] The time seemed ripe to destroy those who obstinately opposed the government's efforts to interpret the Charter in an increasingly royalist sense.

This was accomplished by dissolving the Chamber and setting June 23 and July 3 as dates for new elections. But the elections proved disastrous for the government, which (together with the clergy) had tried to influence their outcome. Instead of the 221 deputies who had formed the opposition in the old Chamber, there were now 274 out of a total of 401 deputies who rejected the policies of Polignac's cabinet to a greater or lesser degree. In view of these results Charles X decided on a coup from above. He intended to prepare for it by issuing four decrees, worked out in utmost secrecy, which would be released in the *Moniteur,* the government paper, on July 26 after being countersigned by his ministers. The contents of the four decrees, which could be said to have started the July Revolution, gave unmistakable notice of the crown's intention to do away with the liberal Charter. As for the details, the decrees eliminated freedom of the press, and reintroduced prior censorship; furthermore, the newly elected Chamber was to be dissolved and new election laws instituted under which the eligibility of active and passive voters was narrowed down still further, and the number of deputies limited to 258.

All in all the four decrees amounted to another 18 Brumaire, which, in the apt words of Louis Blanc, the liberal bourgeoisie dreaded as much as another August 10 [1792, the sacking of the Tuileries].[168] This explains the great confusion and consternation in liberal circles once the decrees became known, though these very circles had been expecting a reaction from the crown following the Chamber elections. But it was characteristic of the political attitude of the liberals that their fears were always counterbalanced by the expectation that the king would give in and accept the fait accompli of the liberal election victory. . . . It was also characteristic of them that hardly had they recovered from the shock produced by the royal intentions, than they began lengthy deliberations that ended in a very subdued resolution of protest.[169]

In view of the moderate attitude of the liberals and the fact that Paris remained calm on July 26 (a very hot day), the government and administration thought they had gained the upper hand.[170] But there was some activity in the Palais-Royal, where a group of younger people had climbed on tables and chairs; they were reading the royal decrees, printed in the *Moniteur*, to the public—very much in the manner of Camille Desmoulins.[171] The Palais-Royal also became the setting for the first signs of unrest that same evening, when the police attempted to confiscate a printing press in one of the shops, attracting a group of protesters. News of these happenings spread like wildfire and within an hour a dense crowd had formed in the gardens of the Palais-Royal. The police arrived at half past ten to clear the gardens and lock the gates, whereupon the crowd moved to the place du Palais-Royal. When they were driven away from there as well, the protesters split up into two demonstrating groups. One proceeded along the rue de Rivoli where they destroyed some streetlights as well as a few windows in the Ministry of Finance. The other group moved along the rue Castiglione, across the place Vendôme and the rue de la Paix, toward the boulevards.[172]

The demonstrators went home about midnight and the city became calm again, so that on the morning of July 27 the authorities were even more certain that they were in control of the situation. This was a fatal mistake, for during the day the passive resistance turned to open protest. Three opposition newspapers, *Le National*, *Le Globe*, and *Le Temps*, gave the signal for outright resistance, despite the ban on publication. Louis Blanc gives a good description of this agitation:

> Hundreds of copies of these papers were distributed in the cafés, the public reading rooms, and restaurants. Journalists went from workshop to workshop, from store to store, to read from the papers and comment on the information. One could see well-dressed, elegant men standing on curbstones addressing the passing crowd, while students, who had been enticed from their quarters by the susceptibility natural to the young, ran through the streets waving their hats and shouting *"Vive la Charte!"*[173]

The confiscation and destruction of the three newspapers' printing presses by detachments of a force of 12,000 men concentrated in Paris and its environs, incited those inclined to revolt still further.[174] In the afternoon of July 27 these troops had to break up crowds gathered at various barricades that had been erected near the rue Saint-Honoré, in the streets around the Bourse, and in the place Vendôme. Around eleven o'clock at night everything was calm again and the troops returned to their barracks.[175]

Though this development pointed to a violent overthrow of the regime, deputies of the liberal opposition continued to remain timid. Meeting at the house of Casimir Périer, they agreed to resist the royal decrees by legal means only. But this reaction was overtaken by what occurred on the following day, when unrest turned to revolution.

During the night of July 27-28 additional barricades were put up, especially in the central and eastern districts of Paris. Workers from the faubourg Saint-Antoine forced their way into stores selling weapons and plundered them; trees were felled in the boulevards and buses were overturned to strengthen the barricades. Demonstrators occupied the Hôtel de Ville and raised the tricolor flag at eleven o'clock on the morning of the 28th, after it had been vacated peacefully by its defenders. Here troops of the royal army began to fraternize more and more with the rebels, whereas elsewhere there was severe fighting, such as in the place des Innocents, the place de Grève and the rue Saint-Antoine.[176] In view of the complex situation—many of the troops were unfamiliar with the topography of Paris and roamed the inner city's maze of streets aimlessly, while the residents pelted them with flowerpots, stones, and other objects—the commander in chief, Marshal Marmont, ordered his troops to withdraw. This retreat decided the outcome, as government troops now controlled only a narrow corridor from the Louvre and the Tuileries in the east to the barrière de l'Etoile in the west. The rest of the city was in the hands of the revolutionaries, who had meantime set up still more barricades in the central and eastern sections.

It was clear that nothing but substantial concessions to the rebels would enable the Bourbons to hold on to the throne. But neither side realized this. While Charles X waited in his palace at Saint-Cloud, far from the bloody fray and hoping that Marmont would gain control of the uprising, the frightened liberal deputies floundered from one embarrassing situation to another, concerned not to compromise themselves. Finally some of them managed to sign a statement protesting the dissolution of the newly elected Chamber, while anxiously trying not to question the king's authority. Because of the cowardice of the liberals—Thiers fled Paris to avoid what he believed was imminent arrest, and Charles de Rémusat hid himself at the duc de Broglie's—blood continued to be shed on July 29.[177]

To begin with the center of that day's fighting was the Louvre, where a battalion of Swiss troops was stationed. When they could no longer withstand the attackers and withdrew along the rue du Carrousel, the troops assigned to defend the Tuileries panicked. They all fled the center of the city, making their way out of Paris via the Champs-Elysées. And once again the sacking of the Tuileries by the *peuple* marked the victory of Paris over the crown.

While the crowd was getting drunk in the wine cellars of the Tuileries, several hundred insurgents captured the barracks of the Swiss Guards in the rue de Babylone, on the Left Bank of the Seine; the archbishop's palace was also raided, and its furniture and books were thrown into the river. In the course of the afternoon the rebels gained complete control of Paris and the revolution was successful—a fact that the participants only gradually understood. Now at last the frightened and confused liberal deputies began to react. Their first concern was to prevent a political radicalization of the revolution and to impose on it their own kind of constitutional framework.[178] It is against this background that the public statement signed by Thiers and several other liberals on July 30 must be read. It rejected Charles X as well as the idea of a republic, which was equated with chaos and war. Circumventing all the rules of succession, it nominated the duc d'Orléans, who, in a move that smacked of Talleyrand, was described for the first time as a "citizen-king."[179]

The document also contained the scenario for what was to take place: on August 2, Charles X abdicated and left for exile in England; on August 3, the Chambers met to revise the Charter; that is, to create the constitutional requirements under which the duc d'Orléans could succeed to the throne. The deputies then went to the Palais-Royal on August 7, to inform the duc d'Orléans officially that he had been elected king of France. He ascended the throne on August 9, as Louis-Philippe I, after having sworn to uphold the revised Charter. Thus the July Monarchy emerged from this peculiar Revolution to take its place in history. It was a strange outcome insofar as the political solution consisted only of a change in dynasty; its representative was considered liberal and at first he was very popular among all sections of the population.[180]

However, beneath the seemingly untroubled surface of the historical events lay the problems contained in the much-debated question of the driving forces of the July Revolution. The famous painting by Eugène Delacroix *Liberty Leading the People* became the icon of the *Trois Glorieuses*. It symbolized the hopes rather than the historical reality of this Revolution that determined the course of the entire nineteenth century. And even the current interpretation of the July Revolution as a "bourgeois revolution" is an inadmissible simplification of the complexity of an event generated by thoroughly diverse motives, causes, and coincidences. First of all, one has to bear in mind that no one had vision enough to foresee the July Revolution. Its outbreak so surprised everyone that even when it was in full swing they were unable to grasp the fact of its occurrence, not to speak of its portent. This was especially true of the liberal opposition, indecisive as it was in its reaction to both crown and *peuple*.

The phenomenology of the July Revolution consists of a mixture of familiar old elements and new ones, whose "chemistry" produced and sustained the chain reaction of the *Trois Glorieuses*. For one last time the Palais-Royal played a special role in the history of Paris, as it had done in the summer of 1789. It was the place where the anger and dissatisfaction of journalists and printers, whose livelihoods were threatened by the new decrees, sparked and stoked the revolutionary fervor of workers, artisans, and petty shopkeepers.[181] The part played on the barricades by insurgents from the central and eastern districts is also familiar.

There were, on the other hand, two new elements: the emergence of modern journalism, and the myth of Napoleon.

As Louis Blanc convincingly describes it, the agitation begun by the journalists and printers on July 27 at first hardly affected the *peuple;* at best it aroused their curiosity. Moreover, the bourgeoisie's concerns over the royal decrees, and especially the significance of their battle cry *"Vive la Charte,"* were far beyond the experiential horizon of the *peuple.* What helped to bring the two completely alien spheres of life closer together was the contagion of violent agitation and unrest, which tends to influence those who are not part of it. But what gave the *peuple* a cause with which they could identify was the appointment of Marshal Marmont, duc de Ragusa, on July 27, as commander of the royal troops. As Louis Blanc maintains, the name of the duc de Ragusa, whose capitulation in 1814 had hastened Napoleon's downfall and the end of the Empire, was synonymous in the eyes of the *peuple* with national humiliation and disgrace: "In appointing Marshal Marmont, duc de Ragusa, to command its defenders, the old monarchy severely compounded the extent of its mistakes; because in doing so, it transformed a dispute that only concerned the bourgeoisie into a matter for the *peuple.*"[182]

Marmont's command of "bourgeois fighting troops" surely activated the latent and growing resentment against the Bourbons, and made the idealized memory of Napoleon stand out more clearly.[183] This may also explain why the unrest at first manifested itself when the crowds tore down and destroyed the royal coats of arms attached to the shops of suppliers to the king. "All of this," writes Louis Blanc, "was nothing but unrest. The tricolor flag was hoisted. Then the revolution began."[184] Such is the power of symbols: the tricolor, which appeared here and there on July 28, was raised on one of the two towers of Notre Dame where it was visible all over the city, fluttering in the breeze. Attention was drawn to it when the big, seldom-heard bell began to ring. For the tricolor was a popular symbol of the Revolution and the Empire, as well as of resistance to the Bourbons and their foreign allies.[185]

And yet this seemingly sudden unity between an infuriated but also hesitant and action-shy bourgeoisie, and the *peuple* who were swayed by symbols and memories and were willing to die at the barricades for a cause they barely understood, actually had a longer history. There had been evidence that the *peuple* identified its own demands and hopes with the political expectations of the liberal backers of the constitutional monarchy since the early 1820s. For instance, prominent liberals like General Foy, whose funeral took place at the end of November 1825 and was attended by an enormous crowd, were very popular. Other well-liked liberals, made familiar to the *classes laborieuses* by the liberal press, included Casimir Périer, Benjamin Constant, or the already all but fossilized Lafayette. The press also helped acquaint the *classes laborieuses* with liberal slogans and demands.[186] As they had done prior to the Revolution of 1789, the *peuple* of the Restoration took their cue from the middle class's attitude toward the Bourbons.[187]

Mercier had already pointed this out.[188] But the present orientation was more political: the press, the cheap political pamphlets, and even the poems and songs of Béranger popularized liberal and national policies and made the lower classes at least superficially aware of them. None of this affected the outcome of the July Revolution, however, as the republican movement was still in its infancy. In fact the working class clung to the myth of Napoleon until the Second Empire, immune to all other political doctrines.

But neither Napoleon's magic influence on the lower classes nor the symbolic importance of the tricolor in which Louis Blanc believed really offers a convincing explanation of why workers, artisans, petty shopkeepers and, in the final hours, a handful of students, were the ones to fight the July Revolution—while the bourgeoisie, portrayed in Delacroix's famous painting as an elegant man wearing a top hat, standing on the barricades holding a musket, watched in fear and indecision. A sociological analysis of the approximately three thousand dead and wounded insurgents of the *Trois Glorieuses* shows that about two-thirds of those fighting were less than thirty-five years old and were not born in Paris or the Department of the Seine. Moreover, most of them were employed in the building trades, which traditionally hired mainly seasonal workers.[189] In contrast, petty artisans like cabinetmakers, goldsmiths, tailors, weavers, wigmakers, and barkeepers did not play a major role in the uprising.[190] Yet these had been the very trades that had produced the *sans-culottes*.[191]

This leads one to conclude, as Prefect of Police Mangin had mistakenly done just before the 1830 Revolution, that the traditional artisan milieu, from which the revolutionary cadre of the Commune of 1792 had come, had turned conservative. It was also because of their fixation on that traditional revolutionary potential that the government and the liberal opposition completely ignored the pathological condition of Paris caused by the rootless seasonal immigrants.[192] Only in the July Revolution—which the liberal middle class had neither wanted nor controlled, but which it used for its own political ends—did this threat become obvious. The *Trois Glorieuses* revealed the outlines of a different revolutionary Paris, that of the *classes dangereuses*, that was to obsess the July Monarchy.

BOOK FIVE

Between Two Revolutions

1830–1848

The capital which is now going so merrily on, increasing with almost American rapidity, will soon ask to be invested; and when this happens, Paris will be seen running out of town with the same active pace that London has done before her; and twenty years hence the Bois de Boulogne may very likely be as thickly peopled as the Regent's Park is now.

Frances Trollope, *Paris and the Parisians in 1835*

Uprising of the Paris workers, June 23–27, 1848, put down by Eugène Cavaignac, the Minister of War. This period lithograph, captioned "The attack on the entrance to the faubourg du Temple," is by A. Provost, and comes from the series Souvenirs des journées de juin, 1848.
ARCHIV FÜR KUNST UND GESCHICHTE, BERLIN

The Great Disillusion

HE OUTCOME OF THE JULY REVOLUTION of 1830 was such that many of its contemporaries asked themselves whether, based on their experience, the *Trois Glorieuses* could even be described as a revolution. That is the gist of Casimir Périer's remarks to the prefect of the Department of the Seine at the time: "It is the misfortune of this country that many people like you believe that a revolution has taken place in France. No, Monsieur, there was no revolution; the only thing that happened was a simple changeover in the head of state."[1]

The Saint-Simonist Prosper Enfantin commented in a similar vein after the July events: "The holy revolt that occurred does not deserve the name of revolution; there was no basic change in the existing social structure; a few names, the national colors, the state's coat of arms, a few amended laws . . . ; such were the achievements of those days of sadness and glory."[2]

It is true that both statements describe the July Revolution as no more than a political upheaval; but while Périer found a satisfactory solution in a mere change in dynasty, Enfantin was clearly disappointed that the *Trois Glorieuses* had no effect on economic or social conditions. These interpretations, whose differences were to shape the physiognomy of the July Monarchy, were representative of two different political and social milieus—the bourgeoisie and the *peuple*.

In fact in social and economic terms, the July Revolution accomplished precisely the opposite of what its participants had expected. Instead of producing an improvement in the recession that had lasted since 1827, the *Trois Glorieuses* made it worse and the bourgeoisie became still more intransigent in its attitude toward the material needs of the *peuple*. The vague, incoherent fears and disorganized expectations of the latter encountered misunderstanding and constant denial on the part of the former.

Whatever disappointment was felt began to be expressed in various peaceful but also ineffective demonstrations and labor conflicts.[3] This ineffectiveness was partially due to the fact that demands and complaints differed according to trade. For instance, in their request to the prefect of police, the saddlers and coach-builders asked that the quota of foreign labor in their trades be lowered so as to deal with unemployment; whereas butcher apprentices demonstrated against a regulation that would prevent many of them from taking advantage of the right to become independent. The cabinet-makers wanted a wage increase, and the printers protested the installation of steam-driven flatbed presses that they feared would cause redundancies. The failure of these attempts at redress was partly due to lack of understanding in the bourgeois press. The latter believed that it recognized signs of a Carlist conspiracy that was making use of the very same elements that had driven Charles X from his throne three weeks earlier.[4] At first only Prefect of Police Girod de l'Ain, who was responsible for law and order, seemed to have some feeling for the Paris workers' complaints; in addition, the government set up a commission in August 1830 that was supposed to study the economic situation of the country and suggest appropriate measures to get trade and commerce going again.[5]

But the initial willingness on the part of the government and city administration to pay attention to the workers' needs gave way to an uncompromising laissez-faire policy once it was firmly established. So when the saddlers demonstrated to have their workday reduced from twelve to eleven hours, and when the cabinetmakers confronted Girod de l'Ain with demands that their wage rates be fixed, he replied that the free play of supply and demand applied to them as well.[6]

The prefect of police emphasized the authorities' intention not to interfere in labor problems by issuing an order on August 25 prohibiting demonstrations and unions, even if organized for peaceful purposes. The only thing permitted was that "if workers in Paris had valid demands they could present them, as individuals . . . to the relevant departments." But the right of individuals to lodge complaints was turned into an empty formula by the concluding paragraph of the order: "Demands that ask us to intervene in negotations between a master and his workers regarding wages or hours, or in work-related conflicts, will not be eligible as they are contrary to the laws, which postulate a free economy."[7]

This defined the basic policy that the government of the July Monarchy was to adopt toward the workers.[8] Sometimes, however, Girod de l'Ain contravened this policy, as when he intervened in favor of the workers in labor conflicts that broke out after August 25.[9]

In spite of increasing violations of the August 25 order, the prefect of the Seine, Odilon Barrot, reacted moderately.[10] Moreover, he tried to deal with social unrest by establishing *ateliers de secours* (public workshops), in which 6,000 people found employment in September.[11] But in a letter to the minister of the interior, dated September 30, 1830, he had to admit the failure of this plan, putting it down to "the sudden invasion of the *ateliers de secours*, organized by the city of Paris, by needy residents from other departments." He goes on:

> The number of individuals from the provinces who seek work here is constantly increasing, and it is therefore to be feared that despite preventive measures taken by the administration, the city will be unable to deal with these elements of misery and dissatisfaction. In view of this, there will be unrest, the city will be financially depleted, and further suffering for the *classe indigente* is inevitable.[12]

The *ateliers de secours* are an example of the initial weakness of the new regime; for instead of closing them down promptly, they were left open over the winter. At the end of December 1830 the number of individuals in these *ateliers* amounted to almost 11,000, of whom 6,000 alone were put to work excavating the Champ de Mars. But by then the authorities were forced to act, being mindful of the potential danger to public security and order caused by such a concentration of paupers. Troops had to be used three times (at the end of November, and the middle and end of December 1830) to break up disturbances caused by the workers in the Champ de Mars. This was sufficient warning for the authorities to close the *ateliers* in January.[13]

Closing the *ateliers de secours* did not provoke the expected unrest. Even the numerous labor conflicts, demonstrations, and attacks on machinery that had occurred since August ceased by November 1830, owing to everyone's preoccupation with a number of strictly political controversies. Furthermore, though Paris was the political capital of France, its industry and economy were not the most developed. The proof came a year later, in November 1831, when a bloody struggle developed in Lyon between the workers, trying to express their social aspirations, and the undiscerning, conservative, propertied bourgeoisie. Paris, which still had a mainly small-business economic structure, was not to see such a confrontation for another seventeen years— the revolution of June 1848.

It was typical of the July Monarchy that the urgent social issue posed by the pauperized lower classes was not recognized by the bourgeoisie. The constant conflicts were either regional or took place in isolated sectors, so that the middle-class public—a group of not even 200,000 voters out of a total of 32 million Frenchmen—and its press were simply able to deny the existence of a "social question." On the other hand, the petit-bourgeois groups among the *classes laborieuses* had no concept of a community of interests; their "class consciousness" developed only very slowly, since at first it was not directly influenced by the development of productive resources.

It was difficult for the *classes laborieuses* to recognize their shared corporative, social, and ultimately political interests because of the way in which they were recruited as an "industrial reserve army." Most of them were simple country folk, who suddenly found themselves confronted by what they saw as the strange and threatening phenomenon of the big city, where they were the victims not only of their bosses but also of landlords, café owners, and foremen—in short, everything connected with life and work. These circumstances contributed to keeping the *classes laborieuses* in a state of dependence and immaturity, and even of existential fear. Quite often this led to a loss of self-confidence that prompted them to protest; their actions were occasionally collective but unorganized, and hence ineffective as revolutionary movements.

Shifting Sands

OR THE RULING BOURGEOISIE the July Monarchy was "the best of all republics," enabling them to worship their two idols: power and profit. The new king, Louis-Philippe, was their ideal representative and was popularly thought of as being a liberal. He owed this reputation to his father "Philippe-Egalité," creator of the *Palais-Marchand*, one-time Jacobin and member of the Convention who, before being guillotined himself, had voted for the death of Louis XVI. Another reason for Louis-Philippe's liberal reputation was that he had fought in the Battle of Jemappes under Dumouriez and thus risked his life for the Revolution of 1789. After the downfall of the Girondins in 1793 Louis-Philippe had at first gone to live in exile in Switzerland; from there he went to the United States and finally to Naples, where he married Marie-Amélie, daughter of the king of the Two Sicilies. Though he had regained his immense fortune in the Restoration, it did not influence his outlook and he distanced himself from all counterrevolutionary activities. The well-known simplicity of his household, the typically bourgeois domestic happiness that he so evidently enjoyed, his reputation as a Voltairean, made Louis-Philippe the personification of the sort of "bourgeois king" that the Paris middle class had envisioned. For they distrusted the supposed disorder of a republic as well as the despotism of the Old Regime.[14]

Even as sovereign, Louis-Philippe maintained this bourgeois appearance during the early months of his reign. With his round hat on the head that Philippon rendered as a pear in his famous caricatures, and an umbrella on his arm, Louis-Philippe strolled through the streets of Paris. As Heinrich Heine writes, he played

> the role of an honest, unassuming paterfamilias with artful guilelessness. . . . He used to shake hands with every spice merchant and artisan, and it is said that he wore a special dirty glove for that purpose, which he always took off and exchanged for a cleaner kid glove when he kept more elevated company and went to see the old aristocrats, his banker-ministers, intriguers, and amaranthine . . . lackeys. When I saw him last, he was strolling up and down among the little gold turrets, marble vases, and flowers on the roof of the Galerie d'Orléans. He was wearing a black frock-coat, and his broad face showed an unconcern that almost makes us shudder when we think of the man's insecure position.[15]

As part of this bourgeois bonhomie, Louis-Philippe continued to live in the Palais-Royal until 1831; it had been given a new lease on life by the July Revolution. Hardly had he been proclaimed king when people flocked there from all over Paris to acclaim him and call out to him to appear at a window or on a balcony. People seeking positions flooded the royal chancellery with petitions and applications, and delegations appeared one after another in the royal apartments. When after a week's time the activity seemed to have become uncontrollable, a "guard of honor" formed spontaneously; but, as it turned out, they were like all the others. "This troop," the Prince de Joinville reports,

> camped on the stairs and in the vestibule day and night. They were nothing but a group of unemployed and layabouts of the worst kind; moreover, they were supplied with stolen weapons belonging to the Musée d'artillerie, from which some of them had even taken some cuirasses and helmets dating from the time of the League. This gang had to be paid and fed. . . . As soon as my father left his

apartments to go to the Chamber of Deputies or elsewhere, the troop presented arms and honored him in their way with drums and trumpets. Each time it
was a scene worthy of the pencil of a Callot.[16]

The picturesque disorder, the constant coming and going of provincial
delegations wanting to express their devotion to Louis-Philippe, who gave
them brand-new tricolor flags bought with his private funds, was an unavoidable tribute to his popular reputation. Then there was the nightly repeated
spectacle of a crowd that gathered outside the railings of the Palais-Royal
loudly expressing the desire to see the sovereign. Hardly had Louis-Philippe
shown himself, when they would begin to sing the Marseillaise, with the king
joining in by tapping his foot in time, as Cuvillier-Fleury reports.[17] All this
came to an end when the royal family moved to the Tuileries, but the bourgeoisie continued to have the right of presentation at court—practically an
exclusive right since the legitimate aristocracy, the *bonne compagnie* of the
faubourg Saint-Germain, strictly refused to socialize with the *roi des barricades*
as they called him.[18] The evenings when Queen Marie-Amélie received the
wives of the "Messieurs les officiers de la milice citoyenne" in the informal
atmosphere of her salon were part of the rituals of the "bourgeois kingdom."
So were the parades of the "époux de ces dames" (husbands of these ladies),
at which the king cordially assured them "Mes chers amis, je suis heureux de
me trouver au milieu de vous" ("My dear friends, I am happy to be with
you").[19]

Such sentiments can hardly be considered hypocritical, for Louis-
Philippe was only too aware that the stability of his throne as well as of the
juste milieu depended on the loyalty of the Paris National Guard. Besides,
there is no doubt that in behaving as he did, the king acted in clear contrast
to the stiff court etiquette observed by Charles X. He achieved real popularity, expressed at the parade of 50,000 National Guardsmen on August 29,
1830, who overwhelmed him with cheers. "They were for him," as S.
Charléty comments, "[it was] a coronation by the people or, if you like, by the
bourgeoisie whose importance could be compared to that of a vote by the
Chamber."[20]

But far more important for Louis-Philippe than the enthusiastic acclaim
given him that day by the National Guard was the motive behind it. The
good citizens who served in the National Guard deeply disliked any confusion that could interfere with their businesses; and the king personified the
concept of order with which they liked to identify. These shared interests created the great political stability of the *juste milieu* that remained unaffected by
disputes and crises. And the agreement between bourgeoisie and crown was
expressed by two laws that came into effect at the end of March 1831: the law
concerning the National Guard and the *loi municipale*. The former, which
Charléty describes as "the most original creation of this period and regime,"
decreed that all French males between twenty and sixty years of age were
subject to military service. But there was an important qualification, namely,
that for the *service ordinaire* (peacetime army) only those men were eligible

who paid a personal income tax. In other words, even membership in the National Guard was tied to a property qualification. Therefore these troops—whose task it was to "guarantee respect for the law, and to maintain peace and order"—were a very homogeneous, bourgeois group who had something to lose.

The *loi municipale* was of special importance to Paris as it decreased somewhat the strict administrative control to which the city had been subject under the Empire and the Restoration. It made clear that the security of the *juste milieu* depended on the propertied bourgeoisie by limiting municipal voting rights to two categories of voters.[21] They consisted of those who "by paying a property qualification tax were considered materially independent and possessed a certain education as a result"; and those who through their service and the esteem they thus earned could provide sufficient guarantees of their suitability and experience.

Both laws contributed decisively to stabilizing the July Monarchy. Until the spring of 1831 the regime had been able to survive only because renewed republican opposition in Paris was still too weak to present a serious challenge. The initial insecurity of the July Monarchy is proven by the fact that there were five different prefects of police in Paris in the period ending in November 1831.[22] A further sign of its feebleness was the fact that despite the constant unrest, labor conflicts, and demonstrations in front of the Palais-Royal—kept in check only by Louis-Philippe's bonhomie—the National Guard was never called on to enforce law and order. That this was a matter of incompetence rather than of wisdom was shown by the trial of four ministers of Charles X who had been arrested for their participation in the failed coup and who were tried by the *Chambre des pairs* in December 1830.

As soon as news was out that the four ministers were being held in the prison at Vincennes, excitement rose to a fever pitch. Mourning for relatives or friends who had been killed during the *Trois Glorieuses* turned to a thirst for revenge: those reponsible for the spilled blood should pay for it. The situation was made even more difficult for Louis-Philippe—who wanted to save the lives of the ministers come what may—by sections of the National Guard who also called for their execution. And the regime was powerless without the unconditional loyalty of these troops.

A wild crowd gathered in front of the Palais-Royal on October 18 demanding the deaths of the ministers. Prevented from entering the building by the National Guard, they set out for Vincennes, armed with clubs, shotguns, and sabers. At the head of the procession someone carried a flag inscribed with the words "Désir du peuple! Mort aux ministres!" ("The people's demand! Death to the Ministers!"). When they reached Vincennes they were met by General Daumesnil, a wooden-legged veteran of the Napoleonic wars, who categorically refused to give up the prisoners. He emphasized his firmness by threatening to blow up the powder stores if the crowd attempted to storm the prison. "That way," he added with grim humor, "we'll all return to Paris through the Porte Saint-Antoine." Impressed by the decisive attitude of the commander of the prison, the crowd returned to Paris crying "Long Live Peg-leg."[23]

The calm outcome of this demonstration did not change the fact that stormy weather still lay ahead. The Austrian attaché in Paris, comte Rodolphe Apponyi, notes in his diary on December 8, 1830: "The entire idle society of Paris is in hiding; the lovely ladies only receive their intimate circle. There are no elegant carriages in the streets of Paris any more; people go on foot or use a hired coach; that is how afraid they are of provoking the *peuple*."[24] In the streets around the Luxembourg Palace, where the trial of the ministers was to take place on December 15, merchants closed their stores for fear of plundering and excesses. According to Apponyi, "Paris is like an encampment; tents have been thrown up everywhere, cannon are in place, and endless columns of troops are marching through the streets in gloomy and threatening silence."[25]

As long as the trial lasted Paris remained tensely calm.[26] But hardly had the verdict been made known—all four defendants were given life sentences—than unrest broke out which Lafayette only barely controlled with the help of the National Guard.[27] That was the first big test of the July Monarchy. But two months later anticlerical demonstrations brought fresh embarrassment, from which the regime only managed to extricate itself because its opponents were not sufficiently strong and resolute to force it out of power.

It was a widely held opinion that the clergy, which had become so powerful under the bigoted Charles X, had been party to the ordinances that caused the July Revolution. That would explain why, especially in the provinces, the political movement controlled by republicans and democrats had such decided anticlerical characteristics as the plundering of theological seminaries and the destruction of mission crosses. In view of this it was insensitive of the Paris clergy to commemorate the eleventh anniversary of the murder of the duc de Berry, on February 14, 1831, with a Requiem Mass in the church of Saint-Germain-l'Auxerrois. This service provoked a far greater disturbance than the events connected with the four ministers. Immediately following the service, attended especially by the faubourg Saint-Germain, an angry mob stormed the church, destroyed the interior furnishings and the presbytery, and plundered the sacristy.

The vandalism, about which the authorities did nothing, set an example. The next day the archbishop's palace near Notre Dame was ransacked by an unruly crowd; furniture, books, and sacred objects were thrown out of the windows into the Seine. Later that evening groups were seen dressed bizarrely in liturgical robes, swinging censers and spraying holy water at passersby in a travesty of sacred rites. The spectacle was made still more objectionable by the fact that it was the climax of carnival, the *fête du boeuf gras*, when it was traditional for masked participants to revel in the streets.[28]

Even the pillaging of the archbishop's palace did not appear to be sufficient grounds for official action. One cannot conclusively prove that the prefect of police and the National Guard were only too glad to see this revolutionary anger spend itself in aggression against the clergy, rather than against the bourgeoisie and its businesses; however, statements by Prefect Baudé and

Foreign Minister Sebastiani, issued on February 16, tend to support this notion.[29]

The excesses of February 14 and 15 formed the epilogue to the *Trois Glorieuses* and used up the revolutionary energies that had been stifled only with great effort on December 21. A similar undertaking this time around would have been much more difficult and its outcome uncertain. Moreover, why would the government risk its precarious position by protecting the clergy, which it did not care for anyway? In this connection it is enlightening that a royal ordinance of February 16 decreed that the Bourbon lilies be removed from the royal coat of arms and the state seal. Thus Louis-Philippe cleverly and quietly approved the political aims that had inspired the preceding revolutionary actions without compromising his regime.

After passing this second test with calculated restraint, the relative stability of the July Monarchy was embodied in the government of Casimir Périer and his *système Périer*. It consisted primarily of a radical refusal to adopt the previous policy of trying to please all movements and parties, which he described as "les prostitutions de la royauté devant l'anarchie."[30] Périer wanted to secure the monarchy within the framework of the Charter and that meant showing the dominant bourgeoisie what governing meant. And as Périer understood it, this meant above all pursuing a strict but legal policy of suppressing the republican movement. It is hardly surprising that with such a policy Périer made enemies on all sides. Louis-Philippe was convinced of his own political competence, as many of his opinions show.[31] It was therefore anything but easy for him to accept the conditions Périer imposed on him and which can be described by the well-known formula, "Le roi regne mais ne gouverne pas" ("the king reigns but does not govern").

Périer was unassailable as well as indispensable because his policy of *fremant dum metuant* was successful although it polarized the country and public opinion. Louis-Philippe suffered the most from this and became the target of popular scorn. Yet it was not only the king's egoism that was wounded by Périer's "system." The vanities of all the celebrities in the Chamber (whatever their persuasion), who confused politics and government with empty declamation, were equally hurt.

Even more fatal than the scorn for the king was the mistrust of him and the royal family, political motives being ascribed to everything they did. For instance, after his move from the Palais-Royal to the Tuileries at the end of 1831, Louis-Philippe expressed the wish that the small section of the gardens still open to the public be closed off for his own and his family's exclusive use. In order to separate the royal family's private section of flowerbeds and ornamental trees from the rest of the gardens and protect the king from curious onlookers, workers began excavating a ditch. Each day the work attracted a group of gaping individuals, who loudly expressed the strangest reasons for it. Some jokers thought the ditch was supposed to accommodate the giraffe— a present from Pasha Mohammed Ali; others teased that it was going to be a hiding place for the column in the place Vendôme, in case there was another invasion of the capital by the Prussians. . . . Even worse than these trite jokes were such calumnies as Louis-Philippe's wanting to build an arcade there like the Palais-Royal, or his wanting to entrench himself in a new Bastille. So the little garden the king had innocently desired—in the way any bourgeois wanted a piece of well-designed nature he could enjoy—became a national affair and provided the incentive for someone with a quick pen to write a play titled *Le Fossé des Tuileries* that was performed in the Théâtre des Variétés.[32]

Périer's liberal-conservative policy—which quite accurately reflected the *juste milieu* and continued to polarize the nation—was condemned to rise or fall with its creator. Once Périer fell victim to the cholera epidemic of 1832, the republicans optimistically seized the opportunity to increase their agitation. Their efforts were helped by the fact that his repressive "system" continued to function after his death; in fact none of his ministers were let go, and even the position of *Président du Conseil* that Périer had held was left vacant. No doubt it gave Louis-Philippe the chance he had been waiting for to prove that Périer was not indispensable and that he, the king, was the one who had influenced the former's policy.

But this was a dangerous and vain assumption on the king's part, for as soon as it was realized that Périer's repressive though legal tactics would endure, an angry protest was mounted by 134 of the left-wing deputies. They sent a letter, studded with invectives, to their voters explaining that, "as long as this regime lasts, France and the July Revolution will be handed over to their enemies."[33] That was a call for open resistance and rebellion, with the aim of defending the July Revolution. What was still missing was a concrete cause, an event that would goad the capital's masses—already made distraught by the raging cholera epidemic—into a fighting mood. It was provided by the funeral of General Lamarque, one of the leaders of the Left, on June 5.

The government, which was expecting unrest, had taken extensive precautions that day. Troops were placed at strategically important points all along the route to be followed by the funeral procession across the boulevards to the Pont d'Austerlitz, from which a carriage was to bear the general's coffin to Mont-de-Marsan, his electoral district. All arrangements for a show of strength had been made so as to prevent the expected demonstration. However, things turned out differently and this was due to the special chemistry described so masterfully by Victor Hugo in *Les Misérables*.[34]

June 5 was an oppressively humid day; the Paris sky was overcast with heavy dark clouds. A cholera epidemic had been raging for weeks and very little was needed to incite the helpless and fearful population to violence. The funeral cortege, consisting of members of secret revolutionary societies, workers, students, political refugees from Poland, Spain, Italy, and Germany, as well as artillery units of the National Guard who were supporters of republicanism, moved through this somber scene.[35] Having arrived at the Pont d'Austerlitz, the procession halted and speakers began to make increasingly wild speeches to the already excited crowd, which reacted with repeated cries of "Vive la République!" The sudden appearance of a rider dressed com-

pletely in black and waving a red flag, as well as the attempt of the municipal cavalry to prevent the crowd from taking Lamarque's coffin to the
Pantheon, were enough to start a general revolt.[36]

Within a very short time the insurgents controlled strategically important points where they put up and manned barricades. By six o'clock they
were in control of the faubourg Saint-Jacques and various adjacent arrondissements all the way to the Jardin des Plantes. It was the same on the Right Bank
where numerous districts stretching eastward from the place des Victoires
were in a state of rebellion.[37]

Two facts sealed the fate of this revolt. The majority of the insurrection-
ists were members of revolutionary societies, who were relatively few in number and unable to win over a sufficient number of workers.[38] Second, the
Paris National Guard troops under the command of General Lobau, as well
as those sent from the suburbs, were loyal and able fighters who managed to
repel the rebels. The fighting ceased around midnight. The next morning,
June 6, renewed fighting broke out around the rue Montmartre, the Passage
du Saumon and the Saint-Merry monastery, but by midday the situation was
sufficiently under control for Louis-Philippe to risk riding alone from the
place de la Concorde to the Bastille, and from there along the *quais* of the
Seine back to the Tuileries. The last of the insurgents, who had entrenched
themselves in the Saint-Merry monastery and who put up a desperate fight
with their last bullets, were shot down mercilessly by the National Guard.[39]
The casualties involved in this unsuccessful rebellion totaled more than eight
hundred dead and wounded.

Louis-Philippe's regime could draw two positive conclusions from the
failed revolt of the Young Turks of the republican movement. In the first
place, the Paris National Guard, so vital to the July Monarchy, had withstood
its baptism of fire. It proved that the bourgeoisie had realized it was in its best
interests to defend the regime against all attacks, its own existence also being
threatened by the *classes laborieuses*. This sentiment is revealed in a letter written by the daughter of a wealthy merchant in the rue Saint-Martin on June 8,
1832: "We closed our store as soon as the tocsin sounded. Papa put on his
uniform and went to join his battalion in the place des Petits-Pères. He
embraced me and Mamma and said: 'We must put an end to these miserable
creatures once and for all!' I've never seen him so angry before."[40]

The second insight that made Louis-Philippe view his rule in a more
hopeful light was that the left wing of the Chamber—the 134 deputies whose
letter had prepared the way for the unrest but who had kept out of sight once
it actually started—were like dogs whose barks were worse than their bites.
Those deputies were an epiphenomenon of the July Revolution, a bourgeois
group that pretended to incorporate the two extremes of being revolutionary
and conservative at the same time. Ironically this was exactly what Louis-
Philippe himself tried to do.

It was now evident that the revolutionary movement had just about
exhausted itself in the *Trois Glorieuses* of July 1830. The events of June 1832
did not bode well for the revival of such a movement in the near future. The

idealism needed for it was allowed no place in the political life of the *juste milieu*. Other forces were required to bring about a republican revolution and their formation was still to come.

But there was one group that wanted to carry on the ideology of republicanism, the *Société des droits de l'homme et du citoyen*, formed at the end of 1832. The success of this society, which quickly acquired more than 3,000 members in Paris and established various affiliates in the provinces, stemmed from its program of combining social questions and political doctrines with a view to revolutionary action.[41] This agenda soon drew public attention to the movement again, despite its setback in June, a fact that the authorities noted with growing distrust.[42] The result was a new wave of repressive regulations with which the government expected to stem the rising tide of republican agitation. However, the prohibition of the society, which then continued its activities underground, proved just as ineffective as the strict control of street sales of newspapers and political brochures. That made the government tighten the screws of repression.

At the end of February 1834, the deputies worked out a new version of the law banning organizations, extending it to include societies of fewer than twenty members. This was done to eliminate a loophole used by the republican movement to set up its groups, and caused a strong reaction. In spite of the government's extensive precautionary measures, unrest broke out in Paris on April 13. This time the incitement came from Lyon, the second most important bastion of republicanism, where a general strike by workers in the silk industry had already caused an upheaval in February. Protest now erupted there on April 9 against the new regulations and was put down only after a dreadful, bloody struggle.

The republicans of Lyon had sent a signal that the Paris *Société des droits de l'homme* felt it was bound to follow. As in Lyon, the Parisian sympathizers threw themselves into battle on April 13 without any plan or leadership. It was obvious from the start that this fight could not be won politically or militarily, and that it was sheer madness to attempt it. A few improvised barricades, which could hardly put up any serious resistance to the advancing troops, were erected by the insurgents in the same area that had seen bitter action in 1832—the Marais, and the rues Beaubourg, Aubry-le-Boucher, and Transnonain. The battles lasted for a few hours and then broke out again briefly the next morning.[43] Hardly had the last rebels been disarmed or dispersed, the barricades captured, and the uneven battle ended, when a rumor broke out that shots had been fired at the departing troops from the house at 12 rue Transnonain. Angry soldiers stormed the house without checking the facts and massacred its various residents.[44] This horrible slaughter of defenseless individuals inspired Daumier's famous lithograph of a man dressed in nothing but a shirt and nightcap, lying at the foot of his bed pierced by bayonets, a work which later became the icon of accusations against the July Monarchy.

The unparalleled carnage in the rue Transnonain was symptomatic of the fact that the republican movement no longer had any credit among the bourgeoisie. Furthermore, the government set about confirming the public impression that the movement stood for disorder and revolution. Additional repressive laws were enacted and more than 2,000 people suspected of republican intrigues were arrested all over the country. One hundred and sixty-four of them were brought to trial in the *Cour des pairs* in Paris on May 5, 1835. However, the trial did not discredit the movement as the regime had hoped; in fact the questionable trial procedure, and the way in which the defendants expressed their republican attitude, aroused considerable sympathy. But for some time to come, republicanism was finished as an effective political movement.

The Cholera Epidemic of 1832

*I*N THE EARLY YEARS OF THE JULY MONARCHY the political development of France was once more inextricably linked to the history of Paris. As always in times of revolutionary upheaval, Paris functioned as the stage for events that cannot be considered in a merely local context. On the other hand these events had their origins and causes in the ever-worsening condition of the city. Its long-ignored problems, aggravated by the tide of immigrants from the provinces, came to a sudden brutal climax in the spring of 1832. It took the form of a cholera epidemic that claimed 18,402 lives.

The epidemic arrived in Paris at the end of March; it was known to be making its way from Asia via Poland, northern Germany, and London. A contemporary pointed out that the closer it got, the more indifferent was the reaction to the threat it presented to the city and its inhabitants:

> This proximity disturbed us far less than the reports from faraway lands, which seemed twice as awful on account of the distance and the newness. All our horror had exhausted itself in the initial descriptions of its fury, in the first figures of its victims; for a Parisian, who so easily grows used to any sort of misfortune, cannot long live in fear of an evil he does not see. Moreover, what should one tell someone who is so convinced of the cleanliness of his city; of the mild and pure air one breathes from the rue de l'Estrapade to the rue du Rocher; of the freshness of the water in the Seine into which endless sewers pour; of the pleasant odors coming from the gutters along our streets. Moreover, as the epidemic took its time in reaching us, it was firmly believed that it had been frightened off by our jokes, our caricatures, and our vigilance. It was already as thoroughly forgotten as last year's celebration, last month's revolt, or yesterday's scandal. Nothing had changed in our lives or habits.[45]

This carefree attitude quickly gave way to panic when cholera claimed its first victim in Paris. The epidemic ran wild soon after it began: by March 31 it had invaded forty-eight of the Paris arrondissements. The authorities were unable to protect the living from the disease and soon the burial of the victims became a problem. The city was unable to deal with the growing numbers of corpses, especially as normal methods of transporting them proved inadequate. The official *Rapport sur la marche et les effets du choléra-morbus dans Paris* issued in 1834 states:

> It was suggested at the time that artillery carriages be used for this purpose. . . . Indeed, they were used one night. But the noise of the metal wheels that is typical of these vehicles, a sound that was only too well-known and made worse by frequent use, disturbed the sleep of the citizens in an unpleasant way; there was an additional, unanticipated difficulty. Since the carriages were not sprung, the coffins opened up with the vigorous bouncing and jolting. The corpses fell out and as they were no longer protected they were mutilated in such a way that the intestines were exposed, releasing a pestilential liquid in the vehicles which then ran onto the streets. The very next day this method of transportation had to be abandoned.
>
> . . . Eventually it was decided to use furniture vans. These vans, being large and well-sprung, did not shake up their contents and could accommodate a large number of coffins. The use of these vans, with which any area in the city was easily reached, eliminated the fear of a terrible piling-up of corpses. But the mere sight of these new hearses, moving slowly through the streets with their heavy loads, created such fear among the inhabitants and especially among the women, that they too soon had to be abandoned.[46]

Indeed, it was these "buses of the dead," which Heinrich Heine described in his report on the epidemic,[47] that epitomized the real terror, as they showed that the city was no more able to deal with its dead than with its living. The almost insoluble problems presented by the epidemic were merely the results of the other difficulties that occupied the hygienists of the period. They ceaselessly criticized the overcrowded hospitals, the inefficient and often blocked sewers, and the revolting knacker's yards and fecal depots of Montfaucon—all of which were due to overpopulation.

The raging disease also emphasized the difference between the classes in society, offering statistical proof that inequality in death was based on inequality in life. It confirmed research that had lately become fashionable among doctors and hygienists, and which was influenced by Louis René Villermé's 1830 study, *De la Mortalité dans les divers quartiers de la ville de Paris*. On the basis of mortality rates in the twelve Paris arrondissements for the years 1817–21 and 1822–26, Villermé concluded that "under prevailing conditions and taking current circumstances into consideration, wealth, prosperity, and poverty are the main causes of the great differences in mortality among the inhabitants of individual arrondissements."[48] In other words, the mere comparison between mortality rates and social class revealed that members of the *classes laborieuses* had a far shorter life expectancy than the bourgeoisie.

In the lottery of life the *classes laborieuses* always had fewer chances. This insight which the cholera disease seemed to confirm, and one often voiced by the frightened bourgeois, is referred to by Bazin, who remarks that "this awful saying" was intended to "reassure any weak spirits who threatened to lose heart. Repeated disdainfully, this sort of arrogant comment consigned the poorest section of the population to their certain ruin, at the same time releasing the wealthy from this fatal tribute."[49]

The cynical confidence expressed in bourgeois circles—that cholera was a sickness confined to the lower classes—seemed at first to be confirmed by the way in which cases occurred. For instance, an article in the *Journal des débats* of March 28, 1832, states:

> Cholera is at our gates. Yesterday a man died in the rue Mazarine. Today nine people were taken to the Hôtel-Dieu, four of whom were already dead. All who have been attacked by this epidemic, which is not supposed to be contagious, belong to the *peuple*. They are saddlers and weavers; they live in the dirty and narrow alleys of the *Cité* and the arrondissements around Notre Dame.[50]

Many of the doctors of the time believed that cholera was not transmitted by contagion, which gave credibility to the opinion that the disease chose its victims mainly from among the lower classes.[51] Though this hope was soon disappointed, the bourgeoisie continued to be convinced of it. They also felt that the *classes laborieuses* were responsible for spreading an illness that embodied the most radical threat to bourgeois society, namely death and destruction.

On the other hand, the diffuse and invisible ubiquity of this deadly menace created panic in the general public. Bazin gives an interesting description of the reactions to the epidemic:

> As soon as the government assured them that all precautions had been taken against the disease, the good citizens almost died of fear and terror. But it got worse when the doctors, the transmitters of official confidence, issued their hygiene instructions.[52] Nothing creates fear more easily than a list of preventive remedies and measures. Any description of what action to take focuses the imagination on a danger that one tries to avoid. What remedy exists for worrying if one is advised to avoid anxiety? What cure is there for trembling, if we are assured that fear kills? Taking action is the only thing that distracts; but everything now undertaken was directly connected with the awful disaster. At home one could follow all the medical advice: one had to fumigate the apartment to disinfect it, to clean out one's room to decontaminate it. One could identify cholera from the graveyard smell of the chlorine, or recognize it from the abdominal flannel bandages or woolen shoes that were worn; everyone dressed according to the requirements of the epidemic. And outside one's own four walls it was lurking in the window of every store, where its name threatened us if we did not go in immediately to buy vials, little pouches, gloves, pomades, pastilles, cakes, Cape wine, tobacco, or whatever—goods the merchants wanted to get rid of. . . . Wherever one went, there was cholera: it dominated conversation in the salon one visited; it was present when two friends met and greeted each other.[53]

All the responses and preventive measures provoked by the threat of cholera were strictly delimited by class; for only the wealthy could afford the nostrums they were offered and were able to alter their diet; the poor, who were equally afraid of the disease, became even more aware of their impotence.[54] The only precautions in which the *classes populaires* could trust were those taken by the authorities, who quickly had the cesspools, the open sewers, and marketplaces sprayed with chlorine. But nothing was done about the filthy streets that were suspected of helping the epidemic to spread.

Those with means could afford the most effective way of escaping the cholera: they could leave the city. At first this privilege was limited to a few families who, as Bazin remarks, "are blessed with leisure and income and whose lives revolve around the Opera and the Bois de Boulogne."[55] But when the number of cholera victims grew much larger at the beginning of April 1832, and had risen to 12,657 people by the end of the month, many showed a greater fear of death than concern for their business interests. Louis Blanc estimates that at that time 700 people left Paris daily on mail coaches.[56] To be sure, among those who fled there were numerous foreigners, like Ludwig Börne, for whom the city had become untenable.[57] The large number of local residents leaving Paris meant that many shops and businesses were closed, which made the situation of the *classes laborieuses* still more desperate. Louis Blanc commented on this with a rhetorical question: "Entre le choléra et la faim qu'allait devenir le peuple?" ("Between cholera and hunger, what was to become of the *peuple?*").[58]

Caught in a situation from which there was no escape, the working class experienced its old collective fears. Just as in 1789, when they suspected that a *pacte de famine* was being planned against them by the rich and powerful, they now worried that the bourgeoisie was using the epidemic to destroy them. In this way insight into the lamentable condition of the city itself provoked by the cholera epidemic was overshadowed by insight into the pathological condition of society. Both had an identical origin: the maladjustment of urban and social structures to the complex demands of a rapidly growing population forced to live in overcrowded conditions.

The suspicion of the working class that it was being singled out as victim found characteristic outlet in rumors and conjectures about a plot by the government and the bourgeoisie to poison it. "The *peuple*," wrote Bazin, "denied the cholera; instead they offered a much simpler and more natural explanation for the outrage."[59] The conjectures and suspicions caused Prefect of Police Gisquet to issue a denial, as unusual as it was unfortunate, which only served to confirm the lower classes' fears:

> The cholera epidemic has given the sworn enemies of public order a new opportunity to spread infamous lies about the government. They dare to maintain that cholera is nothing but a contamination spread about by agents in the government's pay to decimate the population and thus divert attention from politics. I have been informed that to lend credibility to these assertions, certain elements have agreed to visit bars and butcher shops with vials and pouches containing poison—be it to poison wells, wine casks, or meat, or merely to pretend to do so—in order to be arrested *in flagrante* by accomplices. They are then supposed to be released after these accomplices have identified themselves as police agents.[60]

This statement failed to convince those for whom it was intended. But some unfortunate pedestrians, who aroused suspicion by carrying small pouches or vials which very likely contained smelling salts as a protection against the epidemic, had to pay with their lives. They were murdered by an angry crowd, which took them to be the poisoners referred to by the prefect of police.[61]

In reacting this way the *peuple* were accusing the bourgeoisie of trying to square old accounts and destroy them. But they also recognized, as they had done previously, that force could only be met with force. This was a familiar reaction, as shown by a police report on April 23, 1832, that states, "once the tempest of the epidemic has subsided, revolutionary passions will awaken again."[62] And Bazin comments that "the *peuple* has only one way of expressing its fury and there are thousands of poor who can take part."[63]

Such an analysis was not merely based on long experience but was borne out by what took place during demonstrations by ragpickers on April 1. These came about because the *Conseil municipal* had entrusted street cleaning to a new private entrepreneur called Salvette. He was permitted to collect household trash in certain areas of Paris when night fell, instead of at daybreak which had been the usual time for it. This threatened an important source of income of the 1,800 ragpickers whose custom it was to sort through the trash piles for valuable items.[64] Their angry protest culminated in setting fire to several of Salvette's wagons.[65] But this only ignited greater unrest, in which other members of the *peuple* soon participated. The result was that these demonstrations gradually moved from the barriers at the edge of the city, where they had begun, into the center where they smoldered until April 4 when they were finally subdued by the authorities' superior forces.[66]

At any rate the rest of the public had good reasons for not differentiating between acts of violence based on politics and those caused by other grievances. This was especially true at a time when the cholera epidemic was rampant. As Jules Janin characterized it a few months later, "[It is the] pestilence of a *populace* who are the first ones to die of it. With their deaths they provide a terrible and bloody rebuttal of those notions of equality that they have been accused of holding for half a century. . . ." Then, in allusion to the uprisings of June 5 and 6, he adds: "Nothing could be heard in this silence until one day the voice of the *peuple* spoke; and how did this terrible voice speak? It spoke as only the voice of the *peuple* speaks, with iron, with blows, with curses, with murder and blood, with great anger and great force."[67]

Paris and Its Diseases

*O*FFICIAL SCIENTIFIC INVESTIGATIONS of the cholera epidemic revealed that the *peuple* were victimized in death as they had been in life.[68] What must have irritated contemporaries about the findings was that mortality was not as entirely confined to the *classes populaires* as they had wished. Even in bourgeois residential districts, such as the Quartier Saint-Thomas-d'Aquin, 38 per 1,000 residents died of cholera; in the Luxembourg arrondissement 28 per 1,000 succumbed. In contrast, in neighborhoods of the rich and prosperous such as the Chaussée d'Antin only 8 per 1,000, and in the Tuileries only 9 per 1,000 fell victim to the disease. Compared with those figures, loss of life was especially heavy in those parts of the city where the really poor lived, as in the neighborhood of the Hôtel de Ville (53 per 1,000), the *Cité* (52 per 1,000), Arcis (42 per 1,000), and Arsenal (41 per 1,000).

These considerable differences suggested that there was a direct connection between relative population density and cholera mortality. But a comparative study based on the entire city did not confirm this hypothesis. Compared to the average population density of one resident per 43 square meters, sixteen arrondissements were found to be above this average, with 45-186 square meters per resident. The other thirty-two arrondissements were found to have high to extremely high population densities, ranging from 43 down to only 7 square meters; twenty-six of the latter had fewer than 20 square meters per resident. However, a comparison of cholera mortality rates in the two categories of arrondissements revealed that in the thirty-two arrondissements that had fewer than 43 square meters per resident, cholera deaths amounted to 21.62 per 1,000; while the rate in the sixteen arrondissements where the population density was far below the average actually amounted to 22.19 cholera deaths per 1,000.

This rather diffuse and hardly usable conclusion changed as soon as the investigation concentrated on individual houses and their residents. These findings were as follows:

> Except for a small number of houses in which cholera losses had inexplicably been very severe as, for instance, in Grenelle, Gros-Caillou or in the vicinity of the Ecole militaire . . . it was always in the areas where people lived in the worst kind of poverty, herded together in dirty, small rooms, that the epidemic had taken most of its victims.[69]

Having reached these conclusions the same commission then undertook another comparative study, which it summarized as follows:

> Twenty-eight of the forty-eight arrondissements, located in the center of the city, consist of only one-fifth of the entire area of the capital; on the other hand, this is where half of the population lives (383,876 out of a total of 759,135). Thirty-five of the arrondissements hold as many as 146,430 residents in just 180 streets; among these is the Arcis district, where each resident occupies only seven square meters; and in these streets there are buildings containing an average of 73 residents, but never less than 30, 40, or 60 individuals. In these streets there are, without exception, forty-five deaths per thousand, or double the average. (In the first six arrondissements there are up to 6 streets in which the cholera mortality rate is more than double the average, while in the other six arrondissements there are more than 160 such streets.) In these buildings, most of them five storys in height and six to seven meters wide, without open courts, there were as many as ten or eleven deaths. The 146,400 inhabitants of these streets make up one-fifth of the population of Paris; their death rate of 6,492 constituted one-third of all cholera victims. This terrible loss of human life occurred here because nowhere else is the space more confined, the population more crowded, the air more unhealthy, dwellings more perilous, and the inhabitants more wretched.[70]

Having reached these conclusions the commission went a step further in correlating the cholera mortality rate to that of particular professional groups, and then comparing these figures to the normal death rate of specific professions. They therefore divided all professions into four categories: *professions liberales, professions commerciales, professions mécaniques* (including laundresses and all manual trades), and *professions salariées*, which referred to those activities requiring no training, such as street-sweepers, doormen, water-carriers, porters, and ragpickers. The latter group, as the commission proved statistically, differed from the rest in that its cholera mortality rate far exceeded its normal death rate. In this way the epidemic emphasized the group's social disadvantage. The commission drew special attention to this fact in its summary, which created a stir:

> In the capital there is not only one large class of individuals who toil each day to earn their living and whom the authorities should protect at all times from dangers they cannot and do not know how to deal with; there is still another class below this useful and hardworking one, recognizable by its utter indigence and its abject degradation. This class occupies the lowest place in the social hierarchy and is found in our heavily populated manufacturing cities; there it is constantly replenished by the economic fluctuations of industry, by inadequate regulations, and the disorders of moral decay. Nowhere is it as large a group as in Paris, where it is increased by the mass of unemployed who are incessantly drawn there in the hope of finding some sort of work. This class which has no steady abode or assured work, has nothing to call its own save its misery and its vices; after roaming the streets in the daytime, at night these individuals go back to the *maisons garnies* in various parts of the capital, which look as if they had always been intended to harbor members of these classes. . . . There are few older people and children among this roving, nomadic population. These two age groups have difficulty surviving the rigors of a journey; there are also fewer women than men.[71]

With these comments, which corresponded to their statistical findings, the commission stigmatized a whole section of the population which was enlarged by waves of immigrants and which made up a sizable segment of the *classes laborieuses*.[72] The commission's references to the group as *population mobile* and *nomade* reflected their complete marginalization in real life. They were prevented from being integrated into society, the economy, or the life of the capital. In times of economic crisis their number was increased by impoverished artisans. They were the industrial reserve, that gray army of paupers who were considered the greatest danger to society by all the European states who were on the brink of, or had entered the Industrial Revolution. Hence it becomes clear why the *classes laborieuses*—to which this group belonged—were frequently lumped together with the *classes dangereuses*, to form that "ugly secret countersociety beneath public society," of which Victor Hugo writes.[73]

This mingling of *classes laborieuses* and *classes dangereuses*, this Janus-headedness of which bourgeois society accused the lower classes, was considered impossible to eliminate. For the bourgeoisie was convinced that the disgusting conditions in which these classes lived were caused by their moral deficiencies. The commission's report only hinted at this; but the attitude was made much more explicit by commission member Louis-René Villermé, in an article on cholera mortality in the *maisons garnies*. He concludes:

> It is therefore obvious that the epidemic was caused by the very visible uncleanliness of these places, by the poverty and misery of their inhabitants, but above all, by prostitution. . . . From these latter facts it can be seen that cholera had to claim its victims among those who, through their immorality and poverty, are often incited to commit outrages against society. That is surely small comfort compared with the enormous misfortune caused by the disease.[74]

At the same time that the epidemic uncovered the extent of the pathology of Paris and its impenetrable conglomeration of misery and crime, it was also seen as another threat arising from the *classes dangereuses*. Attitudes of this sort influenced the debate carried on in the novels and feuilletons of the times. The picture of Paris evoked there became more gloomy. Descriptions of poverty and misery that had been a picturesque element in the writing of Mercier and his numerous imitators were now replaced by revelations of horror and disgust. The witty wife of Emile de Girardin, the newspaper king of the July Monarchy, who wrote feuilletons under the pseudonym of vicomte de Launay, tells her readers on November 24, 1838:

> How ugly Paris seems after one has been absent for a year. How sad this city of pleasure is! If one returns after a long journey, during which one has breathed pure air, the good air of the mountains, how soon one feels as if one is suffocating in these dark, narrow, and damp thoroughfares that are known simply as the streets of Paris! . . . And thousands of people live, bustle, throng in the damp darkness like reptiles in a swamp. . . . [75]

The title of an 1836 novel by Eugène Roche is *Paris malade*. Its theme is the infirmity of the city, its overpopulation, and the misery, violence, and criminality it produces. There are also numerous examples in Balzac's novels of the way in which the city became more dismal. And in one of Jules Janin's feuilletons, dedicated to the *flâneur* (the stroller), there is one section that includes all the topics and subjects then part of the debate on Paris:

> There are places in Paris known only to the *flâneur*: repulsive passages, labyrinths, ruins, dwellings in which all the city's thieves live. . . . Nighttime Paris is horrible. For that is when the population that lives underground comes out. It is dark everywhere. But, quite faintly, this darkness becomes illuminated by the flickering lantern of a ragpicker; carrying a basket on his back, he looks for his keep in those trash heaps for which there is no description in any language. During the same hours evil-smelling carts stop in front of the sleeping houses to haul away the heaped-up waste. At the corners of dark alleys a wine merchant's weak light shines through curtains that are as red as blood. Thieves steal along the walls, occasionally uttering the call of a night bird, as they make their way to their robberies.[76]

Paris as the capital of crime was a popular literary subject during the July Monarchy, in such works as Eugène Sue's *Mystères de Paris* and Victor Hugo's *Les Misérables*. This interest in crime and its obvious connection to the unwholesome condition of Paris is well documented by Louis Chevalier, in his monumental study, *Classes laborieuses et classes dangereuses*. Clearly the morbid fascination that this topic had for the people of that period reflected their complete passivity toward complex urban problems that were reaching threatening proportions.

Inadequate Measures

*T*HE COMMISSION CHARGED WITH STUDYING the cholera epidemic came to the very brief conclusion "that there are quite specific groups and areas that promote and intensify the spread of cholera, and increase the probability of its virulent progress."[77] It then recommended a comprehensive program for the rehabilitation of Paris that would satisfy sanitary as well as urban requirements and eliminate the unwholesome conditions revealed by the epidemic. Detailed suggestions were given for the improvement of housing; for instance "de construire des habitations destinées surtout aux classes moyennes et laborieuses" ("above all to build dwellings designed principally for the middle and working classes"). They were to be limited to three storys, but of sufficient height to guarantee the satisfactory circulation of air. Furthermore, the report went on: "It would be desirable to introduce a better system for draining household waste, and above all, not to continue laying pipes along stairwells which then become polluted; more care and attention should be paid to the construction of toilets and to the number of cesspools."

The commission's recommendations on housing also included proposals for infrastructural changes. Emphasis was put on widening all inner-city streets to at least forty feet. The report describes existing conditions as follows:

> There are numerous streets in Paris that appear very spacious and well-planned at their point of origin, but which grow more and more cramped as one approaches the center. Such is the case with the rues des faubourgs Saint- Denis, Saint-Martin, Poissonière, du Temple, du Roule, Saint-Honoré, and Saint-Antoine, as well as many others. Too many of these streets are only eight feet wide and some are even narrower, so that there is a strange contrast between the wide roads outside the capital's gates and the much too narrow streets inside its walls. . . . It is especially urgent that the center of Paris be opened up with thoroughfares in all directions by creating big public squares planted with trees, so as to create new avenues which are now definitely scarce in the capital; this will provide light and life to those dark quarters in which half the population vegetates in the most disgusting conditions, where there is so much filth and polluted air, where the streets are so constricted and the mortality rate so high that

there are more dead to mourn here than anywhere else; the residents here are so weak and small that one out of three are unfit for military service.

Along with the construction of new or the enlarging of existing streets, the commission suggested that the very rudimentary, neglected, and clogged sewer system be extended and renovated; in this way it would become capable of accommodating household sewage as well as street drainage. Furthermore, improvement of the fresh-water system was advised: "The number of water faucet connections in the streets should be increased to augment the current inadequate water supply. One can only sigh when one considers that residents of Paris still lack this means of public hygiene and barely consume seven liters of water per day, while every citizen of London has the use of sixty-two liters."[78]

But even these comparatively modest goals were far from adequate, and the problems became still more visible by the end of the July Monarchy. There are various reasons why the government and city administration failed to act, but overall they do not provide a really satisfactory answer. It has to be remembered that the capital's administration paid for its relative independence, gained in the July Revolution, by losing the state subventions that had contributed considerably to its budget. And in Claude-Philibert Barthelot, comte de Rambuteau, who had become prefect of the Seine in June 1833, Paris had to deal with a very thrift-conscious man. His unfortunate predecessor, the comte de Bondy, had run the municipal administration with a view to "obtaining fresh resources irrespective of what he had currently available, so as to speed up and maintain the rehabilitation and beautification of the capital."[79] But Rambuteau aspired to keep the city's expenses in line with his usual underestimation of revenue so as to produce a balanced budget. Only when the revolution of February 1848 was about to end the July Monarchy did he adopt his predecessor's device of obtaining credit or loans for urgent redevelopment.

The political wisdom of this man, who did not realize that unglamorous and troublesome urban renewal—opposed as it was by property owners—was an absolute priority for the future of Paris, is contained in his memoirs:

> Parisians are like children; one constantly has to fill their imagination, and if one cannot give them a victory in battle every month, or a new constitution every year, then one has to offer them daily some new building sites to visit, projects that serve to beautify the city. This is an outlet for their curiosity, for their temperament which is inclined to opposition, and for their passion for debate. . . . That is why I always bore in mind the entertainment as well as the welfare of Parisians by completing important buildings, constructing new streets and gardens, planting trees, and arranging balls, festivals and other amusements. . . . [80]

Rambuteau's plan for Paris resembled the old one of "beautifying" the capital with *embellissements*, with stately monuments and public gardens. He not only ignored the experiences of the cholera epidemic but prided himself on putting his ideas into effect as economically as possible:

My whole system consisted of preventing my chosen *Conseil municipal* from plunging into reforms, whether out of the sheer pleasure of creating something new, or to gain popularity and thus do harm to the budget and the government. I therefore kept the *conseil* busy with important work that was consistent with city revenues, that would not create liabilities for the future nor fail to establish a reserve for sudden expenditures that circumstances might warrant at any time.[81]

This restrictive policy corresponded wholly to the spirit of the July Monarchy, in that the *bourgeoisie règnante* always made sure that their personal interests were not affected by increases in government expenditure. André Morizet's criticism that Rambuteau "administered the budget of Paris according to the same principles he used in his country estate in Burgundy" is therefore too severe.[82] For Rambuteau was merely influenced by the idea of *enrichissez-vous*—which certainly meant setting limits to public expenditures—as was the rest of the *juste milieu*. In terms of Paris, this meant that Rambuteau could only undertake such reforms and projects as met three requirements: they had to have the approval of the *bourgeoisie*, that is, by being promoted by private speculation; they could not interfere with private property; and costs had to be covered by the normal budget.

In this respect Rambuteau's policy concerning the *grands travaux de la voirie* (the construction of streets and organization of trash removal), to which he admits paying the most attention, is very revealing.[83] In the budget years 1834-47, an average of only 15 percent of the total city expenses was used for the upkeep and expansion of the infrastructure.[84] Rambuteau's critics constantly rebuked him for spending too little in view of the rapidly deteriorating condition and overpopulation of Paris.[85] Indeed, part of the expenditure was for the outdated beautification program rather than for much needed urban redevelopment. And while that shows how Rambuteau's initiatives tied in with private speculation, it is also true that he lacked the power to enforce some of the large-scale rehabilitation that would have affected private property.

A prime example of the unanimity between entrepreneurial speculation and decorative urban projects was that of the Champs-Elysées and the place de la Concorde. Both of these properties had been deeded to the city by the crown on August 20, 1828, with the stipulation that Paris build up the area, at its own cost, within a five-year period. The Champs-Elysées, which had been made into a park in the eighteenth century by the marquis de Marigny (*Surintendant des bâtiments de la couronne*), was in an especially neglected condition according to contemporary witnesses:

In the winter one sinks into mud and in the summer one gets covered in dust; at all times of the year, even if there has been little rain, the ditches filled with swampy water pollute the air and cause all sorts of accidents. It is disgustingly dirty under the trees and in the squares. Everyone knows that this place is the notorious haunt of men and women who lead shady lives, and that criminals often meet there as well. There is no place where a tired stroller, children, or old men can rest; there is nothing pleasant to look at or to stimulate the viewer's imagination . . . . [86]

In spite of that the Champs-Elysées park was enjoyed by the public, and along its avenues it featured the sort of popular entertainment that consisted of refreshment booths, ice cream vendors, itinerant merchants, inexpensive garden restaurants, and dance-halls.

The condition of the Champs-Elysées became a thorn in the side of the *bourgeoisie régnante,* especially with the success of new luxury housing being developed in the west of Paris. Toward the end of the 1830s when the new residential area near the Champs-Elysées became more lively, it was considered quite fashionable to live there. This is borne out by a curious inscription on a tombstone, not far from Chopin's grave in the Père-Lachaise cemetery, which reads: "Major General William Cross C.B. . . . who departed this life at his residence in the Champs-Elysées November XXV in the year of the Lord 1843." And Balzac comments in a letter to Mme Hanska: "Within eighteen months Emile [de] G[irardin] has seen an increase in the value of his house [in the rue de Chaillot] of one hundred thousand francs. All of Paris is rushing to the Champs-Elysées."[87]

Only the growing pressure exerted by investors in this arrondissement forced the Paris administration to meet the obligation it had undertaken with the law of August 20, 1828. The Cologne-born architect Jacob Ignaz Hittorf had already been commissioned to work out new plans for the park sections between the place de la Concorde and the rond-point des Champs-Elysées in 1834, but was not given Rambuteau's final approval until the summer of 1838.[88] Once again the delay was due to the prefect's attempts to keep the city budget as low as possible. The solution he came up with was that the city should pay only for landscaping work such as new paths, circular flower beds, and squares, and the installation of a series of new fountains; however, the planned cafés, restaurants, pavilions, *géorama,* panorama, and *cirque d'hiver,* which were to be scattered throughout the park so as to make it more attractive to the public, were to be financed by private investors who would operate these attractions, holding them on hereditary leases.[89] In order to conform to the basic plan, builders had to agree to use Hittorf's designs for the facades.[90]

The restoration of the Champs-Eleseés turned this part of the city into one of the most popular meeting places of the *monde parisien,* as Charles de Forster was later to testify:

> There used to be a repulsive collection of dirty huts and cheap bars there; and rain turned the ground between the trees into muddy swamps, crossed only by those pedestrians who were forced to do so by poverty or business, since one stood to lose one's shoes in them. The pitiful huts have been gone for some years now, thanks to the efforts of the *Conseil municipal;* the two avenues on the right and left sides have been covered in asphalt, and the buildings that were erected according to elegant designs make the tree-framed squares very attractive. . . . Since the fashionable world has adopted the Champs-Elysées, endless barouches pass through it daily. . . . On Sundays society meets there: bourgeois, officer, banker, merchant of the rue Saint-Denis, student, shop assistant, *grisette,* society lady, and good bourgeoise—all of them come there. *C'est là que les parties s'arrangent* (it is there that people pair up).[91]

But in 1834, the park area of the Champs-Elysées and the place de la Concorde, according to *L'Artiste*, was "the least lively public square and also the most uncivilized because of its size . . . where one is buried in summer dust and in winter mud."[92] In his memoirs, Rambuteau says that this area was to be part of his plan to provide "water, air, and shade for Parisians."[93] He certainly tried to fulfill his promise of providing shady trees for Parisian strollers. Along the boulevards, where long stretches still noticeably followed the line of demolished fortifications, he not only replaced the trees felled for barricades during the *Trois Glorieuses*, but had additional trees put in so that "the population could promenade there in greater comfort." The *quais* along the Seine, begun by Napoleon, were also completed by Rambuteau who turned them into avenues by planting trees there, much to the joy of the public. These embellishments, which at least marginally improved the urban image, were supplemented by several prestigious buildings and monuments like the Arc de l'Etoile, the Madeleine, or the church of Notre-Dame-de-Lorette. In addition, an enormous bronze column was erected in the place de la Bastille, which still recalls the July Revolution; and the monument to Napoleon was reinstalled in the place Vendôme.

While some projects such as the Arc de l'Etoile were financed by the state, the most important and impressive one—the new Hôtel de Ville, begun in 1836—was paid for from the normally tightly controlled city budget. Twenty-four million francs were spent on this building, with which the *juste milieu* commemorated itself. That sum was not enough to complete the entire project, but it sufficed to decorate the interior with several sumptuous and extravagantly gilded stucco rooms. Rambuteau held his very popular receptions and balls there in the winter months; they have been well described in Charles Merruau's memoirs.[94]

Other famous projects such as a new Paris Opera, which had already been discussed during the Restoration, were not completed by the July Monarchy either. A similar fate befell Napoleon's plan to complete the Louvre and restore the area around it, something the public never tired of demanding. Balzac gives a detailed description of this slum in *La Cousine Bette*, where he lets the trimmings merchant Rivet, the "oracle of Saint-Denis," express what the public wants. When Cousin Bette tells him that she is about to move away from this poverty-stricken arrondissement, Rivet says to her:

> You're doing the right thing; I have always been very sorry to see you living in this dreadful place which—though I dislike everything that sounds like opposition to the government—dishonors, yes I must say so, dishonors the Louvre and the place du Carrousel. I am a true follower of Louis-Philippe, he is my idol, he is the illustrious and true representative of the class on which his dynasty is based, and I shall never forget what he did for the trimmings business when he reestablished the National Guard. . . . But completion of the Louvre was one of the conditions on which we gave him the crown. . . . [95]

Deplorable Hygiene

*L*ARGE-SCALE URBAN RENEWAL PROJECTS were not what the July Monarchy was interested in; that did not conform to its policy of using public funds prudently. But there were additional motivations, their common denominator being to avoid anything that might cause unrest in the capital and place the regime in jeopardy.[96] These considerations meant that in the fifteen years of Rambuteau's tenure, no more than thirty new streets and a few bridges were built at the city's expense. They contributed little or nothing to easing the disastrous condition of traffic in the inner city. As a matter of fact the Pont Louis-Philippe, which linked the quai de la Grève to the Ile Saint-Louis, collapsed in 1848; and the Pont des Saints-Pères was not connected with any streets on either side of the river. Of the new streets the most important was the one still bearing Rambuteau's name. The rue Rambuteau was designed to provide a direct and convenient thoroughfare between the Marais and the western districts. It was very useful at a time when the rue de Rivoli still ended at what is now the place des Pyramides, a slum section which marred the Louvre area. But construction of the street, which was only thirteen meters wide, was exceedingly costly because of the necessary expropriation payments.[97] Municipal officials therefore gave up the prospect of embarking again on anything of a similar scale.[98]

The example of the rue de Rambuteau shows once again how little latitude there was during the July Monarchy for redevelopment. Rambuteau could proceed with his urban program only where it did not conflict with the private interests of those on whom the regime depended. His few noteworthy achievements—the *quais*, the reorganization of the Champs-Elysées and the place de la Concorde—were of minor importance compared to the vast gaps in the infrastructure. Those problems, highlighted by the loss of almost 20,000 people during the cholera epidemic, grew steadily worse as the population continued to increase.[99]

Yet Rambuteau, encouraged by his contemporaries, genuinely believed that his measures to improve public hygiene were Herculean accomplishments. These consisted mostly of street paving, and the installation of gutters to drain water and make pavements less hazardous. In his memoirs Rambuteau mentions that he had always been especially concerned to upgrade the streets of "Vieux Paris":

> When it rained most of the streets turned into raging streams which one could only cross with the help of wooden planks. There were no pavements, no roof gutters; one was soaked by water running off the roofs. The streets were not sprayed with water in the summer, so that dirty puddles collected in front of the houses, creating that characteristic smell of rotten cabbage by which returning travelers inevitably identify their city. These puddles produced the miasmas, fevers, and sicknesses which sanitation has eliminated. . . . Each year 7 to 8 kilometers of cement drains have been built, which contribute to the cleanliness of the streets; the old-fashioned streets with sewers running down the middle have been replaced by streets with gutters along both sides. . . . In 1833 there was just

221

one 16-kilometer stretch of pavement; in 1848 195 kilometers of pavements edged the streets; and if I were to add the squares, *quais,* and boulevards that were built with sewers, gutters, pavements, and drains, their number would total fourteen hundred thoroughfares, modernized along a length of 260 kilometers.[100]

Everything depends on the point of view, and compared with the previous condition of the Paris streets, which innumerable complaints since the days of Mercier had made a familiar theme for every writer, Rambuteau's efforts represented some minimal progress. The same can be said for his claim to have improved the water supply; according to him, instead of the approximate daily amount of 8 liters of fresh water per person, by the end of his period in office Parisians were able to use 100. But that calculation is pure fiction; in actual fact the fresh water supply for Paris amounted to 86,000 cubic meters, providing each inhabitant with an average of only 85 liters. And even this figure has to be modified considerably according to a report made by Eugène Belgrand, the capital's water supply engineer, to the prefect of the Seine on July 8, 1854. The report stated that two-thirds of the daily amount of water was used for street cleaning, and for filling the various monumental fountains and other public installations. Factories, workshops, laundries, and public baths required 9,000 cubic meters; that left only 14,000 cubic meters for the capital's inhabitants and allowed no more than 13 liters per person each day. However, this is again only an average figure; in reality the distribution of water was blatantly unfair, reflecting as it did the social inequality of the population.

Until the Second Empire no new fresh water reservoirs were created, so that the main supply still came from the Canal de l'Ourcq.[101] Rambuteau's modest contribution to the city's water distribution—aside from a number of public fountains that really belonged in the category of ornamental additions— was to increase to 1,800 the number of *bornes-fontaines* (public fountains) in the streets.[102] These supply points, which were by no means evenly distributed throughout the city, were also rather inefficient. In the summer months, when demand for fresh water increased, it often happened that only a trickle came out of the faucets; the pipes were of such small diameter that they could not deliver a steady supply of water, even though the reservoirs were full.[103]

But however public access was improved, it was hardly an improvement in the distribution to individual households. These, including the Tuileries, still depended on 20,000 water-carriers, who carried their buckets in the same old way.[104] It is hardly surprising, therefore, that the private use of water, especially for personal hygiene, had to be very sparing among all sectors of society.[105] Frances Trollope, who spent some months in Paris in 1835, reports in one of her letters:

> In London, up to the second floor, and often to the third, water is forced, which furnishes an almost unlimited supply of that luxurious article, to be obtained with no greater trouble to the servants than would be required to draw it from a tea-urn. In one kitchen of every house, generally in two, and often in three, the same accommodation is found; and when, in opposition to this, it is

remembered that very nearly every family in Paris receives this precious gift of nature doled out by two buckets at a time, laboriously brought to them by porters, clambering in *sabots*, often up the same stairs which lead to their drawing-rooms, it can hardly be supposed that the use of it is as liberal and unrestrained as with us. . . . Much as I admire the Church of the Madeleine, I conceive that the city of Paris would have been infinitely more benefited, had the sums expended upon it been used for the purpose of constructing pipes for the conveyance of water to private dwellings, than by all the splendour received from the beauty of this imposing structure.[106]

Until 1848 only 5,300 houses were connected to the rudimentary water system, this being a convenience for which one paid and which only the wealthy could afford. But beyond the costs of installation and use, there was another reason why *l'eau à l'étage* (water on every floor) became the standard norm only in the last third of the nineteenth century: namely, the prehistoric drainage system. In contrast to London, where a flush-sewage system which also absorbed household waste had been worked out early on in the nineteenth century, the Paris sewers served mainly as street drains. Household waste was collected in cesspools, which had to be emptied from time to time. This work was rather expensive and involved a disgusting stench that was still thought to cause sickness in the middle of the nineteenth century.[107] A report on the subject of cesspools states:

The emptying of cesspools in Paris has become a great financial burden to house owners, and the burden is constantly growing. This is due to improvements in cesspool construction, the increase in water consumption occasioned by newly installed toilets, and above all by the greater use of bathtubs.[108]

Paris maintained this medieval system until the Second Empire, when construction of an efficient sewage system was undertaken.[109] Meantime the supply of tap water to households was thwarted by building owners who were unwilling to face the greater expenses involved.[110]

The old system had some unpleasant consequences when the cesspools overflowed, draining into cellars and courtyards, or even polluting freshwater wells. As for the area of Montfaucon, where municipal and suburban sewage was still being deposited, it required the genius of a Dante or a Hieronymus Bosch to describe it adequately. It lay to the north of Paris:

. . . five hundred meters from the Bassin de la Villette and the Barrière du Combat, and twenty-five hundred meters from Montmartre, which is across from it to the west. The topographical height of the area is thirty-six meters, taking the Pont de la Tournelle as zero point; that means Montfaucon lies ten meters above the water reservoir of La Villette and forty-six meters below the highest point of the hills of Saint-Chaumont, which it adjoins. Its location shows that the area is more elevated than the highest points on which Paris stands, and this even holds true for the top ridges of the roofs of most of its buildings.[111]

Montfaucon was not only a dark presence in the consciousness of the Parisian population; its pestilential odors spread to the boulevard du Temple, the Marais, and even the Tuileries on mild summer evenings.[112] In 1832 Parent-Duchâtelet had ascribed the problem there to rapid population growth and the accumulation of waste material:

> Two results have been engendered by this increase in the population and, acting concurrently, have ruined all the amenities procured for the city by our ancestors and produced a state of affairs now approaching barbarism, which, both in Paris and in the surrounding villages, has become intolerable to more than one hundred thousand persons.
>
> The two results are the growth of Paris and the increase in the accumulation of matter giving off noxious effluvia. The reservoirs of this cesspool cover an area of 32,000 square meters, not to speak of twelve acres given over to dry refuse and horse-butchers' yards; some 230 to 244 square meters of human excreta are carted there daily and most of the corpses of twelve thousand horses and twenty-five to thirty thousand smaller animals are left to rot on the ground.[113]

The condition and operation of the enormous horse-butcher yards in Montfaucon made it a particularly fearsome place.[114] Again, Parent-Duchâtelet:

> The courtyards of these horse-butcher yards are partially paved but as they are ungraded the liquids cannot run off; it is impossible to imagine the dreadful filth here: the blood of the animals mixes with the guts and covers the ground; in the rain it forms a thick layer of bloody sludge that has to be removed with a hoe to clear a path to the workshops. . . . One can still see that this area was once enclosed by a thick wall; today only two stone gate jambs remain, while the wall itself has come down, undermined by rats.[115]

The rats of Montfaucon, its repugnant trade, its terrible stench, and finally its location directly outside Paris proscribed any further toleration of "what was undoubtedly the greatest center of contagion ever to exist over a considerable period." This was underscored by the experiences of the cholera epidemic.[116] The need to close Montfaucon, and to transfer the horse-butcher yards and the sewage dump to a more outlying area had been recognized as far back as the Old Regime.[117] But nothing had been done, and the problems had meantime become more urgent. The administration kept putting off making any decision; instead it appointed commissions that made recommendations, which were then contradicted by other commissions.[118] This game would probably have continued had the public not exerted so much pressure that the administration finally gave in just prior to the fall of the July Monarchy.[119]

At any rate Rambuteau could claim smugly:

> I managed to move the sewage depot of Montfaucon—that enormous receptacle for city waste that polluted Belleville and La Villette as soon as the wind blew from the north. I designated the forest of Bondy as its location. But it was no small matter to transport an average of 600 cubic meters of refuse over a distance of fifteen kilometers, every night all year round. This problem was solved by the excellent engineer, M. Mary, who suggested installing an intermediate depot at La Villette; a sixteen-kilometer conduit then pumped the waste to its destination with the help of a forty-horsepower steam engine. Furthermore I had a new horse-butcher's yard installed in the plain of Aubervilliers.[120]

It was left to Haussmann, in the Second Empire, to make up for what the July Monarchy had left undone with his own radical concepts of urban redevelopment. To be sure Rambuteau's strategy of paving and draining streets was in keeping with the wisdom of his times; but in other respects he was far behind for reasons discussed earlier. That applies above all to his avoidance of renovating the older parts of the city in which the *classes misérables et laborieuses* were still crowded together, and where sanitary conditions were beyond description.[121] In a paper on those conditions, Dr. Henri Bayard notes an important reason for Rambuteau's neglect. As the memory of the cholera epidemic faded from public attention, so did the interest in a thorough reform of conditions. "The terror induced by the cholera," he writes in 1844,

> and the fear of its return, made house owners as well as tenants observe certain measures of hygiene for a few months; but these fears were soon allayed and in the twelve years since the outbreak of the epidemic, the carelessness and greed of one group, and the misery and filth of the other, have made it possible for this whole swamp to form and fill up again.[122]

This revival of bad habits and carelessness, as well as the self-congratulatory assumption by administration and public that everything humanly possible had been done—there were no further signs of a cholera epidemic—left Paris on the verge of being strangled by problems of its infrastructure.[123] The situation was compounded by the fact that scientific and technological development in the field of sanitation, especially concerning waste and drainage, had reached a standstill. Yet the public was unaware of the severity of the problems, and reports issued by the *Conseil de salubrité* present an unwarranted optimism.[124] The reports stress that the costs of major redevelopment in the city would be diametrically opposed to the investment interests of the bourgeoisie. It took the Revolution of 1848 to bring about a change in attitude; moreover, a second large-scale cholera epidemic, which lasted from March to September 1849 and created 19,184 victims, hastened the process.[125] The acute danger of another outbreak of the disease in Paris lasted until 1854; during this period there were frequent flare-ups of cholera though never again on the scale of 1849.[126] However, more than 1,000 people died in a typhoid epidemic in the spring of 1853.[127]

Rapid Change and Daring Plans

*T*HE BOURGEOISIE CONTINUED TO IGNORE the preposterous conditions of the capital for which they were responsible, their business interests dominating all other considerations.[128] Thus they profited from the needs of a rapidly growing population by developing every last inch of available space. As Balzac puts it, "Infamous, uncontrolled speculation, which from year to year lowers the heights of ceilings, puts an apartment in the space of a drawing-room, and eliminates gardens, will have an influence on Parisian mores. People will soon be forced to live more outside than inside."[129]

This led to a paradoxical economic situation similar to that of the Restoration. Even at the end of the July Monarchy the economy was still dominated by traditional, small-scale craft production. According to a study by the Paris Chamber of Commerce for 1847, the city possessed 64,153 *établissements industriels;* of these only 11 percent employed more than ten workers, while the number of workshops employing more than fifty workers amounted to a mere 0.6 percent.[130]

These enterprises were spread over three areas of the capital: trades specializing in *articles de Paris* were traditionally found in the center; larger metalworking factories were located near the docks of La Villette and the Canal Saint-Martin; and heavier industry, such as engineering and chemical factories, had settled in the municipalities of the northern and northeastern suburbs.[131] However, compared with the textile factories in Lyon and the heavy industry around the coal basin of Lille and Roubaix, Paris, the political and cultural capital of France, played a subordinate, even provincial manufacturing role. It did not become the industrial capital until several decades later when the full impact of the transportation revolution produced by the railroads began to be felt.

Construction of a domestic railroad system was authorized by the Chamber of Deputies on June 11, 1842. The first line, connecting Paris with Saint-Germain, had already been opened on August 26, 1837. The decision to make Paris the terminal for all lines determined its economic future. As center of the system, Paris necessarily became the most important center of the country's economic activity. The city was more radically affected by this change than by anything that had happened previously. But in the July Monarchy only the possibility of this development was discernible.[132]

The promise of unprecedented prosperity from the new transportation system immediately appealed to the imagination of contemporary speculators. Discussions on the location of the central stations revealed two conflicting points of view.

The railroad companies, concerned with their profits, backed the construction of only two stations, the Gare d'Austerlitz on the Left Bank and the Gare Saint-Lazare on the Right Bank of the Seine.[133] These companies were still privately owned by such financiers as the Péreire brothers who, thanks to the Rothschilds, were among France's earliest railroad magnates.[134] For a short time the Péreires even proposed the building of only one terminal station, in the northwest of Paris, to handle the entire rail traffic.[135]

They were opposed by the *Conseil municipal,* which rightly feared that the new centers of economic activity that would develop around the stations were bound to alter radically the urban geography of the capital. On June 29, 1844, the *Conseil* therefore decided on the construction and location of six terminal stations as close to both sides of the Seine as possible.

This decision had an immediate effect on the Paris real estate market.

Thus Balzac, who took part in the parlor game of speculation despite his chronic shortage of money, writes to Madame Hanska on April 3, 1848:

> In six to seven years the remaining 1,400 meters I own will be worth 300,000 to 400,000 *francs.* Monceaux will then be what the neighborhood of Notre-Dame-de-Lorette is today; one can see that it is a dead certainty just by looking at the way Paris is currently developing. There is a reason for this development, whose progress will be so rapid that it may well all happen in three or four years' time. The reason is the train station for the Versailles, Saint-Germain, Rouen, and Le Havre lines, which is located between the future neighborhood of Monceaux and that of Tivoli. . . . Don't expect me to be wrong, for M. d'Aligre has bought considerable property in this area and he will earn millions when the neighborhood develops.[136]

In addition to building a railroad system and making Paris the center of the French rail network, the July Monarchy was responsible for certain other developments whose consequences were soon to become evident. Ever since the Old Regime, the municipal area of Paris had been defined by the wall of the *fermiers-généraux,* which enclosed large undeveloped or thinly populated areas in the west and south. But the population of the suburbs beyond the wall increased at a fast rate, especially after 1840. The greater part of this growth was concentrated in the suburbs closest to the city in the northwest and north.[137] It was encouraged not only by the coming of the railroads, but also by the decision of the Thiers government in 1840 to surround Paris and its suburbs with fortifications. The extensive work, completed by 1845, covered forty kilometers and linked twenty-four municipalities, or parts of them, to the capital.[138] Although these communities did not lose their autonomy until 1860 when they were formally incorporated into Paris, they were unable to withstand the capital's influence even in the earlier years. As rents and the cost of living were considerably lower than in Paris, many who belonged to the poorer classes left the capital to settle in the suburbs. A large number of immigrants from the provinces, especially those employed in constructing the fortifications and who had remained after the work was completed, also settled there.[139] Within very few years hamlets and once-idyllic villages acquired populations of the size of small towns.[140] Rambuteau, thrifty to the point of miserliness, comments as follows:

> The incorporation of those municipalities which lie between the inner and outer suburbs surrounding Paris was often demanded, but I never gave my consent to it. Construction is going on everywhere in the neighboring villages and hamlets, which are growing into populated areas where everything would have to be established—churches, schools, markets, and wells.[141]

Between 1840 and 1860 Paris exported the elements responsible for its own problems at an ever faster rate. For instance, the proportion of poor people living in the suburbs was three times that of Paris; but these municipalities received ten times less in state subsidies for their support. Moreover, their revenues were five times smaller per inhabitant than those of Paris.[142] In view of this, and in the knowledge that sooner or later they would be incorporated into Paris, the communities undertook very little public construction to meet the needs of their rapidly growing population. A report by Haussmann in 1859 gives a rather inadequate impression of conditions there. It mentions

> a solid circle of suburbs, which are subject to more than twenty different administrations; they developed without a plan and are traversed by a tangled network of narrow and twisted roads; a steadily growing nomadic population, which has no roots and cannot be controlled effectively, is crowded together in little alleys and culs-de-sac.[143]

After 1840 there was a growing tendency to shift all the repulsive and unpleasant phenomena and institutions associated with the growth of the capital to its periphery. The earliest examples of this were the vast establishments of Bicêtre and Salpêtrière, which were combination insane asylums, prisons, and hospices for venereal patients—infamous places where "le malheur et le crime" (misfortune and crime) were jumbled together. The trend continued with the removal of such institutions as cemeteries, rubbish dumps, and slaughterhouses to the suburbs, and finally with the settlement of what were considered *établissements insalubres* (unhygienic factories).[144] The inner suburbs acquired their new character in less than a generation; it caused them to lose their former rural aspect and turn into the grimy fringe of the capital.[145] What was especially significant was their function as catch basin for the poorer classes, whose chances of eking out a living in Paris were steadily decreasing. These drifters and nomads, as they were called, were compared by contemporaries to "barbarians" and "natives," and were viewed as the sworn enemies of bourgeois order.[146] Like the lepers of the Middle Ages, they were socially and geographically excluded, and left to their own fate. From 1840 to the end of the Second Empire, before the inner suburbs were incorporated into Paris or joined to the *grande banlieue* (the outer suburbs), the zone between the wall of the *fermiers-généraux* and the new fortifications was like a giant Montfaucon. The social order simply unloaded all its troublesome, dangerous, or insoluble problems there. In *L'Education sentimentale*, Gustave Flaubert describes the physiognomy of this grimy rim of Paris at the end of the July Monarchy:

> The torn-up plain seemed a vague ruin. The enclosure of the fortifications created a horizontal mass; and on the beaten earth pavements edging the street small trees without branches were protected by laths studded with nails. Chemical factories alternated with lumberyards. High doors such as one sees in farms revealed, through their half-open panels, miserable courtyards full of filth, with puddles of dirty water in the middle. Two long cafés, painted blood-red, bore two crossed billiard cues in a wreath of painted flowers between the windows of their upper storys; here and there stood an abandoned, half-built plaster shanty. Then the double line of houses went on and on; and here and there, against the bareness of their facades, a gigantic tin cigar stood out to indicate a tobacco shop. Signs advertising wet-nurses showed a matron in a bonnet cuddling an

infant in an embroidered cover. Torn posters covered the corners of the walls and fluttered in the wind like rags. Workers in smocks, beer carts, laundry carts, and butchers' carts passed. A fine rain fell, it was cold, and the sky was pale. . . . [147]

The frightening growth of the inner suburbs, especially in the north and northwest of Paris, which were directly affected by the routing of the railroad, created an alarming problem.[148] As more and more activities moved there, neighborhoods in the east, south, and center tended to stagnate, or even to suffer losses in population and resources; they also acquired more poor.[149] At the same time tax revenues and ground rents decreased.[150] The further impoverishment of the poorer quarters of Paris signaled an urban disaster that bothered no one as long as bourgeois property interests were satisfied. Once this was no longer the case, because of the location of train terminals and the economic development stimulated by the boulevards, attention began to be paid to the long-existing problems:

> Paris has an abnormal, irregular life rhythm; the proof is that the boulevards, which are the economic centers of trade and commerce on the Right Bank, do not represent axes of normal and regular activity. Indeed, the considerable effect that radiates from them to the north as far as Batignolles and Monceaux is disadvantageous to the neighborhoods south of them. This movement of absorption reaches all the way to the Palais-Royal, where the rents have decreased. It is inevitable, therefore, that if the importance of Batignolles is further increased by the establishment of train stations, the economic balance will shift even more, to the further advantage of that area.[151]

This development was a small foretaste of what was going to happen all over Paris. On October 29, 1839, the *Conseil général de la ville de Paris* asked the prefect to take whatever action was necessary to prevent the uneven distribution of population and commerce:

> . . . for some years now numerous economic activities have moved from their traditional quarters in the capital to arrondissements that are less built-up, where the circulation of traffic is better, and apartments are healthier and more comfortable; this movement has resulted in a grouping of the population that is disadvantageous to the deserted areas; to stop this it is imperative to build wider thoroughfares and eliminate the polluted alleys by completely renovating the blocks of houses situated in them. But as the construction of new streets is progressing slowly, and as this goal will probably not be completed until the distant future . . . it seems expedient not only to expropriate all the properties along the new streets, but also all the houses in the blocks that need to be rehabilitated.[152]

These recommendations by the *Conseil général* contained an implicit criticism of Rambuteau's urban development policy. They also revealed that the *bourgeoisie régnante* was quite aware that the preservation of its capital investments would be threatened if things were allowed to continue as they were.

The overall problems of proceeding with the city's rehabilitation, and of stopping or reversing these troublesome trends, were part of the ongoing debate. For it was clear that "this population displacement will not happen without causing major changes in the life of the arrondissements involved, and hence will also affect the income of property owners there."[153] Of course these concerns were shared by only a very small group of large property owners and real-estate investors, who hoped to profit from a major redevelopment program. At any rate, the main reasons given for the population exodus from the center of Paris were the overcrowding and unsanitary conditions, and the chaotic traffic problems.[154]

This diagnosis determined the cure for the condition, as set out in a study by Ernest de Chabrol-Chaméane:

> Instead of the winding, narrow, and inadequate streets in which the air does not circulate; instead of the miserable houses found in the old neighborhoods on both banks of the Seine, wide streets should be built with low gradients; the main thoroughfares should be generous and even streets of lesser importance should be expanded so that in being connected with the major ones they aid the traffic flow. If this were done, the population would no longer think of leaving these arrondissements; moreover, one could then count on the gradual return of all those who left with regret because need forced them to do so.[155]

But, as Jacques Lanquetin, a prominent member of the *Conseil de la ville*, pointed out, any comprehensive redevelopment and restoration of the city's center had to be complemented by "well-developed and convenient connections with outlying arrondissements." For the latter, he noted, "are separated from the center by bridges that levy tolls, and by a lack of wide and direct streets."[156] Here he was raising another problem, namely that inadequate communication channels within the city threatened its disintegration into numerous autonomous subcenters: " . . . a collection of small market towns of varying character, with distinctive habits and customs that will inevitably lead to rivalry, disagreements, division, and maybe even to outright dispute among them." To prevent this from happening, it was important to develop "a system . . . a comprehensive plan, taking into account future circumstances affecting public structures and street improvements in Paris."[157]

This solution also had an interesting national policy component that expressed a new understanding of the importance of the capital. Paris was the center of the nation's political and cultural activities, and its future development would affect the rest of the country. Hence it was only fair that everyone participate in eliminating the capital's problems. For what had to be prevented, above all, "was that circumstances arise in the seat of government that create unrest and revolt, especially in a capital where the least upheaval has such great influence on the welfare of all of France."[158] Thus it was in the interests of state security to help finance, at least partially, the necessary redevelopment in Paris (see map 2, page 344).

It became possible to do that later, during the Second Empire, as long as the nation's deputies remembered 1848. But during the July Monarchy, as Lanquetin anticipates, it was impossible to get the Chamber's particularist majority to go along with such an idea.[159] Moreover, it was questionable whether the *Conseil général*, which was dominated by property owners fundamentally averse to any kind of rehabilitation, would have been willing and in a position to grant Rambuteau the necessary means. A tax increase was not in the interests of the class the *Conseil* represented; and their bourgeois business sense rejected raising credit as "debt-creating." The grandiose plans of Hippolyte Meynadier or Perreymond, suggesting the revitalization of the city's center to avoid the depopulation of the southern and eastern arrondissements, were therefore published in vain.[160] These plans are worth mentioning because, long before Napoleon III and Haussmann came up with quite different strategies, they offered some plausible solutions for the complex problems that had defeated both the July Monarchy and the Restoration.

Bourgeois Revels

HE BOURGEOIS MONARCHY FIRMLY BELIEVED that what was best for it corresponded with the common good. This illusion was even confirmed by Rambuteau's policy, provided one visited certain city neighborhoods and avoided others; for, as noted earlier, Rambuteau's program of paving, drainage, and the planting of trees had chiefly benefited the western and northwestern quarters. And it was in these arrondissements that commercial investments had had their greatest success during the July Monarchy. The shopping arcades, which had been such a bonanza for the Restoration, were now competing with the profitable stores along the boulevards. This development that followed the July Revolution is interestingly described by Bazin:

> Each time the nation throws off its chains and its oppressive yoke . . . the new political experiences arouse an uncontrollable desire for entertainment from which the boulevards have especially profited. But quite apart from all other changes, here the spirit of the times made effective use of the industry, greed, and prudence that are part of speculation. First the gardens disappeared; the inevitable five-story house with its clumsy facade, its high, narrow windows, its tiny balconies and its stores, replaced those spaces where one once looked on trees and flowers. Where there was no extra building space the stores found a solution by nestling under a terrace, or leaning against a wall; or they were added on to the ground floor. Do not bother to look for "the extravagant buildings, the elegant houses, the English-style garden apartments, the classic pavilions" that once lined this street. All that has been replaced by businesses, stores, and cafés. . . . The habits of the public have changed along with the area; there is no longer a capricious and select social group nervously moving through here at certain hours, expecting something that will excite or entertain them at one or another spot. Now rather there is a general and constant desire to spend time here, without any other attraction than that of the crowd, without any other purpose than that each individual wants to be here along with everyone else.[161]

Commerce burst out of the relatively narrow and intimate arcades and took over the much more spacious, asphalt-covered boulevard. The latter no longer frightened off elegant society as it had formerly done with its dust in the summer, and mud and sludge in other seasons.[162] Moreover, it provided a much larger and more animated stage for a public "that provided entertainment and spectacle for itself."[163] The boulevard became the preferred playground of the *boulevardier*, the *flâneur*, the "one and only sovereign of Paris," as Bazin called him.[164] This individual's whole attitude and behavior embodied his intimate knowledge of a secret that Victor Hugo describes as follows: "Paris expresses the world. For Paris is a whole. Paris is the summit of mankind. . . . Everything found elsewhere is also in Paris."[165] The boulevard, "this promenade truly unique in Europe," was the quintessence of metropolitan life and pleasure.[166] One of these boulevards contained the most famous cafés and restaurants, the Café de Paris, Frascati, and Tortoni, as well as the popular theaters.[167]

Along with the novelty of asphalt, it was gaslight—introduced in grand style after the July Revolution—that added to the popularity of the boulevards.[168] Gaslight not only eliminated those horrors of nighttime Paris, which had become a permanent feature of picturesque literature since Restif de la Bretonne, but lent Paris a new, highly poetic charm. The magic of the Champs-Elysées and the boulevards grew stronger when "all the gas jets strung like a double row of shining pearls as far as the eye could see" bathed everything in a magic light.[169] And even such a superb authority on the pathological condition of the capital as Balzac was impressed by the effect of the boulevards. In a letter to Mme Hanska on September 1, 1837, he writes:

> You have no idea how lovely Paris is becoming; what we needed was this program of building to attain such great results—this splendor that increases daily everywhere, makes us worthy of being the capital of the world. The asphalt-paved boulevards, lit by brass-plated gas lamps, the growing luxury of the stores of this eternal, ever-changing, two-mile-long fair, offer a matchless spectacle. In ten years we shall be clean, we shall no longer talk of the mud of Paris, and then we shall be so magnificent that Paris will truly be seen as a lady of the world, the first among queens, wreathed in walls.[170]

The boulevards, which the petite bourgeoisie saw as its "belt of Venus, of its beloved city," were an important part of the *fête bourgeoise* indulged in by the *juste milieu*.[171] This *fête bourgeoise* is linked in particular to one man, Philippe Musard, as gifted an orchestra conductor as he was an efficient organizer of public balls. His importance in the July Monarchy can only be compared to that of the more famous Jacques Offenbach later on.[172]

There had already been numerous public balls and festivities in Paris during the Restoration. In the summer months outlying garden restaurants like the Jardin de Tivoli at the end of the rue Blanche, or the Jardin de la Grande-Chaumière along the boulevard Montparnasse, as well as Le Ranelagh in the Champs-Elysées—to name the more important ones—were popular places of entertainment.[173] In the autumn and winter dances were held in the mostly uncomfortable *salles d'hiver* in the inner-city neighborhoods. But all of these balls and dances were comparatively modest affairs that contrasted strangely with the enormous settings in which they were held. Generally the dance orchestra consisted of only three or four occasional musicians: one or two violins, a clarinet, and a large drum. A real orchestra of no more than thirty musicians was the exception. The orchestras' musical repertoire was correspondingly modest, so that the dances attended by Parisians during the Restoration were more like family celebrations than uncontrolled saturnalia.[174]

Just as in the period following Thermidor, a dance craze swept through Paris after the *Trois Glorieuses*. Jules Janin comments tersely: "Revolutions turn into entertainment; a ball is the antithesis of an uprising."[175] Indeed there is much to be said for the theory that the dance craze—like all the popular pleasures that promptly became excesses—was a phenomenon complementary to the "time of riots" as Parisians characterized the years 1830–34.[176] An especially crude example of this is the storming and plundering of the archbishop's palace at the height of carnival in 1831. Celebration of carnival had been discontinued under the Empire and Restoration. It was revived with very primitive and hence particularly popular rituals like the *promenade du boeuf* or, on Ash Wednesday morning, the *descente de la courtille*, a wild masked procession from Belleville to the inner city.[177]

An account of carnival in 1833, by Auguste Luchet, illustrates how closely misery was tied to uncontrolled abandonment in a densely populated area like Paris. He writes:

> As soon as all the cholera victims had been buried everyone made ready to celebrate. But civil war followed the cholera epidemic. Then the jubilation was revived again. Yet everyone shared a deep foreboding. Ah well! The *peuple* did not want to be alone because they did not feel comfortable and were afraid. They clapped their hands and stamped their feet, they shouted and sang. When the period of carnival, from February 2 to February 19, was considered too short, it was simply extended by two months; it began five weeks sooner and ended three weeks later. The strange balls of 1833 were the extension of this unique carnival time: hunger and thirst, which increased with this wild entertainment, became part of the seemingly unappeasable craving for movement and noise for which people longed in order to become numb and to forget.[178]

The frenetic craving for entertainment experienced by Parisians in those first, truly dreadful years of the July Monarchy found its outlet in the masked carnivals and big public balls held all year round. Those large dances offered a twofold opportunity, just as the riots and street battles had done: a spectacle as well as the chance to be active, to plunge into the midst of a mass of bodies—whether it was to be heroic or to express the music. Both on the barricades and the dance floor one acted unanimously with the rest of the crowd, was inevitably swept along by its will and momentum. These balls were more like public brawls, athletic games for which one turned up in festive clothes. What made them especially attractive was that social classes were equalized by the common enjoyment. They formed a colorful anonymous crowd in which everyone—a milliner in the arms of a consular attaché, young and old, rich and poor—sought oblivion in music and dance.[179]

It was Philippe Musard who sensed this longing by the public and who intuitively understood the mass psychology behind it. He organized those battles to which everyone flocked, he directed them, and made them extraordinarily effective. The means he used were very simple: a large orchestra of at least forty musicians selected by him, which flooded every nook and cranny of a hall with its sound. Musard was able to turn any ball at which his orchestra performed into an event because he understood how to harmonize the diffuse wishes of a public of two to three thousand individuals. Each ball was a uniquely ecstatic experience, an orgy of bodies and sounds.[180]

Musard was undoubtedly the uncrowned king of the *fête bourgeoise* during the July Monarchy. The great secret of his magic was music—the melodies his baton beat out of his orchestra. The latter consisted of the best musicians he could obtain; the melodies overwhelmed the dense mass of dance enthusiasts and stirred them into an exhibitionist frenzy, an orgiastic madness. The infamous carnival balls that Musard organized in the Théâtre des Variétés were particularly like a combination of orgy and witches' sabbath. That is where the cancan reigned, the dance with brutal and unambiguous movements first seen in Paris in the cholera year of 1832 of all times, and which immediately created a scandal. However, it was not Musard who introduced this dance, considered shameless by most of his contemporaries; rather it was the *jeunesse dorée* who, looking for an antidote to their boredom in the *juste milieu*, had come across the cancan. It was presumably based on a dance from Algeria. The *classes laborieuses* enjoyed the dance on their Sunday excursions to cheap cafés outside the city gates. Count d'Alton Shée, one of the leaders of the *jeunesse dorée*, describes his activities in making the cancan known:

> As with new religions, acceptance of the cancan did not occur without persecution. Distrustful city administrators, astonished policemen, after having participated in the general exhilaration, became enemies of excess and took it upon themselves to expel several of these dangerous innovators. La Curée and Fordié, who were prosecuted, found a home in the Café des Variétés which was connected with the theater. This is where the whole group met, supported by numerous proselytes. They decided to force their way back into the hall. The triumphant rebels began dancing harder than ever; the enthusiasm was at its peak. Monsieur Dartois, the director of the Variétés and a man of wit, understood at a glance that here was a new, lucrative source of income. . . . The success of the balls at the Variétés grew from Sunday to Sunday; newspapers wrote about them, fashion adopted them, and the cancan became all the rage.[181]

It is difficult to form a real impression of the original incredible effect of this dance following its relative domestication by Jacques Offenbach. The cancan was offensive because it revealed passions until then contained by the conventions of the round dances whose stiff elegance bored people after 1830. Because the cancan mocked decency and morals, it embodied a permanent revolt of body and senses. It was an earthshaking event, and an upright man like the German musician Ludwig Rellstab, having seen the cancan on his visit to Paris in the spring of 1843, was filled with horror:

The couples dance in an indecently crowded space, where often the spontaneous contact becomes unavoidably indecorous. But if you notice with what gestures and body movements the males approach the females . . . press themselves against them, and literally throw them from one to the other, and all of it done with shrieks and laughter and obscene jokes, then you are overcome with disgust, yes even more than that, repugnance, a dread of this mass licentiousness, this mockery of all morals and remorse.

As if this were not enough, Rellstab discovered there was worse to come, the cancan became a hellish furioso:

The rhythm of the music grows faster, the movements of the dancers become wilder, more aggressive, more heated; finally the *contredanse* turns into a big galop of paired couples, four in a row, who rush through the hall. Even when the decidedly indecorous individual movements have ceased, the positions and facial expression demonstrate a more aroused lewdness, and the whole wild and ever wilder galop presents a horrible picture of bacchanalian wantonness. In this dance the rhythm also grows faster, and eventually the females look like racing maenads—with glowing cheeks, breathless heaving chests, panting lips, hair that has come undone and is flying—more dragged along with frenzied speed than on their own feet, chasing through the hall until they drop onto the nearest chair as the last chord of the music is heard.[182]

Rellstab, who was so indignant over the obscenity of the cancan, overlooked the fact that it was the *jeunesse dorée*'s way of travestying the values of the *juste milieu*, whose superficiality and dishonesty it laid bare. But once it caught on as a popular public dance, it lost its provocative force. Heine saw through the cancan's polemic intentions, though his understanding of the situation fills him "with inexpressible sadness," as he admits:

It is not only sexual relationships that are the object of wicked dances in the Paris dance halls. It sometimes seems to me as though the dances performed there are a travesty of all that is noble and holy in life, but that has so often been exploited by smart alecks, and made ridiculous by simpletons, that the *peuple* can no longer believe in it as they used to. Yes, the *peuple* have lost their faith in those exalted thoughts of which our political and literary Tartuffes sing and speak so much; indeed the impotent bragging talk so spoiled all ideal things for them that they can no longer see anything in it other than hollow phrases, a so-called *blague* [farce]; and just as Robert Macaire represents this hopeless attitude, it is also revealed in the dance of the *peuple*, which has to be seen as the actual pantomime of Robert Macaire-dom.[183] Whoever has some idea of the latter can now understand those inexpressible dances that as a danced burlesque, not only mock sexual but also bourgeois relationships; in fact they mock everything that is good and beautiful, every kind of inspiration, love of one's country, fidelity, faith, feelings for the family, heroism, the deity.[184]

The Writing on the Wall

USARD'S WELL-ORCHESTRATED DANCE CRAZE and the popular though quasi-illegal cancan were only two among many aspects of the crisis facing the July Monarchy. The glittering mask of the *fête bourgeoise*, so enjoyed by a *juste milieu* proud of its progressive attitudes, could not hide the symptoms of the disease disfiguring its physiognomy. The same gas lamps that cast a magic glow over the boulevards also attracted myriads of itinerant merchants, tricksters, panhandlers, and beggars. They came from that "Greater India," of which Alfred de Musset remarked that it exists only outside of India.[185] Hence it was surely no coincidence, but rather one of those ironies occasionally produced by history, that the July Monarchy fell during the carnival of 1848. It collapsed "without a fight" as Tocqueville writes, "not from blows, but rather from the mere presence of the victors, who were as surprised by their victory as the vanquished were by their fall."[186] It was as though the final, infernolike galop of the cancan had pulled them down.

No other revolution has been predicted so early, with such certainty, and by so many contemporaries as the February Revolution of 1848. Unmistakable signs of its approach could be found in all sections of society from the beginning of the 1840s. The rapid influx of the "floating, nomadic population," which arrived on the trains in ever larger numbers, was particularly disquieting. As always this group was attracted to Paris by the great demand for labor. Karl Gutzkow writes in 1842:

> In this seemingly orderly life four thousand workers daily come to the place de Grève early in the morning, without knowing what they are going to live on that day if they cannot find work; ten thousand who are uncertain of the coming day, twenty thousand who are unsure about the coming week—that is the morbid substance that seeps from the outermost skin of this city, the *barrières* and faubourgs, every day, to infect the inner parts of the social body, the alliance of power and wealth, high rank and possessions.[187]

Gutzkow's observations reflect a tendency that had become more marked since the beginning of the July Monarchy. The number of seasonal workers who arrived in Paris in the spring and who generally returned to their homes in the *morte saison* was constantly growing smaller. It was now customary even for those who were unemployed, or whose families had not come with them, to remain in the capital, a change that affected their integration into the metropolitan milieu.[188] Their presence created a homogeneous working class, leveling previous differences of origin as well as strengthening an overall class consciousness. Traditional rivalries between individual provinces, regions, and villages, which had still caused conflicts and brawls among seasonal workers in the Restoration period, disappeared or were considered of only minor importance.[189] What also contributed to a certain, if very rudimentary class consciousness of the working population was the spread of Saint-

Simonist, socialist, or even communist ideas.[190] The process is described by Heine in a report for the newspaper *Augsburger Allgemeine* on April 30, 1840:

> "Tell me what you sowed today and I shall tell you what you will reap tomorrow!" I thought of this saying by the vigorous Sancho recently, as I was visiting a few workshops in the faubourg Saint-Marceau and discovered what sort of reading material is circulating among the *ouvriers*, the strongest section of the lower class. I found several new editions of old Robespierre's speeches there, as well as pamphlets by Marat; for two sous there were editions of Cabet's history of the Revolution, Cornemin's vicious brochure, Baboeuf's teachings, and Buonarotti's conspiracy, writings that smelled of blood; and I heard songs that seemed to have been written in hell and whose refrains created the wildest excitement. No, in our genteel sphere we cannot conceive of the demonic tones of those songs; one has to have heard them with one's own ears, in those huge workshops where metal is processed and where defiant, half-naked figures beat time on the droning anvil with a large metal hammer as they sing. Such accompaniment is most effective, as is the lighting when angry sparks fly from the forge, nothing but passion and flame! The Republic threatens to burst forth sooner or later as the fruit of this seed.[191]

Indeed, the revolution of February 1848 was unique for having been foretold with such precision.[192] There is Alexis de Tocqueville's famous and oftenquoted statement, made in a speech to the Chamber of Deputies on January 27: "This, gentlemen, is my deep conviction: I believe we are sleeping on a volcano at this hour. I am firmly convinced of it. . . ." [193] But no prophets were needed to make such a forecast; there had been increasing signs of a sudden change, a revolutionary overthrow not only of the regime but of society as well. The crisis that culminated in the events of February 1848 had its origins in various complex problems, but particularly those of a social nature.

With the rapid economic-industrial developments of the 1840s, of which the railroad system and the steam engine were the most conspicuous, the whole question of the working class tended to become more prominent. In contrast to the beginning of the July Monarchy, when the "Saint-Simonist church" flourished only underground and the expression of early socialist ideas was limited to a small group of outsiders, social questions were taken up after 1840 by the press and men of letters. However, one must not overestimate the effects of this discussion; for what came out of it were vague forebodings of a threat to society combined with philanthropic efforts. No coherent socialist doctrine developed that could have successfully organized the overthrow of the existing system. In fact the revolution of 1848 had its banal and rather unheroic origins in a general dissatisfaction experienced by all sections of society. It gave rise to a political opposition that expressed itself in a very vague, undifferentiated, and carping attitude.

The main reason for this general discontent was the economic crisis of 1846. Once again the limited development of the national economy was revealed by the way in which all sectors were affected. Characteristically the problems were preceded by bad harvests: potatoes, which had become a staple food of the *peuple*, were unavailable in Europe for several years because of blight. Moreover, the 1845 wheat crop had only been average. The resulting shortage of basic foods and their high price no longer produced famine in Paris; but the effects were such that at the height of the crisis, in the spring of 1846, various bakeries in faubourg Saint-Antoine were plundered by angry crowds.

What made these difficulties worse—though the authorities tried to alleviate them by issuing bread coupons to the needy—was their concurrence with an industrial crisis. Employers met decreasing demand with layoffs, thereby creating greater unemployment. The effect on the building and railroad construction industries was particularly severe; the metal and textile industries were also hurt, their unemployment rate rising to over 35 percent. Several companies in the latter category were forced into bankruptcy because of insufficient capital reserves and the inability to raise funds in a troubled credit market.[194] Even though commerce and the credit market recovered, social tensions continued after 1847, adding to the general spirit of unhappiness that the press helped articulate.

The influence of public opinion on events was directly related to the escalating predicament of the regime. The *Chambre des pairs* (the upper chamber), which had its seat in the Luxembourg Palace and whose members were appointed for life by the government, soon lost whatever authority it had, and was forgotten by the public. For its part, the *Chambre des députés* (the lower chamber) was thoroughly compromised by numerous cases of corruption.[195]

These problems were exacerbated and increased by a moral crisis that had overcome the bourgeoisie suppporting the regime.[196] There were two particular scandals in 1847 that revealed the moral corruption of the July Monarchy and incensed the public. The first was the Teste-Cubières affair, a bribery and corruption case involving two ministers; the mild verdict by the *Cour des pairs*, to which two of the principal defendants belonged, was equally shocking. The other scandal was that of the murder of the duchesse de Choiseul-Praslin, who was literally butchered with a knife by her husband, the duc de Praslin. Victor Hugo comments on the significance of both of these events to the July Monarchy in these words: "At first the army was stunned by the affair of General Cubières; then it was the turn of the court with the case of President Teste; next comes the aristocracy, which is affected by the murder committed by the duc de Praslin. Now it is necessary for such things to come to an end."[197]

The February Revolution

*T*HE MORAL DECLINE OF THE REGIME, which obstinately refused to make any reforms, occurred against a background of socioeconomic problems, especially pauperism. In fact the convergence of political and economic crises so isolated and weakened the monarchy that its very existence, at least as long as it was represented by Louis-Philippe, became more and more questionable. Yet the opposition was equally impotent and lacked any clear political goals, as shown by the Banquet Campaign begun in July 1847.[198]

Participants in these banquets were exclusively individuals entitled to vote. In other words, the extraparliamentary opposition movement thus formed was restricted to a circle of dissatisfied notables who were anything but radicals, let alone revolutionaries. And yet the Banquet Campaign was decisive in the development of the revolution of February 1848. A final banquet in the series was to have been given in January 1848 by the reform-minded members of the Chamber, who feared they were losing control of the opposition movement. Although it was no different from preceding ones, the prefect of police prohibited it on January 14 on the instructions of the minister of the interior. The organizers reacted to this attack on the legally guaranteed freedom of assembly by postponing the banquet to February 22, and by emphasizing the exclusiveness of their meeting. Originally the banquet was to have taken place in the twelfth arrondissement, an overwhelmingly working-class neighborhood; now it was moved to the western edge of Paris, to the rue du Chemin-de-Versailles. Moreover, the admission price was raised from 3 to 6 francs, and entrance was highly restricted. But despite these concessions the authorities continued to forbid the meeting. In order to avoid further confrontation with the government the majority of the opposition in the Chamber canceled the banquet.[199]

But this conciliatory gesture by an opposition lacking in courage was too late to affect further events. The confrontations between the regime and the overwhelmingly pro-dynasty reform movement, which had found its rallying point in that banquet, were watched with growing suspense by the public. On the morning of that cold and rainy February 22, curious individuals and demonstrators made their way to the place de la Madeleine where the banquet had originally been scheduled. Most of them were unaware that the deputies had given in to the regime, a fact that became known only in the course of the day, and which many were unwilling to believe. Meanwhile more and more people appeared in the boulevards, on the place de la Concorde, and in the streets around the Madeleine. The rain and cold and confirmation that the deputies had canceled the banquet transformed curiosity into anger. Individual calls of "A bas Guizot! Vive la Réforme!" were heard, and here and there the Marseillaise was sung. Toward midday a group of a hundred students, which had formed in the Quartier Latin, arrived in the place de la Concorde. At about the same time demonstrators arrived in front of the Chamber of Deputies in the Palais Bourbon and in front of the Ministry of Foreign Affairs in the boulevard des Capucines, where Guizot had his office. Eventually units of the much-hated *garde municipale* stepped in and chased the demonstrators away from the place de la Concorde. Two people, an old woman and a worker, were killed; their deaths sparked a call for revenge for the first time that day. Demonstrators in front of the Palais Bourbon were also dispersed by troops, while the deputies inside were being bored by a debate on the establishment of a bank in Bordeaux.[200]

All of this happened without more serious incidents and it only became apparent in the evening hours that the situation could grow worse and turn into open rebellion and bloodshed. In the rue de Richelieu an arms dealer was plundered; so was a warehouse in the rue Bondy, where all sorts of theatrical weapons and props belonging to the Théâtre de l'Ambigu were stored; the intruders armed themselves with rapiers, wooden swords, cardboard armor and helmets, and other equipment. The first barricades were also erected. "All of this," writes Daniel Stern, "took place in a very polite and well-mannered way. Hired coaches and private carriages were stopped, their passengers were helped out, the horses were unhitched and given to the coachmen; only then were the vehicles overturned, and the paving stones torn up."[201]

The sum total of all the incidents did not, however, add up to a revolt. At any rate most men of the regime showed no sign of anxiety; to calm the comte de Falloux, who was somewhat anxious about future developments, Thiers said: "A revolution! A revolution! One can see that you know nothing about government and that you understand nothing about its means of power. I, I know what they are! They are ten times more powerful than any conceivable revolt!"[202] The regime could in all good conscience believe itself adequately prepared for all eventualities. Besides the 3,000 men of the *garde municipale*, there were 30,000 additional troops stationed in and around the capital. Moreover, the government had a plan, worked out by Marshal Gérard in 1840, by which any uprising in the city could be quickly put down. That the regime fell within two days, despite these dispositions, was due to the very forces on whose loyalty the regime depended—the middle and petite bourgeoisie, from which the National Guard was drawn.

By the morning of February 23 the physiognomy of Paris was fundamentally changed. Barricades had been put up during the night in the rues Rambuteau, de Tracy, Saint-Denis, Greneta, and Quincampoix. In the early morning hours troop reinforcements began occupying strategic points like the place de la Concorde, the place du Carrousel, and the place de l'Hôtel de Ville, as well as the Porte Saint-Denis and the Porte Saint-Martin, in accordance with the emergency plan. But these measures were of doubtful value in a confrontation between the troops and the population, for soldiers and insurgents were fraternizing everywhere as the barricades continued to go up.[203] Here and there, in the neighborhood of the Halles and elsewhere, groups were supplied with wine and food, and individuals insisted they did not want to shoot each other. The biggest unknown factor was the National Guard, which had also been called up on the 23rd. This troop of petits bourgeois were most annoyed that Guizot's government had refused to reform the voting rights, a reform which would have made them active citizens. Thus, while not exactly opposing the regime, they rejected its political representatives.[204] It was no secret that these petits bourgeois, whose political aspirations had been disappointed and who had suffered from the effects of the economic crisis, were unwilling to give up their lives at the barricades to protect the *juste milieu*. When the National Guard of the twelfth arrondissement arrived at their place of assembly it quickly became clear that if it came to a battle this group would join the insurgents. Cries of "A bas le ministère! Vive la Réforme! A bas Guizot!" could be heard coming from everywhere in their ranks. Five hundred guards of the Fourth Legion from the Halles, the Louvre, and the Banque de France neighborhoods marched to the Palais Bourbon without weapons and followed by a crowd, to hand a petition to the deputies requesting wide-ranging reform.

Similar protests were organized in other parts of the city by guard members. But even if the demonstrations differed according to the district and its social composition, it was clear that the National Guard always had the same concerns. They wanted to keep public peace and order because they knew only too well that violent confrontations were harmful to business; and while they shared anti-Guizot sentiments, they feared socialist activity, seeing it as a threat to their property.

When Louis-Philippe realized in the afternoon of February 23 the extent of the guards' hostile attitude toward Guizot, he decided to sacrifice his minister of foreign affairs and appoint comte Molé to form a new government. Guizot's dismissal, which was a concession to the National Guard, seemed to decrease the tension and to assure the continued loyalty of these troops. The fact that by the evening the protest movement swelled into a major revolt that toppled the monarchy was not the result of a carefully planned coup to establish a republic; rather, it came about because of a tragic incident in the general agitation that produced far-reaching consequences.

When the news of Guizot's ouster became known the streets near the ministries filled with a happy and excited crowd. Cries of "Illuminez! Illuminez!" were heard, as Maxime Du Camp writes, a wish that was immediately fulfilled: "Lamps, rush lights, and candles were put in the windows for lack of lanterns."[205] Gustave Flaubert, who was also there and who included his impressions in his novel *L'Education sentimentale*, notes: "There was joy everywhere. Strollers walked through the streets and lanterns on every floor [of the houses] spread bright light."[206] But at ten o'clock that evening, in the boulevard des Capucines where the Foreign Ministry was located, this festive and relaxed mood changed abruptly into turmoil and fighting. A crowd had made its way there from the eastern parts of the city, and now found themselves blocked off by troops protecting the ministry.[207] As is usually the case, the sight of armed force was seen as a provocation. The crowd demanded to be allowed to pass. In the general confusion that followed a shot suddenly rang out; the increasingly nervous troops interpreted it as a signal to begin firing on the densely packed crowd; fifty-two were killed in the first salvo.[208] Hardly had the shots died down when the troops as well as the crowd fled the area in panic. Only the victims and a few courageous demonstrators, who cared for the wounded, remained.

The *fusillade du boulevard des Capucines* was the spark that ignited the uprising. But the manner in which the news of this senseless slaughter was made known that night added considerably to the excitement and aroused the vengeance of the masses. A coach taking passengers to the Gare du Nord, which passed by shortly after the event, was stopped and sixteen of the corpses were loaded onto it. It was then led slowly through the nocturnal streets.[209]

What must be asked is whether that bloody and macabre event was sheer happenstance, and whether later developments were other than a mere chain reaction. But news of Guizot's dismissal certainly did not put a stop to the agitation in the eastern parts of the city; on the contrary, it was understood there as only the first of further concessions.

Concessions by those in power, a familiar process by now, tended to expedite rather than halt the process of revolutionary fermentation. Basically the decision to dismiss Guizot satisfied the petit-bourgeois elements in the National Guard, who hoped it would lead to the reforms they wanted, though they would not benefit the working class. However, fate decreed that the following day, February 24, would see these two groups united against the July Monarchy. Naturally this sudden unity was not the product of political calculation, but rather a spontaneous reaction to the accidental and sense-less bloodbath on the boulevard des Capucines.

Paris was no longer peaceful after this attack. Numerous barricades blocked the streets on the morning of February 24. Trees had been felled overnight, coaches and buses turned over, paving stones piled up, and con-struction material used to create obstacles for the anticipated troops. There were barricades even in affluent neighborhoods, such as the Champs-Elysées, the avenue Marbeuf, the rue de la Paix, and around the place Vendôme. The Left Bank, which had remained quiet except for the Latin Quarter, also joined the revolutionary movement; the latter was naturally strongest in those areas dominated by the *classes laborieuses*.

As fighting broke out it soon became evident that the situation was beyond the military's control, either because various units deserted to the insurgents or because the strength of the insurrectionaries at the barricades had been underestimated. At midday Louis-Philippe decided to abdicate. Toward one o'clock, the fighting moved closer to the Tuileries and the king fled to Saint-Cloud. An hour later the victors stormed the Tuileries and destroyed all the emblems of the monarchy. Louis-Philippe's throne was car-ried in triumph to the place de la Bastille, where it was burned at the foot of the Colonne de juillet.[210] But despite the destructiveness and confusion of the elated crowd little was plundered, according to Prosper Mérimée's letter to the comtesse de Montijo.[211]

The revolution of 1848 was the least bloody of the nineteenth century. There were only 350 dead and 500 wounded during those three days in February. Alexis de Tocqueville actually felt, as he says in his memoirs,

as if one were still replaying the French Revolution, instead of continuing it. Despite all the naked sabers, the bayonets, and the muskets, I never thought for a moment that I might be in serious danger, nor did anyone else, and I am quite convinced that no one ever actually was in danger. The bloody hatred was only noticeable later on; the special nature of the February Revolution was not yet evident. While they waited, they tried to absorb the passions of their predeces-sors, without managing to do so; they imitated their gestures and posture, as they knew them from the theater, but it was not possible to reproduce their enthusiasm, let alone reexperience their hatred. It was only the tradition of violent acts that these cold souls practiced, without having really understood them. Even though I could definitely foresee that the denouement of this drama would be terrible, I could never take its performers quite seriously; the whole thing seemed a poor tragedy to me, performed by provincial actors.[212]

In fact people were convinced that this revolution had come prematurely, and they also believed, as Tocqueville writes, that "this time a regime was not overthrown, it was simply allowed to fall."[213]

This evaluation explains the astonishment mixed with fear over the unexpected and little-desired outcome of the three days in February. Maxime du Camp puts it this way: "Paris had played with a rebellion and ended with a revolution. . . . Under the pretext of strengthening our institutions we overthrew them, and instead of changing the government, we destroyed the regime."[214] The Republic proclaimed with some tumult on February 25 in the Hôtel de Ville—the place which had served every revolution as organizational center—was a changeling over whose "upbringing" the parties soon fought fiercely. But at first there was confusion, helplessness, and anxiety born of deep forebodings. For the bourgeoisie associated the Republic with disorder, risk, and all sorts of involvements guaranteed to upset the normal course of business. Bourgeois Paris, which had lit its lamps after Guizot had fallen, was now overcome with a leaden numbness. Writing of his encounters with the "losers" of the revolution, the former deputies and peers, the merchants and property owners, Tocqueville reports: "I frequently came across great fear, but little of the real passion that I certainly noticed elsewhere; there was a peculiar resignation. There was no hope anywhere, indeed, I am almost tempted to say there was no thought of returning to the old system; on the contrary, people made haste to distance themselves from it."[215]

Class Struggles and Civil War

*T*HE RESIGNATION OF THOSE WHO HAD SUPPORTED the July Monarchy forms a strange contrast to the elation scattered throughout Paris following the proclamation of the Republic:

Since business was suspended, unrest and curiosity brought everyone out. Inattention to dress blurred class differences, hatred was concealed while hope was plainly demonstrated and the crowds were quiet. Pride in the rights acquired was reflected on all the faces. There was a carnival-like exuberance everywhere and enjoyment of a sort of camp life; nothing was more entertaining than this aspect of Paris during these first days.[216]

Actually this boisterous mood was an anticipation of the great uncertainty ahead, for the February Revolution did more to arouse than to satisfy expectations; it produced more problems than solutions. The battle was by no means over, rather it was to break out again after a short pause and, as soon became evident, with great violence.

However, at first there was much hope, anticipation, and enthusiasm that masked all differences. The walls of houses were covered with notices and announcements celebrating the Revolution and the Republic, or glorifying the French people who were asked to observe unity and brotherhood, as well as respect for property and possessions. Numerous delegations made daily pilgrimages to the Hôtel de Ville to express their demands to the Provisional Government installed there, or to bring a donation for country and Republic.[217] Trees were planted everywhere in the name of freedom, and members of the clergy attended these ceremonies in the naïve belief that holy water would decontaminate such symbols of another revolution.[218]

But very gradually the spirit inspiring the processions, ceremonies, and delegations changed. The earlier conciliatory euphoria receded and instead the activities became expressions of party interests, of the social or economic goals of individual groups. For instance, on March 9 several thousand merchants and bankers from the area around the Bourse went to the Hôtel de Ville to ask for an extension of the legal period allowed for payments of debts to three months. They threatened, in the event that the government refused their request, to dismiss their assistants and workers: "We shall tell them to turn to you for their bread, and we shall see whether they will be satisfied by your patriotism."[219] A week later the *bonnets à poils*, the elite troops of the National Guard known by their bearskin caps, protested against the Provisional Government's intention to abolish their fraternal associations.[220] The following day, March 17, there was a large demonstration of over 100,000 workers, who requested the immediate dissolution of the entire National Guard. Many were unpleasantly surprised by the size of the protest and its radical potential, foreseeing disaster in it. Maxime Du Camp writes: "Paris was dismayed that day and bowed its shoulders under the weight of the misfortune it saw coming. Everyone believed that the battle was about to begin and consequently made his preparations."[221]

This radicalization developed just as new economic difficulties arose. At the beginning of the February Revolution Paris and France had been on the road to economic recovery; but as in 1830, revolutionary upheaval once again turned the economy downward. The number of bankruptcies rose; orders were canceled; money and credit grew scarce and the demand for expensive consumer goods decreased. The wealthy and foreigners left the city in droves, while those who remained dismissed their servants, and sold their horses and carriages. Prosper Mérimée notes in a letter of April 3, 1848: "You have no idea how sad this city, lively just six weeks ago, has become. You see only empty faces and people who are ruined. If you stay at home you see ghosts, but if you mix with society you hear nothing but fear expressed, or news of catastrophes that have overtaken or might overtake friends."[222]

Far more serious was the fact that unemployment had risen to the hitherto unknown figure of 180,000—a social problem that the government had been unable to resolve on February 25 with its proclamation of the right to work.[223] But this proclamation established a legal claim that had to be satisfied immediately if the government was to prevent the political revolution from turning into an even greater social one. It had therefore been decided to institute *ateliers nationaux* in which the unemployed could find work.[224] Louis Blanc, who had appointed himself the legal counsel for these measures, saw to it that the unemployed would receive the necessary capital, through state credits, to buy or create businesses that tied in with their professional qualifications. They could then operate them on a joint basis and live on the proceeds.[225]

However, Alexandre-Thomas Marie, minister of public works, did not carry out the idea of the *ateliers nationaux* as envisaged by the decree; his version of these workshops was more like the former wretched *ateliers de charité*. Still the Provisional Government had approved of them on February 27, wanting to eliminate the issue of mass unemployment as quickly as possible. A *proclamation aux ouvriers* had been issued on the following day, announcing that *ateliers nationaux* would open on March 1, 1848. At the same time regulations had been published for those seeking employment in them.[226]

It soon became obvious that this was not the way to control the problem. For despite strict measures to prevent foreigners and new provincial immigrants from coming to Paris, the number of those seeking employment in the *ateliers* rose from 29,000 on March 5, to over 100,000 by the end of May 1848. Each person admitted to these *ateliers* was paid 2 francs per day; while all other unemployed, who could prove that they had tried to find work, received 1 franc 50, a sum that was reduced to 1 franc after March 15. At first each worker in the *ateliers* was employed for three days per week, and received unemployment compensation for the other three workdays. Until March 15 an unemployed worker therefore received 10 francs 50; this was soon reduced to 9 francs. As of April 16 the workload in the *ateliers* was decreased to two days, so that the weekly benefit payments amounted to 8 francs at best.

The intention behind the establishment of the *ateliers nationaux* was clear from the start. While Louis Blanc's original idea was to find a permanent solution to unemployment, the government found such "socialist experiments" abhorrent. It was concerned only with immobilizing the *masse flottante et dangereuse*, as the unemployed were officially known, and with immunizing them against any radical agitation—or even with turning them into a Praetorian Guard against socialist machinations. At first this Machiavellian calculation worked very well: at the elections of April 23 and 24 for the Constituent Assembly, based on universal and secret adult male suffrage for the first time, an overwhelming majority of the workers from the *ateliers* voted for the government's candidates and thus against Louis Blanc's socialists.[227] The latter were supported by the *Commission du gouvernement pour les travailleurs*, which had its seat in the Palais du Luxembourg, and had great influence on the rest of the workers.

But the *atelier* workers' loyalty had its price, which the Provisional

Government, as well as the Executive Commission which replaced it after the elections, refused to pay. Even worse, the majority of the newly elected Chamber made it unmistakably clear that it intended to close the *ateliers nationaux* as soon as possible. When the new minister of public works, Dr. Trélat, met with Emile Thomas, head of the *Bureau central pour l'organisation des ateliers nationaux du département de la Seine*, for the first time, he explained quite openly: "The Chamber no longer wants the *ateliers nationaux*; many abuses go on there; they are a constant source of insurrection; they have to be closed down as soon as possible."[228] The motivation given by the minister for the decision could hardly be faulted; however, the symptoms had been created by the very people who now wanted to eliminate the *ateliers*. Emile Thomas had repeatedly spoken out against the senseless practice of making everyone employed by the *ateliers*, regardless of their qualifications, work on useless excavations. The pointlessness was aggravated by the fact that there was soon not enough work to go round, so that a hundred workers were doing what ten could easily have done. All appeals to the *Corps des ponts et chaussées* to design a useful public-works program came to nothing. And the reduction of working hours from three to two days was merely a stopgap that made matters still worse.

This occupational therapy ended by making the ever-growing army of the unemployed feel useless, since most of them spent their two paid workdays doing nothing. Various agitators tried to use the disaffected workers' mood to win them over to radical remedies. But what really helped to turn these workers against the Republic were the empty promises and hostile attitude of the Executive Commission toward the *ateliers nationaux*. Hence the alliance between the unemployed and the Parisian *classes laborieuses*—who had gathered under the banner of Louis Blanc's socialism since the February Revolution—developed rapidly. And the *ateliers nationaux* finally turned into the "centers of decay" that the liberal bourgeoisie had long suspected them of being.[229]

Many political clubs had developed since February 25. These were crucial for the politicization of the masses, along with the capital's newspapers, of which there were as many as 171 at one point though many of them were not long-lived.[230] On the other hand, these clubs were by no means the danger to society that many of the frightened bourgeois thought they were. Most of them disbanded after a few meetings, or were only associations of voters whose existence was limited in time. Moreover, several of them were defined by professional or regional connections, in which politics was not the primary concern. Only 20 were actual political clubs with an elected president and enrolled members.[231]

As expected, the moderate republicans had been elected to an overwhelming majority in the Assembly. They were adamantly against the type of *République démocratique et sociale* the socialists were striving for; so it was up to the clubs, with the help of the masses, to organize a political opposition and to exert pressure on the Assembly and the government. On May 15, a date that was to prove significant, a group of democratic socialists organized a demonstration on behalf of Polish freedom as part of the new strategy.[232] In fact the freedom of Poland was only a symbol, already used in the July Monarchy, to protest against reactionary domestic politics. The announced intention was to revive hopes that had been aroused in February; but realists on both sides of the political spectrum suspected there were quite different motivations. While the "moderates" saw the demonstration as a plot by the "reds" to wreak havoc in the Assembly, the leaders of the "reds" suspected a scheme by the police to repudiate the *Démocrates socialistes* and get rid of them.

On the morning of May 15, a crowd of several thousand gathered in the place de la Bastille. It was described as a "loutish parade, a sort of masquerade," by Charles Louis de Freycinet, who went on to say that it was "disorderly from the start and ridiculous to the end."[233] The demonstrators proceeded to the Palais Bourbon, shouting "Vive la Pologne!" without knowing what they would do once they got there. Tocqueville describes the utter confusion: "A demagogic party has so many leaders, chance always plays such a large role and deliberation such a very small one in all its activities, that it is as good as impossible to indicate, before or afterwards, what is or was wanted."[234]

The result of this indecision was disastrous for the Left. Once the crowd reached the Assembly it forced its way in and declared it dissolved, which did not much impress the deputies.[235] After that they moved on to the Hôtel de Ville, as was the custom, convinced they had started another February 24 and forced a government, unwilling to meet their demands, to step down. But that was a false conclusion, as they and their leaders soon realized. The events of May 15 gave the moderates a welcome excuse to take action against the radicals, some of whom like Barbès, Raspail, Blanqui, and Albert, were immediately arrested. Furthermore, the following day the *Commission du Luxembourg*, the government's commission for workers, was disbanded and the most radical political clubs were closed.

May 15 was a *sottise* (a foolish error), as Charles Schmidt called it, insofar as it provoked the final break between the Assembly and the *peuple*, between Paris and the provinces, between the government and the *ateliers nationaux*.[236] It had been a payday in the *ateliers*, and more than 10,000 workers had joined the demonstrators, a fact of which the government was unaware. On May 17 an extraparliamentary commission was appointed to develop plans for a rapid, smooth method for dissolving the *ateliers*. The commission came up with a plan a day later, which the government disliked because it envisaged a gradual and very slow liquidation of the *ateliers*; the plan was therefore abandoned.[237]

Though May 15 seemed on the surface to have had no effect, the political lines had been clearly drawn. It had strengthened the latent notion of a civil war, which had been in the air since the election. The unbridgeable distrust between the opposing groups came into the open precisely on the *Fête de la Concorde*, that grandiose festivity to celebrate the Republic which had long been planned for May 21.[238] Tocqueville writes of it contemptuously, "the revolutionaries of 1848 did not want to or could not imitate the bloody madness of their predecessors, which is why they were often content to imitate their absurdities."[239]

The false peace sworn on May 21 lasted only that one day. Both the government and the moderate majority in the Chamber were more determined than ever to destroy the Left by liquidating the *ateliers nationaux*, the source of the danger as they saw it. On May 24 the *Commission du pouvoir exécutif* issued a decree ordering the conscription of all unmarried workers between the ages of eighteen and twenty-five; those who did not obey "voluntarily" were to be eliminated from the payroll of the *ateliers*. Furthermore, workers who could not prove residence in Paris for six months prior to May 14 were to be sent back to their home regions. The remaining workers were to be put into brigades and sent to work in the regional departments.[240]

Strangely enough, though, there was reluctance to put the decree into effect immediately. This was not because its originators were concerned about violating the proclamation of the right to work. They worried about setting off an explosion for which they were not prepared. It is also possible that by delaying their action they hoped the unrest in the *ateliers* and in Paris generally would peak and put an end to the tension.[241] After much debate the decree was finally signed and released on June 21.

Its publication in the *Moniteur* of June 22, 1848, was a declaration of war by the bourgeoisie against the *classes laborieuses*. The resulting conflict was so unusual that it attracted everyone's attention as none other had done. It is significant that such different thinkers as Alexis de Tocqueville, who was an eyewitness, and Marx and Engels, who followed events from Cologne and developed their theories on class war from them, reach similar conclusions:

> What differentiated the June uprising from all other similar events that have not stopped occurring these sixty years is that its goal was not to change the type of government, but rather to transform the whole of society. Indeed it was not a political confrontation (in the sense we have used the concept up to now) but a class war, a sort of *servile war*.[242]

Moral and Political Bankruptcy

*S*IMULTANEOUS CONFRONTATIONS TOOK PLACE in various parts of the city between June 22 and June 26, 1848; but while the government had a definite strategy, the insurgents had only desperate courage to see them through.[243] The latter spent the first day organizing themselves and setting up barricades. The entire eastern half of the capital on both banks of the Seine, dominated by the *classes laborieuses*, rose up against the bourgeoisie in the western half. Thus the city was divided into two equal halves. The battlefront ran from the barrière Saint-Jacques to the barrière Rochechouart, through the Val-de-Grâce, the rue Saint-Jacques, the rue des Grés, the rue de la Harpe, across the Pont-au-Change, and continued along the Marché des Innocents, the Porte Saint-Denis, the rue Richer, and the rue Cadet to the end of the rue de la Tour-d'Auvergne. To the east of this line all arrondissements, with the exception of the area directly around the Hôtel de Ville, were in rebel hands; almost all the streets were blocked by staggered barricades, of which more than a thousand are said to have been set up.[244]

Many of the barricades were very solid constructions, built under skilled direction with the large paving stones used in street construction in those days. Past experience of barricade fighting in 1830 and in February 1848 was useful this time around. Furthermore, each barricade had its "captain" who had a quasi-military commando control over the fighters. Estimates of how many insurgents participated in the June Days are divided, varying between 10,000 and 15,000, most of whom may well have had their baptism of fire in the February Revolution.[245] A large number of these fighters came from the working class, as well as from the petite bourgeoisie of artisans and small storekeepers. The unemployed from the *ateliers nationaux*, who had originally been so feared, represented only a very small contingent at first. The authorities had decided to continue paying them over this period, and evidently this bribe kept many of them away from the fighting.

What the rebels lacked was leadership. Their insurrection was not a long and secretly well-prepared action; it was a spontaneous hunger strike and revolt against their misery. "Freedom or death," was the battle cry that inspired them; and that freedom, standing for work, adequate pay, and cheap bread, was the essence of the *République démocratique et sociale* of which the bourgeoisie was so afraid. All of this was contained in a memorable dialogue that took place between the opponents in the place du Panthéon immediately before the first fighting broke out. The bourgeoisie were represented by the scientist François Arago, the *peuple* by a nameless insurgent. Arago, whose tall figure was familiar to the workers and who was respected by them, tried at the very last minute to work out some agreement. In answer to his rhetorical question as to how good citizens could rise up against the Republic and the law and put up barricades, he was told: "Monsieur Arago, you are a good citizen; we have great respect for you but that does not give you the right to rebuke us; you have never suffered from hunger, you do not know what deprivation is!"[246]

The government did have a purposeful and deliberate leader in the person of General Louis-Eugène Cavaignac, who had proved his military skill in Algeria and who had become minister of war. Cavaignac was a military type, who was unwilling to subordinate his military convictions to the political demands of his office; he claimed it was his task to give the army back "its dignity," a statement that referred to the army's humiliating failures in 1830 and 1848.[247] A man like this at the head of the government troops, and who requested dictatorial authority during the June battles, was not about to let anything stand in the way of his military principles. Cavaignac gave the deputies Garnier-Pagès, Arago and Ledru-Rollin an example of his obstinacy when they tried to get him to use his troops promptly to prevent the erection of the barricades. He answered rudely: "Do you think I am here to defend the Parisians and their National Guard? Let them defend their city and their businesses themselves! I am not going to break up my troops. I remember 1830 and last February."[248] Though his contempt was unmistakable, he had a plan clearly in mind. In his strategy the National Guard—citizens dressed up as soldiers—played a secondary role at best. After the way they had reacted in February, when large numbers of them defected to the insurgents, they could at most be assigned to guard territory taken by the regular troops. Another uncertainty for Cavaignac to consider was the 16,000 *Gardes mobiles*, paid, trained, and armed troops stationed in barracks, which had been created by decrees of the Provisional Government in February 1848. They were part of the same scheme as the *ateliers nationaux*—to provide paid work for the unemployed—as well as a backup force for the unreliable National Guard. Moreover it was thought to be a good way of ensuring peace and order because these men had been the rebels of the February Revolution.[249] But whatever doubts Cavaignac may have had about their loyalties, coming as they did from the same social class as those manning the barricades, they were soon put to rest. On the contrary, the *Gardes mobiles* fought hard and brutally and their cold-blooded atrocities soon gave them a terrible reputation.

At the start of the fighting Cavaignac depended solely on the 30,000 troops that had to be brought in from outside of Paris, as there was not enough room to accommodate them in the city. It was the first time the railway played an important part in transporting troops, but it took a day to get them there. It was the day the rebels used to set up the barricades. The real fighting and the capture of the barricades—in most cases after preliminary artillery bombardments—only began on June 24, but the resistance was so fierce that despite the government troops' overall superiority it took them two days to capture the Left Bank. The faubourg Saint-Antoine fell the following day.

Now began the victors' relentless revenge; the *Gardes mobiles* were especially zealous in searching out hidden insurgents. There were real manhunts in the suburbs, and houses in the working-class neighborhoods were systematically searched for suspects. Lives counted for little in the sudden rush of power experienced by those who had won. No one knows how many lives were lost in the battles; how many were "shot while escaping," or were summarily liquidated during mass executions in the quarries of Montmartre, the Butte-Chaumont, or in the cemeteries. But it must have been in the hundreds—hundreds of revolutionaries who died for their dream of a different Republic.

On June 28 a police commissioner counted as many as fifteen large furniture vans piled high with corpses, and the rue Blanche was filled with the stench of rotting cadavers interred in the Montmartre cemetery. For days after the end of the fighting the "White Terror" of the *Gardes mobiles* continued to wreak havoc in the eastern half of Paris.[250] Wealthy bourgeois and dandies from the western neighborhoods came to view the damage left by the battles.[251] This repugnant curiosity was titillated for days on end by a different spectacle: troops of prisoners, who had had the doubtful luck to survive the fighting or not to be killed immediately, were led through the streets of Paris before being herded into the outer strongpoints of the fortifications or the cellars of public buildings before being transported to the colonies without trial. Official records give the names, ages, and places of birth of 11,616 individuals captured after the *Journées de juin*.[252]

The June 1848 revolution was a protest against all the changes made by a constitutional monarchy that heedlessly ignored the welfare of Paris. The areas affected by the revolt were the eastern ones in which poverty, cholera, and general urban neglect had taken their toll. The Republic's victory ratified these changes but also engineered its own bankruptcy. This took three-and-a-half years to develop, the years between June 1848 and December 1851 during which Paris was ruled by class hatred and fear.[253] Louis Bonaparte's coup on December 2, 1851, would not have been possible without the memory of the horrible drama of the uprising of June. Paris was not incompatible with a republic, as Henri Lecouturier suggested in his book, *Paris incompatible avec la République;* rather, the bourgeois Republic of 1848 was no longer compatible with Paris.

BOOK SIX

The Second Empire

1852–1870

Je suis étranger à ce qui vient, à ce qui est, comme à ces boulevards nouveaux, qui ne sentent plus le monde de Balzac, qui sentent Londres, quelque Babylone de l'avenir.

I am estranged from what is coming, from what already exists, like these new boulevards that no longer feel like the world of Balzac, that feel like London, like some future Babylon.

Edmond and Jules de Goncourt, *Journal*

Le vieux Paris n'est plus (la forme d'une ville change plus vite, hélas! que le coeur d'un mortel).

Old Paris is gone (the form of a city changes faster, alas, than the heart of man).

Charles Baudelaire, *Le Cygne*

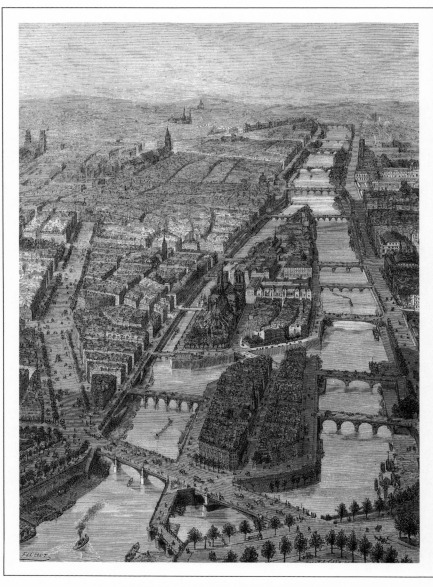

View of the city and the Seine bridges from the Ile de la Cité.
A woodcut based on an 1874 drawing by Fichot.
ARCHIV FÜR KUNST UND GESCHICHTE, BERLIN.

The Weakness of the Republic

*T*HE REVOLUTIONARY EXPERIENCES OF 1848 were deeply etched into the collective memory. Once again it was shown that Paris was the center of revolution; since 1789 three dynasties had been overthrown and the capital had dictated the course of action to the rest of France. Because of its size and prominence the city had to undergo major changes; but the Second Republic was too weak to recognize the possible consequences. As did previous upheavals, the June events merely intensified the regime's powerlessness.

Measures taken by the regime to tame the rebellious dynamics of the capital were clearly inadequate. In July 1848 the elected city administration was abolished; the government continued to depend on the army and the state of emergency until October.[1] Whereas the rest of the country held municipal elections, a commission was appointed in Paris to replace the *Conseil municipal et général* and run the city together with the two prefects. The point was quite obvious: it was feared that a commune elected on the basis of a universal vote would not want to be subordinate to the Constituent Assembly and might even become the organizational center of a new revolutionary movement. In actual fact this provision amounted to a declaration of political bankruptcy, an acknowledgment that now that the June revolt had been suppressed the Republic existed only on a pro forma basis. Victor Hugo characterizes this situation wittily: "The men who have been in charge of the country since February at first thought anarchy was freedom; now they see freedom as anarchy."[2]

How badly the Republic was compromised by the *Journées de juin* was revealed during the ceremonial proclamation of the new Constitution in the place de la Concorde on November 12, 1848. The event was greeted with apparent disinterest by the population, as Victor Hugo reports: "The government asked everyone in Paris to light their lamps. From the rue de la Tour-d'Auvergne to the rue Charlot I noticed only three lamps in one house."[3] One month later, on December 10, 1848, Louis Napoleon Bonaparte was elected president of the Republic by a large majority—another indication of the precarious condition of the Second Republic. While Louis Napoleon received 74 percent of the votes in the country at large—putting him far ahead of his competitors General Cavaignac and the two left-wing representatives, Ledru-Rollin and Raspail—only 58 percent of those eligible voted for him in the Department of the Seine. He still won a majority there, as well as in the suburbs and all twelve Paris arrondissements, which meant that many democrats also voted for him.[4]

Despite the unequivocal result of the election there was no peace for Paris until June 1849. For instance, troops had to be called out in the night of January 29-30, to quell an uprising by the democratic Left. Contradictory rumors made the rounds and stirred people up; but this time the prompt display of strength by the Republican government sufficed to maintain law and order.[5] Three weeks later the authorities were worried about the first anniversary of the February Revolution; then they were concerned about the elections to the Assembly in May, which had been preceded by violent agitation. Indeed, the election results which gave the left-wing *Démocrates-socialistes* ten out of twenty-eight seats in the Department of the Seine alone provided fresh reason for unrest.[6] Several thousand protesters marched from the suburbs to the newly constituted National Assembly on the afternoon of June 13, 1849. When the head of the demonstration reached the Madeleine, General Changarnier moved in suddenly with his troops and dispersed the crowd so quickly that they did not even try to resist.[7] This attempted uprising, planned by Ledru-Rollin and his followers in the Conservatoire des arts et metiers where the *Démocrates-socialistes* held their meetings, ended abruptly and without bloodshed. It sealed the fate of the Left for the next twenty years, for they no longer stood a chance against the army.

Along with all the political upheaval there were still the old economic problems. Though the deprivation in Paris was no longer as brutal as it had been in the past, conditions remained serious.[8] Matters were made worse by a cholera epidemic in 1849, which broke out in March and lasted into the summer. But the authorities had learned from the experience of 1832, and instead of establishing special cholera hospitals they augmented preventive measures.[9] This second epidemic developed much more slowly than that of 1832, though the number of victims was still very high: 19,069 deaths out of a total of 35,449 cases. However, in proportion to the general population of Paris (945,504), there were fewer losses than in 1832, when 18,400 died out of a total of 753,987 residents.[10]

The cholera epidemic, however, prolonged economic difficulties. Revenues from the municipal tax collected on all goods and products passing through the *barrières* are revealing about the course of the recession.[11] The slight upswing in 1850 was due largely to private consumption, speculators being reluctant to use their capital for long-term investments. This had negative effects on the building industry where most of the unemployed, now on welfare following closure of the *ateliers nationaux*, would have found employment.[12] Hence it seems all the more incomprehensible that the major urban redevelopment called for since the early 1840s was not now undertaken.[13]

Many of the projects that the July Monarchy had hoped to complete were halted by the February Revolution.[14] The Provisional Government that held office until June 1848 did not have the funds or the political will to deal with them. It had instead concentrated on taking care of the unemployed in the *ateliers nationaux*. It did pay lip service to two prominent schemes—completion of the Louvre and extension of the rue de Rivoli. Both were elaborated in a decree of May 3, 1848, but that was all.[15] The decree was of some importance at a later date, though, when Haussmann put one of its clauses to good use. This clause revolutionized the ruling on expropriation by permitting the city to acquire properties situated on both sides of the planned extension of the rue de Rivoli, "and to sell those properties lying outside of the planned route, dividing them in such a way that they will be appropriate for the construction of well-ventilated buildings."[16] Thanks to this regulation, the city was able to benefit from the increased value of the property lining the new thoroughfare and thus to finance part of its costs.[17]

In spite of these advantageous arrangements the decree remained ineffective for the time being. The city lacked funds and was unable to attract private capital with municipal bonds. Once Louis Napoleon became president and the Republic experienced greater political stability, the projects were revived. In fact the president let it be known early on that he intended to take a personal interest in the *transformation de Paris*. However, he too soon learned that prompt realization of those long-discussed plans would clash with the stubborn resistance of the National Assembly as well as of the Parisian municipality.[18] The National Assembly, which replaced the Constituent Assembly on May 28, 1849, was dominated by deputies who did not hide their objection to anything that would benefit or embellish Paris. And the twelve arrondissements that made up the Paris municipality were afraid that any requests for funds by the government for the city's transformation would be apportioned very unequally among them. These attitudes meant that a whole year was wasted in fruitless negotiations until the equally time-consuming expropriation procedures could begin in mid-December. The latter concluded at the end of February 1850 with compensation payments determined by a commission. Construction of the first part of the plan was started in March, almost two years after the original decree was issued in 1848. It extended the rue de Rivoli up to the point where the rue du Musée began, about half of the stretch ending at the columns on the east side of the Louvre.[19]

Enforced Transformations

*T*HE OVERALL RESISTANCE TO THE PLANS of Louis Napoleon accurately reflected vested interests and were reinforced by the Constitution of the Republic. They helped accelerate the political developments which culminated in the coup of December 2, 1851. The closer the end of his presidency, the more Louis Napoleon demanded that large public-works projects be started in earnest.[20] He calculated that this would enhance his popularity among the *classes laborieuses* who would thus be assured of bread and wages and remain politically quiet. But vested interests continued to resist his schemes, put off by their magnitude as well as the idea of their hasty execution.

This obstruction put Louis Napoleon under greater pressure; for if he wanted to succeed with his coup—which had been an open secret since the summer of 1850—he had to do more than make demagogic speeches and hold out promises to the *classes laborieuses*. The extent to which his ambition to rebuild Paris was linked to his political plans was shown when he ceremonially laid the foundation stone for the new markets. That event took place just two days prior to the coup, originally planned for September 17, 1851. His statement at the time included this passage:

> The construction of the markets represents a true benefit for mankind because they will improve the provisioning of Paris; the departments will also participate in this, as [the project] does not only affect the city: Paris is the heart of France and the more actively and strongly it beats, the greater will be the gain to the whole country. As I lay the first stone for a building that corresponds so uniquely to the interests of the workers, I confidently express the hope that with the help of well-disposed citizens, and God willing, we shall be able to establish some foundations in the ground of France for a stable social order that will resist violence and the unpredictability of human passions.[21]

With these words Louis Napoleon alluded to a program he worked hard to put into effect after his coup on December 2, 1851, namely, the transformation of Paris. The originality of his vision of transforming and rebuilding Paris has frequently been challenged.[22] Indeed, specific plans had been considered for decades, such as the completion of the Louvre, the generously sized new central markets, or the formation of the *croisée de Paris* by means of the eastward extension of the rue de Rivoli and creation of a north-south axis crossing it.

But aside from the limited projects completed by Napoleon I, the rest had remained a chimera. From this point of view, whatever urban construction Louis Napoleon undertook up to his fall in 1870 was not especially original. The building of wide new streets and squares, renovation of the medieval center of the city and of overpopulated neighborhoods, provision of an efficient sewage system, and development of parks and landscaped areas to break up the stone wasteland—all these had been essential components of various urban plans, or had been suggested by the example of London, the most modern city of the times.

But the question of where Louis Napoleon found his ideas and models for the transformation of Paris continued to be asked. For the opportunity for him to become familiar with the city's problems had existed only since his return from exile in 1848.[23] Yet he managed to create something previously unknown which, when more or less completed, became a worldwide model wherever European influence was felt. Various theories were developed as to how this was possible. Perhaps Louis Napoleon was inspired by the Saint-Simonists, who were the first to make practical suggestions for the improvement of living conditions in urban centers, instead of espousing mere beautification; or perhaps he learned from his exile in London, where he witnessed public debate on the connection between population growth, public hygiene, and urbanization.[24] But the most plausible explanation is that he simply wanted to follow the example of his uncle, Napoleon I, or even outdo him in matters of urban improvement. Louis Napoleon's ambition was quite within the tradition of rulers dating all the way back to the Rome of Augustus. The probability of the latter theory is borne out by the fact that he pursued the renovation of Paris with almost maniacal fervor to the exclusion of just about everything else during his regime.

In his memoirs Charles Merruau, who was general secretary of the Prefecture of the Seine until 1852, describes Louis Napoleon as follows:

> This prince who possessed a rare good faith as well as modern ideas had, thanks to his thorough studies and much reflection, developed an ideal of public works that he wanted to realize in exemplary fashion. He was deeply convinced that he had been given his authority especially to overcome all the obstacles produced by the various interest cliques, by the resistance of the envious, and by the prejudices of routine or the laziness of unimaginative minds that tried to stand in the way of the best and most successful projects intended for the common good. His maxims were: not to condemn anything as daydream without proof; to allow the maturation of fruitful ideas, which officialdom is so often accused of rejecting out of hand; to use his full power to master difficulties; not to stop until the goal was reached; not to postpone anything useful if it could be dealt with immediately; and, finally, not to let other nations exploit those discoveries that so often receive scant regard in his own country. Everything that had been said, written, planned, and already executed in connection with large cities; everything he himself had observed or reflected on in this connection, he immediately wanted to carry out in Paris.[25]

Even if the main idea behind this obsession was part of the traditional inclination of rulers, its execution aimed at more than that. The new splendor of the French capital was to testify to the universal validity of the principles that guided Louis Napoleon's regime. Their modernity proved the progressive spirit of a sovereign who, as Jeanne Gaillard aptly comments, "perhaps rules thanks to the peasants, but who succeeds thanks to industry and the progress of science."[26] To this extent the transformation of Paris was a genuine ideological confession, a political program intended to realize in the capital all the progressive tendencies that had been proclaimed since the Enlightenment. Thus the new Paris—an urban embodiment of civilized progress—became, as Walter Benjamin recognized, the capital of the nineteenth century.

Directly after the coup of December 2 and the elections of December 21, 1851, Louis Napoleon gave his full attention to the projects he had begun earlier. An overwhelming majority of Frenchmen had given Louis Napoleon absolution for his breach of the Constitution and extended his presidency for a further ten years—before he grasped the emperor's crown a year later. Because of his quasi-dictatorial powers he was now able to accelerate the redevelopment program already under way. The obstinate National Assembly had been dissolved and was not replaced until March 1852 by a newly elected legislative assembly, whose majority was strictly pro-Bonapartist. But to ensure that he would not have to depend on the approval of the National Assembly, Louis Napoleon ordered on December 3, 1851, that all future work connected with the transformation of Paris be sanctioned by simple decree.

Despite this admirable instrument, Louis Napoleon decided to limit his energy and new authority to projects already begun, or those he considered especially urgent. A first decree directed the construction of a trolley line to connect the various train stations. On December 13, 1851, the city received credit for over 2 million francs finally to clear the slums between the Louvre and the Tuileries. On March 10, 1852, a decree ordered the development of the thirty-meter-wide boulevard de Strasbourg, which was to lead from the Gare de Strasbourg (now the Gare de l'Est) to the boulevard Saint-Denis, and to become the first section of the north-south corridor; after its completion it formed—together with the axis of the rue de Rivoli, which had been extended to the place du Trône—the *croisée de Paris*, whose intersection was to be the place du Châtelet.

A further decree was issued two days later, setting aside a state subsidy of 26 million francs for the completion of the Louvre. An additional order, on the same day, ruled that the area on which the markets were to be built should be enlarged. Two weeks later, on March 27, 1852, a decree directed the erection of the Palais de l'Industrie on a tract between the Champs-Elysées and the Cours la Reine. Under the next ruling, on July 13, 1852, the state conveyed the Bois de Boulogne, lying on the other side of the fortifications, to the city with the condition that it spend 2 million francs to turn it into a park. Then, on July 24, 1852, came an order establishing the rue des Ecoles and the rue de Rennes on the Left Bank. Finally, on December 23, 1852, the last of that series of important decrees stipulated that the arcades of those houses lining the north side of the rue de Rivoli were to be extended to the place du Palais-Royal.[27]

It was not entirely the quasi-dictatorial authority he held until March 1852 that let Louis Napoleon proceed at such breakneck speed. His coup had been supported by the Bourse as well as by trade and industry, for it was seen as the promise of a strong and politically stable regime.[28] Louis Napoleon tried to reinforce this impression with his decisiveness and eagerness to spend money. In fact he began by mobilizing large, previously unused capital reserves by floating comparatively large loans. The credit demands of the state, which invested funds in public works, were supposed to have a favorable influence on the declining economy, assure full employment, and generally bring about an indefinite period of political and social stability. The disadvantage of this formula was that the frequency and size of state credit demands had to increase as the projects grew; each delay or interruption in this circular flow was bound to lead to the collapse of the regime. In the course of a discussion in 1861 between Nassau William Senior, a professor of political economy, and Gustave de Beaumont, a historian and biographer, the latter refers to a Russian opinion that Napoleon III was "condemned to forced labor for life." Beaumont then adds, "A week's interruption of the building trade would terrify the government."[29]

However, this system worked the way it was intended to almost until the end of the regime. The *fête impériale* of the Second Empire resembled a dance around the golden calf, in which all classes joined. Charles Merruau comments in his memoirs on the success of the policy:

After 1851 the Hôtel de Ville saw its garrison return to its barracks and politics handed back to the administration—its rightful place. No longer did bands of insurgents roam the streets, but troops of masons, carpenters, and other artisans rushed to various building sites. When the paving was torn up it was not to establish barricades but to install gas and water lines. Houses were no longer threatened by artillery or fire, but rather by the well-calculated expropriation compensation. The city budget grew almost automatically from the steady revenues and increasing wealth of taxpayers. Loans were easy to obtain and always yielded at least 5 percent; moreover, they were never spent on anything but the purpose stated at the time of their subscription. Eventually we witnessed the important period in which large projects were carried out under the administration of M. Haussmann, which transformed the capital and made it healthier and bigger. But if one asks what the cost was for all these good deeds, the answer is that the nation sacrificed its freedom and accepted Caesarism.[30]

However, the price was not only the exchange of freedom for Caesarism as Merruau indicates, but also the rapidly increasing burden of debt that Louis Napoleon's construction policy forced on Paris. This was due to two mechanisms working together. One consisted of large-scale public investments that stimulated the economy to produce a greater tax yield (as apologists for the practice of deficit spending *avant la lettre* always predicted they would).[31] The other was the decreasing ability of the surplus from increased tax revenues to cover the debt within a foreseeable period because estimates for the various projects were out of line with actual costs. Furthermore, the longer the regime of Napoleon III lasted, the less willing was the Assembly to approve additional state funds for the transformation of Paris, and after 1858 all new projects had to be funded by the city of Paris itself.[32] However, even this factor was not allowed to slow down or stop the work on which the political fate of Napoleon III depended.[33]

Contemporaries were astounded by the energy with which Louis Napoleon acted, the speed with which entire neighborhoods were razed to the ground, new streets and arrondissements appearing in their stead. "As one speaks," notes Prosper Ménière in his diary,

Paris is changing; demolition is being carried on in grand style, and the city is spending millions to create enormous thoroughfares. It is said that the new rue de Strasbourg, which is supposed to lead to the boulevard between the Portes Saint-Denis and Saint-Martin, is going to be extended to the Seine. In view of all this I ask myself why the old government was incapable of keeping the workers busy the way the prince-president is doing now; for apart from the fact that he is beautifying the city, he has won over the bourgeoisie and is growing more and more popular with artisans and workers. The Louvre will soon be ready and will be, as everyone says, an embellishment of the capital. It is hard to overestimate how much respect the president gains by it: every oak began as an acorn.[34]

Louis Napoleon was not unaware how favorably his actions were viewed. Hence he must have been all the more annoyed that in 1852 his system of credit-financing for public expenditures—which scorned the contemporary practice of cameralistic budgeting—provoked the stubborn opposition of

Jean-Jacques Berger, prefect of the Seine, more and more frequently. Berger belonged to the school of Rambuteau and his most important rule was to maintain a balanced budget. A 50-million-franc loan for the construction of the rue de Rivoli and the markets (luckily it could be placed for over 61 million francs due to favorable economic conditions) was the most to which he and the equally prudent *Conseil municipal* were willing to agree.[35] Because of the unyielding resistance to his other grandiose plans, Louis Napoleon finally dismissed Berger in the spring of 1853.[36] The duc de Persigny, who had been running the Ministry of the Interior since January 1852 and who had to find a successor to Berger, notes in his memoirs:

> Am more determined than ever to help the city administration of Paris to deal with financing the long-term loans; have also learned from my own experience that someone who tends to be political and inclined to generalizations, who is not familiar with details and with bureaucratic procedures, will be confused, hindered, and finally completely outmaneuvered by the freemasonry of the administration; because of this I immediately rejected the idea of looking for a successor to M. Berger within our political assemblies. On the other hand, I think a prefect from a department in the provinces, unacquainted with the Paris salons but familiar with bureaucratic procedures, who would unreservedly accept the proposed system of financing with all its consequences, would assure infinitely better chances of success than would a political figure.[37]

The man who best met these requirements for Persigny and whom he chose from among a number of candidates was Georges-Eugène Haussmann, who was appointed prefect of the Department of the Seine in June 1853.[38] Haussmann was an altogether congenial colleague for Napoleon III. He elaborated and specified the details of the roughly sketched imperial plans, and kept a constant eye on their execution. He also made an immense personal creative contribution to the unprecedented project of the transformation of Paris, so that it is quite appropriate to give him special credit for it.

The Great New Plan

*N*OTHING GIVES A BETTER IDEA of the part played by Napoleon III and Haussmann in the transformation of Paris than an anecdote the latter tells in his memoirs. After he had taken his oath of office in the palace at Saint-Cloud on June 29, 1853, the emperor asked him into his study. There he was handed a map of Paris, where the emperor "had marked in blue, red, or green, depending on their priority, the various new streets whose construction he suggested."[39] Louis Napoleon had been working on his grand design ever since acceding to the presidency; but it was Haussmann who worked out a final plan from which the work could proceed and it was his energy that saw it through to completion. The basic concepts of the plan were those of Louis Napoleon; but it goes without saying that there were certain important modifications, most of which were Haussmann's.[40] Merruau writes:

> Individuals who had access to him [Louis Napoleon] often found him penciling lines on a map of Paris. He paid special attention to the railway terminals as points of departure for what he planned; he saw them as the real approaches to the city instead of the old *barrières* which, though they led to the national highways, would in his opinion eventually become secondary lines of communication. That is why it was of major importance to him to link these new terminals in such a way that the traffic flow between individual stations and hence between the various regions of France could proceed promptly and efficiently through their common center. It also seemed indispensable to him that broad arteries lead from these terminals directly to the center of the metropolis. Furthermore, the president intended to have wide streets connect the administrative buildings, which otherwise could only be brought closer together by means of expensive moves. In this he was motivated by his experience that state administrative offices were always prevented from acting efficiently at decisive moments by being far from their executive organs and the materials they required. . . . It was also necessary to have avenues and wide streets cut through the neighborhoods around the Hôtel de Ville, through the faubourg Saint-Antoine and both sides of the Montagne Sainte-Geneviève, which had until then been enclosed clusters of rebellion. In this connection it was important to indicate sites for barracks, which also had to be connected by streets that would serve as strategic lines of communication in an emergency, permitting the troops to remain in control in all circumstances. Finally, remembering London, Louis Napoleon designed plans for tree-lined squares, parks, and public gardens, as well as open and covered markets. He always thought less in terms of grandiose monuments, unless these had to be completed because work had already been started earlier on, or because he had to satisfy some current need.[41]

Merruau's account reveals the extent to which Louis Napoleon's original urban plans were motivated by the experiences of 1830 and 1848, and by his desire to give his regime a firm basis by transforming the capital as quickly as possible. This intention and its execution by Haussmann were much more complex than their critics have indicated. Even today, the establishment of those broader and straighter streets is explained as meeting artillery requirements. In the fighting at the barricades, the effective use of artillery depended on a clear field of fire over a great distance.[42] But while military-tactical considerations of this sort, and the choice of location for new barracks inside the city, were important to Louis Napoleon's plan for Paris, his concern to obtain and maintain political power was of equal significance. To achieve this he had first of all to make sure that the state gained back the revolutionary sovereignty that Paris had usurped in 1789. And the only means at his disposal was a complete modernization of the capital according to social, political, law-enforcement, traffic-engineering, sanitary, economic, and demographic criteria. He was not solely concerned with being able to control any conceivable emergency through military force. Rather, it was his aim to prevent such a situation from the very start; and this epoch-making concept of urbanism has been characterized as Bonapartism.[43]

When Haussmann was appointed prefect of Paris, he also became the agent for overseeing the transformation of the city. He spent his first year in office preparing the necessary technical and organizational groundwork for such an enormous project. In addition to gathering a group of co-workers, which included such able men as Alphonse Alphand, the creator of the large parks and squares, or Eugène Belgrand, who designed the Paris sewage system, Haussmann concentrated on completing an exact geographical and topographical map of Paris. As it was not possible to refer to older maps for this sort of cartography, the entire city within the *octroi* wall had to be surveyed. The work took over a year to complete and the master plan, drawn on a scale of 1:5,000, was put up on a movable easel in Haussmann's office. It was used to produce maps on a scale of 1:20,000 for practical use and was the most important instrument needed for the transformation of Paris, which continued to be based on the sketch that Napoleon III had given the new prefect at the time of his installation.[44]

As strange as it may sound, no one had a clear idea of what the overall task involved, for nothing was available except this sketch by "a noble hand," nor were the individual projects on which Haussmann and the emperor daily consulted listed in a timetable. Yet what seemed like grandiose and irrational improvisation really had a method. For though the two main protagonists of the plan never had an inkling of the amount of work involved, they thought it best to release information on their intentions one stage at a time. They feared the scope of their undertaking would encounter strong opposition from the National Assembly, which had to approve state subsidies as well as the loans for public works needed by the city.[45] Moreover—and this later became one of Haussmann's main concerns—it was necessary to keep the details of projects confidential for as long as possible to avoid speculation at the expense of the general public.[46] Writing about the streets constructed under his auspices, Haussmann used the term *réseaux*, or networks, developed in the second half of the Second Empire. He spoke of three *réseaux*, which differed only in their financial and technical requirements, as he repeatedly emphasized.[47] Accordingly, all street construction ordered or begun before he came into office and partially subsidized by the state, like that which formed the *croisée* of Paris, belonged to the first network.[48] The second *réseau* included the streets which state and city had agreed upon in the so-called *traité des 180 millions* of March 18, 1858, the state having undertaken to pay up to one-third of the costs or a maximum of 60 million francs.[49] Under the agreement twenty-one new streets totaling twenty-six kilometers in length were laid out within ten years, all of them on the periphery of the city center. This second *réseau* consisted mainly of the thoroughfares sketched out by Napoleon, as Hausmann emphasized in his memoirs.[50]

The main work in this second network was concentrated on the Right Bank, in the eastern half of Paris. where the avenue Daumesnil was established, providing a link between the Bastille and the Château de Vincennes. The boulevard du Prince Eugène (today the boulevard Voltaire) was also added, connecting the place du Trône (now the place de la Nation) in a straight line with the place du Château-d'Eau (place de la République). It made the latter into a large junction, where the boulevard du Prince Eugène and the boulevard Magenta—which handled traffic coming from the Gare du Nord as well as the Gare de l'Est—came together. Furthermore, this was where the rue de Turbigo ended, which came from the Halles quarter to the west and crossed the slum neighborhood of Arts-et-Métiers. Lastly, the rue du faubourg du Temple and the avenue des Amandiers (now the avenue de la République) were built in the direction of Belleville.

No less important was the work done on the Left Bank, where broad streets and boulevards were put through the Gobelins neighborhood, the Montagne Sainte-Geneviève, and the faubourg Saint-Marceau. These were the boulevards Saint-Marcel, Arago, and Port-Royal; the avenue des Gobelins, and the rues Monge, Claude-Bernard and Gay-Lussac, which encircled the Montagne Sainte-Geneviève and connected the Austerlitz and Montparnasse stations. Finally the boulevard du Centre (today the boulevard du Palais) linked the boulevard de Sébastopol on the Right Bank and the boulevard Saint-Michel on the Left Bank, which then connected with the rue Soufflot to lead to the Observatoire.

Construction in the second *réseau* was also concentrated in the west of the city, around the Gare Saint-Lazare. This was where streets like the rue de Rome, the rue Rouen (now the rue Auber), as well as the rue Halévy were put in, whose paths defined the space where the new Opera was to be built in the context of the third network. Other work included the boulevard Malesherbes, which linked the Parc Monceau with the Madeleine, and various streets near the place de l'Etoile, Chaillot, and the Trocadéro.[51] These determined the way in which the fashionable western part of Paris developed after 1860.[52]

The third *réseau* comprised projects financed exclusively by the city of Paris. These were streets that Haussmann could not accommodate under the second network, or whose construction seemed best postponed to a later date.[53]

Despite Haussmann's assurances that he divided the work into three networks merely for financial reasons, there is an obvious coherence to the first and second networks. The first network served to open up the old overpopulated inner city, surrounded by the interior boulevards, which had obstructed through traffic from going north-south and east-west. Work that fell within the second *réseau* added streets to the area lying between the inner boulevards and the tax wall. These streets, which primarily opened up slums in the eastern section, created efficient connections between the center and outlying areas. This was especially important to the regime in terms of relieving the demographic imbalance of the inner city. Moreover, most of these thoroughfares were of more than just local significance, whether they were inner-city extensions of major national highways, or links between the different stations, "the new gates of Paris" as Napoleon III called them.

"The Gutting of Old Paris"

*T*HE NEW SYSTEM OF CITY STREETS certainly improved the flow of traffic, but the work carried out in the first two networks also formed a logical ensemble. Aristide Saccard, the big businessman in Emile Zola's novel *La Curée*, explains the significance and purpose of the construction to his wife as they stand on the hill of Montmartre:

> Yes, the *grande croisée* as they call it. They are making the Louvre and the Hôtel de Ville accessible. That's child's play! It whets the public's appetite. . . . When the first network is finished then the big stuff will begin. The second network will pierce the city everywhere to connect the faubourgs to the first network. . . . From the boulevard du Temple to the Barrière du Trône there will be one slice; then, on this side, another slice from the Madeleine to the Monceau plain; and a third one in this direction, another one in that direction, one over there, one further off, slices everywhere, as if Paris were being hacked with a saber, its veins opened, feeding a hundred thousand demolition workers and masons, and crisscrossed by excellent, strategic avenues that will put the authorities right into the heart of the old neighborhoods.[54]

Zola's Saccard is expressing a truth that applied to more than one or another thoroughfare, such as the extension of the rue de Rivoli which Haussmann himself calls in his memoirs a "direct, spacious, monumental, and above all strategic link."[55] Indeed this was the controlling principle of all the work completed in the category of the first two networks. The *croisée de Paris* literally gutted old Paris, the Paris of revolts and unrest, of cholera and poverty, a process that Haussmann commemorates with these words:

> We ripped open the belly of old Paris, the neighborhood of revolts and barricades, and cut a large opening through the almost impenetrable maze of alleys, piece by piece, and put in cross-streets whose continuations terminated the work. Completion of the rue de Turbigo finally helped to eliminate the rue Transnonain from the map of Paris! In putting in the boulevard de Strasbourg, and extending it to the Seine and beyond, I am certain that the emperor did not have its strategic usefulness in mind; in fact the same is also true for most of the other thoroughfares like the rue de Rivoli, whose direct routing made it no longer suitable for the familiar tactics of local uprisings. But even if this was not his specific intention, though the opposition kept accusing him of it, there is no denying that it was the most opportune result of all the large thoroughfares designed by His Majesty to rehabilitate the old part of the city and open it to traffic. This, along with other good reasons, served to justify the great expense to the state and the rest of France, especially since it must be in the nation's interests that Paris remain peaceful.
>
> As for myself, who encouraged all the additions to the original plan, I can guarantee that their greater or lesser strategic importance was farthest from my mind.[56]

Haussmann's memoirs are no exception to the rule that such works contain apologetic traits.[57] For the whole originality of Napoleon III's and Haussmann's urban policy was primarily to ensure effective governmental control. And in contrast to the timid policy of the constitutional monarchy, which was far too considerate of the opposing interests of the propertied classes, the Second Empire was always exclusively concerned with the national importance of Paris. This fundamentally different approach determined the basic concept of the transformation of Paris. Haussmann's only intentional use of former esthetic policy was that of the "beautiful perspective," and the design of the facades of buildings lining the new streets.[58] Their arrangement and embellishment reflected an eclectic monumentalizing taste which was de rigueur far into the Third Republic. Aside from this formal esthetic tradition, urban planning in the Second Empire made a revolutionary break with older models in its tendency to decentralize.

As of 1789 the development of Paris had been characterized by the fact that all political, bureaucratic, and economic activities were located in the center of the city; that is, between the Palais-Royal in the west, the Hôtel de Ville in the east, the Ile de la Cité in the south, and the Porte Saint-Denis in the north. In the Second Empire the object was to separate these functions, to decentralize them so as to prevent their possibly being blockaded. This intention was especially obvious in the so-called *croisée de Paris*, for besides its strategic importance (which Haussmann admitted), the rue de Rivoli functioned as a *cordon sanitaire* from the Tuileries in the west to the other side of the Hôtel de Ville in the east. Behind it to the south, and including the Ile de la Cité—which in its turn was protected by the Left Bank—there developed an area that was soon limited to executive and administrative business.

Rehabilitation was particularly radical on the Ile de la Cité, where medieval housing conditions had prevailed until then. Haussmann replaced the impenetrable maze of alleys, houses, and courtyards, in which 14,000 people still lived and worked as late as 1856, with an administrative complex.[59] In addition to the Police Prefecture and barracks it included the Palais de Justice, the Tribunal de Commerce, and the Conciergerie prison, as well as a new Hôtel-Dieu (municipal hospital). Of the old buildings, aside from the Sainte-Chapelle and Notre Dame, only a few houses remained in the place Dauphine and parts of the Chanoinesse neighborhood to the north of Notre Dame. Haussmann's plans were for additional administrative buildings to take over this last residential area on the *Cité*, but this was prevented by the end of the Second Empire.[60]

The expansion of the Ile de la Cité into an administrative area created a fortress without walls in the heart of the old city capable of controlling the restless arrondissements on both sides of the river. The Second Empire tried to create a similar situation for the Hôtel de Ville, which had a less favorable location, by building barracks, doing extensive demolition work to clear the large place de l'Hôtel de Ville, and constructing the avenue Victoria and the rue de Lobau—which, together with the rue de Rivoli and the quai de l'Hôtel de Ville, isolated the seat of the city administration and its prefect. The result of these efforts was, as Jeanne Gaillard aptly comments, that "the seat of power remained within the city according to democratic tradition; but this power no longer belonged to the city."[61] Moreover, after the completion of the *croisée de Paris*, this seat of power lay exactly at its intersection. It was the center of that spider's web whose threads spanned the whole city until the end of the Second Empire and sealed its future fate as the prisoner of state power. And it was to this end that relentless demolition was undertaken of old, run-down, and hopelessly overpopulated neighborhoods like Les Arcis or Saint-Honoré, which were among the most awful in the capital. This is evident from figures specifying population growth in those areas traversed by the rue de Rivoli.[62]

The brutal cutting-up of "the old Paris, the neighborhood of revolts and barricades," as Haussmann had remarked apropos the construction of the rue de Rivoli, was conspicuously avoided in the work undertaken in the second and third *réseaux*. Once the administrative center had been insulated, it was possible to use somewhat "gentler" methods to accomplish the same result in the no less overpopulated and unsanitary eastern half of the capital. Thus the faubourg Saint-Antoine was enclosed by a system of wide boulevards, the masterpiece being the boulevard du Prince-Eugène completed in 1862.[63] Haussmann proceeded similarly on the Left Bank, encircling and sealing off the slum of the Montagne Sainte-Geneviève by constructing the rues Monge, Gay-Lussac, and Claude Bernard.[64]

But the suspicion that strategic objectives had motivated the entire renovation program becomes a certainty if one looks into Haussmann's defense of the program. His first argument was that the sole purpose of "the large thoroughfares designed by His Majesty" was to "rehabilitate the old part of the city and open it to traffic."[65] This was not really convincing, as it is obvious that the dividing and isolating function of the new streets could only come about if they also served as broad arteries linking important urban sub-centers.[66] As for the claim of wanting to improve the flow of traffic, it does not satisfactorily explain why the new streets were at first limited to those areas that had become revolutionary strongholds in 1848.

Except for the renovation of the Ile de la Cité and the development of the rue de Rivoli, Haussmann's second argument—that the new streets had the commendable aim of eliminating unwholesome conditions in Paris—is convincingly refuted by his own performance. Much of the work carried out in the second and third *réseaux* left the affected neighborhoods—which were just as slumlike as the *Cité*, Les Arcis, or Saint-Honoré—largely as they were. Other areas, such as the Marais, the neighborhood of Saint-Avoye between the rue de Rivoli and the rue de Turbigo, the Ile Saint-Louis, and the arrondissements of Mail and Bonne Nouvelle, were spared Haussmann's attentions. Their partition or "redevelopment" was not important in terms of politics or security, their population not having been very active in constructing barricades.[67]

It thus becomes clear that the truth was the reverse of Haussmann's declarations. However, when he wrote his memoirs the Second Empire was already a failure in social and political terms; so he had to try to salvage its historical achievement. The major redevelopment that was really needed had never been part of the plan to transform Paris. The same old slums continued to exist unchanged behind the Potemkin-like facades of Haussmann's new rows of houses.[68]

This procedure met the stipulations of the Melun law, passed on April 13, 1850. It made it possible, for the first time, to force landlords of unhygienic lodgings to observe official health regulations.[69] The law was important because it also incorporated the modified expropriation decree of May 3, 1848.[70] The latter measure was later expanded to include all new street construction, under a decree of March 26, 1852. This established the requirements for the uniformity of buildings lining the new streets, which merely hid the neighborhoods behind them.[71]

In view of this practice, there is no basis for the criticism frequently made since then that Haussmann ruthlessly destroyed the old Paris. While he was guilty of some damage in his division of the old neighborhoods, he helped prevent Paris from becoming completely choked. At the same time he managed to provide the old arrondissements with a new lease on life that guaranteed their survival up to the present.

The partitioning of areas of Paris of long historical development found its logical complement in the decentralization that was characteristic of both the second and the third networks. The second network not only rearranged neighborhoods along the periphery of the inner city but linked them with wide thoroughfares that made the city into an interconnected organism. The third *réseau*, begun in 1867, created a series of complementary streets, and provided connections between the old city and suburban areas newly incorporated in 1860.[72] The starlike intersections from which several large streets radiate in different directions, so characteristic of Paris since then, form the nub of this decentralizing pattern.

The two "central stars," between which the Paris street system was developed in the Second Empire, were the place de l'Etoile, where twelve avenues come together, and the place du Trône (now the place de la Nation), from which ten boulevards radiated. Both were situated outside of the old Paris; and because the boulevards and avenues leading from them intersected with so many other streets inside the city, smaller, secondary "stars" had to be created, like the place de la Bastille, the place du Château-d'Eau (now the place de la République), or the place de l'Opéra.[73]

This exemplary traffic network was not determined by the considerations of perspective generally so valued by Haussmann; whatever chance of a view there might have been was spoiled by the abrupt breaking-off of the streets. Only the place de l'Opéra was an exception to this rule, though the intended effect of the complete perspective could have been achieved by different and less complicated means. The decision to construct the place de l'Opéra in the form of a star as well but without placing the opera house itself in an esthetically unsatisfying oblique perspective—if approached, say, from the rue Lafayette, which ran in a straight line over several kilometers—necessitated such an extensive addition of streets that the place had to be enlarged to a double star. Another difficulty was that the hilly terrain of the area around the Opera was not exactly suitable for the symmetrical configuration that the city planners had in mind. An entire thickly populated neighborhood had to make way for the imposing avenue de l'Opéra, which was not completed until the Third Republic.[74] The engineers were also faced with the problem of leveling the Butte des Moulins which stood in the middle of the planned street between the Opera and the Théâtre Français.[75] The establishment of a starlike intersection was therefore unsuitable in terms of perspective and topography, although not of strategy. For the various avenues and streets that came together at the place de l'Opéra established a direct connection with the Gare du Nord (across the rue Lafayette), with the Gare Saint-Lazare (across the rue Auber and rue de Rome), with the Madeleine and Concorde neighborhoods (across the boulevard des Capucines and the rue de la Paix), with the area of the Halles (across the rue du Dix-Décembre, now the rue du Quatre-Septembre) and, finally, with the Left Bank.[76]

Aside from its esthetic intentions, the extravagant development of the place de l'Opéra is a textbook case of decentralizing urbanism.[77] Its strategy is outlined in these words of the guidelines for the second network: "To construct streets that shall provide wide, direct, and numerous communication links between the most important spots in the capital and the military installations that are supposed to protect them."[78] That is to say, the streets between the star intersections served a dual purpose: in the medium term they provided demographic and functional decentralization; in the longer term they allowed the intervention of prompt law–enforcement agencies.

It was obvious to Haussmann's contemporaries that work on the first two *réseaux* was primarily inspired by strategic needs.[79] And yet construction on the third network was concentrated in the fashionable west of the capital, where the boulevards and avenues frequently cut through sparsely populated areas. These thoroughfares now rank among the most splendid of Paris streets, and account for the fact that later interpretations paid less attention to the repressive aspects of Haussmann's plan. Indeed he was astute enough not to undermine the effectiveness of the original, security-oriented purpose of the networks by stressing their practical usefulness. In connection with his overall concern for security, he also undertook the important task of redistributing the population over the entire city, including the suburban municipalities lying within the fortifications and incorporated in 1860. The inner city had reached its demographic peak between 1846 and 1848, and the "gutting" of old Paris had resulted in the brutal eviction of its inhabitants.[80] In addition, a further demographic shift from the overpopulated center— now defined by the place de la République and the place de l'Opéra—was anticipated in connection with the decentralized system of streets.

Among new streets planned in the west of the city, the boulevard Malesherbes—leading from the Madeleine and cutting through the bucolic but barren area of the Plaine Monceau outside the exterior boulevards—was the one most subject to criticism.[81] This arose over a series of topographical anomalies in the location of the boulevard.[82] There was even greater objection to the purchase of the Plaine Monceau by a few large real-estate speculators for what was a negligible sum. They were willing to give Haussmann the land he needed free of charge, knowing that its development would bring enormous profits.[83] The successful urbanization of the Plaine Monceau also necessitated development of the area west of the boulevard Malesherbes. This was accomplished by establishing the avenue de Friedland and the boulevard Haussmann, which connected the place de l'Etoile with the place de l'Opéra, the center of the new business and entertainment district.

Compared with the hectic transformation east and northeast of the place de l'Etoile, the area to the southwest—the sixteenth arrondissement around Passy and Auteuil—made much slower progress at first. Not until the rue Mozart was constructed was urban growth stimulated.[84] Development of the western side of Paris, comprising the eighth, sixteenth, and the southwestern half of the eighteenth arrondissements, at whose center lay the place de l'Etoile, was indeed the "pure folly, the infernal galop of millions," that Zola's speculator Saccard had foreseen.[85] At the beginning of the Second Empire the place de la Concorde still marked the boundary of urban Paris; a few elegant houses and villas did line the Champs-Elysées west of it, but the built-up area was limited. All of this changed abruptly once Haussmann transformed the Champs-Elysées into an English-style park during Napoleon III's Italian campaign. It rapidly increased in desirability as a residential area and appealed to the *grand monde* who built their palaces there. However, this was just the beginning of the urbanization of the fashionable west end of Paris, reaching to Auteuil in the south and beyond the place de Wagram in the north, and expedited after 1860 by Haussmann's network of streets.[86]

Haussmann's Paris

AUSSMANN'S URBANIZATION AND TRANSFORMATION of Paris tended to emphasize social stratification. The sparsely populated and wealthy residential sections in the west contrasted even more now with the overpopulated neighborhoods of the *classes laborieuses* in the east of the capital.[87] In 1863 Anthime Corbon concludes that "the transformation of Paris has evicted the working population from the center to the periphery, so that two cities have developed within the capital: one rich, the other poor; the one encircling the other. The needy class is like an enormous belt enclosing the wealthy class."[88]

There is no doubt that Haussmann bore much responsibility for the famous *ceinture rouge* ("red belt"), because his plan was not only a consequence of but also the cause of further demographic and economic expansion. This expansion took the form of a rapid flow of capital into land within the old city limits, promoting the separation of the classes beyond the Second Empire right up to the present. Increased costs of land and construction produced an intensified use of usable land.[89] The general tendency was to build on all available lots in all neighborhoods, thanks to the comparatively generous expropriation measures that encouraged subdivision of properties lining Haussmann's new streets. The new buildings were all designed in the monumental style of the Second Empire. Their large, wide facades took over much of the expensive ground formerly occupied by the gardens and spacious courtyards of the older houses. Comfort was thus sacrificed to appearance, with facades containing symmetrical lines of balconies, decorated with wrought-iron railings, and supported by caryatids and consoles. There were large entries through which carriages never passed; numerous windows close to a story in height; and finally, sculptured freestone, fluted pilasters, and other ornamental stonework that embellished and subdivided the facades.[90] All of this reflected an attempt to reconcile modern urbanism with the bourgeois way of life, using architectural set pieces to suggest aristocratic luxury.[91]

Interior space in these buildings was designed with an eye to optimum rental income, and provided a marked contrast with the elaborate exteriors.[92] The ground floor was generally given over to commercial use and rented to stores, while the obligatory entryway led to a rear courtyard of at least four square meters according to official regulations. Apartments of more or less the same design were located on the first through sixth floors; the apartment doors opened on to an entry or hallway, which led to the living room and dining room on the street side, while the bedroom, kitchen, and a varying number of other rooms were in the rear of the apartment, where it was generally pitch-black because of the tiny interior courts.

Luxury apartments differed only in their spaciousness; but in them, too, the function of the rooms was determined in advance by their locations: living room, small parlor, dining room, study or library, bedroom and rooms for children and servants, kitchen, toilets, and broom closets. The layout of elegant apartments built after 1850 differed from that of earlier ones, their most important feature being one or two antechambers adjoining the main living rooms. Thus, even if they were larger compared with standard bourgeois apartments of the period, their actual living space was considerably smaller than that of comparable apartments in older houses.[93]

Construction of apartments designed primarily for bourgeois needs and expectations went on everywhere, including the sections east of the boulevard Sébastopol at the periphery of neighborhoods in which the *classes laborieuses* dominated.[94] This development was furthered by a small group of large-scale real-estate and construction companies that controlled and benefited from the property bonanza unleashed by the transformation of Paris. Along entire streets, laid out by them on behalf of the city, they built new buildings that were then sold or rented.[95] The most prominent of these was the Péreire brothers' *Companie immobilière de Paris*, which owned 102 apartment houses along the boulevard du Prince-Eugène alone. However, most of their business interests were concentrated in the west of the capital, where they had numerous properties along the Champs-Elysées, the place de l'Opéra, the rue Lafayette, the boulevard Malesherbes, and the rue de Rivoli.[96]

Smaller firms or individuals stood no chance of competing against these large, financially strong businesses backed by banks and insurance companies and able to invest all over Paris.[97] Moreover, the directors of the large enterprises had close ties to the political establishment, while the smaller ones mostly belonged to the "Orleanist milieu," which was ignored by Bonapartism.[98] The oligopolistic structure of the real-estate market explains the enormous pressure exerted by investors on the capital after 1860.[99] This pressure not only helped Haussmann expedite the urbanization of the fashionable west end, but favored other aspects of his transformation plan.[100]

Those who did not benefit from the transformation were the working class. For whenever one of the older neighborhoods was "haussmannized," its social makeup was inevitably altered.[101] This did not mean that in every instance the *classes laborieuses* were entirely removed from the municipal area of Paris to its outskirts.[102] But it did mean that the bourgeoisie represented a greater percentage of the inner-city population than before the Second Empire, as the endless rows of bourgeois apartment houses still indicate.

Beyond the enormous investment pressure of the Paris real-estate market, this development resulted from a number of motivations. Both the prefect and the real-estate companies wanted to see the costs of the transformation amortized as quickly as possible. This was important to Haussmann because the work could ultimately succeed only if it were carried out speedily. As for the companies, they were interested in obtaining high rents promptly. Their interests converged in the handsome bourgeois apartment houses. The city itself also benefited since building materials, such as freestone, came under the *octroi*, the municipal tax.[103] Finally, what Haussmann most wanted to achieve was a balanced Paris, in which the *classes laborieuses* in the east had their counterpart in the *classes aisées* to the west.

The most radical redevelopment took place in the western and central parts of the city. The latter area was now occupied by government and private administrative offices, banks, and insurance companies, as well as hotels, department stores, and other institutions dealing with large numbers of people. That involved the exodus of its residents; the wealthier ones moved to the new western arrondissements, or to the older neighborhoods west of the boulevards de Strasbourg and Magenta, where they drove out the petit-bourgeois or proletarian population. Rising rents helped the process whereby the *classes laborieuses* were forced to move east to the areas along the periphery. Figures on population density in the eleventh, eighth, and tenth arrondissements, which increased steadily until the end of the Second Empire, illustrate this development.[104]

However, the radical changes undertaken in the center were limited to the area around the new Opera, the Tuileries, the Louvre, and the neighborhoods near the Hôtel de Ville and the markets. In other words, where no new streets were built the old social and economic structure continued as before in the same squalid conditions. That explains why the population density of 600 residents per hectare in the second, third, and fourth arrondissements was still extremely high in 1866 when compared with that of other

Paris neighborhoods.[105] Though the bourgeoisie influenced the social milieu, it was in the minority in relation to the working-class population living there. It is of interest here that the number of reasonably priced older apartments was far greater than that of new, more luxurious ones in the higher tax-yielding arrondissements preferred by the bourgeoisie.[106] Only the sixteenth and seventeenth were exceptions, being decided refuges of the rich, while the new type of apartment house preferred by the bourgeoisie was almost impossible to find in the thirteenth, fourteenth, nineteenth, and twentieth arrondissements.[107] In the east the *embourgeoisement*, presumed to be concurrent with the transformation of Paris, was limited to a few rows of middle-class houses that lined the new streets installed in the working-class neighborhoods.

The social displacement from west to east, which increased noticeably during the Second Empire, was overshadowed by a growing north-to-south development, from the Right Bank to the Left Bank. This was not affected by the complementary axis that Haussmann established on the Left Bank, where the boulevard Saint-Michel intersected with the boulevard Saint-Germain.[108] These arteries were used only by traffic passing through to the Right Bank, and therefore did not offer any particular growth incentives for the rather underdeveloped economy on the Left Bank. However, the Left Bank was not completely ignored; it experienced certain rather minimal and modest changes. Because of its slower economic growth, industries located there were not forced to move to the outskirts as often happened on the Right Bank. Moreover, the capital invested in land was considerably smaller, so that the *classes laborieuses* could continue to live in their traditional neighborhoods near their work. Reasonable rents and relatively low population density on the Left Bank tempted many immigrant workers to settle there, which of course added to the number of inhabitants. The subsequent proletarianization of the fifth and sixth arrondissements impelled the bourgeoisie to move farther south to the area southwest of the Jardin du Luxembourg now made accessible by new streets. However, the aristocratic faubourg Saint-Germain remained unchanged and was completely unaffected by the transformation of the rest of Paris.[109]

The *petite banlieue*, the area between the tax wall and the fortifications, offers the best example of the degree to which the new system of streets eliminated the customary regional geography of communications. On the other hand, the transformation accentuated, differentiated, and enriched this regionalism in economic, demographic, and social terms. Ever since the fortification ring around Paris was completed in 1844, the incorporation of the *petite banlieue* into the capital was merely a question of time.[110] The July Monarchy had shunned a decision, fearing the consequences.[111] The rapid population growth experienced by the suburbs after the mid-1840s, and the unrestrained urbanization that developed in the north and northeast, made their control a political necessity that no regime could permanently avoid.[112] But what must have been particularly alarming was the comparatively high concentration of workshops and factories in the suburbs, which in their turn augmented the proportion of *classes laborieuses* and the poor.[113] For the axiom coined in the days of Napoleon I, that the industrial development of Paris precluded its political security, was still valid.[114] The incorporation of the *petite banlieue* was therefore prompted not as much by economic and urban considerations as by the need for security.

This was confirmed by the relatively late date at which the regime of Napoleon III decided to incorporate the suburbs. Just before the elections of December 2, 1852, it was rumored that the *petite banlieue* would be annexed to the capital and thus become subject to the *octroi* tax. The rumor was energetically denied because it was feared it could lead to a considerable loss of votes in the Department of the Seine.[115] Because the regime was concerned to consolidate its political base, seven more years passed before the legal process for enlarging the city limits including fortifications was set in motion. Not until then was it deemed safe to make decisions that were contrary to the interests of one social group—the owners of workshops and factories around Paris—whose continued support Napoleon III needed.

Railroad-related industries had also developed in France, and their preferred locations were Lyon, Lille, Upper Alsace, and the suburbs of Paris.[116] In the light of the experiences of June 1848 within the city, it was feared that industrial growth on the capital's periphery would add to the potential threat from the working class. The question of municipal and national security fueled a debate on whether further industrialization around the capital would guarantee or endanger social peace.[117]

The decision on January 1, 1860, to incorporate the *petite banlieue* into the capital and thus to expand the *octroi* area made clear which solution the government preferred. For notwithstanding some temporary tax regulations favoring industry, further growth of the *petite banlieue* was held in check by strict fiscal control.[118] This was helped by the fact that the fortifications, and the 370-meter-wide glacis in front of them on which building was not permitted, were absorbed into the capital's administrative territory. It was seriously thought that this no-man's-land would provide an outlet for the growing population, and would also halt industrial expansion within the city.[119] In this the Second Empire harbored the same illusion as the Old Regime which had hoped to stop the growth of Paris by setting legal limits. Beyond the fortifications and outside the area controlled by the *octroi* a new suburban zone developed with more industries, and the population also exploded. The number of inhabitants in the Department of the Seine increased from 257,000 in 1860 to 1 million by the end of the century, and doubled to 2 million by 1931.[120]

Incorporation of the *petite banlieue* was a morsel that took Paris a long time to digest. With the exception of the sixteenth and parts of the seventeenth arrondissements, which belonged to the fashionable west end, the other seven arrondissements, all or parts of which were annexed, remained the stepchildren of urban development. This happened because of their peripheral location and the structure and rapid growth of their inhabitants—all of which had led to the formation of population centers without even the most rudimentary urban and sanitary infrastructure.[121] Furthermore,

Haussmann showed little interest in the needs of these arrondissements which were so far from the real, attractive Paris.

Indeed it would have required an absolutely Herculean effort to integrate the former *petite banlieue* with the older arrondissements of Paris in terms of their urban, economic, and social structure. The new areas remained hermaphrodites until the Third Republic, insofar as they were neither suburbs nor integral parts of Paris. But that, too, was Haussmann's intention, for he had never planned to assimilate the suburbs into the new splendor and wealth of the "capital of the nineteenth century"; he merely wished to have more effective control over the city's mushrooming outskirts. The logical corollary to this was that these new arrondissements generally served the same purpose within the urban organism as they had done before 1860; that is, they continued to be a catchall for the various elements and institutions that would have detracted from the glory of imperial Paris.[122]

The large thoroughfares that Haussmann had built gained him the control he sought by linking the peripheral suburbs with the inner city. These new arrondissements were forced to assume a second-class status, which the demolition of the tax wall did nothing to change. And so the social barriers between the old and the new Paris continued to exist.[123] This deliberate degradation was a logical outcome of the transformation of Paris in the light of its economic, social, political, and strategic policy.

Haussmann tried to mask his neglectful treatment of the former *petite banlieue* by erecting churches and city halls there instead of the needed streets and sewer systems. He was even so generous as to beautify the "far east" of Paris with three large parks, which were supposed to be counterparts to the Bois de Boulogne in the much-preferred west part of the city. They were the Bois de Vincennes and the Parc Montsouris on the southern edge of the city which was not completed until 1878. But the real masterpiece of these political cosmetics was doubtless the Parc des Buttes-Chaumont, built on the wild terrain where the horse abattoir of Montfaucon had been located. Its rocky setting was cleverly transformed into a garden landscape with much romantic charm.

These parks, modeled on London's, together with the majestic avenues, boulevards, and large squares lined with uniform and luxurious buildings, expressed a new and grandiose urban esthetic used by Napoleon III to make Paris the most beautiful city in the world. Not only was the intended effect of important earlier monuments restored by removing obstructions and opening up slum areas, but numerous new buildings were added expressly to mark the historical greatness of the Second Empire. At any rate, one cannot find fault with the overwhelming vista that the "capital of the nineteenth century" offered the observer at the end of that period. Emile Zola tried to render it in the large, naturalistic panoramas that terminate each of the five sections of his novel, *Une Page d'amour*.[124] But these striking prose paintings that capture the *grande ville* as an enormous storm-tossed ocean or evoke a distant and alien Babylon, represent only the surface. Zola comes closer to the essence of the city, to the secret that creates a new urban myth, in a newspaper feuilleton:

I love the horizons of the big city with all my heart. There is an enormously rich source here; we must create a modern art without parallel. The sunny boulevards swarm with people, the squares are luxuriantly green. And depending on whether a ray of sunshine brightens Paris, or a dull sky lets it dream, it resembles a joyful or a melancholy poem. This is art, all around us. A living art, an art still unknown.[125]

Zola's declaration of love for Paris not only indicates the dominant role of the city in his artistic-literary program, but reflects a new and different view of the *grande ville* in literature and art that lasted beyond the fin de siècle. Haussmann's transformation of Paris created the conditions for the great myth in which modernity is fulfilled, the myth of the metropolis as it manifested itself in the Paris of the Second Empire.

Water and Sewage

*N*APOLEON III SAW THE TRANSFORMATION of Paris solely in terms of magnificent new streets and buildings which, aside from their usefulness, were to testify to the glory of his regime. He was not especially interested in other problems of the infrastructure, such as the fresh-water supply, that were becoming more urgent as the population continued to expand.

The capital's fresh water was largely secured from the Seine and the small Ourcq River, which supplied 86,000 cubic meters of water daily in 1854. Two-thirds of this amount was used for street cleaning, for public wells, and for other public needs. Industry, trade, and bathhouses received 9,000 cubic meters daily, which left only 14,000 cubic meters for private households, or 13 liters per inhabitant per day. But such figures tend to gloss over actual conditions; in fact, the 6,230 households directly connected to the rudimentary fresh-water system consumed 9,000 cubic meters of water; another 1,000 cubic meters were sold to affluent individuals from *fontaines marchandes* (commercial water fountains) equipped with special filters. The rest of the inhabitants were left with only 4,000 cubic meters from 68 public wells and 1,779 *bornes-fontaines* (public fountains).[126]

This truly appalling undersupply of fresh water was at first supposed to be improved by the installation of additional and more efficient pumps in the Seine. Napoleon III wanted to entrust the entire water supply to a private consortium under the direction of the banker Charles Laffitte. But Haussmann counseled against it, using two arguments that finally convinced Napoleon III. He warned against giving the monopoly of the water supply to a private company; and he insisted that rather than river water, the capital be supplied with fresh spring water which, though it had to be brought from farther away, was of far better quality.[127] Eugène Belgrand, who was put in charge of the *Direction des eaux de Paris*, estimated the daily water needs at

200,000 cubic meters in his first report of July 1854. Of this volume more than half would have to come from new sources, as the prefect insisted that Seine water only be used for street cleaning in future.[128]

The search for productive water sources around Paris led to the acquisition of the rights to the small Dhuis river in March 1855. An aqueduct was built between 1863 and 1865, to carry this water over a distance of 131 kilometers to a reservoir at the top of Ménilmontant. In 1860 Paris also acquired the rights to all the springs in the Vanne valley; however, completion of the 173-kilometer-long conduit was delayed until 1874 by a long-drawn-out legal battle with the town of Sens. This gave Paris a daily supply of more than 226,000 cubic meters, of which 162,000 cubic meters were needed for public use, whereas private households had to be satisfied with 50,000 cubic meters per day.[129]

After 1854 the system of water mains was greatly expanded and its conduits transferred to the subterranean sewers. By 1874 about 1,370 kilometers of water pipes had been installed and about 83 percent of all buildings were connected to the system.[130] These figures, which would seem to indicate amazingly rapid progress, actually hide some glaring disparities. The eastern half of the capital, and especially its peripheral arrondissements, were at a decided disadvantage. In 1874, 85 percent of all the buildings in the tenth and eleventh arrondissements were connected to the water mains; in the eighteenth, nineteenth, and twentieth arrondissements, the figure was 50 percent; in the thirteenth and fourteenth arrondissements it was only 39 and 32 percent, respectively. In the seventh arrondissement, more than 86 percent of the buildings had mains water supply, and in the fashionable eighth arrondissement, only 29 of the 3,390 buildings remained unconnected. [131]

But these statistics, which Eugène Belgrand proudly made public in 1875, must be carefully analyzed because the amount supplied to individual buildings does not indicate how many of the tenants actually used this convenience. The matter is further complicated by the fact that the supply of water was a joint venture shared by the city and a private company called the *Companie générale des eaux*.[132] The city supplied the water, and developed and maintained the mains network; the *Companie générale* was charged with making the connection to the buildings and collecting the water rates from the users, of which it received 25 percent.[133] This division shows that it was in the city's interest to expand the water system in those areas where their investment costs would be amortized relatively quickly by a large number of private customers. The *Companie générale* charged a basic connection fee of 16 francs per year for each private water connection "à robinet libre" (unmetered) used by up to three people. The fee for each additional person was 4 francs; the charge for the water actually used was based on an estimate.[134]

In addition to these comparatively high costs, water usage was limited by the fact that until 1880 only one connection was permitted in each building. It was installed on the ground floor and served all the tenants. Residents in luxury apartment buildings could obtain connections on each of the floors if they paid for them. Landlords then added the water fees to the rent—a lucrative business for the landlords who usually charged far more than the rates they paid to the *Companie générale.*[135]

It is obvious that a water-supply system for private households based on such a maximization of profits severely limited the number of potential subscribers as well as the amount they used, especially for personal hygiene. This explains why, for example, in Zola's novel *La Curée,* one of the rooms in Saccard's mansion near the Parc Monceau was considered "the wonder of the apartment," and as "the room of which all Paris spoke." This legendary room was nothing but a bathroom, in which a bathtub was set into a sort of alcove.[136]

During the Second Empire and the Third Republic, *l'eau à l'étage* was a luxury that only the wealthy could afford, because of the problem of waste disposal. Some progress had been made in this connection during the July Monarchy and the Second Republic.[137] But Haussmann recognized the need for putting in a new, larger, and more efficient sewage system, as he outlines in his *Premier Mémoire sur les eaux de Paris* of August 4, 1854.[138]

The most complex technical problem associated with a new and efficient sewage system was finding a location outside the city where such a system could drain into the Seine without polluting it, as hitherto, within the city limits. Moreover, the difference in elevation between the main sewer outfall and the water level of the Seine had to be considered so that even at periods of high tide the main sewer would not be flooded. Otherwise, the high water would be carried through the sewers to the city center and inundate the low-lying neighborhoods.[139] This problem was compounded by the very slight fall of the river as it passed through the city, a difficulty Haussmann claims to have solved himself.[140] The primary collector of the Paris sewer system was rerouted to run from the place de la Concorde in a northwesterly direction to the Seine at Asnières, avoiding the large U-shaped bend of the Seine southwest of Paris. This meant that despite the primary collector's incline the elevation difference between it and the Seine's normal water level was 170 centimeters; and it ensured that even under high-water conditions the Paris sewer system was neither blocked nor flooded.[141]

Construction of the collector at Asnières, begun in 1857, and the topography of Paris determined the layout of the rest of the generously built sewer network. By 1872 the length of the system was 172 kilometers.[142] But these improvements mainly benefited Paris within its old boundaries. The former *petite banlieue* was clearly neglected, especially the overcrowded arrondissements of Saint-Vincent-de-Paul, Combat, Belleville, and Ménilmontant in the north and east, and the fourteenth arrondissement in the south.[143] A contemporary report by Vaugirard and Grenelle describes conditions there. Stinking swamps developed next to the houses, and people had to wade through malodorous slime in the unpaved streets.[144] In the west end, however, a dense sewer system took care of the thinly populated districts of Roule and Chaillot.

Despite this obvious preferential treatment for certain arrondissements over others, the Paris sewer system was generally recognized to be one of

Haussmann's achievements. Here, too, he managed to convince his royal master of the need for something in which the latter was supremely disinterested. But the subterranean sewers had a serious drawback, having previously been used solely as street drains. A decree of March 26, 1852, ordered that all new buildings on streets possessing sewers had to install connections for the disposal of household waste at the owners' expense. Within ten years all buildings had to meet this requirement.[145] A further decree issued on December 19, 1854, specified that the connections of private households to the city's sewer lines were to consist of underground galleries, whose minimum height was to be 230 centimeters and the width 130 centimeters. Again, the installation and upkeep were to be paid by the owners.[146] However, the practical effect of these rather severe sanitary measures was limited by two factors.

For one thing, only 20,000 houses complied with the December 1854 regulations, or about one-third of the properties in Paris. Furthermore, these were largely situated in the center and west of the capital, while very few connections were installed in the northern and eastern arrondissements. This was not due to inadequate sewer construction in these areas, but rather to the unwillingness of proprietors to incur expenses that would not increase the value of their properties and would serve a class unable to afford greater water consumption.[147] Hygienic and sanitary conditions therefore deteriorated still further during the Second Empire in neighborhoods populated by the *classes laborieuses*.

Second, only *eaux ménagères*, or kitchen waste, was emptied into the sewer system, while the *eaux vannes*, or bathroom waste, continued to be disposed of in cesspools, holding from twenty to thirty cubic meters, in the cellars of each house.[148] Because the toilets lacked effective ventilation or traps, certain atmospheric conditions produced a pestilential stench in the city.[149] Surprisingly, this antediluvian method, by which everyone alike was made aware of the odors and which detracted from the splendor of the new Paris, seemed to bother no one unduly. This attitude changed only around 1880, when a radically different point of view developed among large sections of the public. Suddenly conditions that had been tolerated for generations were criticized and considered untenable.

In view of the inflexible way in which the old methods were adhered to, Haussmann's statement on April 1, 1859, that in future the *eaux vannes* from private households could be drained directly into the city's sewer system represented a great step forward. The stipulation was that cesspools be provided with an *appareil diviseur* (separator mechanism) that separated water from solid fecal waste which still had to be collected periodically.[150] This informal tolerance of direct drainage of *eaux vannes* into the city sewers was finally made official by decree on July 2, 1867.[151] The measure had a certain success, there being 26,000 toilets in Paris by 1885, used by 500,000 inhabitants. These figures give an indication of how widespread the use of *l'eau à l'étage* had become.[152]

Interim Results

*H*AUSSMANN DOES NOT DESERVE THE BLAME for all the deficiencies in the urban infrastructure of Paris merely because he was an able defender and upholder of bourgeois interests. After all, the city's social fabric had developed before his regime. And the fact that he was a man of his time and of the regime he served was naturally reflected in the new Paris he created. His legacy was so powerful that even the Third Republic found itself forced to continue his work.

At any rate it is beyond question today that Haussmann prevented Paris from being submerged in its unsolved problems. As for the ruthlessness with which he sometimes carried out his work, it cannot simply be explained in terms of the satisfaction he received from venting his "class hatred." It was due rather to the failure of previous regimes to deal with conditions. Haussmann also realized that he had to act quickly to accomplish at least the essentials. One cannot imagine what Paris would have been without Napoleon III and Haussmann. Perhaps it would have become somewhat like the old section of present-day Rome, only much larger, gloomier, and lacking the southern cheerfulness that transfigures even dirt.

Although the authoritarian regime of Napoleon III claimed legitimacy from a plebiscite, it could transform Paris only if it had the support of the wealthy classes. Haussmann was fully aware that their backing generally depended on what they could expect to gain, and he always calculated his projects with their interests in mind. His critics, among whom Zola was the most severe, held this against him time and again. Zola considered the transformation of Paris to be the most representative manifestation of the government's mendacity.[153] In his *Lettres parisiennes*, which appeared in the newspaper *La Cloche* at the beginning of the Third Republic, Zola's criticism grows into a veritable hymn of hate:

> The Empire had the strangest ideas about hygiene. It carried on the way certain housewives do who, though they sweep their parlors, brush the dirt under the furniture. It swept the streets of Paris clean but at the same time pushed all the dirt into the buildings. Moreover, the Empire was like those unfortunate women who wear a silk dress but under it have a dirty slip, stockings with holes, and a torn camisole. The Empire gilded the gullies; its dream was to whitewash the whole city, to line it up and clothe it in ceremonial dress, but it was satisfied with letting the city go barefoot and hide each tear and dirty mark behind lacework. Nothing is more characteristic of this than the care taken to display all the false luxury of the buildings on their facades. It is always thieves who stress their honesty, and the unkempt who protest they are washing their hands. The rue de Rivoli, the rue Lafayette, all of these new streets are much too straight for the Empire. The Paris of M. Haussmann is one enormous deception, the lie of a Jesuitism of gigantic proportions. . . . The squares, the large parks with their flowerbeds, smile a hypocritical smile so as to divert us from the vapors and pestilential stench that constantly drift over the city. All the new plaster, the whitewash, the garish painting are just supposed to hide the gaping cracks, the weakness of the buildings, the incurable wounds, the impending collapse.[154]

Even this criticism, in which Zola retrospectively assumes the role of a cursing prophet, unintentionally admits Haussmann's achievement. Yet one cannot disagree with Zola's objections, for indeed Haussmann concentrated on the facades but failed to regulate the sanitary conditions existing behind them. The *Loi Melun* dated from the Second Republic and the Empire avoided enforcing this law or letting the *Commission de salubrité* be effective.[155] Zola's criticism also demonstrated a new and different understanding of the city produced by Haussmann's work, including a heightened sensibility that was greatly shocked by the revelation of existing urban problems. The *ville malade* was discovered before Koch and Pasteur began working because Haussmann, in transforming Paris, also transformed its inhabitants.

Indeed Haussmann did not produce a model modern city in all respects. But while his modernization had to make allowance for financial and political interests, it still set a trend and served as an example for cities with similar problems. The new Paris that Zola tried to unmask as a fake is still the city of today. Its openness, its well-proportioned monumentality, even its romanticism were all created by Haussmann in the space of seventeen years and they have lasted more than a century. It is not the skyscrapers of New York and Chicago—those blocks of concrete, steel, and glass piled on top of one another with varying degrees of unimaginativeness—that are the architectural symbols of modern times. It is the Paris of Haussmann and Napoleon III, an urban landscape in which man is still the measure of all things.

The Department Stores

*T*HOUGH THE TRANSFORMATION OF PARIS created many problems—which Haussmann was accused of handling inadequately—it led to an even greater concentration of capital in Paris than at the end of the July Monarchy. The sheer scale of the work stimulated the city's economy and promoted considerable structural change. Writing at the beginning of the Third Republic, Maxime Du Camp gives his view of the process:

> The majority of the *peuple parisien* used to be employed in small trades; this is no longer the case today: the great development of science . . . has had a direct influence on the population of large cities; for instead of being content with a relatively modest profit from selling handmade products, they have been led to embark on the adventures of industrial production which, though it often involves great risks, enables competent and intelligent individuals to earn a fortune.[156]

Yet such an interpretation tends to give a false impression. Even under the Second Empire, Paris had by no means developed into an industrial city. An investigation by the Chamber of Commerce in 1860, analyzed by C. Lavollée, shows that there were 101,171 people who were described as *fab-*

ricants (manufacturers); of these only 7,492 employed more than ten workers; 31,480 employed between two and ten workers, while 62,199 had only one employee or worked on their own.[157] These figures clearly indicate that during the Second Empire production was still predominantly artisan-oriented, whereas industrial enterprises—that is factories employing more than fifty or, after 1860, more than one hundred workers—were proportionately extremely few.[158] On the other hand, the number of workshops in Paris grew by 30 percent between 1847 and 1860, the greater part of that growth being due to the incorporation of the *petite banlieue* where, by 1860, 14,067 workshops were located.[159] The absolute increase in commercial and industrial enterprises did not result in larger establishments after 1860, but rather in a greater number of smaller workshops.[160] This was directly related to the fact that industries requiring a great deal of space were forced out of Paris by the rapid increase in real-estate prices; smaller, artisan-oriented businesses manufacturing high-priced finished or luxury goods were able to stay on.[161] At first glance, this may seem like a continuation of the trend during the July Monarchy, when *articles de Paris* made up the greatest percentage of goods produced in the capital. However, there is an important difference; *articles de Paris* had previously been sold primarily in the home market, whereas they were now largely destined for export.[162]

If one compares the sales volume of the different branches of industry in Paris, one makes another suprising discovery: though the building trade experienced an upswing because of the transformation of Paris, it did not rank first. The food industry led with a yearly volume of over 1 billion francs; the *industries diverses* (miscellaneous industries including such artisan-oriented enterprises as fur and leather goods, precision instruments, clocks, and the aforementioned *articles de Paris*) were second with 556 million francs.[163] Next in importance was the clothing trade, with a yearly volume of 455 million francs, followed by the building and furniture industries with 315 million and 200 million francs, respectively.[164]

The great disadvantage of this type of small business, so characteristic of Paris, was that it was very sensitive to seasonal demand because of its specialized nature. Lavollée writes:

> There is only one sector that has a consistent output during the year and that is the food industry. Other branches periodically experience a dead season, which lasts for two to four months and which can be anticipated by customers and workers on account of its almost regular occurrence. . . . This is characteristic of Parisian industry, which produces a considerable amount of fashion and luxury goods and which, apart from any natural loss of production, is exposed to sudden fallings-off in orders caused either by internal political crises or by complications in other countries. The orders placed with Parisian businesses indicate, with thermometer-like precision, the confidence and wealth not only of France but of the whole world.[165]

That is an exact description of the Achilles heel of Parisian industry whose dependence on economic trends made it relatively unstable; such fluctuations also immediately affected the labor market. The few large-scale industrial enterprises on the outskirts of the capital, which were far less susceptible to sudden economic fluctuations, were nevertheless unable to compensate for these structural problems.[166]

Doubtless the most original commercial development during the Second Empire was the rise of the *grands magasins*, or department stores. Their innovative sales techniques attracted a metropolitan and bourgeois clientele. The *grands magasins* were a new type of business, limited to Paris, whose economic success depended on the relative affluence of large sections of the population. They were thus the most prominent expression of the retail boom of the Second Empire. It was a development that emphasized the role of the capital as a center of service industries, and complemented the concept of the imperial city envisaged by Napoleon and Haussmann.[167] Maxime Du Camp saw this phenomenon as a normal function of urban growth, the retail trade being redistributed over the whole city in the wake of its customers.[168] Such a hypothesis may suffice for goods and products needed on a daily basis, but it does not adequately explain the establishment of the *grands magasins*.

The precursors of the *grands magasins* were the *magasins de nouveautés* that developed under the Restoration, the archetype of which was the *Petit matelot* described by Balzac.[169] Here different types of goods were offered under one roof for the first time, especially items of clothing and related accessories that had previously been sold exclusively by a highly specialized retail trade. The habit of purchasing shirt, trousers, jacket, hat, and coat in one rather than five different stores was the big innovation of the *magasins de nouveautés*. The new sales techniques were just as inventive. Prices were lower and geared to large sales, instead of the previous method of overpricing for a small turnover. Individual items now had fixed prices and customers were given the chance to exchange goods once they had bought them.

Such sales methods were taken over and developed still further by the *grands magasins* established in the center of Paris after 1860.[170] This alone would not have sufficed to give the stores their prompt and overwhelming success; it was due rather to a number of external factors.

Among these, the most important was Haussmann's system of streets, which opened the capital to traffic and linked previously self-sufficient neighborhoods.[171] In his novel *Au Bonheur des dames*, which is set in a department store, Zola describes "those new avenues, where the bustling crowds of the fin de siècle moved along in broad sunlit spaces."[172] The department-store magnates saw the streets as large arteries through which passed a constant stream of potential customers.[173] Because of their central location and the new streets, the *grands magasins* had virtually the whole city as a market for their goods—not merely one arrondissement as had been the case for their predecessors, the *magasins de nouveautés*.[174]

But in order to gain access to this market, they had to bring the goods to the attention of the passing crowd, to entice people to enter, to tempt them to buy something. It was important, therefore, for the *grand magasin* to endow the product with a fetishlike quality. A new relationship between the item and an anonymous buying public had to be created that would give the object an illusory quality of uniqueness and exclusivity despite its being mass-produced. In calculating large sales with a relatively small profit margin, the stores were not aiming to democratize their customers. They counted on a bourgeois public in whose breast two souls were in conflict: one desiring the decorative and ostentatious luxury exemplified by Haussmann's facades, and the other upholding the virtues of thrift.[175]

At this prospective female market with its conflicting desires the stores aimed their whole sales psychology (which has changed very little to this day). It consisted of elaborate brochures and posters, newspaper advertisements and catalogs, which supplied details of goods offered and prices. The milling crowds were attracted by the large delivery trucks, with the stores' names on their sides in giant letters, and carrying posters announcing the latest special offers.[176]

The overall appearance of these stores, especially their elaborate architecture, which endowed the ordinariness of the haberdashery trade with the opulence of an opera house, was even more ingenious than advertisements and posters, and transformed the real value of the goods. Here, too, Haussmann's new broad streets created the necessary space for such monumental structures in the cramped center of the city. When Denise, Zola's provincial protagonist in the novel *Au Bonheur des dames*, stands in front of the department store bearing that name for the first time, its unexpected sight takes her breath away:

> Here, exposed to the street, right on the sidewalk, was a veritable landslide of cheap goods; the entrance was a temptation, with bargains that attracted passing customers. From the mezzanine above, woolen and cloth fabrics, merinos, cheviots, and moltons, billowed down like flags in neutral colors of slate gray, marine blue, and olive green, broken up only by their white paper price tags. To one side hung lengths of fur framing the entrance, narrow strips for trimming dresses, delicate ash gray from the backs of lesser sea swallows, pure snow of swan's down, rabbit fur simulating ermine and marten. Below that, set out on tables in flat boxes underneath a pile of remnants, was a large quantity of trimmings for hats sold for next to nothing . . . it looked like the warehouse for a giant fair, the store seemed to be bursting and throwing its surplus into the street.[177]

With its seemingly unlimited and overflowing supply of goods, artfully arranged and displayed behind large windows, the *grand magasin* had an important influence on the development of a new consumer mentality. It accomplished this by turning the prosaic process of purchasing into an addictive experience, as Zola saw. The atmosphere that was indispensable for this experience was created by the architecture of the stores, certain elements of which were familiar because they were eclectic set pieces derived from earlier periods.[178] But the architecture was also revolutionary in its use of new materials, such as iron structures and vast glass surfaces, designed to provide enormous, well-lit and well-ventilated spaces. These, like the markets, train stations, and exposition halls built during the same period, were designed to attract large crowds for a variety of activities that could be carried on speedily and efficiently.[179]

The inventiveness of this architecture consisted in disguising the real, merchandising purpose of these vast emporia by creating a magic atmosphere in which the customer was made to feel like royalty. The interior decoration, which echoed the elaborate facade with stucco work, polished copper decorations, and fluted columns, added to this feeling. The sales space was distributed over several levels connected, as in the new building of the *Bon marché* store, by a wide, double-curving metal staircase reminiscent of the one at the new Opera.[180] And as in the Opera, the staircase did not merely serve the crude purpose of linking two different floors; it was a stage on which the customers were both actors in and observers of a spectacle whose impressive scenery was provided by the profusion of merchandise.[181] This abundance was supposed to enchant customers and confirm their impression of a tempting variety of goods, originally conveyed by the window display.

These *grands magasins* came closer to embodying the transformation of Paris than the train stations, or Victor Baltard's markets.[182] They combined in purest form the functional and esthetic elements that characterized the changes in the capital. As products of the modern metropolis, they were monuments to a new consumer mentality, as well as models of the bureaucratization and rationalization of all aspects of life to which Haussmann made a considerable contribution.

The Condition of the Working Class

*T*HE *CLASSES LABORIEUSES* HAD ONLY a relatively small share in the middle-class prosperity symbolized by the *grands magasins*. Between 1853 and 1871 the average daily wage of a Parisian worker rose from 3 francs 81 to 4 francs 98.[183] In his monograph on *La Vie ouvrière,* Georges Duveau established four different categories for the working class based on their daily wage. The very poorest earned less than 3 francs per day. Those paid between 3 and 5 francs per day were the average wage earners; workers who earned between 5 francs and 6 francs 50 were relatively well-off; while those who received more than 6 francs 50 were considered privileged. By comparing the growth of these four groups between 1847 and 1860, Duveau reached the following conclusion: In 1847 there were 200,000 workers in Paris, a number that rose to 290,000 by 1860. In 1847 there were 160,000 workers who belonged to the group of average wage earners; by 1860 the number had decreased to 132,000. On the other hand, the relatively well-off increased from 11,000 to 19,000; while the privileged group, which was almost nonexistent in 1847, reached 15,000 by 1860. The largest growth took place in the group of those who earned less than the average wage: the figures there grew from 25,000 in 1847 to more than 64,000 in

1860.[184] These statistics indicate two contrasting tendencies: the absolute number of the less-than-average wage earners changed significantly, while the group of workers who had a better-than-average or very good pay scale also increased but to a far smaller extent. It is revealing that the large group of average wage earners decreased considerably. If one considers that women and children were paid far less than men, and that in the Second Empire trade and industry had a one-to-four-month dead season, it follows that more than half of the population lived at a bare subsistence level.[185]

Not only did most of the workers live precariously but so did many of the growing number of employees and state functionaries. As a rule the latter had a higher nominal income than workers who earned a higher-than-average wage, and their conditions of employment were far more stable. But their social status occasioned expenses that did not affect workers.[186] While a worker's wife and children could contribute to the family income, an employee's could not; and whereas a worker could exist in poor housing and wear poor-quality clothing, an employee was expected to spend a certain minimum on both these items.

Aside from stable employment, the second most important advantage for a worker was a supply of basic foods at moderate prices. Bread was still the staple diet of the *classes laborieuses* in the Second Empire, but a greater selection of foods was available and workers now consumed more meat.[187] The consumption of horsemeat, previously considered taboo, was encouraged as of 1866. A *Comité hippophagique* was founded in Paris, which organized several large public dinners where only horsemeat dishes were served.[188] The first *boucherie chevaline* was opened on July 9 of that year; such stores are not uncommon today in the poorer sections of Paris. Although the price of horsemeat was a third lower than that of beef, and moreover was weighed without bones, it was not very popular at first. Old prejudices and taboos were long-lasting and not overcome until times of dire need during the siege of Paris in the winter of 1870–71.

Staple foods became more expensive between 1850 and 1870, and there was a noticeable shortage of bread due to bad harvests between 1853 and 1856.[189] Still, the great supply crises that had regularly led to famines in Paris were now a thing of the past. The French railroad system, which expanded by 18,000 kilometers between 1852 and 1870, made possible the agricultural specialization of entire regions—a development of great importance in keeping the capital regularly supplied.

The *classes laborieuses* profited from these improvements, yet their living conditions deteriorated because of greater isolation, marginalization, and proletarianization. Gradual development of industrial mass production and use of machinery caused a creeping devaluation of manual work. At the same time these changes also permitted increases in productivity, the price of which was greater worker exploitation. As noted earlier, the working class suffered from the consequences of the transformation of Paris, banished as it was to the outskirts, or confined to such overcrowded neighborhoods as the fourth and fifth arrondissements in the inner city.[190] Residents there were considered to be a *population nomade*, living in lodging houses under the most unspeakable sanitary conditions.[191]

Another, quite new phenomenon was the development of a shantytown on vacant land around Chaillot; a report by the *Commission des logements insalubres* in 1857 states: "It is known that at times single individuals, sometimes even communal groups, but more frequently individual speculators, have had the idea of erecting all sorts of dwellings and shacks on previously vacant land, put together in makeshift fashion with wooden frames and fabric salvaged from demolished houses."[192] Slums of this sort even existed near fashionable residential areas, but these were only temporary since empty inner-city lots were quickly developed. However, similar squalid shantytowns for the poorest of the poor sprang up on the edge of Paris, the most famous of which were the Cité Doré, the Cité des Kroumirs, and the Cité Maufry.[193]

Conditions were little better in other working-class arrondissements that formed on the outskirts of Paris. The social plight of their inhabitants was exacerbated by overpopulation and deficiencies in the urban infrastructure.[194] Using Belleville as an example, Max Nordau depicts the horrors of the scene:

> The houses, located along random, dirty, goat path–like alleys, look neglected and flimsy; the plaster is peeling off the dirty fronts; the few stucco ornaments on the rafters are crumbling and fall off piece by piece; the gate hinges are loose; the holes in the windows are covered with waxed paper. The whole impression is one of walking between two rows of ragged beggars, held together with string and adhesive tape, the mere sight of whom is an unexpressed plea for alms. There are not many stores; the few one sees display coarse linen smocks, wooden shoes, clay pipes, and old junk in the windows. . . . Bookstores are just as nonexistent as lending libraries. . . . But almost every building contains a brandy or wine store and a soup kitchen that looks most repulsive; only a few steps further on there is bound to be a dance hall which pompously calls itself *Bal*, and advertises itself with a colored lantern or banner with symbols of music and dance.[195]

Such was the urban ambience in which many of the *classes laborieuses* lived. Typhoid fever and tuberculosis were almost endemic in these places, and so were rickets and other diseases of malnutrition.[196] There were also widespread alcoholism and a high incidence of infant mortality. Anyone who lived to see old age represented an exception that was hardly fortunate, for old age meant abject misery. The material situation of the working class improved only in a few exceptional cases during the Second Empire; the general rule was that conditions grew worse or remained unchanged.[197]

What did change in those years was the mentality of the working class, their view of the world and of the social order in which they lived. The separation of the *classes aisées* and the *classes laborieuses*, their concentration and isolation in two different worlds within the capital, estranged them and created dislike, even enmity and hatred. Michel Chevalier, the Saint-Simonist economist, writes:

There is a gulf between the bourgeoisie on the one hand, and the farmers and workers on the other. The bourgeois finds he has nothing in common with the worker. He has grown used to seeing the worker as a machine that one rents and uses, paying only for useful time. By contrast, large numbers of proletarians look on the bourgeois as an enemy, whose superiority one accepts only because he is the stronger. . . . Today there are two hostile types confronting one another: the bourgeois and the proletarian.[198]

This enmity and division was especially marked in the Second Empire because the factors responsible for the development of both wealth and hopeless poverty were so closely related. The greater the magnificence of the capital in the nineteenth century, the longer and more threatening were the shadows that darkened its horizon.

Monde *and* Demi-Monde

*T*HE WORLD OF POVERTY AND MISERY was very far removed from that of fashionable society. Of course it was considered good form to be active in all sorts of charities, but these were seen as routine duties. As a matter of fact, the daily lives of the upper class—still viewed in a seductive light today—were empty and mainly devoted to idle self-indulgence. The happy few of the *monde parisien* were a bizarre, colorful society, a mixture of the new Napoleonic aristocracy and members of the upper bourgeoisie—bankers, speculators, and industrial magnates. The axis of this world was the imperial court in the Tuileries.

In his book on the Paris of Jacques Offenbach, Siegfried Kracauer notes, "The operetta developed because the society in which it evolved was operettalike."[199] It was operettalike because the parvenus set the tone. One of these newly rich sat on the throne and the lavish court he kept—the many courtiers and dignitaries with their gold-braided uniforms, the elaborate dress mandatory at official receptions, the whole pomp and show—was all sham and tinsel, all part of that artificiality whose greatest enemy is real life. The grand court receptions were planned to give the illusory and beguiling effect of fairy magic, beloved by the imperial couple but entirely unrealistic.[200]

The fashionable life led by Napoleon III and Eugénie, whose beauty and elegance were the ideal of the period, was copied in all the circles of the *monde parisien*. Thousands of guests were invited to the great receptions in Versailles.[201] These were attended by hundreds of bankers and speculators, and even included some of the bourgeoisie who were not part of the moneyed aristocracy.[202] Aside from these large-scale official affairs there was a second, last flowering of salon culture, an endless series of intimate gatherings where gossip and slander provided a certain diversion from the boredom that otherwise would have made social life impossible. Anyone who belonged to this world was condemned to lead what would be for a modern observer an expensive and fatiguing life. This was especially true during the social season, which began in November and lasted until May, the only break being Lent. The balls, dinners, receptions, theater and opera performances, not to mention the afternoon teas, became burdensome to the happy few. As the comte de Grandeffe notes:

> Back in Paris, we have taken up our usual lives again: dinners, outings to the Champs-Elysées and the boulevards, visits during the day and then the soirées. It is unbelievable to what extent these things take up one's time, in spite of which one is left with a void. All of it is absurd, nothing but tumult, always tumult. If one wants to recall something, one cannot remember anything of note, and still one loves this life, perhaps because it goes by so fast and helps to overcome the inevitable boredom that each day brings.[203]

The longer the Second Empire lasted, the more the social life of *monde* and *demi- monde* became intertwined. Society was surrounded by the scandal of an eternal *frou-frou* of loose abandon, which gave Paris a lasting reputation as a hotbed of vice. The *demi-monde* consisted primarily of the scintillating courtesans of the *grande bicherie* (high prostitution) who, like Zola's Nana, had at first made their name—less for their talent than their physical attributes—as actresses and dancers.

What obscured the boundaries so quickly between *monde* and *demi-monde* during the Second Empire was the fact that both shamelessly worshiped the same idol: money. The desire to flaunt one's wealth openly, without any moral scruples, was the catalyst that fused the two groups so thoroughly that it became good form to be noticed by the *chronique scandaleuse* (gossip columns). Who was having an affair with whom was an open secret.[204] It was quite admissible to be seen in public with one's mistress since this helped to demonstrate one's wealth; moreover, depending on the lady's status in the *demi-monde*, such appearances augmented the social standing of her *amant en titre* (chosen lover).

In this parvenu society, whose reality was above all illusion, and in which social reputation was also an object of trade, the women of the *demi-monde* dressed in the same lavish style, used the same luxurious carriages, and attended the same theaters, concerts, balls, and promenades as did the *femmes du monde*.[205] One of these *demimondaines* was Païva, a Polish Jew whose real name was Thérèse Lachmann. Her first marriage was to a Portuguese nobleman, who died shortly after she had relieved him of a large part of his fortune. She was the incarnation of the *lionne* of the Second Empire.[206] Her luxurious mansion in the Champs-Elysées—designed by the architect Pierre Mauguin, it is today appropriately occupied by a Kuwaiti bank—was considered the height of extravagant magnificence by her contemporaries. The monumental bronze door was created by the sculptor Legrain, while the ceiling of the salon was painted by Baudry and was the only one among the lavish decorations that appealed to the Goncourts:

> We are in the famous salon, which is not worth all the hullaballoo it has aroused, in the midst of the finished, or still-to-be-finished paintings that are supposed to represent the destiny of courtesans, beginning with Cleopatra and ending with the lady of the house distributing gold to impoverished Egyptians [*sic*].

In all this wealth there is no art except for Baudry's ceiling. A somewhat thin scattering of gods; an Olympus disjointed but with exquisite coloring, in the midst of which a Venus arises thrusting forward her beautiful left thigh, which is a joyous apotheosis of Veronesean flesh, a most enchanting academic study. The rest of it is an interior decorator's dream, with no sense of the past, without a single piece of furniture, statue, or picture that might save a house from the boredom of the new and give it the interest and enjoyment of the historical.[207]

This criticism is characteristic of Second Empire hypocrisy in that the Goncourts' esthetic taste but not their sense of decency was offended. And that is why hardly anyone who was invited declined the honor of climbing the famous onyx staircase in Païva's house. There was a much-laughed-at saying, "Just as virtue has its staircase, so does vice."[208] Besides the Goncourts, others who gathered in Païva's salon included Théophile Gautier, Sainte-Beuve, Arsène Houssaye, Hippolyte Taine, and Emile de Girardin. This led Viel-Castel, who described the hostess as "the great debauchee of the century," to express the criticism that "once Païva lives in her mansion the upper classes will demean themselves to be admitted there."[209] But such criticism was confined to diaries or memoirs that appeared only after the Second Empire had ended.

According to all the descriptions of her person, Païva was hardly an ideal of beauty even by contemporary standards.[210] Her attraction, like that of many other famous *cocodettes* and *cocottes*, was based largely on a disastrous talent for spending other people's money. For a man of the world, whose Olympus was the Jockey Club, it was a real must to keep a notorious courtesan, to own expensive horses, or to indulge some other luxury. Merely having money was vulgar; what ennobled the parvenu was to spend it lavishly on worldly pleasures. Exaggeration and excess in everything were chic. That applied to the empty display of the houses owned by the rich—Païva's mansion being just one of many—as well as to the parties and banquets at which individuals constantly gathered in monotonous abandon. It also applied to fashion, consisting as it did of such immensely complicated and elaborate outfits that a woman of the world spent hours, helped by her chambermaids, getting ready for a festive event.[211]

The happy few who were able to afford this extravagant life-style, a small circle of perhaps ten thousand people, set the tone that was imitated on the boulevards, the playground of those less blessed with earthly goods. In the Second Empire the great bacchanal, the *grande bouffe parisienne*, became an established feature of the boulevards. The Café de Foy, the Maison Dorée, the Café Anglais, and the Café Riche were among the restaurants whose quality and luxury evoked rhapsodic descriptions.[212] According to the Goncourts, a waiter paid 4,000 francs for a position and there was a waiting list of applicants for years in advance.[213] The boulevards were the promised land of the big city; it was here that the theaters and fashionable clubs were located; even the ladies of the imperial court had their carriages stop at Tortoni's so that their servants could bring them some of his famous ice cream; everyone went there to see and be seen. Around five o'clock in the

afternoon the kiosks received the evening papers fresh off the press; at six
o'clock one could see the residents of the Bréda and Notre-Dame-de-
Lorette neighborhoods set out to conquer the boulevards.[214] These prostitutes descended like a flock of exotic birds and settled down in the cafés along
the boulevards.[215]

During the Second Empire the boulevard was a permanent fair where
bourgeoisie and *bohème, monde* and *demi-monde*, encountered one another.
This mix made up a large part of its charm and attraction, even though it
meant the disappearance of its formerly exclusive public which withdrew to
a few fashionable islands like the Jockey Club or the Café Anglais. This change
in the boulevard was carefully registered by the Goncourts on November
18, 1860:

> In the evening I go to the Eldorado, a big *café-concert* in the boulevard de
> Strasbourg, a columned hall with a profusion of decor and paintings, something
> like the Kroll in Berlin.
>
> Our Paris, the Paris in which we were born, the Paris of 1830 to 1848, is
> disappearing. And it is not disappearing materially, but rather morally. Social life
> is beginning to experience great change. I see women, children, couples, whole
> families in this café. Home life is disappearing. Life is becoming public again.
> The club on the upper levels, the café on the lower levels, that is where society
> and the people are ending up.[216]

The commercialization of the boulevard led to its becoming a democratic entity in the Third Republic, and to its ultimate decline after World War
I. That is, they became victims of Parisian "modernism." In his *Tableaux
parisiens*, Baudelaire speaks of Paris as a "fourmillante cité, cité pleine de
rèves" ("turbulent city, city full of dreams") and as a place where "tout, même
l'horreur, tourne aux enchantements" ("everything, even horror, turns into
magic").[217] But the price that the capital of modernism had to pay, as the
Catholic journalist Louis Veuillot wrote in 1866, was that it developed into
a "ville des multitudes déracinées, mobile amas de poussière humaine" ("city
of rootless multitudes, an unstable pile of human dust"). He warned it: "Tu
pourras t'agrandir et devenir la capitale du monde; tu n'auras jamais de
citoyens!" ("You can grow and become the capital of the world; you will never
have any civic-minded citizens").[218]

Comptes fantastiques

*V*EUILLOT'S PROPHECY REFLECTED the gloomy mood that had
spread since the beginning of the 1860s and that even the brilliance of the *fête impériale* could not dispel. Whatever charisma
the emperor had acquired rested on a few foreign-policy achievements and
his success in resolving the bankruptcy inherited from the Second Republic,

and in banning the fear of revolution and anarchy. But these accomplishments were forgotten as the years went by. The emperor's authoritarian traits, and the transformation of Paris which proved so disadvantageous for the greater part of the population, drew increasing criticism. Moreover, the export of French capital was affected by the beginning of the American Civil War, which coincided with a worldwide economic decline.[219] Prosper Merimée describes the emotional state existing in financial and social circles in a letter to his confidante, Madame de Montijo, on October 16, 1861:

> There is a shortage of bread and money at present. For some time past everyone has been taking the state as his model; that is, spending money freely like sons of good families. Now people are looking back and realizing that everything happened much too fast, and they are afraid. If one starts looking at things more closely one is not in a kindly mood. One asks oneself who is in charge today and how such disturbing things could happen in times of great peace.[220]

The results of the elections to the Legislative Assembly on May 31, 1863, were a nasty shock for the regime. Compared to the previous election of 1857, the number of votes for opposition candidates doubled from 665,000 to close to 2 million, although confidence in the regime was still expressed by a solid majority of over 5 million voters nationwide.[221] On the other hand, it was an obvious alarm signal when all nine Parisian seats were won by the opposition Republican List, which obtained 63 percent of the votes in the capital. Thus Paris again stood at the forefront of a movement that was hostile to the regime and lent the city "an aura of revolt and revolution."[222]

Napoleon III sensed the bourgeoisie's dissatisfaction with his regime early on and sought an effective counterstrategy. He adopted a new, relatively generous social policy with respect to the lower classes so as to gain their support against the *classes supérieures*. This Machiavellian scheme implied a number of accommodating gestures, such as pardoning the printers who had struck in the winter of 1861-62 and been imprisoned. Furthermore, he signed a law on May 25, 1864, permitting workers' unions on the condition that they did not interfere with the *liberté du travail*—the freedom of employers to set wages and work hours.[223] However, despite these and some additional social measures, the overall plan failed. While the *classes laborieuses* enjoyed the new freedoms and used them to organize, to prepare strikes, and to obtain further concessions, they were not misled by the all too obvious paternalism and rejected the regime even more decidedly than before.

Disappointed in his expectation of support from the *classes laborieuses*, Napoleon III was also faced with increasing discontent in the *classes supérieures*, especially among business and financial groups. The latter viewed his friendly overtures to the workers with growing misgiving, and were unhappy with the regime's indecisive handling of foreign-policy setbacks. To put an end to the threat of a liberal, Orleanist opposition in the Assembly, Napoleon III announced at the beginning of 1867 that he was considering a series of concessions. These could, if one wished, be seen as a democratizing of the regime.[224] But as is so often the case, these intended compromises only whetted appetites for more of the same; and after the brief respite of the Paris Exposition in 1867, the regime once more felt opposition from both classes.[225] What complicated and blackened the future of the regime even more was the publication, in 1868, of Jules Ferry's disturbing *Comptes fantastiques d'Haussmann*—a pun on the title of an Offenbach operetta.[226]

The *Comptes fantastiques* have a complicated history that dates back to the 1850s and involves the other important aspect of the transformation of Paris, namely its financing. Haussmann had a free hand as long as the emperor appeared to be all-powerful, since no one dared to contradict his wishes and ideas. It will be recalled that financing of the first network presented no problem, thanks to a state subsidy; the experiences of 1848 were still recent enough so that it was not difficult to convince the deputies from the provinces of the benefit of the gutting of old Paris. However, when it came to the second network, the state, being unwilling to burden the nation with expenditures for the beautification of Paris, only contributed 50 million of the 180 million francs required. Costs of the third network had to be borne by the city itself.

The high-handedness with which Haussmann pursued the transformation of Paris was soon opposed by the Orleanism of Parisian property owners, who in 1858 found two powerful allies in the *Conseil d'état* and the *Cour impériale de cassation*. In December of that year the *Conseil d'état* changed the expropriation law so that the city lost the advantages it had gained in 1852. The benefits now reverted to the owners of the expropriated properties.[227] A decision of the *Cour impériale* on May 7, 1861, created a further difficulty; under this the city had to indemnify the renters and lessees as soon as it expropriated a property, rather than when the building was actually demolished.[228]

Added to these legal measures and interpretations in favor of building- and landowners, renters and lessees, were the rulings of the *jurys d'expropriation*, on which sat representatives of property owners only too willing to back excessive expropriation costs. As Maxime Du Camp writes: "Everything was set in motion to get the jury to award exorbitant payments, a goal that became easier as precedents were created to which any house or property owner could refer once his property was about to be expropriated." And he tells of a popular joke making the rounds in Paris based on the following dialogue. Question to a parvenu: "How did you make your fortune?" Answer: "I was expropriated."[229]

The rulings by the *jurys d'expropriation* helped to increase speculation, with the result that real-estate prices were driven up, especially in those areas of the city that seemed ready for expropriation. In view of this development it was foreseeable that the transformation of Paris would at some point reach the limit of its financial viability.[230] Haussmann found himself more and more in the uncomfortable position of the sorcerer's apprentice. The mechanisms he used to realize the grandiose plans of his imperial lord and master got out of control, threatened to overwhelm him and eventually to prevent him from completing his work. In order to delay this unavoidable end as long as he could, he resorted to ever more complicated and daring maneuvers. One way out, of which Haussmann took full advantage, was to keep the public as uninformed as possible. Another was to undertake the work on a large scale and to complete it quickly, so as to avoid the storms of speculation and to forestall the growing resistance of the assembly. But the question of financing was and remained decisive.

By 1858 at the latest, Haussmann had to be aware that the Legislative Assembly was no longer willing to allot state funds and that the work would have to be financed by the city through domestic capital loans. The only disadvantage was that the government would have to approve each loan. At first this presented no problem. There was plenty of capital available and the growing revenues provided by the transformation of Paris, as well as the negligible outstanding debt, provided sufficient guarantees.[231] In 1855 he asked for a first loan of 60 million francs to finance the first network; this was ratified immediately. It was already more difficult to place a second loan for 130 million francs in 1860, though it was approved by the assembly. The loan only became possible two years later, when the state's *Crédit mobilier* was willing to underwrite one-fifth of it. In 1865 Haussmann finally managed to get the government to agree to a third and final loan of 270 million francs, though this time it was even more difficult to place and was approved only when the *Crédit mobilier* proved willing to take on one-third of it.[232]

Up to 1870 the transformation of Paris consumed 2.5 billion francs, a fantastic sum given prevailing conditions. The surplus from current revenues in the seventeen years of Haussmann's administration as prefect, together with the yield from the resale of expropriated properties and the state's subsidies, amounted to 1.4 billion francs.[233] If the 440 million francs obtained from loans are deducted from this figure, there remains a deficit in the balance of over 600 million francs.

The obvious thing would have been to meet this deficit with a new loan which the French capital market could easily have provided. But there were two factors militating against this: the difficulties experienced in placing the two previous loans in the face of more lucrative foreign investments, such as the building of the Suez Canal; and opposition in the Legislative Assembly, which was increasingly critical of the transformation of Paris and quite willing to use Haussmann to attack Napoleon III. So as not to be held up with his work, Haussmann decided to resort to an illegal trick to obtain financing. Earlier on he had created a *Caisse de la boulangerie*, which paid subsidies to bakers when the price of flour rose beyond the "normal" level and received the sums back when the price fell below it. As a result the price of bread had been kept relatively stable. In 1856, he decided to establish the *Caisse des travaux de Paris*.[234]

This entity was supposed to facilitate payments connected with the rebuilding program, which made sense as the actual costs were often greater than the estimates. Payments were a burden on the city budget, even if only temporary, and required complicated and time-consuming accounting procedures. The *Caisse des travaux* also functioned as a clearinghouse between the city of Paris and its contractors, by providing the latter with short-term financing so as to facilitate the work. Whereas the first network was completed in part by the city and in part by private building syndicates, work on the second and third networks was carried out exclusively by subcontractors in limited partnership with large banks.

The *Caisse des travaux* allocated funds for expropriation payments, and acquired and sold properties. It also received and administered the contractors' execution bonds, refunded with interest upon satisfactory completion of the work. In addition it disbursed subsidies for public-works contracts and supplied credit until the funds became available. Though all these procedures were self-liquidating, and though expenditures were nominally determined by revenues, the *Caisse* needed a working capital which was acquired by the issuance of bonds. Its maximum indebtedness was fixed by law and guaranteed by the city, which thus acquired a floating debt not included in its regular budget.[235]

In this way the *Caisse* set up a financing system that benefited both parties, the city as well as its contractors. Since the contractors financed all the work themselves until completion, the city had effective access to short-term credits for the speedy execution of public works. The city made its payments, including the accrued interest, in installments spread over eight years after the work was completed to the satisfaction of the prefect of Paris. As for the contractors, they were less concerned about the interest they received on their outlays than with the profit they made from the construction of new streets and arrondissements.

As long as the contractors had no trouble in refinancing themselves all was well. But this changed in 1863, when the interest rate rose on the Paris money market and one of the companies found itself in financial straits. The problem was solved when the city, lacking the necessary funds to bail the company out, sought help from the *Crédit foncier* (the government mortgage bank). The latter deposited the exact amount due to the company on completion of its work in the *Caisse des travaux;* in consideration of this and as security, the building company delivered *bons de délégation* (transfer instruments) to the *Crédit foncier*, by which it made over to the bank its claims against the city. Haussmann, for his part, had to recognize the contract as "completed" as soon as the bank had deposited in the *Caisse* the sum agreed on between the city and the company. The transfer instruments, endorsed by Haussmann, then became municipal bonds and could be traded in the money market. A procedure for extended payments by the city and discounting by the bank was set up at the same time.[236]

Haussmann immediately realized the enormous advantage of a financing system that would help him to implement his program without having to depend on the Assembly's approval. He was gambling on the likelihood that the *bons de délégation*, which could be paid off over several years, would be covered by the city's surplus revenues. The advantage for the building companies was that they could obtain credits from the *Crédit foncier* for the full amount right after signing the contract. The bank, for its part, had no trouble raising the needed capital, for small investors in particular were willing to take their savings out from under the mattress to buy its municipal bonds.

The whole arrangement was of course nothing but a way for the city to raise credit for public works without legal authorization. It worked as long as it could be concealed from the Legislative Assembly, or as long as the regime's position was so strong that it could ignore any objections from the deputies. The scheme worked admirably, and until 1868 *bons de délégations* worth 500 million francs were spent, endorsed, and discounted. Repayment did not have to begin until 1869, but it cost the city 450 million francs.[237]

It was certainly too much to expect that financial operations of this magnitude could be kept secret; if nothing else, the municipal bonds with which the *Crédit foncier* refinanced itself in the money market had to draw public attention. Indeed, one of the deputies raised the issue of the *bons de délégation* in the assembly in April 1865. Once the subject was broached it was increasingly referred to both in the assembly and the press, indicating the extent to which public opinion had turned against the Second Empire. Yet despite these well-founded suspicions, nothing changed because Haussmann managed to avoid disclosing his dubious financial practices. Still it did make him concerned enough to sign an agreement with the *Crédit foncier* on November 8, 1867, under which the city's obligations were consolidated into a single long-term debt. The sum amounted to almost 400 million francs, which the city agreed to repay in semiannual instalments over a period of sixty years.[238]

The agreement was the beginning of the end for Haussmann, for it was nothing but a belated attempt to legalize his illegal financial manipulations. Furthermore, it had to be submitted to the *Conseil municipal* and the Legislative Assembly. This was done in April 1868. The latter body then decided to use this "penitential act" by the almighty prefect as the basis for an inquiry into his financial practices before the legislative summer vacation began. In the course of the investigation enough came to light for the government to agree to postpone the plenary debate on the subject for as long as possible.[239]

Approaching the End

*T*HE DATE FOR THE FATAL DEBATE so dreaded by the regime was finally set for February 22, 1869; it came at a very awkward moment for the government and signaled its eventual defeat. By now the aging emperor had forfeited his political assets. His most recent adventure, the Mexican expedition, had ended in a terrible catastrophe and resulted in great public opposition to him and his government. The debate, which was going to come shortly before the Assembly elections scheduled for May, would enable the opposition to uncover and exploit the corruption long associated with the regime. It turned out to be by far the most aggressive confrontation seen in the Legislative Assembly in the Second Empire. Debate lasted until March 6 and was a general settling of accounts with the administration of Napoleon III.[240]

Though the controversy neither brought down the Second Empire nor ended Haussmann's tenure as prefect, both were severely hurt by it. The elections on May 23 and 24 dealt the authoritarian regime, and Haussmann as its most effective exponent, a fatal blow.[241] The opposition obtained 234,000 votes, while the regime's candidates only received 77,000. In view of the majority made up of the broad liberal spectrum to which 147 of the deputies belonged, the regime had no other choice but to become more liberal itself and to recognize its responsiblity to the *Parlement*. For Haussmann the liberal Empire that began with the formation of Emile Ollivier's government on January 2, 1870, meant the bitter end. "The parliamentary Empire," he writes in his memoirs, "is a form of government that is contrary to all my beliefs and with which I did not want to be associated as I suspected that they would throw all of us into the abyss."[242] He was relieved of his position as prefect by decree on January 5, 1870, an event of which Ludovic Halévy writes laconically in his diary: "M. Haussmann's achievement is incomparable; everyone is agreed on this. Paris is a miracle, and M. Haussmann created more in fifteen years than was done in one century. But for now that is enough. There is going to be a twentieth century. Let us leave something for it to do."[243]

Haussmann departed in January 1870. He left a ship whose wheel he had already relinquished with the 1867 agreement between the city and the *Crédit foncier*, when he urged that no further work be undertaken.[244] Since then, especially since the fatal debate of the spring of 1869, his hands had been tied. He devoted his time to organizing the liquidation of the debt, the first payment on which came due in 1869 in the amount of 63 million francs—more than a third of the regular city budget. Haussmann had to admit that this left nothing for financing additional projects.[245]

With the end of the Paris Exposition of 1867 the grand operetta to which the Second Empire was always compared turned into a tragedy with three simultaneous finales. The most austere ending took place on September 4, 1870, when Napoleon III handed his sword to the king of Prussia, whose victorious armies had brought the regime to its knees. The most theatrical ending, but the most dignified and appropriate to his achievements, was the one Haussmann staged on the morning of January 10, 1870. He gives the following description of it in his memoirs:

> I remained in office until I was personally able to hand over all official business to M. Henri Chevreau, whose departure from Lyon had been delayed by a few days, so that I actually did not give up the position of prefect until the evening of January 10, 1870.
> In the period between my dismissal and the end of my service, M. Chevaudier de Valdrôme, the new minister of the interior . . . invited all the heads of the *grands services publics* that came under his jurisdiction, as well as their co-workers, to a reception on the morning of January 10. The letter addressed

to the *préfet de la Seine*, came into my hands, and I asked . . . the *conseil de préfecture*, the *sous-préfets* as well as the directors of the individual *services départementaux* and *municipaux*, to come to the Hôtel de Ville that day; coaches awaited them there, half an hour before the reception was due to begin. . . . Dressed in our official uniforms, we started out at the appointed hour, myself at the head of my cortege of gilded city coaches, each driven by a coachman in gold-trimmed uniform and staffed by a liveried servant; we were escorted by a cavalry unit of the *Garde de Paris*. Our arrival at the ministry in the place Beauvau caused a considerable stir. Followed by my staff I went through the reception rooms where a large crowd was gathered, which parted when I appeared as though I had been Banquo's ghost. The beadles who led the way took me to a separate room, next to the administrative chamber of the minister who, without hesitating, asked me to enter. He, too, was surrounded by his officials, dressed as he was in their gala uniforms. I took my time, had my staff form a semicircle around me on the opposite side of the chamber, and addressed the minister in a dignified way as follows: "*Monsieur le ministre*, I have the honor of presenting to Your Excellency the administrative staff of the *préfecture de la Seine*. In their deep commitment to the Emperor, it was their greatest ambition to be of useful service to His Majesty. Their old head, who considers it a pleasure to express his appreciation to this group, wanted to set his subordinates the example of performing one's duty until the very end."

Not a word from the minister. In his surprise M. Chevaudier took a few steps toward me with outstretched arms, no doubt recalling our relationship in our youth and the few services I had been able to render him later on. Referring to my last words he deplored the callousness of politics; he also expressed his regret at losing the support of such a competent administrator as myself; finally he spoke in terms of admiring recognition of the eminent services I had rendered, especially the *travaux de Paris*, which had called forth the admiration of the whole world— forgetting that he, along with the rest of its sworn enemies in the Legislative Assembly, had voted against the great undertaking he was now praising so volubly. I remained quite unimpressed, stepped back two paces, bowed again and answered: "*Monsieur le ministre*, I am all the more flattered by your appreciation of my career and especially of my achievements in Paris as, I must confess, I did not expect it from you. I began my administrative career in the ministry of the famous Casimir Périer in 1831. Your esteemed father was one of my guarantors at the time. I consider myself extremely fortunate that after thirty-eight years his son, who has also become a minister, openly admits that I have not disappointed that former trust in me."

That was it! Another bow, then I signaled my group and departed, followed by them and the minister's staff, all of whom were very moved and wanted to shake my hand, and to express their sympathy to someone whom, they assured me, they respected as their true head, who stood for the honor and glory of French administration. . . . In this way I relinquished my service just as I had once promised my equals, the *sénateurs de l'Empire*, I would: "with raised head and a clean slate."[246]

The third finale of the Second Empire comes from the pen of Emile Zola, who describes the rise and ignominious fall of the empire of Napoleon III as personified by the great courtesan Nana. At the end of the novel—on the day of France's mobilization against Prussia—she dies of smallpox, a disease that still occurred frequently in those days:

Nana remained alone, her face turned upward in the bright light of the candle. It was only a pitiful remnant, a damp bloody mass, a heap of rotting flesh that lay on the pillows. Smallpox had covered the whole face, one boil next to the other; they had opened and dried up—just as when mold covers the ground—on this shapeless, featureless pulp. One eye, the left one, was completely deformed by the pus seeping from it; the lid of the other was half open, the eye itself sunken and resembling a black rotten hole. Pussy mucus was still flowing from her nose. A reddish crust spread from her cheek to her mouth now stretched into a horrible smile. And on this awful, grotesque mask of nothingness, her hair, her beautiful hair, still flaming like the sun, flowed in a golden stream. Venus was decomposing. It seemed as if the putrescence she had contracted from the tolerated corruption of the gutters, this infection with which she had poisoned an entire people, had now just risen to her face and rotted it.

The room was empty. An enormous wave of desperation rose from the boulevard and made the curtain billow: "To Berlin! To Berlin! To Berlin!"[247]

However, none of these three finales really ended the Second Empire; they only terminated certain careers, each of which had been characteristic of the period. No, the real, the terrible and bloody conclusion, the one that expressed the pent-up reaction to the regime's paradoxes, was the Paris Commune of 1871. It completed the cycle of powerful events set in motion in 1789, when the capital became a unique city whose history was also that of Europe.

BOOK SEVEN

From Commune to Belle Epoque

1871–1914

Des habitations de six à sept étages se joignent
sans discontinuité.
Le sous-sol est encore ménagé en compartiments.
C'est pour loger les habitants qui s'agglomèrent
en foule immense.
Et pour renfermer les richesses que l'industrie
et le commerce produisent dans de vastes
proportions.

Dwellings of six and seven storys are solidly aligned.
The basements are split into compartments.
To lodge the inhabitants who pile up in immense crowds.
And to warehouse the wealth that industry
and commerce produce in vast quantities.

Nguyen-Trong-Hiêp, *Paris Capitale de la France*

Place Vendôme seen from the rue de la Paix.
Pictured is a barricade in the Place Vendôme, for the defense of the the city against the Versailles government troops during the Paris Commune, March 18–28, 1871.
ARCHIV FÜR KUNST UND GESCHICHTE, BERLIN.

The Fall of the Second Empire

*C*ONTRARY TO ITS NORMAL PRACTICE, the regime had not tried to influence the elections of May 1869, which were to prove so calamitous. It merely reorganized the Parisian voting districts to the advantage of the government's candidates. But this manipulation was of no help; even the wealthy bourgeoisie had given up on the Empire. This explains the large majority with which deputies who rejected Napoleon III were elected in the capital. The triumphant liberal opposition (among whom true republicans represented a minority) dreamed of reforming the whole political system.

A similar voting pattern showed up in all other major cities, whereas the countryside and small towns, where the old social structures and authoritarian attitudes predominated, voted overwhelmingly for the status quo. The split electorate expressed a general lack of confidence in the regime, and also indicated a growing difference between urban and rural areas. A gain of 1.2 million votes, which would have been a respectable victory for the government in a two-party, parliamentary system, was practically a defeat under the very different circumstances of the Second Empire. At any rate the results clearly called for prompt and thorough reforms.

But it was soon evident that the reforms of the liberal Empire came too late. Some found them insufficient, others were frightened by them. Instead of uniting within a liberal, parliamentary state, "the two Frances" found the rift between them even deeper.

Social and political agitation grew especially strong in Paris after the Exposition.[1] This was most obvious in the development of the press, after the removal on May 11, 1868, of the most severe of the restrictions imposed on it.[2] Twenty-nine new dailies and weeklies appeared in Paris alone—of course most of them did not survive—all of which opposed Napoleon III to a greater or lesser degree. The most famous and successful of the new publications was the weekly *La Lanterne*, in the format of a brochure, edited by Henri Rochefort. Rochefort's deadliest weapon and the secret of his success was his use of ridicule. For instance he presented the Empire in the form of an operetta. The opening sentence in the first issue of *La Lanterne* set the tone: "According to the Imperial Almanac, France has thirty-six million subjects— not counting the subjects of discontent."[3] The biting barbs that Rochefort fired off in his columns soon had unexpected effect. After very few weeks the regime seriously considered dissolving the Legislative Assembly, ordering new elections, and once again curtailing the new freedom of the press. Though this did not actually come about, Rochefort had to go into exile after the appearance of the eleventh issue of *La Lanterne*. He then attacked the Empire with a still more venomous pen from Brussels.[4]

As restrictions were relaxed, opposition to the regime grew stronger, forcing it into a defensive position. This became clear during the popular festivities to celebrate the hundredth birthday of Napoleon I on August 15, 1869. The comte de Maugny gives a lively account of the mood on that day, clearly showing that even the myth of Napoleon no longer thrilled the masses as it had done before:

> August 15, which is only remotely similar to July 14 and used to be cele-
> brated in a very fashionable and elegant way, has degenerated like everything
> else. The Morel Ball used to be attended by famous society courtesans—of much
> higher quality and status than today's horizontal ones—dressed as *grisettes;* and
> there were men of the world such as Gramont-Caderousse and his clique. This
> time it was quite deserted. The members of clubs, who were much quieter and
> less boisterous than before, did not visit the booths along the Esplanade des
> Invalides as they used to do, and the *peuple* also gave an impression of being
> indifferent, even downcast. There was a certain *tristesse* in the air and great
> emptiness everywhere; from time to time one felt—how should I put it?—a
> fruitlessness and gloom that constricted one's heart.[5]

Even Haussmann was sacrificed as part of the reforms promised by the liberal Empire in the hopes of stabilizing itself, and the elections of May 8, 1870, provided some breathing space. Ostensibly this referendum sought to obtain the voters' consent to the liberalizations that had been enacted. But the republicans and enraged royalists voted against them, so that it became a question of a vote of confidence in the regime. As had been the case in the Legislative Assembly elections the previous year, the majority of voters in the large cities were against the regime; but the rural areas once again gave it their approval and outvoted the opposition.[6]

The regime felt so strengthened by the outcome of the referendum that it increased its repression of republican agitation. By the spring of 1870 the opposition had just about been stifled; Napoleon III's old trick of staking everything on one card seemed to have succeeded yet again.[7] While the threatening clouds had not entirely dispersed there seemed to be a somewhat brighter horizon. Supporters and opponents alike shared the impression that the regime's chances for surviving the crisis were good. They were also agreed that internal consolidation could best be achieved by a succesful war that would erase former setbacks and reversals. The slogan "Revenge for Sadowa!" was still waiting to be put to the test; and a welcome excuse to set-tle old scores arose when a Hohenzollern presented himself as candidate for the vacant Spanish throne.[8] Here was a chance for the Empire to reestablish its autocratic rule without liberal window-dressing.

Napoleon III had to use the opportunity to engage in hostile conflict with Prussia for that was what the French public wanted. Chauvinistic enthu-siasm seemed to make it forget its resentment against the regime.[9] Even the press and surviving radical organizations clamored for war.[10] All of this over-shadowed a basic misgiving as to whether it might not be better to avoid war even at the price of humiliation. As Ludovic Halévy notes in his diary, "That would simply be a bad peace. One would have to fight in one or two years in any case. . . . Then it is better to fight immediately."[11]

As for Napoleon III, he was anything but war-minded; he had aged quickly, had problems with kidney stones, and deep down probably shared Halévy's fatalistic attitude. But like the German statesman who would face a similar situation in August 1914, he saw no possibility other than a "leap in the dark." He left his palace at Saint-Cloud on July 28, 1870; the train carrying him to take over command of the army passed through Paris without stopping. He was never to see it again.

The war with Prussia began with defeats for France; on August 4, 1870, at Weissenburg, on August 6 at Fröschwiller and Forbach. But in Paris rumors told of wonderful achievements by French troops; and at midday on August 6 the city went delirious with joy over victory. Flags hung from windows and in the streets enthusiastic crowds kept singing the Marseillaise.[12] When official news of the defeat and retreat of the imperial troops reached Châlons and Metz in the evening, the effect was devastating. In his telegram to the empress, Napoleon III spoke of the necessity of ordering a state of defensive preparedness in the city. Everyone could guess what this meant in terms of France's chances of victory.

On August 7 the republicans were the first to return to reality, but they tried to pass off an old solution for new: *la patrie* was in danger, it was time to arm the people. For more timorous souls such slogans immediately conjured up the bloody face of the Terror, and even the rational Ludovic Halévy notes in his diary:

> First we must get rid of the Prussians, then—immediately afterwards—the emperor, the empress, the prince-imperial, as well as M. Ollivier, the head of the government. . . . Not a day must be lost. . . . The whole thing smacks of a French Sadowa, of the end of the Empire. That is easy to deal with, but what if it meant the end of France? If the Republic can save us let us have the Republic. Let us have Gambetta, Rochefort, Flourens. All of it, all of it, all of it, rather than the Prussians in Paris.[13]

The only one of Halévy's ideas that became a reality right away was Ollivier's fall. He was replaced by General Cousin-Montauban, comte de Palikao, a professional soldier who was the least suitable man to head a government in this difficult situation. Still, neither the military defeats nor the fall of Ollivier's government on August 9 led to a revolution in Paris. Not that initiatives by certain groups of radical workers were lacking, but republican deputies who were being pushed to proclaim a republic remained passive. An attempt by Blanqui to light the beacon of revolution by storming the fire department in La Villette with sixty of his supporters on August 14 was quickly suppressed by the authorities.[14]

Blanqui's failure showed that Paris was not ready for a revolution. Everyone was much more concerned over a military disaster that would end the Empire in favor of a republic. But until that happened the city had to be prepared for whatever might happen: either a Prussian attack or a peaceful transition to a republic. The Paris National Guard, which had led a shadowy existence as ceremonial troops during the Second Empire, was reactivated to prevent revolt and civil war. Their ranks were increased so much that after a few weeks they numbered 134 battalions of close to 300,000 armed men.[15] But other precautions were also taken. A German journalist by the name of G. Schneider, who was living in Paris at the time, reports on September 1, 1870:

> There are immense supplies of grain stored in the grain markets. The Bois de Boulogne has new residents; instead of carriages and powdered lackeys . . . only four-footed creatures and their keepers are to be found there now. It is said they number 50,000 steers and 300,000 sheep, quite apart from other cattle.[16]

On the evening of September 2, 1870, the government received news of the surrender of the emperor at Sedan.[17] The information was kept secret until the following evening when it was carried in special editions of the major newspapers.[18] Announcement of the capitulation was synonomous with the fall of Napoleon III and the end of the Empire—though naturally the government of comte de Palikao at first refused to accept that conclusion. Instead of doing the only thing it could have done—unite with the moderate republicans—it frittered away the time in useless deliberations. That left the initiative up to the excited crowds, who on September 3 called for the overthrow of the Empire. The Bonapartist administration now found itself in a hopeless position; it was caught without any maneuvering room between the opposition in the Legislative Assembly and the opposition that had formed in the streets.

On a bright Sunday morning, September 4, the administration met once more for a useless session; that same morning the deputies of the Assembly met in the Palais Bourbon. But they, too, hesitated to dissolve the Empire and proclaim the Republic. As in February 1848, the decision was forced on them by the "street." An ever-growing crowd that had gathered outside the Palais Bourbon calling for the overthrow of the Empire and the proclamation of the Republic, finally stormed the hall and broke up the meeting. Assembly members quickly dispersed, except for two republican deputies, Léon Gambetta and Jules Favre, who had the presence of mind to avoid chaos through a symbolic act. They let it be known that the Republic would be proclaimed in the Hôtel de Ville—the "holy place" of all Paris revolutions. Thus these moderate republicans provided a goal for the excited crowd and at the last minute prevented a real and expected uprising from taking place.[19]

The Empire vanished like a ghost; the demonstrators carelessly broke it as if it were a toy. The "operetta" had the ending it merited: the curtain fell, the decor was immediately destroyed, all the symbols of the Napoleonic regime were removed from public buildings. A revolution? Certainly, but a revolution that was more like a boisterous festival of the people. It was ratified by renaming the rue du 10 Décembre as the rue du 4 Septembre.[20]

But this September 4, 1870, the "jour de fête de la grande ville," as Edmond de Goncourt called it, already carried the seeds of tragedy. From the very start the moderate republicans aimed at putting as conservative a government as possible into power. They were influenced by the overwhelmingly conservative and reactionary nature of rural France, and by the fear of a revolt brewing in Paris. Yet they came up with what appeared at the time to be a brilliant idea. They formed a provisional government exclusively of deputies from the Department of the Seine, to be known as the Government of National Defense. It was a way of reviving the old revolutionary myth according to which the fate of France was controlled by Paris. The move was legitimized by the capital's responsibility for bringing down the Empire.

However, the provisional government made a grave mistake in believing that its appointment meant it held power. The atmosphere of carefree celebration that had accompanied the revolution of September 4 was anything but an indication that Paris would simply give its newly won sovereignty to the Government of National Defense. True, the capital reveled in the thought that it had once again helped bring about a revolution; but this one was not intended merely to effect a change of regime. No, this revolution had to make good the losses incurred in the war and to drive the Prussians out of the country by means of a popular revolutionary war.

This enthusiasm was used by the provisional government to secure its own highly precarious situation. It was obvious that this ploy had to end in a tragedy. In his second *Address to the General Council of the International Working Men's Association on the Franco-Prussian War*, Karl Marx analyzes events in Paris from his exile in London:

> The Republic has not overthrown the throne, but only taken its vacant place. It has not been seen as a social victory, but as a measure of national defense. It is in the hands of a provisional government, made up partly of notorious Orleanists, partly of bourgeois Republicans; it includes some upon whom the insurrection of June, 1848, has left its indelible stigma. The division of labor among members of that government promises little good. The Orleanists have seized the positions of power—the army and the police—while the professed republicans have been given the talking assignments. Some of their first acts show rather clearly that they have inherited not only a mass of ruins from the Empire, but also its dread of the working class. If impossible things are now immoderately promised in the name of the Republic, is it not to induce a call for a "possible" government? Is the republic not seen by the bourgeoisie, who would like to be its undertakers, merely as a transition to an Orleanist restoration?
>
> Thus the French working class is in an extremely difficult position. Any attempt to bring the new government down when the enemy is practically knocking at the gates of Paris would be foolhardy. The French workers must do their duty as citizens, but they must not let themselves be dominated by national memories of the First Empire. They must not repeat the past but build the future.[21]

Marx was only too well informed as to the attitudes in Paris. It was not France or the French nation that had begun this unfortunate war, but a regime that had capitulated to the enemy as well as its own people and had been sent packing in disgrace. The Republic had inherited this unwanted war and two contradictory options along with it. Either it had to make peace at any price and then eradicate the legacy of the Second Empire, or it had to continue the war—already lost in military terms—as a popular war modeled on the great Revolution.

The Paris deputies who had so unhesitatingly proclaimed the Republic on September 4 could not afford to act contrary to the popular mood. But as Marx had rightly surmised, the new government was hardly representative of the revolutionary atmosphere. It was given its name, Government of National Defense, to prevent more radical Parisian forces from seizing control.[22] Now it had to negotiate a peace settlement.

To think that this squaring of the circle could succeed was an illusion from the start. Radicals and moderates were united in their rejection of one of Bismarck's demands—cession of Alsace and extensive parts of Lorraine. This unity was reinforced by the hectic preparations for the defense of Paris against an anticipated attack by the Prussian army. This doomsday scenario was awaited in a frenzy of celebration and longing: celebration of freedom and longing for death, the end of the historical process at work in Paris and France since 1792. But the attack never came.[23] The victorious Prussians acted contrary to all expectations by contenting themselves—for reasons that could not be ignored in Paris—with encircling the capital and starving it out.[24] The city was under siege by September 18, 1870, and its almost 2 million inhabitants were sealed off from the rest of France. Paris became a boiler in which the pressure rose quickly.

The Siege of Paris

*T*HE SIEGE OF THE CAPITAL gave the government a respite in which to end a war just about everyone knew to be lost. General Trochu, commander of the defense of Paris, was most insistent that decorum be maintained and that "the honor of France" and the army not be slighted.[25] These contradictory demands led to pretentious statements by the government which nevertheless took no visible action.[26] Meanwhile, conditions in the capital grew worse for the population and famine set in. Edmond de Goncourt, who continued his brother Jules's diary after the latter's premature death in the spring of 1870, chronicles the growing shortage of supplies in minute detail.[27] At first everything seemed to be deceptively plentiful; only oysters disappeared from restaurant menus on September 23. On September 25 there were livestock markets on the boulevards, but the unaccustomed sights were merely illusion and trickery. Just two days later, on September 27, Edmond de Goncourt comments:

> I return from the markets by the rue Montmartre. The marble counters of the Maison Lambert, which in this season are so loaded with saddles of venison, pheasants, and other game, are bare; the fish tanks which are generally full

are empty. And in this little temple of gluttony a very thin man is walking about sadly, while a few steps further on, in the bright light of the gas lamps that make a wall of tin cans shine, a large, jovial young woman is selling Liebig canned meat.

A day later he writes: "None of the butchers have any meat, their grilles are closed, their inside curtains drawn like sinister signs of famine." On October 1, 1870, he notes that horsemeat has almost imperceptibly become part of Paris menus: "Yesterday at Peters I was served a roast whose watery lean meat I studied carefully. It was streaked with white sinews and my painter's eye discerned the difference between its deep red color and the bright pink of beef. The waiter halfheartedly assured me that this horse was beef."

A decree issued October 7, 1870, permitted a market to be held three times a week for horses that were to be butchered.[28] Horsemeat, which so offended Edmond de Goncourt's delicate palate, soon became an extravagant delicacy for most Parisians. Those who could not afford it had to satisfy their hunger with dogs and cats; even rats and sparrows disguised by all sorts of piquant sauces found their way onto the menus of the best restaurants.[29] Once the carp in the Tuileries ponds had been eaten, it was the turn of the exotic animals in the Jardin des Plantes. Six yaks, three zebras, and a buffalo were sold to a butcher for 2,500 francs on October 24. Other animals in the zoo shared their fate in November, and in December even the two beloved pets of the Parisians, the elephants Castor and Pollux, finally had to give up their lives. On December 31, 1870, Edmond de Goncourt remarks in his journal:

> My curiosity made me go to Roos, the English butcher on the boulevard Haussmann. I noticed all sorts of strange animal cadavers. The skinned elephant trunk of young Pollux, the elephant from the Jardin d'Acclimation, hung in its place of honor on the wall; and among the undefinable pieces of meat and strangely formed pairs of horns, an assistant was selling camel kidneys. . . . That evening I ate the famous elephant blood sausage at Voisin's.

The greater part of the population not only suffered from the growing lack of food but also from the extremely cold winter. Firewood supplies were exhausted even faster than food. First the trees disappeared from the Bois de Boulogne and the Bois de Vincennes; then from the boulevards and big public squares and finally, on January 15, 1871, the trees on the Champs-Elysées were sacrificed. Gas supplies also decreased and soon the once brilliantly lit city sank into a pitiful twilight provided by weak kerosene lamps.[30]

Cut off from the outside world, Paris had to suffer many privations.[31] However, this made the masses even more determined to hold out for as long as possible.[32] The small wealthy class, on the other hand, which even now hardly lacked for anything, soon adopted a defeatist attitude.[33] Members of these circles shared the secret aim of bringing the provisional government, the war, and the siege to a quick end, so as to escape the rumbling volcano of Paris in the safety of the provinces.[34]

This treason on the part of the provisional government and the *classes aisées*, which had often and loudly announced their serious intention of fighting the enemy, laid the foundation for the revolution and proclamation of the Commune on March 18. The Commune was the ideal expression of the national-revolutionary patriotism that inspired the capital's masses. It embodied the desire for free elections and a total popular war in which the rest of France would join with Paris to efface the humiliation of the Empire and its lost war.

A foretaste of the future came on October 31, 1870. According to Lissagaray, the historian of the Commune, "Paris received three blows when it awoke that day."[35] The first was the provisional government's official announcement of the previously denied capitulation of Bazain's troops at Metz; the second was the news that Thiers was negotiating a truce with Bismarck at Versailles; and the third was that the plain of Le Bourget which had been taken the previous day had been relinquished again to the enemy. Against this background of two military disasters, the people of Paris saw the negotiations with Bismarck as treason. To them it looked as if the provisional government was following the cowardly example of Bazain. Once more, though, the government managed to avert an insurrection by issuing various lying statements, ceremonial proclamations, and a promise that elections for a Commune would shortly be held.[36]

The outcome of that day's events clearly showed the weakness of the national revolutionary movement. Though it held the upper hand for a few hours, the movement was unable to use the situation and was all too willing to accept the sop it was handed. Its weakness was confirmed by the results of the November 3 election, which the government hoped would end demands for a freely elected Commune. The election, intended as a vote of confidence for the provisional government, demonstrated by 560,000 votes for the government and 63,000 against how little support the republican-socialist Left actually had among the population. Only 15 to 20 percent of Paris residents backed the revolutionary concept of a *guerre à l'outrance* ("war to the finish"). Moreover, this minority was limited to the working-class population of the eleventh, eighteenth, nineteenth, and twentieth arrondissements, whereas an overwhelming majority of the population, fearing the dangers of revolution, opted for the government.[37]

In view of such a majority nothing should have stood in the way of an immediate truce. But when Bismarck heard about the revolt on October 31, he used it as a welcome excuse not to negotiate with a government that could be overthrown at any moment. His reservations, together with the stubborn refusal by Trochu, commander in chief of the French troops, to give the besieging army one of its forts in return for supplying Paris with food, led to a continuation of the hopeless state of affairs.

As of October 31 it could no longer be denied that the defense of the city was an empty gesture designed to preserve the impression of unity. In reality the forces that would confront each other in the spring of 1871 were already formed. It was only because of the besieging troops, the daily deterioration of supplies, and the continued disorganization of those promoting a republic that civil war was averted. Yet the hopelessness and desperation kept the incentives for revolution alive, and new clubs and associations were formed with the aim of politicizing the capital's masses.[38]

For the time being, however, their activities did not affect the balance of power in the city. The provisional government seemed to be in control of the situation and expected that hunger, cold, and the general misery of life in the capital would bring about a speedy truce. This cynical calculation involved the government in a race against time; it needed peace so as to free the manpower it would require to suppress any future agitation.

The famous *affiche rouge* (red poster) that proclaimed the Commune and appeared all over the city on January 6, 1871, showed just how far the revolutionary process had gone.[39] However, the provisional government of September 4 refused to budge, and even the *grand peuple de 89*, who had "destroyed the Bastille and toppled the throne," did not react. They were demoralized by the many deprivations and the bombardment of Paris which had meantime begun. There was one other weak insurrectionary attempt to delay the truce on January 22, 1871, which the government easily put down.[40]

On the morning of January 29 Paris learned that a twenty-one-day truce had been signed the previous day—which in essence amounted to capitulation. In return for supplying food to the capital, the Prussians received control of its ring of fortifications, without which the city could no longer be defended. Of course the provision requiring the disarming of the French troops was even more important. Originally General Moltke, chief of the Prussian General Staff, had insisted that in addition to the regular troops, the 100,000 National Guardsmen also relinquish their arms. The provisional government was to keep only two army divisions for maintaining law and order. When Jules Favre, who had replaced Thiers at the Versailles negotiations, expressed his fears that dismissing the National Guard would bring the government down and result in an insurrection, Bismarck gave him cynical advice: "Then provoke a revolt while you still have an army so that you can suppress it."[41] Eventually it was agreed that the Paris National Guard would not be disarmed and the government was even allowed an extra army detachment.

It looked as if the provisional government had achieved its conflicting goals: a revolution had been prevented, and a truce achieved. The latter applied not only to Paris but to the rest of France, which had conducted a costly winter war under Gambetta's command. It was a strange situation: in the besieged city all parties kept calling for a *guerre à l'outrance*, although the outcome was a few halfhearted, ill-prepared, senseless sorties.[42] The provinces, however, had long become weary of war. Their badly trained troops were pitted against an enemy whose morale and discipline were far superior. But the hopelessness of their condition was not really understood by those confined in Paris who desired a revolution. They were in no position to form an adequate picture of the actual strength of the contending sides.

Even the end of the siege did not change the radicals' view of reality. On the contrary: since September 4, 1870, the various political movements had

had sufficient time to organize clubs and committees, to politicize and win the support of the *peuple* suffering under the siege. The truce had left the government without the means or authority to control the capital effectively, and individual neighborhoods and arrondissements had quickly acquired considerable autonomy. The densely populated working-class arrondissements were controlled by elements whose goal it was to establish a Commune and reintroduce the self-government of which the capital had been deprived since 1795. By the end of January 1871, a weakened government found itself facing an impressively strong and unified opposition.

What made the provisional government's situation especially hopeless was the fact that the *peuple* had arms. In fact, the Paris National Guard, who were paid 30 sous per day, had taken the place of the *ateliers nationaux* in providing for the unemployed. The Guards' morale was unaffected by the truce and they still considered themselves undefeated. Though the final big battle on January 19, 1871, had ended in bloody catastrophe, it had been the National Guards' first chance to demonstrate their bravery. The experience increased their fighting spirit and certainty of victory. It also increased their contempt for a government that they felt had betrayed the nation by signing the truce. The overall public mood was one of disappointed patriotism, for the truce had prevented the popular war that had been so eagerly invoked from taking place. All the sacrifice and deprivation turned out to have been in vain and now caused a general rejection of the government.[43]

The most urgent problem at present was to provide the famine-stricken city with food as quickly as possible. Edmond de Goncourt reports seeing

> a strange procession of men and women returning to Paris by the Pont de Neuilly. Each of them is loaded with sacks containing provisions, even their pockets are bursting with edibles. There are bourgeois with five or six chickens on their shoulders, balanced by two or three rabbits. I also noticed a small, elegantly dressed lady carrying potatoes in a lace handkerchief. And nothing is more revealing than the happiness, I would almost say the tenderness, with which people hold four-pound loaves of bread in their arms, those lovely white loaves that were missed in Paris for so long.[44]

On the other hand, those who had been unable to still their tormenting hunger for so long were shocked when, directly after the cease-fire, hoarded food products began to fill the markets and stores. This happened even before the first transports could reach the capital since merchants were eager to make a profit before prices fell again. Only a few isolated cases of plunder occurred, and without any reaction from the provisional government. Writing in the *Revue des deux mondes*, Gustave de Molinari (a liberal journalist) took the government to task for its indifference and maintained that the merchants "were justified in profiting from their monopoly because of their acumen."[45]

One of the stipulations of the truce—for the time being limited to a period of twenty-one days—was for prompt elections to a National Assembly. Bismarck considered this the only legitimate basis for signing a peace treaty.

The election was scheduled for February 8 and was obviously going to be a referendum on peace and war. It had the result expected by the provisional government and the bourgeoisie: the war-weary rural population voted overwhelmingly for royalist or moderate republican deputies, while Paris, Lyon, and Marseilles opted for the radicals who supported the *guerre à l'outrance*.[46]

What was disastrous about this outcome was the fact that the conservative provincial deputies, who now had the upper hand in the National Assembly, disliked the capital. They equated Paris with the ignominious Empire, and considered it guilty of endangering provincial peace and welfare, of turning the provinces into political and cultural nonentities for its own benefit. This Paris, which after all that had happened would not listen to reason and wanted to continue the war according to the godless, revolutionary precepts of 1789, had to be taught a lesson once and for all.[47] That, at any rate, was the implicit conviction of the majority in the National Assembly, which met in Bordeaux, far from the city of decadent excesses and political passions. And that same conviction was held by Adolphe Thiers, head of the new conservative government.

Impending Drama

*T*HE ELECTION RESULTS OF FEBRUARY 8 created the mood for a drama that was to unfold over the ensuing months. Members of the *classes aisées* had no illusions as to what would follow; they and their families left the city in droves to seek safety in an idyllic country life.[48] Only the 200,000 demobilized soldiers and those who were confined by their poverty to the humiliated and deprivation-marked city remained behind. Du Camp paints a sad picture of what he saw:

> The city had a pitiful appearance: infantrymen, cavalrymen without horses, sailors, irregulars, and volunteers of all sorts in all types of uniforms, National Guards, and members of the *Garde mobile* wandered aimlessly through the streets, hands in their pockets, their guns slung over their shoulders, demoralized by alcohol, defeat and inactivity.[49]

The hopelessness and desperation that followed the siege were further aggravated by persisting economic difficulties; these reached an explosive point in February 1871. The spark that set it off was supplied by the National Assembly, which ratified the truce on March 1, 1871, in ultrabourgeois Bordeaux, a city unaffected by the war. Hardly had that been accomplished— an act that radical republicans saw as sealing the dishonor of France—when the Assembly passed various measures intended to reestablish order and normal economic conditions. On March 7 the moratorium on all goods deposited in the state-run pawnshops was lifted, with the proviso that anything not reclaimed by April 1 would be sold. This decision affected large segments of the population that had resorted to pawning possessions in order to survive. It revealed to what extent the National Assembly misjudged the severity of the situation in Paris. There was unemployment, workshops and factories remained closed, investment and demand were holding back, and even food prices still remained high.

As if this was not bad enough for the *classes laborieuses*, another measure called for the immediate payment of rents owed since the beginning of the siege. (In a further expression of provincial hatred for the capital, the National Guard's daily pay of 30 sous, on which hordes of unemployed depended, had been eliminated. Only those who could prove their need received this small payment after February 15; what had been a modest compensation for patriotic duty had been turned into a charity.)

The National Assembly's policy, inspired by its loathing of Paris, also managed to transform the petite bourgeoisie into its bitter enemy and to drive that group into the arms of the revolutionary movement. This resulted from a law on overdue bills. Much of the business in Paris was based on promissory notes. During the siege repayment was halted and the provisional government had declared a moratorium on such notes. On March 10, 1871, the National Assembly put an end to the moratorium and ordered payment with interest within four months. Thus most small Parisian businesses saw themselves at the mercy of a few large banks which, when willing, extended credit at excessive rates of interest.[50]

These measures were climaxed by a decision (March 10, 1871) to hold future sessions of the Assembly in Versailles instead of Bordeaux.[51] The choice of this location—associated with the monarchy and from which the victorious Prussians had only just departed—made it unmistakably clear just how uninterested in the Republic the Assembly was. The move was also influenced by strategic considerations: the area provided the best opportunity for using military force against the former capital in the event of insurgency.[52]

It is not unlikely that Thiers deliberately intended to provoke an uprising by the Paris masses, so as to establish the *république conservatrice* of his dreams through bloody repression.[53] At any rate, the majority of the National Assembly was very much in favor of such a solution.[54]

A strange situation had developed in Paris following the cease-fire. The provisional government's already fragile authority disappeared altogether, though at first this had no consequences. Once the conditions of the truce were made public they were considered humiliating and created angry feelings—especially the clause by which Prussian-German troops would occupy the western arrondissements prior to their victory parade down the Champs-Elysées. When the parade took place on March 1 and 2, everything remained quiet and the response was one of silent protest.[55] The only action taken by the French was to remove the National Guard's cannon from the west of Paris on February 26 and 27, to prevent their being seized by the victors. Lacking horses, the National Guard, women, and children harnessed themselves to the heavy artillery pieces and dragged them through the city from the place de Wagram to the eastern working-class neighborhoods where they were set up in the place des Vosges and on the hills of Montmartre and Belleville.[56] The cannon had originally been paid for by contributions from residents of various arrondissements, and were now considered "their" property that had to be protected from the foreigners.

Despite agitation by some hotheads the population remained calm, proving that it had not been especially radicalized. This is not surpising, given the long siege which had weakened everyone. Hiding the cannon was the most heroic effort people were willing or able to make. The prevailing calm was an outcome of appeals by the Central Committee of the Federation of National Guards. This was an association of elected delegates of the National Guard formed during the siege, which had developed into the only real authority in Paris.[57] The Central Committee, which merged with the Committee of the Republican Federation on February 24, 1871, provided the political model for the Commune organized a few weeks later.

As of February 24 there were two governments in France: the Central Committee, which had some authority in Paris, and the National Assembly in Bordeaux under the leadership of Adolphe Thiers. From the very start there was a constantly deepening gulf of mutual dislike between the two. The "capitulators of Bordeaux," as Paris radicals called the Assembly after ratification of the truce, went about issuing laws and regulations ostensibly aimed at forcing Paris radicals to their knees. In reality they were intended to accomplish the very opposite: to provoke the capital into revolt, so as to justify a crackdown and bloody and long-sought revenge.

However, the arrows launched by Bordeaux had no effect and things remained peaceful in Paris. The Central Committee proved to be an efficient administrative force whose orders were obeyed; life went on as usual with everyone seeking to eke out a precarious existence. From the vantage point of the capital the situation seemed far less dangerous than from the perspective of the National Assembly. Certain interested parties in Bordeaux kept alive the fear of the cannon in Montmartre, supposedly trained on the city and responsible for preventing businesses from reopening.[58] Such insinuations were given ready credence as the government in Bordeaux had to share its authority with the Prussian occupation forces still in control of a large section of the country. Having also to deal with a kind of opposition government in Paris hurt the Bordeaux government's self-esteem.

Among the endless provocations faced by Paris was the previously mentioned law ending the moratorium on promissory notes. This was especially hard on small businesses, many of which went bankrupt in the space of one week.[59] However, it still did not produce the desired reaction and the Assembly finally resorted to a measure that was bound to arouse opposition. It demanded that the National Guard return their cannon.

The issue of who controlled the cannon was not one of power and impotence, or life and death.[60] It was merely of symbolic value to both sides, but that was what made it all the more dangerous. As long as the cannon remained in the hands of the *classes laborieuses*, they represented the pledge of a socialist revolution feared by the Assembly's rural majority, who were hostile to "modernistic" Paris, and by the influential scandalmongers from the financial and industrial sectors. On the other hand, for the Parisians the cannon bought with their contributions were the best proof that they had not been defeated.

In the first weeks of March the government began negotiating over this conflict-laden issue. At first things seemed to be going well but then came to nothing because of clumsy maneuvers and senseless provocations by individual government representatives.[61] This created mistrust and pressure on both sides. The National Assembly was to have its first meeting in Versailles on March 20, at which time Thiers intended to announce the settlement of the matter of the cannon. But when all attempts at negotiation failed, Thiers decided to attempt a surprise attack.[62]

His plan seemed simple and promised to be successful without excessive bloodshed. But confiscation of the cannon was merely a pretext. At stake was the disbanding of the National Guard and an "arrestation en masse des républicains," as Ferré, a member of the Commune, put it at his trial after the capital was taken.[63] Such a procedure was not illogical; for now that Paris had been robbed of its function as seat of the National Assembly, it was also necessary to deprive the extreme Left of its control of the city. Thiers calculated that he could do this without producing a massacre or civil war in view of the exhaustion of the population. But the action had to be a suprise and conducted with superior force. This had been prepared by the secret concentration of troops in the city. On the evening of March 17 Thiers met with the heads of the military and the police in the Ministry of External Affairs on the quai d'Orsay to discuss his plan. Military units were to occupy the Montmartre, Belleville, and Bastille arrondissements, seize the cannon, and provide cover for the police who were to arrest known republicans in the early morning hours.[64]

At first everything went according to plan, with regular troops occupying the Buttes-Chaumont and Montmartre, and the red flags being removed from the place de la Bastille without resistance. But later in the morning the situation changed when more and more Parisians became aware of what was going on. Barricades were hastily erected, excited groups of individuals surrounded the troops, and those arrested were freed. But what must have been even more alarming to the government was that soldiers refused to obey their officers' orders to shoot into the crowd. Eventually the National Guard and the regular soldiers began to fraternize.[65] By noon Thiers' action had failed.

The explanation lay in the bungled preparation for the whole enterprise. There were too few horses to remove the cannon; nor had provision been made to feed the troops, who put down their arms after some hours to have breakfast in the cafés and stores. But Thiers' most important miscalculation was to count on the support of the *honnêtes gens* and the *bons citoyens*. Posters had suggested that the National Guard cannon were trained on Paris and were ready to "destroy your houses and children." But the good citizens did not react. Nor did they react to a further announcement that characterized members of the Central Committee as "Communists" whose aim was "to plunder Paris," and that closed with the exhortation: "The government asks you to defend your apartments, your families, and your possessions."[66]

But such attempts to revive the experiences of June 1848, when members of the National Guard from affluent neighborhoods had united against the insurgent *canaille*, were now of no avail to the government. The *honnêtes gens*, insofar as they had not left Paris, were largely indifferent or opposed to the "capitulators of Bordeaux"; and the *bonne garde nationale* stayed at home and left the government troops to confront the *fédérés* from the working-class neighborhoods.[67] That must have alerted Thiers to the fact that his plan to tame Paris before the Assembly met in Versailles had miscarried. Still all was not yet lost; hardly any blood had been spilled and the government's "treachery" had surprised rather than angered the population. Now the government had two options: it could give in and calm the excited inhabitants with some concessions; or it could bring in fresh and loyal troops to crush the resistance forming in the working-class areas.[68] However, Thiers decided on still another way out, hardly justified by his supposedly "serious position." The government immediately fled to Versailles, and all troops were removed from Paris which was thus left to its own devices. When he faced the parliamentary committee investigating the events of March 18, 1871, Thiers explained his decision this way:

> I remembered February 24 [1848]. It had been my firm conviction for a long time that we should not waste too much time in Paris if we could not maintain control despite the use of force.
> On February 24 [1848] when our situation grew worse, the king asked me what was to be done. I advised him at the time to leave Paris and then to return together with Marshal Bugeaud and 50,000 men. . . . I also recalled the example of Marshal Windischgratz: after leaving Vienna to its own fate, he returned there victorious. . . . I called my colleagues in for consultation. . . . Then I hesitated no longer and reached a decision. . . . On February 24 [1848] I had been unable to prevail, but on that day [March 18, 1871] I triumphed over all objections.[69]

Though the ex post facto explanation sounded plausible, it is hardly likely that such historical reminiscences actually influenced Thiers' action on March 18; his behavior rather resembled panic-stricken flight.[70] From a military point of view it was certainly an inexcusable mistake for Thiers also to permit the evacuation of the troops occupying the outer fortifications still in French hands.[71] After all, among these units there were some whose loyalty was beyond question; and however little good was served by the fortifications around Paris in keeping a superior attacker at bay, they would have been useful to have if it was intended—as Thiers belatedly tried to claim—to conquer the city behind them.[72]

Thiers' panic reaction contrasted strikingly with the hesitant and confused attitude of the National Guard and the Central Committee. The initial consternation in Paris at the government's flight shows how rudimentary was the organizational level of the republicans. In view of that, all the government's assertions that the events of March 18 were a "criminal insurrection without a convincing reason, without any pretext," to which it had avoided reacting "with a bloody confrontation," were nothing but deliberate propaganda.[73] Nevertheless, it set a logical precedent by which it was not the murderers, but the murdered who bore all the guilt—a logic that influenced the historiography of the Commune for a long time.[74]

It is clear that the government subjugated Paris to the dictatorship of the *Assemblée des ruraux* on March 18. The disparaged radical republicans were now always on the defensive.[75] However, there were a few spontaneous aggressive acts, such as the assassinations of Generals Lecomte and Clément Thomas by an excited mob.[76] Though the Central Committee was kept uninformed about Thiers' flight and the hasty withdrawal of the troops to Versailles until the evening of March 18, it issued the following order: "Erect barricades everywhere. Do not attack."[77] In fact the Committee prevented hotheads from storming the Hôtel de Ville, which had been turned into a fortress and where Jules Ferry, minister of foreign affairs, had taken refuge.[78]

Indeed, March 18 was not comparable to any of the former *journées parisiennes*. What happened that day in Paris was less of an uprising, or even a revolution, than the self-induced collapse of the government after its attempted coup and subsequent flight. Consequently it lost whatever credibility it had had in the capital. The mood of the city is reflected in a letter written by a carpenter, "un homme du peuple," to his sister in the provinces on March 9, 1871: "After that shameful truce [the cease-fire with Prussia], I resigned my commission as captain for it makes one die of shame to know that certain individuals sold us in this way and still believe they have the power to govern and betray us again."[79]

For a long time the propaganda and self-vindication of the eventual victors cast an impenetrable veil over the actual causes of the bloody conflict between Paris and the *gouvernement des capitulards*. The conflict involved an issue that had remained unresolved for centuries. What the capital justly demanded were the same rights and freedoms as every other French city: an elected municipal council and mayor who would be in charge of civic administration. Since the days of Etienne Marcel, the fourteenth-century *prévôt des marchands* who had tried to defend the city's municipal freedom against the demands of the crown, the capital had been under the direct control of the central government. Even the Revolution of 1789 held to this principle until the *Commune insurrectionelle* of 1792-93 abolished it by force. Hence later regimes recognized that Paris could not be granted autonomy like other cities and communities, for there was a permanent danger that it would challenge the authority and functioning of the state.

The fact that Paris possessed fewer rights and less freedom than even the smallest of the 36,000 communities in France was a constant political thorn in the side of its inhabitants. In times of revolution they always tried to gain control of the Hôtel de Ville, the symbol of communal autonomy.

There were various reasons why the traditional slight to Paris in the winter of 1870-71 was taken especially hard. Haussmann's high-handed behavior in his seventeen years as prefect had prepared the ground. Then came the time of deprivation following the fall of the Second Empire when the besieged city found itself in the paradoxical situation of having an enforced autonomy but lacking a *Conseil municipal* and a mayor. The Government of National Defense adamantly opposed such appointments and attempted the impossible task of reconciling its own power and the immediate administrative requirements of the capital. The result was a growing confusion and the erosion of its republican principles—free elections and recognition of civil rights.

A situation fraught with so many contradictions between republican claims and political practice could last only as long as the war created a state of emergency. But even once that was over, Thiers' government prevented a constructive reshaping of the situation by supporting the reactionary *Assemblée des ruraux.* Such a policy was bound to lead to an explosion, something that the reactionary Catholic-Monarchist majority in the Assembly actually desired so that it could destroy Paris and its revolutionary forces.

Seen in this light the conflict that broke out on March 18, 1871, involved much more than municipal rights and the danger of communalism. At issue in reality was the resolution of the process that had begun in 1792 and whose bloody culmination was the end of the Commune of 1871.

And yet despite Thiers' attempt to magnify that event into a revolutionary eruption, there was no evidence that the Bourse—closed between March 23 and 28, the supposed "Reign of Terror"—suffered any price declines. In fact all the stocks traded there stayed firm or even rose.[80] That shows that the capital-owning sector of society did not share the concerns of the government in Versailles, which warned that the insurrection, unless immediately suppressed, spelled the end of bourgeois order.

The Commune

*D*URING THE NIGHT OF MARCH 18-19, the state and all its executive bodies—the army, police, and government—vanished into thin air and Paris became more or less autonomous. That was an unheard-of and unknown situation open to all sorts of developments. Louise Michel, the "Red Virgin" of the Commune, comments in her memoirs: "The victory was complete; it could have been permanent if on the following day we had gone to Versailles, where the government had fled."[81] All those who sympathized with the Commune, from Marx to Trotsky, felt that this was its most decisive mistake, leading to its inevitable failure.

Indeed, what could have been more natural than to take advantage of this unique situation and send the Paris National Guard to Versailles to put an end to the "government of capitulators"? But in terms of actual historic development this argument is unreasonable, for it ignores the real situation faced by those who felt called on to act on March 19.

The power vacuum created by the flight of the government was filled in makeshift fashion by various organizations. Each of these supported the capital's autonomy, the most important being the Central Committee backed by the National Guard from eighteen of the twenty arrondissements. However, the committee was neither a representative organ of the city's population, nor did its members have the time to formulate a common political line that went beyond republican platitudes. What gave the committee a slight edge of legitimacy over other organizations and associations was the measure of recognition it received. Even the central government acknowledged its existence, posters put up on March 18 warning citizens of a "secret committee . . . that . . . wants to form a government in opposition to the legal government."[82] There were also political clubs of varying shades that contributed actively to the politicization of the capital's inhabitants during and after the siege.[83] Finally, there still was some legal authority: the mayors of the twenty arrondissements.

But of all the groups, organizations, and personalities only the Central Committee had real power and could take action. This had been foreseen by those members of the government who, shortly before their flight to Versailles on March 18, had produced and posted an announcement that tried to compromise the committee with a mass of lies and absurd insinuations:

> A committee that calls itself the Central Committee has erected barricades all over Paris and occupied the Ministry of Justice after obtaining some cannon. This Committee coldbloodedly murdered Generals Thomas and Lecomte. No one in Paris has heard of its members; their names are completely new to all. Are they Communists, Bonapartists, or Prussians? Or are they the agents of a triple coalition? In any case, whoever they are, they are the enemies of Paris, willing to let it be plundered; the enemies of France, which they deliver into the hands of Prussia; the enemies of the Republic, which they betray by instituting despotism.[84]

Those accused by Versailles were the very ones who were themselves surprised by events of March 18. When about twenty members of the Central Committee arrived at the Hôtel de Ville at midnight, they encountered complete confusion, a situation that they felt they had no mandate to control. None of the suggestions calling for decisive action, especially those by followers of Blanqui (who had himself been captured by the regime in Versailles some days earlier), gained support. The majority wanted to maintain their legality and avoid civil war; above all, they wished to avoid giving the Prussians any excuse for intervention.[85]

Though no agreement was reached on steps to be taken, nor on whether the committee should become a new governmental body and assume the duties of a city administration, two proclamations were issued on the morning of March 19.[86] They contained three decisions by which the committee legitimized itself. Communal elections were called for (the elected mayors of the twenty arrondissements being ignored), the state of emergency was lifted, and the Hôtel de Ville was designated as the meeting place of the Central Committee in the name of the *peuple*. In taking these actions the committee created a problem for itself, its legitimacy conflicting with that of the legally elected mayors. This led to the temporary development of two competing forces in Paris and prevented firm action from being taken.[87]

The Gordian knot that the committee tied for itself was so intricate that all attempts to undo it were hopeless and played into the hands of the government in Versailles. A delegation of four from the committee was sent to a meeting of the mayors and their representatives on March 19, to resolve the question of legality. After almost forty-eight hours of negotiation, agreement was reached on the text for a further proclamation; it demanded that the National Assembly pass a law sanctioning the previously announced communal elections in Paris.[88]

This compromise was submitted to the *Comités d'arrondissement* for approval but was rejected by an overwhelming majority and not looked on kindly by Versailles. It simply revealed the uncertainties of those who were forced, against their will, to act in a revolutionary manner. A revolution that would lead to civil war and new bloodshed was to be avoided at any cost. As members of the Committee knew only too well from their own experience, Paris was at the end of its strength. It was imperative to provide work and bread for the masses, and to take energetic measures to stem continuing deprivation. But in order to deal with these tasks an elected city administration with communal autonomy was needed, in other words a commune.

From this point of view the compromise was perfectly plausible. Why should not the National Assembly finally allow Paris to be autonomous, so that the announced communal elections would cease to be a revolutionary act? However, such a view was unrealistic, for the government as well as the National Assembly lacked the goodwill for such a compromise; those in Versailles had long since decided to force Paris to its knees. They therefore decided to play on the committee's legalistic scruples by making half-promises while meetings were going on, so as to gain time for a campaign of revenge against the capital.[89]

Though the committee was involved in hopeless negotiations that continued until March 24, it acted firmly in administering the city. Within two days it established order in the midst of what had threatened to turn into chaos.[90] Sheer necessity forced the committee to become more involved than it originally intended until it finally functioned as an actual legislative body.[91] The elections to the Commune, held on March 26 without the consent of the Versailles government, signified that the population was finally willing to consider the events of March 18 as a revolution and to act accordingly.[92]

Neither the "government" of the Central Committee nor the actual Commune—which existed only from the day of its ceremonial proclamation on March 26, 1871, to its dreadful end on May 28—provided the least cause

PARIS

for the bloodthirsty legend with which the victors of Versailles sought to compromise it. The murders of Generals Lecomte and Thomas on the afternoon of March 18 had simply been excesses committed by an angry crowd. A further event made much of by Versailles propaganda was the bloody end to a demonstration on March 22. Testimony by a neutral observer, the American General Sheridan who witnessed the occurrence from his hotel window, generally corroborates the description given by Karl Marx.[93] Marx writes:

> On March 22 a group of "gentlemen" set out from the wealthy neighborhoods, all the dandies in their ranks, led by such well-known figures of the Empire as Heeckeren, Coëtlogon, Henri de Pène, etc. Under the cowardly pretext of a peaceful demonstration, but secretly armed with murderous weapons, this rabble organized itself for action, and disarmed and maltreated the sentries and patrols of the National Guards they encountered. Entering the place Vendôme from the rue de la Paix, they tried to break through the sentries there and gain control of the headquarters of the National Guard behind it, uttering the cry: "Down with the Central Committee! Down with the murderers! Long live the National Assembly!" In reply to their pistol shots, the usual legal requests to desist were made; when these proved ineffective, the general commanding the National Guard gave the order to fire. *One* volley sent packing the silly coxcombs who had expected that the mere sight of "respectable society" would have the same effect on the Paris revolution as Joshua's trumpets had upon the walls of Jericho. They left behind them two dead National Guards and nine severely wounded individuals (among them a member of the Central Committee); and the whole scene of their magnificent achievement was strewn with revolvers, daggers, and sword canes, in testimony of the "unarmed" nature of their "peaceful" demonstration.[94]

Indeed, the Versailles government's accusations of unbridled bloodthirstiness and vandalism were clearly a case of projection. For following its victory its own brutality knew no bounds. At any rate no blood was spilled by the Communards until May 21, when government troops penetrated the west of Paris and slaughtered captured National Guards in broad daylight without even a court-martial.

Moreover, though called a "Commune," it had nothing to do with the concept of "communism," even if its heirs try to perpetuate such a linkage. The Commune was no more a model of socialist rule than it was a dictatorship of the proletariat. It was a freely elected democratic city administration, even if the vote was based largely on the *classes laborieuses*. The majority of its members were republicans or radical democrats, who identified their political beliefs with the traditions of the Jacobin Revolution. This was not altered by the fact that only 83 of the 91 elected members met on March 28 to set it up, and 22 other "moderate" representatives resigned a few days later to join the future victors.[95] Only then was the left wing, to which the remaining 61 members belonged, in control.[96]

The short precarious existence of the Commune and its tragic end created a myth that was embellished with multiple and farfetched speculations on its political aims and intentions. As to actual plans and proclamations of more than immediate significance, and affecting areas other than Paris, the Commune left behind a set of curiously vague, almost naïvely utopian concepts. This applies especially to the document considered to be its "testament," a declaration addressed to the French people on April 19, 1871.[97] It was a radical federalist document, and its central theme of breaking France up into thousands of autonomous communes most likely did not reflect the goal of the revolutionary arrondissements of Paris.[98]

The rather empty sociopolitical message was covered by wordy declamation:

> The communal revolution initiated by the people on March 18 started a new era of experimental, positive, and scientific politics. It marked the end of the old governmental and clerical world, of militarism, officialdom, exploitation, speculation, monopoly, and privilege, which subjugated the proletariat and brought nothing but misfortune to *la patrie*.

Such an accumulation of empty formulas amounted to very little, which is why even Karl Marx declared: "The great social measure of the Commune was its own working existence."[99] The "working existence" lasted from the day it took up its functions on March 28 to the day of its dissolution on May 24. On April 2, five days after its inception, the Commune was forced to wage war when Versailles commenced its attack on Paris. It therefore had to work under abnormal and constraining conditions. There was a further difficulty whose great importance has been pointed out by Henri Guillemin. As of April 5, when the moderates resigned their mandates, the Commune was very much aware that it did not necessarily have the support of the majority of Paris inhabitants, even if they did not actually oppose it. The "practical existence" of the Commune was thus subjected to two conditions that limited its actions to those measures it was certain that most of the population would tolerate.[100]

The first broadly sociopolitical measures concerned the cancellation of edicts issued by the National Assembly in March 1871. The sale of pawned objects in the Mont de Piété ordered for April 1 was postponed indefinitely. Next, repayment of overdue bills was scheduled for July 15; after this deadline payment was to be made in interest-free monthly installments over three years. Finally, it was decreed that landlords had to renounce the arrears of rents due between October 15, 1870, and April 15, 1871—it being decided that capitalists had to make sacrifices as well as other segments of society.[101]

Aside from these rulings, which corresponded to what a large section of the public demanded of the Commune, the *Conseil municipal* passed a number of other decrees that reflected the originality of its political aims.[102] Church and state were separated; priests' stipends no longer came out of tax revenues; and property owned by ecclesiastical institutions became communal. In the area of education, plans were developed for a system of free compulsory primary schools, as well as for a comprehensive system of scholarships and subsidies to enable children from poorer families to benefit from higher education. When the Commune came to an end, it was just on the point of opening two vocational schools, one of which was intended for girls.[103] The changes made in labor laws were particularly impressive. Night work by bakery workers was forbidden, and under a special decree of April 16 workers were permitted to continue operating those businesses and workshops whose owners had fled. This was not intended as a takeover measure; the concerns were to be returned to their rightful owners upon their return. Furthermore, workers were encouraged to form labor unions, and the absurdly severe punishments imposed by employers for breaking discipline in the workplace were abolished.[104]

Compared with other socialist utopias then in existence, what the Commune planned or achieved was incredibly modest. But though the Commune considered property rights sacrosanct and respected them scrupulously, its reforms were unacceptable to the "good citizens" in Versailles. If it had only seized the billions in gold, jewelery, and stocks kept in the safes of the Banque de France, it could have fought its opponents in Versailles far more effectively.[105] Yet at no time did the Commune entertain such an idea and this only hastened its downfall.

It should be borne in mind that what seem today to be modest changes were actually considered revolutionary at the time. The Commune not only questioned established political, economic, and cultural realities but found constructive alternatives for them. Its success in so doing partially explains the still-shocking cruelty used by the victors to defeat it.

The Week of Blood

*T*HE LONG AND DREADFUL DEATH-THROES of the Commune began on Palm Sunday, April 1, 1871. Ever since March 18, revolutionary rhetoric in Paris had been concerned with the government's preparations for civil war. But no one seriously believed it would happen. Nothing was done about the defense of the city, for example training the National Guard and improving its command structure. Such negligence seems all the more incomprehensible in light of the obvious diligence with which those in Versailles were preparing the demoralized troops that had withdrawn from the capital on March 18 and 19 for the planned battle. Moreover, it should have been apparent that these troops were being reinforced by fresh battalions from the provinces. And finally, no one could have been oblivious of Thiers' enthusiasm for this fight; since his flight from Paris he had concentrated all his energies on selecting the generals who were to carry out his revenge. The prospect of war fascinated this historian of the First Empire to the point where he named himself commander in chief. He must have dreamed of assuming a role that would permit him to emulate his idol, Napoleon I, whose campaigns he had studied and analyzed. He so identified with his model that he became its living caricature. General du Barail writes in his memoirs: "Like Napoleon he virtually used to lie on the maps; like him he developed battle plans and called meetings of councils of war at which no one could say anything until he, with inexhaustible energy, had explained the situation and analyzed troop movements."[106]

Thiers felt able to wage war against the Commune, knowing that he had the support of the officers of the former imperial army who wanted to obliterate the dishonor of the defeat by Prussia. He could also count on the *Assemblée des ruraux* who foresaw their own doom in what was happening in Paris. And he had the *honnêtes gens* behind him, the claque that would soon line the streets of Versailles to be entertained by the prisoners paraded before them, beating them with their elegant canes and parasols.[107] Hatred of the Commune to the point of public hysteria was regularly encouraged in newspapers, in church pulpits, and on the speaker's podium in the National Assembly. It eventually found an outlet in the relentless cruelty of the victors, who spared neither women nor children. Such hatred revealed dark depths of the human soul previously unknown in a nineteenth century proud of its civilized behavior. The September 1792 murders of prison inmates had been carried out by a crowd possessed by existential fear. And even the numerous atrocities committed by the revolutionary army against insurgents in the Morbihan and the Vendée pale beside these later violent acts and cold-blooded massacres. The slaughter revealed the rabid class hatred of the victors, which made them view their human opponents as nothing more than dangerous wild animals.[108]

On April 1, 1871, Thiers sent a telegram to the prefects of the various departments, in which he proudly announced: "The Assembly is meeting at Versailles, where one of the best armies France ever had has gathered. All good citizens can therefore be calm and look forward to the end of a battle that will be painful but short."[109] But Thiers was mistaken. Shortly after the fighting began the "best army" became involved in a battle of attrition, organized by two of the Commune's professional officers. They were General Cluseret, who acted as the Commune's delegate to the Ministry of War between April 3 and May 1, and his successor, Louis Rossel, who was forced to give up the position on May 9 because of constant and trying disagreements with the National Guard.[110] Even though the defenders were greatly inferior to their attackers from the start, they managed to hold their own until May 20 by dint of skill and sacrifice, so that the "best army" of which Thiers was so proud remained outside the gates of Paris for some time.[111] But the situation had been changed by the signing of the final peace treaty between France and Germany in Frankfurt-am-Main on May 10, 1871. Though it was merely another capitulation—France having to relinquish Alsace and a large section of Lorraine, and to pay an idemnity of 5 billion gold francs—Thiers had no other choice. It was the only way he could retrieve the French armies in captivity since Sedan and Metz, and now badly needed to destroy the Commune.

Troops from Versailles attacked the weakly defended western arrondissements of Paris on Sunday afternoon, May 21, 1871. After Rossel quit his position as delegate to the Ministry of War, defense arrangements were very poorly organized. For several hours the Commune was completely unaware that the attack had started and undertook no efficient countermeasures.[112] The neighborhoods of the *classes aisées* thus fell easily into the hands of the attackers, who approached from Passy in the southwest in ever greater assault waves, giving their surprised opponents a foretaste of what awaited them. National Guards were captured in droves and shot in the open. News of the atrocities spread like wildfire and helped to strengthen the defenders' flagging spirits. The following morning, Monday, May 22, they tried to stop the advancing attackers in the place de la Concorde and the real battle for Paris began—barricade by barricade. It did not end until May 28, 1871, when the last of the resisting National Guards were shot down in the Père-Lachaise cemetery.[113]

Considerable damage was done in Paris that week by the first widespread use of cannon and machine guns. Even worse than the damage from the cannon were the numerous fires frequently set by the guards to halt the advancing attackers. At times they burned entire rows of houses; certain buildings, like the Tuileries or the Prefecture, were burned down out of sheer destructiveness, to prevent those symbols of hated power from falling undamaged into the assailants' hands. The Hôtel de Ville, which stood for communal freedom, was destroyed for the same reason. Numerous other fires, like that which destroyed the Ministry of Finance, were caused by the artillery of the Versailles troops.[114] In some cases it happened, as Louise Michel reports, that "certain property owners and storekeepers set fires themselves to buildings and goods they no longer knew what to do with, so as to receive compensation later on."[115]

The inferno that Paris became in that *semaine sanglante* was a direct result of the policies adopted by Thiers on the afternoon of March 18. But it is only historically just to emphasize that he had no other choice but to take such action. Thiers could not seriously consider the compromise, which at first had seemed reasonable, of accepting communal elections in the capital. He was a creature of the *Assemblée des ruraux* that did not even consider the Republic proclaimed in Paris on September 4, 1870, as a legitimate form of government. And a regime that had decided to terminate a war lost by its predecessors could not be reconciled to a Paris Commune whose existence depended upon successfully waging a popular revolutionary war against that same enemy.

It was an old, familiar pattern of conflict in that the Commune of 1871 expressed a final attempt by Paris to gain its revolutionary sovereignty. This made the Commune of 1871 part of the long tradition of *journées parisiennes* which, all things considered, were prompted by unchanging motives. But what prevented the Commune from becoming just another episode in the traditional conflict was not so much its politicohistorical importance as the unbelievable cruelty of the victors after its suppression.

Lissagaray, the historian of the Commune, and numerous other contemporary witnesses have described the cold-blooded slaughter of human beings amid the still-smoking ruins of the city in vivid and shocking terms. People were herded together for mass executions in prisons and barracks, in quarries, parks, and fortifications. Even those who surrendered could not count on mercy. The 147 National Guards who participated in the Commune's final battle in the Père-Lachaise cemetery were shot—the wall where this occurred has been a place of pilgrimage for the French Left since the 1880s.[116] Anyone who looked in the least suspicious was sure of certain death without even the pretense of a court-martial. Wearing part of a uniform or army boots, having blackened hands, or just looking defiant meant forfeiting one's life. These unfortunate beings stood in line in the Jardin du Luxembourg until it was their turn; it was the same in the Parc Monceau and the Bois de Boulogne. Supposedly secret massacres occurred in the Lobau barracks and the La Roquette prison, but the blood of the slain seeped out under the gates for days, and the monotonous noise of rifle fire gave the horrible process away.[117]

Long columns of those who avoided the slaughter in the city were taken to Versailles. There they were met at the Porte de la Muette by the cavalry general of the former imperial army, the marquis de Gallifet, a man who owed his military career to the talents of his wife. This man, whom Clemenceau later characterized as a "swine," personified all the cowardly brutality of the victors. Lissagaray describes the rampage of the marquis, who was in charge of the prisoner transports:

> The dead are fortunate for they do not have to undergo the calvary of the prisoners. One can imagine what the arrests must have been like when mass executions occurred. It was a terrible series of raids. Men, women, children, Parisians, provincials, foreigners, the uninvolved, a jumble of individuals of all sexes and ages, all parties and classes. Tenants in buildings, residents in streets were randomly arrested. A suspicion, a word, a dubious attitude were sufficient for someone to be taken into custody. In this way 40,000 people were rounded up between May 21 and 30. The prisoners were lined up in long rows, and tied together so that they formed a single group. Anyone who refused to walk was poked with a bayonet and if he still refused was shot on the spot, or sometimes tied to a horse's tail. The prisoners were forced to kneel outside churches in wealthy neighborhoods before a miserable crowd of lackeys, coxcombs, and streetwalkers, who shouted with one voice: "Death to them! Death to them! Don't let them live! Shoot them on the spot!" In the Champs-Elysées they even wanted to force their way through the guards and draw blood. The columns of prisoners were taken to Versailles. Gallifet awaited them at La Muette. Inside the city he headed the columns and stopped under the windows of the aristocratic clubs to receive their ovations and hurrahs. He took his tithes at the Paris gates; going through the ranks he said to one or another with his look of a hungry wolf: "You look intelligent, fall out." "You have a watch," he said to another, "you must have been an official in the Commune," and he made him fall out as well.

When he had chosen a sufficient number, he had them all immediately shot. Archibald Forbes, the correspondent of the *Daily News*, who was caught up in a raid and had to accompany the column to La Muette, reports what happened during one of these murderous events on June 8:

> The column stopped in the avenue Uhrich and the prisoners were made to stand in four or five rows. General Marquis de Gallifet, who had ridden at the head of us with his general staff, got off his horse and began his inspection close to my left. He walked slowly, reviewed

the rows, touched a prisoner on the shoulder, or ordered him to step out. The individual selected was then led to the middle of the street without further questioning; a second column quickly formed there. They soon realized that their final hour had come and it was gruesomely interesting to observe their behavior. One wounded man, with a bloody shirt, sat down in the street and howled in pain. Others cried quietly. Two soldiers, presumably deserters, implored the other prisoners to state whether they had ever seen them in their ranks. Several smiled stubbornly. What a horrible spectacle to see a human being torn away from his fellow creatures and massacred without any trial! A little distance ahead of me a cavalry officer pointed out to the marquis de Gallifet a man and woman supposedly guilty of something. The woman left the ranks, went down on her knees, and begged for mercy with outstretched arms, protesting her innocence with her tragic gestures. The general observed her for a while and then said with absolute indifference: "Madame, I have been to all the theaters in Paris, it is not worth your while putting on an act." I followed the general, still a prisoner but escorted by two mounted riflemen, and tried to discover what might influence his choice. I noticed that it was not good to be noticeably taller, dirtier, cleaner, older, or uglier than one's neighbor. One individual was released from his suffering on this earth on account of his broken nose. After the general had chosen several hundred prisoners in this way, an execution squad was formed and the column continued on its way. A few minutes later we heard volleys behind us that lasted for a quarter of an hour: the summary execution of these unfortunate people.

On Sunday, May 28, Gallifet said: "All white-haired individuals step out." One hundred and eleven prisoners left the ranks. "You," Gallifet continued, "witnessed June 1848, you are even more guilty than the others." And he had their corpses thrown into the fortification moats.[118]

Problems of odor and the danger of epidemic created by the mountains of corpses piled up all over the city finally ended the mass executions in June. Several streets became practically impassable being covered in human cadavers. Near the Ecole Polytechnique the murdered bodies lay three rows deep in an area that extended for a hundred meters. In the west of Paris, near the Trocadéro, over a thousand bodies awaited burial. The damp, close weather around Pentecost that year hastened decomposition, so that the bodies swelled up and pushed through the thin layer of earth with which they were temporarily covered. An article in the *Temps* asks:

> Who does not recall, even if only for a few minutes, the sight of the square, no the slaughterhouse, of the Tour Saint-Jacques? Here and there heads, arms, feet, and hands stuck up from the recently turned moist earth; on the ground one saw the faces of the corpses dressed in National Guard uniforms; it was awful. A stale, disgusting odor came from the garden; at certain spots it immediately turned into a stench.[119]

In view of these terrible conditions the dead became a danger to the living. The bourgeois press that had at first incited these murders now began to demand that they stop. But removal of the corpses presented fresh problems. Furniture vans and buses transported them to the cemeteries, where a certain number were buried in mass graves; others were thrown into trenches outside the city, which had been dug during the siege. Lissagaray writes:

> The burial of so many corpses was soon more than could be managed and they were cremated in the barracks of the fortifications. But the cremation was only partially completed for lack of sufficient draft, and the flesh was cooked to pulp. The corpses were then piled up on the Buttes-Chaumont, covered with kerosene, and burnt.[120]

It is said that counting up makes no sense. But a comparison of the murders committed by both sides during the liquidation of the Commune is very revealing, the alleged cruelty of the Communards always having served to justify the unparalleled brutality of their conquerors. The Commune was responsible for the deaths of 84 hostages, most of whom were victims of an angry mob. Among them were the archbishop of Paris, a presiding judge, and several Jesuit priests for whom Thiers had stubbornly refused to give up Blanqui—a dead archbishop being of more propaganda value than a live one. Apart from the shooting of Generals Lecomte and Thomas these 84 murders were committed only in the very last days of the Commune, when the victors had long since begun their relentless executions. But they gave rise to the overblown legend of the Commune's abominations, elaborated and popularized by Maxime Du Camp in the four volumes of his *Convulsions de Paris*.

On the other hand, it is impossible to give exact figures for the bloody massacres by the *honnêtes gens*. In a telegram that he sent to the prefects on the evening of May 28, 1871, Thiers wrote that these by no means atoned for the evil deeds and crimes committed. They were intended to make clear to the madmen that one could not challenge and disdain civilization without being punished.[121] The official report made by General Appert estimates the number of those summarily executed to be 17,000.[122] But in reality the number is likely to have been far greater, in the region of 25,000 to 30,000 dead.[123]

Even the number of prisoners, who were still being sentenced by twenty-four military tribunals four years after the end of the Commune, is unknown. Estimates vary between 39,000 and 50,000.[124] But the actual total of those convicted by military tribunals was 10,137; of these 93 were condemned to death, but after the spilling of so much blood only 23 were executed; 251 were sent to do forced labor, 4,586 were deported to New Caledonia, and the rest received prison terms of varying length.[125] The surprising leniency of the military courts is misleading, for the conditions in overcrowded prisons and camps claimed untold other victims.[126] There was little food and indescribable sanitation; the jailers were sadistic and the unfortunate prisoners were exposed to the *honnêtes gens*, whose Sunday pleasure it was to insult them and gape at them as if they were wild animals.

But the incredible display of class hatred, the cruelty, and the massacres worked in the Commune's favor and created a lasting myth of social revolt. It was largely due to the efforts of Karl Marx that this myth was kept alive and developed into an effective tool of revenge. His hastily composed and angry essay *The Civil War in France* was written in his London exile while the Commune was still in its final struggles. Thanks to this essay, perceptions of the Commune differed from those of an anecdote Flaubert told Edmond de Goncourt:

> He [Flaubert] told me of a Chinese delegation that was in Paris during the siege and the Commune, right in the middle of our catastrophe, and who were asked: "What is happening here must surely surprise you?" "Oh no, no! You Westerners are young, you have practically no history. . . . That's the way it always is. . . . Siege, Commune, that's the normal history of mankind."[127]

However, it is a fact that during this "normal history of mankind," that is, between May 22 and June 13, 1871, the authorities were flooded with 379,825 denunciations, most of which were anonymous.[128] It is also true that during this same period the *honnêtes gens* greeted the revenge of the Versailles soldiers with relief and approval; and they gazed at the ruins of Paris with curiosity and esthetic appreciation.[129]

But the end of the Commune was not synonymous with the decline of Paris, and after all the massacres the city soon returned to its customary way of life.[130] Only Edmond de Goncourt seemed to think that it seemed provincial, as he notes in his journal on June 5, 1871.[131] And after the Parisians, who returned in droves once the state of emergency was lifted on June 3, came hordes of English tourists who were enticed by the morbid pleasure of looking at the destruction.[132] Once the theaters and other institutions of mundane entertainment had reopened, fashionable life took possession of the boulevards again. The esthetes and gourmets met at Brébant, one of the best restaurants in Paris, at Tortoni, or one of the other culinary havens. On the surface everything seemed the same as it had been before the war, the siege, and the Commune. The one difference was that those who could afford it devoted themselves even more uninhibitedly to the enjoyment of life.

Thus social life continued uninterruptedly in the Third Republic, and Paris in the 1870s appeared to resemble that of the Second Empire. What detracted from this illusion were the ruins, the damaged or burned public buildings and private houses. And though it was hard to tell at first glance that trade and industry were only gradually picking up again, the great labor shortage showed how many victims had been claimed by the civil war and suppression of the Commune. Entire industrial sectors could not meet the orders that were slowly being placed again, because thousands of skilled workers languished in prisons and camps.[133]

Haussmann's Legacy

AT FIRST IT SEEMED AS IF THE VICTORY of the *honnêtes gens* had condemned Paris to a state of invalidism. For the destruction left by the civil war caused enormous expenses on top of the heavy debts left by Haussmann and the costs of the war with Prussia. It was clear from the start that these expenditures could not come out of the state budget. Nor was it likely that the *transformation de Paris* could be continued under these circumstances; especially since the *Conseil municipal* was controlled by stubborn opponents of Haussmann's policies.

Yet despite negative attitudes and changed political and financial conditions, there was a gradual realization that what had been left as a torso was worth completing. For one thing Haussmann's achievements had by now received universal recognition. The transformation of Paris served as a model wherever similar problems existed in the world, and this helped to silence the criticism. Furthermore, Haussmann's ideas were supported by his staff who continued to hold their positions after his departure and the change in regime. Jean-Charles-Adolphe Alphand succeeded his master as *Directeur des Travaux publics* and not only adopted his methods but soon acquired the same authority.

Finally, the transformation of Paris had long since acquired its own dynamic; to stop the program now made no sense and would not be cost-effective. The completion of various new streets was therefore essential, as was the construction of intersections that determined future traffic planning. Moreover, dispositions for expropriation arranged by Haussmann were still in effect, and to let them expire was neither politically nor economically desirable.[134] Finally, as public pressure to resume the work mounted there was hope that it might revive the economy (see map 3, page 345).

The matter was decided by two factors: the city's finances showed some improvement for the first time in 1875, with a modest budget surplus of 20 million francs. And in April 1876, the government announced a great world exposition to be held in Paris in two years' time. In view of this the city floated two loans totaling 340 million francs for completion of the transformation of Paris.[135] Some of the money was immediately used to continue work on the avenue de l'Opéra, Haussmann's *via triumphalis*; it was officially opened with great pomp on September 21, 1877, by President MacMahon.[136] The final section of the boulevard Saint-Germain (between the place Maubert and the Seine) and its extension as the boulevard Henri IV on the Right Bank of the Seine were also finished. That completed the ring of streets in the south and east, whose northern section was represented by the inner boulevards.[137]

Though construction of the avenue de l'Opéra was an economic success, the costs being partially met by resale of sites not required for its location, its completion marked the end of an era. Construction of the boulevard Haussmann, which promised to be no less profitable, was not begun until after World War I and was finished in the mid-1920s. The initial enthusiasm for continuing Haussmann's program did not pale so quickly merely because of financial and political realities; under the Republic the priorities of urban planning changed.[138]

Strategic considerations that had been central to Haussmann's concepts lost that centrality after the Second Empire and were replaced by greater interest in traffic engineering and public hygiene. The change in priorities was largely due to the fact that instead of fulfilling its defenders' expectations, Haussmann's transformation had produced ever greater contrasts. The narrow, dirty alleys were such an eyesore in the areas where broad, prosperous, and busy streets had been established that the demand for improvements there constantly grew. Moreover, the transformation had not merely reorganized the flow of traffic but had actually increased it. An entire series of side streets was so overloaded that something had to be done promptly. To meet these needs it was decided to widen existing streets, a solution that was compatible with the comparatively modest means available for street construction.[139]

With the exception of the avenue de l'Opéra, the boulevard Saint-Germain, and the boulevard Henri IV, all streets built prior to World War I were at best merely improvements of certain details of Haussmann's plan. The lack of financing for additional work was only of secondary importance, though; primarily the Third Republic lacked the political will and the vision of a grand design to organize the capital's rapid growth. This lack of vision produced the suburban sprawl beyond the fortifications that spread lavalike into the Ile-de-France without any attempt at regional planning.

After 1890 attention was focused on a new mass transportation system, the metro, to the exclusion of any further development of the street network. Horse-drawn buses and trams had not been able able to keep pace with the expansion of Paris and its growing population. The capacity of these vehicles was relatively small, and because of their high fares their operation was limited to such routes as seemed profitable to the privately owned *Compagnie générale des Omnibus*. The city center was therefore not linked to the outskirts and suburbs. A further disadvantage was that the vehicular system increased and complicated circulation in the inner-city streets.[140] These drawbacks, and the example of London's first subway line, opened in 1861, encouraged debate in Paris after 1871 on building its own system.

Discussions lasted for more than twenty years, until construction of the metro became a necessity in view of the exposition planned for 1900.[141] The subterranean lines were generally to follow the most important surface-traffic routes. When the exposition opened, the first metro line from the Porte de Vincennes to the Porte Maillot was partially completed.

By 1914 the system had grown to over eighty kilometers and was entirely financed by the city. The number of passengers increased correspondingly: in 1901 there were 56 million, a figure that almost tripled to 149 million by 1905. In 1914 there were over 400 million passengers.[142]

However, contemporaries soon realized that the metro's great advantages were counterbalanced by its disadvantages. For while the new system improved and speeded up the population's mobility, it increased rather than decreased traffic in the inner city (see map 4, page 345). The result of this unexpected development was that the initial enthusiasm for completion of the metro network began to lessen before the outbreak of World War I. Instead attention was paid to improving surface routes that experienced greater use once the automobile was introduced.

Urban planning in the Third Republic was given a further boost by greater interest in public hygiene on the part of officials and doctors. Conditions that had been tolerated suddenly became unacceptable. The study by Jean Chrétien, *Les Odeurs de Paris,* published in 1881, was symptomatic of a fresh discovery of the *ville malade.* A wealth of statistical investigations now conclusively proved the close relationship between unsanitary living conditions and above-average mortality rates. This connection was brutally revealed during the great typhoid and cholera epidemics of the 1870s, 1880s, and 1890s. Typhoid was endemic to Paris and claimed between 51 (1872-79) and 143 (1882) victims per 10,000 inhabitants annually.[143] Cholera epidemics were especially severe in the years 1873, 1884, and 1892.[144]

Statistics provided clear proof that cholera most particularly affected neighborhoods lacking adequate sewage facilities and still dependent on the Seine for their fresh water. Studies conducted by the *Commission des odeurs de Paris,* appointed in 1880, also offered ammunition in the *bataille du tout-à-l'égout* (battle to get all waste into the sewers), waged by the general public as well as specialists. The dispute was settled by the Law of July 10, 1894, which finally ended the private disposal of excrement and introduced the type of sewage system long since used elsewhere.[145] It required that every household had to be connected to the city's water mains; but as was to be expected, this revolution in public and private hygiene met with the stubborn resistance of building owners. By 1913 only 52,053 houses, or 67 percent, had sewer connections, whereas 43,192 houses still used some type of cesspool.[146]

Still, enormous progress had been made in the field of hygiene. Street cleaning, having become the responsibility of the city administration in 1873, improved notably; it also benefited from the introduction of trash cans in 1883.[147] These and other measures helped to control the epidemics. The only major remaining problem was that of tuberculosis, of which thousands died each year, especially among the *classes laborieuses* who lived in overpopulated slums.[148] Under the Third Republic the contrast in living conditions in the various arrondissements became more marked, according to mortality rates. After 1871 there was a sharp rise in the number of immigrant workers. Their preference for the outskirts of Paris caused further overcrowding in an area where there was normally far less new construction than in wealthy neighborhoods.[149]

The complex relationship between poverty, overpopulation, and deplorable living conditions, along with a higher-than-average mortality rate, was clearly perceived to be dangerous to the whole of society. There were lengthy discussions on the sort of action to be taken, but it was soon recognized that it was not enough merely to complete street construction or improve the sewer system: the slums would have to be cleared as completely as possible and replaced with roomier, more sanitary buildings. At first, however, discussions, investigations, and inquiries focused on the moral effects of the promiscuous living conditions of the *classes laborieuses*. Not until the 1880s was attention paid to the question of hygiene as it affected the lives of the poor, though even then without any practical results.

A law that was supposed to replace the *Loi Melun* of 1850 began to be worked out in 1891 but did not come into force until 1902. It broadened the jurisdiction of the prefect of the Seine and the prefect of police over unsanitary housing. Both authorities were empowered to act where the condition of a building or its tenant density threatened the health of its occupants or of their neighbors. But even by 1914 these regulations still proved ineffective: there was no official and comprehensive slum clearance program yet, or any policy for public housing.[150]

The Belle Epoque

HERE WAS CONFUSION AND INDECISION as to which aspects of Haussmann's plan should be given priority; this was reflected in the political instability of the Third Republic and general lack of purpose on the part of Belle Epoque society.[151] Edmond de Goncourt hoped that the suppression of the Commune would give France a respite of at least twenty years.[152] Unfortunately he was too optimistic. For though the Third Republic exhibited astonishing staying power, it was plagued by numerous crises until World War I, and people lived in expectation of another revolution. Paris experienced all the symptoms of a cold civil war between republicans and monarchists, between Right and Left, between traditional elites and the new bourgeois and rural middle-class voters—not to forget the proletariat with its improved political organization. But it was the rural electorate that was now in control.

Following the political consolidation of the Third Republic in the late 1870s, and a resurgence of national confidence after the success of the exposition of 1878, a new epoch began in the history of Paris. Republicanism developed along with universal suffrage and, in the face of an initial royalist threat, into a broad coalition of the Third Estate. That coalition united the "new social layer," as Gambetta called the middle class, and the rural masses. Thus it not only ended the "France of the notables" but finally eliminated the special political status that Paris had held for almost a century. In a republican France the city lost its former revolutionary sovereignty and its ability to make and break regimes.

As of 1880 the government and National Assembly once again had their seat in Paris, and the city was still the epicenter of the tremors that uninterruptedly shook the Third Republic.[153] But universal suffrage dispersed the political energies that had formerly been almost exclusively concentrated in the capital. Broad ideological conflicts were no longer debated exclusively in Paris but in the whole of France—including both the generalized republican dissatisfaction embodied in the scintillating figure of General Boulanger, and nationalism, anticlericalism, and antisemitism that produced the most serious national crisis of the Third Republic in the Dreyfus affair.[154]

What the capital lost in political and revolutionary sovereignty it gained in cultural and intellectual energy. In the Belle Epoque, as the years between 1880 and 1914 came to be known, Paris developed into the world capital of fashion, art, and literature, and of life's pleasures.[155] This was no coincidence but rather the result of various developments that coalesced, strengthened, and enriched one another. Belle Epoque Paris was a gigantic catalyst for the shrill excitements, the somber fears, and the optimistic expectations that were so characteristic of the fin de siècle, and were expressed by a multitude of views and competing artistic schools and cliques.

The effects of Haussmann's redevelopments on the character of Paris became apparent only after 1880, when France began to recover from the consequences of its defeat and the suppression of the Commune. Destruction of the Commune completed Haussmann's planned expulsion of the *classes laborieuses* to the ghettos of the *ceinture rouge*. It left an overwhelmingly middle-class social milieu in the capital, with a conservative voting pattern in its twenty arrondissements. The social leveling of the population was complemented by a democratizing process of daily life, as exmplified by the success of the *grands magasins*.

Under the auspices of the Republic and universal suffrage, which strengthened and ensured this development, life was lived in public—something that astonished many contemporaries.[156] It was accompanied by what the vicomte d'Avenel described as the *nivellement des jouissances*—the dawn of consumer society and mass culture.[157] In this way the material foundations were laid for the fascinating magic displayed in Paris during the Belle Epoque.

Two phenomena were largely responsible for the *nivellement des jouissances:* the *café-concert* and the music hall, and the expositions. Though the tradition of the former dates further back, they had never before, nor have they since, experienced such success. At the turn of the century there were said to be more than two hundred *café-concerts*, music halls, dance palaces, and *cabarets artistiques*—all places of inexpensive and often very spectacular pleasures.[158] One of their chroniclers called them the "theaters of the poor."[159] But in fact, and this was the secret of their great success, these establishments were frequented not only by the *classes laborieuses*, but by members of all social classes.

Describing what went on in the *cafés-concerts*, a horrified contemporary writes:

> In all of these halls, singing, dancing, and often shameless dramatic performances are given these days in front of princes, wealthy loafers, fashionable ladies, and those who act as if they were. This type of entertainment . . . mani-

fests, above all, a desire for uninhibitedness, languorousness, spectacle, and debasement that is peculiar to our times. However low the theater may have sunk, however little it demands from its audience in terms of behavior and intellectual effort, it still makes certain demands. One may not smoke or keep one's hat on there; moreover, one has to understand the play, or least seem to understand it, and even the actors do not say or mime everything. In the *café-concert*, on the other hand, there are none of these limits! One smokes, drinks, comes and goes as one pleases, while watching highly suggestive acts and listening to incredibly risqué jokes. The *café-concert* is the paradise of libertinism and the most determined bad taste. On top of this the prices are low and the incitement of all the senses is practically free. For a few sous one gets everything that refreshes as well as excites. How then could one avoid coming here to still, or seem to still, the freely admitted or secret desire for dissolute excess that currently plagues the *peuple* as much as good society?[160]

A number of striking parallels and structural similarities existed between the *cafés-concerts* and the department stores. In both of them a socially mixed consumer group could obtain whatever it needed at relatively moderate prices. And as in the department store with its overwhelming choice of goods, the entertainment offered by the *cafés-concerts* and music halls was available to everyone on the same basis. In contrast to theaters, for instance, where the audience sat in reserved seats priced according to their distance from the stage, in the *cafés-concerts* one could stay anywhere for as long as one wanted.

After all, a good part of the entertainment was not what the singers, dancers, acrobats, or magicians offered, but the spectacle provided by the colorful crowd itself as it thronged in the often extravagantly decorated halls. One such was the Folies-Bergère, embellished with stucco and gilt, with allegorical murals and ceiling paintings, and filled with generously upholstered rattan furniture.[161] The alluring effect produced by this crowd was enhanced by numerous wall mirrors and by clever lighting that flattered everything and everyone. The mirrors decorated the *promenoir*, or foyer, of the Folies-Bergère, with its elegant bar commemorated by Manet's famous painting. In his novel *Bel-Ami*, Maupassant gives this description of the bar:

> In the large vestibule that leads to the circular promenade, where elegantly dressed beauties of easy virtue mingle with men in dark suits, a group of women waited for arrivals at one of the three bars, behind which presided three heavily made-up, faded ladies selling drinks and love. The tall mirrors behind them reflected their backs and the faces of the passersby.[162]

Establishments like the Folies-Bergère were meeting places of an anonymous metropolitan public seeking to drown its loneliness in the intoxication of crude sensations. This public is described to Duroy—protagonist of the novel *Bel-Ami*, who is there for first time—in these words:

> Take a look at the orchestra section: nothing but bourgeois with their wives and children; good, stupid types who come to look. In the boxes there are some men-about-town, a few artists, several not quite first-class prostitutes; and behind us [in the foyer] the most peculiar mixture in all of Paris. Who are these men? Look at them. Everything is there, all professions and all classes, but the

rabble dominates. Over there are white-collar types, bank clerks, salesmen, government clerks, journalists, pimps, officers in civilian dress, dandies in tails who dine in cheap restaurants and hurry out of the opera so as to be on time for the [Théâtre des] Italiens; and finally, a crowd of indescribable, dubious types. As for women, there is only one brand: the tart from the [Café] Américain, the two-louis prostitute, who chases five-louis foreigners but falls back on her regulars when she is free. They've been around for ten years now; they've been seen in the same places every evening all year long, except when they have to go to the Saint-Lazare or Lourcine hospitals for treatment.[163]

Because the *cafés-concerts* and music halls offered a continuous program, everyone could do as he liked: drink, eat, or smoke; read the paper, talk with other guests, stand up and walk about; come and go any time; conduct business or keep appointments. In other words these places allowed a kind of freedom that was in sharp constrast to the strict discipline required by the workday routine. And whereas the dramatic action on the legitimate stage developed logically over a specific period of time, these establishments featured a series of totally unconnected segments. This arrangement reflected the accelerated rhythm of modern life, which contemporaries constantly complained of as being "American," and corresponded to the speed of modern production and distribution methods.[164] A growing army of white-collar workers were now expected to spend their days in offices or behind counters, while the workday of the ordinary laborer was increasingly determined by the uniform throb of machines.

The variety of concurrent spectacles that made up the attraction of the *cafés-concerts* and music halls was even greater at the three expositions held in Paris during the Belle Epoque. Along with technical products demonstrating how radically the traditional way of life would be altered, there were carefully displayed historical or exotic idylls.[165] Eugen Weber has commented aptly that each of the three expositions marked the end of a crisis that shook the very foundations of France. Thus the exposition of 1878 signaled the end of the postwar period—the Republic's victory over the strong tendencies toward a royalist restoration. At the same time it demonstrated the renewed political awareness of the nation. The 1889 exposition coincided with the hundredth anniversary of the French Revolution and terminated the Boulanger crisis; that of 1900 not only took place at the start of a new century but after the conclusion of the Dreyfus affair.[166] This observation makes one suspect that these expositions served as substitutes for the revolutions and upheavals anticipated by contemporaries and to which many signs pointed.[167] All three expositions, each bigger and more splendid than its predecessors, counterposed a soaring optimism to the chronic fear of crises in the Belle Epoque. This attitude was epitomized in the iron construction of the Eiffel Tower, erected in conjunction with the exposition of 1889.

These expositions, with their *embarras de richesses* and monumental size, characterized by Walter Benjamin as "places of pilgrimage where goods are fetishized," were highpoints in the life of the Third Republic, but had only an indirect effect on that of the city.[168] Thanks to the hordes of foreign tourists who visited the expositions, the reputation of the French capital as the most dissolute metropolis was spread to the farthest corners of the world. In the 1870s Maxime Du Camp had already noted the following, apropos of the English who traditionally made up the largest contingent of foreign visitors:

> Foreigners admire, fill, and enrich Paris, where they . . . find places of entertainment that they themselves help to flourish by paying the high prices they later boast of having paid. But as soon as they return home and are sitting by their coal fires plagued by boredom, they can be heard to say: "That is the most immoral city in the world," and overlook the fact that they are responsible for at least half of the moral decay of which they accuse us.[169]

Every legend has a basis in fact. And the legend of Belle Epoque Paris as a world capital of pleasure and immorality was not too exaggerated. It was in the Paris of the late nineteenth century that the social and moral phenomena of modern life made their appearance, earlier and more conspicuously than in any other metropolis. That it happened there rather than in London or New York, both of which were then more modern in certain ways, is not surprising. Haussmann's plan had literally leveled and torn apart the old historic sections of the city. The wide new avenues and boulevards now enclosed not only the breeding grounds of disease and revolt, but also the small network of individual neighborhoods so different from one another that each had been almost autonomous. In the light of this development the Commune of 1871 can be interpreted as a drive by the *classes laborieuses* to recapture their old neighborhoods and to reconstruct life as it had been prior to the Second Empire.

These longings and hopes were finally destroyed with the bloody suppression of the Commune. Moreover, the rapid increase in population, which gave Paris close to 2.5 million inhabitants by 1914, firmly established the new functional and demographic organization undertaken by Haussmann. In this sense the transformation of Paris was the only truly successful revolution in Paris during the entire nineteenth century, creating by force the conditions of modern life.

The exuberant, festive whirl of the Belle Epoque, often compared to "a dance on top of a volcano," was society's way of coping with the deeply disturbing alienation of modern life.[170] It was significant that the *fête* was enjoyed not only in areas traditionally associated with entertainment, but became associated with Montmartre in particular.[171] That neighborhood had been a bastion of the Commune, and was still one of the few arrondissements that had been spared transformation. When the literary and artistic bohemians left their chosen cafés in the Latin Quarter in the late 1870s, they discovered the rural idyll of Montmartre with its windmills, vineyards, and gardens. They soon made this sleepy place popular with their artistic cabarets and artists' balls.[172] But Montmartre did not become the center of nightlife until after the Moulin Rouge opened its doors on October 6, 1889—an institution that has since become synonymous with Paris all over the world.[173]

Because of its unique location, the immediate and lasting success of the

Moulin Rouge was unaffected by the rise of similar establishments. Montmartre's narrow, irregular streets, its low houses, and its socially mixed population of bohemians and workers provided a great contrast to Haussmann's monumental, orderly, and alienating Paris. Montmartre fulfilled nostalgic and utopian expectations; it functioned as an antidote to the traumatic experience of modern urban life as manifested by the uniformity of building facades and the emphasis on class differences.

Montmartre's dissolute nightlife of dance-halls, music halls, cabarets, cafés, and restaurants, all open until the small hours, created an area accepted by society as exempt from the usual strict social control. Whoever plunged into this turbulent atmosphere freed himself from the constraints of everyday life and enjoyed the fact that bourgeois norms were actually disdained and mocked here. Montmartre was something like a year-long carnival, where anyone could become a different person for a few hours. One could abandon bourgeois respectability and take pleasure in disappearing in an alien but tempting milieu of bohemians, prostitutes, and criminals.

The great freedom of Montmartre typified the Belle Epoque and corresponded to the Paris of Maupassant's novel *Bel-Ami*, dominated by an avaricious and power-hungry society. The latter even had no scruples about using the atavistic custom of dueling to eliminate competitors and to advance socially. In the witches' sabbath of that "middle-class anarchy," as one Englishman defined the social and political conditions of the period, Montmartre was the last and most iridescent example that Paris was to set the world.[174] It is ironic that in the same city where the nineteenth century came on the heels of a revolution that promised "liberty, equality, and fraternity," it ended in the excesses of the Belle Epoque.

The motto on the Paris coat of arms reads *fluctuat, nec mergitur* (it is tossed by the waves but does not sink); its emblem is a sailing ship. The city's history did not end with the outbreak of World War I. It continued and will continue, for cities generally outlive empires that come and go. What did come to an end was the central role of Paris in the multifaceted drama of revolution and reaction, and its influence on the destiny of Europe.

Appendix

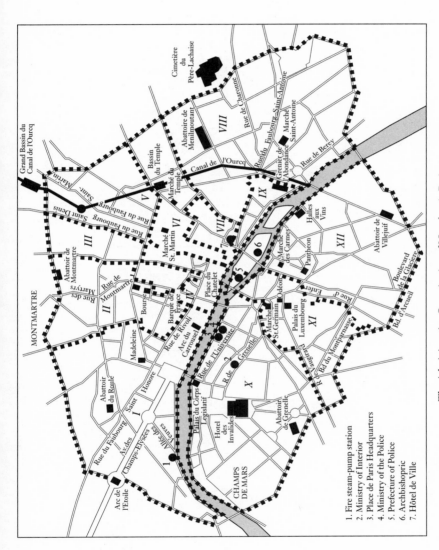

The Administrative Organization of Napoleonic Paris.

From Jean Tulard, Paris et son Administration, 1800–1830 *(Paris: Commission des Travaux Historiques XII, 1976).*

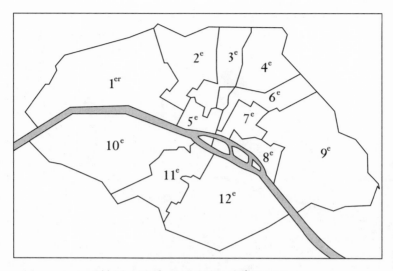

Old (*above*) and new (*below*) arrondissements.
From Louis Girard, La Deuxième République et le Second Empire, 1848–1870
(Paris: Diffusion Hachette, 1881).

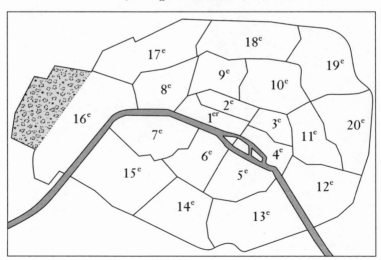

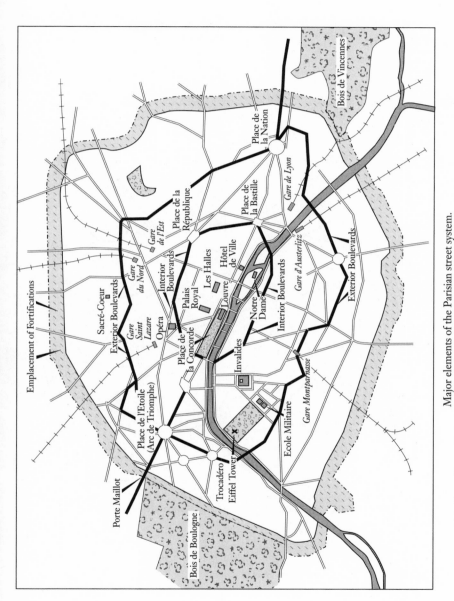

Major elements of the Parisian street system.

From Norma Evenson, *Paris: A Century of Change, 1878–1978 (New Haven and London: Yale University Press, 1979).*

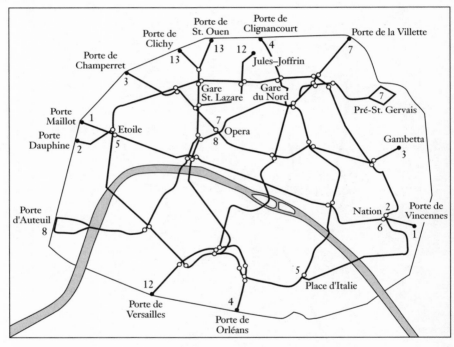

The Paris Metro in 1914.
From Pierre Lavedan, Histoire de l'Urbanisme à Paris *(Paris: Diffusion Hachette, 1975).*

Notes

BOOK ONE. Paris on the Eve of the Revolution

1 Albert Babeau, *Paris en 1789*, 2d ed. (Paris, 1892), p. 4.
2 Hippolyte Monin, *L'Etat de Paris en 1789* (Paris, 1889), pp. 5–9. See also Marcel Reinhard, *Paris pendant la Révolution* (Paris, 1966), 1: 16–19. For a view of the concerns of the Physiocrats, who idealized the life of the peasants and saw the cities as places of moral corruption, see Fougeret de Montbron, *La Capitale des Gaules, ou la Nouvelle Babilonne* (The Hague, 1760).
3 Babeau, *Paris*, p. 12.
4 At the same time the crown lost interest in limiting the city's expansion. The court, now at a considerable distance from the city, in Versailles, was no longer as bothered by the threat of a large population. Instead, it recognized that the sheer size of Paris offered great fiscal advantages. Necker, who was Louis XVI's minister of finance for some time, presented that fact very bluntly: "Taxes and duties of this large city now (in 1784) amount to 77 to 78 million annually, and represent the seventh or eighth part of the kingdom's total revenues. This tax yield is due to the great wealth concentrated in the capital." Jacques Necker, *De l'Administration des finances de la France* (Paris, 1784), 1: 275.
5 For the history and importance of the Quinze-Vingts, see Louis Le Grand, "Les Quinze-Vingts," in *Mémoires de la Société de l'Histoire de Paris* 13 (1887): 179–205. See also Monin, *L'Etat de Paris*, pp. 264–83.
6 Louis-Sébastien Mercier, *Tableau de Paris* (Amsterdam, 1783), 8: 190f. In this period the city developed more actively on the Right than on the Left Bank, mainly for topographical reasons. For discussion of these districts, developed by speculators at the end of the Old Regime, see Jacques-Antoine Dulaure, *Histoire physique, civile et morale de Paris*, 6th ed. (Paris, 1837–38), 7: 8. See also Monin, *L'Etat de Paris*, pp. 15–17.
7 For the history of the Palais-Royal see Victor Champier and G. Roger Sandoz, *Le Palais-Royal d'après des documents inédits* (Paris, 1900), vol. 1.
8 François-Auguste Fauveau baron de Frénilly, *Souvenirs 1768–1828*, 2d ed. (Paris, 1908), p. 24.
9 Henriette-Louise baronne d'Oberkirch, *Mémoires de la Baronne Oberkirch* (Paris, 1853), 2: 63.
10 See the detailed account by Amédée Britsch, *La Maison d'Orleans à la fin de l'Ancien Régime: La jeunesse de Philippe-Egalité 1747–1785* (Paris, 1926), pp. 303–51.
11 See *Exposé des changements à faire au Palais, imprimé par ordre de S.A.S. le duc de Chartres, Prince du Sang* (Paris, 1781).
12 *Ordonnance pour la police de locataires des maisons que l'on construit actuellement au pourtour du jardin du Palais-Royal* (3 mai, 1782), Archives Nationales, R-4, p. 282.

13 Babeau, *Paris*, p. 89.
14 Melchior von Grimm and Denis Diderot, *Correspondance littéraire, philosophique et critique* (Paris, 1813), 2: 535–37. There was still another reason for the prostitutes' preference for the avenues of the Palais-Royal—one directly connected with their profession, as Anne Henri de Dampmartin explained: "The number of the priestesses of Venus seems to increase every day, but especially at twilight. These unhappy victims of vice observe a strange system among themselves. Each avenue has its specific price and every one of these beauties knows how much she can charge. Uncertainty increases in proportion to the extent to which feminine charms are masked by darkness, and the price is lowered accordingly." Anne-Henri de Dampmartin, *Un Provincial à Paris pendant une partie de l'année 1789* (Strasbourg, n.d. [1789]), p. 172.
15 Britsch, *La Maison d'Orléans*, p. 340.
16 Grimm, *Correspondance*, 3: 95–96.
17 A woman who was granted the concession of a florist shop in the Palais-Royal charged more than six francs for a bunch of carnations that cost three to four francs in the flower market. Babeau, *Paris*, p. 95.
18 Mercier, *Tableau*, 10: 232.
19 Nikolai M. Karamzin, *Letters of a Russian Traveller 1789–1790*, ed. Florence Jonas (New York, 1957), p. 215.
20 Alfred Delveau, *Histoire anecdotique des cafés et cabarets de Paris* (Paris, 1862), pp. 57f.
21 See the detailed description of the cafés and restaurants in the Palais-Royal in Champier and Sandoz, *Le Palais-Royal*, 2: 115–34.
22 In his memoirs baron de Frénilly commented on this change in social behavior: "The taste for a comfortable and egoistic way of life created the clubs and multiplied the number of restaurants and cafés, which robbed a family of the chance to have a shared meal. The separation of the sexes caused a great void in gatherings and that was a big drawback, for the worst company for men are other men, and only women for women." Frénilly, *Souvenirs*, p. 82.
23 Marcel Reinhard, *La Révolution 1789–1799: Nouvelle Histoire de Paris* (Paris, 1971), p. 18. Mercier described the Palais-Royal as "a sort of academy, consisting of individuals from all the Estates"; Mercier, *Tableau*, 10: 224.
24 Frénilly, *Souvenirs*, pp. 79f. On hair and fashion in the latter part of the Old Regime, see Comte de Vaublanc, *Mémoires* (Paris, 1857), pp. 132–39.
25 Dampmartin, *Un Provincial à Paris*, p. 172.
26 Mercier, *Tableau*, 10: 220f.; elsewhere Mercier mentioned that the success of the Palais-Royal robbed other parts of the city of their vitality, so that they looked quite provincial, "dismal and uninhabited." Ibid., p. 232.
27 In 1789 Lavallée commented on the way in which construction and land speculation very quickly brought about social differences in the different sections of Paris: "Since Paris has become a completely new city, it is important for the public to realize that there are the better sections and bad ones, streets for duchesses and others for the bourgeoisie; and, finally, *rues perdues* for people who are ignored and for those who hide themselves." Joseph Lavallée, *Les Dernières Adieux du quai des Gesvres à la bonne ville de Paris* (London, 1787), pp. 28f.
28 Restif de la Bretonne described the neighborhood of the rue Saint-Honoré as "the quintessence of French urbanity" which, together with the adjacent Palais-Royal, formed the "brain of the capital." Restif de la Bretonne, *"Les Nuits de Paris," in Oeuvres*, ed. Henri Bachelin (Paris, 1930), 1: 35.
29 Reinhard, *La Révolution*, pp. 29f.
30 Mercier, *Tableau*, pp. 272f. By philosophes, Mercier meant the leading thinkers of the Enlightenment. Anne-Henri de Dampmartin's opinion of the Marais was somewhat more favorable; he described it as "a provincial enclave in the middle of Paris," in

which "the comforts of life on a country estate are combined with the affluence of Paris." See Dampmartin, *Un Provincial à Paris*, p. 31.

31 See George Rudé, *The Crowd in the French Revolution* (Oxford, 1959), pp. 16f. Mercier said of the faubourg Saint-Marcel: "This is the district in which lives the poorest, most restless, and least disciplined mob of all Paris. There is more money in a single house in the faubourg Saint-Honoré than there is in the entire faubourg Saint-Marcel." Mercier, *Tableau*, 1: 268.

32 Friedrich Schulz, *Über Paris und die Pariser* (Berlin, 1791), 1: 46f.

33 See Albert Demangeon, *Paris. La Ville et sa banlieue* (Paris, 1933), p. 16.

34 See description by Schulz, *Über Paris*, 1: 31f.

35 A thirty-six-foot-wide inner patrol road was created along the entire length of the wall, on the other side of which was a boulevard one hundred and eighty feet wide. Furthermore, construction of any type of building within three hundred feet of the wall was forbidden. Reinhard, *La Révolution*, p. 11.

36 Cited by Dulaure, *Histoire de Paris*, 7: 3.

37 See Rudé, *The Crowd*, p. 49.

38 See Reinhard, *La Révolution*, p. 25.

39 Necker, *De l'Administration*, 1: 277.

40 Léon Cahen, "La Population parisienne au milieu du XVIIIᵉ siècle," *La Revue de Paris* (1919), pp. 146–70.

41 Mercier was also horrified to note that cattle were slaughtered right out in the street in front of the butchers in the center of the city. Mercier, *Tableau*, 1: 123. Another example of this was given by Kaplow, who noted that in a very small stretch of the rue Saint-Martin there were no less than fifteen slaughterhouses. See Jeffry Kaplow, *Les Noms des rois: Les Pauvres de Paris à la veille de la Révolution* (Paris, 1974), p. 152.

42 Karamzin, *Letters*, pp. 184f. A new sensitivity to the city's trash and filth developed in the course of the eighteenth century. The first to express it was Jean-Jacques Rousseau. He

recalled his initial impressions of Paris in his *Confessions*, which he began writing in 1760:

My arrival in Paris really disappointed my expectations! The neatness I had seen in Turin, the well-kept streets, the symmetry and orderliness of the houses there, led me to expect still greater treasures. I had pictured a beautiful, large city, a very imposing view that would offer nothing but magnificent streets and palaces of marble and gold. But when I entered the city, coming from the faubourg Saint-Marceau, I saw only narrow, dirty, and fetid streets, miserable houses blackened by smoke, an atmosphere of griminess and poverty, with beggars, cobblers, and peddlers with and without pushcarts selling herbs or old hats. I was so disappointed that everything truly splendid I have seen since has not managed to rid me of my original impression, and has left me with a secret horror of living in this city.

Jean-Jacques Rousseau, *Les Confessions*, ed. Bernard Gagnebin and Marcel Raymond (Paris, 1959), p. 159.

43 Restif de la Bretonne, *Les Nuits*, p. 107.

44 See F. Boudon, A. Chastel, H. Couzy, and F. Hamon, *Système de l'Architecture urbaine: Le Quartier des Halles à Paris* (Paris, 1977).

45 Reinhard, *La Révolution*, p. 91. See also the drastic account of these conditions in J. J. Menuret de Chambaud, *Essais sur l'Histoire médico-topographique de Paris* (Paris, 1786), pp. 93–95.

46 Mercier, *Tableau*, 5: 101f.

47 Voltaire had already fought for a thorough cleanup of the city's center in his 1749 essay "Des Embellisemens de Paris," *Oeuvres complètes de Voltaire* (Kehl, 1786), 39: 163–74.

48 Monin, *L'Etat*, p. 13.

49 Babeau, *Paris*, p. 14.

50 For a discussion of complaints about the acquisition and tearing down of certain houses in the rue de la Pelleterie to make way for one of the quais of the Seine, see Charles-Louis Chassin, ed., *Les Elections et les cahiers de Paris en 1789* (Paris, 1889), 3: 387f.

51 Restitution to the owners of those houses and shops that lined the

Pont-au-Change and the Pont Marie and which were torn down under an edict of September 1786 amounted to the considerable sum of almost 4 million livres; see Babeau, *Paris*, p. 16. However, this sum was paid very reluctantly as shown by a complaint filed with the Estates General by a "Bourgeois de Paris"; see Chassin, *Les Elections*, 3: 389. The complaint was echoed in Article XVIII of the *Cahier du Tiers Etat de Paris*, ibid., p. 362. See also Article VI of the *Cahier particulier de la Ville de Paris*, ibid., pp. 402f.

52   Jacqueline Thibaut-Payen, *Les Morts, l'église et l'état. Recherches d'histoire administrative sur la sépulture et les cimetières dans le ressort du Parlement de Paris au XVIIe et XVIIIe siècles* (Paris, 1977).

53   Jacques Hillairet, *Les 200 Cimetières du vieux Paris* (Paris, 1958).

54   Mercier dedicated a nice essay to the "Ecrivains des Charniers-Innocents." Mercier, *Tableau*, 1: 266–68.

55   Kaplow, *Les Noms des rois*, pp. 181f.

56   Mercier, *Tableau*, 9: 322. These figures given by Mercier appear to be exaggerated. Madeleine Foisil, who based her research on various registers of deaths for the first half of the eighteenth century, calculated that there were on average 1,800 burials a year in the Saints-Innocents cemetery. Madeleine Foisil, "Les Attitudes devant la mort au XVIIIe siècle: Sépultures et suppressions de sépultures dans le cimetière parisien des Saints-Innocents," *La Revue Historique* 251 (1974): 312.

57   Repeated complaints by residents in the Saints-Innocents neighborhood forced the *Parlement de Paris* to commission a committee of scientists to investigate conditions. The committee, which included two doctors and a pharmacist, reported that the strong odors in the area did not come solely from the graves but were also due to an open sewer that ran along the rue de la Ferronerie. This sewer, which carried the contents of toilets as well as the kitchen garbage that residents threw out of their windows, was so small that it overflowed frequently and spilled its reeking contents into the cemetery. The committee recommended first of all that the sewer be closed off immediately; they suggested that the cemetery then be divided into ten sections, each of which was to hold a mass grave, twice as deep as was current practice. Only one of these mass graves was to be used each year, so that the corpses could remain there undisturbed for at least ten years. It was thought that this would give the corpses sufficient time to decompose. Bibliothèque Nationale, Fonds Joly de Fleury 1317, fols. 61r–73v.

58   Mercier, *Tableau*, 9: 323.

59   Bibliothèque Nationale, Fonds Joly de Fleury, 1209 (printed copy of the parliamentary decree of March 12, 1763).

60   Ibid., 1207.

61   *Mémoire des Curés de Paris à l'occasion des arrêts du 12 mars, 21 mai, 23 septembre, 1763, sur le déplacement des cimetières.* Bibliothèque Nationale, Fonds Joly de Fleury, 1207, fol. 19. The royal decree of March 10, 1776, was a typical example of the monarchy's weakness when its laws conflicted with inherited traditions. This law promulgated the closure of all inner-city cemeteries; it prohibited burial in churches and insisted on the establishment of burial sites outside city limits, while expressly providing a separate arrangement for Paris. See also Jacques Michel, *Du Paris de Louis XV à la marine de Louis XVI: L'Oeuvre de monsieur de Sartine* (Paris, 1983), 1: 123f.

62   Archives Nationales, x b 8975.

63   Ibid.

64   Philippe Ariès, *L'Homme devant la mort* (Paris, 1977), p. 489.

65   Archives Nationales, Z.I. O 222, *Informations et procédures relatives à la suppression et extinction du cimetière des Innocents.*

66   A. Thouret, *Rapport sur les exhumations du cimetière et de l'église des Saints-Innocents, Histoire de la Société royale de Médecine* 8 (1786): 238–71. Even at the beginning of the nine-

teenth century excavations for the construction of an aqueduct uncovered further mass graves that were cleared. See Dulaure, *Histoire de Paris*, 7: 227f. And in giving temporary burial to victims of the street fighting during the July Revolution of 1830, various human skeletons were discovered in the place du Marché des Innocents. N. M. Troche, *Notice historique sur les inhumations provisoires faites sur la place du Marché des Innocents* (Paris, 1837), pp. 14f.

67 Jean-Jacques Menuret de Chambaud, *Essai sur l'action de l'air dans les maladies contagieuses* (Paris, 1781).

68 Alain Corbin, *Le Miasme et la jonquille: L'odorat et l'imaginaire sociale XVIIIᵉ–XIXᵉ siècles* (Paris, 1982).

69 For instance, the *Cahier général* of the Third Estate of Paris, for the Estates General of 1789, sets out: "The City Council will investigate whether it might not be advantageous to move all cemeteries, slaughterhouses, tallow presses, and any factories that have large quantities of burnable refuse, outside the city gates, so as to isolate them; the same should be done with all workshops that release dangerous gases." See Chassin, *Les Elections*, 3: 362; see also Art. XII of *Cahier particulier de la ville de Paris*, ibid., p. 405.

70 Mercier, *Tableau*, 3: 137. See also Georges Montorgueil, *Les Eaux et les fontaines de Paris* (Paris, 1928).

71 Mercier, *Tableau*, 3: 141. See also Schulz, *Über Paris*, pp. 63f.

72 The first area to be supplied with tap water by the Périer brothers was, as Mercier observed critically, the faubourg Saint-Honoré. Its generally wealthy inhabitants were those most likely to be able to afford the installation costs in addition to water rates. Mercier, *Tableau*, 3: 139. Friedrich Schulz described the Périer Brothers system in detail:

A building, set firm as a rock over a branch of the Seine, houses two steam engines; each of these daily raises 48,600 buckets of water one hundred feet to the heights of Chaillot, whence it is distributed throughout Paris. The water main runs from Chaillot through the rue du faubourg Saint-Honoré, across the old boulevards to the gate of Saint-Antoine, a distance of over one German mile. The water is stored and purified in four large reservoirs located in four districts of the city before it reaches the public. Conduits run from the reservoirs and from these smaller pipes supply the hotels and bourgeois households that have subscribed to the service....There are several large tubs in the subscribers' houses into which the water flows and which have a sediment of particles because of the purification.

Schulz, *Über Paris*, pp. 60f. The Périer Brothers' water system expanded relatively quickly according to Mercier, who complained that the city's streets were torn up everywhere to repair the burst wooden water conduits, or to lay new ones. Mercier, *Tableau*, 11: 105. For an account of the Périer brothers, see J. Payen, *Les Frères Périer et l'introduction de la machine à vapeur de Watt à Paris* (Paris, 1969).

73 Gérard Jacquemet, "Urbanisme parisien: La bataille du tout-à-l'égout à la fin du XIXᵉ siècle," *La Revue d'Histoire moderne et contemporaine* 26 (1979): 525.

74 Antoine Laurent Lavoisier, *Oeuvres* (Paris, 1868) 3: 255.

75 Mercier, *Tableau*, 3: 139.

76 Ibid., 11: 104.

77 Ibid., 1: 136f. Large pits had been dug out close to the knacker's yard in Montfaucon, in the northeast of Paris, for the disposal of human excrement. In 1789 a group of citizens issued a pamphlet concerning this practice, which stated that these pits did not solve the problems of hygiene and horrible odors. The pamphlet was titled *Mémoire concernant les voiries*, and mentioned the following:

Trash collected daily in Paris is heaped up between the new customs posts of Saint-Denis and des Vertus. Right next to it is the bullfight arena, which constitutes another cesspool. The wild animals on show there are fed with horse cadavers from the knacker's yard nearby. Not far from there, by the new customs post of Saint-Martin and close to the Saint-

Louis Hospital ... is a pit of about four acres in which fecal matter from cesspools is disposed of each day....All the odors and miasmas from waste and decomposing cadavers that add to the pollution of the noxious air are concentrated in a fairly small area.

See Chassin, *Les Elections*, 3: 366. See also Article VIII of the *Cahier particulier de la Ville de Paris*, ibid., pp. 403f. The bullfight arena, which the Abbé Delagrive's city plan of 1728 showed in the rue de Sèvres, was moved to the vicinity of the Saint-Louis Hospital in 1778. According to the few available accounts of this strange spectacle, the arena was used exclusively for all sorts of animal fights: bulldogs against bulls, wild boars, wolves, or bears. Bullfights were prohibited in 1790. Sigismond Lacroix, ed., *Actes de la Commune de Paris et de la Seine pendant la Révolution* (*Collection de documents relatifs à l'histoire de Paris pendant la Révolution française*) (Paris, 1894–1914), 7: 544–50. See also Jacques Hillairet, *Dictionnaire historique des rues de Paris*, 7th ed. (Paris, 1963), 1: 370f., and 2: 521.

78 See Michel, *Du Paris de Louis XV*, p. 127.

79 Mercier, *Tableau*, 7: 231f.

80 Ibid., 1: 129.

81 Ibid., pp. 129f.

82 Ibid., 11: 54f.

83 Ibid., 7: 225f.

84 Ibid., 5: 328.

85 The first Paris street to have a pavement was the rue du Théâtre-Français, newly built in the 1780s, today the rue de l'Odéon. See Babeau, *Paris*, p. 34.

86 Arthur Young, *Voyages en France en 1787, 1788 et 1789*, ed. Henri Sée (Paris, 1931), 1: 201.

87 Schulz, *Über Paris*, p. 37.

88 Waterspouts were forbidden in 1764, but as happened so frequently, the restriction had little effect. According to an estimate, there were still about 50,000 spouts at the end of the Old Regime. See Babeau, *Paris*, p. 37.

89 Young, *Voyages*, 1: 201. Mercier also pointed out the danger of these light carriages, in his *Tableau*, 1: 117, and 6: 81.

90 Ibid., pp. 1–7, and 10: 277–80.

91 There were about 1,000 *fiacres* or hackneys toward the end of the Old Regime—they took their name from the place Saint-Fiacre—that waited for customers at about forty different locations. A ride cost 1 livre 4 sous during the day, and 6 additional sous at night. Young, *Voyages*, 1: 202, n. 3.

92 The oil in these lamps was distilled from animal fat rendered from entrails. Mercier, *Tableau*, 1: 212, and 10: 246. For the operation of these oil lamps and a discussion of the lighting system, see Auguste Philippe Herlaut, *L'Eclairage de Paris à l'époque révolutionnaire* (Paris, 1932), pp. 17, 27. This type of lighting brought numerous complaints. On October 20, Arthur Young protested: "There are endless cafés, music, noise, and prostitutes. There is everything except street sweepers and lights. Your feet get stuck in solid sludge and entire sections of the boulevards are completely unlit." Young, *Voyages*, 1: 196f. Nor were streetlights turned on when the moon was full, an economy severely criticized by Mercier because, he argued, light shed by the moon was ineffective in narrow, overly built-up streets. Mercier, *Tableau*, 1: 212. Similar complaints were voiced by various sources in 1789 in connection with preparations for the Estates General. See Chassin, *Les Elections*, 2: 439, 466, 478.

93 Mercier, *Tableau*, 6: 218f.

94 Ibid., 6: 238, 9: 292–97.

95 Ibid., 2: 267f.

96 Ibid., 5: 283.

97 Ibid., pp. 249–54.

98 Ibid., 6: 82f.

99 Begging in the streets was considered a punishable offense under the Old Regime, as it was thought that all needs were adequately taken care of; consequently, no one had the right to beg with the exception of the inmates of the Quinze-Vingts. For the poor who were able to work

there were a number of *ateliers de charité*, or workhouses, whereas the sick and crippled found refuge in shelters and hospices. Whoever was caught begging was arrested and, if of male sex, was put into the Bicêtre prison; arrested females were incarcerated in the Salpêtrière prison. Characteristically for the Old Regime, both institutions served as hospitals as well as correction facilities and prisons. Despite harsh and repressive police measures, the many unemployed increased the number of street beggars to an extent that shocked contemporaries, who saw this steadily swelling army of the dispossessed as an ever-increasing danger to property, public safety, and order. Mercier, who strongly criticized the severe and barbaric methods used to eliminate this social problem, attested: "The excuse was that poverty necessarily led to crime, and that groups of this size, who had nothing to lose, plotted riots." Ibid., 3: 216f.

100 Babeau, *Paris*, p. 60.
101 Mercier, *Tableau*, 3: 267–73.
102 Ibid., 4: 146–64.
103 Cited by Reinhard, *La Révolution*, p. 41.
104 Jean-Jacques Rousseau, *Julie, ou la nouvelle Héloïse*, ed. Henri Coulet and Bernard Guyon (Paris, 1964), p. 235.
105 Henri (Jacob Heinrich) Meister, *Souvenirs de mon dernier voyage à Paris (1795)*, ed. Paul Usteri and Eugène Ritter (Paris, 1910), pp. 163–65. See also Jacques de Norvins, *Mémorial*, ed. Lanzac de Laborie (Paris, 1897), 1: 160–70.
106 Meister, *Souvenirs*, p. 167.
107 Norvins, *Mémorial*, 1: 208.
108 Quoted by Reinhard, *Paris*, 1: 81.
109 Mercier, *Tableau*, 12: 100.
110 An exact class definition of the *peuple* that tried to differentiate between workers and independent artisans who had their own business would fail to take into account preindustrial social reality. Rudé, *The Crowd*, pp. 18f.
111 Jeffry Kaplow, "Sur la Population flottante de Paris à la fin de l'Ancien

Régime," *Annales Historiques de la Révolution française 39* (1967): 1–14.
112 Albert Soboul, *Les Sans-Culottes parisiens en l'an II: Mouvement populaire et gouvernement révolutionnaire 2 juin 1793–9 thermidor an II* (Paris, 1958), p. 440.
113 Des Essarts, "Ouvrier," in *Dictionnaire de la police . . .* (Paris, 1786), 7: 458–64, cited by Reinhard, *La Révolution*, p. 75. See also Rudé, *The Crowd*, p. 18.
114 Mercier, *Tableau*, 4: 29–38.
115 Ibid., 2: 208–12, and 3: 76–78.
116 In this connection see Alfred Franklin, *Dictionnaire historique des arts, métiers et professions exercés dans Paris depuis le XIIIe siècle* (Paris, 1906).
117 Mercier, *Tableau*, 3: 217–19.
118 Ibid., 9: 317.
119 1 livre = 20 sous; 1 sou = 12 deniers.
120 Reinhard, *La Révolution*, p. 77. See also Kaplow, *Les noms des rois*, p. 100.
121 In addition to Sundays and the traditionally work–free Mondays, there were various other holidays under the Old Regime. This meant a loss of pay on about 150 days a year for the individual worker, so that real wages were less than a third of the nominal amount. George Rudé, "Prices, Wages and Popular Movements in Paris during the French Revolution," *Economic History Review 6*, no. 3 (1954): 248 n.
122 C. E. Labrousse, *Esquisse du mouvement des prix et des revenus en France au XVIIIe siècle* (Paris, 1933), 2: 597–608.
123 A working-class family of five needed a daily bread ration of at least six pounds. Alexander Tuetey, *L'Assistance publique à Paris pendant la Révolution* (Paris, 1895), 1: cxxvi.
124 See Rudé, "Prices, Wages," p. 248, Table I. It is surely unreasonable to assume that a worker spent 80 or 97 percent of his real wages on bread over a period of weeks and months. As a rule up to 50 percent of real wages was spent on this basic food item; 16 percent went for vegetables, fats, and wine, 15 percent for clothing, 5 percent for heating and light, and 10–15 percent for lodging. Georges Lefebvre, "Le Mouvement des prix

et les origines de la Révolution française," *Annales historiques de la Révolution française* 14 (1937): 315. On the miserable conditions in which the *peuple* lived, see Daniel Roche, *Le Peuple de Paris: La Culture populaire au XVIIIᵉ siècle* (Paris, 1981), pp. 66–94.

125 Mercier, *Tableau*, 11: 43.
126 Claude Delasselle, "Les Enfants abandonnées à Paris," *Annales E.S.C.* 30, no. 1 (1975): 187–216.
127 Mercier, *Tableau*, 6: 26.
128 Restif de la Bretonne, *Les Nuits*, p. 103.
129 Mercier, *Tableau*, 10: 3f.
130 Kaplow, *Les Noms des rois*, pp. 192–217.
131 Mercier, *Tableau*, 3: 95–97.
132 Ibid., 1: 62f.
133 See Chassin, *Les Elections*, 3: 424f.
134 Mercier, *Tableau*, 3: 216f.
135 In connection with this see Christian Poultre, *De la Répression de la mendicité et du vagabondage en France sous l'Ancien Régime* (Paris, 1906).
136 Mercier, *Tableau*, 3: 216, 11: 340f.
137 Guillaume François Letrosne, *Mémoire sur les vagabonds et sur les mendiants* (Soissons and Paris, 1764), p. 8.
138 See Kaplow, *Les Noms des rois*, pp. 223f.
139 Cited by Mercier, *Tableau*, 4: 313.
140 Ibid., 8: 2. See also Honoré Gabriel Riquetti Comte de Mirabeau, "Observations d'un Voyageur anglais sur la maison de force appelée Bicêtre," *Oeuvres de Mirabeau* (Paris, 1822), 6: 209–74.
141 Mercier, *Tableau*, 3: 225–27.
142 Dupont de Nemours, *Idées sur les Secours à donner aux pauvres malades dans une grande ville* (Paris, 1786).
143 Mercier, *Tableau*, 3: 233f.
144 Ibid., 1: 54.
145 Ibid., 2: 64.
146 Rudé, *The Crowd*, p. 46.
147 Mercier, *Tableau*, 12: 6.

BOOK TWO. Capital of the Revolution 1789–1799

1 See the description in Arthur Young, *Voyages en France en 1787, 1788 et 1789*, ed. Henri Sée (Paris, 1931), 1:

272–74. See also Camille Desmoulins, *Lettres à son père*, ed. E. Despois (Paris, 1865), 2: 65.
2 Only 11,706 of the 30,000 members of the Third Estate actually voted. See Charles Louis Chassin, ed., *Les Elections et les Cahiers de Paris en 1789* (Paris, 1888–89), 1: 376, 402, 2: 319.
3 See the devious official reason given in ibid., 1: 120.
4 See ibid., 1: 257, 278, 421f.
5 See the text of the *Cahier de doléances du Tiers Etat de Paris*, ibid., 3: 234–37, 333–64.
6 For a detailed account of this unrest see George Rudé, *The Crowd in the French Revolution* (Oxford, 1959), pp. 34–44. See also Chassin, *Elections*, 3: 48–142.
7 Jules Michelet believed that delay in acting on the part of the authorities was intentional rather than incompetent. He argued that a larger demonstration would have given Louis XVI a welcome excuse to postpone the meeting of the Estates General indefinitely. Jules Michelet, *Histoire de la Révolution française*, ed. Gérard Walter (Paris, 1952), 1: 84–87.
8 No mention was made of these events in the minutes of the Paris Assembly. This is all the more surprising as the Réveillon affair caused postponement of the April 28 meeting to April 29. Only those delegates who belonged to the nobility considered the uprising in their meeting on April 29. See Chassin, *Elections*, 3: 144f.
9 Ibid., pp. 245f.
10 George Garrigues, *Les Districts parisiens pendant la Révolution Française* (Paris, 1931).
11 Note the objections raised by the royal administration of Paris; Chassin, *Elections*, 3: 440f., 445.
12 See ibid., p. 442. The complete text of this resolution is contained in Bailly and Duveyrier, eds., *Procès-verbal des séances et déliberations de l'Assemblée Générale des électeurs de Paris* (Paris, 1790), 1: 88–94.
13 Chassin, *Elections*, 3: 475.
14 In fact this motion on a citizens'

militia, proposed by Nicolas de Bonneville on June 25, 1789, was not entered in the minutes until July 10. It was then that the bourgeoisie began to be afraid of the growing unrest among the population of the faubourgs.

15 S. P. Hardy, *Mes Loisirs, ou journal d'événements tels qu'ils parviennent à ma connaissance*, Bibliothèque Nationale, Fonds Français 6687, fol. 365. Hardy's entry was confirmed by the report of a police informer made the same day. See Chassin, *Elections*, 3: 455. On Hardy, see Charles Aubertin, "Le Bourgeois de Paris au dix-huitième siècle," *La Revue des deux mondes* 86 (1871): 199f. For further evidence of public agitation in the Palais-Royal, see Charles-Jean-Dominique de Lacretelle, *Histoire de l'assemblée constituante* (Paris, 1821), 1: 61; and François Louis Comte d'Escherny, *Correspondance d'un habitant de Paris avec ses amis de Suisse et d'Angleterre sur les événements de 1789, 1790 et jusqu'au 4 avril 1791* (Paris, 1791), 17f.

16 Details of this action can be found in *Récit de l'élargissement forcé et la rentrée volontaire des Gardes Françaises dans la prison de l'Abbaye* (Paris, 1789), Bibliothèque Nationale, Lb 39–1883; and in Hardy, *Mes Loisirs*, fols. 373f.

17 *Archives parlementaires de 1787 à 1860. Recueil complet des débats législatifs et politiques des Chambres françaises, imprimé par ordre du Sénat et de la Chambre des députés, fondé par Mavidal et Laurent, continué par L. Lataste, L. Claveau, C. Pionnier, A. Ducom et H. Lemaire, Iʳᵉ série: 1787–1799* (Paris, 1875), 8: 184. See also Chassin, *Elections*, 3: 462–64.

18 Ibid., p. 459.

19 Hardy, *Mes Loisirs*, fols. 377–85.

20 François Louis Comte d'Escherny, *Correspondance d'un habitant de Paris*, pp. 24f.

21 Camille Desmoulins, *Oeuvres*, ed. Jules Claretie (Paris, 1874), 2: 199. See also René Fargé, "Camille Desmoulins au jardin du Palais-Royal," *Annales révolutionnaires* 7 (1914): 646–74.

22 Chassin, *Elections*, 3: 492f.

23 Victor Clerq, "L'Incendie des barrières de Paris en juillet 1789 et le procès des incendiaires," in *Bulletin de la société de l'histoire de Paris et de l'Ile-de-France* (1981), pp. 117–49.

24 Abbé Lamourette, *Désastre de la maison de Saint-Lazare* (Paris, 1789), Bibliothèque Nationale, Lb 39–1942. See also Comte d'Escherny, *Correspondance*, pp. 54f.

25 Chassin, *Elections*, 3: 495.

26 Hardy, *Mes Loisirs*, fol. 386.

27 *Mémoires de Linguet sur la Bastille et de Dusaulx sur le 14 juillet*, ed. MM. Berville and Barrière (Paris, 1821), p. 283.

28 The duc d'Aumont declined to serve (on the morning of July 14) and Lasalle became the sole commander of the citizens' militia. Chassin, *Elections*, 3: 516.

29 Hardy, *Mes Loisirs*, fol. 387.

30 Chassin, *Elections*, 3: 511.

31 Ibid., pp. 513f.

32 Bailly and Duveyrier, *Procès-verbal*, 1: 272.

33 Albert Mathiez, *Les grandes Journées de la Constituante 1789–1791* (Paris, 1913), pp. 22f.

34 The governor of the Hôtel des Invalides later claimed that thirty thousand muskets had been taken by the plunderers. Bailly and Duveyrier, *Procès-verbal*, 1: 371.

35 Ibid., pp. 307–59. There is also a good account in Chassin, *Elections*, 3: 522–35. For a more detailed version see Jacques Godechot, *La Prise de la Bastille, 14 juillet 1789* (Paris, 1965).

36 According to the official report which Jean Dusaulx later made to the Paris Assembly, ninety-eight of the attackers lost their lives and seventy-three were wounded. Jean Dusaulx, *De l'Insurrection parisienne et de la prise de la Bastille* (Paris, 1790) pp. 161f.

37 See the report by Lieutenant de Flue, one of the defenders of the Bastille, in Eugène Fieffe, *Histoire des troupes étrangères au service de la France* (Paris, 1854), 1: 339–56.

38 Hardy, *Mes Loisirs*, p. 398.

39 Comte d'Escherny, *Correspondance*, pp. 75–78.

40 Rudé, *The Crowd*, pp. 56–59. See also Joseph Durieux, *Les Vainqueurs de la Bastille* (Paris, 1911), pp. 261–64.

41 Michelet, *Histoire de la Révolution*, 1: 145.

42 Bailly and Duveyrier, *Procès verbal*, 2: 1–5. A charming description of the dismantlement is given by François René Vicomte de Chateaubriand, *Mémoires d'outre-tombe*, ed. Maurice Levaillant and Georges Moulinier (Paris, 1951), 1: 168f.

43 The actual condition of the city's food supplies was revealed in a decision of the hastily formed *Comité pour la Sûreté publique et la Subsistance de la Ville* (Committee on Public Security), of July 20, appointing a commission to investigate and register grain and flour supplies in all the monasteries in and around Paris. Chassin, *Elections*, 3: 587.

44 In the eyes of the people they were typical of the profiteers in the Old Regime. Foullon, who wanted to become Necker's successor, was supposedly responsible for the dreadful statement going around Paris that, "If they're hungry, let them eat grass! . . . Be patient! When I'm minister, I'll give them hay; my horses live off it as well." Cited by Michelet, *Histoire de la Révolution*, 1: 183f. After July 14, Foullon and Berthier disappeared. Berthier tried to flee, but Foullon thought he could save himself by a macabre comedy. He let it be known that he had had a stroke, and the elaborate burial ceremony he arranged was intended to convince even those who distrusted him. See marquis de Ferrières, *Mémoires*, ed. MM. Berville and Barrière (Paris, 1822), 1: 155. For a detailed description of the lynching of the two men, see Bailly and Duveyrier, *Procès-verbal*, 2: 237–325. See also Jean Sylvain Bailly, *Mémoires*, ed. Saint-Albin Berville and Jean-François Barrière (Paris, 1821), 2: 99–123.

45 *Procès-verbal de la formation et des opérations du Comité militaire de la Ville de Paris: Ire partie, du 16 juillet au 30 septembre 1789* (Paris, 1789), Bibliothèque Nationale, Lf. 133–122.

46 In addition to this National Guard, which was a true citizens' militia, Lafayette also created a paid police regiment that was housed in barracks, divided into companies, and available when needed. These men were recruited from the former Gardes françaises and other military units. Each of the sixty districts had such a *Companie du centre* assigned to it.

47 See Bailly's communication to the districts on July 23, 1789, in Chassin, *Elections*, 3: 629f. But the districts did not agree to this plan. On August 1 it was therefore decided to let each district elect an additional representative to the *Assemblée des Représentants*. See *Actes de la Commune de Paris et de la Seine pendant la Révolution*, ed. Sigismond Lacroix (Paris, 1894–1914), Ire série, 1: 75f. Bailly was not very happy about this; see Bailly, *Mémoires*, 2: 196f.

48 *Les Révolutions de Paris* described the ensuing confusion in its issue of August 9–15, 1789:

    The dissension that exists in the districts, the contradictions between their principles, their decisions and their actions, as well as their intentions that run contrary to those of the city administration, present a picture of dreadful anarchy, now that the immediate danger is past. Imagine an individual whose feet, hands, and limbs have a mind and will of their own; whose one foot wants to walk, while the other wants to stand still; whose gullet closes while his stomach needs nourishment; whose mouth sings while his eyes are heavy with sleep; that corresponds, in all its details, to the pitiful condition of the capital.

49 *Actes de la Commune*, Ire série, 2: 42f.

50 An overview of this communal constitution is given by S. Lacroix, ibid., pp. x–xi.

51 De Capello, the Venetian ambassador in Paris, reported that 200,000 passports were issued between July 14 and September 10. See Maxim Maximovitch Kovalevski, ed., *I Dispacci degli ambasciatori veneti alla corte di Francia durante la Rivoluzione*

(Turin, 1885), 1: 62. The Marquise de la Tour du Pin commented drily in her memoirs: "In France everything is a question of fashion; at that time it was fashionable to emigrate. People took a great deal of money to their country estates, to be able to have a large sum available. Many who had creditors thought it was a way of eluding them." *Mémoires de la marquise de la Tour du Pin, Journal d'une femme de cinquante ans (1778–1815)*, ed. Comte Christian de Liederkerke Beaufort (Paris, 1983), p. 107.

52 Bailly, *Mémoires*, 2: 254. See also Chevalier de Beaurepaire, *Rapport à MM. du district des Pétits Mathurins*, Bibliothèque Nationale, Lb 40–285.

53 *Actes de la Commune*, Iʳᵉ série, 1: 260f.

54 Eric Magnus Baron de Staël-Holstein, *Correspondance diplomatique du Baron de Staël-Holstein et de son successeur le Baron Brinkman*, ed. Léonzun LeDuc (Paris, 1881), p. 126.

55 Hardy notes, for instance, that four hundred domestic servants gathered in the Palais-Royal on August 29, 1789, to demand "their rights as citizens to participate in the various district assemblies, and to request the honor of serving in the National Guard." See Hardy, *Mes Loisirs*, fol. 455.

56 *Actes de la Commune*, Iʳᵉ série, 1: 124.

57 Ibid., pp. 229, 298, 435. See also Bailly, *Mémoires*, 2: 341.

58 See *Actes de la Commune*, Iʳᵉ série, 2: 29, 39f.

59 Cited by François Furet and Denis Richet, *Die Französiche Revolution* (Munich, 1981), 118f.

60 *Actes de la Commune*, Iʳᵉ série, 2: 160–62.

61 Camille Desmoulins, for instance, tried to incite the crowd in the Palais-Royal to do just that. See Mathiez, *Les grandes Journées, p.* 75.

62 A summary of the various reports and accounts is given in Maurice Tourneux, *Bibliographie de l'histoire de Paris pendant la Révolution française* (Paris, 1890), vol. 1, nos. 1405–1573; and Alexandre Tuetey, *Répertoire général des sources manuscrites de l'his-toire de Paris pendant la Révolution française* (Paris, 1890), 1: 947–1039.

63 Rudé, *The Crowd*, pp. 73f.

64 *Actes de la Commune*, Iʳᵉ série, 2: 165.

65 Hardy, *Mes Loisirs*, fol. 502.

66 *Actes de la Commune*, Iʳᵉ série, 2: 171.

67 A good description is provided by the Comte d'Escherny, *Correspondance*, pp. 184–86.

68 For a description of the Tuileries Palace, see Antoine-Nicolas Dezallier d'Argenville, *Voyage pittoresque de Paris ou description de tout ce qu'il y a de plus beau*, 5th ed. (Paris, 1770), pp. 58–71.

69 Comte d'Escherny, *Correspondance*, p. 196.

70 *Actes de la Commune*, Iʳᵉ série, 2: 248, 255–56. See also Comte d'Escherny, *Correspondance*, p. 204.

71 *Adresse de l'Assemblée générale des représentants de la Commune de Paris, présentée à l'Assemblée nationale, le samedi 10 octobre 1789* (Paris, 1789), Bibliothèque Nationale, Lb 40–28; *Actes de la Commune*, Iʳᵉ série, 2: 248.

72 *Adresse de l'Assemblée générale des représentants de la Commune de Paris à tous les habitants de Paris pour le maintien de la tranquilité publique et du respect à l'Assemblée nationale, du 15 octobre 1789* (Paris, 1789), Bibliothèque Nationale, Lb 40–30.

73 *Actes de la Commune*, Iʳᵉ série, 2: 343f., 355–57.

74 The law stated that any assemblies that presented a threat to public law and order were to be broken up. If after three requests by security forces the crowd still refused to obey, a red flag would be hoisted and the crowd would be fired upon. Ibid., pp. 385f.

75 Ibid., pp. 364–67.

76 Maximilien Robespierre, "Discours," in *Oeuvres de Maximilien Robespierre*, ed. Marc Bouloiseau, Georges Lefebvre, and Albert Soboul (Paris, 1950), 6: 122f.

77 A similar stand was taken by Paris districts on Lafayette's suggestion of forming a troop of well-paid *chasseurs des barrières* to supervise and collect customs duties at the Paris city limits. *Actes de la Commune*, Iʳᵉ série, 2: 391f.

78 Robespierre, *Oeuvres*, 6: 349f.

79 Ernest Mellié, *Les Sections de Paris pendant la Révolution française* (Paris, 1898), pp. 9–22, 41f.

80 Mellié, *Les Sections*, pp. 93–143.

81 *Actes de la Commune*, Iᵣₑ série, 4: i–xv; see also *Adresse de la Commune de Paris dans ses soixante sections à l'Assemblée nationale* (Paris, 1790), Bibliothèque Nationale, Lb 40–90. This address was supported by fifty-three of the sixty districts.

82 *Archives parlementaires*, 12: 264f.

83 Details in *Actes de la Commune*, Iᵣₑ série, 5: ii–xv.

84 Talleyrand-Périgord, the recorder of the *Comité de constitution* of the National Assembly, reasoned on June 8 that this limitation was justified because

a free nation is characterized by the ability of everyone who meets the necessary requirements to participate in the legislative process as an active citizen, and to defend it as a soldier. If the nation is called upon to attend the national celebration, it is considered an appeal to all citizens in their capacity as soldiers. Then it is a France that comes ready for battle and not a France prepared for exhaustive discussion (*Archives parlementaires*, 16: 139–41).

In his speech to the National Assembly on June 5, Bailly referred specifically to a "Pact of all Estates and the National Guard." *Actes de la Commune*, Iᵣₑ série, 5: 731. De Charon, Chairman of the *Assemblée des députés pour le pacte fédératif*, who protested the limitation in a letter to Le Chapelier, president of the National Assembly, emphasized that "the city of Paris had not merely proposed an alliance between the troops and the National Guard, but rather a general union of all Frenchmen"; he went on to say: "There is no question that all citizens are soldiers, too; but Frenchmen should be invited to this pact of brotherhood as citizens as well as soldiers." Ibid., p. 734.

85 See the description by Bailli de Virieu in *La Révolution française racontée par un diplomat étranger. Correspondance du Bailli de Virieu*, ed.

Emmanuel vicomte de Grouchy and Antoine Guillois (Paris, 1903), pp. 201–4. See also Louis-Sébastien Mercier, *Paris pendant la Révolution, 1789–1798, ou le Nouveau Paris* (Paris, 1862), 1: 66–72; and marquise de la Tour du Pin, *Mémoires*, p. 129f.

86 Mona Ozouf, *La Fête révolutionnaire, 1789–1799* (Paris, 1976).

87 At the end of December this hiérodrame was given another performance at the Paris Opera and called *La Prise de la Bastille* ("The Taking of the Bastille"). Bailli de Virieu, *Correspondance*, p. 233.

88 Ibid., pp. 204f.

89 G. Lacour-Gayet, *Talleyrand, 1754–1838* (Paris, 1928), 1: 108f.

90 Bailli de Virieu, *Correspondance*, pp. 206f. For the meaning of this oath see Jean Starobinski, *1789: Les Emblèmes de la Raison* (Paris, 1979), pp. 66f.

91 Bailli de Virieu, *Correspondance*, p. 211.

92 Isabelle Bourdin, *Les Sociétés populaires à Paris pendant la Révolution* (Paris, 1937).

93 *Actes de la Commune*, 2ᵉ série, 1: 58. For *unions fraternelles de métier*, see Bourdin, *Les Sociétés populaires*, pp. 109–26.

94 *Actes de la Commune*, 2ᵉ série, 3: 700, 709f.

95 Ibid., 4: 8f.

96 Ibid., pp. 84, 92–94.

97 Ibid., pp. 123f.

98 Ibid., pp. 139, 144.

99 Ibid., pp. 346, 349–52.

100 *Archives parlementaires*, 27:263–73.

101 *Actes de la Comune*, 2ᵉ série, 5: 258–65.

102 Bailli de Virieu, *Correspondance*, p. 273. See also Restif de la Bretonne, *Les Nuits de Paris*, in *Oeuvres*, Henri Bachelin (Paris, 1930), 1: 251; and *Actes de la Commune*, 2ᵉ série, 5: 69f.

103 Michelet, *Histoire de la Révolution*, 1: 610–14.

104 Bailli de Virieu, *Correspondance*, p. 277; and Restif de la Bretonne, *Les Nuits*, pp. 254f.

105 *Actes de la Commune*, 2ᵉ série, 5: 369f.

106 Restif de la Bretonne literally described the two men as *agents provoca-*

teurs. Restif de la Bretonne, *Les Nuits,* p. 257.

107 *Archives parlementaires,* 28: 380.

108 *Mémoires secrets de Fournier l'américain,* ed. F. A. Aulard (Paris, 1890), pp. 45–54.

109 *Actes de la Commune,* 2ᵉ série, 5: 403–6, 428–34.

110 For a detailed account see Michelet, *Histoire de la Révolution,* 1: 705–10.

111 On July 18 the National Assembly issued a very broad law on violation of public peace. See Albert Mathiez, "Le Massacre et le procès du Champ de Mars," *Annales révolutionnaires* 3 (1910): 27f.

112 *Archives parlementaires,* 10: 321.

113 *Actes de la Commune,* 2ᵉ série, 7: 690.

114 Ibid., pp. vi–xiii.

115 Albert Mathiez, *La Vie chère et le mouvement social sous la Terreur* (Paris, 1973) 1:31.

116 Robespierre, *Oeuvres,* 8: 157–84.

117 *Le Moniteur,* 12: 717f.

118 See the description in Bailli de Virieu, *La Révolution,* p. 355.

119 For the text of this speech see Philippe-Joseph-Benjamin Buchez and Prosper-Charles Roux, *Histoire parlementaire de la Révolution française, ou journal des Assemblées nationales, depuis 1789 jusqu'en 1815* (Paris, 1835), 15: 268–99.

120 Buchez and Roux, *Histoire parlementaire,* 16: 247–49.

121 *Le Moniteur,* 13: 324–26.

122 Michelet, *Histoire de la Révolution,* 1: 944.

123 Ibid., p. 968.

124 Frédéric Braesch, *La Commune du 10 août 1792. Etude sur l'histoire de Paris du 10 juin au 2 décembre 1792* (Paris, 1911), p. 339.

125 Alexandre Tuetey, *Répertoire général des sources manuscrites de l'histoire de Paris pendant la Révolution française* (Paris, 1899), 4: xxi–xxxv.

126 It was not possible to determine the professions of the remaining members.

127 Braesch, *La Commune,* pp. 245–81.

128 Ibid., pp. 362–66.

129 Michelet, *Histoire de la Révolution,* 1: 1016–28.

130 Ibid., p. 1026.

131 Braesch, *La Commune,* pp. 484f.

132 Henry Légier Desgranges, "Les Massacres de septembre à la Salpêtrière," *Mémoires de la fédération des sociétés historiques et archéologiques de Paris et de l'Ile de France* 2 (1950): 295–347.

133 Braesch, *La Commune,* pp. 473–82.

134 Henri Calvet, "Les Origines du Comité de l'Evêché," *Annales historiques de la Révolution française* 7 (1930): 12–23.

135 Michelet, *Histoire de la Revolution,* 2: 361f.

136 For the entire wording of this memorandum see *Annales révolutionnaires* 7 (1914): 548–56.

137 Soboul, *Les sans-culottes,* p. 91. See also Mathiez, *La Vie chère,* pp. 237–46.

138 Michelet, *Histoire de la Révolution,* 2: 408.

139 Soboul, *Les sans-culottes,* pp. 109–16.

140 Richard Cobb provides a good description of the mentality of the sansculottes in *Terreur et Subsistances 1793–1795* (Paris, 1965), pp. 3–53.

141 Soboul, *Les sans-culottes,* pp. 139–60.

142 Ibid., pp. 165–70.

143 Ibid., pp. 201–3.

144 Ibid., pp. 183f.

145 Ibid., pp. 633–39.

146 Ibid., pp. 723–59.

147 Ibid., pp. 823–63.

148 Richard Cobb, *Les Armées révolutionnaires. Instrument de la Terreur dans les départements. Avril 1793–floréal an II,* 2 vols. (Paris, 1961–63).

149 Soboul, *Les sans-culottes,* pp. 888–916.

150 Ibid., pp. 944–51. See also George Rudé, "Prices, Wages and Popular Movements in Paris during the French Revolution," *Economic History Review* 6, no. 3 (1954): 260f.

151 As a comparison, in the period from March 1793 to June 1794, there were "only" 1,250 executions. Reinhard, *La Révolution,* p. 325.

152 Soboul, *Les sans-culottes,* pp. 951–74.

153 Michelet, *Histoire de la Révolution,* 2: 923f.

154 Cited by Maxime Du Camp, *Paris, ses organes, ses fonctions et sa vie dans la seconde moitié du XIXᵉ siècle* (Paris, 1894), 4: 133.

155 For the history of this cemetery, located in what is today known as the square Louis XVI, see Jacques

Hillairet, *Dictionnaire historique des rues de Paris,* 7th ed. (Paris, 1963), 1: 89f. See also André Vaquier, "Le Cimitière de la Madeleine et le Sieur Descloseaux," *Mémoires de la Fédération des Sociétés historiques et archéologiques de Paris et de l'Isle-de-France* 12 (1961): 117–34.

156 The rumor caused residents in the area to raise an immediate protest in the firm belief that this practice could cause an epidemic. Michelet, *Histoire de la Révolution,* 2: 924.

157 Ibid., p. 926.

158 Hillairet, *Dictionnaire historique,* 1: 155.

159 The route led from the Conciergerie over the Pont-au-Change, along the quai des Gesvres and across the place de Grève, then through the Arcade Saint-Jean and along the rues de Monceau, du Portour, Saint-Gervais and Saint-Antoine; finally it crossed the place de la Bastille and took the rue du faubourg Saint-Antoine to the place du Trône-Renversé.

160 On the Picpus cemetery see G. Lenotre, "Le Jardin de Picpus 1793–1794," *La Revue des deux mondes* 92 (1927): 46–75. See also G. Lenotre, *Les Pèlerinages de Paris révolutionnaire: Le Jardin de Picpus* (Paris 1928).

161 See Maxime Du Camp, *Paris, ses organes, ses fonctions et sa vie dans la seconde moitié du XIXᵉ siècle,* 7th ed. (Paris, 1884) 4: 134. For information on all the cemeteries used during the Revolution, see Louis Lazare, *La France et Paris* (Paris, 1872), pp. 40–47.

162 Jules Michelet, *Journal,* ed. Paul Viallaneix and Claude Digeon (Paris, 1962), 2: 193f.

163 Wilhelm Adolf Schmidt, *Paris pendant la Révolution, d'après les rapports de la police secrète, 1789–1800* (Paris, 1894), 4: 8–12.

164 Henri Meister, *Souvenirs de mon dernier voyage à Paris* (1795), ed. Paul Usteri and Eugène Ritter (Paris, 1910), p. 79.

165 Frénilly, *Souvenirs,* p. 181.

166 Ibid.

167 Meister, *Souvenirs,* p. 81f.

168 Soboul, *Les sans-culottes,* pp. 650–57.

169 Camille Richard, *Le Comité de Salut public et les fabrications de guerre sous la Terreur* (Paris, 1922).

170 Cited by Louis-Sébastien Mercier, *Paris, pendant la Révolution,* 2: 131.

171 For a description of conditions see Tuetey, *Répertoire,* 5: 20–25.

172 Mercier, *Paris pendant la Révolution,* 1: 357–80.

173 Tuetey, *Repertoire,* 5, no. 3280.

174 Meister, *Souvenirs,* p. 88.

175 Tuetey, *Répertoire* 5, no. 4020.

176 Georges Duval, *Souvenirs Thermidoriens* (Paris, 1844), 2: 67.

177 Mercier, *Paris pendant la Révolution,* 1: 380–98.

178 Duval, *Souvenirs,* 2: 69f.

179 Ibid., p. 74.

180 The gate of which Duval speaks was copied by Godde, the architect, when he created the main gate for the Père Lachaise cemetery in 1825. Godde also used the inscriptions which had been carved into both of the columns and which read: "Fides et pietas erixerunt" ("Faith and piety were the builders") and "Has ultra metas requiescant beatam spem exspectantes" ("May they rest beyond these fears, in blessed hope"). Hillairet, *Dictionnaire historique,* 2: 48.

181 Duval, *Souvenirs,* 2: 76–85. These *Bals des victimes* were described as sheer invention by the Comte d'Allonville. See Comte Armand d'Allonville, *Mémoires secrets* (Paris, 1841), 4: 79f., 84.

182 Alphonse Aulard, *Paris pendant la réaction thermidorienne et sous le Directoire* (Paris, 1898), 1: 21. For conditions in the prisons, see André de Maricourt, *Prisonniers et prisons de Paris pendant la Terreur* (Paris, n.d.). See also Tuetey, *Répertoire,* 6: 1–87.

183 *Le Moniteur,* 21: 402.

184 Ibid., pp. 438f.

185 Charles de Lacretelle, *Dix Années d'épreuves pendant la Révolution* (Paris, 1842), pp. 200f.

186 Ibid., p. 196.

187 On the debate on and enactment of these decrees see *Le Moniteur,* 21:

525–27, 548–50, 581–83. On the social composition and political attitudes of these new committees see Kare D. Tonnesson, *La Défaite des sans-culottes. Mouvement populaire et réaction bourgeoise en l'an III* (Oslo, 1978), pp. 48f. See also Marc Bouloiseau, "Les Comités de surveillance d'arrondissement de Paris sous la réaction thermidorienne," *Archive historique de la Révolution française* 10 (1933): 317–37, 440–53; 11 (1934): 233–49; and 12 (1936): 42–60, 204–17.

188 Reinhard, *La Révolution*, p. 332.
189 For a description of the conflicting parties see Tonnesson, *La Défaite*, p. 52.
190 Françoise Gendron, *La Jeunesse dorée: Episode de la Révolution française* (Quebec, 1979).
191 The *sans-culottes* defined the *Muscadins* as: "ceux qui sont bien habillés" (those who are well-dressed). Cited by Soboul, *Les sans-culottes*, p. 408.
192 Reinhard, *La Révolution*, p. 425.
193 Alphonse Aulard, *La Société des Jacobins. Recueil de documents pour l'histoire du club des Jacobins de Paris . . .* (Paris, 1889–97), 6: 466–74. See also Aulard, *Réaction thermidorienne*, 1: 98f.
194 For information on Carrier and his crimes in Nantes, see Michelet, *Histoire de la Révolution*, 2: 715–44.
195 Aulard, *Réaction thermidorienne*, 1: 120.
196 See Aulard, *Société des Jacobins*, 6: 570f. For public reaction to this law see Aulard, *Réaction thermidorienne*, 1: 179, 182, 185–86.
197 Ibid., 1: 215, 221–28.
198 Ibid., pp. 229f.
199 Ibid., pp. 235–37.
200 Aulard, *Société des Jacobins*, 6: 677.
201 Cited by Gabriel Hanotaux, "La Transformation sociale à l'époque napoléonienne," *La Revue des deux mondes* 33 (1926): 91.
202 Aulard, *Réaction thermidorienne*, 1: 427.
203 Tonnesson, *La Défaite*, pp. 119f. See also Duval, *Souvenirs*, 2: 99.
204 Ibid., p. 116.
205 Ibid., p. 95.
206 Ibid., pp. 110f., 112. See also Lacretelle, *Dix Années*, pp. 210f., Meister, *Souvenirs*, p. 87.

207 Aulard, *Réaction thermidorienne*, 1: 348, 401, 428.
208 Reinhard, *La Révolution*, p. 342. See also Tonnesson, *La Défaite*, p. 126, no. 29.
209 Richard Cobb, *La Mort est dans Paris. Enquête sur le suicide, le meurtre et autres morts subites à Paris au lendemain de la Terreur* (Paris, 1985). See also Duval, *Souvenirs*, 2: 116.
210 Meister, *Souvenirs*, p. 83.
211 Aulard, *Réaction thermidorienne*, 1: 585f.
212 Tonnesson, *La Défaite*, pp. 133–36.
213 Aulard, *Réaction thermidorienne*, 1: 598, 600.
214 Ibid., pp. 588f.
215 Tonnesson, *La Défaite*, pp. 169–71.
216 Ibid., p. 172.
217 Ibid., pp. 176–86.
218 Duval, *Souvenirs*, 2: 128.
219 Ibid., p. 135. See also Tonnesson, *La Défaite*, p. 194.
220 Ibid., pp. 202–5.
221 R. Levasseur, *Mémoires* (Paris, 1831), 4: 218–20.
222 Aulard, *Réaction thermidorienne*, 1: 654, 659, 678, 711f., 714f., 720, 722.
223 Ibid., pp. 660, 662, 691, 710, 714f., 719, 721, 724, 725f., 727.
224 See the extremely biased description of events by Duval, *Souvenirs*, 2: 242–55. See also Tonnesson, *La Défaite*, pp. 253–86.
225 For a description of the events of 2 Prairial, see ibid., pp. 287–305.
226 Duval, *Souvenirs*, 2: 258f. See also Tonnesson, *La Défaite*, pp. 311–14.
227 Ibid., pp. 314–23.
228 Ibid., pp. 324–44.
229 Honoré de Balzac, *Une Ténébreuse Affaire*, in *La Comédie humaine*, ed. Pierre-Georges Castex (Paris, 1977), 8: 509. All further references will be to this edition of Balzac's works.
230 Meister, *Souvenirs*, p. 106.
231 See description by Meister, ibid., pp. 92f.
232 Lynn Hunt, *Politics, Culture, and Class in the French Revolution* (Berkeley, Los Angeles, London, 1984).
233 Edmond and Jules de Goncourt, *Histoire de la société française pendant le Directoire* (Paris, 1864).
234 Médéric-Louis-Elie Moreau de

Saint-Méry, *Voyage aux Etats-Unis de l'Amerique, 1793–1798* (New Haven, Conn., 1913), p. 242.

235 D'Allonville, *Mémoires secrets*, 4: 76f.

236 On the status of women in the Old Regime see Meister, *Souvenirs*, pp. 169f.

237 See Meister on Directory society, ibid., pp. 94f.

238 Frénilly, *Mémoires*, p. 197.

239 See the highly delightful description of events in Lacour-Gayet, *Talleyrand*, 1: 219–34.

240 Aulard, *Réaction thermidorienne*, 2: 215. Mme de Staël's efforts on behalf of the old nobility gained her special attention from police informers who suspected her salon of being a royalist meeting-place. Aulard, 2: 421, 483–84.

241 Etienne-Denis duc de Pasquier, *Histoire de mon temps. Mémoires du Chancelier Pasquier, publiés par M. le duc d'Audiffret-Pasquier* (Paris, 1893), 1: 126.

242 Schmidt, *Paris pendant la Révolution*, 3: 244–51.

243 Complaints by tenants that owners would accept only hard currency in payment of rent are very revealing about the housing situation. Aulard, *Réaction thermidorienne*, 2: 602, 606f., 616, 625, 683.

244 Meister, *Souvenirs*, p. 84. See also Jeanne Pronteau, "La Disparition des espaces verts parisiens: Lotissement des 'marais' des communautés religieuses à la fin du XVIIIᵉ siècle," *Mémoires de la Fédération des Sociétés historiques et archéologiques de Paris et de l'Ile-de-France* 25 (1974): 132–35.

245 The journalist Grimod de la Reynière, who was something of a moral conscience of his time, wrote in the *Censeur dramatique* in 1797:

There is nothing lower, more disgusting or impertinent than these *nouveau riches*. Their speech still reveals their true heritage (some of them were lackeys). Their manners are those of tramps; their politeness is that of thieves. Their wives, who are extravagantly dressed in the latest fashion, do not even have the education of a seamstress or a chambermaid of the good old days (cited by Paul Dacroix, *Directoire, Consulat et Empire. Moeurs et*

usages, lettres, sciences et arts, 1795–1815 [Paris, 1884], p. 17).

246 Aulard, *Réaction thermidorienne*, 3: 50, 94, 188.

247 Ibid., 2: 396. See also Mercier, *Paris pendant la Révolution*, 1: 406, 2: 149f.

248 Reinhard, *La Révolution*, p. 364.

249 Ibid., p. 365.

250 The financial problems of Paris in 1797–1798 were such that the city could no longer even pay for trash collection and street cleaning. Du Camp, *Paris*, 6: 11.

251 "Plan des Artistes, indiquant les rues projetées par la Commission dite des Artistes, en exécution de la loi du 4 avril 1793 pour la division des grandes propriétés nationales, l'embellissement et l'assainissement de la Commune de Paris," in *Les Travaux de Paris, 1789–1889. Atlas dressé sous l'administration de M. E. Poubelle, Préfet de la Seine, sous la direction de M. A. Alphand, inspecteur général des Ponts et Chaussées, directeur des travaux de Paris* (Paris, 1889).

252 Cited by Reinhard, *La Révolution*, p. 432.

BOOK THREE. Capital of Europe 1800–1815

1 Cited by René-André-Polydore Alissan de Chazet, *Mémoires, souvenirs, oeuvres et portraits* (Paris, 1837), 2: 50.

2 Alphonse Aulard, *Etudes et leçons sur la Révolution* (Paris, 1893–98) 2: 223– 225. See also Henry Redhead Yorke, *Paris et la France sous le Consulat* (Paris, 1921), p. 152.

3 Albert Vandal, *L'Avènement de Bonaparte* (Paris, 1902), 1: 196f.

4 Aulard, *Etudes et leçons*, 2: 223.

5 André-François comte de Miot de Melito, *Mémoires* (Paris 1858), 1: 267.

6 François-René vicomte de Chateaubriand, *Mémoires d'outre–tombe*, ed. Maurice Levaillant and Georges Moulinier (Paris, 1951), 1: 443. See also Vandal, *L'Avènement*, 2: 63–69.

7 Miot de Melito, *Mémoires*, 1: 228.

8 Henriette–Lucy, marquise de La

Tour du Pin, *Mémoires. Journal d'une femme de cinquante ans* (1778–1815), ed. Comte Christian de Liederkerke Beaufort, (Paris, 1983), pp. 282f.

9 Etienne-Denis duc de Pasquier, *Histoire de mon temps. Mémoires du chancelier Pasquier,* ed. M. le duc d'Audiffret-Pasquier (Paris, 1893–95), 1: 206.

10 François-Auguste Fauveau baron de Frénilly, *Souvenirs (1768–1828),* ed. Arthur Chuquet, 2d ed. (Paris, 1908), p. 310.

11 Comte Armand d'Allonville, *Mémoires secrets de 1770 à 1830,* (Paris, 1838–45), 4: 320f.

12 Adèle Comtesse de Boigne, *Récits d'une Tante. Mémoires de la comtesse de Boigne* (Paris, 1921) 1: 209f. See also D'Allonville, *Mémoires,* 5: 26f. The duc de Rovigo claimed credit for reconciling the society of the faubourg Saint-Germain with that of the Empire. See Anne-Jean-Marie-René Savary duc de Rovigo, *Mémoires du duc de Rovigo, pour servir à l'histoire de l'empereur Napoléon* (Paris, 1900), 4: 395.

13 Victorine comtesse de Chastenay, *Mémoires de madame de Chastenay, 1771–1815* (Paris, 1896), 2: 8.

14 Fifty-eight percent of the nobles created by Napoleon came from the ranks of the bourgeoisie; 22 percent belonged to the old aristocracy, and 20 percent were from the lower, popular levels. Jean Tulard, *Le Consulat et l'Empire 1800–1815, Nouvelle Histoire de Paris* (Paris, 1970), p. 35, n. 24.

15 Frénilly, *Souvenirs,* p. 324. See also Constance Cazenove d'Arlens, *Deux Mois à Paris et à Lyon sous le Consulat* (Paris, 1903), p. 21. It also worked in reverse, deserters from the old nobility being "cut" socially by the new aristocracy. See Chastenay, *Mémoires,* 2: 68.

16 D'Arlens, *Deux Mois à Paris,* pp. 118f. See also Laure duchesse d'Abrantes, *Mémoires ou souvenirs historiques sur Napoléon* (Paris, 1832), 5: 186.

17 Some curious examples are given in Léon de Lanzac de Laborie, *Paris sous Napoléon* (Paris, 1906), 3: 173–74. See also Chateaubriand, *Mémoires d'outre-tombe,* 1: 442.

18 Georges Lacour-Gayet, *Talleyrand,* (Paris, 1928–34), 2: 17f.; and Alphonse Aulard, *Paris sous le Consulat* (Paris, 1903), 1: 180.

19 The composer Johann Friedrich Reichardt, who was in Paris in 1802 and 1803 and had access to many salons, writes about this in amazement and amusement in *Vertraute Briefe aus Paris, geschrieben in den Jahren 1802 und 1803* (Hamburg, 1804), 2: 143f.

20 When it became known in 1807 that a *cour des comptes* was going to be established, 2,000 applicants applied for 80 positions! See Pierre Marot, *Recherches sur la vie de François de Neufchâteau* (Nancy, 1966), p. 272.

21 See the description in Reichardt, *Vertraute Briefe,* 2: 368f.

22 Chateaubriand, *Mémoires d'outre-tombe,* 1: 443.

23 Reichardt, *Vertraute Briefe,* 1: 227f.

24 For instance, Juliette Récamier introduced a fashionable accessory, the cashmere shawl, that became an indispensable item for feminine elegance. Jouy parodies the origins of this "frénésie pour la mode nouvelle" ("frenzy for the new fashion") in a wonderful story recounted in *L'Hermite de la Chaussée d'Antin ou observations sur les moeurs et les usages parisiens au commence-ment du XIXe siècle* (Paris, 1814), 2: 304–6. Stendhal describes this book as a work "si bien adapté à l'esprit du bourgeois de France et à la curiosité bête de l'Allemand" ("so suited to the spirit of the French bourgeois and the stupid curiosity of the German") in *Souvenirs de l'égotisme, Oeuvres intimes,* ed. V. del Litto, (Paris, 1982), 2: 503.

25 D'Arlens, *Deux Mois à Paris,* p. 70.

26 Reichardt, *Vertraute Briefe,* 1: 222–24.

27 Mathieu Molé, *Souvenirs d'un témoin de la Révolution et de l'Empire (1791–1803)* (Paris, 1943), p. 306.

28 D'Arlens, *Deux Mois à Paris,* p. 59.

29 Jouy, *L'Hermite,* 4: 312.

30 Aulard, *Paris sous le Consulat,* 1: 164.

31 Miot de Melito, *Mémoires*, 2: 43–45
32 Chateaubriand, *Mémoires d'outre-tombe*, 1: 438.
33 Aulard, *Paris sous le Consulat*, 1: 149.
34 Lanzac de Laborie, *Paris sous Napoléon*, 1: 111.
35 Aulard, *Paris sous le Consulat*, 1: 224.
36 Lanzac de Laborie, *Paris sous Napoléon*, 1: 112. For a description of the dissolute behavior, see Reichardt, *Vertraute Briefe*, 2: 379–90.
37 Aulard, *Paris sous le Consulat*, 1: 263.
38 Jean-Paul Aron, *Le Mangeur du XIXᵉ siècle* (Paris, 1973), pp. 5–24.
39 Saint-Aubin, *L'Expedition de Don Quichotte contre les moulins à vent* (n.p., 1795), p. 10.
40 Edmond and Jules de Goncourt, *Histoire de la société française pendant le Directoire* (Paris, 1864),p. 74–79. A lively description of the Palais-Royal during the Empire is also given by Docteur Louis Véron, *Mémoires d'un bourgeois de Paris* (Paris, 1853), 1: 57–60.
41 Pierre Jouhaud, *Paris dans le XIXᵉ siècle* (Paris, 1809), pp. 135–42. See also August von Kotzebue, *Erinnerungen aus Paris im Jahre 1804* (Berlin, 1804), 1: 161–77; and Johann Friedrich Castelli, *Memoiren meines Lebens. Gefundenes und Empfundenes, Erlebtes und Erstrebtes* (Munich, n.d.), 1: 343–45.
42 See the panorama of refined gourmandism presented by Jean-Paul Aron in *Le mangeur du XIXᵉ* (Paris, 1973), pp. 25–48.
43 Alexandre-Balthazar-Laurent Grimod de la Reynière, *Almanach des Gourmands servant de guide dans les moyens de faire excellente chére*, 8 vols. (Paris, 1804–11).
44 Ibid., 2: 122f.
45 Jouy, *L'Hermite*, 2: 398.
46 Aulard, *Paris sous le Consulat*, 1: 724.
47 Louis Prudhome, *Miroir historique, politique et critique de l'ancien et du nouveau Paris et du département de la Seine* (Paris, 1804), 1: 237.
48 *Almanach des gourmands*, 2: 275.
49 Ibid., 1: 176.
50 Ibid., 1: 59, and 2: 44f.
51 Jean Robiquet, *La Vie quotidienne au temps de Napoléon* (Paris, 1942), p. 149.
52 D'Abrantes, *Mémoires*, 2: 149–52. See also Jouhaud, *Paris dans le XIXᵉ siècle*, p. 287f.
53 On these childish games see Henri d'Almeras, *La Vie parisienne sous le Consulat et l'Empire* (Paris, n.d.), pp. 148–60.
54 Johann Konrad Friedrich, *Der Glückssoldat. Wahrheit und Dichtung oder vierzig Jahre und noch fünfzehn Jahre aus dem Leben eines Toten* (Munich, 1920), 2: 542–45.
55 See the witty comments by Kotzebue, *Erinnerungen aus Paris*, 1: 181–85.
56 Ibid., 1: 185–87. See also D'Almeras, *La Vie parisienne*, pp. 462f.
57 Sir John Dean Paul, *Journal d'un voyage à Paris au mois d'août 1802* (Paris, 1913), p. 50.
58 See Stendhal's revealing diary entry in *Oeuvres intimes*, ed. V. del Litto, 2 vols. (Paris, 1981), 1: 237f.
59 Louis Madelin, *Histoire du Consulat et de l'Empire* (Paris, 1948), 11: 12.
60 Cited by Goncourt, *Histoire de la société française pendant le Directoire*, p. 174.
61 Kotzebue, *Erinnerungen aus Paris*, 1: 188–91.
62 John Scott described the curious practice resorted to by some families, who wanted to find a good match for their daughters. They would rent a luxurious apartment for a short time and throw extravagant parties there to give the impression of wealth, which in fact did not exist. John Scott, *A Visit to Paris in 1814* (London, 1816), pp. 145–46.
63 Stendhal, *Correspondance*, ed. Henri Martineau and V. del Litto, (Paris, 1968), 1: 78.
64 Rovigo, *Mémoires*, 4: 375.
65 Aulard, *Paris sous le Consulat*, 2: 632.
66 Lanzac de Laborie, *Paris sous Napoléon*, 3: 238.
67 Ibid., 3: 239.
68 Aulard, *Paris sous le Consulat*, 2: 195f.
69 François-René vicomte de Chateaubriand, *Le Génie du Christianisme*, ed. Maurice Regard (Paris, 1978), p. 233n.
70 A saying coined by Brunet, a well-known vaudeville entertainer of the time, has survived: "Mon Dieu, pour

être enterré comme ça, j'aimerais autant ne pas mourir." Quoted by Lanzac de Laborie, *Paris sous Napoléon*, 3: 344.

71 "Anyone was entitled to bury all the dead he wanted on his property. No formality was required other than a permit issued by the police on submission of a doctor's death certificate. The only restriction was that the property be situated outside the Paris city limits." Paul Lacroix, *Directoire, Consulat et Empire. Moeurs et usages, lettres, sciences et arts, 1795–1815* (Paris, 1884), p. 246.

72 François-Valentin Mulot, *Vues d'un citoyen ancien député de Paris à l'Assemblée législative sur les sépultures* (Paris, n.d.); E. Pastoret, *Rapport sur la violation des sépultures et des tombeaux* (Paris, year IV); and Charles Henrion, *Encore un tableau de Paris* (Paris, year VIII), pp. 68–70. See also the megalomaniac project of an enormous necropolis suggested by Pierre Giraud, *Les Tombeaux ou essai sur les sépultures* (Paris, 1801).

73 Antoine-Chrysostôme Quatremère de Quincy, *Département de la Seine: Rapport fait au Conseil général, le 15 thermidor an VIII, sur . . . le scandale des inhumations actuellles, l'érection des cimetières, la restitution des tombeaux, mausolées etc.* (Paris, n.d.), pp. 22–40.

74 Lanzac de Laborie, *Paris sous Napoléon*, 3: 349.

75 For a detailed account of the suggestions see Pascal Hintermeyer, *Politiques de la mort, tirées du concours de l'Institut, Germinal an VIII–Vendémiaire an IX* (Paris, 1981).

76 Du Camp, *Paris*, 6: 111.

77 Lanzac de Laborie, *Paris sous Napoléon*, 3: 351.

78 Aulard, *Paris sous le Consulat*, 2: 263.

79 Some of these plans and projects can be found in the Archives Nationales, F8, 92.

80 Alfred des Cilleuls, *Histoire de l'administration parisienne au XIXᵉ siècle* (Paris, 1900), 1: 413f.

81 C. Cambry, *Rapport sur les sépultures présenté à l'administration centrale du département de la Seine* (Paris, year VII), p. 63.

82 *Mémoires de l'Academie . . . des sciences morales et politiques de l'Institut* (Paris, 1799) 2: 696.

83 Lanzac de Laborie, *Paris sous Napoléon*, 3: 368.

84 Ibid.

85 Ibid., pp. 368f.

86 Des Cilleuls, *Histoire*, 1: 417f.

87 Frochot acquired twenty–six hectares of land here for the eastern cemetery.

88 Lanzac de Laborie, *Paris sous Napoléon*, 3: 371.

89 Ibid., p. 377.

90 Jacques-Antoine Dulaure, *Histoire physique, civile et morale de Paris* (Paris, 1837), 7: 235; L. E. Chennechot, *Promenades philosophiques et sentimentales au Père Lachaise* (Paris, 1823); J. P. G. Viennet, *Promenades historiques au cimetiére du Père Lachaise* (Paris 1824); and Felix MacDonough, *The Wandering Hermit* (Paris, 1823), 2: 1–11. The description of Père Lachaise in Balzac's novel *Ferragus* closes with the words: "It is a scandalous comedy! Here is Paris over again—streets, store signs, industries, houses, and all complete; but it is a Paris seen through the wrong end of the perspective glass, a microscopic city, a Paris diminished to a shadow of itself, and shrunk to the measure of these chrysalids of the dead, this human species that has dwindled so much in everything save vanity." Honoré de Balzac, *Ferragus, Chef des devorants*, 5: 898.

91 *Compte rendu de l'administration du département de la Seine et de la ville de Paris pendant l'année 1836 par M. le comte de Rambuteau* (Paris, 1837), p. 73.

92 Lanzac de Laborie, *Paris sous Napoléon*, 3: 374.

93 Ibid., p. 373.

94 *Recherches statistiques sur la ville de Paris et le département de la Seine* (Paris, 1826), vol. 3, table XX.

95 Héricart de Thury, *Description des catacombes de Paris* (Paris, 1815); Jouy, *L'Hermite*, 2: 358–66; and Emile Gerards, *Paris souterrain* (Paris, n.d.).

96 Adrien-Cyprien Duquesnoy, *Rapport sur les secours à domicile* (Paris, 1801), pp. 38f.

97   Auguste Luchet, *Paris. Esquisses dédiées au peuple parisien* (Paris, 1830), pp. 11f.

98   Jouy, *L'Hermite*, 2: 137–45; Scott, *A Visit to Paris*, p. 69. See also Johann Georg Heinzmann, *Voyage d'un Allemand à Paris et retour par la Suisse* (Lausanne, 1800), pp. 10f.

99   Alphonse Aulard estimated the number of workers then living in Paris at 92,000, *Paris sous l'Empire* (Paris, 1923), 3: 827–47. Jean Tulard gives a figure of 350,000, which includes their families, in *Le Consulat et l'Empire*, p. 87. As for the size of the Paris population, in 1801 there were 546,846 inhabitants; in 1807 there were 580,609, and only in 1817, at 713,966, was it comparable to what it had been at the end of the Old Regime. See Louis Chevalier, *La Formation de la population parisienne au XIXe siècle* (Paris, 1950), p. 40.

100 See the charming anecdote in Emile Tersen, *Napoléon* (Paris, 1959), p. 371.

101 Tulard, *Le Consulat et l'Empire*, p. 95. See also Alexandre Chabert, *Essai sur les mouvements des revenus et de l'activité économique en France de 1798 à 1820* (Paris, 1949), pp. 173–264.

102 Tulard, *Le Consulat et l'Empire*, p. 90.

103 Ibid., p. 263. See also Chabert, *Essai sur les mouvements des revenus*, pp. 166–69.

104 Reichardt, *Vertraute Briefe*, 1: 251f.

105 Henrion, *Encore un tableau*, p. 130. See also Claude Anthelme Costaz, *Essai sur l'administration de l'agriculture, du commerce, des manufactures et des subsistances, suivi de l'historique des moyens qui ont amené le grand essor pris par les arts depuis 1793, jusqu'à 1815* (Paris, 1818), p. 150.

106 Tulard, *Le Consulat et l'Empire*, p. 265.

107 Ibid., pp. 269–72.

108 Jouy, *L'Hermite*, 5: 77–81.

109 Jean-Jacques Menuret de Chambaud, *Essais sur l'histoire médico-topographique de Paris* (Paris, 1804), pp. 28f.

110 Jean Jaurés, *Le Consulat et l'Empire, histoire socialiste de la Révolution française* (Paris, 1922), 6: 534–35.

111 Jean-Antoine-Claude Chaptal, *Mes Souvenirs sur Napoléon* (Paris, 1893), pp. 284f.

112 Lanzac de Laborie, *Paris sous Napoléon*, 5: 157f.

113 Aulard, *Paris sous le Consulat*, 2: 353.

114 Napoléon, *Corréspondance de Napoléon Ier, publiée par ordre de l'Empereur Napoléon III* (Paris, 1861), 8: 520.

115 Napoléon, *Corréspondance*, 22: 148, 375, 383.

116 Tulard, *Le Consulat et l'Empire*, pp. 93f. See also Chabert, *Essai sur les mouvements des revenus*, pp. 155–58.

117 Lanzac de Laborie, *Paris sous Napoléon*, 6: 320.

118 Ibid., 6: 336–52. See also Chabert, *Essai sur les mouvements des revenus*, pp. 158–60.

119 Napoléon, *Corréspondance*, 19: 107f.

120 Lanzac de Laborie, *Paris sous Napoléon*, vol. 1.

121 Jean Tulard, *Paris et son administration, 1800–1830* (Paris, 1976), pp. 73–79.

122 Cited by Tulard, *Le Consulat et l'Empire*, p. 173.

123 Tulard, *Paris et son administration*, pp. 205–7.

124 Lanzac de Laborie, *Paris sous Napoléon*, 2: 60–66.

125 See the numerous contemporary reports cited by Albert Vandal, *L'Avènement de Bonaparte* (Paris, 1902), 1: 50–60, 446–59. See also the drastic account by Docteur Poumiès de la Siboutie, *Souvenirs d'un médecin de Paris* (Paris, 1910), pp. 82–86.

126 Reichardt, *Vertraute Briefe*, 1: 250f.

127 Jouy, *L'Hermite*, 1: 311.

128 See Stendhal's diary entry for September 10, 18ll, in *Oeuvres intimes*, 1: 743.

129 Menuret de Chambaud, *Essais sur l'histoire médico-topographique*, p. 82.

130 An impression of the grandiose but vague plans conceived by Napoleon for the transformation of Paris is contained in the speech of Prefect Frochot of December 1, 1808, given to the legislative body. *Archives parlementaires*, 2e sèrie, 10: 184.

131 Lanzac de Laborie, *Paris sous Napoléon*, 2: 271. See also Tulard, *Paris et son administration*, pp. 221–25.

132 Tulard, *Le Consulat et l'Empire*, p. 188.

133 Lanzac de Laborie, *Paris sous Napoléon*, 5: 135–37, and 326–28.

134 Ibid., 2: 274f.

135 Napoléon, *Corréspondance*, 16: 161f.

136 Lanzac de Laborie, *Paris sous Napoléon*, 2: 280f. See also Charles Durand, *Le Régime juridique de l'expropriation pour utilité publique sous le Consulat et le Premier Empire* (Aix-en-Provence, 1948).

137 Bonaparte had discovered that "in order to beautify Paris it was more necessary to demolish than to construct. Because how else can those buildings achieve recognition that remain hidden away today? Why not simply pull down the entire area of the *Cité*? After all, it is nothing more than an enormous ruin that merely serves to harbor the rats of the old Lutetia." Cited by Paul Léon, *Paris. Histoire de la rue* (Paris, 1947), p. 112. During an interview in 1981, Jacques Chirac, then mayor of Paris, said concerning the rehabilitation of the old Les Halles section, "But what can you do? This was a neighborhood of food, rats, and poor people."

138 Napoléon, *Corréspondance*, 6: 549f.

139 Lanzac de Laborie, *Paris sous Napoléon*, 2: 172.

140 Ibid., 2: 134.

141 All but one of the houses adjacent to the wall were demolished along with it. The exception was the restaurant owned by Very, who owed this special favor to the Empress Josephine. D'Almeras, *La Vie parisienne*, pp. 124–26. A detailed description of Very's restaurant is contained in Reichardt, *Vertraute Briefe*, 3: 196–209. See also *Almanach des gourmands*, 1: 185f.

142 Lanzac de Laborie, *Paris sous Napoléon*, 2: 136.

143 Chateaubriand, *Mémoires d'outre-tombe*, 1: 853.

144 Napoléon, *Corréspondance*, 21: 116f.

145 Marie-Louise Biver, *Le Paris de Napoléon* (Paris, 1963), pp. 199–207.

146 Ibid., p. 62.

147 Lucien Dubech and Pierre d'Espezel, *Histoire de Paris* (Paris, 1931), 2: 73f.

148 Cited by Lanzac de Laborie, *Paris sous Napoléon*, 2: 157.

149 Ibid., p. 158.

150 Ibid., p. 114.

151 Biver, *Le Paris de Napoléon*, pp. 87f.

152 Ibid., pp. 90–92.

153 Ibid., pp. 93–99.

154 Lanzac de Laborie, *Paris sous Napoléon*, 2: 123.

155 See the description in Scott, *A Visit to Paris*, p. 90.

156 Simon Lacordaire, *Les Inconnus de la Seine. Paris et les métiers de l'eau du VIIIᵉ au XIXᵉ siècle* (Paris, 1985).

157 Napoléon, *Corréspondance*, 12: 145.

158 Lanzac de Laborie, *Paris sous Napoléon*, 2: 125.

159 Ibid., 2: 126.

160 Napoléon, *Corréspondance*, 7: 504.

161 Lanzac de Laborie, *Paris sous Napoléon*, 2: 127–31. See also Pierre Lavedan, *Histoire de l'urbanisme à Paris: nouvelle histoire de Paris* (Paris, 1975), pp. 348f.

162 Charles Percier and Pierre Fontaine, *Résidences des souverains, Parallèle entre plusieurs résidences des souverains de France, d'Allemagne, de Suède, de Russie, d'Espagne et d'Italie* (Paris, 1833), p. 48.

163 Biver, *Le Paris de Napoléon*, p. 310.

164 Percier and Fontaine, *Résidences des souverains*, p. 49.

165 Ibid., p. 66.

166 Ibid., p. 153.

167 Lanzac de Laborie, *Paris sous Napoléon*. 2: 166f.

168 Percier and Fontaine, *Résidences des souverains*, p. 42.

169 Cited by Biver, *Le Paris de Napoléon*, p. 196. See also the hair–raising description given by Frédéric comte de Clarac, *Description historique et graphique du Louvre et des Tuileries*, ed. Alfred Maury (Paris, 1853), pp. 397f. See also Louis–François Bausset, *Mémoires anecdotiques sur l'interieur du Palais et sur quelques événements de l'Empire, dépuis 1806 jusqu'à 1816, pour servir à l'histoire de Napoléon* (Paris, 1827), 4: 162f.

170 Napoléon, *Correspondance*, 9: 138.

171 For details see Biver, *Le Paris de Napoléon*, pp. 296–301.

172 Napoléon, *Correspondance*, 12: 103.

173 Bausset, *Mémoires anecdotiques*, 4: 105f.

174 Charles prince de Clary et Aldringen, *Trois Mois à Paris lors du mariage de l'Empereur Napoléon Iᵉʳ et de l'archi-*

duchesse Marie-Louise (Paris, 1914), pp. 57f.

175 See the assessment in Biver, *Le Paris de Napoléon*, pp. 214–91.

176 Lanzac de Laborie, *Paris sous Napoléon*, 2: 234.

177 Ibid., 1: 103.

178 Ibid., 2: 234; a contrary view is held by Biver, *Le Paris de Napoléon*, pp. 154f.

179 Lanzac de Laborie, *Paris sous Napoléon*, 2: 235.

180 Pierre Lelièvre, *Vivant Denon, directeur des beaux-arts de Napoléon* (Paris, 1942), p. 39.

181 Bausset, *Mémoires anecdotiques*, 4: 183.

182 The Arc de Triomphe was not completed until 1836; see Lanzac de Laborie, *Paris sous Napoléon*, 2: 255f; Biver, *Le Paris de Napoléon*, pp. 187–98. The arch in the place de l'Etoile, designed by Chalgrin, was originally supposed to be erected at the intersection of the rue Saint-Antoine and the place de la Bastille! Minister Champagny pointed out that such an enormous construction at that location would only prove to be an obstruction and suggested placing it in the empty area near the barrière de Chaillot, where it stands today. See André Morizet, *Du Vieux Paris aux Paris moderne. Haussmann et ses prédécesseurs* (Paris, 1932), p. 75.

183 Napoléon, *Correspondance*, 12: 373.

184 Reichardt, *Vertraute Briefe*, 1: 132f.

185 Ferdinand Boyer, "Les Responsabilités de Napoléon dans le transfert à Paris des oeuvres d'art de l'étranger," *La Revue d'Histoire moderne et contemporaine*, 11 (1964): 241–62. See also Karl August Varnhagen von Ense, *Denkwürdigkeiten des eignen Lebens*, ed. Konrad Feilchenfeldt (Frankfurt-am-Main, 1987), 2: 93–100.

186 Reichardt, *Vertraute Briefe*, 1: 121–30.

187 Lanzac de Laborie, *Paris sous Napoléon*, 8: 428–51.

188 Jean-Antoine-Claude Chaptal, *Mes Souvenirs sur Napoléon* (Paris, 1893), p. 355.

189 See the water analyses in Dulaure, *Histoire de Paris*, 8: 210–15; for con-

trary findings see d'Abrantes, *Mémoires*, 6: 16f.

190 Henrion, *Encore un tableau*, pp. 140–42.

191 Napoléon, *Correspondance*, 12: 265.

192 Lanzac de Laborie, *Paris sous Napoléon*, 2: 300.

193 For details see ibid., pp. 303–14. See also Dulaure, *Histoire de Paris*, 7: 190–95.

194 Biver, *Le Paris de Napoléon*, p. 108.

195 Tulard, *Le Consulat et l'Empire*, p. 230.

196 Aulard, *Paris sous le Consulat*, 2: 34.

197 Napoléon, *Correspondance*, 15: 253, 260.

198 Tulard, *Le Consulat et l'Empire*, pp. 235f.

199 Jouy, *L'Hermite*, 1: 117f.

200 Lanzac de Laborie, *Paris sous Napoléon*, 2: 328f.

201 Jeanne Pronteau, *Les Numérotages des maisons de Paris du XVᵉ siècle à nos jours* (Paris, 1966).

202 Henrion, *Encore un tableau*, p. 49.

203 Tulard, *Le Consulat et l'Empire*, p. 257.

204 Lanzac de Laborie, *Paris sous Napoléon*, 3: 281–83.

205 Chastenay, *Mémoires*, 2: 120f.

206 Lanzac de Laborie, *Paris sous Napoléon*, 3: 290–95.

207 Gaspard Gourgaud, *Journal de Sainte-Hélène* (Paris, 1947), 1: 530.

208 Lanzac de Laborie, *Paris sous Napoléon*, 5: 329.

209 Jean-Baptiste Poujoulx, *Paris à la fin du XVIIIᵉ siècle* (Paris, year VIII), pp. 245f.

210 Pierre Lavedan, "Napoléon Iᵉʳ Les Halles de Paris," *Archives de l'art français* 24 (1969): 23–29.

211 Lanzac de Laborie, *Paris sous Napoléon*, 5: 315f.

212 Thomas Richard Underwood, *Paris en 1814* (Paris, 1907), p. 121.

213 Richard Boxhall Grantham, "Description of the Abattoirs of Paris," *Proceedings of the Institution of Civil Engineers* 8 (1849): 66–81.

214 Lanzac de Laborie, *Paris sous Napoléon*, 5: 317.

215 Bertrand Gille, *Documents sur l'état de l'industrie et du commerce de Paris et du département de la Seine (1778–1810)* (Paris, 1963), p. 49.

216 Prudhomme, *Miroir historique*, 2: 107.

217 Pierre Jouhaud, *Paris dans le dix-neuvième siècle* (Paris, 1809), pp. 55f.;

Almanach des Gourmands, 1: 192–95. Sometimes even extravagant advertisements were used to attract customers. See the delightful description of cunning methods used, in Varnhagen von Ense, *Denkwürdigkeiten,* 2: 122–25.

218 Figures given by the prefect of the department of the Seine in 1801 make this very clear: in that year only 1,722 workers were employed in larger factories of this sort, while ten years earlier there had been 7,053 workers. Lanzac de Laborie, *Paris sous Napoléon,* 6: 236.

219 On the shortage of workers see Aulard, *Paris sous le Consulat,* 2: 240f., 565, 573; on the subject of orders received, ibid., pp. 17, 193, 488, 580, 611f., 620, 738.

220 Odette Viennet, *Une Enquête économique dans la France impériale. Le voyage du hambourgois Nemnich* (Paris, 1947), p. 57, cited in Tulard, *Le Consulat et l'Empire,* p. 76.

221 David H. Pinkney, "Paris, Capitale du coton sous le Premier Empire," *Annales E.S.C.* 5 (1950): 56–60.

222 Lanzac de Laborie, *Paris sous Napoléon,* 6: 161–78.

223 Ernest d'Hauterive, *La Police secrète du Premier Empire* (Paris, 1913), 2: 117.

224 Ibid., 1: 380.

225 Lanzac de Laborie, *Paris sous Napoléon,* 6: 50f.

226 Ibid., p. 52.

227 Ibid., p. 54.

228 Tulard, *Le Consulat et l'Empire,* p. 341.

229 Lanzac de Laborie, *Paris sous Napoléon,* 6: 72–75.

230 Ibid., pp. 328f.

231 Ibid., 5: 212.

232 Ibid., p. 213.

233 Ibid., p. 216.

234 Ibid., p. 244.

235 Pasquier, *Mémoires,* 1: 503.

236 Lanzac de Laborie, *Paris sous Napoléon,* 5: 258–64.

237 Tulard, *Le Consulat et l'Empire,* pp. 352f.

238 Chastenay, *Mémoires,* 2: 200f.

239 Boigne, *Mémoires,* 1: 262f. See also Varnhagen von Ense, *Denkwürdigkeiten,* 2: 126.

240 Charles Joseph Minard, *Carte figurative des pertes successives en hommes de l'armée française dans la campagne de Russie 1812–1813* (Paris, 1869), cited in Edward R. Tufte, *The Visual Display of Quantitative Information* (Cheshire, Conn., 1983), p. 176.

241 Emile Tersen, *Napoléon* (Paris, 1959), p. 371.

242 Victor duc de Broglie, *Souvenirs 1785–1870* (Paris, 1886), 1: 252.

243 Pasquier, *Mémoires,* 2: 225.

244 An eyewitness report on the course of the battle, from the perspective of a Paris resident, is given in Underwood, *Paris en 1814,* pp. 158–71.

245 Henri Houssaye, *1814* (Paris, 1888), p. 547.

246 Cited by Marie-Louise Biver, *Pierre Fontaine* (Paris, 1964), p. 182. See also the description in Chastenay, *Mémoires,* 2: 312f; and Underwood, *Paris en 1814,* pp. 217–21.

247 Houssaye, *1814,* pp. 549–51. See also Underwood, *Paris en 1814,* pp. 213–16.

248 Broglie, *Souvenirs,* 1: 256f.

249 Pasquier, *Mémoires,* 2: 255.

250 Houssaye, *1814,* pp. 553f. See also Robert Margerit, *Waterloo* (Paris, 1964), pp. 14f.

251 Heinrich Ritter von Srbik, *Metternich. Der Staatsmann und der Mensch* (Munich, 1925), 1: 176f; and Margerit, *Waterloo,* p. 13.

252 Lacour-Gayet, *Talleyrand,* 2: 363–75. See also Houssaye, *1814,* pp. 558–61.

253 Tulard, *Paris et son administration,* pp. 366–74. See also Margerit, *Waterloo,* p. 23. Talleyrand wrote mockingly to Tsar Alexander on June 13, 1814: "Sire, I assume that you encountered much dissatisfaction in Paris. But aside from the suddenness of the most recent revolution, as well as the surprise experienced by so many heated passions, what—taken all in all—remains of Paris? Nothing but a town of officialdom and offices. It was only once appointments ceased to be made that Parisians became aware of the despotism of a Bonaparte." See Talleyrand, *Mémoires 1754–1815,* ed. Jean-Paul Couchoud (Paris, 1982), p. 668.

254 See the examples given in Georges Firmin-Didot, *Royauté ou Empire,*

Les rapports inédits du comte Anglès (Paris, n.d.), pp. 27, 36, 57 and 59. See also Margerit, *Waterloo*, pp. 23–25.

255 Tulard, *Le Consulat et l'Empire*, p. 379.

256 In connection with other measures see Pasquier, *Mémoires*, 2: 335f.

257 Tulard, *Le Consulat et l'Empire*, p. 380. See also Margerit, *Waterloo*, p. 17.

258 Henry Houssaye, *1815. La Première Restauration. Les Cent-Jours* (Paris, 1896), p. 63.

259 Broglie, *Souvenirs*, pp. 291f.

260 See examples given in Emile Le Gallo, *Les Cent-Jours* (Paris, 1923), p. 108. See also Margerit, *Waterloo*, pp. 55–57.

261 Broglie, *Souvenirs*, 1: 295–97.

262 Ibid., p. 295.

263 Le Gallo, *Les Cent-Jours*, pp. 109f; see also Margerit, *Waterloo*, pp. 65f.

264 Le Gallo, *Les Cent-Jours*, pp. 110ff.

265 See the account of the mixed feelings of the public in Charles Beslay, *1830–1848–1870. Mes souvenirs* (Paris, 1873), p. 47.

266 For details on the extent of the reorganization see Tulard, *Paris et son administration*, pp. 377–79. See also Margerit, *Waterloo*, pp. 67–70.

267 Biver, *Pierre Fontaine*, p. 186.

268 Margerit, *Waterloo*, pp. 71f.

269 Le Gallo, *Les Cent-Jours*, p. 302.

270 Napoléon, *Correspondance*, 28: 30, 38.

271 Chateaubriand, *Mémoires d'outre-tombe*, 1: 953–59.

272 John Hobhouse, *Lettres écrites de Paris pendant le dernier règne de l'Empereur Napoléon* (Ghent and Brussels, 1817), 1: 192. See also Le Gallo, *Les Cent-Jours*, pp. 303–6.

273 Tulard, *Paris et son administration*, pp. 381f. See also Margerit, *Waterloo*, pp. 119–22.

274 Chateaubriand, *Mémoires d'outre-tombe*, 1: 952.

275 Frédéric Bluche, *Le Plébiscite des Cent-Jours* (Paris and Geneva, 1974) pp. 81–87.

276 Firmin-Didot, *Royauté ou Empire*, p. 294.

277 Le Gallo, *Les Cent-Jours*, pp. 305f.

278 Antoine Thibaudeau, *Mémoires 1799–1815* (Paris, 1913), p. 489.

279 Le Gallo, *Les Cent-Jours*, p. 305.

280 Ibid., p. 309.

281 Tulard, *Le Consulat et l'Empire*, pp. 402–4.

282 Margerit, *Waterloo*, pp. 440–45.

283 Thibaudeau, *Mémoires*, p. 535; for the intrigues behind the scenes see Margerit, *Waterloo*, pp. 496–528.

284 Tulard, *Le Consulat et l'Empire*, p. 407.

285 For details see Hobhouse, *Lettres écrites de Paris*, 2: 135–59. See also Margerit, *Waterloo*, pp. 541–65.

286 Tulard, *Le Consulat et l'Empire*, p. 409.

287 Emmanuel comte de Las Cases, *Le Mémorial de Saint–Hélène*, ed. Ernest Dunan (Paris, 1951), 2: 120.

288 Gille, *Documents sur l'état de l'industrie*, p. 50.

BOOK FOUR. Growth and Stagnation 1815–1830

1 Adèle comtesse de Boigne, *Récits d'une tante. Mémoires de la comtesse de Boigne* (Paris, 1921–23), 2: 90.

2 Comte Armand d'Allonville, *Mémoires secrètes de 1770 à 1830* (Paris, 1838–45), 5: 351.

3 See Jean Tulard, "Du Paris impérial au Paris de 1830 d'après les bulletins de police," *Bulletin de la Société de l'histoire de Paris et de l'Ile de France* 96 (1971): 160.

4 Louis XVIII used to say to those who wanted Chabrol replaced: "M. Chabrol is married to the city of Paris and I have done away with divorces." Cited in André Morizet, *Du Vieux Paris au Paris moderne. Haussmann et ses prédécesseurs* (Paris, 1932), p. 86.

5 See Tulard, *"Du Paris impérial,"* p. 161. See also Jean Tulard, *Paris et son administration (1800–1830)* (Paris, 1976), pp. 427–39.

6 See Guillaume de Bertier de Sauvigny, *La Restauration 1815–1830. Nouvelle Histoire de Paris* (Paris, 1977), pp. 19–21. See also Tulard, *Paris et son administration*, pp. 422–25.

7 Charles de Remusat, *Mémoires de ma vie*, ed. Charles H. Pouthas (Paris, 1958), 1: 255.

8   See Tulard, *Paris et son administra-tion*, pp. 441–47.

9   Alexandre Chabert, *Essai sur les mouve-ments des revenus et de l'activité économique en France de 1789 à 1820* (Paris, 1949), pp. 389–421.

10 Tulard, *Paris et son administration*, p. 385.

11 Bertier de Sauvigny, *La Restauration*, p. 123.

12 Tulard, *Paris et son administration*, p. 386.

13 Conseil municipal, session of December 22, 1816 (ibid.).

14 See Chabrol's report to the king in *Le Moniteur*, February 7, 1818.

15 Tulard, *Paris et son administration*, pp. 390–93.

16 Honoré de Balzac, *La Vendetta*, in *La Comédie humaine*, ed. Pierre-Georges Castex (Paris, 1976), 1: 1,097.

17 Pierre Debofle, "Les Travaux de Paris (1814–1830). Recherches sur la politique d'urbanisme de la ville de Paris sous la Restauration" (the-sis, Ecole Normale des Chartes, Paris, 1974), p. 67.

18 Tulard, *Paris et son administration*, p. 394.

19 Tulard, *"Du Paris impérial,"* p. 168.

20 See the masterly depiction in Balzac's *La Vendetta*, 1: 1,035–1,102.

21 William Dorset Fellowes, *Paris dur-ing the Interesting Month of July 1815. A Series of Letters Addressed to a Friend in London* (London, 1815), p. 76.

22 See the estimate of costs in Bertier de Sauvigny, *La Restauration*, p. 476.

23 Louis Barron, *Paris pittoresque. La vie, les moeurs, les plaisirs, 1800–1900* (Paris, 1900), pp. 99–100.

24 Boigne, *Mémoires*, 2: 96.

25 Poumiès, *Souvenirs d'un médecin de Paris* (Paris, 1910), p. 183.

26 Victor duc de Broglie, *Souvenirs* (Paris, 1886), 1: 316.

27 Tulard, *Paris et son administration*, p. 403.

28 For details see ibid., pp. 404–8: for the unequivocal preference given to property owners see Adeline Daumard, *La Bourgeoisie parisienne de 1815 à 1848* (Paris, 1963), pp. 32f.

29 Poumiès, *Souvenirs*, pp. 174f.

30 Bertier de Sauvigny, *La Restauration*, p. 156.

31 For a critical analysis of population growth see Louis Chevalier, *Classes laborieuses et classes dangereuses à Paris pendant la première moitié du XIXe siècle* (Paris, 1958), pp. 209–13.

32 *Recherches statistiques sur la Ville de Paris et le Département de la Seine* (Paris, 1829), 4: 18–37.

33 Ibid., pp. 23f.

34 Ibid., vol. 4; See also Chevalier, *Classes laborieuses*, pp. 220–22, 225–28.

35 *Recherches statistiques*, 4: 16.

36 Adeline Daumard, *Maisons de Paris et propriétaires parisiens au XIXe siècle, 1809–1880* (Paris, 1965), p. 23.

37 Chevalier, *Classes laborieuses*, pp. 267–77.

38 See the statistical tables in Bertier de Sauvigny, *La Restauration*, p. 161. See also Chevalier, *Classes laborieuses*, pp. 277–91.

39 George D. Sussman, *Selling Mother's Milk: The Wet-Nursing Business in France 1715–1914* (Urbana, Ill., and London, 1982). See also Bertier de Sauvigny, *La Restauration*, pp. 158f.

40 See the moving description in Balzac, *Pierrette*, ed. Castex, 5: 40f. The sug-gestions for reform made by con-temporaries deliberately overlooked the cruelties of this practice. See Boys de Loury, "Mémoires sur les modifications à apporter dans le ser-vice de l'administration des nour-rices," in *Annales d'Hygiène publique*, 27 (1842): 5–35.

41 For a comparison in infant mortality in the first and twelfth districts of Paris see Louis-René Villermé, "De la Mortalité dans les divers quartiers de la Ville de Paris," ibid. 3 (1830): 328–32. See also Edmonde Vedrenne-Villeneuve, "L'Inégalité sociale devant la mort dans la première moitié du XIXe siécle," *Population* 16 (1961), 665–98.

42 Balzac, *Le Colonel Chabert*, ed. Castex, 3: 373.

43 Heinrich von Kleist, *Sämtliche Werke und Briefe*, ed. Wilhelm Herzog (Leipzig, 1911), 6: 226.

44 Balzac, *La Fille aux yeux d'or*, ed. Castex, 5: 1,039–41.

45 See Balzac, *Le Cabinet des antiques*, (Preface to the 1839 edition), ed. Castex, 4: 960.

46   Adeline Daumard, *La Bourgeoisie parisienne de 1815 à 1948* (Paris, 1963), p. 7.

47   Ibid., p. 8.

48   *Journal de la Société de Statistique* (October 1836), p. 228, cited in Daumard, *La Bourgeoisie parisienne*, p. 11. See also *Recherches statistiques* 3 (1826), table 58, and 4 (1829), table 69.

49   Chevalier, *Classes laborieuses*, p. 444.

50   See the statistics given in Bertier de Sauvigny, *La Restauration*, p. 142.

51   Ibid., pp. 236f.

52   Ibid., p. 239.

53   Ibid., pp. 121, 124f.

54   Tulard, "Du Paris impérial," p. 167.

55   Hubert and Georges Bourgin, *Les Patrons, les ouvriers et l'Etat. Le régime de l'industrie en France de 1814 à 1830. Recueil de textes publiés pour la Société d'Histoire contemporaine* (Paris 1941), 3: 216.

56   Tulard, "Du Paris impérial," p. 168.

57   Bertier de Sauvigny, *La Restauration*, p. 261.

58   Jean-Louis-Henri Bertin, *Biographie de M. De Belleyme* (Paris, 1863), pp. 26–29.

59   See the description of these dwellings in C. de Beauregard, *Nouveaux Tableaux de Paris ou Observations sur les moeurs et usages des parisiens au commencement du XIXᵉ siècle* (Paris, 1828), 1: 46f.

60   *Collection officielle des ordonnances de police (1800–1848)* (Paris, 1880).

61   An example that strikingly confirms this assumption is contained in *Compte d'Administration des dépenses de la Préfecture de Police* (Paris, 1819), p. xxvii.

62   See Jill Harsin, *Policing Prostitution in Nineteenth-Century Paris* (Princeton, 1985), pp. 72–80.

63   See Dumard, *La Bourgeoisie parisienne*, pp. 182f.

64   Donald J. Olsen, *The City as a Work of Art: London, Paris, Vienna* (New Haven and London, 1986), pp. 135f.

65   Balzac, *La Cousine Bette*, ed. Castex, 8: 436f.

66   Auguste Luchet, *Paris. Esquisses dédiées au peuple parisien* (Paris, 1830), pp. 11–13.

67   Pierre-Joseph-Spiridiou Dufey, *Mémorial parisien, ou Paris tel qu'il fut, tel qu'il est* (Paris, 1821), p. 3.

68   Luchet, *Paris*, pp. 159f; see also Balzac's description of the rue Greneta in *César Birotteau*, ed. Castex, 6: 257f.

69   See Adeline Daumard, *Maisons de Paris et propriétaires parisiens au XIXᵉ siècle* (Paris, 1965), p. 86.

70   See Bertrand Gille, *La Banque et le crédit en France de 1815 à 1848* (Paris, 1959), pp. 183–94.

71   Bertier de Sauvigny, *La Restauration*, p. 300.

72   Antoine Caillot, *Mémoires pour servir à l'histoire des moeurs* (Paris, 1827), 2: 87f. See also Louis-Gabriel Montigny, *Le Provincial à Paris. Esquisses des moeurs parisiennes* (Paris, 1825), vol. 3, chap. 13.

73   Daumard, *La Bourgeoisie parisienne*, p. 206.

74   See the charming vignette "Die Läden," in Ludwig Börne, *Schilderungen aus Paris (1822 und 1823), Gesammelte Schriften* (Hamburg and Frankfurt-am-Main, 1862), 3: 45–51. See also Eduard Kolloff, *Schilderungen aus Paris* (Hamburg, 1839), 2: 65–102.

75   Jean-Baptiste Gouriet, *Panorama parisien* (Paris, 1827), p. 17.

76   See the detailed description of the Passage des Panoramas, in Montigny, *Le Provincial*, 1: 158–72.

77   The prospectuses used by Balzac's César Birotteau to advertise his cosmetics are a good example. See *César Birotteau*, pp. 65–67, 156f. See also Jean-Hervé Donnard, *Balzac. Les réalités économiques et sociales dans la Comédie humaine* (Paris, 1961), pp. 253–58.

78   Balzac, *La Maison du chat-qui-pelote*, ed. Castex, 1: 44.

79   Balzac, *César Birotteau*, pp. 42f.

80   See *Collection des Maisons de commerce de Paris et des intérieurs les mieux décorés* (Paris, 1926; rpr.).

81   Bertier de Sauvigny, *La Restauration*, p. 314.

82   Montigny, *Le Provincial*, 2: 102f.

83   [Auguste Luchet], *Nouveau Tableau de Paris* (Paris, 1835), 6: 107f. The Passage Delorme, erected in 1808 and demolished in 1896, was the first glass-covered arcade to be built. See Johann

Friedrich Geist, *Passagen. Ein Bautyp des 19. Jahrhunderts* (Munich, 1978), p. 267.

84 See Louis Bonnier, "Les Passages couverts," *Commission du Vieux Paris, Procés-verbal, séance du samedi 9 décembre 1916*, p. 272.

85 Geist, *Passagen*, p. 278.

86 Ibid., pp. 30f. See also [Luchet], *Nouveau Tableau*, 6: 103.

87 Geist, *Passagen*, pp. 32f.

88 Thiollet and Roux, *Nouveau Recueil de menuisérie et décorations intérieures et exterieures*, cited in Geist, *Passagen*, p. 279.

89 For a detailed description of these two arcades see ibid., pp. 273–78.

90 Bonnier, "Les Passages couverts," pp. 271–73.

91 Geist, *Passagen*, pp. 268–71.

92 A detailed description is given ibid., pp. 262–67.

93 On the panoramas see Stephan Oettermann, *Das Panorama. Die Geschichte eines Massenmediums* (Frankfurt-am-Main, 1980), pp. 113–15.

94 Amédée Kermel, "Les Passages de Paris," in *Paris ou le livre de cent-et-un* (Paris, 1833), 10: 70. See also the charming description of the goods displayed in the Passage des Panoramas, in Ludwig Rellstab, *Paris im Frühjahr 1843: Briefe, Berichte und Schilderungen* (Leipzig, 1844), 1: 19f.

95 Balzac, *César Birotteau*, pp. 257f.

96 August Lewald, "Ein Menschenleben," in *Gesammelte Schriften* (Leipzig, 1844), 6: 57.

97 Kermel, "Les Passages," p. 69.

98 Charles de Forster, *Quinze Ans à Paris (1832–1848). Paris et les parisiens* (Paris, 1848), 1: 120f.

99 Kermel, *Les Passages*, pp. 70f.

100 Other arcades that lay to the east of these were the Passage du Saumon (1827–1899), the Passage du Grand Cerf (1825), the Passage Bourg l'Abbé (1825–1852), the Passage du Caire (1799), the Passage Ponceau (1826), the Passage du Prado (1830), and the Passage Brady (1828).

101 See the frequently reproduced lithograph by Bertall, "Coupe d'une maison parisienne le 1er janvier 1845," in Max von Boehn, *Vom Kaiserreich zur Republik. Eine französische Kultur-geschichte des 19. Jahrhunderts* (Berlin, 1917), p. 249.

102 *The Architect: A Journal of Art, Civil Engineering and Building* 10 (1873): 141, cited in Donald J. Olsen, *The City as a Work of Art: London, Paris, Vienna* (New Haven and London, 1986), pp. 137f.

103 Jean-Hervé Donnard, *Les Réalités économiques et sociales dans la Comédie humaine* (Paris, 1961), pp. 279–84.

104 Guillaume-Tell Doin and Edouard Thomas Charton, *Lettres sur Paris* (Paris, 1830), p. 15.

105 Daumard, *Maisons de Paris*, p. 92, and *La Bourgeoisie parisienne*, p. 209.

106 This was a type of store that became very fashionable during the Restoration. The former sales space on the ground floor was replaced by two windows a full story high; these defined a small passage in the middle of the facade at the end of which stairs led to the first floor where the salesrooms were now located. See Léon Cahen, "L'Enrichissement de la France sous la Restauration," *La Revue d'histoire moderne* 5 (1930): 192.

107 Caillot, *Mémoires*, 2: 87–89.

108 Daumard, *Maisons de Paris*, pp. 21f.

109 Ibid., p. 35.

110 See *Recherches statistiques*, 4: 48–50.

111 *Mémoire adressé par une réunion de propriétaires, architectes et constructeurs de la ville de Paris à Messieurs les membres de la Commission d'enquête* (Paris, 1829), p. 7 [Bibliothèque Nationale, 8°Z Le Senne 6550].

112 *Recherches statistiques*, 4: 71. Between 1812 and 1833 the increase in the ground rent was 63 percent. Daumard, *Maisons de Paris*, pp. 123, 129f.

113 Caillot, *Mémoires*, 2: 90. See also Gérard Jacquemet, "Lotissement et construction dans la proche banlieue parisienne, 1820–1840," *Paris et l'Ile-de-France* 25 (1974): 207–56.

114 See the statistics in Bernard Rouleau, *Villages et faubourgs de l'ancien Paris, histoire d'un espace urbain* (Paris, 1985), pp. 197f.

115 Chabrol, "Rapport du 24 août," *Budget de la ville de Paris pour 1822*, cited by Jeanne Pronteau, "Construction et aménagement des nouveaux

quartiers de Paris (1820–1826)," *Histoire des entreprises* (November 1958), p. 9.

116 For details see ibid., pp. 17–19.

117 Ibid., pp. 19–22.

118 Ibid., pp. 22–24.

119 Gabriel-Julien Ouvrard, *Mémoires de Gabriel-Julien Ouvrard sur sa vie et ses diverses opérations financières* (Paris, 1827), 3: 96f.

120 It is not surprising, therefore, that speculation in these areas was especially lucrative, as Balzac notes in various of his works. See *Béatrix*, ed. Castex, 2: 838f., and *Le Colonel Chabert*, 3: 332.

121 Balzac, *Beatrix*, 2: 896f.

122 Morizet, *Du vieux Paris*, p. 87. See also Pierre Debofle, "Les Travaux de Paris (1814–1830). Recherches sur la politique d'urbanisme de la ville de Paris sous la Restauration" (thesis, Ecole Normale des Chartes, Paris, 1974), pp. 68–71.

123 Bertier de Sauvigny, *La Restauration*, p. 51.

124 *Recherches statistiques sur la Ville de Paris* (Paris, 1823), 2: 8.

125 Bertier de Sauvigny, *La Restauration*, p. 54.

126 *Recherches statistiques*, 4: 44f.

127 Alfred des Cilleuls, *Histoire de l'administration parisienne au XIXᵉ siècle* (Paris, 1900), 1: 312.

128 L. Alphonse, *De la salubrité de la ville de Paris* (Paris, 1826), pp. 8f.

129 Tulard, *Paris et son administration*, p. 463.

130 Etienne-Jean Delécluze, *Journal 1824–1828*, ed. Robert Baschet (Paris, 1948), pp. 79, 91, 116, 130.

131 For a detailed description of this "battle" see Henri d'Almeras, *La Vie parisienne sous la Restauration* (Paris, n.d.), pp. 405–18.

132 Alfred de Musset, *La Confession d'un enfant du siècle*, in *Oeuvres complètes en prose*, ed. Maurice Allem and Paul Courant (Paris, 1960), p. 67.

133 Louis Véron, *Mémoires d'un bourgeois de Paris* (Paris, 1853), pp. 202–22.

134 See the delightful description of an *ancien salon* in Victor Hugo, *Les Misérables*, ed. Maurice Allem (Paris, 1951), pp. 623–26.

135 See Jules Bertaut, *Le Faubourg Saint-Germain sous l'Empire et la Restauration* (Paris, 1949).

136 On the salons of the Romantics, see Frantz Funck-Brentano, "Salons et cénacles romantiques. La Vie parisienne à l'époque romantique," *Conférence du Musée Carnavalet 1930* (Paris, 1931), pp. 9–48.

137 The *Journal des débats*, a most important paper with 23,000 subscribers, had a subscription rate of 15 francs for three months, 30 francs for six months, and 60 francs for a year. See Charles Ledré, "La Press nationale sous la Restauration et la Monarchie de Juillet," in *Histoire générale de la presse française de 1815 à 1871* (Paris, 1969), 2: 33f., n. 1.

138 Stendhal, *"Souvenirs d'Egotisme,"* *Oeuvres intimes*, ed. V. del Litto (Paris, 1982), 2: 512. See also the description of the reading rooms in Ludwig Börne, *Gesammelte Werke*, 3: 73–79. See also Claude Pichois, "Les Cabinets de lecture à Paris durant la première moitié du XIXᵉ siècle," *Annales E.S.C.*, 14, no. 3 (1959): 521–34.

139 Etienne Delécluze, *Journal de Delécluze 1824–1828*, ed. Robert Baschet (Paris, 1948), pp. 286f.

140 Victor-Joseph Etienne de Jouy, *L'Hermite de la Guiane ou observations sur les moeurs et les usages français au commencement du XIXᵉ siècle* (Paris, 1817), 3: 122f.

141 Stendhal, *Souvenirs d'Egotisme*, p. 438.

142 Popular humor named the stretch of boulevard between the rue Taitbout and the rue Le Peletier "boulevard Gand," because that is where the deposed monarch's followers met— the king being exiled in Ghent (Gand). At the time of Napoleon this section was known as the boulevard de Coblentz.

143 Stendhal, *Souvenirs d'Egotisme*, p. 469.

144 François Fosca, *Histoire des cafés de Paris* (Paris, 1934), pp. 96–126.

145 Delécluze, *Journal*, p. 269.

146 Philarète Chasles, *Mémoires* (Geneva, 1973), 2: 2f.

147 Alfred-Auguste Cuvillier-Fleury, *Journal intime*, ed. Edouard Bertin (Paris, 1900–3), 1: 51.

148 Chateaubriand went so far as to claim that this Chapelle Expiatoire was "le monument peut-être le plus remarquable de Paris." Chateaubriand, *Mémoires d'outre-tombe*, 1: 905.

149 Véron, *Mémoires*, 1: 354.

150 Ibid., 2: 2.

151 Balzac, *Le Père Goriot*, 2: 151. The duc d'Escars was master of the king's household. He died in 1822, supposedly from a digestive problem, and Louis XVIII is said to have commented on his death as follows: "Le pauvre d'Escars! J'ai pourtant meilleur estomac que lui!" ("Poor d'Escars! I've got a stronger stomach than he!"). The fact that behind the magnificent facades things were at times less than magnificent is established by Ludwig Börne, who lived in a room overlooking a restaurant kitchen in the Palais-Royal during his second visit to Paris: "The unwashed cooks start being creative and inspired early in the morning, and if one watches how the refinement that is part of all French dishes is achieved, one could lose one's appetite for a whole week." Ludwig Börne, *Briefe aus Paris* (1830–1833), letter no. 5, in *Gesammelte Schriften*, 8: 32.

152 Jean-Paul Aron, *Le Mangeur du XIXᵉ siècle* (Paris, 1973), pp. 59–62.

153 A. Trebuchet, "Recherches sur l'éclairage public de Paris," *Annales d'hygiène publique* 31 (1844): 108–26.

154 The proverbial immobility of Parisians, who often never left their neighborhoods during their lifetime, provided the incentive for a series of humorous sketches based on Louis-Balthasar Néel's *Voyage de Paris à Saint-Cloud par mer et retour de Saint-Cloud à Paris par terre* (Paris, year X).

155 D'Almeras, *La Vie parisienne sous la Restauration*, p. 94.

156 Ibid., pp. 103–6. See also Bertier de Sauvigny, *La Restauration*, pp. 104–6. See also Ernest Fouinet, "Un Voyage en Omnibus. De la barrière du Trône à la barrière de l'Etoile," in *Paris, ou le livre des cent-et-un* (Paris, 1831), 2: 59–82.

157 Wilhelm Heinrich Riehl, *Land und Leute*, 3rd ed. (Stuttgart and Augsburg, 1856), p. 61.

158 Tulard, *Paris et son administration*, p. 490.

159 *Recherches statistiques*, 4: 48.

160 Ibid., p. 47.

161 Pierre Gonnet, "Esquisse de la crise économique en France de 1827 à 1832," *La Revue d'histoire économique et sociale* 9 (1955): 249–92.

162 David H. Pinkney, *The French Revolution of 1830* (Princeton, N.J., 1972), p. 60.

163 Tulard, *Paris et son administration*, p. 491.

164 Ibid., p. 492.

165 See Pinkney, *The French Revolution of 1830*, p. 65. See also Benoiston de Chateauneuf, "Sur les Enfants trouvés," *Annales d'hygiène publique* 21 (1839): 88–123.

166 Tulard, *Paris et son administration*, p. 508.

167 Pinkney, *The French Revolution of 1830*, p. 62.

168 Louis Blanc, *Histoire de dix ans 1830–1840*, 6th ed. (Paris, 1846), 1: 153.

169 Remusat, *Mémoires*, 2: 313–16. Louis Blanc comments on the first of these meetings as follows: "Par une assez triste bizarrerie, cette révolution qui devait faire tomber la couronne dans le greffe, commença précisément par une consultation d'avocats" ("Sadly and bizarrely, this revolution which was to embroil the crown in litigation began as a lawyers' consultation"). Blanc, *Histoire de dix ans*, 1: 176, 179–81.

170 Pinkney, *The French Revolution of 1830*, pp. 89f.

171 Blanc, *Histoire de dix ans*, 1: 175.

172 Pinkney, *The French Revolution of 1830*, p. 91.

173 Blanc, *Histoire de dix ans*, 1: 186.

174 Events at *Le Temps* (in the lively rue de Richelieu), whose owner Jean-Jacques Baude faced the police with much personal courage, raised the general excitement. See the description in Louis Blanc, *Histoire de dix ans*, 1: 188f.

175 For a detailed account see Pinkney, *The French Revolution of 1830*, pp. 103–8.

176 Ibid., pp. 109–21.

177 On the behavior of the liberals, see ibid., pp. 123–29.

178 See the delightful description of the intrigues centered in the house of the banker Laffitte in Louis Blanc, *Histoire de dix ans*, 1: 271–76.

179 Georges Lacour-Gayet, *Talleyrand* (Paris, 1928–34), 3: 225–32.

180 Blanc, *Histoire de dix ans*, 2: 37.

181 Ibid., 1: 192.

182 Ibid., p. 187.

183 Jean-Lucas Dubreton, *Le Culte de Napoléon 1815–1848* (Paris, 1960), pp. 271– 97.

184 Blanc, *Histoire de dix ans*, 1: 200.

185 Pinkney, *The French Revolution of 1830*, p. 267.

186 Edgar Leon Newman, "The Blouse and the Frock Coat: The Alliance of the Common People of Paris with the Liberal Leadership and the Middle Class during the last Years of the Bourbon Restoration," *Journal of Modern History* 46 (1974): 38–59.

187 Ernest Labrousse, *Le Mouvement ouvrier et les théories sociales en France de 1815 à 1848* (Paris, 1947), pp. 87f.

188 Louis-Sébastien Mercier, *Tableau de Paris* (Amsterdam, 1782–88; repr. Geneva, 1979), 12: 6.

189 Tulard, *Paris et son administration*, 508. See also Pinkney, *The French Revolution of 1830*, 257ff.

190 Soboul, *Les Sans-Culottes*, 402–405.

191 Pinkney, *The French Revolution of 1830*, 253ff.

192 Claude-Philibert Barthelot, Comte de Rambuteau, *Mémoires*, ed. Georges Lequin (Paris, 1905), 374.

Book Five. Between Two Revolutions 1830–1848

1 S. Charléty, *La Monarchie de juillet (1830–1848)*, in *Histoire de France contemporaine depuis la Révolution jusqu'à la paix de 1919*, ed. Ernest Lavisse (Paris, 1921), 5: 5.

2 Edouard Dolléans, *Histoire du Mouvement ouvrier (1830–1871)* (Paris, 1936), 1: 44.

3 Octave Festy, *Le Mouvement ouvrier au début de la Monarchie de Juillet (1830–1834)* (Paris, 1908), pp. 38–44. See also Jean-Pierre Aguet, *Les Grèves sous la Monarchie de Juillet (1830–1847)* (Geneva, 1954), pp. 14–25.

4 See Georges Bourgin, "La Crise ouvrière à Paris dans la seconde moitié de 1830," in *La Revue Historique* 198 (1947): 205. See also Festy, *Le Mouvement ouvrier*, p. 42.

5 Bourgin, "La Crise ouvrière," p. 205.

6 Ibid., p. 207.

7 Festy, *Le Mouvement ouvrier*, p. 44.

8 Jean Tulard, *La Préfecture de police sous la monarchie de juillet* (Paris, 1964), pp. 93–96.

9 David Pinkney, "Laissez-faire or Intervention? Labor Policy in the First Months of the July Monarchy," in *French Historical Studies* 3 (1963): 123–28.

10 Festy, *Le Mouvement ouvrier*, pp. 62f.

11 David H. Pinkney, "Les Ateliers de secours à Paris (1830–1831). Précurseurs des ateliers nationaux de 1848," *La Revue d'histoire moderne et contemporaine* 12 (1965): 66.

12 Bourgin, "La Crise ouvrière," p. 207.

13 Pinkney, "Les Ateliers de secours," pp. 69f.

14 A nice "physiology" of the Paris bourgeoisie is given in Anaïs de Raucou [Bazin, pseud.], "Le Bourgeois de Paris," in *Paris ou le livre des cent-et-un* (Paris, 1831), 1: 39–57.

15 Heinrich Heine, "Französiche Zustände," in *Sämtliche Schriften*, ed. Klaus Briegleb (Munich, 1975), 3: 108.

16 Prince de Joinville, *Vieux Souvenirs* (Paris, 1894), p. 51.

17 Alfred Auguste Cuvillier-Fleury, *Journal intime*, ed. Edouard Bertin (Paris 1900–3), 1: 261–63.

18 Comte Rodolphe Apponyi, *Vingt-Cinq ans à Paris (1826–1850). Journal du Comte Rodolphe Apponyi*, ed. Ernest Daudet (Paris, 1913), 1: 397f.

19 Cited in Jean-Lucas Dubreton, *La Royauté bourgeoise 1830* (Paris, 1930), p. 25.

20 Charléty, *La Monarchie de Juillet*, p. 17. See also Cuvillier-Fleury, *Journal intime*, 1: 272f.

21 Louis Blanc, *Histoire de dix ans, 1830–1840* (Paris, 1846), 2: 264f.

22 Tulard, *La Préfecture de police*, pp. 40–45.

23 Dubreton, *La Royauté bourgeoise*, pp. 47f. See also Blanc, *Histoire de dix ans*, 2: 121f.

24 Apponyi, *Vingt-Cinq ans*, 1: 377.

25 Ibid., p. 384.

26 Ibid., pp. 389–91.

27 Blanc, *Histoire de dix ans*, 2: 204–7.

28 Ibid., pp. 269–77.

29 Charléty, *La Monarchie de Juillet*, pp. 23f.

30 Dubreton, *La Royauté bourgeoise*, p. 60.

31 He once commented to the Austrian attaché in Paris: "I know the French! Don't worry! I know how to deal with them!" See Appponyi, *Vingt-cinq ans*, 3: 64.

32 Jules Bertaut, *Le Roi bourgeois (Louis-Philippe intime)* (Paris, 1936), p. 91.

33 Charléty, "La Monarchie de Juillet," p. 77.

34 Victor Hugo, *Les Misérables*, ed. Maurice Allem (Paris, 1951), pp. 1072f.

35 Apponyi, who was watching the scene, reports: "The coffin was promptly decorated with the flags of foreign refugees, among which one could discern those of Poland and of the new Germany in red, black, and gold colors." Apponyi, *Vingt-cinq ans*, 2: 206.

36 Henri Gisquet, *Mémoires de M. Gisquet, ancien préfet de police* (Paris, 1840), 2: 205–14.

37 Ibid., pp. 214–19.

38 Ibid., pp. 224f.

39 For a description of the desperate fight, see ibid., pp. 236f. See also Blanc, *Histoire de dix ans*, 3: 307–12; and Apponyi, *Vingt-cinq ans*, 2: 210–12.

40 Dubreton, *La Royauté bourgeoise*, p. 99.

41 For details, see Charléty, *La Monarchie de Juillet*, pp. 98f.

42 Gisquet, *Mémoires*, 1: 327–34.

43 Ibid., 3: 381–94.

44 Ibid., pp. 396–99. See also Blanc, *Histoire de dix ans*, 4: 280–85; and Alexandre-Auguste Ledru [Ledru-Rollin], *Mémoire sur les évènements de la rue Transnonain dans les jour-nées des 13 et 14 avril 1834* (Paris, 1834).

45 Anaïs de Raucou [Bazin], "Le Choléra-Morbus à Paris," in *Paris ou le livre des cent-et-un* (Paris, 1831–34), 5: 349f; for details on official preventive measures, see Gisquet, *Mémoires*, 1: 421–37.

46 *Rapport sur la marche et les effets du choléra-morbus dans Paris et les communes rurales du département de la Seine* (Paris, 1834), pp. 45f.

47 Heine, "Französiche Zustände," 3: 179.

48 Louis-René Villermé, "De la Mortalité dans les divers quartiers de la ville de Paris et des causes qui la rendent très différente dans plusieurs d'entre eux, ainsi que dans les divers quartiers de beaucoup des grandes villes," *Annales d'hygiène publique* 3 (1830): 311f. See also William Coleman, *Death Is a Social Disease: Public Health and Political Economy in Early Industrial France* (Madison, Wis., 1982), pp. 149–71.

49 Bazin, "Le Choléra-Morbus," pp. 356f.

50 Cited by Louis Chevalier, *Le Choléra. La première épidémie du XIXe siècle* (La Roche-sur-Yon, 1958), pp. 14f. Louis Blanc comments on such newspaper reports: "Papers close to the court hastened to establish the preferences of the pestilence by listing the names and professions of the victims, to allay the fears of the lucky ones, or to flatter their pride. It was always those in waistcoats or rags who were the ones to head the awful procession from Paris toward death." See Blanc *Histoire de dix ans*, 3: 206.

51 See the explanation of the doctors who worked in the Hôtel-Dieu in *Le Moniteur*, April 1, 1832, pp. 939f.

52 See "Instruction populaire sur les principaux moyens à employer pour se garantir du choléra-morbus, et sur la conduite à tenir lorsque cette maladie se déclare," ibid., March 30, 1832, pp. 911f.

53 Bazin, "Le Choléra-Morbus," pp. 352–55.

54 Apponyi reports in his diaries: "The only precautions that people took, and which became somewhat fashionable, were those of carrying little camphor pouches that lovely ladies

offered their companions; or one had a little box that contained a scented pastille made of mint and camomile; it was customary to carry such a little box in one's vest pocket and to sniff it from time to time." See Apponyi, *Vingt-cinq ans*, 2: 162f.

55 Bazin, "Le Choléra-Morbus," p. 356.

56 Blanc, *Histoire de dix ans*, 3: 213.

57 However, many of the seasonal workers also appear to have left; see Louis-René Villermé, "Note sur les ravages du choléra-morbus dans les maisons garnies de Paris," in *Annales d'hygiène publique* 11 (1834): 38. See also Martin Nadaud, *Mémoires de Léonard, ancien garçon maçon* (Bourganeuf, 1895), p. 62.

58 Blanc, *Histoire de dix ans*, p. 213.

59 Bazin, "Le Choléra-Morbus," p. 358.

60 Chevalier, *Le Choléra*, p. 19.

61 Gisquet, *Mémoires*, 1: 464–67. See also Blanc, *Histoire de dix ans*, 3: 214–16.

62 Tulard, *La Préfecture de police*, p. 132.

63 Bazin, "Le Choléra-Morbus," p. 359.

64 According to Frégier, ragpickers made their rounds three times a day: in the morning, at noon, and at night. See H. A. Frégier, *Des Classes dangereuses de la population dans les grandes villes et des moyens de les rendre meilleures* (Paris, 1840), 1: 104f.

65 Gisquet, *Mémoires*, 1: 458–63.

66 Ibid., p. 469.

67 Jules-Gabriel Janin, *Paris depuis la révolution de 1832* (Brussels, 1832), cited in Chevalier, *Le Choléra*, p. 12.

68 A synopsis of the findings contained in the *Rapport sur la marche et les effets du choléra-morbus* is given in Chevalier, *Le Choléra*, pp. 25–45; a critical appraisal of the report is given in Coleman, *Death Is a Social Disease*, pp. 172–80.

69 *Rapport . . . du choléra-morbus*, p. 120.

70 Ibid., pp. 195f.; on the development of population density in Paris, see C. H. Pouthas, "La Population française pendant la première moitié du XIXe siècle," *I.N.E.D.*, *Travaux et documents*, cahier no. 25 (Paris, 1956), pp. 160–62.

71 *Rapport . . . du choléra-morbus*, pp. 191f.

72 Frégier calculated that an average of 30,000 individuals came to Paris each year looking for work. *Des Classes dangereuses*, 1: 24. See also the discussion in Louis Chevalier, *Classes laborieuses et classes dangereuses à Paris pendant la première moitié du XIXe siècle* (Paris, 1958), pp. 267–71.

73 Hugo, *Les Misérables*, p. 963.

74 Villermé, *Notes sur les ravages du choléra-morbus*, pp. 403f. See also Gisquet, *Mémoires*, 1: 450.

75 Delphine de Girardin [vicomte de Launay], *Lettres parisiennes* (Paris, 1857), 2: 22f.

76 Jules-Gabriel Janin, *Un Hiver à Paris* (Paris, 1847), pp. 201f.

77 *Rapport . . . du choléra-morbus*, p. 124.

78 Ibid., pp. 196–202.

79 Alfred des Cilleuls, *Histoire de l'administration parisienne au dix-neuvième siècle* (Paris, 1900), 2: 98.

80 Claude-Philibert Barthelot comte de Rambuteau, *Mémoires du comte de Rambuteau publiés par son petit-fils*, ed. Georges Lequin (Paris, 1905), pp. 269f.

81 Ibid., p. 291.

82 André Morizet, *Du Vieux Paris au Paris moderne. Haussmann et ses prédécesseurs* (Paris, 1932), p. 109.

83 Rambuteau, *Mémoires*, p. 371.

84 See Chevalier, *Classes laborieuses*, p. 245, n. 2.

85 Morizet, *Du Vieux Paris*, p. 110.

86 Emile Bères, H. Dronsart, and Hector Horeau, *Mémoire sur l'embellissement des Champs-Elysées et les avantages que le gouvernement et la population parisienne doivent en retirer* (Paris, 1836), p. 7.

87 Honoré de Balzac, *Lettres à Madame Hanska*, ed. Roger Pierrot (Paris, 1969), 3: 365.

88 See Karl Hammer, *Jacob Ignaz Hittorf. Ein Pariser Baumeister 1792–1867* (Stuttgart, 1968).

89 See Jules Janin, *Un Hiver à Paris* (Paris, 1847), pp. 33–39.

90 Thomas von Joest, "Hittorf et les embellissements des Champs-Elysées," in *Catalogue de l'exposition Hittorf (1792–1867)*, (Paris, 1986), pp. 153–62. See also Joest, "Des Restaurants, des cafés, d'un théâtre jadis célèbre du Géorama et de la grandeur de quelques projets," ibid., pp. 189–206.

91 Charles de Forster, *Quinze Ans à Paris (1832–1848). Paris et les parisiens* (Paris, 1848), 1: 111f. See also Gustave Flaubert, *L'Education sentimentale*, in *Oeuvres*, ed. A. Thibaudet and R. Dumesnil (Paris, 1968), 2: 54f.

92 *L'Artiste*, 1834, p. 26. The park in the place de la Concorde was also designed by Hittorf. See Jean-Marie Bruson, "La place de la Concorde," in *Catalogue de l'exposition Hittorf*, pp. 75–109.

93 Rambuteau, *Mémoires*, p. 368.

94 Charles Merruau, *Souvenirs de l'Hotel de Ville de Paris 1848–1852* (Paris, 1875), pp. 32–35.

95 Honoré de Balzac, *La Cousine Bette*, ed. Castex, 7: 154f.

96 Rambuteau, *Mémoires*, pp. 373f.

97 Rambuteau took advantage of the expropriation law modified in 1841, which stipulated that "if property is acquired for public construction but is not used for that purpose, its former owners or their heirs can claim its return." In other words, only the width of the street could legally be expropriated, with the result that property owners could make a profit on their real estate now adjacent to a widened street. See Merruau, *Souvenirs*, p. 77.

98 For a detailed survey of Rambuteau's urban accomplishments, see ibid., pp. 339–49.

99 For instance, nothing was done to clean up the pestiferous Halles area or to move its functions to another part of the city. See Dr. Henri Bayard, "Mémoire sur la topographie médicale du IVᵉ arrondissement de la ville de Paris," in *Annales d'Hygiène publique* 28 (1842): 251–309. See also Jacques Lanquetin, *Observations sur un travail de l'administration municipale de Paris, intitulé "Etudes sur les Halles"* (Paris, 1843); and Auguste Tessereau, *Etudes hygiéniques sur les Halles centrales de Paris* (Paris, 1847).

100 Rambuteau, *Mémoires*, pp. 375f.

101 Eugène Belgrand, *Recherches statistiques sur les sources du bassin de la Seine qu'il est possible de conduire à Paris* (Paris, 1854), pp. 25–28.

102 Rambuteau, *Mémoires*, p. 378. It was to his credit that twenty-eight public *pissoirs*, the famous *Vespasiennes*, were erected, which only disappeared in recent times. See Gisquet, *Mémoires*, 4: 429–31.

103 Georges-Eugène Haussmann, *Mémoires du baron Haussmann*, 3rd ed. (Paris, 1893), 3: 237.

104 Eduard Devrient, *Briefe aus Paris* (Berlin, 1840), p. 288.

105 It is interesting to note that contemporaries praised the great care that courtesans lavished on their personal hygiene. See De Forster, *Quinze Ans à Paris*, 2: 296.

106 Frances Trollope, *Paris and the Parisians in 1835* (London, 1836), 1: 231f.

107 Alphonse Guérard, "Observations sur le méphitisme et la désinfection des fosses d'aisances," *Annales d'hygiène publique* 32 (1844): 343f.

108 A. Trébuchet, "Rapports généraux des travaux du Conseil de Salubrité depuis 1829 jusqu'en 1839," ibid., 25 (1841): 82. On the problem of toilets *"dites à l'anglaise"* ("the so-called English toilets"), as well as household bathtubs, used especially by the sick for therapeutic purposes, see Alexandre-Jean-Baptiste Parent-Duchâtelet, "Rapport sur les améliorations à introduire dans les fosses d'aisances, leur mode de vidange et les voiries de la ville de Paris," ibid., 14 (1835): 260–62. The piping of sewage from households into the public sewers was prohibited, under penalty, by an order of the *Conseil d'état* on January 22, 1795. See Gérard Jacquemet, "Urbanisme parisien: La Bataille du tout-à-l'égout à la fin du XIXᵉ siècle," *La Revue d'histoire moderne et contemporaine* 26 (1979): 507. See also *Rapports généraux des travaux du Conseil de salubrité pendant les années 1840 à 1845 inclusivement* (Paris, 1847).

109 See the suggestions, modeled on London's system, in A. Chevallier, "Mémoires sur les égouts de Paris, de Londres, de Montpellier," in *Annales d'hygiène publique* 19 (1838): 366–409.

110 The attitude of house owners is explained as follows:

But if we look more closely at this attitude, we must recognize that it is full of wisdom and corresponds to rather understandable calculations. Indeed there is not one house owner who does not think of his cesspool with horror. The mere thought of its scheduled emptying-out fills him with dread. This operation and its expense often have an adverse effect on the sales value of the property. In view of this attitude, does anyone really believe it is possible to convince them to subscribe to water-main connections? The inevitable consequence would be that the number of cesspool cleanings, which everyone dreads so much, would greatly increase and so would the costs. That is why we consider the current customary installation of cesspools, and the way in which they are emptied, to be the greatest hindrance to individuals who wish to become part of the water distribution system (Parent-Duchâtelet, "Rapport sur les améliorations," p. 306).

111 Alexandre-Jean-Baptiste Parent-Duchâtelet, *Les Chantiers d'écarrisage* [sic] *de la ville de Paris, envisagés sous le rapport de l'hygiène publique* (Paris, 1832), p. 45.

112 *Rapport . . . du choléra-morbus*, p. 38.

113 Cited by Chevalier, *Classes laborieuses*, p. 251. See also the descriptions in Louis Roux, *De Montfaucon, de l'insalubrité de ses établissements et de la necessité de leur suppression immédiate* (Paris, 1841); and Jules Garnier, *Une Visite à la voirie de Montfaucon considerée sous le point de vue de la salubrité publique* (Paris, 1844).

114 Parent-Duchâtelet, *Les Chantiers*, pp. 46–103.

115 Ibid., p. 48.

116 Ibid., pp. 97f.

117 Fourcroy, Hallé, and Thouret, *Rapport sur la voirie de Montfaucon* (Paris, 1788).

118 P. S. Girard, "Du Déplacement de la voirie de Montfaucon," *Annales d'hygiène publique* 9 (1833): 59–82. See also Parent-Duchâtelet, "Des Obstacles que les préjugés medicaux apportent dans quelques circonstances à l'assainissement des villes," ibid., 13 (1835): 243–303.

119 "Montfaucon must be abolished," writes Parent-Duchâtelet. "It is repugnant to the population of Paris and its environs, and public opinion has become more outspoken about it; this sewage dump is an embarrassment to the city and causes visiting foreigners to reproach us." See Parent-Duchâtelet, "Rapport sur les améliorations . . . ," pp. 262f.

120 Rambuteau, *Mémoires*, p. 370.

121 In summarizing Rambuteau's improvements, and in order to present an account of conditions in the twelfth arrondissement in 1844, Dr. Henri Bayard quoted a report by the *Commission sanitaire du quartier du Jardin-des-Plantes et la commission de salubrité du XIIe arrondissement*, which he introduced with these words: "Since that time some paving has been done, and a number of water-main connections have been installed, but nothing has changed in conditions in the inner city." See Dr. Henri Bayard, "Mémoire sur la topographie médicale des Xe, XIe et XIIe arrondissemens [sic] de la ville de Paris. Recherches historiques et statistiques sur les conditions hygiéniques des quartiers qui composent ces arrondissemens [sic]," *Annales d'hygiène publique* 32 (1844): 257–59.

122 Ibid., p. 284.

123 An 1844 report on epidemics states: "It is obvious that to the extent that we make progress in public hygiene the threat of epidemics will decrease. The widening of streets, their cleanliness, paving, and drainage; the relocation of cemeteries, and the draining of damp areas, etc., have either eliminated or at least made less dangerous the epidemic disasters that threatened our ancestors." See M. Bricheteau, "Extrait d'un rapport de la Commission des Epidémies de l'Académie royale de Médecine pour l'année 1839 et une partie de 1840," *Annales d'hygiène publique* 25 (1841): 270.

124 See the *Rapports généraux des travaux du Conseil de salubrité pendant les années 1840 à 1845 inclusivement* (Paris, 1847). See also A. Trébuchet, "Rapports généraux des travaux du Conseil de salubrité pendant les années 1846, 1847 et 1848," *Annales d'hygiène publique*, 2nd ser. 7 (1857): 303–49.

125 Ferdinand Blondel, *Rapport sur les épidémies cholériques de 1832 et 1849 dans les établissements dépendant de l'administration générale de l'Assistance publique de la ville de Paris* (Paris, 1850), p. 81; and Dr. Camille Candy, *Rapport sur le choléra-morbus de Paris* (Lyon, 1849); see also Merruau, *Souvenirs*, pp. 198–200.

126 Alphonse Guérard, "Sur l'épidemie du choléra qui sévit en ce moment à Paris," *Annales d'hygiène publique*, 2nd ser. 1 (1854): 79–101.

127 Louis-René Villermé, "De l'Epidémie typho[ï]de qui a frappé la ville de Paris pendant les cinq premiers mois de 1853," ibid., pp. 83–95.

128 Henri Lecoutourier, *Paris incompatible avec la République. Plan d'un nouveau Paris où les révolutions seront impossibles* (Paris, 1848).

129 Balzac, *Les Petits Bourgeois*, ed. Castex, 8: 22.

130 Centre de documentation d'histoire de technique, *Evolution de la géographie industrielle de Paris et sa proche banlieue au XIXᵉ siècle* (Paris, 1976), 1: 47; Chambre de Commerce de Paris, *Statistiques de l'industrie à Paris resultant de l'enquête faite par la Chambre de Commerce pour les années 1847–1848* (Paris, 1851). See also Bertrand Gille, "Fonctions économiques de Paris," in *Paris, Fonctions d'une capitale. Colloques: Cahiers de civilisation*, ed. Guy Michaud (Paris, 1962), 115–51.

131 Centre de documentation, *Evolution de la géographie industrielle*, 1: 116. See also Maurice Levy-Leboyer, *Les Banques européennes et l'industrialisation internationale dans la première moitié du XIXᵉ siècle* (Paris, 1964), pp. 116–18, 345– 48.

132 David H. Pinkney, *Decisive Years in France, 1840–1847* (Princeton, N.J., 1986), p. 55. Despite the speed with which the European railroad system developed in the 1840s, the old mail coaches continued to coexist with it for quite some time. Victor Fournel comments in amazement in 1858:

As for mail coaches, there is one last remarkable relic left. In the year of grace 1857, at a time of steamships, balloons, and trains, a real mail coach was still in service between Paris and Venice! It needed six weeks for this journey and it never lacked passengers. This mail coach, to which I herewith draw the public's admiring attention and which I recommend to all friends of the good old days, is located in the rue Pavée-Saint-André, where one can see it every two or three days at about six o'clock in the morning as it sets out on its distant expedition. (Victor Fournel, *Ce qu'on voit dans les rues de Paris* [Paris, 1858], p. 273).

133 Michel Mollat, ed., *Histoire de l'Ile-de-France et de Paris* (Toulouse, 1971), p. 460.

134 Egon Caesar Conte Corti, *Das Haus Rothschild in der Zeit seiner Blüte 1830–1871* (Leipzig, 1928), pp. 127f.

135 René Clozier, *La Gare du Nord* (Paris, 1940), pp. 25f. See also C. Polonceau and Victor Bois, "De la Disposition et du service des gares et stations sur les chemins de fer," in *La Revue générale de l'architecture et des travaux publics* 1 (1840): 513–43.

136 Balzac, *Lettres à Mme Hanska*, 2: 606.

137 Bernard Rouleau, *Villages et faubourgs de l'ancien Paris. Histoire d'un espace urbain* (Paris, 1985), pp. 198f.

138 A total of fourteen municipalities were split by the fortifications. See Jean Bastié, *La Croissance de la banlieue parisienne* (Paris, 1964), p. 179. For a detailed description of the Paris fortifications see Félix Pigeory, *Les Monuments de Paris au dix-neuvième siècle. Histoire architectonique de Paris ancien et moderne* (Paris, 1849), pp. 329–37.

139 Around 1840 the seasonal influx of workers decreased; there was a definite trend instead for provincial immigrants to remain in Paris. See Chevalier, *La Formation de la population parisienne*, pp. 219f.

140 See the figures in Rouleau, *Villages et faubourgs*, p. 197.

141 Rambuteau, *Mémoires*, p. 369.

142 See *Préfecture du département de la Seine. Commission d'extension de Paris. Considérations techniques préliminaires* (Paris, 1913), 1: 147.

143 Cited by Bastié, *La Croissance*, p. 180; for a detailed description of the

infrastructural deficits, see *Commission d'extension de Paris*, 1: 150–66. See also Dr. Henri L. Meding, *Essai sur la topographie médicale de Paris* (Paris, 1852), p. 81.

144 See *Evolution de la géographie industrielle*, 1: 101f., 110–17.

145 In 1826 James Fenimore Cooper could still describe the *petite banlieue* as a rural idyll:

Unlike English and American towns, Paris has scarcely any suburbs. Those parts which are called its *Faubourgs* are in truth integral parts of the city, and, with the exception of a few clusters of wine-houses and *guinguettes*, which have collected near its gates to escape the city duties, the continuity of houses ceases suddenly with the *barrières*, and, at the distance of half a mile from the latter, one is as effectually in the country, so far as the eye is concerned, as if a hundred leagues in the provinces. The unfenced meadows, vineyards, lucerne, oats, wheat and vegetables, in many places, literally reach the walls.(James Fenimore Cooper, *Gleanings in Europe: France* [Albany, N.Y., 1983], p. 66).

146 For a systematic analogy between the *classes laborieuses* and nomads and barbarians, see Eugène Buret, *De la Misère des classes laborieuses en Angleterre et en France* (Paris, 1840), 2: 2–14, 49.

147 Flaubert, *l'Education sentimentale*, pp. 133f.

148 Bastié, *La Croissance*, p. 107.

149 Ernest de Chabrol-Chaméane, *Mémoire sur le déplacement de la population dans Paris et sur les moyens d'y remédier présenté par les trois arrondissements de la rive gauche de la Seine à la Commission établie près le ministère de l'Interieur* (Paris, 1840). See also Jacques-Séraphim Lanquetin, *Ville de Paris. Question du déplacement de la population. Etat des études sur cette question* (Paris, 1842).

150 But the fact that the train stations were dispersed over the entire city area did not at first alter the situation. In the north of Paris, the price per square meter around the Gare Saint-Lazare and Tivoli neighborhoods in 1840 was 200 francs; whereas in the south, in the area of the Gare d'Orléans, it was only 13 francs. See Perreymond, "Régénération du vieux Paris," *La Revue générale de l'architecture* 3 (1842): 571n.

151 Ibid.," 573f.

152 On property expropriation, see above, n. 97; the citation is in Chabrol Chaméane, *Mémoire*, pp. 1f.

153 Ibid., p. 2.

154 Ibid., p. 7; see also Lanquetin, *Question du déplacement de la population*, p. 2.

155 Chabrol-Chaméane, *Mémoire*, pp. 9f. See also Lanquetin, *Question du déplacement de la population*, p. 10.

156 Ibid., p. 12.

157 Lanquetin, *Observations sur un travail de l'administration*, p. 9.

158 Lanquetin, *Question du déplacement de la population*, pp. 23f. How large a role the question of security played in these considerations is shown by the concepts developed by Rabusson, who conceives of Paris as "a large battlefield," and which suggest that

the western part be reserved for the bourgeoisie; after all, care must be taken that the working class does not advance any further, but rather that they settle in the east, in the direction of the plain of Vincennes, where the Marne flows into the Seine. . . . Furthermore, the bourgeoisie must be supported and encouraged, and installed as a buffer zone between the working-class arrondissements and the seat of the government. The bourgeoisie should preferably live in the areas adjoining the government district, to the north and east of it, so that the bourgeois arrondissements and apartments resemble a fortification that has to be attacked and overcome before the government is reached (A. Rabusson, *Affaire du déplacement de la population dans Paris. Deuxième note relative au coté politique de ce déplacement* [Paris, 1843], pp. 11–17).

159 "The administrators of this large city should beware of harboring any illusions that they will soon receive a subsidy from the Chamber. Who is unaware that the majority of the deputies, who have forgotten the fable of the limbs and the stomach, act as if they were jealous of the wealth in Paris." Lanquetin, *Question du déplacement de la population*, p. 24.

160 Hippolyte Meynadier, *Paris sous le point de vue pittoresque et monumental, ou Eléments d'un plan général d'ensemble de ses travaux d'art et d'utilité publique* (Paris, 1843). See also the review of this plan, Perreymond, "De la grande circulation dans Paris, et du livre de M. Hippolyte Meynadier, *Paris sous le point de vue . . .*," *La Revue générale de l'architecture* 5 (1844): 184–88, 232–35; and Perreymond, "Régénération du vieux Paris," ibid., 4 (1843): 25–37, 72–88, 413–29, 449–69. Théophile Gautier also offered a fantastic suggestion in "Paris futur," in *Caprices et zigzags* (Paris, 1852), pp. 318–23.

161 Anaïs de Raucou [Bazin], *L'Epoque sans nom, esquisses de Paris 1830–1833* (Paris, 1833), 2: 152f.

162 Delphine de Girardin, *Lettres parisiennes*, 3: 10.

163 Bazin, *l'Epoque sans nom*, 2: 142.

164 Ibid., 2: 298.

165 Hugo, *Les Misérables*, p. 603.

166 Edouard-Ferdinand vicomte de Beaumont-Vassy, *Les Salons de Paris et la société parisienne sous Louis-Philippe Ier* (Paris, 1866), p. 152.

167 Only the boulevard des Italiens was considered fashionable and *comme il faut* by strollers and dandies of the Jockey Club. It ran from the beginning of the rue Drouot up to where the Opera is today, so it was just a few meters long. A charming and detailed account of the life along this boulevard, of the types who went there, of its cafés and other places of entertainment, can be found in Gustave Claudin, *Mes souvenirs, les Boulevards de 1840–1870* (Paris, 1884), pp. 5–45. See also Henri de Villemessant, *Mémoires d'un journaliste* (Paris, 1867–78), 1: 277–92. For a description of the boulevards running from the boulevard de la Madeleine to the place de la Bastille, see Ludwig Rellstab, *Paris im Frühjahr 1843: Briefe, Berichte und Schilderungen* (Leipzig, 1844), 1: 64–80.

168 Delphine de Girardin, *Lettres parisiennes*, 1: 220.

169 Flaubert, *L'Education sentimentale*, p. 384.

170 Balzac, *Lettres à Mme Hanska*, 1: 534.

171 Balzac, *La Fille aux yeux d'or*, ed. Castex, 5: 1045.

172 François Gasnault, "Un Animateur des bals publics parisiens: Philippe Musard (1792–1859)," in *Bulletin de la Société de l'histoire de Paris et de l'Ile-de-France 108* (1982): 117–49.

173 Claude Ruggieri, *Précis historique sur les fêtes, les spectacles et les réjouissances publiques jusqu'au sacre de Charles X* (Paris, 1830); descriptions of the Jardin de la Grande-Chaumière and the Jardin du Tivoli are also given in Auguste Luchet [Pourcelt de Baron], *Paris. Esquisses dédiées au peuple parisien et à M. J. A. Dulaure* (Paris, 1830), pp. 47–63; and in Felix MacDonough, *The Wandering Hermit* (Paris, 1823), 1: 212–16.

174 Gasnault, *Un Animateur des bals publics*, p. 120.

175 Jules Janin, "Les Bals (1832)," in *Oeuvres diverses*, ed. A. de la Fizelière (Paris, 1883), 2nd ser., 5: 292.

176 Hugo, *Les Misérables*, p. 1080.

177 See Auguste Luchet [Pourcelt de Baron], "La Descente de la Courtille en 1833," in *Paris ou le livre des cent-et-un*, 11: 29–55. See also the delightful depiction of the carnival and the "Descente de la Courtille" in 1835, in Apponyi, *Vingt-cinq ans*, 3: 37–46; and Benjamin Gastineau, *Le Carnaval* (Paris, 1855); see also Alain Faure, *Paris Carême-prenant. Du Carnaval a Paris au XIXe siècle* (Paris, 1978).

178 Auguste Luchet [Pourcelt de Baron], *Nouveau Tableau de Paris* (Paris, 1834), 2: 367f.

179 Delphine de Girardin writes on February 15, 1839:

The balls organized by Musard are still very popular. The Bal Musard is of course an old attraction already, hallowed by time and custom. Young people from the best circles of society, who bear the most famous names, display feverish activity heightened still further by their inner emigration and political aversions. They dance, they galop, they waltz with ardor, with passion, the way they would fight if we had a war, the way they would love if people today still had poetry in their hearts. They do not attend the parties at court, ugh! There they would meet their lawyer or their banker; instead they prefer to go to Musard; there they might at least meet their valet or their groom; wonderful! It is possible to dance in front of such people without compromising oneself (Delphine de Girardin, *Lettres parisiennes*, 2: 94f).

180 "Those who were orgiastically inflamed by Romanticism met at the Bal Musard and the Bal des Variétés for wild waltzes, infernal *galops*, and the quadrille, which created real havoc. Today's moderate exuberances are in the tradition of Père Lachaise [the cemetery] if one compares them to that delusory madness created by Musard with his devilish violins. That was a gust of wind, a storm, a gale. A witches' sabbath, a revolt of giants, the eruptions of Vesuvius hardly manage to give the vaguest idea of these dizzying surges. Nothing, not even a raging ocean could have stopped Musard's infernal *galop* once it had started." Arsène Houssaye, *Les Confessions. Souvenirs d'un demi-siècle* (1830–1880) (Paris, 1885), 2: 290f.

181 Edmond de Lignères, comte d'Alton Shée, *Mémoires du vicomte d'Aulnis* (Paris, 1868), pp. 190–92.

182 Rellstab, *Paris im Frühjahr 1843*, 1: 88–90; a similar account is given in Carl Ferdinand Gutzkow, *Paris und Frankreich in den Jahren 1834–1874*, in *Gesammelte Werke* (Jena, 1879), 1st ser., 7: 206–7. See also the delightful description of a carnival ball at the Opéra comique in February 1842 in Heinrich Heine, *Lutetia*, in *Sämtliche Schriften*, ed. Klaus Briegleb, 2d ed., (Munich, 1975), 5: 395.

183 Robert Macaire was the cynical thief in the novel *L'Auberge des Adrets*, by Charles Rabou. He became known through a melodrama with the same title, by Benjamin Antier, published in 1823. But he only became a social type through the caricatures of Daumier, which began to appear in the mid-1830s in the comic magazine *Charivari*.

184 Heine, *Lutetia*, pp. 394f.

185 Cited in Delphine de Girardin, *Lettres parisiennes*, 1: 220f.

186 Alexis de Tocqueville, *Souvenirs*, in *Oeuvres complètes*, ed. J. P. Mayer (Paris, 1964), 12: 83.

187 Gutzkow, *Paris und Frankreich*, pp. 93f.

188 See Nadaud, *Mémoires de Léonard*, pp. 80f.

189 Chevalier, *La Formation de la population parisienne*, pp. 219f.

190 Bernard H. Moss, "Parisian Producer's Associations (1830–51): The Socialism of Skilled Workers," in *Revolution and Reaction. 1848 and the Second French Republic*, ed. Roger Price (London and New York, 1975), pp. 73–86. See also Nadaud, *Mémoires de Léonard*, pp. 193–206.

191 Heine, *Lutetia*, p. 251.

192 Theodore Zeldin, *France 1848–1945* (Oxford, 1973), 1: 468. See also the maréchal de Castellane's diary entry of January 26, 1847, where he notes: "We are threatened by a social upheaval," *Journal du Maréchal de Castellane 1804–1862* (Paris, 1896), 3: 378.

193 Tocqueville, *Souvenirs*, p. 38.

194 Ernest Labrousse, *Aspects de la crise et de la dépression de l'économie française au milieu du XIXᵉ siècle*, Bibliothèque de la Révolution de 1848, vol. 19 (La Roche-sur-Yon, 1956); see also Charles Seignobos, *La Révolution de 1848—Le Second Empire*, in *Histoire de la France contemporaine depuis la Révolution jusqu'à la paix de 1919*, ed. Ernest Lavisse, vol. 6 (Paris, 1921), pp. 31–33.

195 P. and T. Higonnet, "Class Corruption and Politics in the French Chamber of Deputies 1846–1848," *French Historical Studies* 5 (1967): 204–24.

196 Tocqueville aptly described the deeper causes of the corruption of this group in his *Souvenirs*, p. 31.

197 Victor Hugo, *Choses vue, Souvenirs, Journaux, Cahiers 1847–1848*, ed. Hubert Juin (Paris, 1972), p. 156.

198 J. J. Bingham, "The French Banquet Campaign of 1847–1848," *Journal of Modern History* 21 (1959): 1–15.

199 For a full account of these events see the detailed study in Albert Crémieux, *La Révolution de février. Etude critique sur les journées des 21, 22, 23, 24 février 1848* (Paris, 1912).

200 Tocqueville, *Souvenirs*, p. 51.

201 Marie Comtesse d'Agoult [Daniel Stern], *Histoire de la Révolution de 1848* (Paris, 1850–53), 1: 173, n. 2.

202 Alfred-Frédéric-Pierre comte de Falloux, *Mémoires d'un royaliste* (Paris, 1888), 1: 265. In his *Souvenirs*, Maxime Du Camp ends his report of the events of February 22, 1848, with the following anecdote: "As I was returning to my apartment, my doorman—who had been a *gendarme des chasses* under Charles X—asked what the news was. 'They're burning the chairs in the parks.' 'Ah,' he answered, 'that's how the July Revolution began too!'" Maxime Du Camp, *Souvenirs de l'année 1848*, ed. Maurice Agulhon (Paris and Geneva, 1979), p. 38.

203 On the role of the army during the February Revolution see Jonathan M. House, "Civil-Military Relations in Paris, 1848," in *Revolution and Reaction*, ed. Roger Price (London and New York, 1975), p. 150.

204 House, "Civil-Military Relations," pp. 151f. See also Louis Girard, *La Garde nationale 1814–1871* (Paris, 1964), pp. 261–86.

205 Du Camp, *Souvenirs*, p. 53.

206 Flaubert, *L'Education sentimentale*, p. 315.

207 See interesting details in Marie comtesse d'Agoult, *Histoire*, 1: 196f.

208 There is a detailed eyewitness report in Du Camp, *Souvenirs*, pp. 63–67. See also Crémieux, *La Révolution de février*, pp. 191–96; and Albert Crémieux, "La Fusillade du boulevard des Capucines le 23 février 1848," *La Révolution de 1848* 8 (1911): 99–124.

209 Marie comtesse d'Agoult, *Histoire*, 1: 202.

210 There is a description in Flaubert, *L'Education sentimentale*, pp. 320f.

211 Prosper Mérimée, *Corréspondance générale*, ed. Maurice Parturier (Paris and Toulouse, 1946), 5: 253.

212 Tocqueville, *Souvenirs*, p. 75. See also Du Camp, *Souvenirs*, pp. 72–74.

213 Tocqueville, *Souvenirs*, p. 61. Prosper Mérimée comments similarly: "Truly, the July Monarchy has been brought down by whistles rather than musket shots." See Mérimée, *Correspondance*, 5: 252.

214 Du Camp, *Souvenirs*, p. 109.

215 Tocqueville, *Souvenirs*, p. 99.

216 Flaubert, *L'Education sentimentale*, p. 325.

217 See the delightful account of these activities in Du Camp, *Souvenirs*, pp. 120f.

218 Ibid., pp. 126f.; and Flaubert, *L'Education sentimentale*, p. 325. See also Merruau, *Souvenirs*, pp. 285–88.

219 Charles Schmidt, *Les Journées de Juin 1848* (Paris, 1926), p. 24.

220 Du Camp, *Souvenirs*, pp. 133–36. See also Girard, *La Garde nationale*, pp. 293–97.

221 Du Camp, *Souvenirs*, pp. 137f.

222 Mérimée, *Correspondance*, 5: 274f.

223 Charles Schmidt, *Des Ateliers nationaux aux barricades du juin* (Paris, 1948), pp. 9–13.

224 On the *ateliers nationaux* see Donald Cope MacKay, *The National Workshops: A Study in the French Revolution of 1848* (Cambridge, Mass., 1933).

225 Seignobos, *La Révolution de 1848*, p. 44.

226 Schmidt, *Des Ateliers nationaux*, pp. 15–17.

227 Seignobos, *La Révolution de 1848*, p. 46.

228 Cited by Schmidt, *Des Ateliers nationaux*, p. 27.

229 A typical example of this "bourgeois" attitude is the description given by Dr. Poumiès de la Siboutie in his memoirs:

I often had a chance to visit these so-called *ateliers nationaux*. No doubt there were many decent people there, who were well-behaved and were reliable workers, who were willing to work for what they were paid; but there was a rebellious and corrupt minority there as elsewhere, who had nothing in mind but to cause agitation and unrest, who did not want to work, and who could not stand seeing others work. They spent their days making noise, singing, and gossiping. At times individual groups of them played bingo or cards; and they danced like savages. They referred to the *ateliers* as *râteliers* (troughs). In the Girondin anthem, instead of the refrain "To die [mourir] for the fatherland," they sang: "To be nourished [nourri] by the fatherland / That is the best lot" etc.

Occasionally they organized lectures; thus they heard a talk on Lamartine's *History of the Gironde*, commented on from their point of view. See Dr. Poumiès de la Siboutie, *Souvenirs d'un médecin de Paris* (Paris, 1910), pp. 311f. See also Mark Traugott, *Armies of the Poor: Determinants of Working-class Participation in the Parisian Insurrection of June 1848* (Princeton, N.J., 1985), pp. 127–47.

230 Rémi Gossez, "La Presse parisienne à destination des ouvriers, 1848–1851," in *La Presse ouvrière, 1819–1850*, ed. Jacques Godechot, Bibliothèque de la Révolution de 1848, vol. 23 (La Roche-sur-Yon, 1966), pp. 123–90.

231 Peter Amann, "The Paris Club Movement," in *Revolution and Reaction*, ed. Roger Price (London and New York, 1975), pp. 115–32. See also the account of club life in Flaubert, *L'Education sentimentale*, pp. 332–40. Though this club movement had a decidedly middle-class clientele, the *classes laborieuses* had their own organizations. See Rémi Gossez, *Les Ouvriers de Paris, I: L'Organisation 1848–1851*, in Bibliothèque de la Révolution de 1848, vol. 24 (La Roche-sur-Yon, 1967).

232 Peter Amann, "A *journée* in the Making: May 15, 1848," *Journal of Modern History* 42, no. 1 (1970): 42–69. See also *Rapport de la commission d'enquête sur l'insurrection qui a éclaté dans la journée du 23 juin et sur les évènements du 15 mai* (Paris, 1848).

233 Cited by Schmidt, *Les Journées*, p. 26.

234 Tocqueville, *Souvenirs*, p. 131.

235 See the eyewitness reports ibid., pp. 132–42; and Du Camp, *Souvenirs*, pp. 165–97.

236 Schmidt, *Les Journées*, p. 27. See also Tocqueville, *Souvenirs*, p. 148.

237 Schmidt, *Des Ateliers nationaux*, pp. 27–29.

238 Tocqueville, *Souvenirs*, pp. 144–47; see also Balzac, *Lettres à Mme Hanska*, 4: 363; and Henri d'Almeras, *La Vie parisienne sous la République de 1848* (Paris, n.d.), pp. 195–204.

239 Tocqueville, *Souvenirs*, p. 143.

240 Schmidt, *Des Ateliers nationaux*, pp. 29f.

241 Maurice Agulhon, *1848 ou l'Appren-*

tissage de la République 1848–1852, in *Nouvelle histoire de la France contemporaine*, vol. 8 (Paris, 1973), pp. 65f.

242 Tocqueville, *Souvenirs*, p. 151.

243 See details in Marie comtesse d'Agoult, *Histoire*, 2: 372–469. See also Pierre de la Gorce, *Histoire de la Seconde République française* (Paris, 1887), 1: 321–96; and Schmidt, *Les Journées*, pp. 38–114.

244 See the plan of the barricades in Louis Girard, "La Deuxième République et le Second Empire 1848–1870," in *Nouvelle histoire de Paris* (Paris, 1981), pp. 36f. See also Agulhon, *1848*, p. 71. For a detailed description of the eastern battlefield, see Merruau, *Souvenirs*, pp. 184–88.

245 Charles Tilly and Lynn H. Lees, "The People of June 1848," in Roger Price, ed., *Revolution and Reaction*, p. 186.

246 Cited by Agoult, *Histoire*, 2: 384.

247 Cited ibid., p. 376.

248 Cited by Schmidt, *Des Ateliers nationaux*, p. 47.

249 Pierre Caspard, "Aspects de la lutte des classes en 1848: Le recrutement de la Garde nationale mobile," *La Revue historique* 252 (1974): 81–106. See also Pierre Chalmin, "Une Institution militaire de la Seconde République: La Garde nationale mobile," *Etudes d'Histoire moderne et contemporaine* 2 (1948): 37–82; and Traugott, *Armies of the Poor*, pp. 34–113.

250 Ernest and Henriette Renan, *Nouvelles lettres intimes, 1846–1850* (Paris, 1923), pp. 209f.

251 See the revealing letter by Mérimée, who was one of the *badauds de la bataille* ("battle-curious"), in Mérimée, *Correspondance*, 5: 335–53.

252 See the discussion of the "Liste générale en ordre alphabétique des inculpés de juin 1848," in Tilly and Lees, "The People of June 1848," pp. 186–201.

253 See the numerous references in Victor Hugo, *Choses vues*, pp. 103–217. See also Merruau, *Souvenirs*, pp. 188–90.

BOOK SIX. The Second Empire
1852–1870

1 Charles Merruau, *Souvenirs de l'Hôtel de Ville de Paris, 1848–1852* (Paris, 1875), p. 84.
2 Victor Hugo, *Choses vues. Souvenirs, journaux, cahiers 1830–1885,* ed. Hubert Juin (Paris, 1972), vol. 2 (1847–1848), p. 380.
3 Ibid., p. 388.
4 André-Jean Tudesq, *L'Election présidentielle de Louis-Napoléon. 10 décembre, 1848* (Paris, 1965), p. 210.
5 See the account in Hugo, *Choses vues 1849–1869,* pp. 120–22.
6 Merruau, *Souvenirs,* p. 183.
7 Ibid., pp. 188f.
8 See the statistics on welfare in Armand Husson, *Les Consommations de Paris* (Paris, 1856), pp. 32–39.
9 Merruau, *Souvenirs,* p. 197.
10 Ibid., p. 198. As in 1832, the disease again emphasized social inequality, there being considerably more victims in the eastern and poorer areas of the city than in the wealthier, western neighborhoods. See Ferdinand Blondel, *Rapport sur les épidémies cholériques de 1832 et 1849 (de 1853 et de 1854) dans les établissements dépendant de l'administration générale de l'assistance publique de la ville de Paris* (Paris, 1850–55), p. 83; see also *Recherches statistiques sur la ville de Paris et le Département de la Seine* (Paris, 1823–60), 6: 455–71.
11 See the figures given in Maxime Du Camp, *Paris, ses organes, ses fonctions et sa vie dans la seconde moitié du XIXᵉ siècle,* 7th ed. (Paris, 1884), 6: 400.
12 "Rapport du Directeur des Contributions directes de la Seine au préfet, 10 octobre 1850," cited in Adeline Daumard, *Maisons de Paris et propriétaires parisiens au XIXᵉ siècle 1809–1880* (Paris, 1965), p. 23.
13 The population of Paris grew from 785,000 in 1831 to 1,053,300 in 1851. See *Département de la Seine. Service de la statistique municipale. Résultats statistiques du dénombrement pour la ville de Paris et le département de la Seine* (Paris, 1899), p. 426.
14 Louis Girard, *La Deuxième République et le Second Empire 1848–1870. Nouvelle Histoire de Paris* (Paris, 1981), p. 53.
15 See Alfred Des Cilleuls, *Histoire de l'administration parisienne au XIXᵉ siècle* (Paris, 1900), 2: 192.
16 Merruau, *Souvenirs,* pp. 77f.
17 Jeanne Gaillard, *Paris La Ville (1852–1870)* (Paris, 1977), p. 23.
18 Ibid., pp. 24f.
19 Merruau, *Souvenirs,* pp. 149–56. Financing of this work was settled by a law of October 4, 1849, that determined that two-thirds of the costs be paid by the city and the remaining third by the State. See Gaillard, *Paris,* p. 31.
20 As the Constitution of the Republic precluded the reelection of an acting president, Louis Napoleon's presidency ended in May 1852. Jasper Ridley, *Napoleon III and Eugenie* (London, 1979), p. 279. See also Merruau, *Souvenirs,* pp. 375–78.
21 Ibid., p. 443.
22 Pierre Lavedan, *Histoire de l'urbanisme à Paris. Nouvelle Histoire de Paris* (Paris, 1975), pp. 404–11.
23 Victor Hugo provides an anecdote that is indicative of Louis Napoleon's ignorance about the city of his birth: "Louis Napoleon knew Paris so little that when we met for the first time he told me, 'I often looked for you. I went to your old apartment. What sort of a square is this place des Vosges?' 'It is the place Royale,' I responded. 'Ah,' he answered, 'is that an old square?'" Hugo, *Choses vues 1849–1869,* pp. 103f.
24 David H. Pinkney, *Napoleon III and the Rebuilding of Paris* (Princeton, N. J., 1958), pp. 29–34.
25 Merruau, *Souvenirs,* pp. 363f.
26 Gaillard, *Paris,* p. 30.
27 Merruau, *Souvenirs,* pp. 486–90. See also André Morizet, *Du Vieux Paris au Paris moderne. Haussmann et ses prédécesseurs* (Paris, 1932), p. 150.
28 Merruau, *Souvenirs,* pp. 482f.
29 William Nassau Senior, *Conversations with Distinguished Persons during the Second Empire from 1860 to 1863* (London, 1880), 1: 193. Senior's compatriot, Bayle St. John, remarked apropos of the building boom: "I cannot help meditating whether this

system of employing a third of the population in knocking down and building up the capital, with the professed object of giving work to the classes that make *émeutes*, is not a coarse form of Communism." Bayle St. John, *Purple Tints of Paris: Character and Manners in the New Empire* (London, 1854), p. 11. Between 1852 and 1869 a total of 19,726 houses containing 117,553 apartments were demolished; in the same period 34,160 new buildings with 215,304 apartments were put up. See Françoise Marnata, *Les Loyers des bourgeois de Paris 1860–1958* (Paris, n.d.), p. 14.

30 Merruau, *Souvenirs*, p. 496.

31 From 1852 to 1870 tax revenues increased from 53 million to 172 million francs. See A. Bailleux de Marisy, "La Ville de Paris devant le Corps législatif," *La Revue des deux mondes* 86 (1870): 420. See also the pertinent explanations of this financing system in Jean-Gilbert-Victor Fialin, duc de Persigny, *Mémoires*, ed. H. de Laire comte d'Espagny (Paris, 1896), pp. 244f.

32 See Morizet, *Du Vieux Paris*, pp. 201f.

33 On the financial balance of the transformation of Paris, see Louis Girard, *La Politique des travaux publics du Second Empire* (Paris, 1952), pp. 261–358.

34 Prosper Ménière, *Journal*, ed. Dr. E. Ménière (Paris, 1903), p. 26.

35 See Persigny, *Mémoires*, pp. 240–43. See also Morizet, *Du Vieux Paris*, p. 152.

36 Persigny, *Mémoires*, pp. 248f.

37 Ibid., p. 250.

38 Among the numerous biographies of Haussmann, see especially J. M. and Brian Chapman, *The Life and Times of Baron Haussmann; Paris in the Second Empire* (London, 1957); and Gérard-Noël Lameyre, *Haussmann, Préfet de Paris* (Paris, 1958). See also the remarkable characterization of Haussmann in Persigny, *Mémoires*, pp. 253–55.

39 Georges-Eugène Haussmann, *Mémoires du Baron Haussmann* (Paris, 1890), 2:

53. On the fate of Napoleon's sketch-map, see Morizet, *Du Vieux Paris*, p. 130.

40 See David H. Pinkney, *Napoleon III*, pp. 27–29.

41 Merruau, *Souvenirs*, pp. 364f.

42 In 1854 Bayle St. John understood the motivation for the new construction in Paris: "Whole quarters, refuges of poverty and democracy, have been cut down; broad streets, by which fresh air and artillery may penetrate in every direction, have been opened; public buildings, capable of being used as fortresses, are rising everywhere." Bayle St. John, *Purple Tints of Paris*, pp. 4–5.

43 On the theory of Bonapartism, see Theodore Zeldin, *France 1848–1945*, 1: 504–60. See also Dieter Groh, "Caesarismus," in *Geschichtliche Grundbegriffe. Historisches Lexikon zur politisch-sozialen Sprache in Deutschland*, ed. O. Brunner, W. Conze, and R. Koselleck (Stuttgart, 1972), 1: 726–71. For an analysis of the transformation of Paris, see Marcel Cornu, *La Conquête de Paris* (Paris, 1972), pp. 55–78.

44 Haussmann, *Mémoires*, pp. 13–16.

45 The to-do over the plans for the new opera house, whose very mention had to be avoided if one did not want to frighten the National Assembly, is a good example. See Pinkney, *Napoleon III*, p. 60.

46 Haussmann, *Mémoires*, 3: 9.

47 Ibid., 2: 202f., 3: 55.

48 For details on work contained in the first *réseau*, see ibid., pp. 59–64.

49 Eventually the state's share of the costs of the second *réseau* was decreased to a maximum of 50 million francs. See Morizet, *Du Vieux Paris*, p. 202.

50 Haussmann, *Mémoires*, 3: 66.

51 For details on the second réseau, see Haussmann, *Mémoires*, 3: 66–86. See also Henri Malet, *Le Baron Haussmann et la rénovation de Paris* (Paris, 1973), pp. 185– 202; and Pinkney, *Napoleon III*, pp. 60–68.

52 Between 1861 and 1872, 4,268 new buildings were erected in the seventh, eighth, fifteenth, and sixteenth

arrondissements alone, a figure that represents 30 percent of all dwellings put up in Paris in this period. See Centre de documentation d'histoire et de technique, *Evolution de la Géographie industrielle de Paris et sa proche banlieue au XIXᵉ siècle* (Paris, 1976), 1: 302.

53 Haussmann, *Mémoires*, 3: 86–100. See also Malet, *Le Baron Haussmann*, pp. 233– 51.

54 Émile Zola, *La Curée*, in *Les Rougon-Macquart. Histoire naturelle et sociale d'une famille sous le Second Empire*, ed. Armand Lanoux (Paris, 1960), 1: 389. All further references will be to this edition.

55 Haussmann, *Mémoires*, 3: 21.

56 Ibid., pp. 54f.

57 Persigny's failure to mention the strategic importance of the transformation of Paris is seen by Pinkney as an indication that such motives were indeed only of secondary importance! But Pinkney overlooks the fact that Persigny, "the least of all men [to] dissimulate the government's intent to use force in maintaining order" (Pinkney, *Napoleon III*, p. 36) could also have written his memoirs with thoroughly apologetic intentions.

58 Haussmann, *Mémoires*, 3: 29, 60.

59 *Recherches statistiques*, 6: 10.

60 Haussmann, *Mémoires*, 3: 554. See also Morizet, *Du Vieux Paris*, pp. 206–8.

61 Gaillard, *Paris*, p. 33.

62

Arrondissement	1800	1848	1856
Tuileries	10,540	14,207	8,534
Saint-Honoré	9,764	12,639	8,076
Marches	8,861	10,936	5,205
Lombards	11,844	16,881	11,451
Les Arcis	8,741	13,046	3,761

Cited in *Recherches statistiques*, 6: 10. According to Louis Lazare, fifty-seven streets and passages, as well as 2,227 houses, were sacrificed to the *croisée de Paris*; he also gives a figure of 25,000 inhabitants who were driven away on account of the construction. See Louis Lazare, *Etudes Municipales. Les quartiers pauvres de Paris* (Paris, 1869), pp. 51, 83–90.

63 For the special strategic significance of the boulevard du Prince Eugène, see Pinkney, *Napoleon III*, pp. 65–66.

64 For a description of this slum, see Abel Transon and Dublanc, "Observations sur quelques industries et, en particulier sur le commerce des chiffons dans le XII arrondissement de Paris," *Annales d'hygiène publique*, 2nd ser., 1 (1854): 63–78.

65 For full text see above, p. 266; Haussmann, *Mémoires*, 3: 54f.

66 For an interpretation of Haussmann's claims of "blamelessness" in connection with traffic improvements, see Louis Réau et al., *L'Oeuvre du Baron Haussmann, préfet de la Seine (1853–1870)* (Paris, 1954), pp. 31–36. See also Anthony Sutcliffe, *The Autumn of Central Paris: The Defeat of Town Planning 1850–1870* (London, 1970), pp. 27– 29, 33–39.

67 See the general map of barricade construction in June 1848 in Girard, *La Deuxième République et le Second Empire*, p. 37. See also Maurice Halbwachs, *La Population et les tracées de voies à Paris depuis un siècle* (Paris, 1928), pp. 76–78.

68 This conclusion is borne out by the fact that the cholera epidemics of 1854 and 1856 were most severe in the fourth arrondissement (corresponding to the new division of 1860), in the Arcis, Lombards, Marché-Saint-Jean and Hôtel de Ville neighborhoods, whereas the areas to the west of the rue Saint-Denis were mostly spared. Préfecture du Département de la Seine. Secrétariat général. Service de la statistique municipale, *Tableaux statistiques de l'épidémie cholérique de 1884 à Paris et étude statistique des épidémies antérieures* (Paris, 1886), pp. 45–47.

69 Joseph-Antoine Bouvard and Gustave Jourdan, eds., *Recueil de règlements concernant le service des alignements et de la police de constructions dans la ville de Paris* (Paris, 1900), pp. 175–77. On the importance of the law see Jeanne Hugueney, "Un Centenaire oublié: La première loi française d'urbanisme, 13 avril 1850," in *La vie urbaine* (1950), pp.

241–49. See also Ann Louise Shapiro, *Housing the Poor of Paris, 1850–1902* (Madison, Wis., 1985), pp. 18f; and Gustave Jourdan, *Législation sur les logements insalubres, traité pratique* (Paris, 1879). For criticism of this law, see Emile Laurent, *Les Logements insalubres, la loi de 1850, son application, ses lacunes* (Paris, 1882).

70 Article 13 of the Law of April 13, 1850. See also A. Bailleux de Marisy, "La Ville de Paris: Ses finances et ses travaux publics depuis le commencement du siècle," *Revue des deux mondes* 47 (1863): 806.

71 Under Article 4 of the Decree of March 26, 1852, "each building owner was expected to provide an architect's plan and blueprints and to adhere to the regulations required for public security and hygiene." Cited in Robinet and Trébuchet (Rapporteurs), "Rapport général sur les travaux de la Commission des logements insalubres pendant les années 1852, 1853, 1854, 1855 et 1856," *Annales d'hygiène publique*, 2nd ser., 8 (1857): 470.

72 Haussmann, *Mémoires*, 3: 86.

73 It seems almost unnecessary to point out that each of these "stars" with its radiating streets also ensured the strategic control of the arrondissements around it.

74 See the charming account of this neglected arrondissement and the demolition work begun there in 1877 in Max Nordau, *Aus dem wahren Milliardenlande: Pariser Studien und Bilder* (Leipzig, 1878), 1: 16–19.

75 Adeline Daumard, "L'Avenue de l'Opéra de ses origines à la Guerre de 1914," *Bulletin de la Société de l'Histoire de Paris et de l'Ile-de-France*, (1970), p. 161.

76 In this connection it is revealing to read the criticism of the extension of the rue Lafayette made by Ferdinand de Lasteyrie, one of Haussmann's tenacious critics, in 1861:

What sort of an idea is it to extend the rue Lafayette to the boulevard des Capucines and thus cut at an angle into all the affluent streets of the Chaussée d'Antin area; to destroy the wealthiest

houses and the last gardens there; and at the same time to pay large compensations for dislodging rich financial companies located there; and all of that just to have the steady traffic from two or three train stations converge in the neighborhood of the future opera, already overburdened by traffic. (Ferdinand de Lasteyrie, *Les Travaux de Paris: Examen critique* [Paris, 1861], pp. 82f)

77 Haussmann, *Mémoires*, 3: 87–89.

78 Cited by Gaillard, *Paris*, pp. 37f.

79 The best and most detailed contemporary analysis of strategic motivations for the transformation of Paris is in Victor Fournel, *Paris nouveau, Paris futur* (Paris, 1865), pp. 29–40.

80 The number of tenants per house in the first six arrondissements had decreased to such an extent that it approximated the Paris average. *Evolution de la Géographie industrielle de Paris*, 1: 301.

81 Lasteyrie, *Les Travaux de Paris*, pp. 75–77.

82 Haussmann, *Mémoires*, 3: 72f.

83 Préfecture du Département de la Seine. Commission d'extension de Paris, *Considérations techniques préliminaires* (Paris, 1913), p. 29. See also Gaillard, *Paris*, pp. 45f; and the criticism of Louis Lazare in *Les Quartiers pauvres*, pp. 71–75.

84 Préfecture du Département de la Seine. Commission d'extension de Paris, *Aperçu historique* (Paris, 1913), pp. 199f.

85 Zola, *La Curée*, pp. 389f.

86 For a detailed description of the development of the west end of Paris see Lucien Dubech and Pierre d'Espezel, *Histoire de Paris* (Paris, 1931), 2: 144f.

87 On the population density of the eastern arrondissements see *Evolution de la géographie industrielle de Paris*, 1: 303.

88 Anthime Corbon, *Le Secret du peuple de Paris* (Paris, 1863), p. 200.

89 See Daumard, *Maisons de Paris*, pp. 203–5.

90 The symmetry of the facades was Hausssmann's idée fixe. See his circular, "Aux Commissaires-voyers de Paris, rélativement à l'harmonie a établir entre les façades des maisons

neuves, 5 octobre 1855," in *La Revue générale de l'architecture et des travaux publics* 13 (1855): 406–7. See also Haussmann, *Mémoires*, 3: 24f., 76, 215. Moreover, the administration had to see the plans for a facade before it would issue a building permit. See Charles Lortsch, *La Beauté de Paris et la loi* (Paris, 1912), pp. 33–35, 95–110; see also the description of the facade of Saccard's house built near the Parc de Monceau in Zola, *La Curée*, p. 331.

91 See François Loyer, *Paris XIXe siècle. L'Immeuble et la rue* (Paris, 1987), pp. 233–60; and Gaillard, *Paris*, pp. 72f. The uniform monumentality of Haussmann's facades upset many of his contemporaries. Perhaps the most amusing criticism comes from the pen of Victor Fournel, who writes in 1865:

The appearance of Paris has become a question of cadastral survey administered by surveyors and in the hands of an inflexible bureaucracy; Paris resembles a material appendix to the Code Napoléon. The big city is being disciplined according to the wishes of its colonel, as if it were a regiment; its houses stand at attention in rank and file, according to size and facing front; they wear uniforms and are shiny from head to toe like soldiers on parade. The bourgeoisie, whose greatest joy it is to watch the infantry parade on the Champ-de-Mars for as far as the eye can see . . . admire this sight as well, for it gives them almost the same wealth of perspective and variety of aspects. We only have one street now in Paris: the rue de Rivoli. Not content with cutting through the entire city from one end to the other, it also appears in other places, just hiding under different names. Fournel, *Paris nouveau*, pp. 14f.

See also the late Romantic gothicizing criticism of Stéphane Gachet, *Paris tel qu'il doit être* (L'Ile-de-la-Cité, Paris, 1856), pp. 11f. What emphasized the monotony of bourgeois apartment houses still more was the height of each story, officially limited to 2 meters 60; moreover, depending on the width of the street, seven floors were the maximum allowed. See Charles Magny, *Des*

Moyens juridiques de sauvegarder les aspects esthétiques de la ville de Paris (Paris, 1911), pp. 48f.

92 See the criticism in Léon Colin, *Paris, sa topographie, son hygiène, ses maladies* (Paris, 1885), pp. 133f.

93 Daumard, *Maisons de Paris*, p. 206.

94 Georges Duveau, *La Vie ouvrière en France sous le Second Empire* (Paris, 1946), p. 344.

95 On the role of financial companies in the transformation of Paris, see A. Bailleux de Marisy, "Des Sociétés foncières et leur rôle dans les travaux publics," *Revue des deux mondes*, 2e période, 34 (1861): 193–216.

96 Pinkney, *Napoleon III*, pp. 90f.

97 Daumard, *Maisons de Paris*, pp. 220–29.

98 Gaillard, *Paris*, pp. 121–26.

99 Girard, *La Politique des travaux publics*, p. 206.

100 Gaillard, *Paris*, pp. 75–79.

101 Louis Chevalier, *La Formation de la population parisienne au XIXe siècle* (Paris, 1950), p. 83.

102 The number of residents in the lodging houses in the center of the city increased noticeably after 1851. See Gaillard, *Paris*, pp. 208–14.

103 See the statistics on the import of freestone into Paris in the years 1847–1869 in Girard, *La Deuxième République et le Second Empire*, p. 198.

104 Ibid., p. 162.

105 Ibid., p. 145.

106 However, rents increased in these old apartment buildings as well. See Elsie Canfora-Argandona and Roger H. Guerrand, *La Répartition de la population. Les conditions de logement des classes ouvrières à Paris au XIXe siècle* (Paris, 1977), pp. 48–52.

107 Gaillard, *Paris*, p. 84. See also Henri Bonnet, "La Carte des pauvres à Paris," *Revue des deux mondes*, 5e période, 35 (1906): 381–420.

108 The boulevard Saint-Germain, especially, met the needs of the bourgeoisie living on the Left Bank. See A. Husson, *De la Régénération de la rive gauche de la Seine* (Paris, 1856), pp. 7f.

109 On the development of the entire Left Bank see Gaillard, *Paris*, pp. 85–100.

110 See the description in Morizet, *Du Vieux Paris*, pp. 222–24.

111 See above, pp. 225–31.

112 This is shown by the population growth in some communes of the *petite banlieue*, which grew as large as medium-size towns:

	1800	1846	1856
Belleville	1,684	27,556	57,699
Monceaux	—	19,864	44,094
Montmartre	609	14,710	36,450
La Chapelle	788	14,398	33,355

Cited in Commission d'Extension de Paris, *Aperçu historique*, p. 136, table I.

113 Ibid., pp. 145–47.

114 Bernard Rouleau, *Villages et faubourgs de l'ancien Paris. Histoire d'un espace urbain* (Paris, 1985), p. 215.

115 Commission d'Extension de Paris, *Aperçu historique*, pp. 142f.

116 Chevalier, *La Formation de la Population*, p. 126.

117 For a detailed discussion of this controversy, see Gaillard, *Paris*, pp. 49–53. See also Michel Chevalier, *L'Industrie et l'octroi de Paris*, 2d ed. (Paris, 1867).

118 Commission d'Extension de Paris, *Aperçu historique*, pp. 183f; see also Gaillard, *Paris*, pp. 55–61, 466f.

119 Ibid., pp. 191f.

120 Commission d'Extension de Paris, *Considérations techniques préliminaires*, pp. 45f. See also Morizet, *Du Vieux Paris*, pp. 239f.

121 Commission d'Extension de Paris, *Aperçu historique*, pp. 151–58.

122 It is revealing to note what Haussmann has to say in this connection to the *Conseil général du département de la Seine*, on December 3, 1866: "The construction of streets all over the city is being carried out to decrease population density in the old arrondissements, and also to open these up to traffic; this also applies to all the new arrondissements that have been incorporated into Paris, so as to make them habitable." Cited in Girard, *La Deuxième République et le Second Empire*, p. 171.

123 Chevalier, *La Formation de la Population*, pp. 241–44.

124 Emile Zola, *Une Page d'amour. Les Rougon-Macquart*, 2: 850–53, 904–9, 972f., 1,026–33, 1,091.

125 Marie Claire Bancquart, *Images littéraires du Paris "fin-de-siècle"* (Paris, 1979), p. 71.

126 *Evolution de la Géographie industrielle*, 1: 192f.

127 Haussmann, *Mémoires*, 3: 292–96.

128 *Evolution de la Géographie industrielle*, 1: 304f.

129 See Haussmann, *Mémoires*, 3: 303–17, 327–46. See also Maurice Block and Henri de Pontich, *Administration de la ville de Paris et du département de la Seine* (Paris, 1884), 463–69; and Pinkney, *Napoleon III*, pp. 105–26.

130 *Evolution de la Géographie industrielle*, 1: 307.

131 Ibid., p. 308.

132 On the Companie générale des eaux, see Jean-Pierre Goubert, *La Conquête de l'eau* (Paris, 1986), pp. 177–79, 181f.

133 Block and Pontich, *Administration de la ville de Paris*, pp. 474f.

134 The price for a cubic meter of fresh water was between 0.30 and 0.40 francs. See Gérard Jacquemet, "Urbanisme parisien: La bataille du tout-à-l'égout à la fin du XIXe siècle," in *Revue d'Histoire moderne et contemporaine* 26 (1979): 506.

135 Not until modification of the contract in 1880 did the Compagnie générale become responsible for installing water pipes on all floors of a building at its own expense. See Block and Pontich, *Administration de la ville de Paris*, pp. 480, 481. Yet it took until 1940(!) for 97.6 percent of all apartments in Paris to have a water connection. See Goubert, *La Conquête de l'eau*, p. 241. This explains why water-carriers were still around at the end of the Second Empire. See Du Camp, *Paris*, 5: 260.

136 Zola, *La Curée*, pp. 478f. The care that courtesans lavished on their personal hygiene at that time was proverbial, as even members of the bourgeoisie were still very cursory in such matters. This was due not only to the expense of obtaining and getting rid of the water, but also to a traditional dislike of water. See

Goubert, *La Conquête de l'eau,* pp. 65–121. A diary entry (May 29, 1867) by Jules Michelet, on the daily morning toilet of his wife, is very revealing: "She takes care of her personal hygiene early in the morning between five and seven o'clock. Hardly any other woman uses as much water as she does. I admire her for it. She does this even when she is in a hurry. . . . She has a barely perceptible body odor in the evening or morning." See Jules Michelet, *Journal,* ed. Paul Villaneix and Claude Dignon (Paris, 1959–76), 3: 470.

137 *Evolution de la Géographie industrielle de Paris,* 1: 197.

138 *Premier Mémoire sur les eaux de Paris presenté par le Préfet de la Seine au Conseil municipal (4 août 1854)* (Paris, 1858), pp. 42–53.

139 *Second Mémoire sur les eaux de Paris presenté par le Préfet de la Seine au Conseil municipal (16 juillet 1858)* (Paris, 1858), pp. 102f.

140 Haussmann, *Mémoires,* 3: 299.

141 *Second Mémoire sur les eaux de Paris,* pp. 106f. See also Haussmann, *Mémoires,* 3: 298f.

142 *Evolution de la Géographie industrielle de Paris,* 1: 311; for details on the route of this sewer system, see *Second Mémoire sur les eaux de Paris,* pp. 93–106. See also Haussmann, *Mémoires,* 3: 350–66; and Eugène Belgrand, *Les Travaux souterrains de Paris* (Paris, 1887), vol. 5 (atlas), plate II, and "Deuxième Partie: Les Egouts." Further information can be found in Emile Gérards, *Paris souterraine* (Paris, 1909), pp. 487–504; and Alfred Mayer, "La Canalisation souterraine de Paris," in *Paris-Guide par les principaux écrivains et artistes de la France,* 2 vols. (Paris, 1867), 2: 1,605–14.

143 *Evolution de la Géographie industrielle de Paris,* 2: 311f.

144 *Commission d'Extension de Paris. Aperçu historique,* p. 153.

145 Préfecture de la Seine. Direction des Travaux de Paris, "Décret relatif aux rues de Paris, 16 mars 1852, art. 6," in *Recueil de règlements* (Paris, 1875), p. 70.

146 Préfecture de la Seine, "Arrêté réglementaire pour l'exécution du décret du 26 mars, 1852, 19 décembre 1854, art. 1," in *Recueil de règlements,* p. 72.

147 *Evolution de la Géographie industrielle de Paris,* 1: 312.

148 A royal decree of June 5, 1834, permitted mobile cesspools as well. These had a lesser capacity but had the advantage of being interchangeable, while the installed cesspools, of which there were 70,000 in 1880, had to be emptied at night by sewage collectors. The costs of such collection varied from 4 to 8 francs per cubic meter, which explains why so many proprietors were loath to pay water connections. See Jacquemet, "Urbanisme parisien," p. 506.

149 This stench was more or less obvious depending on the social geography of Paris. See J. Chrétien, *Les Odeurs de Paris. Etude analytique des causes qui concourent a l'insalubrité de la ville et des moyens de les combattre* (Paris, 1881), pp. 5f.

150 Belgrand, *Les Travaux souterrains,* 5: 277.

151 However, house owners had to meet five requirements: they had to install a connection to the city water system; order a connection to the sewer system; have a separator installed in the cesspool; have the separate chamber for fecal matter provided with a trap; and finally, pay a yearly fee of 30 francs for each toilet.

152 Jacquemet, "Urbanisme parisien," p. 507.

153 Karl Korn, *Zola in seiner Zeit* (Frankfurt-am-Main, 1980), pp. 141–48.

154 Emile Zola, "Lettres Parisiennes," *La Cloche,* June 8, 1872, cited in *Oeuvres complètes,* ed. Henri Mitterand (Paris, 1976), 14: 77f.

155 The "Melun Law" was amended once during the Second Empire by the Law of May 25, 1864. This amendment only increased the personnel of the *Commission de la salubrité.* See Préfecture de la Seine, *Recueil des règlements,* p. 178. See also Bouvard and Jourdan, eds., *Recueil des règlements concernant le service des aligne-*

ments et de la police de construction dans la ville de Paris (Paris, 1900), pp. 181–88.

156 Du Camp, *Paris*, 6: 234.

157 C. Lavollée, "Statistique industrielle de Paris," *Revue des deux mondes* 55 (1865): 1037. See also *Evolution de la géographie industrielle de Paris*, 1: 167, table 15.

158 Ibid., p. 83.

159 Ibid., p. 127.

160 Gaillard, *Paris*, p. 433. See also Du Camp, *Paris*, 6: 255.

161 Ibid., p. 446. See also Chambre de Commerce de Paris. *Enquête sur les conditions du travail en France pendant l'année 1872* (Paris, 1875), p. 54.

162 Gaillard, *Paris*, pp. 440–43.

163 This does not include establishments working with precious metals, which alone had a volume of 183 million francs.

164 Lavollée, "Statistique industrielle," p. 1,034.

165 Ibid., pp. 1,042f.

166 This makes it very clear why the concept "Industrial Revolution" must be used very carefully. On the industrial geography of Paris, see *Evolution de la géographie industrielle de Paris*, 1: 129–66; and Gaillard, *Paris*, pp. 457–82.

167 Statistics for various professional groups, based on population figures for 1872, show that of 1.8 million Paris inhabitants, over 400,000 were active in trade, while those employed by the *industrie parisienne* amounted to 816,000, about double that number. See Toussaint Loua, *Atlas Statistique de la population de Paris* (Paris, 1873), p. 59. Similar figures for 1872 are given by Du Camp, *Paris*, 6: 255–57. That means that store clerks formed a new social group among the capital's population. On the development of professional group statistics in the years 1856–86, see Chevalier, *La Formation de la population*, pp. 74–79.

168 Du Camp, *Paris*, 6: 256.

169 See Bertrand Gille, "Recherches sur l'origine des grands magasins parisiens. Note d'orientation," *Paris et l'Ile-de-France* 7 (1955): 251–64.

170 Once the *grands magasins* were established, the relationship between production and sales experienced radical change dictated by trade and described by G. d'Avenel as follows:

One and the same trend . . . today forces production to specialize and trade to become diversified. Each manufacturer tends to manufacture only one or else very few different products so as to improve their quality, to produce them in larger quantity, and to be able to sell them more cheaply. On the other hand, each merchant tends to carry more and more different items so as to sell as many as possible, to make them move faster, and at the same time to sell them more cheaply while still making a considerably larger profit. (G. d'Avenel, "Le Mécanisme de la vie moderne," in *Revue des deux mondes* 124 (1894): 330)

171 "The new streets of Haussmannic Paris were indeed midwives to the department store." Philip G. Nord, *Paris Shopkeepers and the Politics of Resentment* (Princeton, N. J., 1986), p. 132.

172 Emile Zola, *Au Bonheur des dames*, in *Les Rougon-Macquart*, 3: 687.

173 This explains the reason for the great concentration of *grands magasins* in the new center of Paris: Le Louvre in the rue de Rivoli; La Samaritaine and La Belle Jardinière near the *croisée de Paris*; Au Printemps near the place de l'Opéra; the Réunis in the place du Château d'Eau and Au Bon Marché in the rue de Bac on the Left Bank. The history of the founding of Le Louvre shows how difficult the initial phase was for these enterprises, see d'Avenel, "Le Mécanisme," pp. 339–41. A public transportation system also developed at the same time and in connection with the transformation of Paris. The eleven bus companies operating in Paris merged in 1855 to become the *Compagnie générale des omnibus;* it had 660 horse-drawn buses in 1866, each of which had twenty-six seats, and they operated mainly in the central and western arrondissements of Paris. See Du Camp, *Paris*, 1: 202; see also *Evolution de la géographie industrielle de Paris*, 1: 323–25; and Ghislaine Bouchet,

"La Traction hippomobile dans les transports publics parisiens (1855–1914)," *Revue Historique* 271 (1984): 125–34.

174 But mail-order business with the provinces or foreign countries was also important. See d'Avenel, "Le Mécanisme," pp. 354f.

175 In his novel *Au Bonheur des dames* (pp. 466–68), Zola masterfully describes, in the character of Mme Marty, the conflict in the bourgeois soul provoked by a *grand magasin*.

176 d'Avenel, "Le Mécanisme," p. 347. See also Marc Martin, "Presse, publicité et grandes affaires sous le Second Empire," *Revue historique* 256 (1976): 343–83.

177 Zola, *Au Bonheur des dames*, pp. 390f.

178 Louis Hautecoeur, "De l'Echoppe aux grands magasins," *Revue de Paris* 54 (1933): 827f.

179 See the carefully worked-out organization of labor in the *grands magasins* in d'Avenel, "Le Mécanisme," pp. 352–54.

180 Hautecoeur, "De l'Echoppe," pp. 829, 830.

181 See the descriptions of the fantastic effects achieved with the rebuilding of *Au Bonheur des dames* in Zola, *Au Bonheur des dames*, pp. 611–46.

182 Zola describes the great fascination experienced by Denise at the mere sight of the store *Au Bonheur des dames:* "In the big city, black and silent in the rain, in this strange and unfamiliar Paris, it shone like a beacon, it alone seemed to be the light and life of the city." Ibid., p. 414.

183 Duveau, *La Vie ouvrière*, p. 319.

184 Ibid., p. 320. Duveau based his findings on the 1847 and 1860 surveys by the Paris Chamber of Comerce.

185 According to Du Camp, sixty-three out of one hundred burials during the Second Empire involved paupers, who were buried in the *fosse commune* at the expense of the city of Paris. See Du Camp, *Paris*, 6: 141.

186 See Paul-François Dupont, *Insuffisance des traitements en général et de la necessité d'une prompte augmentation* (Paris, 1859). See also the enlightening itemization of expenses of a mar-

ried employee with three children, who had a yearly nominal income of 1,900 francs, but whose household budget showed a yearly deficit of over 700 francs despite a most economical life-style, in Maurice Allem, *La Vie quotidienne sous le Second Empire* (Paris, 1948), pp. 102f.

187 Gaillard, *Paris*, pp. 233–38.

188 Anthony B. North–Peat gives the menu of the *Grand Banquet hippophagique* that took place September 30, 1866, at the invitation of M. Lauze, President of the *Societé pour la protection des animaux*, to which ladies were also invited:

Potage
Consommé de cheval

Hors-d'Oeuvre
Saucisson de cheval

Relevé
Cheval nature (bouilli)

Entrée
Cheval à la mode

Légumes
Flageolets sautés à l'huile de cheval

Roti
Filet de cheval sauce poivrade
Salade à l'huile de cheval
Demi-litre de vin par couvert

Anthony B. North-Peat, *Paris sous le Second Empire. Femmes, la mode, la cour. Correspondance (1864–1869)* (Paris, 1911), pp. 227f.

189 Toshio Horii, "La Crise alimentaire de 1853 à 1856 et la Caisse de la Boulangerie de Paris," *Revue historique* 272 (1984): 375–401.

190 Gaillard, *Paris*, pp. 208–14.

191 The *Commission des logements insalubres* repeatedly found that their "good advice came up against the unchangeable habits, the indifference of people unable to grasp the significance of this advice and for whom the word UNCLEANLINESS is of no importance whatsoever." Robinet and Trébuchet (Rapporteurs), "Rapport général sur les travaux de la Commission des Logements insalubres pendant les années 1852 . . .

1856," in *Annales d'Hygiène publique et de Médecine légale*, 2nd ser., 8 (1857): 473. See also Octave du Mesnil, "Les Garnis insalubres de la ville de Paris," ibid., 49 (1878): 193–232; and Pierre Mazerolle, *La Misère de Paris, les mauvais gîtes* (Paris, 1875), pp. 23–113.

192 Robinet and Trébuchet (Rapporteurs), "Rapport général," p. 471.

193 The Cité Doré, named for an investor by that name, who had bought the land and leased the lots on which this slum formed, was primarily used by the ragpickers as storage area and living quarters. See Alain Faure, "Classe malpropre, classe dangereuse. Quelques remarques à propos des chiffoniers parisiens au XIXᵉ siècle et de leurs cités," in *Haleine des faubourgs: Ville, habitat et santé au XIXᵉ siècle* (Fontenay-sous-Bois, 1978), pp. 79–103. For a description of the Cité des Kroumirs, see Octave du Mesnil, "La Cité des Kroumirs," *Annales d'Hygiène publique et de Médecine légale*, 3rd ser., 7 (1889): 209–19. On the Cité Maufry, see Emile Zola, *Les Trois Villes*, in *Les Oeuvres complètes*, ed. Maurice Le Blond (Paris, n.d.), 26: 18–25.

194 Eugène Belgrand, *Transformation de la vidange et suppression de la voirie de Bondy. Achèvement des égouts et emploi de leurs eaux dans l'agriculture* (Paris, 1875), pp. 4f.

195 Nordau, *Aus dem wahren Milliardenlande*, 1: 64. See also Jacques Rougerie and Louis Girard Belleville, eds., *Les Elections de 1869* (Paris, 1960), pp. 30–35.

196 Typhoid mortality rates in Paris, 1865–84:

	Number of Deaths	% per 10,000 Inhabitants
1865	1,161	6.4
1869	1,080	5.4
1873	1,021	4.3
1877	1,201	4.0
1881	2,121	14.9
1884	1,619	7.2

Cited in Préfecture du Département de la Seine. Direction des Travaux

de Paris. *Commission supérieure de l'assainissement de Paris, séance du 26 mars 1885* (Paris, n.d.), p. 142.

197 Mortality rates provide an indication of the social inequality of the poor even in death. Deaths per 10,000 inhabitants were as follows:

Arrondissement	1880	1881	1882
I.	19.7	18.9	18.1
II.	19.4	19.0	17.9
III.	23.5	21.2	20.3
IV.	24.7	23.8	23.6
V.	28.7	24.2	25.0
VI.	21.4	20.3	21.0
VII.	25.6	23.9	23.2
VIII..	16.5	15.4	15.3
IX.	18.2	15.3	16.5
X.	25.4	22.8	22.5
XI.	31.7	27.0	26.0
XII.	31.1	27.9	29.9
XIII.	45.5	34.5	36.3
XIV.	36.6	30.3	37.8
XV.	34.8	29.6	29.7
XVI.	24.8	20.8	21.2
XVII.	28.2	22.4	23.8
XVIII.	30.5	26.8	28.5
XIX.	33.8	29.6	31.9
XX.	37.4	30.5	31.6
Average	27.9	24.2	25.0

Cited in Léon Colin, *Paris, sa topographie, son hygiène, ses maladies* (Paris, 1885), pp. 325–27.

198 Duveau, *La Vie ouvrière*, pp. 411f.

199 Siegfried Kracauer, *Jacques Offenbach und das Paris seiner Zeit*, in *Schriften*, ed. Karsten Witte (Frankfurt-am-Main, 1976), 8: 186.

200 Edmond and Jules de Goncourt, *Journal. Mémoires de la vie littéraire*, ed. Robert Ricatte (Paris, 1956), 2: 263f.

201 Albert comte de Maugny, *Souvenirs du Second Empire. La fin d'une société* (Paris, 1889), pp. 31–38.

202 Maugny, *Souvenirs*, p. 107. The Michelets gave a masked ball on March 3, 1864, to which 100 persons were invited. See Michelet, *Journal*, 3: 243. The Goncourts noted in their diary: "We went to the Michelets' ball dressed as Chinese; all the women wore costumes of oppressed peoples and nations, such as the Poles, Hungarians, Venetians. It seemed as though future

European revolutions were dancing before my eyes." Ibid., 2: 25.

203 Arthur comte de Grandeffe, *Paris sous Napoléon III, mémoires d'un homme du monde de 1857 à 1870* (Paris, 1879), p. 53. See also the complaints by the Goncourts, *Journal*, 2: 487f.

204 For instance, Horace comte de Viel-Castel, whose memoirs list the most important events of the *Chronique scandaleuse*, notes on March 8, 1859: "Prince Napoleon, who is as dissolute a husband as he is a nasty cousin, has not broken off his relationship with Anna Deslion; all of Paris is talking about it. There is a joke making the rounds about this engaging prince. What is the similarity, one asks, between him and a capon? A capon [*chapon*] is an impotent cock [*coq impuissant*], but the prince is a potent rascal [*coquin puissant*]." See Horace comte de Viel-Castel, *Mémoires sur le règne de Napoléon III 1851–1864*, ed. Pierre Josserand (Paris, 1942), 2: 107. The special tactfulness of this relationship was that Anna Deslion had previously been the mistress of Napoleon III for some time. See also Goncourt, *Journal*, 1: 312–13, 1,040f.

205 See the comment by the Goncourts, ibid., p. 321.

206 Frédéric Loliée, *La Païva. La légende et l'histoire de la Marquise de Païva. D'après les pages retrouvées de sa vie* (Paris, 1913). See also Marcel Boulenger, *La Païva* (Paris, 1930).

207 Goncourt, *Journal*, 2: 347.

208 Ludovic Halévy, *Carnets*, ed. Daniel Halévy (Paris, 1935), 1: 77, n. 1.

209 Viel-Castel, *Mémoires*, 2: 45f. See also Eugène Delacroix, *Journal*, ed. André Joubin (Paris, 1932), 2: 326.

210 See Goncourt, *Journal*, 2: 348. On the other hand, Aglaé-Joséphine Savatier, who became famous as Apollonie Sabatier and was called the "lady president," was a real beauty. Proof of this is a nude statue, sculpted by Clésinger in 1847 as "La Femme piquée par un serpent," which is now in the Musée d'Orsay. The Goncourts' journal transmits the following dialogue between the writer

George Sand and Auguste Clésinger, which can be understood in relation to the scandal raised by that sculpture: "Mme Sand: 'I shall make your behavior public.' Clésinger: 'And I shall sculpt your behind. The whole world will recognize it.'" Ibid., 1: 77.

211 Allem, *La Vie quotidienne*, pp. 135–56.

212 Auguste Luchet, "Les Grands cuisines et les grands caves," *Paris-Guide*, 2: 1545–54. See also Henri de Villemessant, *Mémoires d'un journaliste* (Paris, 1873), 3: 106–227; and Jean-Paul Aron, *Le Mangeur du XIXe siècle* (Paris, 1973), pp. 79–94.

213 Goncourt, *Journal*, 2: 105.

214 E. de la Bédollière, "Les Boulevards de la Porte Saint-Martin à la Madeleine," *Paris-Guide*, 2: 1296.

215 "I have noticed a great change in prostitution. Until now it was ambulatory, until now floating, walking, half-hidden. . . . Today Paris has stationary prostitution—sitting in the bright glare of the gas lamps, at café tables along the boulevards, several rows deep facing the passersby, cheeky with the public and familiar with the waiters in their white aprons." Goncourt, *Journal*, 2: 11.

216 Ibid., 1: 835.

217 Baudelaire, "Les Sept vieillards," and "Les Petites vieilles," *Tableaux parisiens*, in *Oeuvres complètes*, ed. Claude Pichois (Paris, 1975–76), pp. 87, 89.

218 Louis Veuillot, *Les Odeurs* (Paris, 1866), p. ix.

219 Alain Plessis, *De la Fête impériale au mur des fédérés 1852–1871 (Nouvelle histoire de la France contemporaine, vol. 9)* (Paris, 1973), pp. 110–12.

220 Prosper Merimée, *Correspondance générale*, ed. Maurice Parturier (Paris and Toulouse, 1941–64), 10: 377.

221 Plessis, *De la Fête impériale*, p. 209.

222 Halévy, *Carnets*, 1: 36.

223 Adrien Dansette, *Histoire du Second Empire* (Paris, 1972), 2: 250–59.

224 Plessis, *De la Fête impériale*, pp. 214–16.

225 On the Paris Exposition of 1867 see Allem, *La Vie quotidienne*, pp. 185–88. See also Patricia Mainardi, *Art and Politics of the Second Empire: The Universal Expositions of 1855 and*

1867 (New Haven and London, 1988). The Goncourts describe this event as follows: "The Exposition, the final blow against everything we have, the Americanization of France, industry displacing art, the steam thresher competing with a painting [probably a reference to a painting of a man winnowing grain, by Jean-François Millet], chamber pots with lids . . . in a word, the Federation of Materialism." Goncourt, *Journal,* 2: 317. See also Chapman, *The Life and Times of Baron Haussmann* (London, 1957), pp. 199-212.

226 Jules Ferry, *Comptes fantastiques d'Haussmann, lettre adressé à MM. les membres de la Commission du Corps législatif chargés d'examiner le nouveau projet de l'emprunt de la ville de Paris* (Paris, 1868).

227 Haussmann, *Mémoires,* 2: 310–12. See also Daumard, *Maisons de Paris,* p. 210.

228 Gaillard, *Paris,* p. 28. See also Daumard, *Maisons de Paris,* p. 213; and Du Camp, *Paris,* 6: 254.

229 Ibid., p. 255.

230 Sutcliffe, *The Autumn of Central Paris,* pp. 40–42.

231 Morizet, *Du vieux Paris,* pp. 284f.

232 Pinkney, *Napoleon III,* pp. 187–88. See also Girard, *La Politique des travaux publics,* p. 332.

233 For an exact statement of costs, see Haussmann, *Mémoires,* 2: 337–40.

234 Morizet, *Du Vieux Paris,* p. 286.

235 Pinkney, *Napoleon III,* p. 191. See also Girard, *La Politique des travaux publics,* p. 332.

236 The best account of this method of financing is in Pinkney, *Napoleon III,* pp. 193f. See also Girard, *La Politique des travaux publics,* pp. 333–37; and Haussmann, *Mémoires,* 2: 328–33.

237 Pinkney, *Napoleon III,* pp. 195f.

238 Ibid., pp. 197–99.

239 The compromise, on which legislators reached agreement prior to the debate, spelled the end of Haussmann's transformation of Paris. It was agreed in principle that all expenditures for public works by the city of Paris had to be submitted to the Legislative Assembly for approval. Ibid., p. 201.

For further developments, see Girard, *La Politique des travaux publics,* pp. 372–75; and *La Deuxième Republique et le Second Empire,* pp. 347–49.

240 See the vivid account of this debate in Morizet, *Du Vieux Paris,* pp. 296–302. See also Girard, *La Politique des travaux publics,* pp. 375–79.

241 On the Paris elections of 1869, see Dansette, *Histoire du Second Empire,* 2: 343–49. See also Girard, *La Deuxième République et le Second Empire,* pp. 395–403; and Plessis, *De la Fête impériale,* p. 217f.

242 Haussmann, *Mémoires,* 2: 537.

243 Halévy, *Carnets,* 2: 40f.

244 Pinkney, *Napoleon III,* p. 200.

245 Ibid., pp. 205–6.

246 Haussmann, *Mémoires,* 2: 558–61.

247 Zola, *Nana,* in *Les Rougon-Macquart,* 2: 1,485.

BOOK SEVEN. From Commune to Belle Epoque 1871–1914

1 See Adrien Dansette, *Histoire du Second Empire* (Paris, 1972–76), 2: 317–23; on the great influence of the *Association Internationale des Travailleurs* on the political radicalization of Paris workers, see Jacques Rougerie, "L'A.I.T. et le mouvement ouvrier à Paris pendant les événements de 1870–1871," in Jacques Rougerie, ed., *1871: Jalons pour une histoire de la Commune de Paris* (Paris, 1973), pp. 3–14.

2 See Dansette, *Histoire du Second Empire,* 2: 293–98.

3 Cited in ibid., 2: 326.

4 Though Rochefort did not bring about the downfall of the Second Empire, the effect of his articles showed how weak the regime was. In his poetry cycle *L'Année terrible,* which is dedicated "A Paris, Capital des Peuples," Victor Hugo outlines Rochefort's importance: "Rochefort, the unafraid, the powerful archer, whose arrow is embedded in the flank of the Empire." See Victor Hugo. *Les Pamphlétaires d'église. L'Année terrible,* in *Oeuvres poétiques,* ed. Pierre Albouy (Paris, 1974), 3: 456.

5   Albert comte de Maugny, *Souvenirs du Second Empire. La fin d'une société* (Paris, 1889), pp. 200f.

6   There were 7,358,000 yes votes as against 1,572,000 no votes, a result that Napoleon III commented on as follows: "If we had been in the minority I would have abdicated. But what should I have done if we had only received five million votes? Then we would have been in a rather embarrassing position." Cited in Dansette, *Histoire du Second Empire*, 2: 377. Out of 400,000 voters in Paris, 184,000 voted no and only 138,000 voted yes, so that a majority voted against the Empire even in its new liberal guise. If one compares the results with those of the 1869 election, it is clear that 60,000 voters who then voted for an opposition candidate now opted for the Empire. Louis Girard interprets this as being due to the fact that "the liberal bourgeoisie gave up its united stand with the *peuple*, and thus left a coalition without which revolution was impossible in Paris." See Girard, *La Deuxième République et le Second Empire* (Paris, 1981), p. 407.

7   See Dansette, *Histoire du Second Empire*, 2: 379–83.

8   See Johannes Willms, *Nationalismus ohne Nation. Deutsche Geschichte 1789–1914* (Düsseldorf, 1983), pp. 398f., 407–13.

9   See G. Schneider, *Pariser Briefe* (Leipzig, 1872), 2: 525–35.

10 Except for three newspapers, *Siècle*, *Journal des Debats*, and *Reveil*. See Jasper Ridley, *Napoleon III and Eugenie* (London, 1979), p. 559.

11 Ludovic Halévy, *Carnets*, ed. Daniel Halévy (Paris, 1935), 2: 172.

12 Ibid., p. 212. See also Schneider, *Pariser Briefe*, 2: 577–80.

13 Halévy, *Carnets*, 2: 213f.

14 Dansette, *Histoire du Second Empire*, 2: 303f.

15 See Stewart Edwards, *The Paris Commune 1871* (London, 1971), pp. 45–47.

16 Schneider, *Pariser Briefe*, 2: 629.

17 On the part of the French, the capitulation document was signed not by General MacMahon who com-
manded the armies surrounded at Sedan but by his second in command, General Baron de Wimpffen. He never lived down this humiliation, as his tombstone in Père Lachaise testifies. All the campaigns in which he participated are engraved there, including the name of Sedan, but with a question mark. A protest *d'outre-tombe* and presumably the only question mark in a cemetery, the place of final certainty.

18 See the account of such scenes in Schneider, *Pariser Briefe*, 2: 631.

19 On these events, see Dansette, *Histoire du Second Empire*, 2: 416–27.

20 Edmond and Jules de Goncourt, *Journal. Mémoires de la vie littéraire*, ed. Robert Ricatte (Paris, 1956), 2: 589–92. See also Schneider, *Pariser Briefe*, 2: 633–40.

21 Karl Marx and Friedrich Engels, "The Civil War in France. Second Address," in *Writings on the Paris Commune*, ed. Hal Draper (New York and London, 1971), pp. 47–48.

22 See Henri Guillemin, *L'Avènement de M. Thiers. Réflexions sur la Commune* (Paris, 1971), p. 25.

23 See Goncourt, *Journal*, 2: 597–607.

24 See Willms, *Nationalismus ohne Nation*, pp. 415–21.

25 See Edwards, *The Paris Commune*, pp. 58f.

26 Ibid., pp. 69–71.

27 Goncourt, *Journal*, 2: 615–743. See also Schneider, *Pariser Briefe*, 3: 99–110, 197–99.

28 See Henri d'Almeras, *La Vie parisienne pendant le Siège et sous la Commune* (Paris, n.d.); see also Goncourt, *Journal*, 2: 682f.

29 On December 4, 1870, the Paris paper *Les Nouvelles* published the courses served at a formal dinner for a group of well-known gourmets:

Consommé de cheval au millet
Brochettes de foie de chien à la maître d'hotel
Emincés de râble de chat sauce mayonnaise
Epaule de filet de chien sauce tomate
Civet de chat aux champignons
Côtelettes de chien aux petits pois
Salmis de rats à la Robert
Gigot de chien flanqué de ratons
Salade d'escarolles

Bégonia au jus
Plum Pudding au jus et à la moelle de cheval
Dessert et vins

Cited in d'Almeras, *La Vie Parisienne pendant le Siège*, p. 9.

30   On October 15, 1870, Edmond de Goncourt notes in his journal:

Driven from the boulevard by the forced rationing of gas; unable to enjoy modern life in this city where everyone retires early; unable to read any more; prevented from rising to the realm of pure ideas and thoughts by the reduction of those ideas and thoughts to the miserable subject of nourishment; to be robbed of all that was once part of the intellectual relaxation of an educated Parisian; to have to do without all news and gossip; finally, condemned to vegetate under the brutal and monotonous conditions of the war, a Parisian is seized by boredom only comparable to that experienced in a provincial city. (Goncourt, *Journal*, 2: 638).

31   Mail-pigeons and fifty-four balloons were released during the siege and transported 2.5 million letters; they were the only means of communication with the outside world in this period. See d'Almeras, *La Vie parisienne pendant le siège*, pp. 31–38. See also Schneider, *Pariser Briefe*, 3: 37–40.

32   "The worse the situation became, the greater was the desire to fight." See Louise Michel, *La Commune* (Paris, 1978), p. 89.

33   Shortly before the end of the siege, on January 13, 1871, Edmond de Goncourt writes: "One has to do justice to the population of Paris—and to marvel at them! That in spite of the brazen displays in the food stores—which reminded the famine-stricken inhabitants in most inappropriate fashion that for their money the rich could always have poultry, game, and choice delicacies—they did not break the windows, upset the goods, and manhandle the sales staff." See Goncourt, *Journal*, 2: 716. When the siege ended, fourteen habitués of Brébant's restaurant, one of whom was Edmond de Goncourt, had the Paris Mint inscribe a medallion as follows:

Pendant
le siège de Paris
quelques personnes ayant
accoutumé [sic]de se réunir chez M. Brébant
tous les quinze jours ne sont pas une seule
fois aperçues qu'elles dînaient dans
une ville de deux millions
d'âmes assiégées
1870–1871

Cited in d'Almeras, *La Vie parisienne pendant le Siège et sous la Commune*, pp. 17f.

34   On November 10, 1870, Edmond de Goncourt notes: "At the moment everyone I see needs spiritual and intellectual peace, needs to leave Paris. Everyone is saying: 'As soon as this is over I am leaving.' And then they mention some corner of France, a vague bit of countryside where, far from Paris and everything that recalls it, they will be able to stop thinking, stop reflecting, stop remembering, at least for a short while." See Goncourt, *Journal*, 2: 671.

35   Prosper-Olivier Lissagaray, *Geschichte der Kommune von 1871*, 2d ed. (Stuttgart, 1894), p. 20.

36   For a detailed account of events see Edwards, *The Paris Commune*, pp. 77–84.

37   Ibid., pp. 85, 87f.

38   Ibid., pp. 89–94.

39   For the wording of the proclamation see Jacques Rougerie, *Paris libre 1871* (Paris, 1971), pp. 61–63.

40   See Edwards, *The Paris Commune*, pp. 108–10.

41   Moritz Busch, *Tagebuchblätter. Graf Bismarck und seine Leute während des Krieges mit Frankreich 1870–1871 bis zur Rückkehr nach Berlin Wilhelmstrasse 76* (Leipzig, 1899), 2: 97.

42   The best contemporary analysis of this *drôle de guerre* is given in Francis Garnier, *Le Siège de Paris, journal d'un officier de marine* (Paris, 1887).

43   Even Edmond de Goncourt, who was anything but a revolutionary, notes on January 30, 1871: "But what makes me more angry than anything is the Jesuitism—and never was a word more apt—the Jesuitism of the current government which, because it obtained the word *Agreement*

instead of *Surrender* at the beginning of this dishonorable treaty, hopes like evil and cowardly rogues to keep secret the extent of France's misfortune and shame." Goncourt, *Journal*, 2: 733.

44 Ibid., pp. 736f.

45 Gustave de Molinari, "Les Approvisionnements de Paris à la fin du Siège," in *La Revue des deux mondes* 91 (1871): 746.

46 See Charles Seignobos, *Le Declin de l'Empire et l'établissement de la Troisième République* (1859–1875), (*Histoire de France contemporaine depuis la Révolution jusqu'à la paix de 1919*, ed. Ernest Lavisse [Paris, 1921], vol. 8), pp. 282–84. See also Guillemin, *L'Avènement de M. Thiers*, pp. 35–65.

47 See Emile Beaussire, "Le Procès entre Paris et la Province," *Revue des deux mondes* 93 (1871): 114–37. Conversely, Paris regarded the provinces with the utmost contempt, as shown by the famous exclamation of Deputy Gaston Crémieux at the first session of the newly elected National Assembly: "Assemblée de ruraux, honte de la France!" ("Assembly of country bumpkins, shame of France!"). Cited in Maxime Du Camp, *Les Convulsions de Paris* (Paris, 1881), 1: 20.

48 Guillemin, *L'Avènement de M. Thiers*, pp. 116f.

49 Du Camp, *Les Convulsions*, 1: 22.

50 Edwards, *The Paris Commune*, pp. 118f. See also Guillemin, *L'Avènement de M. Thiers*, pp. 134f.

51 Ibid., pp. 133f.

52 Edwards, *The Paris Commune*, p. 120.

53 Guillemin, *L'Avènement de M. Thiers*, pp. 140–44.

54 Ibid., pp. 145–48.

55 See the account in Schneider, *Pariser Briefe*, 3: 475–92; and Goncourt, *Journal*, 2: 740–42.

56 Edwards, *The Paris Commune*, p. 125.

57 See Charles Rihs, *La Commune de Paris. Sa structure et ses doctrines (1871)* (Geneva, 1955), pp. 15–20; and Edwards, *The Paris Commune*, pp. 126–28. See also Henri Lefebvre, *La Proclamation de la Commune 26 mars 1871* (Paris, 1965), pp. 195–203; and Rougerie, *Paris libre 1871*, pp. 84–100.

58 Edwards, *The Paris Commune*, p. 129.

59 Lissagaray mentions 150,000 notes protested between March 13 and 17. Lissagaray, *Geschichte der Kommune*, p. 68.

60 Guillemin has collected a number of testimonies from members of the government who considered the supposed "threat" of the cannon as "more ridiculous than dangerous," as Jules Favre put it to Thiers on March 6. See Guillemin, *L'Avènement de M. Thiers*, pp. 149–51.

61 Lefebvre, *La Proclamation de la Commune*, pp. 219–32. See also Edwards, *The Paris Commune*, pp. 130f.

62 Jules Favre later maintained before the parliamentary committee investigating the events of March 18, 1871, that he had encouraged Thiers to use force because it was planned to demobilize the Paris National Guard, which cost the state over 600,000 francs daily, to avoid national bankruptcy. The fact that the suppression of the Commune cost 260 million francs showed the absurdity of his argument. See Guillemin, *L'Avènement de M. Thiers*, pp. 151f.

63 Jacques Rougerie, ed., *Procès des Communards* (Paris, 1964), p. 86.

64 See Guillemin, *L'Avènement de M. Thiers*, pp. 152f.; and Edwards, *The Paris Commune*, pp. 135–37. See also the detailed description in Lefebvre, *La Proclamation de la Commune*, pp. 233–86.

65 See the documents in Jacques Rougerie, *Paris libre 1871* (Paris, 1971), pp. 103f. See also Lissagaray, *Geschichte der Kommune*, pp. 73–77; and Edwards, *The Paris Commune*, pp. 138–40.

66 Guillemin, *L'Avènement de M. Thiers*, p. 155.

67 In his memoirs Thiers refers to all of 600 members of the National Guard from bourgeois arrondissements who were willing to help the government on March 18. See Adolphe Thiers, *Notes et Souvenirs (1870–1873)* (Paris, 1903), p. 140.

68 On suitable suggestions made by the mayor of the twentieth arrondisse-

ment, see Edwards, *The Paris Commune*, pp. 147f.

69 *Enquête parlementaire sur l'insurrection du 18 mars 1871* (Paris, 1872), p. 177, cited in Rougerie, *Paris libre 1871*, p. 102.

70 Guillemin, *L'Avènement de M. Thiers*, pp. 156–59.

71 According to the clauses of the cease-fire treaty, the Prussian troops held only the forts between Saint-Denis in the north and Charenton in the southwest of Paris. See the map in Lefebvre, *La Proclamation de la Commune*, pp. 412f.

72 This mistake was rectified when the Mont-Valérien, the most strategic of the forts, was occupied by government troops on March 20. See Edwards, *The Paris Commune*, p. 150.

73 From a comment made by Jules Grevy, president of the National Assembly, at its first session in Versailles on March 20, 1871. Guillemin, *L'Avènement de M. Thiers*, p. 160.

74 For instance, Maxime Du Camp's presentation of events is characteristic of the pro-government attitude: "After the cease-fire, when each one of us, bowed by the weight of our defeat, fought against his own despondency, took heart again and resumed his work so as to give to the country what was left of his energy, goodwill, and knowledge, the future members of the Commune and conspirators of the revolt met in small circles, exchanged words, watched in delight as the army disbanded, and aimed at the heart of civilization." See Du Camp, *Les Convulsions*, 4: 2.

75 For a detailed account of further events in Paris on March 18, see Edwards, *The Paris Commune*, pp. 143–47.

76 Government propaganda immediately turned the murder of the two generals into a cause célèbre, for which the Central Committee was blamed. See Guillemin, *L'Avènement de M. Thiers*, p. 159; and Edwards, *The Paris Commune*, pp. 141f.

77 Ibid., p. 150.

78 Guillemin, *L'Avènement de M. Thiers*, pp. 161f.

79 Rougerie, ed., *Procès des Communards*, p. 175.

80 See Lefebvre, *La Proclamation de la Commune*, pp. 302–4.

81 Michel, *La Commune*, p. 167.

82 Gustave Lefrançais, *Etude sur le mouvement communaliste à Paris en 1871* (Neuchâtel, 1871), pp. 137–39.

83 On the clubs see Gustave de Molinari, *Les Clubs rouges pendant le Siège de Paris* (Paris, 1871); and Rihs, *La Commune de Paris*, pp. 37–57.

84 Cited in Lefebvre, *La Proclamation de la Commune*, p. 277.

85 Ibid., pp. 281f.

86 See the text of the proclamations in Lefebvre, *La Proclamation de la Commune*, p. 282f. See also André Découflé, *La Commune de Paris (1871). Révolution populaire et pouvoir révolutionnaire* (Paris, 1969), pp. 122–25.

87 Lefebvre, *La Proclamation de la Commune*, p. 284.

88 Ibid., pp. 285f.

89 On the much-discussed role played by the mayors of the twenty arrondissements at the negotiations, see Guillemin, *L'Avènement de M. Thiers*, pp. 175–84. See also Lefebvre, *La Proclamation de la Commune*, pp. 325–39, 166–72; and Edwards, *The Paris Commune*, pp. 161–64.

90 Ibid., p. 189.

91 See Lefebvre, *La Proclamation de la Commune*, pp. 292–317. See also Edwards, *The Paris Commune*, pp. 164–66; and Rougerie, *Paris libre 1871*, pp. 112–35.

92 On the elections see Edwards, *The Paris Commune*, pp. 183–86. See also Guillemin, *L'Avènement de M. Thiers*, p. 184; and Rougerie, *Paris libre 1871*, pp. 135–47.

93 Guillemin, *L'Avènement de M. Thiers*, p. 185.

94 Marx, *Der Bürgerkrieg in Frankreich*, p. 62.

95 Edwards, *The Paris Commune*, pp. 203f. By this time the *honnêtes gens* had long since fled Paris; see Goncourt, *Journal*, 2: 749.

96 Guillemin, *L'Avènement de M. Thiers*, pp. 211–14. On the sociology and political differentiation of the Com-

mune, see Edwards, *The Paris Commune*, pp. 205–7, 210f.

97 For the text of this document see Rougerie, *Paris libre 1871*, pp. 153–56.

98 See the explanation of the declaration in Edwards, *The Paris Commune*, p. 218. See also, Rihs, *La Commune de Paris*, pp. 134–42; and Découflé, *La Commune de Paris*, pp. 229–41.

99 Marx, *Der Bürgerkrieg in Frankreich*, p. 84.

100 Guillemin, *L'Avènement de M. Thiers*, p. 219.

101 Ibid., p. 227. See also Edwards, *The Paris Commune*, pp. 253–56. The decree resulted in many tenants moving out of apartments on which they owed rent before the deadline of April 15—a process commented on by Edmond de Goncourt in these words: "The only movement and signs of life visible in Paris are people moving their belongings in the twilight hours, for which they use wagons pulled by members of the National Guard. Democratic tenants hurry to profit from the Commune's rent decree." See Goncourt, *Journal*, 2: 761.

102 The decree concerning the remission of rent payments assured the Commune the permanent support of the *classes laborieuses*. See Edwards, *The Paris Commune*, 190f. See also the surly comments on this matter in Goncourt, *Journal*, 2: 755.

103 Edwards, *The Paris Commune*, pp. 266–75.

104 Ibid., pp. 257–66.

105 Guillemin, *L'Avènement de M. Thiers*, pp. 234–43. See also Edwards, *The Paris Commune*, pp. 251f.

106 Général François-Charles Du Barail, *Mes Souvenirs* (1864–1879) (Paris, 1896), 3: 260. See also Xavier Marmier, *Journal (1848–1890)*, ed. Eldon Kaye (Geneva, 1968), 2: 225.

107 Henri Rochefort, *Les Aventures de ma vie*, ed. Jean Guichard-Meili (Paris, 1980), p. 159. See also Marie-Camille-Alfred vicomte de Meaux, *Souvenirs politiques 1871–1877* (Paris, 1905), p. 52.

108 On May 28, the last day of the battles, Xavier Marmier notes in his journal: "I know that after being driven from one barricade to another, and from street to street, they had fled to the area around the Père Lachaise cemetery and their hideouts in Belleville, where they fought on without the least hope of victory. Like rabid dogs, their madness increased with their death-throes." Marmier, *Journal*, 2: 259.

109 Cited in Lissagaray, *Geschichte der Kommune von 1871*, p. 152.

110 Découflé, *La Commune de Paris*, pp. 119–84.

111 For a detailed account of the battles see Lissagaray, *Geschichte der Kommune von 1871*, pp. 153–280. See also the detailed chronology of events in Lefebvre, *La Proclamation de la Commune*, pp. 367–88.

112 Lissagaray, *Geschichte der Kommune von 1871*, pp. 280–87.

113 For an impartial account of the *semaine sanglante*, see Edwards, *The Paris Commune*, pp. 313–39.

114 See the interesting description of the fire that raged during the night of May 23–24 in Lissagaray, *Geschichte der Kommune von 1871*, pp. 308f.

115 Michel, *La Commune*, p. 319.

116 Madeleine Rebérioux, "Le Mur des Fédérés," in *Les Lieux de mémoire. La République*, ed. Pierre Nora (Paris, 1984), 1: 619–49.

117 Goncourt, *Journal*, 2: 818.

118 Lissagaray, *Geschichte der Kommune von 1871*, pp. 361–63.

119 Cited in ibid., p. 359.

120 Ibid., p. 360.

121 Rougerie, *Paris libre 1871*, p. 255.

122 Guillemin, *L'Avènement de M. Thiers*, p. 277.

123 Edwards, *The Paris Commune*, p. 346.

124 Ibid., p. 347.

125 Rougerie, *Paris libre 1871*, p. 257.

126 See the hair-raising descriptions of conditions in the prison camps in Michel, *La Commune*, pp. 346–52.

127 Goncourt, *Journal*, 2: 844.

128 Guillemin, *L'Avènement de M. Thiers*, p. 283.

129 Goncourt, *Journal*, 2: 817.

130 The Commune was only a revolutionary episode for the *classe aisée*, a

bleeding that was necessary from time to time, as Edmond de Goncourt notes in his journal on May 31, 1871:

It's fine. There has been neither reconciliation nor compromise. The solution was brutal. It was naked force. . . . The outcome has restored confidence to the army, which learned in the blood of the *Communaux* that it was still able to fight. [The Commune] was bled white; and bleedings like this one, by killing the combative part of the population, postpone a new revolution for a generation. There are easily twenty years of peace ahead of the old society, provided the rulers have the courage to do what is necessary (Goncourt, *Journal*, 2: 819).

131 Ibid., 2: 821.
132 See d'Almeras, *La Vie parisienne pendant le Siège*, pp. 539–41.
133 Edwards, *The Paris Commune*, pp. 349f.
134 Anthony Sutcliffe, *The Autumn of Central Paris: The Defeat of Town Planning (1850–1970)* (London, 1970), pp. 44f.
135 Ibid., pp. 46f.
136 Adeline Daumard, "L'Avenue de l'Opéra de ses origines à la Guerre de 1914," *Bulletin de la Société de l'Histoire de Paris et de l'Ile-de-France* (1970), pp. 162–68. See also Sutcliffe, *The Autumn of Central Paris*, pp. 49–53.
137 Ibid., p. 54.
138 Ibid., pp. 55–59.
139 Ibid., pp. 59–77.
140 Norma Evenson, *Paris: A Century of Change, 1878–1978* (New Haven and London, 1979), pp. 76–85.
141 Sutcliffe, *The Autumn of Central Paris*, pp. 83–85; and Evenson, *Paris*, pp. 91–105.
142 Emile Gérards, *Paris souterrain* (Paris, 1909), pp. 574–81; and Evenson, *Paris*, pp. 105–9.
143 Jacques Bertillon, "De l'Augmentation de fréquence des principales maladies épidémiques à Paris pendant la période 1865–1883 et de leurs saisons d'élection," *Annuaire statistique de la ville de Paris* (Paris, 1883). See also Paul-Camille-Hyppolyte Brouardel, "Note sur la mortalité par quelques maladies épidémiques à Paris, pendant les douze dernières années," *Revue d'Hygiène et de Police sanitaire* 4 (1882): 951–54.

144 See Préfecture du Département de la Seine. Service de la statistique municipale, *Tableaux statistiques de l'épidémie cholérique de 1884 à Paris et étude statistique des épidémies antérieures* (Paris, 1886), pp. 48–55; and Préfecture de Police. Conseil d'hygiène publique et de salubrité, *L'Epidémie cholérique de 1892 dans le département de la Seine* (Paris, 1893).
145 Gérard Jacquemet, "Urbanisme parisien: La bataille du tout-à-l'égout à la fin du XIXᵉ siècle," *Revue d'histoire moderne et contemporaine* 26 (1979): 509–27.
146 Ibid., pp. 535–45.
147 A decree by Prefect Eugène Poubelle of November 24, 1883, stipulated that house owners had to provide sufficient trash cans for household refuse. The regulation was a heavy blow for the ragpickers, who revenged themselves by calling the trash cans *poubelles* after the prefect. Since then the term has become standard usage. See Gustave Jourdan, *Etudes d'hygiène publique* (Paris, 1892), pp. 13–17.
148 Jacques Bertillon, *De la Fréquence des principales causes de décès à Paris* (Paris, 1906). See also Bertillon, "Mouvements de population et causes de décès selon le degré d'aisance à Paris, Berlin, Vienne," in *Comptes-rendu. Dixième Congrès international d'hygiène et de démographie à Paris en 1900* (Paris, 1901), pp. 961–80.
149 Ann Louise Shapiro, *Housing the Poor of Paris 1850–1902* (Madison, Wis., 1985), pp. 55–83.
150 Sutcliffe, *The Autumn of Central Paris*, pp. 105–14; and Shapiro, *Housing the Poor*, pp. 84–164.
151 See Zeldin's analysis of the Third Republic as "one of the most confusing and paradoxical of political regimes." See Zeldin, *France 1848–1945* (Oxford, 1973), 1: 570–604.
152 See above, note 130.
153 See John Edward Courtenay Bodley, *France* (London, 1898), 2: 272–317; and Eugen Weber, *France: Fin de Siècle* (Cambridge, Mass. and London, 1986), pp. 105–29.
154 On the Boulanger crisis, see Adrien

Dansette, *Le Boulangisme* (Paris, 1938), and F. H. Seager, *The Boulanger Affair* (New York, 1969); on the Dreyfus crisis see Joseph Reinach, *Histoire de l'affaire Dreyfus* (Paris, 1907).

155 For a brief but excellent description of the Belle Epoque, see Roger Shattuck, *The Banquet Years: The Arts in France 1885–1918* (London, 1959).

156 "Fashionable women, in gowns with plunging necklines, sat at public restaurant tables as though they were in a private apartment. And this was by no means in a spa or seaside resort, where no one is really at home and everyone naturally spends time at the casino, but in a capital and in a country where the rules of traditional etiquette are observed like religious commandments." See vicomte Georges d'Avenel, *Le Mécanisme de la vie moderne*, 5ème série (Paris, 1905), p. 47.

157 Vicomte Georges d'Avenel, *Le Nivellement des jouissances* (Paris, 1913).

158 See Maurice Talmeyr, "Cafés-Concerts et Music-Halls," *Revue des deux mondes*, 5ème période, 10 (1902): 159.

159 André Chadourne, cited in Charles Rearick, *Pleasures of the Belle Epoque: Entertainment and Festivity in Turn-of-the-Century France* (New Haven and London, 1985), p. 83.

160 Talmeyr, "Cafés-Concerts," pp. 160f.

161 See the charming description of the Folies-Bergère in 1879, in Joris-Karl Huysmans, *Croquis parisiens, Les Folies-Bergère en 1879*, in *Oeuvres complètes*, vol. 8 (Paris, 1919), pp. 7–28.

162 Guy de Maupassant, *Bel-Ami*, ed. Gérard Delaisement (Paris, 1959), pp. 14f.

163 Maupassant, *Bel-Ami*, p. 16.

164 "Around six o'clock Paris seems to me like an American Babylon; in the fierce rush of the crowds to their entertainments, in the ruthlessness of coachmen insured against running over old men, there is no longer the friendly, mild, and polite behavior of the old Paris." See Goncourt, *Journal*, 3: 603.

165 See Jean-Jacques Bloch and Marianne Delort, *Quand Paris allait "à l'Expo"* (Paris, 1980), pp. 61–120. See also Rearick, *Pleasures*, pp. 119–46; and Debora L. Silverman, "The 1889 Exhibition: The Crisis of Bourgeois Individualism," *Oppositions* 8 (1977): 71–91.

166 Weber, *France*, p. 110.

167 Ibid., pp. 105–41.

168 See Walter Benjamin, *Das Passagen-Werk, Gesammelte Schriften*, ed. Rolf Tiedemann, vol. 5/1 (Frankfurt-am-Main, 1982), p. 50.

169 Du Camp, *Paris*, p. 290.

170 See Georges Montorgueil, *La Vie des boulevards* (Paris, 1896), p. 226.

171 Simon Arbellot, *La Fin du boulevard* (Paris, 1965).

172 See Louis Chevalier, *Montmartre du plaisir et du crime* (Paris, 1980), pp. 151–63; and Jacques Castelnau, *La Belle Epoque* (Paris, 1962), pp. 81–122. See also Rearick, *Pleasures*, pp. 55–79; and Jerrold Seigel, *Bohemian Paris: Culture, Politics and the Boundaries of Bourgeois Life, 1830–1930* (New York, 1987), pp. 215–41.

173 See Chevalier, *Montmartre*, pp. 163–66.

174 Bodley, *France*, 2: 366.

BIBLIOGRAPHY

Abrantès, Laure Junot, duchesse d'. *Mémoires de Mme la duchesse d'Abrantès, ou souvenirs historiques sur Napoléon, la Révolution, la Directoire, le Consulat, l'Empire et la Restauration.* 18 vols. Paris, 1831–35.

Actes de la Commune de Paris et de la Seine pendant la Révolution. Edited by Sigismond Lacroix. 15 vols. Paris, 1894–1914.

Additions aux différents projects de cahier. Paris, 1789.

Adresse de l'Assemblée générale des Représentants de la Commune de Paris pour le maintien de la tranquilité publique et du respect du à l'Assemblée nationale, du 15 octobre 1789. Paris, 1789.

Adresse de l'Assemblée générale des Représentants de la Commune de Paris, presentée à l'Assemblée nationale, le samedi 10 octobre 1789. Paris, 1789.

Adresse de la Commune de Paris dans ses soixante sections à l'Assemblée nationale. Paris, 1790.

Aguet, Jean-Pierre. *Les Grèves sous la Monarchie de Juillet (1830–1847).* Geneva, 1954.

Agulhon, Maurice. *1848 ou l'Apprentissage de la République 1848–1852.* Paris, 1973.

Allem, Maurice. *La Vie quotidienne sous le Second Empire.* Paris, 1948.

Allonville, comte Armand d'. *Mémoires secrets de 1770 à 1830, par M. le comte d'Allonville.* 6 vols. Paris, 1838–45.

Alméras, Henri d'. *La Vie parisienne pendant le Siège et sous la Commune.* Paris, n.d.

———. *La Vie parisienne sous le Consulat et l'Empire.* Paris, n.d.

———. *La Vie parisienne sous la République de 1848.* Paris, n.d.

———. *La Vie parisienne sous la Restauration.* Paris, n.d.

Alton Shée, Edmond de Liguère, comte d'. *Mémoires du vicomte d'Aulnis.* Paris, 1868.

Amann, Peter. "A Journée in the Making: May 15, 1848." *Journal of Modern History* 42 (1970).

———. "The Paris Club Movement." In *Revolution and Reaction*, edited by Roger Price. London and New York, 1975.

Annuaire statistique de la ville de Paris. Paris, 1883.

Apponyi, comte Rodolphe. *Vingt-cinq ans à Paris (1826–50): Journal du comte Rodolphe Apponyi.* Edited by Ernest Daudet. 4 vols. Paris, 1913–26.

Arbellot, Simon. *La Fin du boulevard.* Paris, 1965.

Archives parlementaires de 1787 à 1860. Recueil complet des débats législatifs et politiques des Chambres françaises, imprimé par ordre du Sénat et de la Chambre des députés, fondé par Mavidal et Laurent, continué par L. Lataste et al. 1st series, 1787–99. 91 vols. Paris, 1867–1913.

Archives parlementaires de 1800 à 1860. 2nd series, Paris, n.d.

Ariès, Philippe. *L'Homme devant la mort.* Paris, 1977.

Ariste, Paul d'. *La Vie et le monde du boulevard (1830–1870)*. Paris, 1930.

Arnault, Antoine-Vincent. *Souvenirs d'un sexagénaire*. 4 vols. Paris, 1833.

Aron, Jean-Paul. *Le Mangeur du XIXe siècle*. Paris, 1973.

Aubertin, Charles. "Le Bourgeois de Paris au dix-huitième siècle." *Revue des deux mondes* 86 (1871).

Aulard, François-Alphonse. *Etudes et leçons sur la Révolution française*. 2 vols. Paris, 1893–98.

———. *Paris pendant la réaction thermidorienne et sous le Directoire: Recueil de documents pour l'histoire de l'esprit public à Paris*. 5 vols. Paris 1898–1902.

———. *Paris sous le Consulat*. 4 vols. Paris, 1903–13.

———. *Paris sous le premier Empire*. 3 vols. Paris, 1912–23.

———. *La Société des Jacobins: Recueil de documents pour l'histoire du club des Jacobins de Paris*. 6 vols. Paris, 1881–97.

Avenel, vicomte Georges d'. "Le Mécanisme de la vie moderne." *Revue des deux mondes* 124 (1894).

———. *Le Mécanisme de la vie moderne*. 5th series. Paris, 1905.

———. *Le Nivellement des jouissances*. Paris, 1913.

Babeau, Albert. *Paris en 1789*. 2nd ed. Paris, 1892.

Bailleux de Marisy, A. "Des Sociétés foncières et de leur rôle dans les travaux publics." *Revue des deux mondes* 34 (1861).

———. "La Ville de Paris devant le Corps législatif." *Revue de deux mondes* 86 (1870).

———. "La Ville de Paris: Ses finances et ses travaux publics depuis le commencement du siècle." *Revue des deux mondes* 47 (1863).

Bailli de Virieu. *La Révolution française racontée par un diplomat étranger: Corréspondance du Bailli de Virieu*. Edited by Emmanuel vicomte de Grouchy and Antoine Guillois. Paris, 1903.

Bailly, Jean-Sylvain. *Mémoires de Bailly, avec une notice sur sa vie, des notes et des éclaircissements historiques*. Edited by Saint-Albin Berville and Jean-François Barrière. 3 vols. Paris, 1821–22.

———, and Honoré-Nicolas-Marie Duveyrier. *Procès-verbal des séances et déliberations de l'Assemblée générale des électeurs de Paris réunis à l'Hôtel de Ville, le 14 juillet 1789, rédigé depuis le 26 avril jusqu'au 21 mai 1789, par M. Bailly . . . et depuis le 22 mai jusqu'au 30 juillet 1789 par M. Duveyrier*. 3 vols. Paris, 1790.

Balzac, Honoré de. *La Comédie humaine*. Edited by Pierre-Georges Castex. 12 vols. Paris, 1976–81.

———. *Lettres à Madame Hanska*. Edited by Roger Pierrot. 4 vols. Paris, 1967–71.

Bancquart, Marie Claire. *Images littéraires du Paris "fin-de-siècle."* Paris, 1979.

Barron, Louis. *Paris pittoresque, 1800–1900: La vie, les moeurs, les plaisirs*. Paris, 1900.

Barrot, Odilon. *Mémoires posthumes de Odilon Barrot*. 4 vols. Paris, 1875–76.

Bastié, Jean. *La Croissance de la banlieue parisienne*. Paris, 1964.

Baudelaire, Charles. *Oeuvres complètes*. Edited by Claude Pichois. 2 vols. Paris, 1975–76.

Bausset, Louis-François-Joseph, baron de. *Mémoires anecdotiques sur l'intérieur du Palais et sur quelques évenements de l'Empire, depuis 1805 jusqu'au 1er mai 1816 pour servir à l'histoire de Napoléon*. 4 vols. Paris, 1827–29.

Bayard, Henri. "Mémoire sur la topographie médicale du IVe arrondissement de la ville de Paris." *Annales d'hygiène publique et de médecine légale* 28 (1842).

———. "Mémoire sur la topographie médicale des Xe, XIe et XIIe arrondissements de la ville de Paris: Recherches historiques et statistiques sur les conditions hygiéniques des quartiers qui composent ces arrondissements." *Annales d'hygiène publique et de médecine légale* 32 (1844).

Bazin, Anaïs de Raucou. "La Choléra-Morbus à Paris." In *Paris ou le livre des cent-et-un*. Paris, 1832.

———. *L'Epoque sans nom, esquisses de Paris 1830–1833*. 2 vols. Paris, 1833.

Beaumont-Vassy, Edouard-Ferdinand, vicomte de. *Les Salons de Paris et la société parisienne sous Louis-Philippe 1er*. Paris, 1866.

Beauregard, C. de. *Nouveaux Tableaux de Paris ou observations sur les moeurs et usages des parisiens au commencement du XIXe siècle, faisant suite à la collection des moeurs françaises, anglaises, italiennes, espagnoles de J. Pain et C. de Beauregard.* 2 vols. Paris, 1828.

Beaurepaire, Chevalier de. *Rapport à MM. du district des Petits Mathurins.* N.p., n.d.

Beaussire, Emile. "Le Procès entre Paris et la Province." *Revue des deux mondes* 93 (1871).

Belgrand, Eugène. *Recherches statistiques sur les sources du bassin de la Seine qu'il est possible de conduire à Paris.* Paris, 1854.

―――. *Transformation de la vidange et suppression de la voirie de Bondy: Achèvement des égouts et emploi de leurs eaux dans l'agriculture.* Paris, 1875.

―――. *Les Travaux souterrains de Paris.* 5 vols. Paris, 1872–87.

Benjamin, Walter. *Das Passagen-Werk.* Edited by Rolf Tiedemann. 2 vols. Frankfurt-am-Main, 1982.

Benoiston de Châteauneuf, Louis-François. "Sur les enfants trouvés." *Annales d'hygiène publique et de médecine legale* 21 (1839).

Bères, Emile, H. Dronsart, and H. Horeau. *Mémoire sur l'embellissement des Champs Elysées et les avantages que le gouvernement et la population parisienne doivent en retirer.* Paris, 1836.

Bertaut, Jules. *Le Faubourg Saint-Germain sous l'Empire et la Restauration.* Paris, 1949.

―――. *Paris 1870–1935.* New York, 1936.

―――. *Le Roi bourgeois (Louis-Philippe intime).* Paris, 1936.

Bertier de Sauvigny, Guillaume de. *La Restauration 1815–1830.* Paris, 1977.

Bertillon, Jacques. "De l'Augmentation de fréquence des principales maladies épidémiques à Paris pendant la période 1865–1883 et de leurs saisons d'élection." *Annuaire statistique de la ville de Paris.* Paris, 1883.

―――. *De la Fréquence des principales causes de décès à Paris.* Paris, 1906.

―――. "Mouvements de population et causes de décès selon le degré d'aisance à Paris, Berlin, Vienne." *Comptes-rendus: Dixième Congrès international d'hygiène et de démographie à Paris en 1900.* Paris, 1901.

Bertin, Jean-Louis-Henri. *Biographie de M. de Belleyme, préfet de police, député, président du Tribunal de la Seine.* Paris, 1863.

Berville, Saint-Albin, and Jean-François Barrière, eds. *Mémoires de Linguet sur la Bastille et de Dusaulx sur le 14 juillet, avec des notices, des notes, et des éclaircissemens historiques.* Paris, 1821.

Beslay, Charles. *1830–1848–1870. Mes souvenirs.* Paris, 1873.

Bingham, J. J. "The French Banquet Campaign 1847–1848." *Journal of Modern History* 21 (1959).

Biver, Marie-Louise. *Le Paris de Napoléon.* Paris, 1963.

―――. *Pierre Fontaine.* Paris, 1964.

Blanc, Louis-Jean-Joseph. *Histoire de dix ans, 1830–1840.* 5 vols. Paris, 1846.

Blayau, Noël. *Billault, Ministre de Napoléon III, d'après ses papiers personnels, 1805–1863.* Paris, 1969.

Bloch, Jean-Jacques, and Marianne Delort. *Quand Paris allait "à l'Expo."* Paris, 1980.

Block, Maurice, and Henri de Pontich. *Administration de la ville de Paris et du département de la Seine.* Paris, 1884.

Blondel, Ferdinand. *Rapport sur les épidémies cholériques de 1832 et de 1849 (de 1853 et de 1854) dans les établissements dépendant de l'administration générale de l'assistance publique de la ville de Paris.* 2 vols. Paris, 1850–55.

Bluche, Frédéric. *Le Plébiscite des Cent-Jours.* Paris and Geneva, 1974.

Bodley, John Edward Courtenay. *France.* 2 vols. London, 1898.

Boehn, Max von. *Vom Kaiserreich zur Republik: Eine Französische Kulturgeschichte des 19. Jahrhunderts.* Berlin, 1917.

Boigne, Adèle, comtesse de. *Récits d'une tante: Mémoires de la comtesse de Boigne.* 5 vols. Paris, 1921–23.

Bonnet, Henri. "La Carte des pauvres à Paris." *Revue des deux mondes* 35 (1906).

Bonnier, Louis. *Les Passages couverts*. Commission du Vieux Paris, procès-verbal, séance du samedi 9 decembre, 1916.

Börne, Ludwig. *Gesammelte Schriften*. 12 vols. Hamburg and Frankfurt-am-Main, 1862.

Bouchet, Ghislaine. "La Traction hippomobile dans les transports publics parisiens (1855–1914)." *Revue historique* 271 (1984).

Boudon, F., A. Chastel, H. Couzy, and F. Hamon. *Système de l'architecture urbaine. Le quartier des Halles à Paris*. Paris, 1977.

Boulenger, Marcel. *La Païva*. Paris, 1930.

Bouloiseau, Marc. "Les Comités de surveillance d'arrondissement de Paris sous la réaction thermidorienne." *Archive historique de la Révolution française* 10 (1933), 11 (1934), and 12 (1936).

Bourdelais, P., and J. Y. Roulot. "Le Choléra en France au XIXᵉ siècle." *Annales E.S.C.* 33 (1978).

Bourdin, Isabelle. *Les Sociétés populaires à Paris pendant la Révolution*. Paris, 1937.

Bourgin, Georges. "La Crise ouvrière à Paris dans la seconde moitié de 1830." *Revue historique* 198 (1947).

Bourgin, Hubert, and Georges Bourgin. *Les Patrons, les ouvriers et l'état: Le régime de l'industrie en France de 1814 à 1830. Recueil de textes publiés pour la Société d'histoire contemporaine*. 3 vols. Paris, 1912–41.

Boutet, Henri. *Les Curiosités de Paris*. Paris, n.d.

Bouvard, Joseph-Antoine, and Gustave Jourdan, eds. *Recueil de règlements concernant le service des alignements et de la police des constructions dans la ville de Paris (dressé sous la direction de M. Bouvard)*. Paris, 1900.

Boxhall-Grantham, Richard. "Description of the Abattoirs of Paris." *Proceedings of the Institution of Civil Engineers* 8 (1849).

Boyer, Ferdinand. "Les Responsabilités de Napoléon dans le transfert à Paris des oeuvres d'art de l'étranger." *Revue d'histoire moderne et contemporaine* 11 (1964).

Boys de Loury. "Mémoires sur les modifications à apporter dans le service de l'administration des nourrices." *Annales d'hygiène publique et de médecine légale* 27 (1842).

Braesch, Frédéric. *La Commune du 10 août 1792: Etude sur l'histoire de Paris du 10 juin au 2 décembre 1792*. Paris, 1911.

Bricheteau, M. "Extrait d'un rapport de la Commission des épidémies de l'Académie royale de médecine pour l'année 1839 et une partie de 1840." *Annales d'hygiène publique et de médecine légale* 25 (1841).

Britsch, Amédée. *La Maison d'Orléans à la fin de l'Ancien Régime: La jeunesse de Philippe-Egalité (1747–1785)*. Paris, 1926.

Broglie, Victor, duc de. *Souvenirs*. 4 vols. Paris, 1886.

Brouardel, Paul-Camille-Hippolyte. "Note sur la mortalité par quelques maladies épidémiques à Paris, pendant les douze dernières années." *Revue d'hygiène et de police sanitaire* 4 (1882).

Bruson, Jean-Marie. "La Place de la Concorde." In *Catalogue de l'exposition Hittorf (1792–1867): Un architecte du XIXᵉ siècle*. Paris: Musée Carnavalet, 1986.

Buchez, Philippe-Joseph-Benjamin, and Prosper-Charles Roux. *Histoire parlementaire de la Révolution française, ou Journal des assemblées nationales depuis 1789 jusqu'en 1815 contenant la narration des événements . . . précédée d'une introduction sur l'histoire de France jusqu'à la convocation des Etats généraux*. 40 vols. Paris, 1834–38.

Buret, Eugène. *De la Misère des classes laborieuses en Angleterre et en France: de la nature de la misère, de son existence, de ses effets, de ses causes, et de l'insuffisance des remèdes qu'on lui a opposés jusqu'ici, avec les moyens propres à en affranchir les sociétés*. 2 vols. Paris 1840.

Burger, W. [Thoré, Etienne-Joseph-Théophile]. *Salons (1861–1868)*. 2 vols. Paris, 1870.

Busch, Moritz. *Tagebuchblätter: Graf Bismarck und seine Leute während des Krieges mit Frankreich 1870–1871 bis zur Rückkehr nach Berlin Wilhelmstrasse 76*. 3 vols. Leipzig, 1899.

Cahen, Léon. "L'Enrichissement de la France sous la Restauration." *Revue d'histoire moderne* 5 (1930).

———. "La Population parisienne au milieu du XVIIIe siècle. *La Revue de Paris* (1919).

Caillot, Antoine. *Mémoires pour servir à l'histoire des moeurs et usages des Français, depuis les plus hautes conditions jusqu'aux classes inférieures de la société, pendant le regne de Louis XVI, sous le Directoire exécutif, sous Napoléon Bonaparte, et jusqu'à nos jours.* 2 vols. Paris, 1827.

Calvet, Henri. "Les Origines du Comité de l'Echêvé." *Annales historiques de la Révolution française* 7 (1930).

Cambry, C. *Rapport sur les sépultures présenté à l'administration centrale du département de la Seine.* Paris, year VII.

Candy, Camille. *Rapport sur le choléra-morbus de Paris.* Lyon, 1849.

Canfora-Argandoña, Elsie, and Roger H. Guerrand. *La Répartition de la population: Les conditions de logement des classes ouvrières à Paris au 19e siècle.* Paris, 1977.

Caspard, Pierre. "Aspects de la lutte des classes en 1848: Le recrutement de la garde nationale mobile." *Revue historique* 252 (1974).

Castellane, Esprit-Victor-Elizabeth-Boniface, maréchal comte de. *Journal du maréchal de Castellane 1804–1862.* 5 vols. Paris, 1895–97.

Castelli, Johann Friedrich. *Memoiren meines Lebens: Gefundenes und Empfundenes, Erlebtes und Erstrebtes.* Munich, n.d.

Castelnau, Jacques. *Belle Epoque.* Paris, 1962.

Catalogue de l'exposition Hittorf (1792–1867): Un architecte du XIXe siècle. Paris: Musée Carnavalet, 1986.

Cazenove d'Arlens, Constance de. *Deux Mois à Paris et à Lyon sous le Consulat.* Paris, 1903.

Centre de documentation d'histoire de technique. *Evolution de la géographie industrielle de Paris et sa proche banlieue au XIXe siècle.* 2 vols. and atlas. Paris, 1976.

Chabert, Alexandre. *Essai sur les mouvements des revenus et de l'activité économique en France de 1789 à 1820.* Paris, 1949.

Chabrol-Chaméane, Ernest de. *Mémoire sur le déplacement de la population dans Paris et sur les moyens d'y rémedier, présenté par les trois arrondissements de la rive gauche de la Seine à la Commission établie près le ministère de l'Interieur.* Paris, 1840.

Chalmin, Pierre. "Une Institution militaire de la Seconde République: La Garde nationale mobile." *Etudes d'histoire moderne et contemporaine* 2 (1948).

Chambre de Commerce de Paris. *Enquête sur les conditions du travail en France pendant l'année 1872.* Paris, 1875.

———. *Statistique de l'industrie à Paris résultant de l'enquête faite par La Chambre de Commerce pour les années 1847–1848.* Paris, 1851.

———. *Statistique de l'industrie à Paris résultant de l'enquête faite par la Chambre de Commerce pour l'année 1860.* Paris, 1864.

Champier, Victor, and G. Roger Sandoz. *Le Palais-Royal d'après des documents inédits (1629–1900).* 2 vols. Paris, 1900.

Chapman, J. M., and Brian Chapman. *The Life and Times of Baron Haussmann: Paris in the Second Empire.* London, 1957.

Chaptal, Jean-Antoine-Claude. *Mes Souvenirs sur Napoléon, par le Cte Chaptal, publiés par son arrière-petit-fils le Vte A. Chaptal.* Paris, 1893.

Charlety, S. *La Monarchie de juillet (1830–1848).* In *Histoire de France contemporaine depuis la Révolution jusqu'à la paix de 1919*, edited by Ernest Lavisse. Paris, 1921.

Chasles, Philarète. *Mémoires.* 2 vols. Geneva, 1973.

Chassin, Charles-Louis, ed. *Les Elections et les cahiers de Paris en 1789.* 4 vols. Paris, 1888–89.

Chastenay, Victorine, comtesse de. *Mémoires (1771–1815), publiés par Alphonse Roserot.* 2 vols. Paris, 1896.

Châteaubriand, François-René. *Génie du christianisme ou beautés de la religion chrétienne.* Edited by Maurice Regard. Paris, 1978.

———. *Mémoires d'outre-tombe.* Edited by Maurice Levaillant and Georges Moulinier. 2 vols. Paris, 1951.

Chazet, René-André-Polydore Allisan de. *Mémoires, souvenirs, oeuvres et portraits.* Paris, 1837.

Chennechot, L. E. *Promenades philosophiques et sentimentales au cimitière du Père Lachaise.* Paris, 1823.

Chevalier, Louis, ed. *Le Choléra. La première épidémie du XIX\u1d49 siècle.* La Roche-sur-Yon, 1958.

―――. *Classes laborieuses et classes dangereuses à Paris pendant la première moitié du XIX\u1d49 siècle.* Paris, 1958.

―――. *La Formation de la population parisienne au XIX\u1d49 siècle.* Paris, 1950.

―――. *Montmartre du plaisir et du crime.* Paris, 1980.

Chevalier, Michel. *L'Industrie et l'octroi de Paris.* 2 vols. Paris, 1867.

Chevallier, A. "Mémoires sur les égouts de Paris, de Londres, de Montpellier." *Annales d'hygiène publique et de médecine légale* 19 (1838).

Chrétien, Jean. *Les Odeurs de Paris, étude analytique des causes qui concourent à l'insalubrité de la ville et des moyens de les combattre.* Paris, 1881.

Clarac, Frédéric, comte de. *Description historique et graphique du Louvre et des Tuileries, publiées dans son Musée de sculpture de 1826–1828, précédée d'une notice biographique sur l'auteur, par Alfred Maury.* Edited by Alfred Maury. Paris, 1853.

Clary et Aldringen, Charles, prince de. *Trois Mois à Paris lors du mariage de l'Empereur Napoléon I\u1d49\u02b3 et de l'Archiduchesse Marie-Louise.* Paris, 1914.

Claudin, Gustave. *Mes Souvenirs, les boulevards de 1840–1870.* Paris, 1884.

Clerq, Victor. "L'Incendie des barrières de Paris en juillet 1789 et le procès des incendiaires." *Bulletin de la société de l'histoire de Paris et de l'Ile-de-France,* 1981.

Clozier, René. *La Gare du Nord.* Paris, 1940.

Cobb, Richard. *Les Armées révolutionnaires: Instrument de la terreur dans les départements. Avril 1793–floréal an II.* 2 vols. Paris, 1961–63.

―――. *La Mort est dans Paris: Enquête sur le suicide, le meurtre et autres morts subites à Paris au lendemain de la Terreur.* Paris, 1985.

―――. *Terreur et subsistances 1793–1795.* Paris, 1965.

Cochin, Augustin. *De la Condition des ouvriers français d'après les derniers travaux.* Paris, 1862.

―――. *Paris, sa population, son industrie: Mémoire lu à l'Académie des sciences morales et politiques, les 18 et 25 juin 1864.* Paris, 1864.

Coleman, William. *Death Is a Social Disease: Public Health and Political Economy in Early Industrial France.* Madison, Wis., 1982.

Colin, Léon. *Paris, sa topographie, son hygiène, ses maladies.* Paris, 1885.

Collection des maisons de commerce de Paris et des intérieurs les mieux décorés. Reprint. Paris, 1926.

Collection officielle des ordonnances de police (1800–1848). Paris, 1880.

Conseil de salubrité. *Rapports généraux des travaux du Conseil de salubrité pendant les années 1840 à 1845 inclusivement.* Paris, 1847.

Cooper, James Fenimore. *Gleanings in Europe: France.* Albany, N.Y., 1983.

Corbin, Alain. *Le Miasme et la jonquille: L'odorat et l'imaginaire social XVIII\u1d49–XIX\u1d49 siècles.* Paris, 1982.

Corbon, Anthime. *Le Secret du peuple de Paris.* Paris, 1863.

Cornu, Marcel. *La Conquête de Paris.* Paris, 1972.

Corti, Egon Caesar Conte. *Das Haus Rothschild in der Zeit seiner Blüte 1830–1871.* Leipzig, 1928.

Costaz, Claude-Anthelme. *Essai sur l'administration de l'agriculture, du commerce, des manufactures et des subsistances, suivi de l'historique des moyens qui ont amené le grand essor pris par les arts depuis 1793 jusq'à 1815.* Paris, 1818.

Crémieux, Albert. "La Fusillade du boulevard des Capucines le 23 février 1848." *La Révolution de 1848,* 8 (1911).

―――. *La Révolution de février: Etude critique sur les journées des 21, 22, 23, 24 février 1848.* Paris, 1912.

Cuvillier-Fleury, Alfred-Auguste. *Journal intime*. Edited by Edouard Bertin. 2 vols. Paris, 1900–1903.

Dampmartin, Anne-Henri, vicomte de. *Un Provincial à Paris pendant une partie de l'année 1789*. La Villette, n.d.

Dansette, Adrien. *Le Boulangisme*. Paris, 1938.

―――――. *Histoire du Second Empire*. 3 vols. Paris, 1972–76.

Daumard, Adéline. "L'Avenue de l'Opéra de ses origines à la guerre de 1914." *Bulletin de la société de l'histoire de Paris et de l'Ile-de-France*, 1970.

―――――. *La Bourgeoisie parisienne de 1815 à 1848*. Paris, 1963.

―――――. *Maisons de Paris et propriétaires parisiens au XIXe siècle*. Paris, 1965.

Debofle, Pierre. "Les Travaux de Paris (1814–1830): Recherches sur la politique d'urbanisme de la ville de Paris sous la Restauration." Dissertation, Ecole Normale des Chartes. Paris, 1974.

Découflé, André. *La Commune de Paris (1871): Révolution populaire et pouvoir révolutionnaire*. Paris, 1969.

Delacroix, Eugène. *Journal*. Edited by André Joubin. Paris, 1932.

Delasselle, Claude. "Les Enfants abandonnés à Paris." *Annales E.S.C.* 30 (1975).

Delécluze, Etienne-Jean. *Journal de Delécluze 1824–1828*. Edited by Robert Baschet. Paris, 1948.

Delveau, Alfred. *Histoire anecdotique des cafés et cabarets de Paris*. Paris, 1862.

Demangeon, Albert. *Paris. La ville et sa banlieue*. Paris, 1933.

Département de la Seine. Service de la statistique municipale. *Résultats statistiques du dénombrement pour la ville de Paris et le département de la Seine*. Paris, 1899.

Des Cilleuls, Alfred. *Histoire de l'administration parisienne au XIXe siècle*. 2 vols. Paris, 1900.

Desgranges, Henry Légier. *Les Massacres de septembre à la Salpêtrière: Mémoires de la fédération des sociétés historiques et archéologiques de Paris et de l'Ile-de- France*, vol 2. 1950.

Desmoulins, Camille. *Oeuvres*. Edited by Eugène Despois. 3 vols. Paris, 1865.

―――――. *Oeuvres*. Edited by Jules Claretie. 2 vols. Paris, 1874.

Devrient, Eduard. *Briefe aus Paris*. Berlin, 1840.

Dézallier d'Argenville, Antoine-Nicolas. *Voyage pittoresque de Paris ou Indication de tout ce qu'il y a de plus beau dans cette grande ville en peinture, sculpture et architecture*. 5th ed. 2 vols. Paris, 1770.

Doin, Guillaume-Tell, and Edouard Thomas Charton. *Lettres sur Paris*. Paris, 1830.

Dolléans, Edouard. *Histoire du mouvement ouvrier (1830–1871)*. Paris, 1936.

Donnard, Jean-Hervé. *Balzac: Les Réalités économiques et sociales dans La Comédie humaine*. Paris, 1961.

Du Barail, Général François-Charles. *Mes Souvenirs (1864–1879)*. 3 vols. Paris, 1894–96.

Dubech, Lucien, and Pierre d'Espezel. *Histoire de Paris*. 2 vols. Paris, 1931.

Dubreton, Jean-Lucas. *Le Culte de Napoléon 1815–1848*. Paris, 1960.

―――――. *La Royauté bourgeoise 1830*. Paris, 1930.

Du Camp, Maxime. *Les Convulsions de Paris*. 5th ed. 4 vols. Paris, 1881.

―――――. *Paris, ses organes, ses fonctions et sa vie dans la seconde moitié du XIXe siècle*. 7th ed. Paris, 1883–84.

―――――. *Souvenirs de l'année 1848: la révolution de février, le 15 mai, l'insurrection de juin*. Edited by Maurice Agulhon. Paris and Geneva, 1979.

Dufey, Pierre-Joseph-Spiridiou. *Mémorial parisien, ou Paris tel qu'il fut, tel qu'il est*. Paris, 1821.

Dulaure, Jacques-Antoine. *Histoire physique, civile et morale de Paris*. 8 vols. Paris, 1837–38.

Dupont, Paul-François. *Insuffisance des traitements en général et de la nécessité d'une prompte augmentation*. Paris, 1859.

Dupont de Nemours, Pierre-Samuel. *Idées sur les secours à donner aux pauvres malades dans une grande ville*. Philadelphia and Paris, 1786.

Duquesnoy, Adrien-Cyprien. *Rapport sur les secours à domicile.* Paris, 1801.

Durand, Charles. *Le Régime juridique de l'expropriation pour utilité publique sous le Consulat et le Premier Empire.* Aix-en-Provence, 1948.

Durieux, Joseph. *Les Vainqueurs de la Bastille.* Paris, 1911.

Dusaulx, Jean. *De l'Insurrection parisienne et de la prise de la Bastille, discours historique, prononcé par extrait dans l'Assemblée nationale.* Paris, 1790.

Duval, Georges-Louis-Jacques. *Souvenirs thermidoriens.* 2 vols. Paris, 1844.

Duveau, Georges. *La Vie ouvrière en France sous le Second Empire.* Paris, 1946.

Edwards, Stewart. *The Paris Commune 1871.* London, 1971.

Escherny, François-Louis, comte d'. *Correspondance d'un habitant de Paris avec ses amis de Suisse et d'Angleterre sur les événements de 1789, 1790 et jusqu'au 4 avril 1791.* Paris, 1791.

Evenson, Norma. *Paris: A Century of Change: 1878-1978.* New Haven and London, 1979.

Exposé des changements à faire au Palais-Royal: Imprimé par ordre de S. A. S. le duc de Chartres, prince du sang. Paris, 1781.

Falloux, Alfred-Frédéric-Pierre, comte de. *Mémoires d'un royaliste.* 2 vols. Paris, 1888.

Farge, Arlette, ed. *Vivre dans la rue à Paris au XVIIIᵉ siècle.* Paris, 1979.

Farge, René. "Camille Desmoulins au jardin du Palais-Royal." *Annales révolutionnaires* 7 (1914).

Faure, Alain. "Classe malpropre, classe dangereuse: Quelques remarques à propos des chiffoniers parisiens au XIXᵉ siècle et de leurs cités." In *Haleine des faubourgs: Ville, habitat et santé au XIXᵉ siècle.* Fontenay-sous-Bois, 1978.

————. *Paris Carême prenant. Du carnaval à Paris au XIXᵉ siècle.* Paris, 1978.

Fellowes, William Dorset. *Paris during the Interesting Month of July 1815: A Series of Letters Addressed to a Friend in London.* London, 1815.

Ferrières, Marquis de. *Mémoires.* Edited by Saint-Albin Berville and Jean-François Barrière. 3 vols. Paris, 1822.

Ferry, Jules. *Comptes fantastiques d'Haussmann, lettre adressée à MM. les membres de la Commission du Corps legislatif chargés d'examiner le nouveau projet d'emprunt de la ville de Paris.* Paris, 1868.

Festy, Octave. *Le Mouvement ouvrier au début de la Monarchie de Juillet (1830–1834).* Paris, 1908.

Fieffée, Eugène. *Histoire des troupes étrangères au service de France, depuis leur origine jusqu'à nos jours, et de tous les régiments levés dans les pays conquis sous la première République et l'Empire.* 2 vols. Paris, 1854.

Firmin-Didot, Georges. *Royauté ou Empire: La France en 1814 d'après les rapports inédits du comte Anglès.* Paris, 1897.

Flaubert, Gustave. *L'Education sentimentale.* Edited by A. Thibaudet and R. Dumesnil. *Oeuvres*, vol. 2. Paris, 1968.

Foisil, Madeleine. "Les Attitudes devant la mort au XVIIIᵉ siècle: Sépultures et suppressions de sépultures dans le cimetière parisien des Saints-Innocents." *Revue historique* 251 (1974).

Forster, Charles de [Karol]. *Quinze Ans a Paris (1832–1848): Paris et les parisiens.* 2 vols. Paris, 1848–94.

Fosca, François. *Histoire des cafés de Paris.* Paris, 1934.

Fouinet, Ernest. "Un voyage en omnibus: De la barrière du Trône à la barrière de l'Etoile." In *Paris, ou le livre des cent-et-un.* Paris, 1831.

Fournel, Victor. *Ce qu'on voit dans les rues de Paris.* Paris, 1858.

————. *Paris nouveau, Paris futur.* Paris, 1865.

Fournier l'Héritier, Claude, dit l'Américain. *Mémoires secrets de Fournier l'Américain, publiés pour la première fois d'après le manuscrit des Archives nationales.* Edited by F. A. Aulard. Paris, 1890.

Franklin, Alfred. *Les anciens plans de Paris, notices historiques et topographiques.* 2 vols. Paris, 1878–80.

_____. *Dictionnaire historique des arts, métiers et professions exercés dans Paris depuis le XIIIe siècle*. Paris, 1906.

_____. *La Vie privée d'autrefois: l'hygiène*, Paris, 1890.

Frégier, H. A. *Des Classes dangereuses de la population dans les grandes villes et des moyens de les rendre meilleures*. 2 vols. Paris, 1840.

Frenilly, Auguste-François Fauveau, baron de. *Souvenirs (1768–1828)*. Edited by Arthur Chuquet. 2d ed. Paris, 1908.

Fribourg, E. E. *Du Pauperisme parisien*. Paris, 1872.

Friedrich, Johann Konrad. *Der Glückssoldat: Wahrheit und Dichtung oder vierzig Jahre und noch fünfzehn Jahre aus dem Leben eines Toten*. 4 vols. Munich, 1920–23.

Funck-Brentano, Frantz. *Salons et cénacles romantiques. La vie parisienne à l'époque romantique*. Conférence du Musée Carnavalet 1930. Paris, 1931.

Furet, François, and Denis Richet. *Die Französische Revolution*. Munich, 1981.

Gachet, Stéphane. *Paris tel qu'il doit être: L'Ile de la Cité*. Paris, 1856.

Gaillard, Jeanne. *Paris, la ville (1852–1870)*. Paris, 1977.

Garnier, Francis. *Le Siège de Paris, journal d'un officier de marine*. 3rd ed. Paris, 1887.

Garnier, Jules. *Une Visite à la voirie de Montfaucon considérée sous le point de vue de la salubrité publique*. Paris, 1844.

Garrigues, Georges. *Les Districts parisiens pendant la Révolution française*. Paris, 1931.

Gasnault, François. "Un Animateur de bals publics parisiens: Philippe Musard (1792–1859)." *Bulletin de la société de l'histoire de Paris et de l'Ile-de-France* 108 (1982).

Gastineau, Benjamin. *Le Carnaval*. Paris, 1855.

Gautier, Théophile. "Paris-futur." In *Caprices et zigzags*. Paris, 1852.

Geist, Johann Friedrich. *Passagen: Ein Bautyp des 19. Jahrhunderts*. Munich, 1978.

Gendron, Françoise. *La Jeunesse dorée: Episode de la Révolution française*. Quebec, 1979.

Gérards, Emile. *Paris souterrain: Formation et composition du sol de Paris, les eaux souterraines, carrières et catacombes, les égouts, voies ferrées souterraines, métropolitain, municipal, chemin de fer électrique Nord-Sud, souterrains divers, fauna et flore souterraines de Paris*. Paris, 1909.

Gille, Bertrand. *La Banque et le crédit en France de 1815 à 1848*. Paris, 1959.

_____. *Documents sur l'état de l'industrie et du commerce de Paris et du département de la Seine (1778–1810)*. Paris, 1963.

_____. "Fonctions économiques de Paris." In *Paris, fonctions d'une capitale: Colloques: Cahiers de civilisation*, edited by Guy Michaud. Paris, 1962.

_____. "Recherches sur l'origine des grands magasins parisiens: Note d'orientation." In *Paris et l'Ile-de-France*, vol. 7. Paris, 1955.

Girard, Louis. *La Deuxième République et le Second Empire 1848–1870*. Paris, 1981.

_____. *La Garde nationale 1814–1871*. Paris, 1964.

_____. *La Politique des travaux publics du Second Empire*. Paris, 1952.

_____. *Les Elections de 1869*. Paris, 1960.

Girard, Pierre-Simon. "Du Déplacement de la voirie de Montfaucon." *Annales d'hygiène publique et de médecine légale* 9, 1 (1833).

_____. *Recherches sur les établissements de bains publics à Paris depuis le VIe siècle jusqu'à present*. Paris, 1832.

Girardin, Delphine de [Le Vicomte de Launay]. *Lettres parisiennes*. 3 vols. Paris, 1856.

Giraud, Pierre. *Les Tombeaux ou essai sur les sépultures*. Paris, 1801.

Gisquet, Henri. *Mémoires de M. Gisquet, ancien préfet de police, écrits par lui-même*. 4 vols. Paris, 1840.

Godechot, Jacques, ed. *Bibliothèque de la Révolution de 1848*. La Roche-sur-Yon, 1967.

_____. *La Prise de la Bastille, 14 juillet 1789*. Paris, 1965.

Goncourt, Edmond and Jules de. *Histoire de la société française pendant le Directoire*. 3rd ed. Paris, 1864.

_____. *Journal. Mémoires de la vie littéraire*. Edited by Robert Ricatte. 4 vols. Paris, 1956.

Gonnet, Pierre. "Esquisse de la crise économique en France de 1827 à 1832." *Revue d'histoire économique et sociale* 9 (1955).

Gossez, Rémi. *Les Ouvriers de Paris, I: L'Organisation 1848–1851*, edited by Jacques Godechot. Bibliothèque de la Révolution de 1848, vol. 14. La-Roche-sur-Yon, 1967.
_____. "La Presse parisienne à destination des ouvriers, 1848–1851." In *La Presse ouvrière, 1819–1850*, edited by Jacques Godechot. Bibliothèque de la Révolution de 1848, vol. 13. La Roche-sur-Yon, 1966.
Goubert, Jean-Pierre. *La Conquête de l'eau*. Paris, 1986.
Gourgaud, Gaspard, baron. *Journal de Sainte-Hélène*. Edited by Gustave Aubry. 2 vols. Paris, 1947.
Gouriet, Jean-Baptiste. *Panorama parisien*. Paris, 1827.
Grandeffe, Arthur, comte de. *Paris sous Napoléon III, mémoires d'un homme du monde de 1857 à 1870*. Paris, 1879.
Grimm, Melchior von, and Denis Diderot. *Correspondance littéraire, philosophique et critique*. 16 vols. Paris, 1813.
Grimod de la Reynière. *Almanach des gourmands servant de guide dans les moyens de faire excellente chère; par un vieil amateur*. 8 vols. Paris 1804–11.
Groh, Dieter. "Caesarismus." In *Geschichtliche Grundbegriffe. Historisches Lexikon zur politisch-sozialen Sprache in Deutschland*, edited by O. Brunner, W. Conze, and R. Koselleck. Stuttgart, 1972.
Guérard, Alphonse. "Observations sur le méphitisme et la désinfection des fosses d'aisances." *Annales d'hygiène publique et de médecine légale* 32 (1844).
_____. "Sur l'épidemie du choléra qui sévit en ce moment à Paris." *Annales d'hygiène publique et de médecine légale*, 2nd series, 1 (1854).
Guerrand, Roger. *Mémoires du métro*. Paris, 1961.
Guillemin, Henri. *L'Avènement de M. Thiers: Reflexions sur la Commune*. Paris, 1971.
Gutzkow, Carl-Ferdinand. *Paris und Frankreich in den Jahren 1834–1874*. In *Gesammelte Werke*, 1st series, vol. 7. Jena, 1879.
Halbwachs, Maurice. *Les Expropriations et le prix des terrains à Paris 1860–1900*. Paris, 1909.
_____. *La Population et les tracés des voies à Paris depuis un siècle*. Paris, 1928.
Halévy, Ludovic. *Carnets*. Edited by Daniel Halévy. 2 vols. Paris, 1935.
Hammer, Karl. *Jacob Ignaz Hittorf. Ein Pariser Baumeister 1792–1867*. Stuttgart, 1968.
Hanotaux, Gabriel. "La Transformation sociale à l'époque napoléonienne." *Revue des deux mondes* 33 (1926).
Hardy, S. P. "Mes Loisirs, ou journal d'événements tels qu'ils parviennent à ma connaissance." Bibliothèque Nationale, Fonds français 6687.
Harsin, Jill. *Policing Prostitution in Nineteenth Century Paris*. Princeton, N.J., 1985.
Haussmann, Georges-Eugène. "Aux Commissaires-voyers de Paris, relativement à l'harmonie à établir entre les façades des maisons neuves." *Revue générale de l'architecture et des travaux publics* 13 (1855).
_____. *Mémoires*. 3 vols. Paris, 1893.
_____. *Premier Mémoire sur les eaux de Paris présenté par le préfet de la Seine au Conseil municipal (4 août 1854)*. Paris, 1858.
_____. *Second Mémoire sur les eaux de Paris présenté par le préfet de la Seine au Conseil municipal (16 juillet 1858)*. Paris, 1858.
Hautecoeur, Louis. "De l'Echoppe aux grands magasins." *Revue de Paris* 54 (1933).
Hauterive, Ernest d'. *La Police secrète du Premier Empire: Bulletins quotidiens adressés par Fouché à l'Empereur*. 2 vols. Paris, 1908–13.
Heine, Heinrich. *Sämtliche Schriften*. Edited by Klaus Briegleb. 6 vols. Munich, 1975.
Heinzmann, Johann Georg. *Voyage d'un Allemand à Paris et retour par la Suisse*. Lausanne, 1800.
Henrion, Charles. *Encore un tableau de Paris*. Paris, year VIII.
Héricart de Thury, L. E. F., vicomte. *Description des catacombes de Paris*. Paris, 1815.
Herlaut, Auguste Philippe. *L'Eclairage de Paris à l'époque révolutionnaire*. Paris, 1931.
Higonnet, P., and T. Higonnet. "Class, Corruption and Politics in the French Chamber of Deputies 1846–1848." *French Historical Studies* 5 (1967).

Hillairet, Jacques. *Dictionnaire historique des rues de Paris.* 7th ed. 3 vols. Paris, 1963.
_____. *Les 200 Cimetières du vieux Paris.* Paris, 1958.
Hintermeyer, Pascal. *Politiques de la mort.* Paris, 1981.
Hobhouse, John. *Lettres écrites de Paris pendant le dernier règne de l'Empereur Napoléon.* 2 vols. Ghent and Brussels, 1817.
Horii, Toshio. "La Crise alimentaire de 1853 à 1856 et la Caisse de la boulangerie de Paris." *Revue historique* 272 (1984).
House, Jonathan M. "Civil-Military Relations in Paris, 1848." In *Revolution and Reaction: 1848 and the Second French Republic,* edited by Roger Price. London and New York, 1975.
Houssaye, Arsène. *Les Confessions. Souvenirs d'un demi-siècle (1830–1880).* 6 vols. Paris, 1885–91.
Houssaye, Henri. *1814.* Paris, 1888.
_____. *1815. La Première Restauration. Les Cent-Jours.* Paris, 1896.
Hugo, Victor. *Choses vues: Souvenirs, journaux, cahiers 1830–1885.* Edited by Hubert Juin. 4 vols. Paris, 1972.
_____. *Les Misérables.* Edited by Maurice Allem. Paris, 1951.
_____. *Oeuvres poétiques.* Edited by Pierre Albouy. 3 vols. Paris, 1974.
Hugueney, Jeanne. "Un Centenaire oublié: La première loi française d'urbanisme, 13 avril 1850." *La Vie urbaine* (1950).
Hunt, Lynn. *Politics, Culture and Class in the French Revolution.* Berkeley, Los Angeles, and London, 1984.
Husson, Armand. *Les Consommations de Paris.* Paris, 1856.
_____. *De la Regénération de la rive gauche de la Seine.* Paris, 1856.
Huysmans, Joris-Karl. *Croquis parisiens: Les Folies-Bergère en 1789.* In *Oeuvres complètes de J. K. Huysmans,* vol. 8. Paris, 1929.
"Instruction populaire sur les principaux moyens à employer pour se garantir du choléra-morbus, et sur la conduite à tenir lorsque cette maladie se déclarée." *Le Moniteur* (March 30, 1832).
Jacquemet, Gérard. "Lotissement et construction dans la proche banlieue parisienne 1820–1840." *Paris et l'Ile-de-France* 24 (1974).
_____. "Urbanisme parisien: La bataille du tout-à-l'égout à la fin du XIXᵉ siècle." *Revue d'histoire moderne et contemporaine* 26 (1979).
Janin, Jules-Gabriel. "Les Bals (1832)." In *Oeuvres diverses,* edited by A. de la Fizelière. 2nd series, vol. 5. Paris, 1883.
_____. *Paris depuis la révolution de 1832.* Brussels, 1832.
_____. *Un Hiver à Paris.* Paris, 1847.
Jaurès, Jean. *L'Histoire socialiste de la Révolution française.* 2 vols. Paris, 1922.
Joest, Thomas von. "Des Restaurants, des cafés: d'un théâtre jadis célèbre du géorama et de la grandeur de quelques projets." *Catalogue de l'exposition Hittorf (1792–1867).* Paris: Musée Carnavalet, 1986.
_____. "Hittorf et les embellissements des Champs Elysées." *Catalogue de l'exposition Hittorf (1792–1867).* Paris: Musée Carnavalet, 1986.
Joinville, Prince de. *Vieux Souvenirs.* Paris, 1894.
Jouhaud, Pierre. *Paris dans le XIXᵉ siècle, ou réflexions d'un observateur sur les nouvelles institutions, les embellissements, l'esprit public, la société.* Paris, 1809.
Jourdan, Gustave. *Etudes d'hygiène publique.* Paris, 1892.
_____. *Législation sur les logements insalubres, traité pratique.* Paris, 1879.
Jouy, Victor-Joseph-Etienne [de Jouy]. *L'Hermite de la Chaussée-d'Antin ou observations sur les moeurs et les usages parisiens au commencement du XIXᵉ siècle.* 5 vols. Paris, 1814.
_____. *L'Hermite de la Guiane ou observations sur les moeurs et les usages français au commencement du XIXᵉ siècle.* 3 vols. Paris, 1816–17.
Kaplow, Jeffry. *Les Noms des rois: Les pauvres de Paris à la veille de la Révolution.* Paris, 1974.
_____. "Sur la Population flottante de Paris à la fin de l'Ancien Régime." *Annales historiques de la révolution française* 39 (1967).

Karamzin, Nikolai M. *Letters of a Russian Traveller 1789–1790.* Edited by Florence Jonas. New York, 1957.

Kleist, Heinrich von. *Sämtliche Werke und Briefe.* Edited by Wilhelm Herzog. 6 vols. Leipzig, 1911.

Kock, Paul de. *La Grande Ville: Nouveau tableau de Paris, comique, critique et philosophique.* 2 vols. Paris, 1842.

Kolloff, Eduard. *Schilderungen aus Paris.* 2 vols. Hamburg, 1839.

Korn, Karl. *Zola in seiner Zeit.* Frankfurt-am-Main, 1980.

Kotzebue, August Friedrich Ferdinand von. *Erinnerungen aus Paris im Jahre 1804.* 2 vols. Berlin, 1804.

Kovalevski, Maksim Maksimovitch, ed. *I Dispacci degli ambasciatori veneti alla corte di Francia durante la rivoluzione.* Turin, 1895.

Kracauer, Siegfried. *Jacques Offenbach und das Paris seiner Zeit.* In *Schriften*, vol. 8. Edited by Karsten Witte. Frankfurt-am-Main, 1976.

L., Alphonse. *De la Salubrité de la ville de Paris.* Paris, 1826.

Labrousse, Camille Ernest. *Aspects de la crise et de la dépression de l'économie française au milieu du XIXᵉ siècle.* La Roche-sur-Yon, 1956.

———. *Esquisse du mouvement des prix et des revenus en France au XVIIIᵉ siècle.* 2 vols. Paris, 1933.

———. *Le Mouvement ouvrier et les théories sociales en France de 1815 à 1848.* Paris, 1947.

Lacordaire, Simon. *Les Inconnus de la Seine: Paris et les métiers de l'eau du XIIIᵉ au XIXᵉ siècle.* Paris, 1985.

Lacour-Gayet, Georges. *Talleyrand.* 4 vols. Paris, 1928–34.

Lacretelle, Charles-Jean-Dominique de (le jeune). *Dix années d'épreuves pendant la Révolution.* Paris, 1842.

———. *Histoire de l'Assemblée constituante.* 2 vols. Paris, 1821.

Lacroix, Paul. *Directoire, Consulat et Empire: Moeurs et usages, lettres, sciences et arts, 1795–1815.* Paris, 1884.

La Gorce, Pierre de. *Histoire de la Seconde République française.* 2 vols. Paris, 1887.

Lambeau, Lucien. *Histoire des communes annexées à Paris en 1859.* Paris, 1923.

Lameyre, Gérard-Noël. *Haussmann, préfet de Paris.* Paris, 1958.

Lamourette, Abbé Antoine-Adrien. *Désastre de la maison de Saint-Lazare.* Paris, 1789.

Lanquetin, Jacques. *Observations sur un travail de l'administration municipale de Paris, intitulé "Etudes sur les Halles."* Paris, 1843.

———. *Ville de Paris: Question du déplacement de la population. Etat des études sur cette question.* Paris, 1842.

Lanzac de Laborie, Léon de, ed. *Mémorial de J. de Norvins.* 3 vols. Paris, 1896–97.

———. *Paris sous Napoléon.* 8 vols. Paris, 1905–13.

Las Cases, Emmanuel, comte de. *Le Mémorial de Sainte-Hélène.* Edited by Ernest Dunan. 2 vols. Paris, 1951.

Lasteyrie du Saillant, Ferdinand-Charles, comte de. *Les Travaux de Paris: examen critique.* Paris, 1861.

Laurent, Emile. *Les Logements insalubres, la loi de 1850, son application, ses lacunes, réformes désirables, projet de loi.* Paris, 1882.

Lavallée, Joseph. *Les dernières adieux du quai des Gesvres à la Bonne Ville de Paris.* London, 1787.

Lavedan, Pierre. *Histoire de l'urbanisme à Paris.* Paris, 1975.

———. "Napoléon Iᵉʳ. Les Halles de Paris." *Archives de l'art français* 24 (1969).

Lavisse, Ernest, ed. *Histoire de France contemporaine depuis la Révolution jusqu'à la paix de 1919.* 10 vols. Paris, 1920–22.

Lavoisier, Antoine Laurent. *Oeuvres.* Edited by J. B. Dumas, E. Grimaux, and F. A. Fouque. 6 vols. Paris, 1864–93.

Lavollée, C. "Statistique industrielle de Paris." *Revue des deux mondes* 55 (1865).

Lazare, Louis. *Etudes municipales: Les quartiers pauvres de Paris.* Paris, 1869.

———. *La France et Paris.* Paris, 1872.

Lecouturier, Henri. *Paris incompatible avec la république, plan d'un nouveau Paris où les révolutions seront impossibles.* Paris, 1848.

Ledré, Charles. *La Presse nationale sous la restauration et la Monarchie de Juillet. Histoire générale de la presse française de 1815 à 1871,* vol. 2. Paris, 1969.

Ledru, Alexandre-Auguste [Ledru-Rollin]. *Mémoire sur les événements de la rue Transnonain dans les journées des 13 et 14 avril 1834.* Paris, 1834.

Lefebvre, Georges. "Le Mouvement des prix et les origines de la révolution française." *Annales historiques de la révolution française* 14 (1937).

Lefebvre, Henri. *La Proclamation de la Commune, 26 mars 1871.* Paris, 1965.

Lefrançais, Gustave. *Etude sur le mouvement communaliste à Paris en 1871.* Neuchâtel, 1871.

Le Gallo, Emile. *Les Cent-Jours.* Paris, 1923.

Le Grand, Louis. "Les Quinze-Vingts." *Mémoires de la société de l'Histoire de Paris* 13 (1887).

Lelièvre, Pierre. *Vivant Denon: Directeur des Beaux-Arts de Napoléon.* Paris, 1942.

Lenotre, G. "Le Jardin de Picpus 1793–1794." *Revue des deux mondes* 92 (1927).

————. *Les Pèlerinages de Paris révolutionnaire: Le jardin de Picpus.* Paris, 1928.

Léon, Paul. *Paris. Histoire de la rue.* Paris, 1947.

Lescauriet, Auguste. *Histoire des agrandissements de Paris.* Paris, 1860.

Le Trosne, Guillaume-François. *Mémoire sur les vagabonds et sur les mendiants.* Soissons and Paris, 1764.

Leuret, François. "Notice historique sur A. J. B. Parent-Duchâtelet." *Annales d'hygiène publique et de médecine légale* 16 (1836).

Levasseur, René. *Mémoires.* 4 vols. Paris, 1829–31.

Lévy-Leboyer, Maurice. *Les Banques européennes et l'industrialisation internationale dans la première moitié du XIXᵉ siècle.* Paris, 1964.

Lewald, August. *Ein Menschenleben.* In *Gesammelte Schriften,* vol. 6. Leipzig, 1844.

Lissagaray, Prosper-Olivier. *Geschichte der Kommune von 1871.* 2nd ed. Stuttgart, 1894.

Loliée, Frédéric. *La Païva: La légende et l'histoire de la marquise de Païva. D'après les pages retrouvées de sa vie.* Paris, 1913.

Londiche, René. *Les Transports en commun à la surface dans la région parisienne.* Paris, 1929.

Lortsch, Charles. *La Beauté de Paris et la loi.* Paris, 1912.

Loua, Toussaint. *Atlas statistique de la population de Paris.* Paris, 1873.

Loyer, François. *Paris XIXᵉ siècle: L'immeuble et la rue.* Paris, 1987.

Luchet, Auguste [Pourcelt de Baron]. "La Descente de la courtille en 1833." In *Paris ou le livre des cent-et-un.* Paris, 1834.

————. "Les Grandes Cuisines et les grandes caves." In *Paris-Guide.* Paris, 1867.

————. *Nouveau Tableau de Paris.* Paris, 1834.

————. *Paris: Esquisses dediées au peuple parisien et à M. J. A. Dulaure.* Paris, 1830.

MacDonough, Felix. *The Wandering Hermit.* 2 vols. Paris, 1823.

McKay, Donald Cope. *The National Workshops: A Study in the French Revolution of 1848.* Cambridge, Mass., 1933.

Madelin, Louis. *Histoire du Consulat et de l'Empire.* 16 vols. Paris, 1937–48.

Magny, Charles. *Des Moyens juridiques de sauvegarder les aspects esthétiques de la ville de Paris.* Paris, 1911.

Mainardi, Patricia. *Art and Politics of the Second Empire: The Universal Expositions of 1855 and 1867.* New Haven and London, 1988.

Malet, Henri. *Le Baron Haussmann et la rénovation de Paris.* Paris, 1973.

Margerit, Robert. *Waterloo.* Paris, 1964.

Maricourt, baron André Du Mesnil de. *Prisonniers et prisons de Paris pendant la Terreur.* Paris, n.d.

Marmier, Xavier. *Journal (1848–1890).* Edited by Eldon Kaye. 2 vols. Geneva, 1968.

Marnata, Françoise. *Les Loyers des bourgeois de Paris 1860–1958.* Paris, n.d.

Marot, François. *Recherches sur la vie de François de Neufchâteau.* Nancy, 1966.

Martin, Marc. "Presse, publicité et grandes affaires sous le Second Empire." *Revue historique* 256 (1976).

Marx, Karl. *Der Bürgerkrieg in Frankreich.* East Berlin, 1970.

Mathiez, Albert. *Les Grandes journees de la Constituante 1789–1791.* Paris, 1913.

―――. "Le massacre et le procès du Champ de Mars." *Annales révolutionnaires* 3 (1910).

―――. *La Vie chère et le mouvement social sous la Terreur.* 2 vols. Paris, 1973.

Maugny, comte Albert de. *Souvenirs du Second Empire: La fin d'une société.* Paris, 1889.

Maupas, Charlemagne-Emile de. *La présidence de Louis-Napoléon. Mémoires sur le Second Empire,* vol. 1. Paris, 1884.

Maupassant, Guy de. *Bel-Ami.* Edited by Gérard Delaisement. Paris, 1959.

Mayer, Alfred. "La Canalisation souterraine de Paris." In *Paris-Guide.* 2 vols. Paris, 1867.

Mazerolle, Pierre. *La Misère de Paris, les mauvais gîtes.* Paris, 1875.

Meaux, vicomte Marie-Camille-Alfred de. *Souvenirs politiques 1871–1877.* Paris, 1905.

Meding, Henri L. *Essai sur la topographie médicale de Paris, examen général des conditions de salubrité dans lesquelles cette ville est placée.* Paris, 1852.

Meister, Henri [Jacob Heinrich]. *Souvenirs de mon dernier voyage à Paris (1795).* Edited by Paul Usteri and Eugène Ritter. Paris, 1910.

Mellié, Ernest. *Les Sections de Paris pendant la Révolution française (21 mai 1790–19 vendémiaire an IV).* Paris, 1898.

Mémoire adressé par une réunion de propriétaires, architectes et constructeurs de la ville de Paris à Messieurs les membres de la Commission d'enquête. Paris, 1829.

Ménière, Prosper. *Journal: Mémoires anecdotiques sur les salons du Second Empire.* Paris, 1903.

Menuret de Chambaud, Jean-Jacques. *Essai sur l'action de l'air dans les maladies contagieuses, qui a remporté le prix proposé par la Société royale de médecine.* Paris, 1781.

―――. *Essais sur l'histoire médico-topographique de Paris.* Paris, 1786.

Mercier, Louis-Sébastien. *Paris pendant la Révolution, 1789–1798, ou le nouveau Paris.* 2 vols. Paris, 1862.

―――. *Tableau de Paris.* 12 vols. Amsterdam, 1782–88. Reprint. Geneva, 1979.

Mérimée, Prosper. *Correspondance générale.* Edited by Maurice Parturier. 17 vols. Paris and Toulouse, 1941–64.

Merruau, Charles. *Souvenirs de l'Hôtel de Ville de Paris 1848–1852.* Paris, 1875.

Mesnil, Octave du. "La Cité des Kroumirs." *Annales d'hygiène publique et de médecine légale,* 3rd series, 7 (1889).

―――. "Les Garnis insalubres de la ville de Paris." *Annales d'hygiène publique et de médecine légale,* 2nd series, 50 (1878).

Meynadier, Gabriel-Louis-Hippolyte, baron de Flamalens. *Paris sous le point de vue pittoresque et monumental, ou éléments d'un plan général d'ensemble de ses travaux d'art et d'utilité publique.* Paris, 1843.

Michel, Jacques. *Du Paris de Louis XV à la marine de Louis XVI: L'Oeuvre de Monsieur de Sartine.* 2 vols. Paris, 1983.

Michel, Louise. *La Commune.* Paris, 1978.

Michelet, Jules. *Histoire de la Révolution française.* Edited by Gérard Walter. 2 vols. Paris, 1952.

―――. *Journal.* Edited by Paul Villaneix and Claude Digeon. 3 vols. Paris, 1959–76.

Miot de Melito, André-François, comte de. *Mémoires.* 3 vols. Paris, 1858.

Mirabeau, Honoré-Gabriel de Riquetti, comte de. *Oeuvres.* Paris, 1822.

Molé, Mathieu. *Souvenirs d'un témoin de la Révolution et de l'Empire (1791–1803).* Paris, 1943.

Molinari, Gustave de. "Les Approvisionnements de Paris à la fin du siège." *Revue des deux mondes* 91 (1871).

―――. *Les Clubs rouges pendant le siège de Paris.* Paris, 1871.

Mollat, Michel, ed. *Histoire de l'Ile-de-France et de Paris.* Toulouse, 1971.

Monin, Hippolyte. *L'Etat de Paris en 1789, études et documents sur l'Ancien Régime à Paris.* Paris, 1889.

Montigny, Louis-Gabriel. *Le Provincial à Paris, esquisses des moeurs parisiennes.* 3 vols. Paris, 1825.

Montorgueil, Octave Lebesgue [Georges]. *Les Eaux et les fontaines de Paris*. Paris, 1928.
_____. *La Vie des boulevards, Madeleine-Bastille*. Paris, 1896.
Moreau de Saint-Méry, Médéric-Louis-Elie. *Voyage aux Etats-Unis de l'Amérique, 1793–1798*. New Haven, Conn., 1913.
Morizet, André. *Du Vieux Paris au Paris moderne. Haussmann et ses prédécesseurs*. Paris, 1932.
Moss, Bernhard H. "Parisian Producers' Associations (1830–1851): The Socialism of Skilled Workers." In *Revolution and Reaction: 1848 and the Second French Republic*, edited by Roger Price. London and New York, 1975.
Mulot, François-Valentin. *Vues d'un citoyen ancien député de Paris à l'Assemblée législative sur les sépultures*. Paris, n.d.
Musset, Alfred de. *La Confession d'un enfant du siècle*. In *Oeuvres complètes en prose*, edited by Maurice Allem and Paul Courant. Paris, 1960.
Nadaud, Martin. *Mémoires de Léonard, ancien garçon maçon*. Bourganeuf, 1895.
Napoléon Ier. *Correspondance de Napoléon Ier publiée par ordre de l'Empereur Napoléon III*. 32 vols. Paris, 1858–70.
Necker, Jacques. *De l'Administration des finances de la France*. 3 vols. Paris, 1784.
Néel, Louis-Balthazar. *Voyage de Paris à Saint-Cloud par mer et retour de St. Cloud à Paris par terre*. Paris, year X.
Newman, Edgar Leon. "The Blouse and the Frock Coat: The Alliance of the Common People of Paris with the Liberal Leadership and the Middle Class during the Last Years of the Bourbon Restoration." *Journal of Modern History* 46 (1974).
Nguyen-Trong-Hiêp. *Paris capitale de la France: Recueil de vers*. Hanoi, 1897.
Nord, Philip G. *Paris Shopkeepers and the Politics of Resentment*. Princeton, N.J., 1986.
Nordau, Max. *Aus dem wahren Milliardenlande, Pariser Studien und Bilder*. 2 vols. Leipzig, 1878.
North-Peat, Anthony B. *Paris sous le Second Empire: Femmes, la mode, la cour: Correspondance (1864–1869)*. Paris, 1911.
Nouveau Tableau de Paris aux XIXe siècle. 7 vols. Paris 1814–35.
Oberkirch, Henriette-Louise Waldner de Freundstein, baronne d'. *Mémoires de la baronne d'Oberkirch*. 2 vols. Paris, 1853.
Oettermann, Stephan. *Das Panorama. Die Geschichte eines Massenmediums*. Frankfurt-am-Main, 1980.
Olsen, Donald J. *The City as a Work of Art: London, Paris, Vienna*. New Haven and London, 1986.
Ordonnance pour la police des locataires des maisons que l'on construit actuellement au pourtour du jardin du Palais-Royal. May 3, 1782.
Ouvrard, Gabriel-Julien. *Mémoires de G. J. Ouvrard sur sa vie et ses diverses opérations financières*. 3 vols. Paris, 1826–27.
Ozouf, Mona. *La Fête révolutionnaire, 1789–1799*. Paris, 1976.
Pacroix, Paul. *Directoire, Consulat et Empire: Moeurs et usages, lettres, sciences et arts, 1795–1815*. Paris, 1884.
Parent-Duchâtelet, Alexandre-Jean-Baptiste. *Les Chantiers d'écarrisage [sic] de la ville de Paris, envisagés sous le rapport de l'hygiène publique*. Paris, 1832.
_____. "Des Obstacles que les préjugés médicaux apportent dans quelques circonstances à l'assainissement des villes et à l'établissment de certaines manufactures." *Annales d'hygiène publique et de médecine légale* 13/2 (1835).
_____. "Projet d'un rapport demandé par M. le préfet de la Seine sur le projet de construction d'un clos central d'écarrisage [sic], pour la ville de Paris." *Annales d'hygiène publique et de médecine légale* 16/1 (1836).
_____ (Rapporteur). "Rapport sur les améliorations à introduire dans les fosses d'aisance, leur mode de vidange et les voiries de la ville de Paris." *Annales d'hygiène publique et de médecine légale* 14/2 (1835).
Paris-Guide, par les principaux écrivains et artistes de la France. 2 vols. Paris, 1867.
Paris-Hachette 1900: Annuaire complet commercial, administratif et mondain. Paris,1900.
Paris, ou le livre des cent-et-un. 15 vols. Paris, 1831–34.

Pasquier, Etienne-Denis, duc de. *Histoire de mon temps: Mémoires du chancelier Pasquier.* Edited by M. le duc d'Audiffret-Pasquier. 6 vols. Paris, 1893–95.

Pastoret, Claude-Emmanuel-Joseph-Pierre. *Rapport sur la violation des sépultures et des tombeaux, fait au nom de la commission de la classification et de la révision des lois.* Paris, year IV.

Paul, Sir John Dean. *Journal d'un voyage à Paris au mois d'août 1802.* Paris, 1913.

Payen, J. *Les Frères Périer et l'introduction de la machine à vapeur de Watt à Paris.* Paris, 1969.

Percier, Charles, and Pierre Fontaine. *Résidences de souverains: Parallèle entre plusieurs résidences de souverains de France, d'Allemagne, de Suède, de Russie, d'Espagne et d'Italie.* Paris, 1833.

Pereire, Isaac. *La Question des chemins de fer de Paris.* Paris, 1879.

Perreymond. *Le Bilan de la France ou la misère et le travail.* Paris, 1849.

_____. "De la grande circulation dans Paris, et du livre de M. Hippolyte Meynadier, *Paris sous le point de vue etc.*" *Revue générale de l'architecture et des travaux publics* 5 (1844).

_____. *Paris monarchique et Paris républicain, ou une page de l'histoire de la misère et du travail.* Paris, 1849.

_____. "Régénération du vieux Paris." *Revue générale de l'architecture et des travaux publics* 4 (1843).

Persigny, Jean-Gilbert-Victor Fialin, duc de. *Mémoires.* Edited by H. de Laire, comte d'Espagny. Paris, 1896.

Pichois, Claude. "Les Cabinets de lecture à Paris durant la première moitié du XIXe siècle." *Annales E.S.C.* 14 (1959).

Picot, Georges. *Les Logements d'ouvriers: Un devoir social.* Paris, 1885.

Pigeory, Félix. *Les Monuments de Paris au dix-neuvième siècle: Histoire architectonique de Paris ancien et moderne.* Paris, 1849.

Pinkney, David. "Les Ateliers de secours à Paris (1830–1831). Précurseurs des ateliers nationaux de 1848." *Revue d'histoire moderne et contemporaine* 12 (1965).

_____. *Decisive Years in France, 1841–1847.* Princeton, N.J., 1986.

_____. *The French Revolution of 1830.* Princeton, N.J., 1972.

_____. "Laissez-faire or Intervention? Labor Policy in the First Months of the July Monarchy." *French Historical Studies* 3 (1963).

_____. *Napoleon III and the Rebuilding of Paris.* Princeton, N.J., 1958.

_____. "Paris, capitale du coton sous le Premier Empire." *Annales* 5 (1950).

Plessis, Alain. *De la fête impériale au mur des fédérés, 1852–1871.* Paris, 1973.

Polonceau, C., and Victor Bois. "De la Disposition et du service des gares et stations sur les chemins de fer." *Revue générale de l'architecture et des travaux publics* 1 (1840).

Poubelle, M. E. *Les Travaux de Paris, 1789–1889.* Paris, 1889.

Poujoulx, Jean-Baptiste. *Paris à la fin du XVIIIe siècle.* Paris, year VIII.

Poultre, Christian. *De la répression de la mendicité et du vagabondage en France sous l'Ancien Régime.* Paris, 1906.

Poumiès de la Siboutie. *Souvenirs d'un médecin de Paris.* Paris, 1910.

Pouthas, Charles H. "La Population française pendant la première moitié du XIXe siècle." *I. N. E. D., Travaux et documents,* cahier no. 25. Paris, 1956.

Préfecture de Police. *Compte d'administration des dépenses de la préfecture de police.* Paris, 1819.

Préfecture de Police. Conseil d'hygiène publique et de salubrité. *L'Epidémie cholérique de 1892 dans le département de la Seine.* Paris, 1893.

Préfecture du departement de la Seine. Commission d'extension de Paris. *Aperçu historique.* Paris, 1913.

_____. *Considérations techniques préliminaires.* Paris, 1913.

Préfecture du département de la Seine. Direction des travaux de Paris. Commission supérieure de l'assainissement de Paris. *Séance du 26 mars 1885.* Paris, n.d.

_____. *Recueil de reglements.* Paris, 1875.

Préfecture du département de la Seine. Secrétariat général. Service de la statistique municipale. *Tableaux statistiques de l'épidémie cholérique de 1884 à Paris et étude statistique des épidémies antérieures.* Paris, 1886.

Price, Roger, ed. *Revolution and Reaction: 1848 and the Second French Republic*. London and New York, 1975.

Procès-verbal de la formation et des opérations du Comité militaire de la ville de Paris: Ire partie du 16 juillet au 30 septembre 1789. Paris, 1789.

Pronteau, Jeanne. "Construction et aménagement des nouveaux quartiers de Paris (1820–1826)." *Histoire des entreprises* 2 (1958).

_____. "La Disparition des espaces verts parisiens: Lotissement des 'marais' des communautés religieuses à la fin du XVIIIe siècle." *Mémoires de la fédération des sociétés historiques et archéologiques de Paris et de l'Ile-de-France* 25 (1974).

_____. *Les Numérotages des maisons de Paris du XVe siècle à nos jours*. Paris, 1966.

Proust, Marcel. *A la recherche du temps perdu*. Edited by Pierre Clarac and André Ferré. 3 vols. Paris, 1954.

Prudhomme, Louis-Marie. *Miroir historique, politique et critique de l'ancien et du nouveau Paris et du département de la Seine*. 6 vols. Paris, 1804.

Quatremère de Quincy, Antoine-Chrysostôme (Rapporteur). *Rapport fait au conseil général, le 15 Thermidor an VIII, sur l'instruction publique, le rétablissement des bourses, le scandale des inhumations actuelles, l'érection des cimetières, la restitution des tombeaux, mausolées, etc*. Paris, 1800.

Rabusson, A. *Affaire du déplacement de la population dans Paris: Deuxième note relative au côté politique de ce déplacement*. Paris, 1843.

Rambuteau, Claude-Philibert-Barthelot, comte de. *Compte rendu de l'administration du département de la Seine et de la ville de Paris, pendant l'année 1836*. Paris, 1837.

_____. *Mémoires du comte de Rambuteau publiés par son petit-fils*. With an introduction and notes by Georges Lequin. Paris, 1905.

Rapport de la commission d'enquête sur l'insurrection qui a éclaté dans la journée du 23 juin et sur les événements du 15 mai. Paris, 1848.

Rapports généraux des travaux du conseil de salubrité pendant les années 1840–1845 inclusivement. Paris, 1847.

Rapport sur la marche et les effets du choléra-morbus dans Paris et les communes rurales du département de la Seine. Paris, 1834.

Rearick, Charles. *Pleasures of the Belle Epoque: Entertainment and Festivity in Turn-of-the-Century France*. New Haven and London, 1985.

Réau, Louis et al. *L'Oeuvre du baron Haussmann, préfet de la Seine (1853–1870)*. Paris, 1954.

Rébérioux, Madeleine. "Le Mur des fédérés." In *Les Lieux de mémoire: La République*, vol. 1., edited by Pierre Nora. Paris, 1984.

Recherches statistiques sur la ville de Paris et le Département de la Seine. 6 vols. Paris, 1823–60.

Récit de l'élargissement forcé et la rentrée volontaire des gardes françaises dans la prison de l'Abbaye. Paris, 1789.

Reichardt, Johann Friedrich. *Vertraute Briefe aus Paris, geschrieben in den Jahren 1802 und 1803*. 3 vols. Hamburg, 1804.

Reinach, Joseph. *Histoire de l'affaire Dreyfus*. 7 vols. Paris, 1907.

Reinhard, Marcel. *Paris pendant la Révolution*. 2 vols. Paris: Les Cours de la Sorbonne, 1966.

_____. *La Révolution 1789–1799*. Paris, 1971.

Rellstab, Ludwig. *Paris im Frühjahr 1843: Briefe, Berichte und Schilderungen*. 3 vols. Leipzig, 1844.

Remusat, Charles de. *Mémoires de ma vie*. Edited by Charles H. Pouthas. 3 vols. Paris, 1958–67.

Renan, Ernest, and Henriette Renan. *Nouvelles Lettres intimes 1846–1850*. Paris, 1923.

Restif de la Bretonne. *Oeuvres*. Edited by Henri Bachelin. 9 vols. Paris, 1930–32.

Richard, Camille. *Le Comité de salut public et les fabrications de guerre sous la terreur*. Paris, 1922.

Ridley, Jasper. *Napoleon III and Eugenie*. London, 1979.

Riehl, Wilhelm Heinrich von. *Land und Leute*. 3rd ed. Stuttgart and Augsburg, 1856.

Rihs, Charles. *La Commune de Paris. Sa structure et ses doctrines (1871)*. Geneva, 1955.

Robespierre, Maximilien. *Discours*. In *Oeuvres complètes*, edited by Marc Bouloiseau, Georges Lefebvre, and Albert Soboul. Paris, 1950–67.

Robinet and Trebuchet (Rapporteurs). "Rapport général sur les travaux de la Commission des logements insalubres pendant les années 1852 . . . 1856." *Annales d'hygiène publique et de médecine légale*, 2nd series, 8 (1857).

Robiquet, Jean. *La Vie quotidienne au temps de Napoléon*. Paris, 1942.

Roche, Daniel. *Le Peuple de Paris: La culture populaire au XVIIIe siècle*. Paris, 1981.

Rochefort, Henri. *Les Aventures de ma vie*. Edited by Jean Guichard-Meili. Paris, 1980.

Rodenberg, Julius. *Paris bei Sonnenschein und Lampenlicht*. Leipzig, 1867.

Rougerie, Jacques. "L'A. I. T. et le mouvement ouvrier à Paris pendant les événements de 1870–1871." In *1871: Jalons pour une histoire de la commune de Paris*, edited by Jacques Rougerie. Paris, 1973.

_____. *Paris libre 1871*. Paris, 1971.

_____, ed. *Procès des Communards*. Paris, 1964.

Rouleau, Bernard. *La Tracé des rues de Paris*. Paris, 1967.

_____. *Villages et faubourgs de l'ancien Paris: Histoire d'un espace urbain*. Paris, 1985.

Rousseau, Jean-Jacques. *Les Confessions*. Edited by Bernard Gagnebin and Marcel Raymond. Paris, 1959.

_____. *Julie, ou la nouvelle Héloïse*. Edited by Henri Coulet and Bernard Guyon. Paris, 1964.

Roux, Louis. *De Montfaucon, de l'insalubrité de ses établissements et de la necessité de leur suppression immédiate*. Paris, 1841.

Rudé, George. *The Crowd in the French Revolution*. Oxford, 1959.

_____. "Prices, Wages and Popular Movement in Paris during the French Revolution." *Economic History Review* 6 (1954).

Ruggieri, Claude-Fortuné. *Précis historique sur les fêtes, les spectacles et les réjouissances publiques jusqu'au sacre de Charles X*. Paris, 1830.

Saint-Aubin, Camille. *L'Expédition de Don Quichotte contre les moulins à vent, ou l'absurdité de la guerre qu'on fait aux agioteurs et à l'agiotage*. N.p., 1795.

St. John, Bayle. *Purple Tints of Paris: Character and Manners in the New Empire*. London, 1854.

Savary, Anne-Jean-Marie-René, duc de Rovigo. *Mémoires du duc de Rovigo, pour servir à l'histoire de l'Empereur Napoléon*. 8 vols. Paris, 1828.

Schmidt, Charles. *Des Ateliers nationaux aux barricades de juin*. Paris, 1948.

_____. *Les Journées de juin 1848*. Paris, 1926.

Schmidt, Wilhelm Adolf. *Paris pendant la Révolution d'après les rapports de la police secrète, 1789–1800*. 4 vols. Paris 1880–94.

Schneider, G. *Pariser Briefe*. 4 vols. Leipzig, 1872.

Schulz, Friedrich. *Über Paris und die Pariser*. Berlin, 1791.

Scott, John. *A Visit to Paris in 1814, Being a Review of the Moral, Political, Intellectual and Social Condition of the French Capital*. London, 1816.

Seager, F. H. *The Boulanger Affair*. New York, 1969.

Seigel, Jerrold. *Bohemian Paris: Culture, Politics, and the Boundaries of Bourgeois Life, 1830–1930*. New York, 1986.

Seignobos, Charles. *Le Declin de l'Empire et l'établissement de la Troisième République (1859–1875)*. Histoire de France contemporaine depuis la Révolution jusqu'à la paix de 1919, vol. 8. Edited by Ernest Lavisse. 10 vols. Paris, 1921.

_____. *La Revolution de 1848—Le Second Empire*. Histoire de France contemporaine depuis la Révolution jusqu'à la paix de 1919, vol. 6. Edited by Ernest Lavisse. 10 vols. Paris, 1921.

Senior, Nassau William. *Conversations with Distinguished Persons during the Second Empire from 1860–1863*. 2 vols. London, 1880.

Seyffarth, Woldemar. *Wahrnehmungen in Paris, 1853 und 1854*. Gotha, 1855.

Shapiro, Ann Louise. *Housing the Poor of Paris 1850–1902*. Madison, Wis., 1985.

Shattuck, Roger. *The Banquet Years: The Arts in France 1885–1918*. London, 1959.
Silverman, Debora L. "The 1889 Exhibition: The Crisis of Bourgeois Individualism." *Oppositions* 8 (1977).
Soboul, Albert. *Les Sans-Culottes parisiens en l'an II: Mouvement populaire et gouvernement révolutionnaire 2 juin 1793–9 thermidor an II*. Paris, 1958.
Srbik, Heinrich Ritter von. *Metternich: Der Staatsmann und der Mensch*. 2 vols. Munich, 1925.
Staël, Germaine de. *Considérations sur les principaux événements de la Révolution françoise*. 3 vols. Paris, 1818.
Staël-Holstein, Erik Magnus, baron de. *Correspondance diplomatique du baron de Staël-Holstein . . . et de son successeur . . . le baron Brinkman: Documents inédits sur la Révolution (1783–1799) recueillis aux archives royales de Suède*. Edited by Léozun le Duc. Paris, 1881.
Stahr, Adolf. *Nach fünf Jahren, Pariser Studien aus dem Jahre 1855*. 2 vols. Oldenburg, 1857.
Starobinski, Jean. *1789. Les Emblèmes de la raison*. Paris, 1979.
Stendhal, *Correspondance*. Edited by Henri Martineau and V. del Litto. 3 vols. Paris, 1982.
––––––. *Oeuvres intimes*. Edited by V. del Litto. 2 vols. Paris, 1981.
Stern, Daniel [Agoult, Marie de Flavigny, comtesse d']. *Histoire de la Révolution de 1848*. 3 vols. Paris, 1850–53.
Sussman, George D. *Selling Mother's Milk: The Wet-Nursing Business in France 1715–1914*. Urbana, Ill., and London, 1982.
Sutcliffe, Anthony. *The Autumn of Central Paris: The Defeat of Town Planning 1850– 1970*. London, 1970.
Talleyrand. *Mémoires 1754–1815*. Edited by Jean-Paul Couchond. Paris, 1982.
Talmeyr, Maurice. "Cafés-Concerts et Music-Halls." *Revue des deux mondes* 10 (1902).
Tersen, Emile. *Napoléon*. Paris, 1959.
Tessereau, Auguste. *Etudes hygiéniques sur les Halles centrales de Paris*. Paris, 1847.
Texier, Edmond-Auguste [Kel–Kun, Peregrinus, Sylvius]. *Tableau de Paris*. 2 vols. Paris, 1852–53.
Thibaudeau, Antoine C. *Mémoires 1799–1815*. Paris, 1913.
Thibaut-Payen, Jacqueline. *Les Morts, l'église et l'état: Recherches d'histoire administrative sur la sépulture et les cimetières dans le ressort du Parlement de Paris au XVIIᵉ et XVIIIᵉ siècles*. Paris, 1977.
Thiers, Adolphe. *Notes et souvenirs (1870–1873)*. Paris, 1903.
Thiollet and Roux. *Nouveau Recueil de menuiserie et décorations intérieures et exterieures*. Paris, 1837.
Thouret, Michel A.. *Rapport sur la voirie de Montfaucon lu dans la séance de la sociète royale de médecine du 11 novembre 1788*. Paris [1788].
––––––. *Rapport sur les exhumations du cimetière et de l'église des Saints-Innocents*. Histoire de la Société royale de médecine, vol. 8 (1786).
Tilly, Charles, and Lynn H. Lees. "The People of June 1848." In *Revolution and Reaction. 1848 and the Second French Republic*, edited by Roger Price. London and New York, 1975.
Tite, William. "On the Paris Street Improvements and Their Cost." *Journal of the Statistical Society* 27 (1864).
Tocqueville, Alexis de. *Souvenirs. Oeuvres complètes*, vol. 12. Edited by J. P. Mayer. Paris, 1964.
Tønnesson, Kåre D. *La Défaite des Sans-Culottes: Mouvement populaire et réaction bourgeoise en l'an III*. 2nd ed. Oslo, 1978.
Tour du Pin, Henriette-Lucy, marquise de la. *Mémoires: Journal d'une femme de cinquante ans (1778–1815)*. Edited by Christian comte de Liederkerke Beaufort. Paris, 1983.
Tourneux, Maurice. *Bibliographie de l'histoire de Paris pendant la Révolution française*. 5 vols. Paris, 1890–1913.

Transon, Abel and Dublanc. "Observations sur quelques industries et en particulier sur le commerce des chiffons dans le XIIᵉ arrondissement de Paris." *Annales d'hygiène publique et de médecine légale*, 2nd series, 1 (1854).

Traugott, Mark. *Armies of the Poor: Determinants of Working-Class Participation in the Parisian Insurrection of June 1848*. Princeton, N.J., 1985.

Les Travaux de Paris, 1789–1889. Atlas dressé sous l'administration de M. E. Poubelle, préfet de la Seine, sous la direction de M. Jean-Charles-Adolphe Alphand, Inspecteur Général des Ponts et Chaussées, Directeur des Travaux de Paris. Paris, 1889.

Trébuchet, A. "Rapports généraux des travaux du Conseil de salubrité depuis 1829 jusqu'en 1839." *Annales d'hygiène publique et de médecine légale* 25 (1841).

———. "Rapports généraux des travaux du Conseil de salubrité pendant les années 1846, 1847 et 1848." *Annales d'hygiène publique et de médecine légale*, 2nd series, 7 (1857).

———. "Recherches sur l'éclairage public de Paris." *Annales d'hygiène publique et de médecine légale* 31 (1844).

Troche, Nicholas-Michel. *Notice historique sur les inhumations provisoires faites sur la place du Marché des Innocens, devant la colonnade du Louvre*. Paris, 1837.

Trollope, Frances. *Paris and the Parisians in 1835*. 2 vols. London, 1836.

Tudesq, André-Jean. *L'Election présidentielle de Louis-Napoléon Bonaparte. 10 décembre 1848*. Paris, 1965.

Tuetey, Alexandre, *L'Assistance publique à Paris pendant la Révolution, documents inédits recueillis et publiées par Alexandre Tuetey*. 4 vols. Paris, 1895–97.

———. *Répertoire général des sources manuscrites de l'histoire de Paris pendant la Révolution française*. 11 vols. Paris, 1890–1914.

Tufte, Edward R. *The Visual Display of Quantitative Information*. Cheshire, Conn., 1983.

Tulard, Jean. *Le Consulat et l'Empire 1800–1815*. Paris, 1970.

———. "Du Paris impérial au Paris de 1830 d'après les bulletins de police." *Bulletin de la société de l'histoire de Paris et de l'Ile-de-France*, 1971.

———. *Paris et son administration (1800–1830)*. Paris, 1976.

———. *La Préfecture de police sous la Monarchie de Juillet*. Paris, 1964.

Underwood, Thomas Richard. *Paris en 1814*. Paris, 1907.

Vandal, Louis-Jules-Albert. *L'Avènement de Bonaparte*. 2 vols. Paris, 1902.

Vaquier, André. "Le Cimetière de la Madeleine et le Sieur Descloseaux." In *Mémoires de la Fédération des societés historiques et archéologiques de Paris et de l'Ile-de-France* 12 (1961).

Varnhagen von Ense, Karl August. *Denkwürdigkeiten des eignen Lebens*. Edited by Konrad Feilchenfeldt. Frankfurt-am-Main, 1987.

Vaublanc, B. V. M. Viennot de [comte de Vaublanc]. *Mémoires*. Paris, 1857.

Vedrenne-Villeneuve, Edmonde. "L'Inégalité sociale devant la mort dans la premiére moitié du XIXᵉ siècle." *Population* 16 (1961).

Véron, Louis. *Mémoires d'un bourgeois de Paris*. 6 vols. Paris, 1853–55.

Veuillot, Louis. *Les Odeurs de Paris*. Paris, 1866.

Viel-Castel, Horace, comte de. *Mémoires sur le règne de Napoléon III, 1851–1864*. Edited by Pierre Josserand. 2 vols. Paris, 1942.

Viennet, Jean-Pons-Guillaume. *Promenade philosophique au cimetière du Père Lachaise*. Paris, 1824.

Viennet, Odette. *Une Enquête économique dans la France impériale: Le voyage du hambur-geois Nemnich*. Paris, 1947.

Villemessant, Henri de. *Mémoires d'un journaliste*. 6 vols. Paris, 1867–78.

Villermé, Louis-René. "De la mortalité dans les divers quartiers de la ville de Paris et des causes qui la rendent très différente dans plusieurs d'entre eux, ainsi que dans les divers quartiers de beaucoup des grandes villes." *Annales d'hygiène publique et de médecine légale* 3 (1830).

———. "De l'épidemie typhoïde qui a frappé la ville de Paris pendant les cinq premiers mois de 1853." *Annales d'hygiène publique et de médecine légale*, 2nd series, 2 (1854).

_____ "Note sur les ravages du choléra-morbus dans les maisons garnies de Paris." *Annales d'hygiène publique et de médecine légale* 11 (1834).

Voltaire. *Oeuvres complètes*. Gotha, 1786.

Weber, Eugen. *France: Fin de Siècle*. Cambridge, Mass., and London, 1986.

Willms, Johannes. *Nationalismus ohne Nation: Deutsche Geschichte 1789–1914*. Düsseldorf, 1983.

Yorke, Henry Redhead. *Paris et la France sous le Consulat*. Paris, 1921.

Young, Arthur. *Voyages en France en 1787, 1788 et 1789*. Edited by Henri Sée. Paris, 1931.

Zeldin, Theodore. *France 1848–1945*. 2 vols. Oxford, 1973.

Zola, Emile. *Oeuvres complètes*. Edited by Maurice Le Blond. Paris, 1927–29.

_____. *Oeuvres complètes*. Edited by Henri Mitterand. 15 vols. Paris, 1966–70.

_____. *Les Rougon-Macquart*. Edited by Armand Lanoux. 5 vols. Paris, 1960–65.

Index